AMMO
AND BALLISTICS

By
Bob Forker

Safari Press Inc.

P.O. Box 3095, Long Beach, California 90803

The trademark Safari Press ® is registered with the U.S. Patent and Trademark Office and in other countries.

Forker, Robert

First edition

Safari Press Inc.

2000, Long Beach, California

ISBN 1-57157-161-2

Library of Congress Catalog Card Number: 98-71025

10 9 8 7 6 5 4 3 2 1

Readers wishing to receive the Safari Press catalog, featuring many fine books on big-game hunting, wingshooting, and sporting firearms, should write to Safari Press Inc., P.O. Box 3095, Long Beach, CA 90803, U.S.A. Tel: (714) 894-9080 or visit our Web site at www.safaripress.com.

Contents

Dedication

Dedicated to the memory of
Frank C. Barnes,
whose useful book,
Cartridges of the World*,*
set the standard by which all other data books are judged.

Acknowledgments

We wish to thank all the people who have contributed to this database. The list is long, but without the cooperation of these contributors, the book would be less useful:

A-Square Company, Inc., Black Hills Ammunition, Inc., CCI/Speer (Blount Sporting Equipment Division), Federal Cartridge Company, Fiocchi, Hansen Cartridge Company, Hornady Manufacturing Company, Patria Lapua Oy, Lazzeroni Arms Company, Kynoch (Kynamco Limited), MagTech, Norma Precision AB, PMC (Eldorado Cartridge Corporation), Remington Arms, Weatherby, and Winchester Ammunition.

A very special thank you goes to Bob Nosler of Nosler bullets who has so generously allowed us to use Nosler's cartridge drawings in this book.

Most of the ballistic calculations in this book were done using Dr. Ken Oehler's (Oehler Research, Inc.) Ballistic Explorer program.

FOREWORD

In the course of the last quarter-century or so I have written a dozen books and hundreds of magazine articles that directly or indirectly have something to do with shooting. This is my life as much as my hobby, and I've been fortunate to have turned it into a profession of sorts. Mind you, I enjoy sitting down and doing the writing almost as much as the "research"—the shooting and hunting—it requires. Most of my work is designed, as Bob Petersen always says, to "entertain and instruct," probably in that order; I am not of a technical bent, and have no background in any scientific discipline. However, it is possible that some of my writings have been of some help to my readers in making sound choices in firearms and ammunition for various purposes.

If that is so, it is largely because I have received similar help from others who do have technical knowledge and expertise. As shooters, we all need help. The world of cartridges, calibers, bullets, ballistics, and trajectories is ever more diverse, and although the basic theories don't change, the myriad choices available today makes choosing the right tool ever more complex. I also need help as a writer for shooters and about shooting. Like most writers, I have a fairly extensive reference library. Some books I refer to once in a while, and others fairly frequently. A very few are referred to almost daily and are literally coming apart from use.

Those hard-used volumes include the reloading manuals from the major bullet makers, plus two more prized references: Frank Barnes's *Cartridges of the World*; and Bill Matthews's *Shoot Better II*. This book by Bob Forker is going to be one of those books that will be used regularly and will soon become dog-eared. In fact, I intend to buy two of them—one for my bookcase, and one for my travel kit!

I will not say that Bob Forker's book replaces, supplants, or renders obsolete my other favorite resources. This book deals with current factory-loaded cartridges, but the various excellent reloading manuals must remain a primary source for loading recipes. Frank Barnes's timeless work remains *the* reference for thumbnail sketches of cartridges of all ages, especially the obsolete and obscure. Bill Matthews's landmark work provides excellent and detailed ballistics and trajectory data on cartridges from the major manufacturers, and essentially popularized the concept of sighting in for "Maximum Point-Blank Range." These works remain invaluable.

However, Bob Forker has compiled a mountain of data and information into one volume, data that has *never* been available in one place. Yes, this book is about factory ammunition, but that's a lot like saying *The Old Man and the Sea* is about fishing. There is much more here. In addition to data from the major ammunition manufacturers, he has included data from literally every manufacturer, large or small, who markets "ready-made" ammunition in the United States.

Naturally you will find ballistics figures and trajectory curves, but you will also find detailed cartridge diagrams; pressure and ballistic coefficients; standard rifling twists; recoil index; and even Taylor's "Knock-Out" (KO) values. These are the kinds of things that we shooters love to argue about around a campfire, and in the past I have spent countless hours running from one reference to another looking for these priceless crumbs of information. Now I will have them all in one place. Be warned: If you and I engage in a campfire argument, I'll have Forker's book in my duffel bag to back me up!

Of course, you will find much more than raw data in this volume. You will also find clear and concise writing that clarifies the complexities of ballistics coefficients, energy versus momentum, and so much more. Over the years a number of readers have suggested that I compile a volume similar to this one. I never would for two good reasons. First, I am not qualified to do so. Second, it would entail *TOO MUCH WORK*! I don't want to delay you much longer in getting past the traditional necessity of a foreword so you can delve into the meat of this book, but let me just elaborate on these two considerations.

Unlike myself and most other gunwriters of this and every other generation, Bob Forker is truly a "technical gunwriter." He has contributed to *Guns & Ammo* for over thirty-five years, and more importantly, he has a genuine engineering background. During his career in the aerospace industry Bob's specialty was gun and ammunition development and weapons system installation in fixed and rotary-wing aircraft. He designed the under-ground ballistics laboratory at Bob Petersen's ranch that has contributed so much to *G&A* and other Petersen publications. During my own long tenure at Petersen Publishing, the rules were very simple: If you had a really knotty problem dealing with ballistics, you called Bob Forker! He usually had the answer, but if he didn't he would find it. Quickly.

I've known Bob Forker some twenty years. We've shot together, hunted together, done shows together, and commiserated over the vagaries of editors and publishers. His is the finest "gun mind" I know, the kind required to distill a mountain of raw data from innumerable sources into a cohesive whole. I couldn't have done it and, moreover, I wouldn't have wanted to. You are holding in your hands a work unequaled by anything Hercules had to tackle. I am awed by the scope and breadth of this work, and, above all, I am most grateful to Bob Forker for having done this for all of us. This is not a "read and enjoy" book. Rather, it is a "read, study, and revisit" book. You will revisit it often, as will I.

Colonel Craig T. Boddington
U.S.M.C.

Introduction

There was a time when someone who needed ammunition went to his local hardware store and said he wanted a box of, let's say, .30-30 ammunition. That was it. He was lucky to find any ammo in the right caliber, let alone to have any choice of different bullets, brands, performance levels, etc. He took his box of cartridges and went hunting. Life was simple.

Today we "suffer" from just the opposite problem; we have far more variations than any one person can remember. For the .30-30 Winchester alone there are at least seventy-five different combinations of bullet weight, brand, etc., available for retail sale in the U.S. That may be a problem, but it's a good kind of problem. This book enables you to see just what factory ammunition is available, in what caliber, in what bullet styles, and with enough detailed performance data so you can make meaningful comparisons.

As we started to collect this data, we immediately ran into the question of how much to include and where to stop. That's not an easy decision, and it will not please everyone. We started with the fundamental decision to include only factory-made ammunition, excluding custom reloaders and wildcat calibers. A lot of factory ammunition sold in the U.S. is not actually made here (Hansen, Kynoch, Lapua, MagTech, and Norma come quickly to mind), so we decided to include foreign manufacturers with distribution systems in this country. To keep the size of this book within reasonable bounds, we have limited the listings to calibers that are well known in the U.S.

As soon as you get past the calibers that are standardized in the U.S. by the Small Arms and Ammunition Manufacturers' Institute (SAAMI), you get into a large gray area. Weatherby's cartridges provide an excellent example. When the Weatherby line of cartridges was first introduced, you either bought your ammunition from the Weatherby factory or loaded your own, because no other manufacturer offered loaded ammunition in Weatherby calibers.

The concept of proprietary cartridges furnished by custom gunmakers is not at all new. Around 1900 in England, that practice was the rule rather than the exception, and such classics as the .375 Holland & Holland Magnum were once proprietary cartridges. Like the .375 H&H, over time, several of the Weatherby calibers were standardized by SAAMI. Ammunition for these calibers is now produced by independent ammunition makers, which removes them from the "proprietary" category. For other Weatherby calibers, the only factory ammunition that gets to the dealers' shelves still comes exclusively through Weatherby. That isn't bad; it's just the way things are. As of this writing, I believe that all Weatherby calibers not covered by SAAMI standards are controlled by Commission Internationale Permanente (CIP), the agency that oversees ammunition producers in Western Europe.

Relatively recently, several U.S. companies have developed their own lines of proprietary calibers. In general, these companies provide a source of factory-loaded ammunition for their own calibers. Although most of these cartridges have not received formal standardization in the U.S. or elsewhere, these folks are building their products under their own closely controlled conditions, which quite often includes outside testing by independent laboratories. Deciding which of these calibers to include in the listings wasn't easy. We did our best to make the book as inclusive as possible.

A comprehensive list of what's offered just gets you started. The performance data allows you to compare velocity, energy, Taylor KO Index ("Knock-Out" values), bullet path, and wind drift for various ranges. With that information you can quickly see the tradeoffs between light and fast bullets and the heavier and slower offerings.

In compiling this comparison data we have, wherever possible, used the manufacturer's own data. Where the manufacturer was unable to supply specific data, we have done our best to construct the missing items, using the best supporting information we could find.

HOW TO USE THIS BOOK

The listings in this book are divided into four sections: Small and Medium Centerfire Cartridges, African Cartridges, Pistol Cartridges, and Rimfire Cartridges. Within these four sections the listings begin with the smallest and end with the largest caliber. If you refer to the sample listing on page XIII you will see that there is ❶ description (with short historical notes) and a ❷ drawing of each caliber.

For each caliber we list a ❸ Relative Recoil Factor to give you some idea of the recoil the caliber will generate. Most shooters can handle the recoil of a .30-06 reasonably well with some practice; it has a relative recoil factor of 2.19. Should you carry a .700 Nitro Express, you will note that its relative recoil factor is 9.00, more than three times what a .30-06 generates! On the same line as the relative recoil factor you will find the controlling agency for standardization of this cartridge. In the Author's Notes there is a discussion of standardization and what it means to the shooter.

Item ❹ gives the standard performance numbers that have been established for this caliber. We list both the Maximum Average Pressures obtained by both the Copper Crusher and the Transducer methods. Number ❺ gives two figures. The first is the standard barrel length the factories use to create their velocity figures. If you shoot a .300 Weatherby Magnum with a 22-inch barrel, do not be surprised if your chronograph shows velocities significantly below the factory figures provided here; the reason for this is that this caliber is tested in the factory with a 26-inch barrel. The second number is the twist rate of the rifling the factories use in the factory test barrels.

Starting below the heavy black line are the listings of all the factory loads currently available in this caliber. The listings start with the lightest bullet and progress down to the heaviest bullet available in factory loadings for this caliber. Within each bullet weight there are listings for the bullet styles available. Within each bullet style, the listings run from the highest muzzle velocity to the lowest.

Under each specific loading you will find ❻ manufacturer, ❼ bullet weight, ❽ the manufacturer's name for his loading, and ❾ the factory stock number (in parenthesis) that can be used to order that particular cartridge and load. The individual cartridge listings also provide ❿ velocity, ⓫ energy, and ⓬ Taylor Knockout values. (See "The 'Great' Debate" in the Author's Notes for a discussion of the significance of these factors.) ⓭ The figures for the category of path - inches show the bullet's position relative to the line of sight at ranges up to 500 yards (depending on the listings section). For small and medium centerfire listings the figures assume a scope-sighted rifle that is set at a 200-yard "zero." For the African calibers the figures are based on iron sights and a 150-yard "zero." The rimfire listings are based on scope sights with a 100-yard "zero." Note that for handgun cartridges the path - inches listing is replaced by figures for mid-range trajectory height in inches.

⓮ The category of wind drift - inches shows how much the bullet is pushed off-course by a direct crosswind of 10 mph at ranges out to 500 yards. The G1 Ballistic Coefficient value ⓯ is useful for those shooters who want to calculate their own ballistic data.

Find the cartridge you want and locate the desired bullet weight; then look through the entries to see who makes what. Check the performance numbers to see whether a particular load is what you need. If you aren't quite satisfied, you can check the listings for the next higher or lower bullet weight in this caliber. If you are just playing "What if," you can also try other calibers to see if you can find a load that would do your job. If you cannot find a load with the performance you want, it probably isn't available as a factory product.

❶ .223 Remington

When the .223 Remington cartridge was adopted by the US Army as M193 5.56mm Ball ammunition in 1964, that action ensured that the .223 would become the most popular .22 centerfire in the list. Every cartridge that becomes a US Army standard, with the possible exception of the .30 Carbine, has gone on to a long and useful commercial life. Just look at the .45-70, the .45 Colt, the .30-06, and the .45 ACP. The .223 case has been "necked" to every possible size, the TCU series of cartridges and the .30 Whisper being examples.

Even without the military application, the .223 Remington had plenty of potential to become popular. Based on the .222 and the .222 Remington Magnum, the .223 provides an excellent balance of accuracy and performance with good case and barrel life. It has become the standard by which all other .22s are judged.

Most guns chambered for the .223 have a barrel twist of 1 turn in 14 inches. That twist provides enough stability for bullets up to 55 grains but begins to be marginal above that level. Today there are bullets weighing as much as 75 grains available in loaded ammunition (80-grain bullets for the handloader). It takes a faster twist to stabilize these heavier bullets and some gunmakers offer barrel twists as fast as 1 turn in 7 inches in this caliber. If you have one of the fast-twist barrels you may have problems with the very light varmint loads. The high velocities attained and the quick twist combine to produce a bullet spin rate that can literally rip thin-jacketed bullets apart. Guns equipped with quick twist barrels will usually do better with 55-grain and heavier bullets.

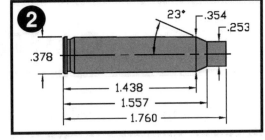

❸ Relative Recoil Factor = 0.80   Controlling Agency: SAAMI

❹ Weight Grains	Velocity fps	Maximum Average Pressure		❺ Standard barrel for velocity testing:
		Copper Crusher	Transducer	
53	3305	52,000 cup	55,000 psi	24 inches long - 1 turn in 12 inch twist
55	3215	52,000 cup	55,000 psi	
60	3200	52,000 cup	55,000 psi	
64	3000	52,000 cup	55,000 psi	

❻ Hornady   ❼ 40-grain   ❽ V-Max Moly ❾   (83253)

❿ Distance - Yards	Muzzle	100	200	300	400	500	
⓫ Velocity - fps	3800	3305	2845	2424	2044	1715	
Energy - ft-lb	1282	970	719	502	371	261	
⓬ Taylor KO values	4.9	4.2	3.6	3.1	2.6	2.2	
⓭ Path - inches	-1.5	0.9	0.0	-5.2	-16.4	-36.0	⓯ G1 Ballistic Coefficient = 0.218
⓮ Wind Drift - inches	0.0	1.0	4.4	10.7	20.4	34.7	

Winchester 40-grain Ballistic Silvertip (SBST223A)

Distance - Yards	Muzzle	100	200	300	400	500	
Velocity - fps	3700	3166	2693	2245	1879	1540	
Energy - ft-lb	1216	891	644	456	314	211	
Taylor KO values	4.7	4.1	3.5	2.9	2.4	2.0	
Path - inches	-1.5	1.0	0.0	-5.8	-18.4	-40.9	
Wind Drift - inches	0.0	1.2	5.0	12.1	23.5	40.3	G1 Ballistic Coefficient = 0.202

American Eagle (Federal) 50-grain Jacketed Hollow Point (AE223G)

Distance - Yards	Muzzle	100	200	300	400	500	
Velocity - fps	3400	2910	2460	2060	1700	1390	
Energy - ft-lbs	1285	940	875	470	320	215	
Taylor KO values	5.4	4.7	3.9	3.3	2.7	2.2	
Path - inches	-1.5	1.3	0.0	-7.1	-22.6	-50.2	
Wind Drift - inches	0.0	1.3	5.5	13.4	26.2	45.3	G1 Ballistic Coefficient = 0.204

CAUTION & WARNING!

Common sense needs to be used when handling and discharging a firearm. **Always keep the following in mind:** Always point a firearm in a safe direction; never point a firearm at another person. Treat all firearms as though they were loaded. Wear eye and hearing protection at all times when handling firearms. Only adults competent in handling firearms and ammunition should ever attempt to load or discharge a firearm.

Do not attempt to use this book to handload your own ammunition up to the bullet velocities listed on these pages. Your firearm may not be able to withstand the pressures generated by the loads listed in this book. The handloading of ammunition and the discharging of a firearm should never be attempted without the supervision of an adult experienced in both handloading and firearms. Do not attempt to handload ammunition without knowing how to read signs of (excessive) pressure in both guns and ammunition. Keep these principles of safety in mind so as to provide a safe environment for everyone.

DISCLAIMER

The reader may notice certain discrepancies in spellings in this book. Unlike most books where consistency is paramount, the author and the publisher decided to reproduce the actual word usage for the cartridges exactly as they appear in the manufacturers' catalogs. This is where the discrepancies arose. One manufacturer may use *Soft Nose* as part of its description for the ammunition in its catalog, while another might use *Softnose, soft nose, or softnose.* (Safari Press's style is to combine the two words and lowercase it—softnose.) Furthermore, when you go to your local shop to buy any ammunition, you may find the word usage on the box differs slightly from what you will find in this book. This further discrepancy is the result of a manufacturer failing to replicate exactly the wording in its catalog to that found on its cartridge boxes. For the purpose of this book, we have listed the information supplied from the manufacturer's catalog, which may differ slightly from what is printed on the cartridge box.

AUTHOR'S NOTES

How to Select Ammunition

When you set out to buy ammunition you usually know at least two things right at the start. You know what caliber you want, and you generally know whether the ammunition will be used for target shooting or hunting. If the use is target shooting, the process is relatively easy because once you select the caliber, your primary concern is accuracy.

Selecting hunting ammunition is considerably more complicated. The ultimate goal in the hunt is to obtain a reliable, clean kill, so the first step is to get a hit. A hit is a necessary condition for a kill, but after the initial hit, the bullet must also finish the job. Until about fifty years ago little was done to design bullets for specific hunting jobs. Most of the attention paid to bullet performance was in the African calibers. Of course, the direct consequences to the shooter of poor bullet performance on an African hunt are much easier to visualize.

In the U.S., John Nosler developed the partition bullet and brought it into general usage. But Nosler's bullets were available only to reloaders, and as late as the mid-60s, no major manufacturer used Noslers in factory ammunition.

I remember getting letters back then asking whether any other bullets performed like Noslers without costing as much. After all, Nosler partition bullets cost about a dime each at that time. That seemed like a lot to folks who were used to paying no more than a nickel for any other bullet of the same weight. These folks didn't seem to realize that it's the worst sort of economy to accept poor performance to save a few cents per bullet. Thirty years ago it amazed me to see how many hunters couldn't understand that.

The results obtained with the Nosler, and other premium performance hunting bullets that followed, gradually convinced hunters that these "expensive" bullets were a bargain because they produced good kills. But the benefits of these bullets were still limited to the hunters who loaded their own ammo. As time went on the benefits of good bullets became clearer to an increasing percentage of hunters. With a market established, it wasn't long before the custom reloaders began offering ammunition loaded with premium bullets.

When the ammo factories saw custom reloaders cutting into their sales they began to get the picture. Maybe a market really existed for ammunition loaded with premium bullets. From a tentative start with one premium loading, the mainline factories now offer more and more choices of premium bullets. Today these choices include not only specialty bullets furnished by individual makers, but improved performance bullet designs produced by the ammo factories themselves. The increased availability of premium bullets is mostly responsible for the quantum jump in the variety of ammunition offered today.

The question of *which* premium bullet to use goes beyond the scope of this book. So many specialized high-performance bullets are now available in factory ammunition that it isn't possible to give meaningful advice about which bullet might work best for you without testing them in your specific hunting conditions. Several different brands might very well give you nearly identical performance, but that's a good kind of problem. If you can't tell the difference, it really comes down to which of two or three brands is the easiest to locate.

This book can help narrow your choices to a few promising candidates. With the list narrowed down you can check with manufacturers or with gun shops in your area for more information. When you find a bullet that works well for you, my advice is to stick with it. There's no point switching around if you are getting good results unless you just enjoy trying new things.

Standardization

Only about 140 years have passed since breechloading guns that fired ammunition contained in metal cartridge cases came into common use. The first of these cartridges were rimfire rounds with about .50 caliber projectiles. Soon after, the centerfire primer system took over and continues to dominate. All the early centerfire cartridges were loaded with black powder, but after about 1890 nitro (smokeless) powders made their appearance and soon became the product of choice.

Smokeless powder resulted in greatly increased performance and made cleaning your gun after firing less critical. This improved performance came at the price of significantly increased working pressures. As the government became more and more intrusive, U.S. ammunition makers of the early 1900s recognized that sooner or later they would have to adopt industry standards or be subject to the same type of government regulation that was beginning in Europe.

Ultimately, the Small Arms and Ammunition Manufacturers' Institute was formed in the U.S. SAAMI, as the group is called, is a voluntary organization. You don't have to be a member of SAAMI to manufacture ammunition in the U.S. Members need not conform to SAAMI standards. However, for liability reasons, a manufacturer would be extremely foolish to make a product that did not follow the collective experience of SAAMI with regard to chamber pressure.

Besides velocity and chamber pressure standards, SAAMI also distributes dimensional standards for both cartridges and chambers. It's easy to see the value of the dimensional standards. When you go out to buy ammunition for your gun you want it to fit in that gun's chamber. This is an important cooperative effort. Imagine the chaos that would result if every gun and ammunition manufacturer worked to its own idea of the correct dimensions. A proprietary cartridge doesn't undergo this level of formal control and doesn't need to until it ceases to be proprietary and more than one company makes guns and ammunition for the caliber.

In Europe, an organization called Commission Internationale Permanente (CIP) controls most ammunition. CIP's approach to the standardization of ammunition performance seems to be that they will mandate maximum average chamber pressures, but allow individual manufacturers to load any bullet weight to any velocity desired as long as the company observes the maximum average pressure limits. From a pure "blow up the gun" standpoint, controlling maximum average pressure is all that matters. For European manufacturers, conforming to CIP standards is often a matter of law; it's not voluntary in many countries.

Unlike CIP, SAAMI specifications do control velocities and in doing so, specify the bullet weights associated with each of these standard velocities. The tolerance on the velocities is a whopping 90 feet per second (fps). This means that if a particular cartridge and bullet weight have a nominal velocity of 2,700 fps, the ammunition conforms to the standard if the average velocity for the lot is between 2,610 and 2,790 fps. No ammunition I know of has shot-to-shot variations of 180 fps. It would be pretty awful stuff. But if a manufacturer makes up a run of ammunition that turns out to have an average velocity of, let's say, 2,615 fps when the nominal is 2,700 fps, and other characteristics (especially pressure) are nominal, the ammunition still conforms to SAAMI standards.

Several ammunition companies have developed new high energy propellants or highly specialized loading techniques that allow them to load some calibers to as much as 200 fps faster than standard velocity levels without exceeding allowable pressures. This high performance ammunition offers a way to get near-magnum performance from a "standard" rifle.

Energy vs. Momentum —
The "Great" Debate

It started with hunters. There exists a genuine difference of opinion between those who believe that high velocity is "everything" (the higher the striking velocity the better), and those who believe that the best measure of effectiveness is bullet weight (and perhaps the size of the hole the bullet makes), provided the striking velocity meets some minimum standard. It's pretty obvious that neither position, as simplified above, is a perfect measure of effectiveness. Within the last fifteen years or so, this debate has spilled over from the hunting fields into the city streets and has become an important factor in selecting ammunition for self-defense application.

Because the user has a choice of bullet weight for almost every specific factory cartridge, this debate has become a problem for everyone who buys ammunition. The debate can be characterized as "light and fast" vs. "heavy and slow." In physics terminology, it comes down to whether a cartridge's effectiveness is more nearly comparable to its energy than to its momentum. Let's take a closer look at these terms. Energy is defined as one-half of mass times the square of velocity. As long as we confine our discussion to the earth (I understand there's not much to hunt on the moon), we can think of mass as being the same as weight. Momentum is defined as mass times velocity. When you look at these two definitions, you see that energy is proportional to velocity squared (multiplied by itself), and momentum is proportional to velocity *to the first power* (no multiplier). Thus, energy puts a premium on velocity, and momentum does not. So, if you are on the side of light and fast, you believe that energy is the better measure of effectiveness when choosing a hunting cartridge.

In the early days, the heavy and slow school seems to have dominated professional British African hunters. This school of thought was responsible for pushing the African guns into some impressively large calibers. John "Pondoro" Taylor wanted a measure of cartridge effectiveness that he believed reflected his real world. He finally settled on a measure that is bullet weight (pounds) times velocity (fps) times the bullet diameter (inches), which became known as the Taylor Knock-Out Values. The data for each individual cartridge in the book shows both the energy and the Taylor KO Values of the bullet at various ranges.

If you take either measure to extremes you will find that they both fall apart. The particles (electrons or some such little things) fired into patients to break up kidney stones are more energetic than bullets because they are traveling tens or even hundreds of thousands of feet per second. These highly energetic but very light particles break up the stones but don't kill the patient, clearly demonstrating that energy isn't a perfect measure of killing power. At the same time, a professional football quarterback can put more momentum (or Taylor Index for that matter) on a thrown football than many guns can put onto their bullets. Since we don't lose a dozen or so wide receivers each weekend, momentum is obviously not a perfect measure of killing power. Part of the explanation is that neither measure—energy or momentum—by itself takes bullet construction into account. The terminal performance of the bullet on the target is at least as important as which measure you prefer.

When the military looks at the effectiveness of weapon systems, one factor that enters the calculation is the probability of a kill for each shot. However, the probability of a kill depends upon two factors: the probability of a hit and the probability of a kill, given a hit. The probability of a hit depends upon many things, including the accuracy of the shooter and his equipment and, of course, the accuracy of the bullet. Velocity plays a part in the probability of a hit because higher velocity results in flatter trajectory and reduced wind drift.

Given a hit, the probability of a kill depends heavily on bullet construction and striking velocity. It is generally accepted that a bullet must penetrate deeply enough to reach a vital organ for it to be effective. It must also leave a bullet path large enough to provide a conduit for blood to "drain." This definition of how the bullet should perform leads us to favor our current crop of high-performance hollow point and controlled expansion bullets.

At least two hunting applications seem to contradict conventional wisdom. The first is light varmint hunting. In varmint hunting, a hit is not a foregone conclusion. A two-inch target at three hundred yards isn't all that easy to hit, and it takes an accurate bullet to even get a hit. Still, almost any hit with nearly any bullet will produce a kill.

In the foregoing example, bullet performance after the hit isn't nearly as important as getting a hit in the first place. When we go through the probability of a kill equation, we find that—in this application—the hit probability is the controlling factor.

A certain class of heavy, and by implication, dangerous, game is so tough-skinned that conventional expanding bullets can't achieve the required penetration. Getting a hit is not as difficult as penetrating a vital organ. For this class of game, most hunters conclude that solid bullets or bullets with exceptionally thick jackets, possibly with a core of compressed powdered tungsten, give the best performance. Within broad limits, accuracy doesn't matter.

It isn't possible to generalize about the "best" bullet for every application, or to come up with a single "best" caliber. In the final analysis, the shooter has to do his homework. He should look at the printed data and talk to other shooters to see what they are using. Then he should try his selection under his own field conditions. After all, performance in the field is the only thing that really matters.

Ballistics—Trajectory and All That Good Stuff

If you never take a shot beyond one hundred yards or so, you can skip this chapter. But anyone, whether hunter or target shooter, who is even thinking about firing at longer ranges, should have at least a basic idea of why a bullet flies the way it does. Let's begin with the concept of a bullet that is fired in a more or less horizontal direction—the way 99.9 percent of all bullets are fired. After the bullet leaves the gun it encounters two major external forces. One is the resistance of air to the passage of the bullet, and the other is the force of gravity. As you can undoubtedly guess, air resistance slows the bullet, and gravity pulls it down. The big question is how much of each.

If we start with the gravity business, the classic comparison is a bullet fired horizontally and another bullet dropped from the height of the gun at the same time the gun is fired. According to theory, they would both reach the ground at the same time. This is true only in an oversimplified sense. In the real world, the fired bullet ends up getting "lift" from the air much as a modern ski-jumper gets "lift" by laying out his body over the tips of his skis. Lift reduces the rate of bullet drop, but air resistance plays a much more important role than simply reducing the amount of bullet drop. Air resistance slows the bullet soon after it leaves the muzzle. The rate of slowing—deceleration—at any time during the flight depends on the speed of the bullet at that moment. Near the muzzle, deceleration is relatively significant, but as the bullet goes down the range the rate of deceleration diminishes. Near the maximum range of the gun, or if the bullet is fired in a near-vertical direction, the bullet slows until it reaches the top of its trajectory. As it starts down, the bullet

speeds up again. As the bullet continues downward, it encounters a denser atmosphere and may start to slow down again, even as it continues to fall. All that happens at distances far beyond any that are useful for either hunting or target work, so we don't need to concern ourselves with those very long trajectories.

Around 1890, when smokeless powder came into general use by the military, the performance of military rifles and cannon took a quantum leap. The world's military powers began to study the flight of projectiles. Some data, mostly empirical, already existed, but suddenly the ranges and times of flight to be studied were much larger than in the days of black powder. At approximately the same time, heavier-than-air flying machines were developed, first gliders, then powered aircraft. Ballistics and aerodynamics both involve things flying through the air, so you might wonder why the two sciences proceeded down very separate paths for the best part of seventy years. There's no explanation that satisfies me, but I suppose it boils down to the fact that the two groups didn't talk to each other. In fairness, the velocity ranges of concern for each group were very different. Today, at the professional level, the speed of aeronautical things has caught up with bullet speeds, and the science of ballistics is slowly moving closer to the aerodynamic approach.

For the average shooter, the older ballistics work is still valid and probably easier to use. Let's take a look at how some of this science evolved and what it means to you today. The first big breakthrough came when various countries began to conduct firing programs with "standard" projectiles. These programs were carried out separately and each country jealously protected its own data. The concept of a "standard" projectile was a big breakthrough. The problems resulting from trying to draw meaningful comparisons of data from numerous shots is difficult even if all the projectiles are alike, so it's understandable that it becomes impossible when the data is for different projectiles. In the United States, Captain James M. Ingalls led the work. Working with his own data and earlier work by a Russian, Colonel Mayevski, Ingalls produced a table that showed what happened to the speed of a bullet as it proceeded downrange. This data started with the highest velocity Ingalls could obtain from his test gun and documented the projectile's speed as a function of time. The tables also showed how far the bullet had traveled in the previous time increments. Ingalls's second breakthrough came when he recognized that regardless of original launch speed, if the standard projectile is moving at 2,000 feet per second, the standard bullet will always slow down from 2,000 fps to 1,900 fps in the same elapsed time, covering the same distance as it does so.

Those two insights allowed the use of Ingalls's tables to predict trajectory data for any gun firing the standard projectile, no matter what the muzzle velocity. Ingalls's standard projectile was one inch in diameter and weighed one pound. It was pretty clear that something more was needed if the concept was to be useful for more than just the standard projectile, which set the stage for Ingalls's third breakthrough. That came when he saw he could "adjust" his tables by a factor that compensated for changes in bullet size, shape, and weight. This factor became known as the Ingalls's Ballistic Coefficient (C_I). If you knew a bullet's ballistic coefficient and

muzzle velocity, you could do a pretty fair job of predicting downrange performance. It wasn't long before some other bright lad found a way to predict the bullet drop when the downrange time, distance, and velocity factors were known.

Shortly after the turn of the century, a group called the Gavre Commission combined Ingalls's ballistic work with work from other countries to produce some new, slightly improved tables. The new tables recognized that the velocity decay for a flat-based projectile differed from that of a boattail projectile. The different projectile shapes were assigned to tables designated as G1, G2, G3, etc.; the "G" is for Gavre. These new tables improved the precision of the performance predictions by a small amount. The multiple forms of ballistic coefficient generated a new problem. The ballistic coefficient for a projectile that uses the G1 table cannot be compared with the coefficient for a projectile that uses the G2 table. That isn't too bad if you are working with one or two different bullets, but it becomes a nightmare as the number of different bullet shapes increases.

Within the last ten or fifteen years, the various ammunition and bullet manufacturers have agreed to standardize the equivalent of G1 coefficients for all bullets because any ballistic prediction is never absolutely perfect. The error that results is quite small for all realistic ranges. As they say in aerospace, the results are "close enough for government work." By sticking to one type of coefficient, you can look at the coefficients for a variety of bullets and know that a coefficient of 0.400 is always " better" than a coefficient of 0.300. All performance tables in this book are based on G1 coefficients.

Maximum Effective and Point-Blank Ranges

Two ballistic concepts are much more important to hunters than to target shooters: Maximum Effective Range (MER) and Maximum Point-Blank Range (MPBR). These two ranges are not the same. MPBR is the maximum range at which a gun will keep its bullets within a given distance of the aim point without changing the sights or "holding off." In its pure form it really doesn't depend on the ability of the shooter, only his equipment.

MER, on the other hand, depends heavily on the shooter. By my definition, MER is the longest range at which a shooter can keep his bullets within a circle of given size. To do this he can adjust the sights, hold off, or use any other means at his disposal to get his hit. Any shooter has a variety of MERs depending on the equipment he is using, the type of rest he has available, and what the weather—especially the wind—is doing.

Maximum Effective Range

Let's look at Maximum Effective Range (MER) in more detail. I've done this test along with other shooters of different skill levels. Take a paper plate of any convenient size (six- or eight-inches diameter will do for a start) and staple the plate to a stick. Start by using any gun with iron sights from a freestanding position and see how far out can you can go and still keep 9 out of 10 shots on the plate. If you are an "average" shot you may have trouble keeping nine out of ten on the plate at fifty yards. This test is most valid if done under simulated hunting conditions, starting with a cold gun and without any shooting prior to your first shot. If you use a gun with a scope instead of the iron sights you might move the plate out a bit farther.

Now, let's take another step. If you fire from a good rest with a flat-shooting gun using a scope you might be able to do the nine out of ten thing out to 200 or even 300 yards. If you aren't a practiced long-range shooter it's unlikely you'll be able to get out much beyond 300 yards. These tests are only for a stationary target. Could you do better on a moving target? Few of us can! If the target is presented at ranges other than the even 50- or 100-yard increments, the problem gets a lot harder especially when the range is over 200 yards, and is nearly impossible beyond 300 yards.

What does this test represent? The size of the plate represents the lethal area of deer-size game. If you can't reliably put your shots into the lethal area beyond a given range then you shouldn't be taking a shot at game under those conditions. It is bad enough to miss completely, but it is far worse to gut-shoot a buck and have it run off too fast and too far to track, only to die somewhere in the brush and be wasted. Maximum Effective Range depends far more on the shooter, his equipment, and the conditions under which the shot was taken than on the details of the cartridge's ballistics.

Maximum Point-Blank Range

The concept of Maximum Point-Blank Range (MPBR) is that for any given lethal zone diameter, any gun can be "zeroed" for a certain distance so the trajectory between the first crossing of the sight line (for practical purposes, from the gun) and the zero range never rises above the sight line by more than the radius of the lethal area. Then from the zero range to MPBR, the bullet's trajectory descends below the sight line until the impact point at MPBR is one lethal area radius below the sight line. The idea is that for any range out to the MPBR, the bullet will always strike within this lethal radius.

7

The shooter will not have to hold high or low; instead he can always hold dead on. For example, using a .22-250 for varmints with a two-inch diameter lethal circle, the bullet will strike one inch high at about 125 yards if you have the rifle zeroed for 200 yards. The MPBR for this example is 230 yards. If you have a lethal circle eight inches in diameter, the four-inch-high point is at about 170 yards with a 275 yard zero and a MPBR of 370 yards. You can see that the MPBR depends heavily on the size of the lethal circle.

MPBR is not without controversy. The controversy is not about the concept itself or even the actual MPBR numbers; it's about what happens in the field. I know two professional guides who are 180 degrees apart on this subject. One loves the idea. He has the client demonstrate where the client's gun is zeroed before the hunt. The guide judges the range to the target and instructs the client to hold dead on if the guide decides the range is within MPBR. The idea of Maximum Effective Range also affects his decision whether to tell the client to shoot. For most shooters with modern guns, the Maximum Effective Range is shorter than the MPBR, sometimes very much shorter.

The second professional guide says that in his experience the MPBR idea may be technically correct, but is terrible in practice. No matter where he tells the client to hold, the client makes his own adjustment for range. Furthermore, the client almost always overestimates the range. Holding high when the real range is shorter (often much shorter) than the estimated range and shorter than the zero range (where the trajectory is above the sight line) far too often means a miss over the back of the game.

This clearly tells me that if the shooter can determine the range accurately—by lots of practice, by using a range finder, or by listening to his guide—AND if he knows where his gun will shoot at that range, AND if he can hold well enough, he will get good hits. If you don't hold off, the MPBR concept puts an upper limit on how far you should attempt to shoot. If you want to hold off, you need to know both the range to the target and how high you must hold to get hits at that range. That knowledge doesn't come without lots and lots of practice. Finally, given a good hit, the rest depends on the quality of the bullet. If the bullet doesn't perform, everything else is wasted.

The tables below list MPBRs for bullets with assorted ballistic coefficients at different muzzle velocities, and for two- and six-inch lethal areas. You may wonder why we haven't listed bullet weight in the tabulated data. The fact is that any bullet with a ballistic coefficient of 0.350, for example, launched at any given muzzle velocity will fly along the same trajectory path regardless of its weight. Bullet weight does affect ballistic coefficient to the extent that ballistic coefficient equals sectional density divided by the bullet's form (shape) factor, and sectional density is bullet weight divided by the bullet diameter squared. The caliber of the gun doesn't matter in the table, but it's also indirectly involved in two ways. Small calibers have lighter bullets that need better form factors to achieve the same ballistic coefficient as a heavier bullet. Also, smaller caliber guns generally produce higher velocities than the larger calibers. These tables are calculated using a sight height above the bore line of 1.5 inches, which is pretty standard for most scope-sighted rifles. A third table shows what happens if the gun has iron sights 0.9 inches above the bore line.

Start with the table for the correct lethal zone diameter (two-inch or six-inch). Find the approximate ballistic coefficient for your bullet and pick the line closest to your muzzle velocity. Read across the table to find the range where the bullet first crosses the line of sight (going up), the distance to the high point of the trajectory, the range at which you should zero your rifle (where the bullet comes down to cross the line of sight for the second time), and finally, the Maximum Point-Blank Range.

For example, let's look at MPBR for a .300 Winchester firing 180-grain Hornady ammunition. The ballistic coefficient of the ammunition is 0.436 and the nominal muzzle velocity is 2,960 fps. We will use the chart for scope sights and a six-inch lethal zone. In the six-inch table we use a ballistic coefficient (BC) of 0.400. If you look at the listing for a BC of 0.500 you will find that large changes in the BC number don't make a huge difference in the MPBR data. Likewise, use the line for 3,000 fps. Again that's close enough to 2,960. The first crossing occurs at 25 yards (all data are rounded to the closest five yards), the high point is at 140 yards, the zero range is 250 yards, and the MPBR is 290 yards.

If the rifle had iron sights the numbers would be: first crossing—15 yards, high point—130 yards, zero range—240 yards, and MPBR—285 yards. As you can see, the height of the sight above the bore line does change the numbers a little. I wonder how many people can keep nine or ten shots in six inches at 325 yards using a rifle with open iron sights. I'll wager there aren't many. I sure can't.

There's Always a Trade-off

When we select ammunition for a specific application there's always a trade-off. If we can have the luxury of selecting the very "best" gun for the application the trade-offs are lessened, but few of us are fortunate enough to have guns for every possible situation. For certain applications, such as varmint shooting or target work, we can trade a hunting bullet's effectiveness for accuracy. For general hunting, the last little bit of accuracy, or for that matter, the last little bit of ballistic coefficient, doesn't justify trading away bullet performance.

In the final analysis only you can decide which way to lean on each of these trades. You can get help from various sources—friends, gun shop employees, and especially professional guides. You then have to evaluate just what the advice from each source is worth. The guide probably has the most to lose if he gives you bad advice. If your hunt isn't successful you won't be back.

This book provides the technical information on cartridge performance you need to help you decide, from a purely technical standpoint, which trades are best. We don't even attempt to take a stand on light and fast vs. heavy and slow. That's a fundamental choice you must make for yourself: Good luck and good shooting!

Maximum Point-Blank Range
Scope Sight
Use This Table For 2-inch-Diameter Lethal Zone (Varmint Shooting)

Ballistic Coefficient	Muzzle Velocity fps	First LOS Crossing yards	High Point yards	"Zero" Range yards	Max. Point Blank Range yards
0.200	2000	25	70	110	125
	2500	35	85	135	155
	3000	40	105	160	185
	3500	45	120	185	210
	4000	50	135	210	235
0.300	2000	25	75	115	130
	2500	35	85	140	160
	3000	40	105	165	190
	3500	45	120	195	220
	4000	50	140	220	250
0.400	2000	25	75	115	135
	2500	35	85	145	170
	3000	40	110	170	200
	3500	45	125	200	230
	4000	55	140	225	260
0.500	2000	25	75	120	135
	2500	35	90	145	170
	3000	40	110	175	230
	3500	45	125	200	230
	4000	55	145	230	265

Maximum Point-Blank Range
Scope Sight
Use This Table For 6-inch-Diameter Lethal Zone (Large-Game Shooting)

Ballistic Coefficient	Muzzle Velocity fps	First LOS Crossing yards	High Point yards	"Zero" Range yards	Max. Point Blank Range yards
0.200	2000	20	90	155	180
	2500	20	110	190	220
	3000	25	130	225	260
	3500	30	150	260	300
	4000	35	165	290	335
0.300	2000	20	95	165	195
	2500	20	115	205	235
	3000	25	140	240	280
	3500	30	160	275	320
	4000	35	180	310	360
0.400	2000	20	95	170	200
	2500	20	115	210	245
	3000	25	140	250	290
	3500	30	160	285	335
	4000	35	185	325	375
0.500	2000	20	100	175	205
	2500	25	120	215	250
	3000	25	140	255	300
	3500	30	165	295	345
	4000	35	190	330	390

Maximum Point-Blank Range
Iron Sights
Use This Table For 6-inch-Diameter Lethal Zone (Large-Game Shooting)

Ballistic Coefficient	Muzzle Velocity fps	First LOS Crossing yards	High Point yards	"Zero" Range yards	Max. Point Blank Range yards
0.200	2000	10	85	150	175
	2500	15	105	185	220
	3000	15	125	220	255
	3500	20	140	250	290
	4000	20	160	280	325
0.300	2000	10	85	160	185
	2500	15	110	195	230
	3000	15	130	235	275
	3500	20	150	270	315
	4000	20	170	300	355
0.400	2000	10	90	165	195
	2500	15	110	200	240
	3000	15	130	240	285
	3500	20	150	275	325
	4000	20	175	310	370
0.500	2000	10	90	165	200
	2500	15	115	205	245
	3000	15	130	245	290
	3500	20	155	285	335
	4000	25	175	320	380

CARTRIDGES FOR DEER AND ELK

by
Colonel Craig T. Boddington

The author used a .375 H&H to take this bull elk on the Jicarilla Apache Reservation. The .375's level of power is needed, and there are certainly flatter-shooting cartridges, but the .375 drops elk with authority and should not be overlooked as a viable choice.

Deer and elk cartridges is a large subject, but you can make it as simple or as complex as you like. The vast majority of American hunters are deer hunters. This is because our North American deer are the most plentiful and readily available big-game animals in the entire world. Millions of eastern hunters are whitetail hunters, and hundreds of thousands of westerners pursue the mule deer and other western varieties. After the various deer, the American elk or wapiti is the most-pursued North American game. So if we find a way to encapsulate sound guidance on choosing cartridges for hunting elk and deer in the next few pages, we will probably serve the needs of the vast majority of our readers.

Actually, we'll do a whole lot more than that. North America's deer, from the small Coues whitetails up through the blacktails, average-sized whitetails, average-sized mule deer, on up to really large white-tailed and mule deer range from about 100 pounds on up to 350 pounds or more. The country they inhabit and in which they are hunted varies from dense underbrush and forest to plains, deserts, and high mountains. We can talk about deer rifles and cartridges, but in reality the requirements are the same for hunting thin-skinned non dangerous game throughout the world. A good eastern whitetail rifle is a pretty good choice for hunting the full range of small and mid-sized African antelope in relatively thick country, such as the heavy thornbush that covers most of southern Africa. A rifle that is ideal for the small Coues white-tailed in the Southwest's desert mountains will be excellent for pronghorn on the Great Plains and springbok on the Kalahari. A rifle that is ideal for mule deer in the high country is probably equally ideal for wild sheep and goats anywhere in the world.

Similarly, when we talk about perfect elk rifles and cartridges, we do not imply that an elk rifle is only an elk rifle. Our wapiti is just a big deer, but he is also very strong and tenacious; he is a tough customer and often requires hard hunting. We pick our elk rifles based not only on the animal, but also on the terrain. An elk rifle that's ideal for jackpine jungles, oakbrush thickets, and the Pacific Northwest's rainforests is probably not the ideal elk rifle for high Alpine meadows and sagebrush foothills. You must always match the cartridge to the terrain, but a cartridge adequate for elk is almost certainly a good moose cartridge. Also, it is probably not a bad choice for most bear hunting, and will be well-suited for the larger African plains game, such as wildebeest, zebra, sable, roan, kudu, oryx, and such.

First we'll talk about deer cartridges; then we'll talk about elk cartridges. Just keep in mind that in place of deer, you can think about the myriad other game that range from about 100 to 300 pounds. This game may be hunted in country that requires short, medium, and long shots, which influences cartridge selection just as much, if not more, than the size of the game. Likewise, when we speak of elk cartridges, we're talking about big, tough game

ranging from 400 pounds to upwards of half a ton—the only restriction being that we're talking about nondangerous game. Again, you'll find elk cartridges for close cover and for open country, and some that will cover the gamut of normal hunting situations.

Whether we're talking about deer or elk, your choice should be dictated by the kind of shooting opportunity, your hunting technique, and the terrain. The late great gunwriter, Colonel Townsend Whelen, once theorized that you should have 1000 ft-lbs of energy at the target to take deer cleanly. Bullet weight, caliber, and design also come into play, and shot placement is far more critical than any data that can be gleaned from any chart in this or any other volume. Even so, Whelen's "1000 ft-lbs at the animal" rule has always seemed a sensible minimum for deer. For elk, I figure that number should be doubled. I have always used these rules when choosing my own cartridges, and they are reflected in the following general guidelines.

WHITE-TAILED DEER

Approximately 25 million white-tailed deer inhabit North America, ranging from Mexico almost to Canada's treeline, and from the Atlantic almost to the Pacific in some 30 recognized subspecies. There are another eight subspecies in Central and South America. As mentioned, white-tailed deer vary greatly in size, and hunting them spans almost the full gamut of potential habitat, the only possible exception being very high mountains above the timberline.

Whitetail cartridges generally start at about 6mm and go on up to around .30 caliber. However, in order to talk intelligently about cartridges for white-tailed deer, it is necessary to

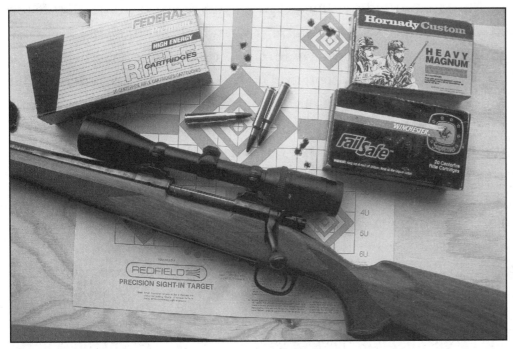

This Winchester Model 70 in .338 Winchester Magnum is the author's idea of a perfect all-around elk rifle. The .338 has the advantage of a good selection of factory loads featuring superb elk bullets.

that the blunt-nosed, large-caliber slugs associated with brush cartridges may not be quite as good at getting through obstructions as sharp-pointed bullets from more versatile calibers. Even so, the legend of the brush cartridges persists, and they do have a purpose in whitetail hunting.

A list of brush cartridges generally starts with the time-honored .30-30 and includes other old favorites like the .35 Remington and .45-70, along with a very few newer cartridges like the .356 and .375 Winchester and the .444 Marlin. These are generally short-range cartridges for two reasons. First, all of these rounds share high arcing trajectory curves that make shot placement very difficult at even medium range. Second, because of low initial velocity and poor bullet aerodynamics, energy figures also drop rapidly.

Obviously, the larger calibers in this group hit very hard, but even the .30-30, despite its modest paper ballistics, is extremely effective on deer-sized game. Part of the reason for this is the flat-nosed or very blunt, round-nosed bullets traditionally loaded in these cartridges (mandatory in tubular-magazine rifles!) transfer energy very rapidly, delivering a heavy blow that often seems disproportionate to ballistics charts.

These cartridges are at their best within 100 yards, and are difficult to use at much

find out exactly where the hunt will take place, what the local habitat is like, what hunting technique will be employed, and what the object is. For instance, centerfire .22s are legal in many states. Their use is controversial, but cartridges such as the .223 and .22-250, loaded with the heavy-for-caliber bullets available today are extremely effective if you pick your shots. I think the .22s are poor choices for serious trophy hunters. "Big buck" hunters must also pick their shots, of course, but a trophy hunter wants to be able to take any reasonable shot, so he needs a bigger cartridge firing a heavier bullet. Hunters who expect to take smaller-bodied deer and don't mind waiting for an ideal shot presentation will find the .22 center-fires dramatically effective, but they are not general-purpose whitetail cartridges.

On the other end of the spectrum, neither are the so-called "brush cartridges." This is a misnomer. No bullet is particularly good at "bucking brush," and tests usually suggest more than 150 yards, so they are not suited to open country or mixed cover where a longish shot is possible. On the other hand, these cartridges are excellent for stand hunting or still hunting in very thick cover. Most hunters who use them swear by them because they drop deer with dramatic efficiency, especially the larger calibers in this group.

Under most circumstances, however, whitetail hunters are best-served by a versatile cartridge that can handle a wide range of shooting opportunities. Again, to my thinking this starts with the 6mms—.243 Winchester and 6mm Remington—and goes up to the magnum .30s. This is a wide spectrum, and exactly where *your* best choice lies depends in part on where you hunt your whitetails. I think the 6mms, .25s, and milder 6.5s (like the .260 Remington and 6.5x55) are best for smaller-bodied deer in mixed cover. To me, this means that even a big buck is unlikely to exceed 200 pounds, and while longish shots may be necessary, they are not likely to have to reach much beyond 250 or 300 yards. Texas is a good example. Texas whitetails can grow wonderful antlers, but they are small-bodied. Most hunting is done from stands, and whether in the rolling hill country or overlooking the endless *senderos* of the brush country, the typical Texas whitetail stand offers a variety of shots. The .25-06 is one of the most popular cartridges among Texas whitetail hunters, and it is ideal indeed.

Although the fast 6mms and .25s shoot quite flat, I don't see them as good choices for the largest-bodied whitetails, especially in open country. This also applies to "smaller" 6.5s such as the .260 Remington and 6.5x55. The reason is simple. At some point on the near or far side of 300 yards, the energy levels are

either below or very close to that 1000 ft-lbs minimum. I want at least that much energy carried to whatever distance I am likely to shoot, and on big-bodied northern and plains whitetails that can weigh 300 pounds and more, I prefer even more energy.

This takes us to the other side of the general eligibility range of whitetail cartridges— the fast, large-cased "magnum" .30s. Before you start howling, I agree that you don't *need* a magnum, .30 or otherwise, to hunt whitetails or any other deer. However, there exist some combinations of extra-large-bodied deer and very open country where the additional downrange energy from a fast .30 can come in handy. Good examples are the wheat fields and prairie pothole country of Alberta and Saskatchewan, and the wide-open spaces of the Great Plains. This past fall I was offered a long and difficult cross-canyon shot in western Kansas. A host of cartridges could have done the job, but the simple fact that I was carrying a .300 Weatherby Magnum made the "shoot-don't shoot" decision simple, and I got the buck.

The combination of big bucks and big country isn't especially rare as whitetails continue to flourish in agricultural areas and to expand westward. Even so, most terrain does not necessitate the added reach that a magnum .30 offers. Under most conditions, the indomitable triad—the .270, .280, and .30-06— can handle any shooting opportunity likely to present itself. These three cartridges stand out in my mind as the ideal choices for hunting "any deer under any conditions," especially whitetails. You could certainly add a number of only slightly *less* capable cartridges, such as the 7mm-08 Remington, 7x57 Mauser, and .308 Winchester. You could also add some slightly *more* capable cartridges, such as the .264 Winchester Magnum, .270 Weatherby Magnum, and all of the 7mm magnums. Collectively, this makes a broad group. All, with the proper choice of bullet and load, are capable of projecting 1000 foot/pound and more to at least 400 yards. Very few of us really need more than that—and even fewer have any business attempting shots at longer distances.

COUES WHITETAILS

The Coues whitetail of the arid Southwest desert mountains is only one of the many whitetail subspecies singled out for a separate category by all the trophy record books. In terms of choosing cartridges, I agree with this, because hunting the Coues whitetail is indeed a special and unique set of circumstances. A few paragraphs earlier I mentioned some scenarios where big deer are hunted in very big country. However, the Coues whitetail is a *very small* deer that is hunted in big country. It is not necessary to stretch a barrel out of proportion to take a Coues whitetail, but in my experience shots at Coues whitetail are, on average, longer than shots at all the rest of our deer. The bigger the buck, the longer the shot is likely to be.

I have hunted Coues whitetails with the .270, .280, .30-06, 7mm Remington Magnum, .300 Winchester and Weatherby Magnums, and even the 8mm Remington Magnum. Any of the faster, flatter shooting "whitetail cartridges" will work, but serious Coues deer hunters are very likely to carry fast .30s. This is not necessarily because they need the bullet energy, but simply because an aerodynamic 180-grain, .30-caliber bullet does such a wonderful job of bucking those

hard-to-judge mountain breezes.

That said, I am not at all convinced that a magnum .30 is the best choice, but I am convinced that the farther you can shoot with confidence and accuracy, the better off you are with Coues whitetails. Very fast 6.5s, such as the .264 Winchester Magnum and Lazzeroni's 6.71 Blackbird, are ideal. Likewise are the very fast 7mms, from the 7mm Remington Magnum on up to Lazzeroni's 7.21 Firehawk, the 7mm Dakota Magnum, and the 7mm STW. One mustn't leave out the superb .270 Weatherby Magnum, another ideal choice for these very small deer in very big country.

MULE DEER

The largest whitetails are every bit as big as the largest mule deer. However, the average mule deer buck taken by hunters will surely outweigh the average white-tailed buck harvested. Special circumstances occur where shooting opportunities at whitetails are longer than most shooting opportunities at mule deer. However, throughout their range, the average shot at a mule deer is considerably longer than the average shot at a whitetail. What does that mean? Simply that mule deer hunting generally entails longer shots at bigger-bodied deer than the average whitetail hunter is used to. Relatively little mule deer hunting is done in the close cover that characterizes quite a lot of white-tail hunting.

This does not mean that mule deer hunting is generally long-range shooting. If you're a serious long-range shooter, you can always find a way to employ your skills, but in my experience mule deer are generally more "stalkable" than whitetails. In their typically open country with a lot of up-and-down relief,

The author's David Miller 7mm Remington Magnum was used to take this desert mule deer in Sonora.

there is often a limit to how close you can stalk. I have taken a few mule deer at very long range, and a few at very close range, but to my mind the "normal" shot is somewhere between 200 and 300 yards. This means my general-purpose whitetail cartridges, represented by the .270, .280, and .30-06, but including a host of slightly slower and faster cartridges, are also suitable for hunting mule deer.

Although I have taken mule deer at long range, in my experience the necessity for long-range shooting is much rarer than it is with whitetails. If that is the case, and I believe it is, then your need for a magnum .30 is no greater with mule deer than it is with whitetails. That said, mule deer hunt-ing—especially for the millions of eastern whitetail hunters—takes us into big, open, and often unfamiliar country where judging range is difficult and confidence in your rifle is at a premium. A good .270, .280, or .30-06 will handle almost all mule deer hunting situations, shooting flat enough and carrying as much bullet energy as far as most of us have any business shooting. However, in that big, open country something a bit faster and flatter can give you immeasurable and invaluable confidence. A magnum .30 will do that, but all things considered, I believe the fast 7mms, from the 7mm Remington Magnum upward, are probably the most ideal for hunting mule deer.

COLUMBIAN BLACK-TAILED DEER

For some years now, the various record books have separated the Columbian black-tailed deer of coastal California, Oregon, and Washington from the Sitka black-tailed deer of northwestern B.C., southeastern Alaska, and the offshore islands. I will do the same because the deer are very different. The "southern" black-tailed deer are small-bodied, not as small as Coues whitetails, but much smaller than mature whitetails and average-sized mule deer.

The country is also "smaller" than most mule deer country throughout the West. Blacktails are homebodies, and although some herds make significant migrations from summer to winter range, on average their territories are smaller. Their country is also generally more compact, ranging from very heavy forests in the Pacific Northwest to oak grassland ridges cut by poison-oak-choked canyons in California. Blacktail hunters in the rain forests of coastal Washington and Oregon often hunt blacktails just like close-cover whitetails, by stand-hunting along known trails with shots very close or not at all. Farther inland, and in most of California's blacktail range, hunting is generally by glassing and stalking, just like mule deer hunting except the country is such that long shots are fairly unusual.

The size of the deer and the distance of the shots generally call for lighter calibers, but this is not universal. In the really thick stuff of coastal Washington and Oregon, hunters often use large-caliber "brush cartridges," which makes a lot of sense. In California and central Oregon, the .243 is probably the favorite blacktail cartridge. It's a good choice, as is just about any "deer cartridge" between 6mm and 7mm. My own favorites include the .270 and 7x57, but even these great cartridges are really overpowered (if there is such a thing!) for most blacktail hunting. Mild-mannered cartridges like the .250 Savage, .257 Roberts, .260 Remington, and 6.5x55 are also excellent for Columbian blacktail.

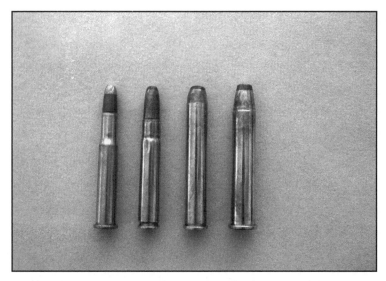

Left to right: .30-30 Winchester, .358 Winchester, .444 Marlin, .45-70. These are a few of the so-called "brush cartridges." They don't really buck brush any better than anything else, but their heavy, blunt-nosed slugs deliver a heavy blow and anchor deer with authority.

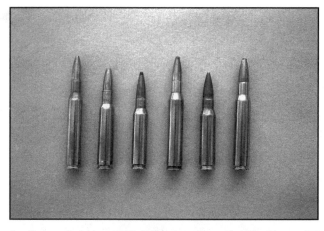

Left to right: .270 Winchester, 7x57, 7mm-08 Remington, .280 Remington, .308 Winchester, .30-06 Springfield. Campfire ballistics arguments are an enjoyable pastime, but the truth is that these fine cartridges are so similar in performance on deer-sized game that they could be used interchangeably without their user ever knowing the difference.

SITKA BLACK-TAILED DEER

I understand that the black-tailed deer of northern B.C. and coastal Alaska are smallish deer. This I can't say for sure, but I *can* say that the Sitka blacktails of Kodiak and some of Alaska's other islands are absolute brutes. These are stocky deer that look like barrels with legs, and their size is about twice that of the Columbian blacktails I am more familiar with. Also, there are at least two altogether different kinds of Sitka blacktail hunting. Farther south, the forest is incredibly thick and grows almost to the beach. Shooting is close. This is also true farther north in the early season, when the grasses and other annuals are lush and thick. Later on, when winter sets in, the grass and shrubs turn brown and are beaten down by wind and snow. Then the slopes become wide open, and shooting distances are much farther.

There is yet another consideration throughout this country: Sitka blacktails share their habitat with coastal grizzlies and Alaskan brown bear. In thick cover you always face the chance of a close encounter with a bear, and you can be in real danger when you're packing meat. Later on, when the vegetation is down, a sharp eye and common sense should be enough to avoid trouble, but you may need to reach out quite a distance to anchor a very substantial deer. So, guns and loads for Columbian blacktails are simply too light for Sitka deer. Early in the season something on the order of a .35 Whelen or .358 makes a lot of sense. Later, when shots can be much farther, a flat-shooting cartridge like a fast 6.5 or 7mm is far better. For all-around use, a magnum .30 makes a pretty good choice—with heavy bullets early in the season and lighter, flatter-shooting loads later on.

Left to right: .240 Weatherby Magnum, .264 Weatherby Magnum, .270 Weatherby Magnum, 7mm Weatherby Magnum, .300 H&H Magnum, .308 Norman Magnum, .300 Winchester Magnum, .300 Weatherby Magnum. A belted magnum isn't essential for any deer hunting, but the smaller magnums are useful for smaller deer in open country, while those from the 7mm on up are excellent for even the largest deer in country where shots can be long.

ELK

When you step up to elk, you take a giant leap upward from the largest deer. It is quite possible for a huge whitetail or mule deer to weigh just about as much as a cow elk or spike, but a mature bull elk is a vastly different creature. Weights of 800 pounds are not uncommon, and you might find a 1000-pound elk. More important, elk are also tough creatures, generally much more tenacious of life than the much larger moose.

I don't want my words to be misconstrued; elk are not impressed by velocity, bullet weight, foot/pounds, Knock-Out Values, or whatever. The only thing that impresses an elk is shot placement, for which there is no substitute. Regardless of what you hit him with, a poorly hit elk can go a very long way. Given proper shot placement, a well-constructed bullet from a .270 can dispatch any elk ever calved. But neither the .270 nor any of the other normal deer calibers are my idea of elk cartridges.

This is a controversial subject, but I prefer significantly larger cartridges for elk. I don't base my preference on the theory that a marginal hit with a bigger cartridge will do the trick.

It will not. I base it on two concepts. First, when it comes to elk I'm not a meat hunter. An old bull is a very different animal from a cow or spike, and different from a 3½-year-old five-by-five. He's bigger, stronger, and much harder to put down. Second, knowing how difficult it is to get a shot at such a bull, I want a cartridge that can drive a bullet into the vitals from any reasonable angle. This does not mean shooting at the north end of a southbound elk. That's no shot at all on an unwounded bull. It does mean strong quartering angles, and it means shooting through small windows in the timber.

Elk hunting varies as much as deer hunting. In heavy forest, the more potent "brush cartridges" are wonderful. The old .348 Winchester and almost equally obsolete .358 Winchester are both fine choices, and after 125 years there are still no flies on the .45-70 as a close-cover elk cartridge. Most elk hunters, however, need a bit more reach. The .35 Whelen is wonderful for mixed cover and bugling hunts.

For all-around use, and in high timberline basins where shots can be long, the best elk cartridges are found among the magnums from .30 caliber up to .375. Best of the best, to me, are the .33's—.338 Winchester Magnum, .340 Weatherby Magnum, .330 Dakota, Lazzeroni's 8.59 Titan, and so forth. To these you could add the 8mm Remington Magnum and the very few fast .35s—the almost defunct .358 Norma Magnum and the wildcat (at this writing) .358 Shooting Times Alaskan (STA). These are my idea of elk cartridges. As a minimum, the 7mm magnums with 175-grain bullets, along with the .308 and .30-06 with 180-grain bullets make good starting points. Given a choice, however, I much prefer a .300 with 200-grain bullets, or even better, an 8mm Remington Magnum or one of the .33s.

BULLETS FOR DEER AND ELK

If an ideal bullet for deer *and* elk has ever been designed, I have never seen it. Compared to an elk, even the largest deer is a small, light-boned game animal. Today we have wonderful bullets, and many of us have become enamored of them. You do not need today's super-tough, deep-penetrating, ultra-controlled-expansion designs for deer hunting. You don't want a bullet that will come apart, and there are certainly bullets that are too fragile for use on deer. But you do want a bullet that will open up and do some damage. It's okay if a bullet penetrates completely. Given a choice, I'd just as soon have both an entrance and an exit wound, but I don't want the entrance and the exit to be the same diameter, indicating minimal expansion. It's also okay if a deer bullet doesn't exit on deer. As long as the bullet reaches the vitals it'll work.

Elk bullets are a different story. A bullet suited for elk *must* penetrate completely on deer-sized game (and from almost any angle); otherwise you simply won't have enough penetration for game several times larger. It's as simple as that. Elk bullets must be very tough to penetrate much heavier hide, muscle, and bone. Expansion must ultimately limit penetration, so elk bullets generally can't expand as much as ideal deer bullets. They need to stay together and retain weight in order to drive as deeply as they must.

Hunters in search of both deer and elk—or hunters who take their favorite deer or elk rifle to Africa to hunt the diverse plains game—simply cannot have the perfect bullet for everything they might encounter. Under such circumstances, common sense dictates selecting a bullet designed for the largest game you expect to encounter. Some of the very best deer bullets range from marginal to altogether unsuitable for elk-sized game. Regrettably, these distinctions cannot be found on any ballistics chart, regardless of detail. No one has yet devised a formula that properly takes bullet performance into account, and it is probably not possible to create one. Although you must sort through a fair amount of hype, most of the manufacturers today are pretty honest about the kind of performance their bullets are designed to give. Pay attention. When you select bullets for game—especially large, tough game—the best choice isn't always the fastest or the most aerodynamic!

VARMINT CARTRIDGES
by
Colonel Craig T. Boddington

A few groups shot with a factory Model 112 Savage using factory ammo. The level of accuracy delivered by today's varmint loads is simply astonishing, but you always need to experiment to discover what your rifle likes best.

The sport of varmint hunting is now at an all-time high. The reasons for this are fairly obvious. Although there are many specialists among us—sheep hunters, elk hunters, bear hunters, safari hunters, you name it—hunters as a group tend to pursue the game that is most available. In the 1920s waterfowlers comprised America's largest group of sportsmen. Market hunting, the Dust Bowl, and loss of wetlands changed that. In the postwar years, upland game was the primary pursuit across most of the land, but changing agricultural practices ended that era. Over the last 30 years the white-tailed deer's amazing population explosion has made the average American hunter a deer hunter, resulting in some 10 million deer hunters.

I don't predict a change in that anytime soon, but varminting is coming on strong. As license fees increase and bag limits and seasons shrink, more hunters are enjoying the long seasons and high-volume shooting that only varminting allows. The class of game that we call "varmints" is also increasing dramatically, creating greater opportunity. With the fur market in the basement and trapping politically incorrect, predator numbers are reaching an all-time high. With poisoning also on the outs, prairie dogs, woodchucks, and other rodents are also more plentiful than has been the case for many a year. In fact, whether for rodent or predator control, shooting is just about the only viable option, which creates opportunity. Landowners who wouldn't dream of admitting big-game or upland bird hunters are very likely to welcome a wintertime predator caller or a summer 'chuck shooter. Mind you, I am not predicting that varminting will ever catch up with deer hunting, but it is more popular now than ever, and serious varminters are among the most avid shooters in the country.

The class of cartridges that we call "varmint cartridges" is hardly new. Mild-mannered cartridges useful for dispatching pests have been with us since the dawn of the self-contained cartridge. The English called them "rook rifles," the rook being a type of crow.

23

The British form was of larger caliber and lower velocity than we are used to, but the intent was the same—a cartridge too mild for big game, but useful for dispatching rooks, badgers, and other pests.

Our first varmint cartridges—although we didn't use that term for some decades—started in the black powder era with rounds such as the .25-20 and .32-20. These cartridges achieved greater popularity after conversion to smokeless powder and still retain some following today. They are not powerful enough to be reliable on even small deer, and the lever-action rifles they were traditionally chambered for are not accurate enough for precision varminting as we know it today. Still, these old-timers are just fine for predator calling in relatively close cover.

The first cartridge that really looked like a modern varmint cartridge was the .22 Savage Hi-Power. Developed by Charles Newton for Arthur Savage's Model 99 lever action, this 1912 cartridge was probably ahead of its time. Woodchuck hunters loved it, but there weren't many of them in 1912. It propelled a heavy-for-caliber 70-grain bullet at a then-awesome 2800 fps, and the cartridge got a bad rap when too many hunters used it on game that was too large. We know today that a well-constructed .22 bullet of that weight, though probably not ideal, is quite effective on small and mid-sized deer, but 1912-vintage softpoints were not nearly as reliable as the bullets we have today. The .22 Savage Hi-Power got a lot of people thinking about centerfire .22s, but its commercial life was limited.

The .22 Hornet, which is still with us, was probably the first genuine varmint cartridge. Based on an existing black powder case, it appeared on the scene in 1932 and had the

This coyote was taken with the very fast Lazzeroni 6.71. Blackbird. Cartridges like this buck the wind well and shoot unbelievably flat, but recoil levels are too high for constant use in high-volume shooting such as plinking prairie dogs and ground squirrels.

great advantage of being chambered to accurate bolt actions. The .22 Hornet was and is a very useful little cartridge, but with its tiny case and moderate velocity, it is hardly a red-hot number. The next factory varmint cartridge to come along was a screamer. The .220 Swift, introduced in 1935, was the first cartridge to break the 4000 fps barrier, and it is still one of the fastest commercial cartridges.

The .220 Swift, along with parallel wildcat developments, enabled long-range varminting as we know it today. In the past 65 years no factory cartridge has been introduced that surpasses the .220 Swift's velocity. On the other hand, it achieved and still maintains a reputation for burning out barrels much too quickly. This reputation was probably more deserved with the barrel steels of the 1930s than it is today, but as you approach 4000 fps barrel life shortens very rapidly.

Winchester introduced two more .22 centerfires in the 1930s—the .218 Bee, based on the .25-20 case and the .219 Zipper, based on the .25-35. The former was housed in the small Winchester Model 92 action, the latter in the Model 94. Winchester obviously didn't learn much from their .220 Swift. In lever action form, neither the .218 nor the .219 offered the accuracy the budding community of varmint hunters demanded. The .218 has seen some resurgence in bolt-actions, but the fast, large-cased .219 is virtually forgotten.

Twenty years passed before another important development in varmint cartridges. In 1955, in an interesting coincidence, Winchester introduced their .243 and Remington introduced their .244. Both were and are exceptionally effective varmint cartridges, especially well-suited for use in the windy West. The .244, with somewhat greater case capacity, is actually the better of the two. However, there was a big difference in how they were introduced. In 1955, Winchester correctly viewed the .243 as a "dual-purpose" cartridge, well-suited for varminting, but equally well-suited for pronghorn and small deer. They introduced the matching .243 rifles with a 1-in-10-inch rifling twist, able to stabilize 80-grain varmint bullets as well as 100-grain big-game bullets. On the other hand, Remington guessed wrong. They introduced their .244 as a long-range varmint cartridge into a world in which long-range varminting was not yet popular.

The author's Rod Herrett-customized XP-100 in .233 delivers groups that will rival most bull-barreled rifles. The short, inherently stiff barrels of these specialty pistols often deliver wonderful accuracy and are great fun to use in varmint hunting.

Their rifles had a 1-in-12-inch twist, too slow to stabilize 100-grain bullets. The .243 took off like a rocket while the .244 was left at the launching pad. In 1963, Remington corrected the error. They renamed the cartridge "6mm Remington" and switched to a 1-in-9-inch rifling twist. The 6mm did a bit better than the .244, but in spite of being a faster and often more accurate cartridge than the .243, it never caught up. In recent years Remington has quit chambering rifles for it.

Although we've seen some recent developments, the world of varmint cartridges became quite complete in the 1950s and

1960s. First conceived as a benchrest cartridge by Remington's great engineer, Mike Walker, the .222 Remington proved a wonderful boon to varminters. Introduced in 1950 with a 50-grain bullet at 3200 fps, the .222 was as mild-mannered as it was accurate, nicely splitting the difference between the limited range of the .22 Hornet and the extremely high velocity of the barrel-burning .220 Swift. Military experimentation resulted in the .222 Remington Magnum in 1958, and a few years later, the winner of this experimentation, the 5.56mm NATO, now known as the .223 Remington. The .222 Remington Magnum is a wee bit faster than the .223, which is a wee bit faster than the .222 Remington, but they are so close that no prairie dog would ever know the difference. In popularity, however, the .223 has emerged as the long-term winner.

With the .220 Swift languishing—probably because of its reputation as a barrel burner—there seemed a need for a faster .22 though maybe not quite as fast as the .220. Three came along in 1963, 1964, and 1965 respectively. The first was Roy Weatherby's .224 Weatherby Magnum, the only belted .22 centerfire. Next came Winchester's .225 Winchester, a fast and efficient cartridge, but also a bit odd with its rimmed case. Then Remington changed the varminter's world forever. Ever since the 1930s, .22 wildcats based on the .250 Savage case had been popular. In fact, the .22 Varminter, as the most popular version was called, was almost a cult cartridge. It is unclear why it took so long for a factory to snap it up, but Remington's 1965 introduction of the .22-250 Remington was a stroke of genius and market gold.

Although fully 35 years have passed since the debut of the .22-250, and despite the increasing popularity of varminting, no truly significant varmint cartridges have been introduced with the possible exception of the .17 Remington in 1971. The .220 Swift has made a strong comeback, and specialty cartridges like the accurate .22 PPC and Lazzeroni's fast, new, short-cased 6mm have hit the market. Varmint rifles have changed significantly, growing ever more accurate. Factory ammo, too, has gotten ever more accurate. Despite an increased market, part of the problem is that the varmint cartridges we have are extremely good. Some wildcat developments probably deliver a bit more accuracy, but it takes careful handloading to produce that accuracy, so they are not of interest to ammunition manufacturers. Even today we can't go significantly faster without reducing barrel life drastically, and varmint hunters don't want that. Most modern .220 Swift loads have actually been reduced to the near side of 4000 fps, and few handloaders push to the max. I suspect we will see new varmint cartridges coming down the pike, but I doubt we will embrace many of them. Indeed, we have a perfectly adequate selection right now.

Left to right: .22 WMR, .22 Hornet, .218 Bee, .17 Remington, .222 Remington, .222 Remington Magnum, .223 Remington, .224 Weatherby Magnum, .22-250 Remington, .220 Swift. This lineup includes most factory varmint cartridges available today. None are new, the 1971-vintage .17 Remington being the most recent.

I tend to group varmint cartridges into those best-suited for short, medium, and long range. In varminting terms, I don't mean bayonet range when I say "short." In this context, short range, is about 150 yards or less. Medium range goes out to 250 or 300 yards, and long range is anything beyond that.

SHORT-RANGE VARMINT CARTRIDGES

Although we tend to think of centerfires, it would be a huge mistake to overlook the .22 rimfires. The lowly .22 Long Rifle (LR) is very short-ranged. Even in superbly accurate rifles, wind drift and drop make 100-yard shooting with a .22 LR very difficult, and the power to take anything larger than a prairie dog cleanly is lacking at that distance. That said, no serious varminter should be without a good .22. Wandering the fields after gophers or jackrabbits, or strolling along the edges of a prairie dog town is some of the most fun—and best shooting practice—the world of varminting can offer. Low report and inexpensive ammo are additional bonuses.

This spectacular group was delivered by a .222 Remington Magnum. Not all rifles can produce groups like this and certainly not with factory loads, but that is the goal all serious varminters strive for.

The .22 Winchester Magnum Rimfire (WMR) is vastly more effective and new loads make it even more so. Only in cool hands on a calm day can the .22 WMR reach much past 125 yards, but it has a flatter trajectory than the .22 LR and hits with a whole lot more authority. At close range, the .22 WMR is adequate for coyotes, but the .22 LR never is.

The .22 Hornet is another giant step upward in performance. Although it's a tiny-cased little cartridge, it propels the traditional 45-grain bullet at a very credible 2690 fps. It is sufficiently flat-shooting to use well beyond 150 yards, but the reality is that few Hornets can hit small varmints beyond this distance. Although it's a fun little cartridge, the Hornet rarely has the accuracy of the faster centerfires. Another drawback is that those tiny cases are difficult to reload, and of course Hornet ammo is far more expensive than .22 WMR ammo. All that aside, the .22 Hornet is a wonderful little cartridge, particularly useful for the varminter who likes to prowl the hills and fields and hunt varmints like big game. The .218 Bee is very similar, but in bolt-action rifles it is often, but not always, a bit more accurate.

MEDIUM-RANGE VARMINT CARTRIDGES

The efficient .22 PPC has a following, and many shooters cling to the wonderfully accurate .222, but this territory is virtually owned by the .223 Remington. The reason for this is obvious. The .223 is our military cartridge, and America's military cartridges have always become popular in the sporting market. Although it's plenty accurate, it is not as inherently accurate as the ballistically similar .222. Over the years the .223 has blown the very similar .222 Remington

Magnum off the market, and has almost destroyed the .222 Remington.

Today no American rifles are chambered for the .222 Remington Magnum, and darned few for the .222. Because of the great variety of factory loads, availability of military brass, and almost universal chambering by firearms manufacturers, the .223 is the odds-on choice for a mid-range varminter, but if you run into a .222 or .222 Remington Magnum, don't be afraid of either one. Both are extremely fine cartridges.

With a 55-grain bullet at something between 3200 and 3300 fps, all three of these cartridges are effective to at least 300 yards, even on very small varmints. Barrel life is quite good, and serious varminters like the fact that recoil is so slight you can "call your shots" through the scope. Add a few hundred fps, and muzzle jump takes you off the target.

Although this kind of rifle is perfectly useful in a heavy-barreled varminter, these cartridges also do well in sport-weight rifles intended for predator calling or more casual varminting. Faster cartridges don't make nearly as much sense when mated to light barrels because of much more rapid barrel heating.

The other mid-range varmint rifle we must mention is the little .17 Remington. This is another of very few cartridges that exceeds 4000 fps. However, despite its great speed the tiny 25-grain bullet starts to shed velocity quickly, and doesn't buck wind particularly well. It is not a long-range number, but it is devastatingly effective on small varmints. The .17 has never been particularly popular, but it has hung in for nearly thirty years. Most .17s are quite accurate, but barrel fouling is a problem that necessitates frequent cleaning to maintain accuracy.

LONG-RANGE VARMINT CARTRIDGES

The .223 owns the middle ground and the .22-250 is the long-range champ, at least in popularity. It is accurate and fast, but it is not necessarily better than the other options. The .224 Weatherby Magnum, chambered only by Weatherby and using ammo offered only by Weatherby, is a fine cartridge that is ballistically identical to the .22-250. It never had much of a chance in the popularity race, and even Weatherby has stopped chambering for it. The .225 Winchester, also virtually

The coyote is unquestionably America's number one predator. Coyotes are extremely tough creatures; at very close range a .22 WMR will work, but the .22 center-fires from .222 Remington on up are the best medicine.

identical, is another very fine cartridge. It had the bad luck to be introduced in 1964, when Winchester changed from the pre-1964 to the post-1964 Model 70. It might have had a chance, but that ended when Remington "legitimized" the legendary .22-250 a year later.

The .220 Swift is not always as accurate as the .22-250, but that depends on the rifle. The Swift's saving grace is that, albeit by a small margin, it is faster than the .22-250. It has not only survived, but has made quite a comeback. Today more rifles are being chambered to .220 Swift—and a greater variety of factory loads—than ever before.

All of these very fast .22s shoot as flat as a .22 centerfire, flat enough to make hitting even small targets relatively simple at very long range. They all share a problem, too. By their very nature, .22 bullets have lower ballistic coefficients than bullets of larger caliber and greater mass. They are susceptible to wind, and the western prairies are always windy. The option is to go to larger calibers, and many varminters do. The primary requirement for varminting is accuracy. Being "overgunned" is not really an issue, and .22 centerfires don't have a patent on accuracy.

Many varminters rely on 6mms, from the .243 up to the .240 Weatherby Magnum, and even faster wildcats such as the 6mm-284. A few go a step farther, up to the fast .25s. A very few rely on the wind-bucking properties of the long-for-caliber 6.5s, from the .260 Remington on up to Lazzeroni's red-hot 6.71

Blackbird. All of these cartridges are wonderfully effective. The problem is that they have more recoil than most serious varminters are comfortable with. Mind you, this is not a problem for predator calling and woodchuck shooting. In high-volume varminting like prairie dogs or California ground squirrels, many dozens—even hundreds—of shots may be fired in a day. Even the recoil of a mild .243 can make one jumpy at day's end. The bigger .25s and 6.5s are simply too much for most shooters.

Many modern varminters are very serious people. They may bring a variety of rifles and handguns on a varmint shoot. The primary arm is usually a heavy-barreled .22 centerfire, the caliber depending on preference and terrain, but you'll often see a "walkaround" .22 rimfire or Hornet, or both! You may also see a fast 6mm or 6.5 taken out every now and then while other barrels are cooling. Others who are less serious about the sport, or more restricted in budget, treat themselves to just one varmint rifle. If it is to be just one, then the obvious choice is a long-range rig in one of the fast .22 centerfires. Unlike the others, this rifle can handle all varmint hunting situations, close or far, prairie dog town, or predator calling. But don't forget that neither the rifle nor the caliber are all-important. Unlike most other kinds of hunting, the first and foremost requirement for varminting is accuracy, and you need all you can get!

Data for Small and Medium Centerfire Rifle Cartridges

.17 Remington

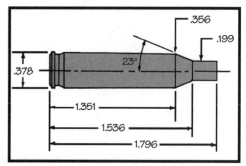

The .17 Remington was introduced in 1971. While it is based on the .222 Remington case this design isn't just a .222 necked to .17 caliber. The case body was lengthened and the neck shortened to provide just a little more case volume than a simple necking down of the .222 would have created. The .17 Remington has never become as popular as some of its larger cousins, the .222 and .223 for instance, and as a result there is only one factory loading available for this caliber.

Relative Recoil Factor = 0.45   **Controlling Agency : SAAMI**

Bullet Weight Grains	Velocity fps	Maximum Average Pressure Copper Crusher	Transducer	Standard barrel for velocity testing:
25	4000	52,000 cup	N/S	24 inches long - 1 turn in 9 inch twist

Remington 25-grain Hollow Point (HP) Power-Lokt (R17REM)

Distance - Yards	Muzzle	100	200	300	400	500
Velocity - fps	4040	3284	2644	2086	1606	1235
Energy - ft-lb	906	599	388	242	143	85
Taylor KO values	2.5	2.0	1.6	1.3	1.0	0.8
Path - inches	-1.5	+1.0	0.0	-6.0	-20.3	-47.3
Wind Drift - inches	0.0	1.4	6.3	15.7	31.5	56.2

G1 Ballistic Coefficient = 0.151

.218 Bee

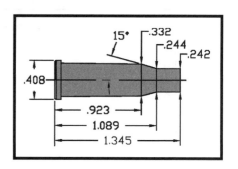

The .218 Bee can be thought of as a slight improvement over the .22 Hornet. Introduced in 1938, the Bee was created from the .25-20 Winchester case especially for the Model 65 Winchester (a lever-action rifle). It does have about 30 percent more case capacity than the Hornet, which allows the Bee to get about 50 fps more velocity from its 46-grain bullet. While the Bee could have been an excellent little cartridge in an accurate gun, the factory loading has just about run out its lifetime, as evidenced by the fact that only Winchester makes a factory loading, and only loads a single bullet choice. Today, there are just too many good centerfire .22s to spend very much time, money, or effort to build up a new rifle chambered for this cartridge.

Relative Recoil Factor = 0.56   **Controlling Agency : SAAMI**

Bullet Weight Grains	Velocity fps	Maximum Average Pressure Copper Crusher	Transducer	Standard barrel for velocity testing:
46	2725	40,000 cup	N/S	24 inches long - 1 turn in 16 inch twist

Winchester 46-grain HP (X218B)

Distance - Yards	Muzzle	100	200	300	400	500
Velocity - fps	2760	2102	1550	1156	961	850
Energy - ft-lb	778	451	245	136	94	74
Taylor KO value	4.1	3.1	2.3	1.7	1.4	1.3
Path - inches	-1.5	+3.4	0.0	-18.8	-63.6	-142.5
Wind drift - inches	0.0	2.8	13.0	33.6	65.4	104.4

G1 Ballistic Coefficient = 0.130

.22 Hornet

The oldest of the centerfire .22s in use today is the .22 Hornet. The Hornet was developed from an old black powder number called the .22 WCF (Winchester Center Fire). Winchester introduced the Hornet as a factory cartridge in the early 1930s. The initial success of the .22 Hornet probably came because there wasn't any competition. Hornets have a very mixed reputation for accuracy. Some guns do very well while others are terrible. Part of this seems to be the result of some strange chambering practices in factory guns produced in the U.S. Unlike the .218 Bee, the Hornet appears to be showing some new life. It's still an excellent little varmint cartridge when fired from a "good" gun as long as the range is limited to about 200 yards.

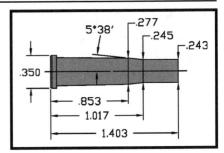

Relative Recoil Factor = 0.54   **Controlling Agency: SAAMI**

Bullet Weight Grains	Velocity fps	Maximum Average Pressure		
		Copper Crusher	Transducer	
45	2655	43,000 cup	N/S	
46	2655	43,000 cup	N/S	

Standard barrel for velocity testing:
24 inches long - 1 turn in 16 inch twist

Winchester 34-grain Jacketed HP (JHP) (S22H1)

Distance - Yards	Muzzle	100	200	300	400	500
Velocity - fps	3050	2132	1415	1017	852	741
Energy - ft-lb	700	343	151	78	55	41
Taylor KO values	3.3	2.3	1.5	1.1	0.9	0.8
Path - inches	-1.5	+3.3	0.0	-21.2	-75.8	178.2
Wind drift - inches	0.0	3.4	16.5	44.1	83.9	113.2

G1 Ballistic Coefficient = 0.097

Hornady 35-grain V-MAX (8031)

Distance - Yards	Muzzle	100	200	300	400	500
Velocity - fps	3100	2278	1601	1135	929	811
Energy - ft-lb	747	403	199	100	67	51
Taylor KO values	3.5	2.6	1.8	1.3	1.0	0.9
Path - inches	-1.5	+2.8	0.0	-16.9	-60.4	-144.7
Wind drift - inches	0.0	2.9	13.5	36.2	71.3	115.5

G1 Ballistic Coefficient = 0.110

Remington 45-grain Pointed Soft Point (SP) (R22HN1)

Distance - Yards	Muzzle	100	200	300	400	500
Velocity - fps	2690	2042	1502	1128	948	840
Energy - ft-lb	723	417	225	127	90	70
Taylor KO values	3.9	2.9	2.2	1.6	1.4	1.2
Path - inches	-1.5	+3.6	0.0	-20.0	-66.9	-148.6
Wind drift - inches	0.0	2.9	13.5	34.8	66.7	106.4

G1 Ballistic Coefficient = 0.130

Winchester 45-grain SP (X22H1)

Distance - Yards	Muzzle	100	200	300	400	500
Velocity - fps	2690	2042	1502	1128	948	840
Energy - ft-lb	723	417	225	127	90	70
Taylor KO values	3.9	2.9	2.2	1.6	1.4	1.2
Path - inches	-1.5	+3.6	0.0	-20.0	-66.9	-148.6
Wind drift - inches	0.0	2.9	13.5	34.8	66.7	106.41

G1 Ballistic Coefficient = 0.130

Remington 45-grain HP (R22HN2)

Distance - Yards	Muzzle	100	200	300	400	500
Velocity - fps	2690	2042	1502	1128	946	840
Energy - ft-lb	723	417	225	127	90	70
Taylor KO values	3.9	2.9	2.2	1.6	1.4	1.2
Path - inches	-1.5	+3.6	0.0	-20.0	-66.9	-148.6
Wind drift - inches	0.0	2.9	13.5	34.8	66.7	106.4

G1 Ballistic Coefficient = 0.130

Winchester 46-grain HP (X22H2)

Distance - Yards	Muzzle	100	200	300	400	500
Velocity - fps	2690	2042	1502	1128	948	841
Energy - ft-lb	739	426	230	130	92	72
Taylor KO values	3.9	2.9	2.2	1.6	1.4	1.2
Path - inches	-1.5	+3.6	0.0	-20.0	-66.9	-148.6
Wind drift - inches	0.0	2.9	13.5	34.8	66.7	106.4

G1 Ballistic Coefficient = 0.130

.222 Remington

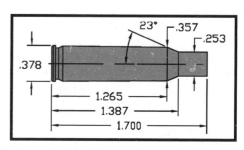

The .222 Remington, when introduced in 1950, was a whole new cartridge design. This new cartridge, which was an instant hit, would drive a 50-grain bullet in excess of 3100 fps. The design combined a rimless 0.378-inch head diameter with a bottlenecked case, a conservative 23 degree shoulder and a 0.3127-inch neck length to produce a cartridge that had all the elements needed to be superbly accurate. The .222 soon caught on as varmint rifle and for many years was the caliber of choice in benchrest competitions. Today, its popularity has been somewhat diluted by the .223 Remington (5.56 NATO), which is the US standard infantry cartridge, but the .222 remains an excellent little cartridge. Most of the ammunition manufacturers load for this caliber. There are a wide range of ammunition choices.

Relative Recoil Factor = 0.74   **Controlling Agency: SAAMI**

Weight Grains	Velocity fps	Maximum Average Pressure	
		Copper Crusher	Transducer
50-52	3110	46,000 cup	50,000 psi
55	3000	46,000 cup	50,000 psi

Standard barrel for velocity testing:
24 inches long - 1 turn in 14 inch twist

Hornady 40-grain V-MAX Moly (83103)

Distance - Yards	Muzzle	100	200	300	400	500
Velocity - fps	3600	3117	2673	2269	1911	1596
Energy - ft-lb	1151	863	634	457	324	226
Taylor KO values	4.6	4.0	3.4	2.9	2.4	2.0
Path - inches	-1.5	+1.1	0.0	-6.1	-18.9	-41.2
Wind drift - inches	0.0	1.1	4.7	11.4	22.0	37.5

G1 Ballistic Coefficient = 0.219

Winchester 40-grain Ballistic Silvertip (SBST222)

Distance - Yards	Muzzle	100	200	300	400	500
Velocity - fps	3370	2915	2503	2127	1786	1487
Energy - ft-lb	1009	755	556	402	283	196
Taylor KO values	4.3	3.7	3.2	2.7	2.3	1.9
Path - inches	-1.5	+1.3	0.0	-6.9	-21.5	-47.2
Wind drift - inches	0.0	1.2	5.1	12.3	23.8	40.6

G1 Ballistic Coefficient = 0.22

Norma 50-grain SP (15711)

Distance - Yards	Muzzle	100	200	300	400	500
Velocity - fps	3199	2667	2193	1771	1452	1156
Energy - ft-lb	1136	790	534	348	224	148
Taylor KO values	5.1	4.3	3.5	2.8	2.3	1.8
Path - inches	-1.5	+1.7	0.0	-9.1	-29.3	-67.1
Wind drift - inches	0.0	1.6	6.9	17.2	33.9	58.9

G1 Ballistic Coefficient = 0.185

Federal 50-grain SP (222A)

Distance - Yards	Muzzle	100	200	300	400	500
Velocity - fps	3140	2600	2120	1700	1350	1110
Energy - ft-lb	1095	750	500	320	200	135
Taylor KO values	5.0	4.2	3.4	2.7	2.2	1.8
Path - inches	-1.5	+1.9	0.0	-9.7	-31.6	-71.3
Wind drift - inches	0.0	1.7	7.3	18.3	36.3	62.9

G1 Ballistic Coefficient = 0.176

Remington 50-grain Pointed SP (R222R1)

Distance - Yards	Muzzle	100	200	300	400	500
Velocity - fps	3140	2602	2123	1700	1350	1107
Energy - ft-lb	1094	752	500	321	202	136
Taylor KO values	5.0	4.2	3.4	3.2	2.2	1.8
Path - inches	-1.5	+1.9	0.0	-9.7	-31.7	-72.3
Wind drift - inches	0.0	1.7	7.3	18.3	36.3	62.9

G1 Ballistic Coefficient = 0.176

Winchester 50-grain Pointed SP (X222R)

Distance - Yards	Muzzle	100	200	300	400	500
Velocity - fps	3140	2602	2123	1700	1350	1107
Energy - ft-lb	1094	752	500	321	202	136
Taylor KO values	5.0	4.2	3.4	3.2	2.2	1.8
Path - inches	-1.5	+2.2	0.0	-10.0	-32.3	-73.8
Wind drift - inches	0.0	1.7	7.3	18.3	36.3	62.9

G1 Ballistic Coefficient = 0.176

PMC 50-grain SP (222B)

Distance - Yards	Muzzle	100	200	300	400	500
Velocity - fps	3040	2727	2354	2012	1651	1269
Energy - ft-lb	1131	908	677	494	333	197
Taylor KO values	4.9	4.4	3.8	3.2	2.6	2.0
Path - inches	-1.5	+1.6	0.0	-7.9	-24.5	-54.3
Wind drift - inches	0.0	1.4	6.1	14.9	29.1	49.8

G1 Ballistic Coefficient = 0.299

Remington 50-grain HP (R222R3)

Distance - Yards	Muzzle	100	200	300	400	500
Velocity - fps	3140	2635	2182	1777	1432	1172
Energy - ft-lb	1094	771	529	351	228	152
Taylor KO values	5.0	4.2	3.5	2.8	2.3	1.9
Path - inches	-1.5	+1.8	0.0	-9.2	-29.8	-67.1
Wind drift - inches	0.0	1.6	6.8	16.8	33.1	57.2

G1 Ballistic Coefficient = 0.188

Hornady 50-grain V-MAX Moly (83153)

Distance - Yards	Muzzle	100	200	300	400	500
Velocity - fps	3140	2729	2362	2008	1710	1450
Energy - ft-lb	1094	827	614	448	325	233
Taylor KO values	5.0	4.4	3.8	3.2	2.7	2.3
Path - inches	-1.5	+1.5	0.0	-7.9	-24.4	-52.9
Wind drift - inches	0.0	1.2	5.1	12.4	23.9	40.6

G1 Ballistic Coefficient = 0.233

Remington 50-grain V-Max, Boattail (PRV222RA)

Distance - Yards	Muzzle	100	200	300	400	500
Velocity - fps	3140	2744	2380	2045	1740	1471
Energy - ft-lb	1094	836	629	464	336	240
Taylor KO values	5.0	4.4	3.8	3.3	2.8	2.4
Path - inches	-1.5	+1.5	0.0	-7.8	-23.9	-51.7
Wind drift - inches	0.0	1.2	5.0	12.2	23.4	39.6

G1 Ballistic Coefficient = 0.242

Norma 50-grain Full Metal Jacket (FMJ) (15715)

Distance - Yards	Muzzle	100	200	300	400	500
Velocity - fps	3199	2693	2240	1833	1481	1208
Energy - ft-lb	1136	805	557	373	244	167
Taylor KO values	5.1	4.3	3.6	2.9	2.4	1.9
Path - inches	-1.5	+1.6	0.0	-8.7	-28.0	-63.2
Wind drift - inches	0.0	1.5	6.5	16.0	31.7	54.8

G1 Ballistic Coefficient = 0.192

Norma 50-grain FMJ (15713)

Distance - Yards	Muzzle	100	200	300	400	500
Velocity - fps	2790	2330	1917	1554	1263	1069
Energy - ft-lb	864	603	403	263	177	127
Taylor KO values	4.5	3.7	3.1	2.5	2.0	1.7
Path - inches	-1.5	+2.2	0.0	-12.2	-39.2	-88.8
Wind drift - inches	0.0	1.8	7.9	19.6	38.6	65.5

G1 Ballistic Coefficient = 0.192

Lapua 55-grain SP (4315030)

Distance - Yards	Muzzle	100	200	300	400	500
Velocity - fps	2890	2402	1968	1581	1273	1070
Energy - ft-lb	1020	705	471	305	198	140
Taylor KO values	5.1	4.2	3.5	2.8	2.2	1.9
Path - inches	-1.5	+2.3	0.0	-11.5	-37.1	-84.2
Wind drift - inches	0.0	1.0	4.1	9.7	18.3	30.4

G1 Ballistic Coefficient = 0.184

Hansen 55-grain Posi-Feed SP (HCC222B)

Distance - Yards	Muzzle	100	200	300	400	500
Velocity - fps	3020	2620	2254	1917	1612	1351
Energy - ft-lb	1115	839	620	449	317	223
Taylor KO values	4.8	4.2	3.6	3.1	2.6	2.2
Path - inches	-1.5	+1.5	0.0	-8.5	-26.6	-58.5
Wind drift - inches	0.0	1.3	5.6	13.6	26.2	44.6

G1 Ballistic Coefficient = 0.232

Federal 55-grain FMJ Boattail (222B)

Distance - Yards	Muzzle	100	200	300	400	500
Velocity - fps	3020	2740	2480	2230	1990	1780
Energy - ft-lb	1115	915	750	610	485	385
Taylor KO values	5.3	4.8	4.4	3.9	3.5	3.1
Path - inches	-1.5	+1.6	0.0	-7.7	-22.7	-45.3
Wind drift - inches	0.0	0.9	3.7	8.7	16.2	26.8

G1 Ballistic Coefficient = 0.338

Lapua 55-grain FMJ (4315020)

Distance - Yards	Muzzle	100	200	300	400	500
Velocity - fps	2890	2475	2096	1752	1455	1218
Energy - ft-lb	1020	748	536	375	259	181
Taylor KO values	5.1	4.4	3.7	3.1	2.6	2.1
Path - inches	-1.5	+2.1	0.0	-10.1	-31.7	-69.9
Wind drift - inches	0.0	0.9	3.9	9.2	17.2	28.4

G1 Ballistic Coefficient = 0.218

Norma 62-grain SP (15716)

Distance - Yards	Muzzle	100	200	300	400	500
Velocity - fps	2887	2457	2067	1716	1413	1181
Energy - ft-lb	1148	831	588	405	275	192
Taylor KO values	5.7	4.9	4.1	3.4	2.8	2.3
Path - inches	-1.5	+2.1	0.0	-10.4	-32.8	-72.8
Wind drift - inches	0.0	1.5	6.5	16.5	32.2	54.9

G1 Ballistic Coefficient = 0.214

.222 Remington Magnum (Discontinued)

Remington's .222 Magnum is a cartridge that never really had a good chance to become popular. The .222 RM started life as an experimental military cartridge based on the .222 Rem. case. Remington began to load for this "Improved" .222 in 1958 but the .223 Remington, which was adopted as a military cartridge signed its death warrant in 1964. There's nothing wrong with the .222 Remington Magnum as a cartridge; in fact, the slightly greater volume and longer neck makes it a bit "better" than the .223 on a technical basis. But historically, a cartridge that's almost identical to a standard military cartridge is going nowhere. The .222 Remington Magnum has dropped out of the catalogs in 1998 and is unlikely to be available after the present stocks are exhausted.

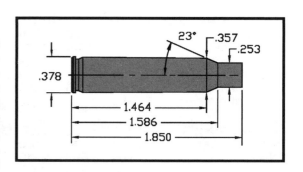

Relative Recoil Factor = 0.79   **Controlling Agency: SAAMI**

Bullet Weight Grains	Velocity fps	Maximum Average Pressure		Standard barrel for velocity testing:
		Copper Crusher	Transducer	
55	3215	50,000 cup	N/S	24 inches long - 1 turn in 14 inch twist

Remington 55-grain SP (R222M1)

Distance - Yards	Muzzle	100	200	300	400	500
Velocity - fps	3240	2748	2305	1906	1556	1272
Energy - ft-lb	1282	922	649	444	296	198
Taylor KO values	5.7	4.8	4.1	3.4	2.7	2.2
Path - inches	-1.5	+1.6	0	-8.5	-26.7	-59.5
Wind drift - inches	0.0	1.4	6.1	15.0	29.5	51.0

G1 Ballistic Coefficient = 0.197

.223 Remington

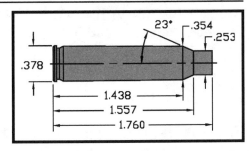

When the .223 Remington cartridge was adopted by the US Army as M193 5.56mm Ball ammunition in 1964, that action ensured that the .223 would become the most popular .22 centerfire in the list. Every cartridge that becomes a US Army standard, with the possible exception of the .30 Carbine, has gone on to a long and useful commercial life. Just look the .45-70, the .45 Colt, the .30-06, and the .45 ACP. The .223 case has been "necked" to every possible size, the TCU series of cartridges and the .30 Whisper being examples.

Even without the military application, the .223 Remington had plenty of potential to become popular. Based on the .222 and the .222 Remington Magnum, the .223 provides an excellent balance of accuracy and performance with good case and barrel life. It has become the standard by which all other .22s are judged.

Most of guns chambered for the .223 have a barrel twist of 1 turn in 14 inches. That twist provides enough stability for bullets up to 55 grains but begins to be marginal above that level. Today there are bullets weighing as much as 75 grains available in loaded ammunition (80-grain bullets for the handloader). It takes a faster twist to stabilize these heavier bullets and some gunmakers offer barrel twists as fast as 1 turn in 7 inches in this caliber. If you have one of the fast-twist barrels, you may have problems with the very light varmint loads. The high velocities attained and the quick twist combine to produce a bullet spin rate that can literally rip thin-jacketed bullets apart. Guns equipped with quick-twist barrels will usually do better with 55-grain and heavier bullets.

Relative Recoil Factor = 0.80   **Controlling Agency: SAAMI**

Bullet Weight Grains	Velocity fps	Maximum Average Pressure		Standard barrel for velocity testing:
		Copper Crusher	Transducer	
53	3305	52,000 cup	55,000 psi	24 inches long - 1 turn in 12 inch twist
55	3215	52,000 cup	55,000 psi	
60	3200	52,000 cup	55,000 psi	
64	3000	52,000 cup	55,000 psi	

Hornady 40-grain V-Max Moly (83253)

Distance - Yards	Muzzle	100	200	300	400	500
Velocity - fps	3800	3305	2845	2424	2044	1715
Energy - ft-lb	1282	970	719	502	371	261
Taylor KO values	4.9	4.2	3.6	3.1	2.6	2.2
Path - inches	-1.5	0.9	0.0	-5.2	-16.4	-36.0
Wind drift - inches	0.0	1.0	4.4	10.7	20.4	34.7

G1 Ballistic Coefficient = 0.218

Winchester 40-grain Ballistic Silvertip (SBST223A)

Distance - Yards	Muzzle	100	200	300	400	500
Velocity - fps	3700	3166	2693	2245	1879	1540
Energy - ft-lb	1216	891	644	456	314	211
Taylor KO values	4.7	4.1	3.5	2.9	2.4	2.0
Path - inches	-1.5	1.0	0.0	-5.8	-18.4	-40.9
Wind drift - inches	0.0	1.2	5.0	12.1	23.5	40.3

G1 Ballistic Coefficient = 0.202

American Eagle (Federal) 50-grain JHP (AE223G)

Distance - Yards	Muzzle	100	200	300	400	500
Velocity - fps	3400	2910	2460	2060	1700	1390
Energy - ft-lb	1285	940	875	470	320	215
Taylor KO values	5.4	4.7	3.9	3.3	2.7	2.2
Path - inches	-1.5	1.3	0.0	-7.1	-22.6	-50.2
Wind drift - inches	0.0	1.3	5.5	13.4	26.2	45.3

G1 Ballistic Coefficient = 0.204

Winchester 50-grain Ballistic Silvertip (SBST223)

Distance - Yards	Muzzle	100	200	300	400	500
Velocity - fps	3410	2982	2593	2235	1907	1613
Energy - ft-lb	1291	987	746	555	404	289
Taylor KO values	5.5	4.8	4.1	3.6	3.1	2.6
Path - inches	-1.5	1.2	0.0	-6.4	-19.8	-42.8
Wind drift - inches	0.0	1.1	4.6	11.1	21.2	35.8

G1 Ballistic Coefficient = 0.238

Black Hills 50-grain V-Max (M223N7)

Distance - Yards	Muzzle	100	200	300	400	500
Velocity - fps	3300	2909	2626	2173	1850	1562
Energy - ft-lb	1231	940	708	524	380	271
Taylor KO values	5.3	4.7	4.2	3.5	3.0	2.5
Path - inches	-1.5	1.3	0.0	-6.8	-21.1	-45.6
Wind drift - inches	0.0	1.1	4.7	11.4	21.9	37.1

G1 Ballistic Coefficient = 0.238

Federal 50-grain Speer TNT HP (P223V1)

Distance - Yards	Muzzle	100	200	300	400	500
Velocity - fps	3300	2860	2450	2080	1750	1460
Energy - ft-lbs	1210	905	670	480	340	235
Taylor KO Index	5.3	4.6	3.9	3.3	2.8	2.3
Path - Inches	-1.5	1.4	0.0	-7.3	-22.6	-49.7
Wind Drift - Inches	0.0	1.2	5.2	12.5	24.2	41.3

G1 Ballistic Coefficient = 0.223

PMC 50-grain BlitzKing (223BKA)

Distance - Yards	Muzzle	100	200	300	400	500
Velocity - fps	3300	2874	2484	2130	1809	1530
Energy - ft-lbs	1209	917	685	504	363	260
Taylor KO Index	5.3	4.6	4.0	3.4	2.9	2.4
Path - Inches	-1.5	1.4	0.0	-7.0	-21.8	-47.0
Wind Drift - Inches	0.0	1.1	4.8	11.7	22.4	38.1

G1 Ballistic Coefficient = 0.236

Remington 50-grain V-Max (PRV223RA)

Distance - Yards	Muzzle	100	200	300	400	500
Velocity - fps	3300	2889	2514	2168	1851	1586
Energy - ft-lb	1209	927	701	522	380	273
Taylor KO values	5.3	4.6	4.0	3.5	3.0	2.5
Path - inches	-1.5	1.6	0.0	-7.8	-22.9	-51.7
Wind drift - inches	0.0	1.1	4.7	11.4	21.8	36.9

G1 Ballistic Coefficient = 0.239

Black Hills 52-grain Match HP (M223N3)

Distance - Yards	Muzzle	100	200	300	400	500
Velocity - fps	3300	2876	2466	2091	1752	1456
Energy - ft-lb	1281	956	702	505	354	245
Taylor KO values	5.5	4.8	4.1	3.5	2.9	2.4
Path - inches	-1.5	1.4	0.0	-7.1	-22.3	-49.0
Wind drift - inches	0.0	1.2	5.2	12.6	24.3	41.6

G1 Ballistic Coefficient = 0.220

Federal 52-grain Sierra MatchKing BTHP (P223K)

Distance - Yards	Muzzle	100	200	300	400	500
Velocity - fps	3300	2860	2460	2090	1790	1470
Energy - ft-lbs	1255	945	700	505	360	250
Taylor KO Index	5.5	4.8	4.1	3.5	2.9	2.4
Path - Inches	-1.5	1.4	0.0	-7.2	-22.4	-49.2
Wind Drift - Inches	0.0	1.2	5.1	12.4	23.9	40.8

G1 Ballistic Coefficient = 0.225

PMC 52-grain BTHP Match (223SMA)

Distance - Yards	Muzzle	100	200	300	400	500
Velocity - fps	3200	2808	2447	2117	1817	1553
Energy - ft-lbs	1182	910	691	517	381	278
Taylor KO Index	5.6	4.9	4.3	3.7	3.2	2.7
Path - Inches	-1.5	1.5	0.0	-7.3	-22.4	-47.9
Wind Drift - Inches	0.0	1.1	4.7	11.3	21.7	36.6

G1 Ballistic Coefficient = 0.185

Hornady 53-grain HP (8023)

Distance - Yards	Muzzle	100	200	300	400	500
Velocity - fps	3330	2882	2477	2106	1710	1475
Energy - ft-lb	1306	978	722	522	369	256
Taylor KO valuies	5.6	4.9	4.2	3.6	3.0	2.5
Path - inches	-1.5	1.7	0.0	-7.4	-22.7	-49.1
Wind drift - inches	0.0	1.2	5.1	12.4	23.9	40.8

G1 Ballistic Coefficient = 0.223

Winchester 53-grain HP (X223RH)

Distance - Yards	Muzzle	100	200	300	400	500
Velocity - fps	3330	2882	2477	2106	1710	1475
Energy - ft-lb	1306	978	722	522	369	256
Taylor KO values	5.6	4.9	4.2	3.6	3.0	2.5
Path - inches	-1.5	1.7	0.0	-7.4	-22.7	-49.1
Wind drift - inches	0.0	1.2	5.1	12.4	23.9	40.8

G1 Ballistic Coefficient = 0.223

Black Hills 55-grain SP (M223N2)

Distance - Yards	Muzzle	100	200	300	400	500
Velocity - fps	3250	2848	2480	2140	1829	1552
Energy - ft-lb	1290	991	751	560	409	294
Taylor KO values	5.7	5.0	4.4	3.8	3.2	2.7
Path - inches	-1.5	1.4	0.0	-7.1	-21.9	-47.1
Wind drift - inches	0.0	1.1	4.7	11.4	21.9	37.0

G1 Ballistic Coefficient = 0.245

Hansen 55-grain Posi-Feed SP (HCC223B)

Distance - Yards	Muzzle	100	200	300	400	500
Velocity - fps	3247	2811	2415	2052	1724	1439
Energy - ft-lb	1287	965	712	515	363	253
Taylor KO values	5.7	4.9	4.3	3.6	3.0	2.5
Path - inches	-1.5	1.5	0.0	-7.5	-23.3	-51.0
Wind drift - inches	0.0	1.2	5.2	12.7	24.5	41.8

G1 Ballistic Coefficient = 0.225

Federal 55-grain Hi-Shok SP (223A)

Distance - Yards	Muzzle	100	200	300	400	500
Velocity - fps	3240	2750	2300	1910	1550	1270
Energy - ft-lb	1260	920	650	445	295	195
Taylor KO values	5.7	4.8	4.0	3.4	2.7	2.2
Path - inches	-1.5	1.6	0.0	-8.2	-26.1	-58.3
Wind drift - inches	0.0	1.4	6.1	15.0	29.3	50.6

G1 Ballistic Coefficient = 0.198

Remington 55-grain Pointed SP (R223R1)

Distance - Yards	Muzzle	100	200	300	400	500
Velocity - fps	3240	2750	2300	1910	1550	1270
Energy - ft-lb	1260	920	650	445	295	195
Taylor KO values	5.7	4.8	4.0	3.4	2.7	2.2
Path - inches	-1.5	1.6	0.0	-8.2	-26.1	-58.3
Wind drift - inches	0.0	1.4	6.1	15.0	29.3	50.6

G1 Ballistic Coefficient = 0.198

Winchester 55-grain Pointed SP (X223R)

Distance - Yards	Muzzle	100	200	300	400	500
Velocity - fps	3240	2750	2300	1910	1550	1270
Energy - ft-lb	1260	920	650	445	295	195
Taylor KO values	5.7	4.8	4.0	3.4	2.7	2.2
Path - inches	-1.5	1.6	0.0	-8.2	-26.1	-58.3
Wind drift - inches	0.0	1.4	6.1	15.0	29.3	50.6

G1 Ballistic Coefficient = 0.198

Lapua 55-grain SP (4315050)

Distance - Yards	Muzzle	100	200	300	400	500
Velocity - fps	3133	2708	2321	1966	1648	1376
Energy - ft-lb	1199	896	658	472	332	231
Taylor KO values	5.5	4.8	4.1	3.5	2.9	2.4
Path - inches	-1.5	0.9	0.0	-8.2	-25.4	-55.6
Wind drift - inches	0.0	1.3	5.5	13.4	25.9	44.1

G1 Ballistic Coefficient = 0.225

PMC 55-grain Pointed SP (223B)

Distance - Yards	Muzzle	100	200	300	400	500
Velocity - fps	3112	2767	2431	2100	1806	1516
Energy - ft-lb	1182	935	715	539	398	281
Taylor KO values	5.5	4.9	4.3	3.7	3.2	2.7
Path - inches	-1.5	0.9	0.0	-7.5	-22.9	-49.1
Wind drift - inches	0.0	1.1	4.8	11.6	22.1	37.3

G1 Ballistic Coefficient = 0.255

Hansen 55-grain Posi-Feed HP (HCC223E)

Distance - Yards	Muzzle	100	200	300	400	500
Velocity - fps	3247	2811	2415	2052	1724	1439
Energy - ft-lb	1287	965	712	515	363	253
Taylor KO values	5.7	4.9	4.3	3.6	3.0	2.5
Path - inches	-1.5	1.5	0.0	-7.5	-23.3	-51.0
Wind drift - inches	0.0	1.2	5.2	12.7	24.5	41.8

G1 Ballistic Coefficient = 0.225

Federal 55-grain Sierra Gameking Boattail HP (P223E)

Distance - Yards	Muzzle	100	200	300	400	500
Velocity - fps	3240	2770	2340	1950	1610	1330
Energy - ft-lb	1280	935	670	465	315	215
Taylor KO values	5.7	4.9	4.1	3.4	2.8	2.3
Path - inches	-1.5	1.4	0.0	-6.7	-20.5	-43.4
Wind drift - inches	0.0	1.3	5.8	14.1	27.3	47.4

G1 Ballistic Coefficient = 0.207

PMC 55-grain Boattail HP (223VB)

Distance - Yards	Muzzle	100	200	300	400	500
Velocity - fps	3240	2717	2250	1832	1473	1196
Energy - ft-lb	1282	901	618	410	265	175
Taylor KO values	5.7	4.8	4.0	3.2	2.6	2.1
Path - inches	-1.5	0.9	0.0	-8.6	-27.7	-62.2
Wind drift - inches	0.0	1.5	6.6	16.3	32.3	56.0

G1 Ballistic Coefficient = 0.185

Remington 55-grain HP Power-Lokt (R223R2)

Distance - Yards	Muzzle	100	200	300	400	500
Velocity - fps	3240	2773	2352	1969	1627	1341
Energy - ft-lb	1282	939	675	473	323	220
Taylor KO values	5.7	4.9	4.1	3.5	2.9	2.4
Path - inches	-1.5	1.5	0.0	-7.9	-24.8	-55.1
Wind drift - inches	0.0	1.3	5.7	14.0	27.2	46.7

G1 Ballistic Coefficient = 0.209

Federal 55-grain Nosler Ballistic Tip (P223F)

Distance - Yards	Muzzle	100	200	300	400	500
Velocity - fps	3240	2870	2530	2220	1920	1660
Energy - ft-lb	1280	1005	780	600	450	336
Taylor KO values	5.7	5.1	4.5	3.9	3.4	2.9
Path - inches	-1.5	1.4	0.0	-6.8	-20.8	-44.2
Wind drift - inches	0.0	1.0	4.3	10.3	19.6	32.8

G1 Ballistic Coefficient = 0.267

Federal 55-grain Sierra BlitzKing (P223J)

Distance - Yards	Muzzle	100	200	300	400	500
Velocity - fps	3240	2870	2520	2200	1910	1640
Energy - ft-lb	1280	1005	775	590	445	330
Taylor KO values	5.7	5.1	4.4	3.9	3.4	2.9
Path - inches	-1.5	1.4	0.0	-6.9	-20.9	-45.0
Wind drift - inches	0.0	1.0	4.4	10.5	19.9	33.5

G1 Ballistic Coefficient = 0.264

Hornady 55-grain V-Max Moly (83273)

Distance - Yards	Muzzle	100	200	300	400	500
Velocity - fps	3240	2859	2507	2181	1891	1628
Energy - ft-lb	1282	998	767	581	437	324
Taylor KO values	5.7	5.0	4.4	3.8	3.3	2.9
Path - inches	-1.5	1.4	0.0	-7.1	-21.4	-45.2
Wind drift - inches	0.0	1.0	4.4	10.6	20.2	34.0

G1 Ballistic Coefficient = 0.258

Federal 55-grain Trophy Bonded Bear Claw (P223T2)

Distance - Yards	Muzzle	100	200	300	400	500
Velocity - fps	3100	2630	2210	1830	1500	1240
Energy - ft-lb	1175	845	595	410	275	185
Taylor KO values	5.5	4.6	3.9	3.2	2.6	2.2
Path - inches	-1.5	1.8	0.0	-8.9	-28.7	-64.5
Wind drift - inches	0.0	1.4	6.3	15.5	30.3	52.0

G1 Ballistic Coefficient = 0.203

Hansen 55-grain FMJ - M193 (HCC223A)

Distance - Yards	Muzzle	100	200	300	400	500
Velocity - fps	3247	2914	2605	2316	2045	1795
Energy - ft-lb	1288	1037	829	655	511	393
Taylor KO values	5.7	5.1	4.6	4.1	3.6	3.2
Path - inches	-1.5	0.9	0.0	-6.4	-19.4	-40.8
Wind drift - inches	0.0	0.9	3.8	9.1	17.1	28.4

G1 Ballistic Coefficient = 0.298

American Eagle (Federal) 55-grain FMJ Boattail (AE223)

Distance - Yards	Muzzle	100	200	300	400	500
Velocity - fps	3240	2950	2670	2410	2170	1940
Energy - ft-lb	1280	1060	875	710	575	460
Taylor KO values	5.7	5.2	4.6	4.2	3.8	3.4
Path - inches	-1.5	0.9	0.0	-6.1	-18.3	-37.8
Wind drift - inches	0.0	0.8	3.3	7.8	14.6	24.0

G1 Ballistic Coefficient = 0.342

Federal 55-grain FMJ Boattail (223B)

Distance - Yards	Muzzle	100	200	300	400	500
Velocity - fps	3240	2950	2670	2410	2170	1940
Energy - ft-lb	1280	1060	875	710	575	460
Taylor KO values	5.7	5.2	4.6	4.2	3.8	3.4
Path - inches	-1.5	0.9	0.0	-6.1	-18.3	-37.8
Wind drift - inches	0.0	0.8	3.3	7.8	14.6	24.0

G1 Ballistic Coefficient = 0.342

Remington 55-grain Metal Case (R223R3)

Distance - Yards	Muzzle	100	200	300	400	500
Velocity - fps	3240	2759	2326	1933	1587	1301
Energy - ft-lb	1282	929	660	456	307	207
Taylor KO values	5.7	4.9	4.1	3.4	2.8	2.3
Path - inches	-1.5	1.6	0.0	-8.1	-25.5	-57.0
Wind drift - inches	0.0	1.4	5.9	14.6	28.5	49.1

G1 Ballistic Coefficient = 0.202

UMC (Remington) 55-grain Metal Case (L223R3)

Distance - Yards	Muzzle	100	200	300	400	500
Velocity - fps	3240	2759	2326	1933	1587	1301
Energy - ft-lb	1282	929	660	456	307	207
Taylor KO values	5.7	4.9	4.1	3.4	2.8	2.3
Path - inches	-1.5	1.6	0.0	-8.1	-25.5	-57.0
Wind drift - inches	0.0	1.4	5.9	14.6	28.5	49.1

G1 Ballistic Coefficient = 0.202

PMC 55-grain FMJ-Boattail (223A)

Distance - Yards	Muzzle	100	200	300	400	500
Velocity - fps	3195	2882	2525	2169	1843	1432
Energy - ft-lb	1246	1014	779	574	415	250
Taylor KO values	5.6	5.0	4.4	3.8	3.2	2.5
Path - inches	-1.5	1.4	0.0	-6.8	-21.1	-46.0
Wind drift - inches	0.0	1.2	5.2	12.7	24.5	41.8

G1 Ballistic Coefficient = 0.266

Lapua 55-grain FMJ (4315040)

Distance - Yards	Muzzle	100	200	300	400	500
Velocity - fps	3133	2896	2671	2457	2253	2058
Energy - ft-lb	1197	1022	870	736	619	517
Taylor KO values	5.5	5.1	4.7	4.3	4.0	3.6
Path - inches	-1.5	1.3	0.0	-6.2	-18.2	-37.0
Wind drift - inches	0.0	0.7	2.8	6.6	12.2	19.8

G1 Ballistic Coefficient = 0.412

Black Hills 60-grain SP (M223N4)

Distance - Yards	Muzzle	100	200	300	400	500
Velocity - fps	3150	2782	2442	2127	1837	1575
Energy - ft-lb	1322	1031	795	603	450	331
Taylor KO values	6.0	5.3	4.7	4.1	3.5	3.0
Path - inches	-1.5	1.6	0.0	-7.5	-22.5	-48.1
Wind drift - inches	0.0	1.1	4.6	11.0	21.0	35.3

G1 Ballistic Coefficient = 0.264

Hornady 60-grain SP (8028)

Distance - Yards	Muzzle	100	200	300	400	500
Velocity - fps	3150	2782	2442	2127	1837	1575
Energy - ft-lb	1322	1031	795	603	450	331
Taylor KO values	6.0	5.3	4.7	4.1	3.5	3.0
Path - inches	-1.5	1.6	0.0	-7.5	-22.5	-48.1
Wind drift - inches	0.0	1.1	4.6	11.0	21.0	35.3

G1 Ballistic Coefficient = 0.264

Black Hills 62-grain "Heavy" FMJ

Distance - Yards	Muzzle	100	200	300	400	500
Velocity - fps	3150	2778	2436	2119	1827	1564
Energy - ft-lb	1366	1063	817	618	459	337
Taylor KO values	6.2	5.5	4.8	4.2	3.6	3.1
Path - inches	-1.5	1.5	0.0	-7.4	-22.6	-48.4
Wind drift - inches	0.0	1.1	4.6	11.1	21.2	35.7

G1 Ballistic Coefficient = 0.260

Hansen 62-grain FMJ SC-SS109 (HCC223C)

Distance - Yards	Muzzle	100	200	300	400	500
Velocity - fps	3000	2694	2407	2139	1888	1658
Energy - ft-lb	1239	999	798	630	491	379
Taylor KO values	6.0	5.4	4.8	4.2	3.7	3.3
Path - inches	-1.5	1.7	0.0	-7.7	-23.0	-48.1
Wind drift - inches	0.0	1.0	4.1	9.8	18.5	30.7

G1 Ballistic Coefficient = 0.307

Hansen 62-grain FMJ Match - SS109 Equivalent (HCC223M)

Distance - Yards	Muzzle	100	200	300	400	500
Velocity - fps	3000	2694	2407	2139	1888	1658
Energy - ft-lb	1239	999	798	630	491	379
Taylor KO values	6.0	5.4	4.8	4.2	3.7	3.3
Path - inches	-1.5	1.7	0.0	-7.7	-23.0	-48.1
Wind drift - inches	0.0	1.0	4.1	9.8	18.5	30.7

G1 Ballistic Coefficient = 0.307

Remington 62-grain HP Match (R223R6)

Distance - Yards	Muzzle	100	200	300	400	500
Velocity - fps	3025	2572	2162	1792	1471	1217
Energy - ft-lb	1260	911	643	442	298	204
Taylor KO values	6.0	5.2	4.3	3.6	2.9	2.4
Path - inches	-1.5	1.9	0.0	-9.4	-29.9	-66.6
Wind drift - inches	0.0	1.5	6.4	15.8	31.0	53.2

G1 Ballistic Coefficient = 0.205

Winchester 64-grain Power Point Plus (SHV223R2)

Distance - Yards	Muzzle	100	200	300	400	500
Velocity - fps	3090	2684	2312	1971	1664	1398
Energy - ft-lb	1357	1024	760	552	393	278
Taylor KO values	6.3	5.5	4.7	4.0	3.4	2.8
Path - inches	-1.5	1.5	0.0	-8.2	-25.4	-55.1
Wind drift - inches	0.0	1.2	5.4	13.0	25.0	42.6

G1 Ballistic Coefficient = 0.234

Winchester 64-grain Power Point (X223R2)

Distance - Yards	Muzzle	100	200	300	400	500
Velocity - fps	3020	2656	2320	2009	1724	1473
Energy - ft-lb	1296	1003	765	574	423	308
Taylor KO values	6.2	5.4	4.8	4.1	3.5	3.0
Path - inches	-1.5	1.7	0.0	-8.2	-25.1	-53.6
Wind drift - inches	0.0	1.2	5.0	11.9	22.8	38.5

G1 Ballistic Coefficient = 0.258

PMC 64-grain Pointed SP (223C)

Distance - Yards	Muzzle	100	200	300	400	500
Velocity - fps	2775	2511	2261	2026	1806	1604
Energy - ft-lb	1094	896	726	583	464	366
Taylor KO values	5.7	5.1	4.6	4.1	3.7	3.3
Path - inches	-1.5	2.0	0.0	-8.8	-26.1	-54.1
Wind drift - inches	0.0	1.0	4.1	9.8	18.4	30.4

G1 Ballistic Coefficient = 0.340

Black Hills 68-grain "Heavy" Match HP (M223N5)

Distance - Yards	Muzzle	100	200	300	400	500
Velocity - fps	2850	2581	2327	2088	1863	1656
Energy - ft-lb	1227	1006	818	658	524	414
Taylor KO values	6.2	5.6	5.1	4.5	4.1	3.6
Path - inches	-1.5	1.9	0.0	-8.3	-24.6	-51.0
Wind drift - inches	0.0	0.9	4.0	9.4	17.6	29.2

G1 Ballistic Coefficient = 0.330

Federal 69-grain Sierra Matchking HP Boattail (GM223M)

Distance - Yards	Muzzle	100	200	300	400	500
Velocity - fps	3000	2720	2460	2210	1980	1760
Energy - ft-lb	1379	1135	926	749	600	475
Taylor KO values	6.6	6.0	5.4	4.9	4.4	3.9
Path - inches	-1.5	1.6	0.0	-7.4	-21.9	-45.4
Wind drift - inches	0.0	0.9	3.7	8.8	16.4	27.1

G1 Ballistic Coefficient = 0.338

Hornady 75-grain Boattail HP Match (8026) (Moly - 80263)

Distance - Yards	Muzzle	100	200	300	400	500
Velocity - fps	2790	2554	2330	2119	1926	1744
Energy - ft-lb	1296	1086	904	747	617	506
Taylor KO values	6.7	6.1	5.6	5.1	4.6	4.2
Path - inches	-1.5	2.4	0.0	-8.8	-25.1	-50.8
Wind drift - inches	0.0	0.8	3.5	8.2	15.4	25.2

G1 Ballistic Coefficient = 0.390

Black Hills 75-grain "Heavy" Match HP (M223N6)

Distance - Yards	Muzzle	100	200	300	400	500
Velocity - fps	2750	2520	2302	2094	1898	1714
Energy - ft-lb	1259	1058	883	731	600	489
Taylor KO values	6.6	6.0	5.5	5.0	4.6	4.1
Path - inches	-1.5	2.0	0.0	-8.6	-25.1	-51.3
Wind drift - inches	0.0	0.9	3.6	8.4	15.7	25.8

G1 Ballistic Coefficient = 0.390

.22-250 Remington

The .22-250, which became a standardized factory cartridge in 1965, has a history that starts about 1915 when Charles Newton designed the .250 Savage. In the late 1920s and early 1930s a number of people began experimenting with the .250 Savage necked to .22 caliber. One early number was the .220 Wotkyns Original Swift. J. E. Gebby and J. Bushnell Smith called their version the .22 Varminter and copyrighted the name. Most gunsmiths, when chambering guns for the .22 caliber version of the .250 Savage simply called the cartridge the .22-250 to avoid any copyright troubles.

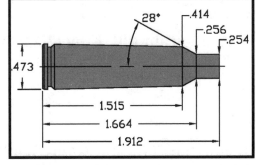

Remington's introduction of the .22-250 finally brought this fine cartridge its deserved recognition as a standardized factory caliber. In the fastest loading today, the .22-250 is only 50 fps slower than the .220 Swift. Some of the wildcat loadings from the 1950s produced velocities about 200 fps higher than today's factory standards. They also produced pressures to match and that fact explains why the factories are sometimes slow to adopt wildcat designs and seldom achieve the velocity claims of the wildcat inventors.

Relative Recoil Factor = 0.90   **Controlling Agency: SAAMI**

Bullet Weight Grains	Velocity fps	Maximum Average Pressure Copper Crusher	Transducer
40	3975	53,000 cup	65,000 psi
52	3740	53,000 cup	65,000 psi
53-55	3650	53,000 cup	65,000 psi
60	3600	53,000 cup	65,000 psi

Standard barrel for velocity testing:
24 inches long - 1 turn in 14 inch twist.

Federal 40-grain Sierra Varminter HP (P22250V)

Distance - Yards	Muzzle	100	200	300	400	500
Velocity - fps	4000	3320	2720	2200	1740	1360
Energy - ft-lb	1420	980	680	430	265	164
Taylor KO values	5.1	4.2	3.5	2.8	2.2	1.7
Path - inches	-1.5	0.8	0.0	-5.6	-18.4	-42.8
Wind drift - inches	0.0	1.2	5.0	12.2	23.7	40.7

G1 Ballistic Coefficient = 0.166

Hornady 40-grain V-Max Moly (83353)

Distance - Yards	Muzzle	100	200	300	400	500
Velocity - fps	4150	3631	3147	2699	2293	1932
Energy - ft-lb	1529	1171	879	647	467	331
Taylor KO values	5.3	4.6	4.0	3.5	3.0	2.5
Path - inches	-1.5	0.5	0.0	-4.2	-13.3	-28.9
Wind drift - inches	0.0	0.9	4.0	9.5	18.0	30.4

G1 Ballistic Coefficient = 0.220

Winchester 40-grain Ballistic Silvertip (SBST22250A)

Distance - Yards	Muzzle	100	200	300	400	500
Velocity - fps	4150	3591	3099	2658	2257	1893
Energy - ft-lb	1530	1146	853	628	453	318
Taylor KO values	5.3	4.6	4.0	3.4	2.9	2.4
Path - inches	-1.5	0.6	0.0	-4.2	-13.4	-29.5
Wind drift - inches	0.0	1.0	4.1	9.8	18.6	31.4

G1 Ballistic Coefficient = 0.215

Winchester 50-grain Ballistic Silvertip (SBST22250*)

Distance - Yards	Muzzle	100	200	300	400	500
Velocity - fps	3810	3341	2919	2536	2182	1859
Energy - ft-lb	1611	1239	946	714	529	384
Taylor KO values	6.1	5.4	4.7	4.1	3.5	3.0
Path - inches	-1.5	0.8	0.0	-4.9	-15.2	-32.9
Wind drift - inches	0.0	1.0	4.0	9.6	18.2	30.6

G1 Ballistic Coefficient = 0.238

Hornady 50-grain V-Max Moly (83363)

Distance - Yards	Muzzle	100	200	300	400	500
Velocity - fps	3800	3349	2925	2535	2178	1862
Energy - ft-lb	1603	1245	950	713	527	385
Taylor KO values	6.1	5.4	4.7	4.1	3.5	3.0
Path - inches	-1.5	0.8	0.0	-5.0	-15.6	-33.3
Wind drift - inches	0.0	1.0	4.0	9.5	18.0	30.3

G1 Ballistic Coefficient = 0.240

PMC 50-grain BlitzKing (22-250BKA)

Distance - Yards	Muzzle	100	200	300	400	500
Velocity - fps	3725	3264	2641	2455	2103	1785
Energy - ft-lb	1540	1183	896	669	491	354
Taylor KO values	6.0	5.2	4.2	3.9	3.4	2.9
Path - inches	-1.5	0.8	0.0	-5.0	-15.5	-33.6
Wind drift - inches	0.0	1.0	4.2	10.0	19.0	32.1

G1 Ballistic Coefficient = 0.235

Remington 50-grain V-Max Boattail (PRV2250A)

Distance - Yards	Muzzle	100	200	300	400	500
Velocity - fps	3725	3272	2864	2491	2147	1832
Energy - ft-lb	1540	1188	910	689	512	372
Taylor KO values	6.0	5.2	4.6	4.0	3.4	2.9
Path - inches	-1.5	0.8	0.0	-5.0	-15.5	-33.6
Wind drift - inches	0.0	1.0	4.1	9.8	18.6	31.3

G1 Ballistic Coefficient = 0.234

Norma 53-grain SP (15733)

Distance - Yards	Muzzle	100	200	300	400	500
Velocity - fps	3707	3272	2809	2425	2070	1748
Energy - ft-lb	1618	1231	928	690	504	360
Taylor KO values	6.3	5.5	4.8	4.1	3.5	3.0
Path - inches	-1.5	0.9	0.0	-5.4	-16.7	-36.2
Wind drift - inches	0.0	1.0	4.3	10.3	19.6	33.1

G1 Ballistic Coefficient = 0.231

Hornady 53-grain HP (8030)

Distance - Yards	Muzzle	100	200	300	400	500
Velocity - fps	3680	3185	2743	2341	1974	1646
Energy - ft-lb	1594	1194	886	645	459	319
Taylor KO values	6.2	5.4	4.7	4.0	3.3	2.8
Path - inches	-1.5	1.1	0.0	-5.7	-17.8	-38.8
Wind drift - inches	0.0	1.1	4.6	11.1	21.4	36.4

G1 Ballistic Coefficient = 0.218

Federal 55-grain Sierra BlitzKing (P22250C)

Distance - Yards	Muzzle	100	200	300	400	500
Velocity - fps	3680	3270	2890	2540	2220	1920
Energy - ft-lb	1655	1300	1020	790	605	450
Taylor KO values	6.5	5.8	5.1	4.5	3.9	3.4
Path - inches	-1.5	0.9	0.0	-5.1	-15.6	-33.1
Wind drift - inches	0.0	0.9	3.7	8.9	16.8	28.0

G1 Ballistic Coefficient = 0.263

Federal 55-grain Hi-Shok SP (22250A)

Distance - Yards	Muzzle	100	200	300	400	500
Velocity - fps	3680	3140	2660	2220	1830	1490
Energy - ft-lb	1655	1200	860	605	410	270
Taylor KO values	6.5	5.5	4.7	3.9	3.2	2.6
Path - inches	-1.5	1.0	0.0	-6.0	-19.1	-42.8
Wind drift - inches	0.0	1.2	5.2	12.5	24.3	41.9

G1 Ballistic Coefficient = 0.198

Remington 55-grain Pointed SP (R22501)

Distance - Yards	Muzzle	100	200	300	400	500
Velocity - fps	3680	3137	2656	2222	1832	1493
Energy - ft-lb	1654	1201	861	603	410	272
Taylor KO values	6.5	5.5	4.7	3.9	3.2	2.6
Path - inches	-1.5	1.0	0.0	-6.0	-19.1	-42.8
Wind drift - inches	0.0	11.2	5.2	12.5	24.3	41.8

G1 Ballistic Coefficient = 0.198

Winchester 55-grain Pointed SP (X222501)

Distance - Yards	Muzzle	100	200	300	400	500
Velocity - fps	3680	3137	2656	2222	1832	1493
Energy - ft-lb	1654	1201	861	603	410	272
Taylor KO values	6.5	5.5	4.7	3.9	3.2	2.6
Path - inches	-1.5	1.0	0.0	-6.0	-19.1	-42.8
Wind drift - inches	0.0	11.2	5.2	12.5	24.3	41.8

G1 Ballistic Coefficient = 0.198

Federal 55-grain Trophy Bonded Bear Claw (P22250T1)

Distance - Yards	Muzzle	100	200	300	400	500
Velocity - fps	3600	3080	2610	2190	1810	1490
Energy - ft-lb	1585	1155	835	590	400	270
Taylor KO values	6.3	5.4	4.6	3.9	3.2	2.6
Path - inches	-1.5	1.1	0.0	-6.2	-19.8	-44.5
Wind drift - inches	0.0	1.2	5.2	12.5	24.3	41.8

G1 Ballistic Coefficient = 0.203

PMC 55-grain Pointed SP (22-250B)

Distance - Yards	Muzzle	100	200	300	400	500
Velocity - fps	3586	3203	2852	2505	2178	1877
Energy - ft-lb	1570	1253	993	766	579	430
Taylor KO values	6.3	5.6	5.0	4.4	3.8	3.3
Path - inches	-1.5	1.0	0.0	-5.2	-16.0	-34.2
Wind drift - inches	0.0	0.9	3.8	9.1	'17.1	28.6

G1 Ballistic Coefficient = 0.266

Federal 55-grain Sierra GameKing HP Boattail (P22250B)

Distance - Yards	Muzzle	100	200	300	400	500
Velocity - fps	3680	3280	2929	2590	2280	1990
Energy - ft-lb	1655	1315	1040	815	630	480
Taylor KO values	6.5	5.8	5.1	4.6	4.0	3.5
Path - inches	-1.5	0.9	0.0	-5.0	-15.1	-32.0
Wind drift - inches	0.0	0.8	3.6	8.4	15.8	26.3

G1 Ballistic Coefficient = 0.276

PMC 55-grain HP Boattail (22-250VB)

Distance - Yards	Muzzle	100	200	300	400	500
Velocity - fps	3680	3104	2596	2141	1737	1395
Energy - ft-lb	1654	1176	823	560	368	238
Taylor KO values	6.5	5.5	4.6	3.8	3.1	2.5
Path - inches	-1.5	1.1	0.0	-6.3	-20.2	-45.8
Wind drift - inches	0.0	1.3	5.6	13.6	26.6	46.0

G1 Ballistic Coefficient = 0.190

Remington 55-grain HP Power-Lokt (R22502)

Distance - Yards	Muzzle	100	200	300	400	500
Velocity - fps	3680	3209	2785	2400	2046	1725
Energy - ft-lb	1654	1257	947	703	511	363
Taylor KO values	6.5	5.6	4.9	4.2	3.6	3.0
Path - inches	-1.5	1.0	0.0	-5.5	-17.0	-37.0
Wind drift - inches	0.0	1.0	4.3	10.4	19.9	33.7

G1 Ballistic Coefficient = 0.230

Hornady 55-grain V-Max Moly (83373)

Distance - Yards	Muzzle	100	200	300	400	500
Velocity - fps	3680	3265	2876	2517	2183	1887
Energy - ft-lb	1654	1302	1010	772	582	433
Taylor KO values	6.5	5.7	5.1	4.4	3.8	3.3
Path - inches	-1.5	0.9	0.0	-5.3	-16.1	-34.1
Wind drift - inches	0.0	0.9	3.8	9.1	17.3	28.9

G1 Ballistic Coefficient = 0.258

Hornady 60-grain SP (8039)

Distance - Yards	Muzzle	100	200	300	400	500
Velocity - fps	3600	3195	2826	2485	2169	1878
Energy - ft-lb	1727	1360	1064	823	627	470
Taylor KO values	6.9	6.1	5.4	4.8	4.2	3.6
Path - inches	-1.5	1.0	0.0	-5.4	-16.3	-34.8
Wind drift - inches	0.0	0.9	3.8	9.1	17.2	28.7

G1 Ballistic Coefficient = 0.264

.225 Winchester

The .225 Winchester was introduced in 1964, with the idea that it was a replacement for the .220 Swift. It is classified as semi-rimmed, rather than rimmed, and can be used in Model 70s and other box-magazine guns. Remington's standardization of the .22-250 in 1965 dealt the .225 a severe, but not fatal, blow. The cartridge continues to hang on by the skin of its teeth in Winchester's 1998 ammo catalog with one single bullet listed, but one wonders if it will live to see the millennium.

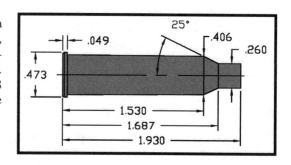

Relative Recoil Factor = 0.90   **Controlling Agency: SAAMI**

Bullet Weight Grains	Velocity fps	Maximum Average Pressure		Standard barrel for velocity testing:
		Copper Crusher	Transducer	
55	3650	N/A	60,000 psi	24 inches long - 1 turn in 14 inch twist.

Winchester 55-grain Pointed SP (X2251)

Distance - Yards	Muzzle	100	200	300	400	500
Velocity - fps	3570	3066	2616	2208	1838	1514
Energy - ft-lb	1556	1148	836	595	412	280
Taylor KO values	6.2	5.4	4.6	3.9	3.2	2.7
Path - inches	-1.5	1.1	0.0	-6.3	-19.8	-43.7
Wind drift - inches	0.0	1.2	5.0	12.2	23.7	40.7

G1 Ballistic Coefficient = 0.208

.224 Weatherby Magnum

Weatherby's .224 Magnum, introduced in 1963, is a miniaturized version of the .300 Weatherby, belt, venturi shoulder, and all. This nifty little cartridge provides just a shade less performance than the current king of the centerfire .22s, the .22-250. At one time Norma loaded a 53-grain bullet in this case but that loading was dropped a couple years ago. The only loading in 1998 is the Weatherby factory's 55-grain soft-point bullet. Weatherby no longer lists new rifles in this caliber.

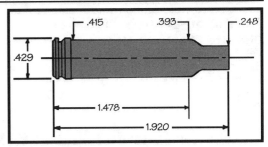

Relative Recoil Factor = 0.90   **Controlling Agency: CIP**

Bullet Weight Grains	Velocity fps	Maximum Average Pressure		Standard barrel for velocity testing:
		Copper Crusher	Transducer	
N/S	N/S	3800 bar	4370 bar	26 inches long - 1 turn in 14 inch twist

Weatherby 55-grain Pointed - Expanding (H 224 55 SP)

Distance - Yards	Muzzle	100	200	300	400	500
Velocity - fps	3650	3192	2780	2403	2056	1741
Energy - ft-lb	1627	1244	944	705	516	370
Taylor KO values	6.4	5.6	4.9	4.2	3.6	3.1
Path - inches	-1.5	1.0	0.0	-5.5	-17.1	-37.0
Wind drift - inches	0.0	1.0	4.3	10.2	19.6	33.0

G1 Ballistic Coefficient = 0.220

.220 Swift

When it was introduced in 1935, the .220 Swift was the "swiftest" cartridge in the factory inventory. Today, the Swift still claims the "record" (4200 fps with a 40-grain bullet), but by only 50 fps over the .22-250 with the same bullet weight. Much of what has been written about the Swift is a direct steal from the stories about King Arthur's sword, mostly myth. The .220 Swift doesn't need any fiction. It's a very high velocity .22, one suitable for all varmint applications. Part of the Swift's bad press has resulted from shooters using thin-jacketed varmint bullets on deer-sized game. The results are seldom satisfactory, but it is unfair to blame the cartridge for the foolishness of a few uninformed people.

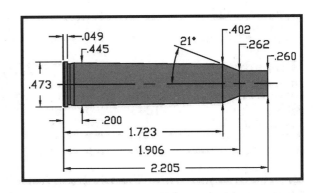

Relative Recoil Factor = 0.90   **Controlling Agency: CIP**

Bullet Weight Grains	Velocity fps	Maximum Average Pressure		Standard barrel for velocity testing:
		Copper Crusher	Transducer	
55	3650	54,000 cup	N/A	24 inches long - 1 turn in 14 inch twist
60	3600	54,000 cup	N/A	

Hornady 40-grain V-Max Moly (83203)

Distance - Yards	Muzzle	100	200	300	400	500
Velocity - fps	4200	3678	3190	2739	2329	1962
Energy - ft-lb	1566	1201	904	666	482	342
Taylor KO values	5.4	4.7	4.1	3.5	3.0	2.5
Path - inches	-1.5	0.5	0.0	-4.0	-12.9	-27.4
Wind drift - inches	0.0	0.9	3.9	9.4	17.8	29.9

G1 Ballistic Coefficient = 0.220

Winchester 40-grain Ballistic Silvertip (SBST220)

Distance - Yards	Muzzle	100	200	300	400	500
Velocity - fps	4050	3518	3048	2624	2238	1885
Energy - ft-lb	1457	1099	825	611	445	316
Taylor KO values	5.2	4.5	3.9	3.4	2.9	2.4
Path - inches	-1.5	0.7	0.0	-4.4	-13.9	-30.4
Wind drift - inches	0.0	1.0	4.1	9.7	18.5	31.2

G1 Ballistic Coefficient = 0.221

Norma 50-grain SP (15701)

Distance - Yards	Muzzle	100	200	300	400	500
Velocity - fps	4019	3380	2826	2335	1895	1516
Energy - ft-lb	1794	1268	887	605	399	255
Taylor KO values	6.4	5.4	4.5	3.7	3.0	2.4
Path - inches	-1.5	0.7	0.0	-5.1	-16.9	-38.4
Wind drift - inches	0.0	1.2	5.2	12.6	24.6	42.6

G1 Ballistic Coefficient = 0.180

Winchester 50-grain Pointed SP (X220S)

Distance - Yards	Muzzle	100	200	300	400	500
Velocity - fps	3870	3310	2816	2373	1972	1616
Energy - ft-lb	1663	1226	881	625	432	290
Taylor KO values	6.2	5.3	4.5	3.8	3.2	2.6
Path - inches	-1.5	0.8	0.0	-5.2	-16.7	-37.1
Wind drift - inches	0.0	1.1	4.8	11.6	22.4	38.4

G1 Ballistic Coefficient = 0.200

Hornady 50-grain SP (8121)

Distance - Yards	Muzzle	100	200	300	400	500
Velocity - fps	3850	3327	2862	2442	2060	1716
Energy - ft-lb	1645	1228	909	662	471	327
Taylor KO values	6.2	5.3	4.6	3.9	3.3	2.7
Path - inches	-1.5	0.8	0.0	-5.1	-16.1	-35.3
Wind drift - inches	0.0	1.0	4.5	10.7	20.6	35.0

G1 Ballistic Coefficient = 0.213

Remington 50-grain Pointed SP (R220S1)

Distance - Yards	Muzzle	100	200	300	400	500
Velocity - fps	3780	3158	2617	2135	1710	1357
Energy - ft-lb	1586	1107	760	506	325	204
Taylor KO values	6.0	5.1	4.2	3.4	2.7	2.2
Path - inches	-1.5	1.0	0.0	-6.2	-20.1	-46.2
Wind drift - inches	0.0	1.3	5.7	14.1	27.8	48.6

G1 Ballistic Coefficient = 0.175

Hornady 50-grain V-Max Moly (83213)

Distance - Yards	Muzzle	100	200	300	400	500
Velocity - fps	3850	3396	2970	2576	2215	1894
Energy - ft-lb	1645	1280	979	736	545	398
Taylor KO values	6.2	5.4	4.8	4.1	3.5	3.0
Path - inches	-1.5	0.7	0.0	-4.8	-15.1	-32.2
Wind drift - inches	0.0	0.9	3.9	9.4	17.7	29.8

G1 Ballistic Coefficient = 0.233

Remington 50-grain V-Max Boattail (PRV220SA)

Distance - Yards	Muzzle	100	200	300	400	500
Velocity - fps	3780	3321	2908	2532	2185	1866
Energy - ft-lb	1586	1224	939	711	530	387
Taylor KO values	6.0	5.3	4.7	4.1	3.5	3.0
Path - inches	-1.5	0.8	0.0	-5.0	-15.4	-33.2
Wind drift - inches	0.0	0.9	4.0	9.5	18.0	30.2

G1 Ballistic Coefficient = 0.239

Federal 52-grain Sierra MatchKing HP Boattail (P220V)

Distance - Yards	Muzzle	100	200	300	400	500
Velocity - fps	3830	3370	2960	2600	2230	1910
Energy - ft-lb	1690	1310	1010	770	575	420
Taylor KO values	6.4	5.6	4.9	4.3	3.7	3.2
Path - inches	-1.5	0.8	0.0	-4.8	-14.9	-31.9
Wind drift - inches	0.0	0.9	3.9	9.2	17.4	29.2

G1 Ballistic Coefficient = 0.250

Federal 55-grain Trophy Bonded Bear Claw (P220T1)

Distance - Yards	Muzzle	100	200	300	400	500
Velocity - fps	3700	3170	2690	2270	1880	1540
Energy - ft-lb	1670	1225	885	625	430	290
Taylor KO values	6.5	5.8	4.7	4.0	3.3	2.7
Path - inches	-1.5	1.0	0.0	-5.8	-18.5	-40.3
Wind drift - inches	0.0	1.2	5.0	12.1	23.5	40.3

G1 Ballistic Coefficient = 0.202

Federal 55-grain Sierra BlitzKing (P220A)

Distance - Yards	Muzzle	100	200	300	400	500
Velocity - fps	3800	3370	2990	2630	2310	2000
Energy - ft-lb	1765	1390	1090	850	650	490
Taylor KO values	6.7	5.9	5.3	4.6	4.1	3.5
Path - inches	-1.5	0.8	0.0	-4.7	-14.4	-30.7
Wind drift - inches	0.0	0.9	3.6	8.5	16.1	26.8

G1 Ballistic Coefficient = 0.263

Hornady 55-grain V-Max Moly (83243)

Distance - Yards	Muzzle	100	200	300	400	500
Velocity - fps	3680	3215	2876	2517	2183	1887
Energy - ft-lb	1654	1302	1010	772	582	435
Taylor KO values	6.5	5.7	5.1	4.4	3.8	3.3
Path - inches	-1.5	0.9	0.0	-5.3	-16.1	-34.1
Wind drift - inches	0.0	0.9	3.8	9.1	17.2	28.8

G1 Ballistic Coefficient = 0.258

Hornady 60-grain HP (81122)

Distance - Yards	Muzzle	100	200	300	400	500
Velocity - fps	3600	3199	2824	2475	2156	1868
Energy - ft-lb	1727	1364	1063	816	619	465
Taylor KO values	6.9	6.1	5.4	4.8	4.1	3.6
Path - inches	-1.5	1.0	0.0	-5.4	-16.3	-34.8
Wind drift - inches	0.0	0.9	3.9	9.2	17.3	29.0

G1 Ballistic Coefficient = 0.264

.243 Winchester

The .243 Winchester was the first (1955) of the spinoffs of the .308 cartridge after the .308s military adoption in 1954. There were few other 6mm cartridges to compete against. Except for the 6mm Navy, which was very much unloved and effectively obsolete, the 6mm size didn't go anywhere in the United States until after the announcement of the .243 Win. Today the 6 mm calibers have taken over the middle ground between the .22s and the 7mms from the .25 caliber guns. The .243 is a truly versatile cartridge, one that's an excellent varmint caliber with the lighter bullets while retaining a very good capability against deer-sized game with bullets in the 100-grain weight class.

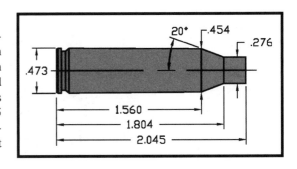

Relative Recoil Factor = 1.25   **Controlling: SAAMI**

Bullet Weight Grains	Velocity fps	Maximum Average Pressure		
		Copper Crusher	Transducer	
75	3325	52,000 cup	60,000 psi	
80	3325	52,000 cup	60,000 psi	
85-87	3300	52,000 cup	60,000 psi	
100	2950	52,000 cup	60,000 psi	

Standard barrel for velocity testing:
24 inches long - 1 turn in 10 inch twist

Winchester 55-grain Ballistic Silvertip (SBST243)

Distance - Yards	Muzzle	100	200	300	400	500
Velocity - fps	4025	3597	3209	2853	2525	2220
Energy - ft-lb	1978	1579	1257	994	779	602
Taylor KO values	7.7	6.7	6.1	5.4	4.8	4.2
Path - inches	-1.5	0.6	0.0	-4.0	-12.3	-26.0
Wind drift - inches	0.0	0.0	3.2	7.5	14.0	23.2

G1 Ballistic Coefficient = 0.277

Hornady 58-grain V-MAX Moly (83423)

Distance - Yards	Muzzle	100	200	300	400	500
Velocity - fps	3750	3319	2913	2539	2195	1889
Energy - ft-lb	1811	1469	1107	820	595	425
Taylor KO values	7.2	6.7	5.9	5.1	4.4	3.8
Path - inches	-1.5	1.2	0.0	-5.5	-16.4	-34.5
Wind Drift - inches	0.0	0.9	3.9	9.3	17.5	29.4

G1 Ballistic Coefficient = 0.249

Federal 70-grain Speer TNT HP (P243V1)

Distance - Yards	Muzzle	100	200	300	400	500
Velocity - fps	3400	3040	2700	2390	2100	1830
Energy - ft-lb	1795	1435	1135	890	685	520
Taylor KO values	8.4	7.4	6.6	5.8	5.1	4.4
Path - inches	-1.5	1.1	0.0	-5.9	-18.0	-37.9
Wind Drift - inches	0.0	0.9	3.8	9.1	17.1	28.5

G1 Ballistic Coefficient = 0.213

Federal 70-grain Nosler Ballistic Tip (P243F)

Distance - Yards	Muzzle	100	200	300	400	500
Velocity - fps	3400	3070	2760	2470	2200	1950
Energy - ft-lb	1785	1465	1185	950	755	590
Taylor KO values	8.3	7.5	6.7	6.0	5.3	4.7
Path - inches	-1.5	1.1	0.0	-5.7	-17.1	-35.7
Wind Drift - inches	0.0	0.8	3.4	8.1	15.2	25.2

G1 Ballistic Coefficient = 0.310

Remington 75-grain V-Max Boattail (PRV243WC)

Distance - Yards	Muzzle	100	200	300	400	500
Velocity - fps	3375	3065	2775	2504	2248	2008
Energy - ft-lb	1897	1564	1282	1044	842	671
Taylor KO values	8.8	8.0	7.2	6.5	5.9	5.2
Path - inches	-1.5	1.1	0.0	-5.6	-16.8	-34.9
Wind Drift - inches	0.0	0.0	3.2	7.6	14.2	23.4

G1 Ballistic Coefficient = 0.331

Hornady 75-grain HP (8040)

Distance - Yards	Muzzle	100	200	300	400	500
Velocity - fps	3400	2970	2578	2219	1890	1595
Energy - ft-lb	1926	1469	1107	820	595	425
Taylor KO values	8.9	7.7	6.7	5.8	4.9	4.2
Path - inches	-1.5	1.2	0.0	-6.5	-20.3	-43.8
Wind Drift - inches	0.0	1.1	4.7	11.2	21.5	36.4

G1 Ballistic Coefficient = 0.236

Federal 80-grain Sierra Pro-Hunter SP (243AS)

Distance - Yards	Muzzle	100	200	300	400	500
Velocity - fps	3350	2960	2590	2260	1950	1670
Energy - ft-lb	1995	1550	1195	905	675	495
Taylor KO values	9.3	8.2	7.2	6.3	5.4	4.6
Path - inches	-1.5	1.3	0.0	-6.4	-19.7	-42.2
Wind Drift - inches	0.0	1.0	4.3	10.4	19.8	33.2

G1 Ballistic Coefficient = 0.256

Remington 80-grain Pointed SP (R243W1)

Distance - Yards	Muzzle	100	200	300	400	500
Velocity - fps	3350	2955	2593	2259	1951	1670
Energy - ft-lb	1993	1551	1194	906	676	495
Taylor KO values	9.3	8.2	7.2	6.3	5.4	4.6
Path - inches	-1.5	1.2	0.0	-6.5	-19.8	-42.4
Wind Drift - inches	0.0	1.0	4.4	10.4	19.9	33.4

G1 Ballistic Coefficient = 0.256

Winchester 80-grain Pointed SP (X2431)

Distance - Yards	Muzzle	100	200	300	400	500
Velocity - fps	3350	2955	2593	2259	1951	1670
Energy - ft-lb	1993	1551	1194	906	676	495
Taylor KO values	9.3	8.2	7.2	6.3	5.4	4.6
Path - inches	-1.5	1.2	0.0	-6.5	-19.8	-42.4
Wind Drift - inches	0.0	1.0	4.4	10.4	19.9	33.4

G1 Ballistic Coefficient = 0.256

PMC 80-grain Pointed SP (243A)

Distance - Yards	Muzzle	100	200	300	400	500F
Velocity - fps	2940	2684	2444	2215	1999	1796
Energy - ft-lb	1535	1280	1060	871	709	574
Taylor KO values	8.2	7.5	6.8	6.2	5.6	5.0
Path - inches	-1.5	1.7	0.0	-7.5	-22.1	-45.3
Wind Drift - inches	0.0	0.8	3.5	8.2	15.4	25.3

G1 Ballistic Coefficient = 0.364

Remington 80-grain HP Power-Lokt (R243W2)

Distance - Yards	Muzzle	100	200	300	400	500
Velocity - fps	3350	2955	2593	2259	1951	1670
Energy - ft-lb	1933	1551	1194	906	676	495
Taylor KO values	9.3	8.2	7.2	6.3	5.4	4.6
Path - inches	-1.5	1.2	0.0	-6.4	-19.8	-42.3
Wind Drift - inches	0.0	1.0	4.3	10.4	19.8	33.2

G1 Ballistic Coefficient = 0.256

Federal 85-grain Sierra GameKing HP Boattail (P243D)

Distance - Yards	Muzzle	100	200	300	400	500
Velocity - fps	3320	3070	2830	2600	2380	2180
Energy - ft-lb	2080	1770	1510	1280	1070	890
Taylor KO values	9.8	9.1	8.4	7.7	7.0	6.4
Path - inches	-1.5	1.1	0.0	-5.5	-16.1	-32.8
Wind Drift - inches	0.0	0.6	2.7	6.2	11.6	18.8

G1 Ballistic Coefficient = 0.402

PMC 85-grain HP Boattail (243VA)

Distance - Yards	Muzzle	100	200	300	400	500
Velocity - fps	3275	2922	2596	2292	2009	1748
Energy - ft-lb	2024	1611	1272	991	761	577
Taylor KO values	9.7	8.6	7.7	6.8	5.9	5.2
Path - inches	-1.5	1.3	0.0	-6.5	-19.7	-41.4
Wind Drift - inches	0.0	1.0	4.0	9.6	18.0	30.1

G1 Ballistic Coefficient = 0.282

Remington 90-grain Pointed SP, Ballistic Tip (PRT243WC)

Distance - Yards	Muzzle	100	200	300	400	500
Velocity - fps	3120	2871	2636	2411	2199	1997
Energy - ft-lb	1945	1647	1388	1162	966	797
Taylor KO values	9.7	8.5	7.8	7.1	6.5	5.9
Path - inches	-1.5	1.4	0.0	-6.4	-18.8	-38.4
Wind Drift - inches	0.0	0.7	3.0	7.0	13.0	21.3

G1 Ballistic Coefficient = 0.390

Lapua 90-grain FMJ (4316050)

Distance - Yards	Muzzle	100	200	300	400	500
Velocity - fps	2904	2659	2427	2206	1998	1801
Energy - ft-lb	1686	1413	1117	973	798	649
Taylor KO values	9.1	8.3	7.6	6.9	6.2	5.6
Path - inches	-1.5	1.7	0.0	-7.6	-22.4	-46.0
Wind Drift - inches	0.0	0.8	3.4	8.1	15.0	24.7

G1 Ballistic Coefficient = 0.378

Winchester 95-grain Ballistic Silvertip (SBST243A)

Distance - Yards	Muzzle	100	200	300	400	500
Velocity - fps	3100	2854	2626	2410	2203	2007
Energy - ft-lb	2021	1719	1455	1225	1024	850
Taylor KO values	10.2	9.4	8.7	7.9	7.3	6.6
Path - inches	-1.5	1.4	0.0	-6.4	-18.9	-38.4
Wind Drift - inches	0.0	0.7	3.0	6.9	18.9	38.4

G1 Ballistic Coefficient = 0.400

Hornady 100-grain SP Boattail - Light Magnum (8546)

Distance - Yards	Muzzle	100	200	300	400	500
Velocity - fps	3100	2839	2592	2358	2138	1936
Energy - ft-lb	2133	1790	1491	1235	1014	832
Taylor KO values	10.8	9.9	9.0	8.2	7.4	6.7
Path - inches	-1.5	1.5	0.0	-6.8	-19.8	-40.2
Wind Drift - inches	0.0	0.8	3.2	7.5	13.9	22.8

G1 Ballistic Coefficient = 0.373

Winchester 100-grain Power Point Plus (SHV2432)

Distance - Yards	Muzzle	100	200	300	400	500
Velocity - fps	3090	2818	2562	2321	2092	1877
Energy - ft-lb	2121	1764	1458	1196	972	782
Taylor KO values	10.7	9.8	8.9	8.1	7.3	6.5
Path - inches	-1.5	1.3	0.0	-6.7	-20.0	-41.1
Wind Drift - inches	0.0	0.8	3.4	7.9	14.8	24.4

G1 Ballistic Coefficient = 0.355

Lapua 100-grain Mega SP (4316054)

Distance - Yards	Muzzle	100	200	300	400	500
Velocity - fps	2986	2788	2598	2417	2242	2075
Energy - ft-lb	1980	1726	1499	1297	1117	956
Taylor KO values	10.4	9.7	9.0	8.4	7.8	7.2
Path - inches	-1.5	1.5	0.0	-6.6	-19.3	-38.8
Wind Drift - inches	0.0	0.6	2.6	5.9	11.0	17.7

G1 Ballistic Coefficient = 0.479

Norma 100-grain SP (16003)

Distance - Yards	Muzzle	100	200	300	400	500
Velocity - fps	3018	2747	2493	2252	2026	1813
Energy - ft-lb	2023	1677	1380	1126	912	730
Taylor KO values	10.5	9.5	8.7	7.8	7.0	6.3
Path - inches	-1.5	1.5	0.0	-7.1	-21.2	-43.8
Wind Drift - inches	0.0	0.8	3.5	8.3	15.5	25.6

G1 Ballistic Coefficient = 0.471

Federal 100-grain Sierra GameKing SP Boattail (P243C)

Distance - Yards	Muzzle	100	200	300	400	500
Velocity - fps	2960	2760	2570	2380	2210	2040
Energy - ft-lb	1950	1690	1460	1260	1080	925
Taylor KO values	10.3	9.6	8.9	8.3	7.7	7.1
Path - inches	-1.5	1.5	0.0	-6.8	-19.8	-39.9
Wind Drift - inches	0.0	0.6	2.6	6.1	11.3	18.3

G1 Ballistic Coefficient = 0.471

Federal 100-grain Nosler Partition (P243E)

Distance - Yards	Muzzle	100	200	300	400	500
Velocity - fps	2960	2730	2510	2300	2100	1910
Energy - ft-lb	1945	1650	1395	1170	975	805
Taylor KO values	10.3	9.5	8.7	8.0	7.3	6.6
Path - inches	-1.5	1.6	0.0	-7.1	-20.8	-42.5
Wind Drift - inches	0.0	0.7	3.1	7.2	13.4	22.0

G1 Ballistic Coefficient = 0.406

Federal 100-grain Hi-Shok SP (243B)

Distance - Yards	Muzzle	100	200	300	400	500
Velocity - fps	2960	2700	2450	2220	1990	1790
Energy - ft-lb	1945	1615	1330	1090	880	710
Taylor KO values	10.3	9.4	8.5	7.7	6.9	6.2
Path - inches	-1.5	1.6	0.0	-7.9	-22.0	-45.4
Wind Drift - inches	0.0	0.8	3.5	8.4	15.6	25.7

G1 Ballistic Coefficient = 0.358

Hornady 100-grain SP Boattail (8046)

Distance - Yards	Muzzle	100	200	300	400	500
Velocity - fps	2960	2728	2508	2299	2099	1910
Energy - ft-lb	1945	1653	1397	1174	979	810
Taylor KO values	10.3	9.5	8.7	8.0	7.3	6.6
Path - inches	-1.5	1.6	0.0	-7.2	-21.0	-42.8
Wind Drift - inches	0.0	0.7	3.1	7.2	13.4	22.0

G1 Ballistic Coefficient = 0.406

PMC 100-grain SP Boattail (243HB)

Distance - Yards	Muzzle	100	200	300	400	500
Velocity - fps	2960	2742	2534	2335	2144	1964
Energy - ft-lb	1945	1669	1426	1211	1021	856
Taylor KO values	10.3	9.5	8.8	8.1	7.4	6.8
Path - inches	-1.5	1.6	0.0	-7.0	-20.5	-41.4
Wind Drift - inches	0.0	0.7	2.9	6.8	12.5	20.4

G1 Ballistic Coefficient = 0.431

Remington 100-grain Pointed SP, Boattail (PRB243WA)

Distance - Yards	Muzzle	100	200	300	400	500
Velocity - fps	2960	2720	2492	2275	2069	1875
Energy - ft-lb	1945	1642	1378	1149	950	780
Taylor KO values	10.3	9.4	8.7	7.9	7.2	6.5
Path - inches	-1.5	1.6	0.0	-7.2	-21.2	-43.3
Wind Drift - inches	0.0	0.8	3.2	7.6	14.0	23.0

G1 Ballistic Coefficient = 0.391

Remington 100-grain Pointed SP Core-Lokt (R243W3)

Distance - Yards	Muzzle	100	200	300	400	500
Velocity - fps	2960	2697	2449	2215	1993	1786
Energy - ft-lb	1945	1615	1332	1089	882	708
Taylor KO values	10.3	9.4	8.5	7.7	6.9	6.2
Path - inches	-1.5	1.6	0.0	-7.5	-22.0	-45.4
Wind Drift - inches	0.0	0.8	3.6	8.4	15.7	25.9

G1 Ballistic Coefficient = 0.356

Winchester 100-grain Power-Point (X2432)

Distance - Yards	Muzzle	100	200	300	400	500
Velocity - fps	2960	2697	2449	2215	1993	1786
Energy - ft-lb	1945	1615	1332	1089	882	708
Taylor KO values	10.3	9.4	8.5	7.7	6.9	6.2
Path - inches	-1.5	1.6	0.0	-7.5	-22.0	-45.4
Wind Drift - inches	0.0	0.8	3.6	8.4	15.7	25.9

G1 Ballistic Coefficient = 0.356

Speer 100-grain Grand Slam (24500)

Distance - Yards	Muzzle	100	200	300	400	500
Velocity - fps	2950	2684	2434	2197	1975	1766
Energy - ft-lb	1932	1600	1315	1072	866	693
Taylor KO values	10.2	9.3	8.4	7.6	6.9	6.1
Path - inches	-1.5	1.7	0.0	-7.6	-22.4	-46.1
Wind Drift - inches	0.0	0.9	3.6	8.6	16.0	26.4

G1 Ballistic Coefficient = 0.352

PMC 100-grain Pointed SP (243B)

Distance - Yards	Muzzle	100	200	300	400	500
Velocity - fps	2743	2507	2283	2070	1869	1680
Energy - ft-lb	1670	1395	1157	951	776	626
Taylor KO values	9.5	8.7	7.9	7.2	6.5	5.8
Path - inches	-1.5	2.0	0.0	-8.7	-25.5	-52.3
Wind Drift - inches	0.0	0.9	3.7	8.8	16.4	26.9

G1 Ballistic Coefficient = 0.378

Norma 100-grain Full Jacket (16002)

Distance - Yards	Muzzle	100	200	300	400	500
Velocity - fps	3018	2747	2493	2252	2026	1813
Energy - ft-lb	2023	1677	1380	1126	912	730
Taylor KO values	10.5	9.5	8.7	7.8	7.0	6.3
Path - inches	-1.5	1.5	0.0	-7.1	-21.2	-43.8
Wind Drift - inches	0.0	0.8	3.5	8.3	15.5	25.6

G1 Ballistic Coefficient = 0.282

6mm Remington

Remington's 6mm was introduced in 1963 as a replacement for a basically identical 1955 cartridge called the .244 Remington. Remington expected that cartridge (the .244) to be a formidable competitor for Winchester's .243 but their guns were built with a 1-turn-in-12-inch twist (vs. the .243's 1 turn in 10 inches). This left the .244 unable to reliably stabilize 100- and 105-grain bullets. In 1963 the caliber was renamed 6mm Remington, and the rifles were manufactured with a twist rate of 1 turn in 9 inches. The popularity of this cartridge now approaches that of the .243.

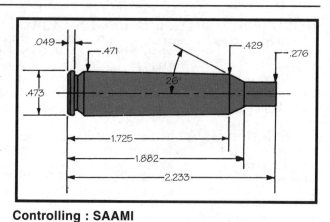

Relative Recoil Factor = 1.40

Controlling : SAAMI

Bullet Weight Grains	Velocity fps	Maximum Average Pressure	
		Copper Crusher	Transducer
80	3400	52,000 cup	65,000 psi
90	3175	52,000 cup	65,000 psi
100	3090	52,000 cup	65,000 psi

Standard barrel for velocity testing:
24 inches long - 1 turn in 9 inch twist

Remington 75-grain V-Max Boattail (PRV6MMRC)

Distance - Yards	Muzzle	100	200	300	400	500
Velocity - fps	3400	3088	2795	2524	2267	2026
Energy - ft-lb	1925	1587	1303	1061	856	683
Taylor KO values	8.8	8.0	7.3	6.6	5.9	5.3
Path - inches	-1.5	1.1	0.0	-5.5	-16.5	-34.3
Wind Drift - inches	0.0	0.8	3.2	7.5	14.1	23.2

G1 Ballistic Coefficient = 0.331

Federal 80-grain Sierra Pro-Hunter (6AS)

Distance - Yards	Muzzle	100	200	300	400	500
Velocity - fps	3470	3060	2690	2350	2040	1750
Energy - ft-lb	2140	1665	1290	980	735	540
Taylor KO values	9.6	8.5	7.5	6.5	5.7	4.9
Path - inches	-1.5	1.1	0.0	-5.9	-18.2	-38.4
Wind Drift - inches	0.0	1.0	4.1	9.9	18.8	31.6

G1 Ballistic Coefficient = 0.256

Hornady 100-grain SP Boattail - Light Magnum (8566)

Distance - Yards	Muzzle	100	200	300	400	500
Velocity - fps	3250	2997	2756	2526	2311	2105
Energy - ft-lb	2345	1995	1687	1418	1186	984
Taylor KO values	11.3	10.4	9.6	8.8	8.0	7.3
Path - inches	-1.5	1.6	0.0	-6.3	-18.2	-36.0
Wind Drift - inches	0.0	0.7	2.8	6.6	12.2	19.9

G1 Ballistic Coefficient = 0.394

Federal 100-grain Nosler Partition (P6C)

Distance - Yards	Muzzle	100	200	300	400	500
Velocity - fps	3100	2860	2640	2420	2220	2020
Energy - ft-lb	2135	1820	1545	1300	1090	910
Taylor KO values	10.8	9.9	9.2	8.4	7.7	7.0
Path - inches	-1.5	1.4	0.0	-6.4	-18.8	-38.2
Wind Drift - inches	0.0	0.7	2.9	6.8	12.6	20.5

G1 Ballistic Coefficient = 0.406

Federal 100-grain Hi-Shok SP (6B)

Distance - Yards	Muzzle	100	200	300	400	500
Velocity - fps	3100	2830	2570	2330	2100	1890
Energy - ft-lb	2135	1775	1470	1205	985	790
Taylor KO values	10.8	9.8	8.9	8.1	7.3	6.6
Path - inches	-1.5	1.4	0.0	-6.7	-19.8	-40.8
Wind Drift - inches	0.0	0.8	3.3	7.8	14.6	24.1

G1 Ballistic Coefficient = 0.357

Hornady 100-grain SP Boattail (8186)

Distance - Yards	Muzzle	100	200	300	400	500
Velocity - fps	3100	2861	2634	2419	2231	2018
Energy - ft-lb	2134	1818	1541	1300	1068	904
Taylor KO values	10.8	9.9	9.1	8.4	7.7	7.0
Path - inches	-1.5	1.4	0.0	-6.4	-18.8	-38.3
Wind Drift - inches	0.0	0.7	2.9	6.8	12.6	20.6

G1 Ballistic Coefficient = 0.405

Remington 100-grain Pointed SP, Boattail (PRB6MMRA)

Distance - Yards	Muzzle	100	200	300	400	500
Velocity - fps	3100	2852	2617	2394	2183	1982
Energy - ft-lb	2134	1806	1621	1273	1058	872
Taylor KO values	10.8	9.9	9.1	8.3	7.5	6.8
Path - inches	-1.5	1.4	0.0	-6.5	-19.1	-38.5
Wind Drift - inches	0.0	0.7	3.1	7.2	13.4	22.0

G1 Ballistic Coefficient = 0.383

Remington 100-grain Pointed SP Core-Lokt (R6MM4)

Distance - Yards	Muzzle	100	200	300	400	500
Velocity - fps	3100	2829	2573	2332	2104	1889
Energy - ft-lb	2133	1777	1470	1207	983	792
Taylor KO values	10.8	9.8	8.9	8.1	7.3	6.6
Path - inches	-1.5	1.4	0.0	-6.7	-19.8	-40.8
Wind Drift - inches	0.0	0.8	3.3	7.9	14.7	24.1

G1 Ballistic Coefficient = 0.356

Winchester 100-grain Power Point (X6MMR2)

Distance - Yards	Muzzle	100	200	300	400	500
Velocity - fps	3100	2829	2573	2332	2104	1889
Energy - ft-lb	2133	1777	1470	1207	983	792
Taylor KO values	10.8	9.8	8.9	8.1	7.3	6.6
Path - inches	-1.5	1.5	0.0	-7.0	-20.4	-41.7
Wind Drift - inches	0.0	0.8	3.3	7.9	14.7	24.1

G1 Ballistic Coefficient = 0.356

6.17mm (.243) Lazzeroni Spitfire

Lazzeroni has two lines of high-performance cartridges. The smallest of these is the 6.17mm Spitfire. This is factory-production ammunition, not a wildcat caliber (although like many cartridges it started as one). The Spitfire is a "short" magnum, suitable for adaptation to all actions designed for the .308 case. Performance levels of this and other Lazzeroni calibers are impressive.

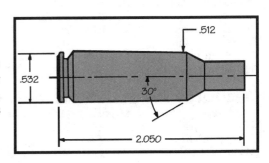

Relative Recoil Factor = 1.36   **Controlling Agency : Factory**

Lazzeroni 85-grain Nosler Partition (617SF085P)

Distance - Yards	Muzzle	100	200	300	400	500
Velocity - fps	3550	3284	3034	2798	2574	2360
Energy - ft-lb	2379	2036	1738	1478	1251	1052
Taylor KO values	10.5	9.7	9.0	8.3	7.6	7.0
Path - inches	-1.5	0.9	0.0	-4.6	-13.8	-28.1
Wind Drift - inches	0.0	0.6	2.4	5.7	10.5	17.1

G1 Ballistic Coefficient = 0.404

.240 Weatherby Magnum

Weatherby's .240 Magnum fills the 6mm line in their extended family of cartridges. The .240 is a belted case (many people think that's what makes it a "magnum") with Weatherby's trademark venturi shoulder. If you look closely at the dimensions you will see that this cartridge comes very, very close to duplicating the .30-06's dimensions, making it for talking purposes a 6mm-06. That's plenty of cartridge to give the .240 Weatherby the best performance on the 6mm list. The .240 drives a 100-grain bullet about 300 fps faster than the 6mm Remington and 450 fps faster than the .243 Winchester with the same bullet. Rifles chambered for the .240 Weatherby have dropped off the current Weatherby inventory.

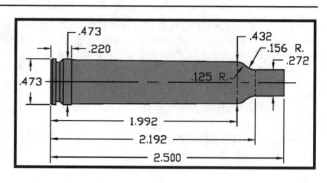

Relative Recoil Factor = 1.46

Controlling Agency : CIP

Bullet Weight grains	Velocity fps	Maximum Average Pressure		Standard barrel for velocity testing:
		Copper Crusher	Transducer	
N/S	N/S	3800 bar	4370 bar	26 inches long - 1 turn in 10 inch twist

Weatherby 87-grain Pointed-Expanding (H 240 87 SP)

Distance - Yards	Muzzle	100	200	300	400	500
Velocity - fps	3523	3199	2898	2617	2352	2103
Energy - ft-lb	2399	1977	1622	1323	1069	855
Taylor KO values	10.6	9.7	8.8	7.9	7.1	6.4
Path - inches	-1.5	0.7	0.0	-4.7	-15.3	-31.8
Wind Drift - inches	0.0	0.7	3.1	7.3	13.6	22.3

G1 Ballistic Coefficient = 0.328

Weatherby 90-grain Barnes-X Bullet (B 240 90 XS)

Distance - Yards	Muzzle	100	200	300	400	500
Velocity - fps	3500	3222	2962	2717	2484	2264
Energy - ft-lb	2448	2075	1753	1475	1233	1024
Taylor KO values	10.9	10.1	9.3	8.5	7.8	7.1
Path - inches	-1.5	0.9	0.0	-5.0	-14.5	-29.8
Wind Drift - inches	0.0	0.6	2.6	6.2	11.4	18.6

G1 Ballistic Coefficient = 0.328

Weatherby 95-grain Nosler Ballistic Tip (N 240 95 BST)

Distance - Yards	Muzzle	100	200	300	400	500
Velocity - fps	3420	3146	2888	2645	2414	2195
Energy - ft-lb	2467	2087	1759	1475	1229	1017
Taylor KO values	11.3	10.4	9.5	8.7	8.0	7.2
Path - inches	-1.5	1.2	0.0	-5.6	-15.4	-31.5
Wind Drift - inches	0.0	0.7	2.8	6.4	11.9	19.4

G1 Ballistic Coefficient = 0.379

Weatherby 100-grain Pointed-Expanding (H 240 100 SP)

Distance - Yards	Muzzle	100	200	300	400	500
Velocity - fps	3406	3134	2878	2637	2408	2190
Energy - ft-lb	2576	2180	1839	1544	1287	1065
Taylor KO values	11.8	10.9	10.0	9.2	8.4	7.6
Path - inches	-1.5	0.8	0.0	-5.1	-15.5	-31.8
Wind Drift - inches	0.0	0.7	2.8	6.4	11.9	19.4

G1 Ballistic Coefficient = 0.381

Weatherby 100-grain Nosler Partition (N 240 100 PT)

Distance - Yards	Muzzle	100	200	300	400	500
Velocity - fps	3406	3136	2882	2642	2415	2199
Energy - ft-lb	2576	2183	1844	1550	1294	1073
Taylor KO values	11.8	10.9	10.0	9.2	8.4	7.6
Path - inches	-1.5	0.8	0.0	-5.0	-15.4	-31.6
Wind Drift - inches	0.0	0.7	2.7	6.4	11.7	19.1

G1 Ballistic Coefficient = 0.385

.250 Savage

The .250 Savage is another cartridge that's nearing the end of a long and useful life. Announced in 1915, it was intended for the Savage 99 lever-action rifle. Because the 87-grain bullet would reach 3000 fps (at least in the advertising literature) the cartridge became known as the .250-3000. While the introduction of the .243 Winchester has cut deeply into the popularity of the .250 Savage, it will live for many more years in the form of the .22-250, which was based on the .250 case.

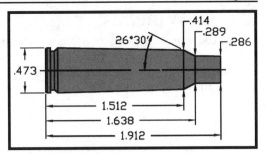

Relative Recoil Factor = 1.27   **Controlling Agency: SAAMI**

| Bullet Weight Grains | Velocity fps | Maximum Average Pressure | | Standard barrel for velocity testing: |
		Copper Crusher	Transducer	
87	3010	45,000 cup	N/S	24 inches long - 1 turn in 14 inch twist
100	2800	45,000 cup	N/S	

Remington 100-grain Pointed SP (R250SV)

Distance - Yards	Muzzle	100	200	300	400	500
Velocity - fps	2820	2504	2210	1836	1684	1461
Energy - ft-lb	1765	1392	1084	832	630	473
Taylor KO values	10.4	9.2	8.1	6.7	6.2	5.4
Path - inches	-1.5	2.0	0.0	-9.2	-27.7	-58.6
Wind Drift - inches	0.0	1.2	4.7	11.7	22.2	37.1

G1 Ballistic Coefficient = 0.286

.25-20 Winchester

The .25-20 Winchester is an outgrowth of the .25-20 Single Shot. At the time of its introduction in 1893 for Winchester's Model 92 Rifle it was considered radical because of its "sharp" 16-degree shoulder. This has almost reached the end of its commercial life.

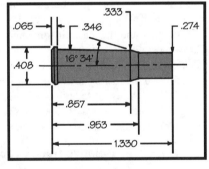

Relative Recoil Factor = 0.57   **Controlling Agency : SAAMI**

| Bullet Weight Grains | Velocity fps | Maximum Average Pressure | | Standard barrel for velocity testing: |
		Copper Crusher	Transducer	
86	1445	28,000 cup	N/S	24 inches long - 1 turn in 14 inch twist

Remington 86-grain SP (R25202)

Distance - Yards	Muzzle	100	200	300	400	500
Velocity - fps	1460	1194	1030	931	858	797
Energy - ft-lb	407	272	203	165	141	122
Taylor KO values	4.6	3.8	3.3	3.0	2.7	2.5
Path - inches	-1.5	11.4	0.0	-44.1	-128.3	-259.9
Wind Drift - inches	0.0	4.0	15.7	33.7	56.7	84.5

G1 Ballistic Coefficient = 0.191

Winchester 86-grain SP (X25202)

Distance - Yards	Muzzle	100	200	300	400	500
Velocity - fps	1460	1194	1030	931	858	798
Energy - ft-lb	407	272	203	165	141	122
Taylor KO values	4.6	3.8	3.3	3.0	2.7	2.5
Path - inches	-1.5	11.4	0.0	-44.1	-128.3	-259.9
Wind Drift - inches	0.0	4.0	15.7	33.7	56.7	84.5

G1 Ballistic Coefficient = 0.191

.25-35 Winchester

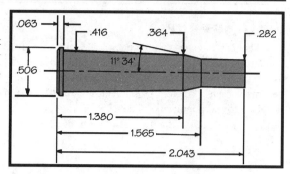

Introduced in 1895, the .25-35 Winchester has enough terminal performance at short ranges to be effective on deer-sized game. The 117-grain bullet at 2230 fps certainly isn't the same class as a .30-30 but this caliber continues to hang on in Winchester's catalog. This cartridge is also on its last legs, with only one loading offered.

Relative Recoil Factor = 1.18   **Controlling Agency: SAAMI**

Bullet Weight Grains	Velocity fps	Maximum Average Pressure		Standard barrel for velocity testing:
		Copper Crusher	Transducer	
117	2210	37,000 cup	N/S	24 inches long - 1 turn in 8 inch twist

Winchester 117-grain SP (X2535)

Distance - Yards	Muzzle	100	200	300	400	500
Velocity - fps	2230	1866	1545	1282	1097	985
Energy - ft-lb	1292	904	620	427	313	252
Taylor KO values	9.6	8.0	6.7	5.5	4.7	4.2
Path - inches	-1.5	4.3	0.0	-19.0	-59.2	-128.1
Wind Drift - inches	0.0	2.2	9.6	23.5	44.5	71.8

G1 Ballistic Coefficient = 0.214

.25-06 Remington

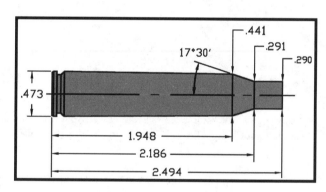

The history of the conversion of wildcat cartridges to factory numbers is rather spotty. Part of this is because, until recently, wildcatters almost never had a numerical way to measure pressures, and kept loading the charges (pressures) higher and higher until something looked like it was going to let go. That almost always led to factory velocities (at rational pressures) that were substantially lower than the wildcatters' claims. In 1969 Remington made the .25-06 into a factory cartridge. As a wildcat it had been around since the early 1920s. A few of today's .25-06 factory loadings list velocities for the 117-grain bullet in excess of 3000 fps. By comparison, some old wildcat data lists velocities well over 3200 fps with the same bullets.

Relative Recoil Factor = 1.57   **Controlling Agency : SAAMI**

Bullet Weight Grains	Velocity fps	Maximum Average Pressure		Standard barrel for velocity testing:
		Copper Crusher	Transducer	
87	3420	53,000 cup	63,000 psi	24 inches long - 1 turn in 10 inch twist
90	3420	53,000 cup	63,000 psi	
100	3210	53,000 cup	63,000 psi	
117	2975	53,000 cup	63,000 psi	
120	2975	53,000 cup	63,000 psi	

Winchester 85-grain Ballistic Silvertip (SBST2506A)

Distance - Yards	Muzzle	100	200	300	400	500
Velocity - fps	3470	3156	2864	2590	2332	2089
Energy - ft-lb	2273	1880	1548	1266	1026	824
Taylor KO values	10.8	9.8	8.9	8.1	7.3	6.5
Path - inches	-1.5	1.0	0.0	-5.2	-15.7	-32.5
Wind Drift - inches	0.0	0.7	3.1	7.3	13.5	22.2

G1 Ballistic Coefficient = 0.334

Winchester 90-grain Positive Expanding Point (X25061)

Distance - Yards	Muzzle	100	200	300	400	500
Velocity - fps	3440	3043	2680	2344	2034	1749
Energy - ft-lb	2364	1850	1435	1098	827	611
Taylor KO values	11.4	10.1	8.9	7.7	6.7	5.8
Path - inches	-1.5	1.4	0.0	-6.0	-18.4	-39.3
Wind Drift - inches	0.0	1.0	4.1	9.8	18.6	31.3

G1 Ballistic Coefficient = 0.260

Federal 90-grain Sierra GameKing HP Boattail (P2506V)

Distance - Yards	Muzzle	100	200	300	400	500
Velocity - fps	3440	3040	2680	2340	2030	1750
Energy - ft-lb	2365	1850	1435	1100	825	610
Taylor KO values	11.4	10.0	8.9	7.7	6.7	5.8
Path - inches	-1.5	1.1	0.0	-6.0	-18.3	-38.2
Wind Drift - inches	0.0	.0	4.1	9.8	18.6	31.3

G1 Ballistic Coefficient = 0.260

Remington 100-grain Pointed SP Core-Lokt (R25062)

Distance - Yards	Muzzle	100	200	300	400	500
Velocity - fps	3230	2893	2580	2287	2014	1762
Energy - ft-lb	2316	1858	1478	1161	901	689
Taylor KO values	12.0	10.6	9.5	8.4	7.4	6.5
Path - inches	-1.5	1.3	0.0	-6.6	-19.8	-41.7
Wind Drift - inches	0.0	0.9	3.9	9.3	17.6	29.2

G1 Ballistic Coefficient = 0.293

Federal 110-grain Nosler Ballistic Tip (P2506D)

Distance - Yards	Muzzle	100	200	300	400	500
Velocity - fps	3210	2960	2720	2490	2289	2070
Energy - ft-lb	2290	1940	1640	1380	1150	955
Taylor KO values	11.8	10.9	10.0	9.1	8.4	7.6
Path - inches	-1.5	1.2	0.0	-6.0	-17.5	-35.8
Wind Drift - inches	0.0	0.7	2.9	6.7	12.4	20.3

G1 Ballistic Coefficient = 0.393

Winchester 115-grain Ballistic Silvertip (SBST2506)

Distance - Yards	Muzzle	100	200	300	400	500
Velocity - fps	3060	2825	2603	2390	2188	1996
Energy - ft-lb	2391	2038	1729	1459	1223	1017
Taylor KO values	12.9	11.9	11.0	10.1	9.2	8.4
Path - inches	-1.5	1.4	0.0	-6.6	-12.6	-20.6
Wind Drift - inches	0.0	0.7	2.9	6.8	12.6	20.6

G1 Ballistic Coefficient = 0.410

Federal 115-grain Nosler Partition (P2506E)

Distance - Yards	Muzzle	100	200	300	400	500
Velocity - fps	2990	2750	2520	2300	2100	1900
Energy - ft-lb	2285	1930	1620	1350	1120	915
Taylor KO values	12.6	11.6	10.6	9.7	8.9	8.0
Path - inches	-1.5	1.6	0.0	-7.0	-20.8	-42.2
Wind Drift - inches	0.0	0.8	3.2	7.4	13.8	22.6

G1 Ballistic Coefficient = 0.392

Federal 115-grain Trophy Bonded Bear Claw (P2506T1)

Distance - Yards	Muzzle	100	200	300	400	500
Velocity - fps	2990	2740	2500	2270	2050	1850
Energy - ft-lb	2285	1910	1590	1310	1075	870
Taylor KO values	12.6	11.6	10.6	9.6	8.7	7.8
Path - inches	-1.5	1.6	0.0	-7.2	-21.1	-43.2
Wind Drift - inches	0.0	0.8	3.4	7.9	14.7	24.1

G1 Ballistic Coefficient = 0.372

Hornady 117-grain SP Boattail - Light Magnum (8545)

Distance - Yards	Muzzle	100	200	300	400	500
Velocity - fps	3110	2855	2613	2384	2168	1968
Energy - ft-lb	2512	2117	1774	1475	1220	1006
Taylor KO values	13.4	12.3	11.2	10.2	9.3	8.5
Path - inches	-1.5	1.6	0.0	-7.1	-20.3	-40.4
Wind Drift - inches	0.0	0.7	3.1	7.2	13.4	22.0

G1 Ballistic Coefficient = 0.382

Federal 117-grain Sierra GameKing SP Boattail (P2506C)

Distance - Yards	Muzzle	100	200	300	400	500
Velocity - fps	2990	2770	2570	2370	2190	2000
Energy - ft-lb	2320	2000	1715	1465	1240	1045
Taylor KO values	12.8	11.9	11.0	10.2	9.4	8.6
Path - inches	-1.5	1.5	0.0	-6.8	-19.9	-40.4
Wind Drift - inches	0.0	0.7	2.8	6.6	12.1	19.8

G1 Ballistic Coefficient = 0.437

Federal 117-grain Sierra Pro-Hunter SP (2506BS)

Distance - Yards	Muzzle	100	200	300	400	500
Velocity - fps	2990	2730	2480	2250	2030	1830
Energy - ft-lb	2320	1985	1645	1350	1100	885
Taylor KO values	12.8	11.7	10.7	9.7	8.7	7.9
Path - inches	-1.5	1.6	0.0	-7.2	-21.4	-44.0
Wind Drift - inches	0.0	0.8	3.4	8.1	15.1	24.8

G1 Ballistic Coefficient = 0.364

Hornady 117-grain SP Boattail (8145)

Distance - Yards	Muzzle	100	200	300	400	500
Velocity - fps	2990	2749	2520	2302	2096	1900
Energy - ft-lb	2322	1962	1649	1377	1141	938
Taylor KO values	12.8	11.8	10.8	9.9	9.0	8.2
Path - inches	-1.5	1.6	0.0	-7.0	-20.7	-42.2
Wind Drift - inches	0.0	0.8	3.2	7.4	13.8	22.6

G1 Ballistic Coefficient = 0.391

Speer 120-grain Grand Slam (24514)

Distance - Yards	Muzzle	100	200	300	400	500
Velocity - fps	3130	2835	2558	2298	2054	1826
Energy - ft-lb	2610	2141	1743	1407	1125	888
Taylor KO values	13.8	12.5	11.3	10.1	9.0	8.0
Path - inches	-1.5	1.4	0.0	-6.8	-20.1	-41.7
Wind Drift - inches	0.0	0.9	3.6	8.5	15.9	26.3

G1 Ballistic Coefficient = 0.329

Remington 120-grain Pointed SP Core-Lokt (R25063)

Distance - Yards	Muzzle	100	200	300	400	500
Velocity - fps	2990	2730	2484	2252	2032	1825
Energy - ft-lb	2383	1995	1644	1351	1100	887
Taylor KO values	13.2	12.0	10.9	9.9	9.0	8.0
Path - inches	-1.5	1.6	0.0	-7.2	-21.4	-44.1
Wind Drift - inches	0.0	0.8	3.4	8.1	15.1	24.9

G1 Ballistic Coefficient = 0.363

Winchester 120-grain Positive Expanding Point (X25062)

Distance - Yards	Muzzle	100	200	300	400	500
Velocity - fps	2990	2730	2484	2252	2032	1825
Energy - ft-lb	2382	1985	1644	1351	1100	887
Taylor KO values	13.2	12.0	10.9	9.9	8.9	8.0
Path - inches	-1.5	1.9	0.0	-7.5	-22.0	-44.8
Wind Drift - inches	0.0	0.8	3.4	8.1	15.2	25.0

G1 Ballistic Coefficient = 0.362

.257 Roberts

Remington adopted the .257 Roberts as a factory number in 1934 and Winchester followed a year later. The design of the .257 cartridge stemmed from work done as early as 1909 by Griffin & Howe, A. O. Niedner, and Major Ned Roberts. Their work culminated in the early '30s with a cartridge called the .25 Roberts. The .25 Roberts was a little different from the .257 Roberts, hence the two different descriptions. Both cartridges were certainly closely related to the 7x57 Mauser (as was the .30-06). The .257 Roberts is an "Oldie but Goodie" and still provides a useful capability, both as a varmint rifle and a gun for deer-sized game.

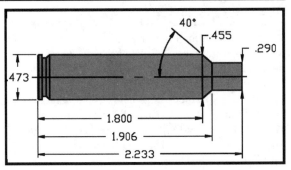

Relative Recoil Factor = 1.47   **Controlling Agency : SAAMI**

Bullet Weight Grains	Velocity fps	Maximum Average Pressure		Standard barrel for velocity testing:
		Copper Crusher	Transducer	
87	3150	45,000 cup	54,000 psi	24 inches long - 1 turn in 10 inch twist
100	2880	45,000 cup	54,000 psi	
117	2630	45,000 cup	54,000 psi	
+ P Loads				
100	2980	50,000 cup	58,000 psi	
117	2760	50,000 cup	58,000 psi	

Hornady 117-grain SP Boattail - Light Magnum (8535)

Distance - Yards	Muzzle	100	200	300	400	500
Velocity - fps	2940	2694	2460	2240	2031	1844
Energy - ft-lb	2245	1885	1572	1303	1071	883
Taylor KO values	12.6	11.6	10.6	9.6	8.7	7.9
Path - inches	-1.5	1.7	0.0	-7.6	-21.8	-44.7
Wind Drift - inches	0.0	0.8	3.3	7.8	14.5	23.8

G1 Ballistic Coefficient = 0.384

Hornady 117-grain SP Boattail (8135)

Distance - Yards	Muzzle	100	200	300	400	500
Velocity - fps	2780	2550	2331	2122	1925	1740
Energy - ft-lb	2007	1689	1411	1170	963	787
Taylor KO values	11.9	11.0	10.0	9.1	8.3	7.5
Path - inches	-1.5	1.9	0.0	-8.3	-24.4	-49.9
Wind Drift - inches	0.0	0.8	3.5	8.2	15.4	25.3

G1 Ballistic Coefficient = 0.392

Remington 117-grain SP Core-Lokt (R257)

Distance - Yards	Muzzle	100	200	300	400	500
Velocity - fps	2650	2291	1961	1663	1404	1199
Energy - ft-lb	1824	1363	999	718	512	373
Taylor KO values	11.4	9.8	8.4	7.1	6.0	5.2
Path - inches	-1.5	2.6	0.0	-11.7	-36.1	-78.2
Wind Drift - inches	0.0	1.5	6.5	15.9	30.6	51.5

G1 Ballistic Coefficient = 0.240

Federal 120-grain High Velocity + P, Nosler Partition (P257B)

Distance - Yards	Muzzle	100	200	300	400	500
Velocity - fps	2780	2560	2360	2160	1970	1790
Energy - ft-lb	2060	1750	1480	1240	1030	855
Taylor KO values	12.2	11.3	10.4	9.5	8.7	7.9
Path - inches	-1.5	1.9	0.0	-8.2	-24.0	-48.9
Wind Drift - inches	0.0	0.8	3.3	7.8	14.4	23.6

G1 Ballistic Coefficient = 0.414

.257 Weatherby Magnum

If you want the highest velocity from any .25-caliber gun firing factory ammunition, the .257 Weatherby is the gun for you. In the latter part of WW II, Roy Weatherby shortened a .300 Magnum case and necked it to .25 caliber, thereby creating a case with significantly more volume than the .25-06. All other things being equal, a larger case volume translates directly into higher velocity. With the same bullet, the .257 Weatherby Magnum is about 200 fps faster than the .25-06 and at least 400 fps faster than the .257 Roberts. The .257 Weatherby is certainly the king of the .25 caliber hill.

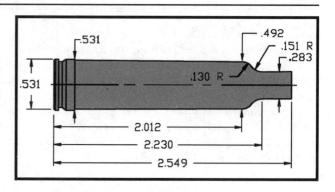

Relative Recoil Factor = 1.76   **Controlling Agency: CIP**

Bullet Weight Grains	Velocity fps	Maximum Average Pressure Copper Crusher	Transducer	Standard barrel for velocity testing:
N/S	N/S	3800 bar	4370 bar	26 inches long - 1 turn in 10 inch twist

Weatherby 87-grain Pointed-Expanding (H 257 87 SP)

Distance - Yards	Muzzle	100	200	300	400	500
Velocity - fps	3825	3472	3147	2845	2563	2297
Energy - ft-lb	2826	2328	1913	1563	1269	1019
Taylor KO values	12.2	11.1	10.1	9.1	8.2	7.3
Path - inches	-1.5	0.7	0.0	-4.2	-12.7	-26.6
Wind Drift - inches	0.0	0.7	2.9	6.7	12.4	20.4

G1 Ballistic Coefficient = 0.323

Weatherby 100-grain Pointed-Expanding (H 257 100 SP)

Distance - Yards	Muzzle	100	200	300	400	500
Velocity - fps	3602	3298	3016	2750	2500	2020
Energy - ft-lb	2881	2416	2019	1515	1260	1040
Taylor KO values	13.2	12.1	11.1	10.1	9.2	8.3
Path - inches	-1.5	0.8	0.0	-4.7	-14.0	-28.8
Wind Drift - inches	0.0	0.7	2.7	6.4	11.9	19.4

G1 Ballistic Coefficient = 0.358

Federal 115-grain Nosler Partition (P257WBA)

Distance - Yards	Muzzle	100	200	300	400	500
Velocity - fps	3150	2900	2660	2420	2220	2020
Energy - ft-lb	2535	2145	1810	1515	1260	1040
Taylor KO values	13.3	12.2	11.2	10.2	9.4	8.5
Path - inches	-1.5	1.3	0.0	-6.2	-18.4	-37.5
Wind Drift - inches	0.0	0.7	3.0	6.9	12.8	21.0

G1 Ballistic Coefficient = 0.391

Federal 115-grain Trophy Bonded Bear Claw (P257WBT1)

Distance - Yards	Muzzle	100	200	300	400	500
Velocity - fps	3150	2890	2640	2400	2180	1970
Energy - ft-lb	2535	2125	1775	1470	1210	990
Taylor KO values	13.3	12.2	11.1	10.1	9.2	8.3
Path - inches	-1.5	1.4	0.0	-6.3	-18.8	-38.5
Wind Drift - inches	0.0	0.8	3.1	7.3	13.6	22.3

G1 Ballistic Coefficient = 0.372

Weatherby 115-grain Nosler Ballistic Tip (N 257 115 BST)

Distance - Yards	Muzzle	100	200	300	400	500
Velocity - fps	3400	3170	2952	2745	2547	2357
Energy - ft-lb	2952	2566	2226	1924	1656	1419
Taylor KO values	14.4	13.4	12.5	11.6	10.8	10.0
Path - inches	-1.5	1.0	0.0	-5.0	-14.6	-29.6
Wind Drift - inches	0.0	0.6	2.3	5.3	9.8	15.8

G1 Ballistic Coefficient = 0.393

Weatherby 115-grain Barnes-X Bullet (B 257 115 XS)

Distance - Yards	Muzzle	100	200	300	400	500
Velocity - fps	3400	3158	2929	2711	2504	2306
Energy - ft-lb	2952	2546	2190	1877	1601	1358
Taylor KO values	14.4	13.3	12.4	11.4	10.6	9.7
Path - inches	-1.5	1.0	0.0	-5.1	-14.8	-30.2
Wind Drift - inches	0.0	0.6	2.4	5.6	10.4	16.8

G1 Ballistic Coefficient = 0.430

Weatherby 117-grain Round Nose-Expanding (H 257 117 RN)

Distance - Yards	Muzzle	100	200	300	400	500
Velocity - fps	3402	2984	2595	2240	1921	1639
Energy - ft-lb	3007	2320	1742	1302	956	690
Taylor KO values	14.6	12.8	11.1	9.6	8.3	7.0
Path - inches	-1.5	1.2	0.0	-6.4	-19.7	-42.4
Wind Drift - inches	0.0	1.1	4.5	10.8	20.6	34.7

G1 Ballistic Coefficient = 0.256

Weatherby 120-grain Nosler Partition (N 257 120 PT)

Distance - Yards	Muzzle	100	200	300	400	500
Velocity - fps	3305	3046	2801	2570	2350	2141
Energy - ft-lb	2910	2472	2091	1760	1471	1221
Taylor KO values	14.6	13.4	12.3	11.3	10.4	9.4
Path - inches	-1.5	1.1	0.0	-5.6	-16.4	-33.6
Wind Drift - inches	0.0	0.7	2.8	6.5	12.0	19.5

G1 Ballistic Coefficient = 0.392

6.53mm (.257) Lazzeroni Scramjet

The 6.53mm Scramjet is the .25 caliber entry in the Lazzeroni line of high-performance cartridges. The cases in the Lazzeroni line are not based on any existing cartridge. Three different case head sizes are used (see the case drawings for details). With a muzzle velocity of 3750 fps, the 6.53 comes very close to duplicating the performance of the .257 Weatherby.

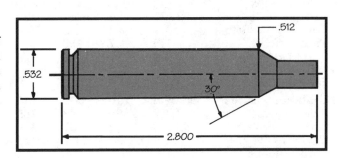

Relative Recoil Factor = 1.69

Controlling Agency : Factory

Lazzeroni 100-grain Nosler Partition (653SJ100P)

Distance - Yards	Muzzle	100	200	300	400	500
Velocity - fps	3750	3501	3266	3044	2833	2631
Energy - ft-lb	3123	2722	2370	2058	1782	1537
Taylor KO values	13.8	12.9	12.0	11.2	10.4	9.7
Path - inches	-1.5	0.7	0.0	-3.9	-11.6	-23.7
Wind Drift - inches	0.0	0.5	2.0	4.7	8.6	13.9

G1 Ballistic Coefficient = 0.454

.260 Remington

Perhaps the story of the .260 Remington should start out, "Where have you been?" That's because the .260 Remington is simply a 6.5mm-308. Since the .243 Win. (1955) is a 6mm-08 and Remington began offering the 7mm-08 in 1980, the only logical reason the 6.5 mm-08 didn't develop sooner is that the 6.5mm caliber has only recently had a good selection of bullets for the reloader. Time will tell if the .260 Remington has what it takes to become a popular "standard."

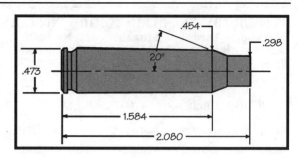

Relative Recoil Factor = 1.73   Controlling Agency : SAAMI

Bullet Weight Grains	Velocity fps	Maximum Average Pressure		Standard barrel for velocity testing:
		Copper Crusher	Transducer	
140	2725	N/A	60,000 psi	24 inches long - 1 turn in 9 inch twist

Remington 120-grain Pointed SP, Ballistic Tip (R260R1)

Distance - Yards	Muzzle	100	200	300	400	500
Velocity - fps	2890	2688	2494	2309	2131	1962
Energy - ft-lb	2225	1924	1657	1420	1210	1025
Taylor KO values	13.1	12.2	11.3	10.4	9.6	8.9
Path - inches	-1.5	1.7	0.0	-7.3	-21.1	-42.5
Wind Drift - inches	0.0	0.7	2.8	6.5	12.0	10.6

G1 Ballistic Coefficient = 0.460

Remington 125-grain Nosler Partition (PRT260RA)

Distance - Yards	Muzzle	100	200	300	400	500
Velocity - fps	2875	2669	2473	2285	2105	1934
Energy - ft-lb	2294	1977	1697	1449	1230	1037
Taylor KO values	13.6	12.6	11.7	10.8	9.9	9.1
Path - inches	-1.5	1.7	0.0	-7.4	-21.4	-43.4
Wind Drift - inches	0.0	0.7	2.9	6.7	12.4	20.5

G1 Ballistic Coefficient = 0.450

Federal 140-grain Sierra GameKing (P260A)

Distance - Yards	Muzzle	100	200	300	400	500
Velocity - fps	2750	2570	2390	2220	2060	1900
Energy - ft-lb	2350	2045	1775	1535	1315	1125
Taylor KO values	14.5	13.6	12.6	11.7	10.9	10.0
Path - inches	-1.5	1.9	0.0	-8.0	-23.1	-46.1
Wind Drift - inches	0.0	0.7	2.8	6.5	12.1	19.6

G1 Ballistic Coefficient = 0.489

Federal 140-grain Trophy Bonded Bear Claw (P260T1)

Distance - Yards	Muzzle	100	200	300	400	500
Velocity - fps	2750	2540	2340	2150	1970	1800
Energy - ft-lb	2350	2010	1705	1440	1210	1010
Taylor KO values	14.5	13.4	12.4	11.4	10.4	9.5
Path - inches	-1.5	1.9	0.0	-8.4	-24.1	-48.8
Wind Drift - inches	0.0	0.8	3.2	7.5	14.0	22.8

G1 Ballistic Coefficient = 0.431

Remington 140-grain Pointed SP Core-Lokt (PRT260R1)

Distance - Yards	Muzzle	100	200	300	400	500
Velocity - fps	2750	2544	2347	2158	1979	1810
Energy - ft-lb	2352	2011	1712	1488	1217	1021
Taylor KO values	14.5	13.4	12.4	11.4	10.4	9.6
Path - inches	-1.5	1.9	0.0	-8.3	-24.0	-47.2
Wind Drift - inches	0.0	0.8	3.2	7.4	13.8	22.5

G1 Ballistic Coefficient = 0.436

Remington 140-grain Nosler Ballistic Tip (PRT260RC)

Distance - Yards	Muzzle	100	200	300	400	500
Velocity - fps	2890	2688	2494	2309	2131	1962
Energy - ft-lb	2597	2246	1935	1658	1413	1198
Taylor KO values	15.3	14.2	13.2	12.2	11.3	10.4
Path - inches	-1.5	1.7	0.0	-7.3	-21.1	-42.5
Wind Drift - inches	0.0	0.7	2.8	6.5	12.0	19.6

G1 Ballistic Coefficient = 0.459

Speer 140-grain Grand Slam (24554)

Distance - Yards	Muzzle	100	200	300	400	500
Velocity - fps	2750	2518	2297	2087	1890	1705
Energy - ft-lb	2351	1970	1640	1354	1111	904
Taylor KO values	14.5	13.3	12.1	11.0	10.0	9.0
Path - inches	-1.5	2.3	0.0	-8.9	-25.8	-51.6
Wind Drift - inches	0.0	0.9	3.6	8.5	15.9	26.1

G1 Ballistic Coefficient = 0.386

6.5x55mm Swedish Mauser

One of the oldest cartridges in the factory inventory, the 6.5x55mm Swedish Mauser was adopted as a military cartridge over 100 years ago. The cartridge has been very popular in Europe and still ranks somewhere like 15th in the list of American reloading die sales (only a couple places behind the .30-30). Performance wise, this cartridge is virtually identical to the .257 Roberts. Because it is used in many military surplus guns with a wide range of strength characteristics, the factory specifications have been set very much on the mild side.

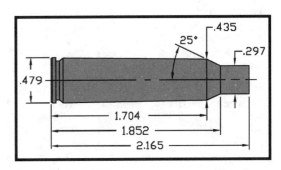

Relative Recoil Factor = 1.72   **Controlling Agency : SAAMI**

Bullet Weight Grains	Velocity fps	Maximum Average Pressure		Standard barrel for velocity testing:
		Copper Crusher	Transducer	
160	2380	46,000 cup	N/S	24 inches long - 1 turn in 7.87 inch twist

Lapua 100-grain FMJ (4316033)

Distance - Yards	Muzzle	100	200	300	400	500
Velocity - fps	2725	2360	2057	1723	1458	1241
Energy - ft-lb	1647	1238	912	659	472	342
Taylor KO values	10.3	8.9	7.8	6.5	5.5	4.7
Path - inches	-1.5	2.4	0.0	-11.0	-33.6	-72.8
Wind Drift - inches	0.0	1.4	6.2	15.0	29.0	49.0

G1 Ballistic Coefficient = 0.242

Norma 100-grain HP (16527)

Distance - Yards	Muzzle	100	200	300	400	500
Velocity - fps	2625	2354	2100	1862	1645	1449
Energy - ft-lb	1530	1232	980	771	601	446
Taylor KO values	9.9	8.9	7.9	7.0	6.2	5.5
Path - inches	-1.5	2.4	0.0	-10.3	-30.7	-64.0
Wind Drift - inches	0.0	1.3	4.8	11.4	21.4	35.5

G1 Ballistic Coefficient = 0.322

Lapua 108-grain Scenar HP Boattail (4316031)

Distance - Yards	Muzzle	100	200	300	400	500
Velocity - fps	2953	2753	2562	2379	2203	2034
Energy - ft-lb	2092	1818	1575	1357	1164	993
Taylor KO values	12.0	11.2	10.4	9.7	9.0	8.3
Path - inches	-1.5	1.6	0.0	-6.8	-19.9	-40.0
Wind Drift - inches	0.0	0.6	2.6	6.2	11.3	18.4

G1 Ballistic Coefficient = 0.471

Lapua 123-grain Scenar HP Boattail (4316032)

Distance - Yards	Muzzle	100	200	300	400	500
Velocity - fps	2855	2682	2516	2356	2202	2053
Energy - ft-lb	2225	1965	1729	1517	1324	1152
Taylor KO values	13.2	12.4	11.7	10.9	10.2	9.5
Path - inches	-1.5	1.7	0.0	-7.2	-20.6	-41.2
Wind Drift - inches	0.0	0.9	3.6	8.4	15.7	25.6

G1 Ballistic Coefficient = 0.535

Hornady 129-grain SP-Light Magnum (8550)

Distance - Yards	Muzzle	100	200	300	400	500
Velocity - fps	2750	2548	2355	2171	1995	1827
Energy - ft-lb	2166	1860	1589	1350	1139	956
Taylor KO values	13.4	12.4	11.5	10.6	9.7	8.9
Path - inches	-1.5	2.2	0.0	-8.5	-24.4	-49.6
Wind Drift - inches	0.0	0.8	3.1	7.3	13.5	22.0

G1 Ballistic Coefficient = 0.444

PMC 139-grain Pointed SP (6.5MB)

Distance - Yards	Muzzle	100	200	300	400	500
Velocity - fps	2550	2348	2156	1975	1803	1645
Energy - ft-lb	2007	1701	1435	1204	1004	835
Taylor KO values	13.4	12.3	11.3	10.4	9.5	8.6
Path - inches	-1.5	2.4	0.0	-9.9	-28.7	-58.2
Wind Drift - inches	0.0	0.9	3.6	8.4	15.7	25.6

G1 Ballistic Coefficient = 0.430

Norma 139-grain Vulcan HP (16558)

Distance - Yards	Muzzle	100	200	300	400	500
Velocity - fps	2854	2569	2302	2051	1818	1604
Energy - ft-lb	2515	2038	1636	1298	1021	794
Taylor KO values	15.0	13.5	12.1	10.8	9.5	8.4
Path - inches	-1.5	1.8	0.0	-8.4	-25.2	-52.6
Wind Drift - inches	0.0	1.0	4.2	10.0	18.8	31.2

G1 Ballistic Coefficient = 0.325

Lapua 139-grain Scenar HP (4316030)

Distance - Yards	Muzzle	100	200	300	400	500
Velocity - fps	2625	2478	2337	2200	2068	1940
Energy - ft-lb	2127	1896	1680	1494	1320	1162
Taylor KO values	13.8	13.0	12.3	11.5	10.8	10.2
Path - inches	-1.5	2.1	0.0	-8.4	-24.1	-47.9
Wind Drift - inches	0.0	0.6	2.4	5.6	10.2	16.5

G1 Ballistic Coefficient = 0.601

Norma 139-grain Full Jacket "Electron" (16525)

Distance - Yards	Muzzle	100	200	300	400	500
Velocity - fps	2625	2474	2327	2186	2050	1918
Energy - ft-lb	2127	1889	1672	1475	1297	1136
Taylor KO values	13.8	13.0	12.2	11.5	10.7	10.1
Path - inches	-1.5	2.0	0.0	-8.5	-24.3	-48.4
Wind Drift - inches	0.0	0.6	2.5	5.8	10.6	17.1

G1 Ballistic Coefficient = 0.583

Norma 140-grain Nosler (16559)

Distance - Yards	Muzzle	100	200	300	400	500
Velocity - fps	2790	2594	2407	2227	2055	1892
Energy - ft-lb	2420	2093	1801	1543	1314	1113
Taylor KO values	14.7	13.7	12.7	11.8	10.9	10.0
Path - inches	-1.5	1.8	0.0	-7.8	-22.7	-45.8
Wind Drift - inches	0.0	0.7	2.9	6.8	12.5	20.4

G1 Ballistic Coefficient = 0.467

Hornady 140-grain SP-Light Magnum-E (8575)

Distance - Yards	Muzzle	100	200	300	400	500
Velocity - fps	2740	2541	2361	2169	1999	1842
Energy - ft-lb	2333	2006	1717	1463	1242	1054
Taylor KO values	14.5	13.4	12.5	11.5	10.6	9.7
Path - inches	-1.5	2.4	0.0	-8.7	-24.0	-49.3
Wind Drift - inches	0.0	0.7	3.0	7.0	13.0	21.2

G1 Ballistic Coefficient = 0.459

Federal 140-grain Hi-Shok SP (6555B)

Distance - Yards	Muzzle	100	200	300	400	500
Velocity - fps	2600	2400	2220	2040	1860	1700
Energy - ft-lb	2100	1795	1525	1285	1080	900
Taylor KO values	13.7	12.7	11.7	10.8	9.8	9.0
Path - inches	-1.5	2.3	0.0	-9.4	-27.2	-55.0
Wind Drift - inches	0.0	0.8	3.4	8.0	14.8	24.2

G1 Ballistic Coefficient = 0.440

PMC 140-grain SP Boattail (6.5HB)

Distance - Yards	Muzzle	100	200	300	400	500
Velocity - fps	2560	2386	2218	2057	1903	1757
Energy - ft-lb	2037	1769	1529	1315	1126	960
Taylor KO values	13.5	12.6	11.7	10.9	10.0	9.3
Path - inches	-1.5	2.3	0.0	-9.4	-27.1	-54.2
Wind Drift - inches	0.0	0.7	3.1	7.2	13.2	21.5

G1 Ballistic Coefficient = 0.495

Federal 140-grain Trophy Bonded Bear Claw (P6555T2)

Distance - Yards	Muzzle	100	200	300	400	500
Velocity - fps	2550	2350	2160	1980	1810	1650
Energy - ft-lb	2020	1720	1450	1220	1015	845
Taylor KO values	13.5	12.4	11.4	10.5	9.6	8.7
Path - inches	-1.5	2.6	0.0	-12.0	-37.6	-81.7
Wind Drift - inches	0.0	0.9	3.6	8.4	15.5	25.4

G1 Ballistic Coefficient = 0.434

Remington 140-grain Pointed SP Core-Lokt (R65SWE1)

Distance - Yards	Muzzle	100	200	300	400	500
Velocity - fps	2550	2353	2164	1984	1814	1655
Energy - ft-lb	2022	1720	1456	1224	1023	850
Taylor KO values	13.5	12.4	11.4	10.5	9.6	8.7
Path - inches	-1.5	2.4	0.0	-9.8	-27.0	-57.8
Wind Drift - inches	0.0	0.8	3.5	8.3	15.4	25.2

G1 Ballistic Coefficient = 0.436

Speer 140-grain Grand Slam (24520)

Distance - Yards	Muzzle	100	200	300	400	500
Velocity - fps	2550	2318	2099	1892	1699	1523
Energy - ft-lb	2021	1670	1369	1112	898	721
Taylor KO values	13.5	12.2	11.1	10.0	9.0	8.0
Path - inches	-1.5	2.5	0.0	-10.4	-30.6	-62.8
Wind Drift - inches	0.0	1.0	4.2	10.0	18.8	30.9

G1 Ballistic Coefficient = 0.370

Winchester 140-grain SP (X6555)

Distance - Yards	Muzzle	100	200	300	400	500
Velocity - fps	2550	2359	2176	2002	1836	1680
Energy - ft-lb	2022	1731	1473	1246	1048	878
Taylor KO values	13.5	12.5	11.5	10.6	9.7	8.9
Path - inches	-1.5	2.4	0.0	-9.7	-28.1	-56.8
Wind Drift - inches	0.0	0.8	3.4	8.0	14.8	24.2

G1 Ballistic Coefficient = 0.370

PMC 140-grain HP Boattail Match (6.5SMA)

Distance - Yards	Muzzle	100	200	300	400	500
Velocity - fps	2560	2398	2243	2093	1949	1811
Energy - ft-lb	2037	1788	1563	1361	1181	1020
Taylor KO values	13.5	12.7	11.8	11.1	10.3	9.6
Path - inches	-1.5	2.3	0.0	-9.2	-26.4	-52.7
Wind Drift - inches	0.0	0.7	2.8	6.6	12.1	19.6

G1 Ballistic Coefficient = 0.536

PMC 144-grain FMJ (6.5MA)

Distance - Yards	Muzzle	100	200	300	400	500
Velocity - fps	2650	2370	2110	1870	1650	1450
Energy - ft-lb	2246	1803	1431	1122	871	673
Taylor KO values	14.4	12.9	11.5	10.2	9.0	7.9
Path - inches	-1.5	2.4	0.0	-10.5	-30.9	-64.0
Wind Drift - inches	0.0	1.1	4.8	11.4	21.5	35.7

G1 Ballistic Coefficient = 0.316

Lapua 155-grain Mega SP (4316021)

Distance - Yards	Muzzle	100	200	300	400	500
Velocity - fps	2559	2421	2288	2159	2033	1913
Energy - ft-lb	2253	2017	1801	1603	1423	1259
Taylor KO values	15.0	14.2	13.4	12.6	11.9	11.2
Path - inches	-1.5	2.2	0.0	-8.9	-25.2	-50.0
Wind Drift - inches	0.0	0.6	2.4	5.5	10.2	16.2

G1 Ballistic Coefficient = 0.630

Norma 156-grain Oryx SP (16562)

Distance - Yards	Muzzle	100	200	300	400	500
Velocity - fps	2559	2245	1953	1687	1450	1254
Energy - ft-lb	2269	1746	1322	986	728	545
Taylor KO values	15.1	13.2	11.5	9.9	8.5	7.4
Path - inches	-1.5	2.7	0.0	-11.9	-36.2	-77.0
Wind Drift - inches	0.0	1.4	6.0	14.5	27.6	46.2

G1 Ballistic Coefficient = 0.348

Norma 156-grain Alaska SP (16552)

Distance - Yards	Muzzle	100	200	300	400	500
Velocity - fps	2559	2245	1953	1687	1450	1254
Energy - ft-lb	2269	1746	1322	986	728	545
Taylor KO values	15.1	13.2	11.5	9.9	8.5	7.4
Path - inches	-1.5	2.7	0.0	-11.9	-36.2	-77.0
Wind Drift - inches	0.0	1.4	6.0	14.5	27.6	46.2

G1 Ballistic Coefficient = 0.276

Norma 156-grain TXP Line, Swift (16541)

Distance - Yards	Muzzle	100	200	300	400	500
Velocity - fps	2526	2226	2040	1818	1615	1432
Energy - ft-lb	2211	1794	1441	1145	903	710
Taylor KO values	14.9	13.1	12.0	10.7	9.5	8.4
Path - inches	-1.5	2.6	0.0	-10.4	-32.6	-67.6
Wind Drift - inches	0.0	1.1	4.7	11.3	21.2	35.0

G1 Ballistic Coefficient = 0.345

Norma 156-grain Vulcan HP (16556)

Distance - Yards	Muzzle	100	200	300	400	500
Velocity - fps	2644	2395	2159	1937	1730	1540
Energy - ft-lb	2422	1987	1616	1301	1037	822
Taylor KO values	15.6	14.1	12.7	11.4	10.2	9.1
Path - inches	-1.5	2.2	0.0	-9.7	-28.9	-59.6
Wind Drift - inches	0.0	1.0	4.3	10.1	19.0	31.4

G1 Ballistic Coefficient = 0.354

.264 Winchester Magnum

Winchester's .264 Magnum was touted to be a world beater when it was introduced in 1958. It never quite reached the popularity that was anticipated. This generally isn't because it lacked performance. The .264 WM could reach factory velocities well in excess of 3000 fps even with the heavier bullet offerings. Nothing else in the 6.5mm class came close. Barrel life and a general shortage of good 6.5mm bullets for reloading didn't help its popularity. Today only Remington (who have dropped their own 6.5mm Remington Magnum) makes factory ammo for the .264 WM and they only offer one loading, a 140-grain bullet.

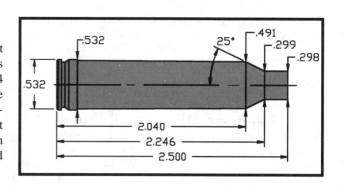

Relative Recoil Factor = 1.91

Controlling Agency: SAAMI

Bullet Weight Grains	Velocity fps	Maximum Average Pressure	
		Copper Crusher	Transducer
100	3300	54,000 cup	64,000 psi
140	3015	54,000 cu	64,000 psi

Standard barrel for velocity testing:
24 inches long - 1 turn in 9 inch twist

Remington 140-grain SP (R25202)

Distance - Yards	Muzzle	100	200	300	400	500
Velocity - fps	3030	2782	2548	2326	2114	1914
Energy - ft-lb	2854	2406	2018	1682	1389	1139
Taylor KO values	16.0	14.7	13.5	12.3	11.2	10.1
Path - inches	-1.5	1.5	0.0	-7.2	-20.8	-42.2
Wind Drift - inches	0.0	0.8	3.2	7.4	13.9	22.7

G1 Ballistic Coefficient = 0.384

.270 Winchester

When Winchester took the .30-06 in 1925 and necked it to .270, I doubt if they even guessed that it would become one of the most popular non-military calibers sold in the US. The popularity of the cartridge is demonstrated by the fact that there are over 40 different factory loadings available for the .270. That's a larger number than any other cartridge that is not a military standard. This popularity isn't an accident. The .270 drives 130-grain bullets to just over 3000 fps, providing an excellent flat shooting capability that's bettered only by the magnums.

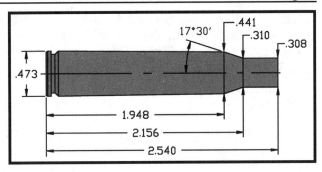

Relative Recoil Factor = 1.82   **Controlling Agency : SAAMI**

Bullet Weight Grains	Velocity fps	Maximum Average Pressure	
		Copper Crusher	Transduce
100	3300	52,000 cup	65,000 psi
130	3050	52,000 cup	65,000 psi
140	2950	52,000 cup	65,000 psi
150	2830	52,000 cup	65,000 psi
160	2650	52,000 cup	65,000 psi

Standard barrel for velocity testing:
24 inches long - 1 turn in 10 inch twist

Remington 100-grain Pointed SP (R270W1)

Distance - Yards	Muzzle	100	200	300	400	500
Velocity - fps	3320	2924	2561	2225	1916	1636
Energy - ft-lb	2448	1898	1456	1099	815	594
Taylor KO values	13.1	11.6	10.1	8.8	7.6	6.5
Path - inches	-1.5	1.2	0.0	-6.2	-20.3	-43.6
Wind Drift - inches	0.0	1.0	4.4	10.7	20.3	34.2

G1 Ballistic Coefficient = 0.253

Hornady 130-grain SST-LM (8554)

Distance - Yards	Muzzle	100	200	300	400	500
Velocity - fps	3215	2998	2790	2590	2400	2218
Energy - ft-lb	2983	2594	2246	1936	1662	1420
Taylor KO values	16.6	15.5	14.4	13.4	12.4	11.5
Path - inches	-1.5	1.2	0.0	-5.8	-17.0	-34.2
Wind Drift - inches	0.0	0.6	2.4	5.7	10.4	16.9

G1 Ballistic Coefficient = 0.457

Winchester 130-grain Power-Point Plus (SHV2705)

Distance - Yards	Muzzle	100	200	300	400	500
Velocity - fps	3154	2881	2628	2388	2161	1946
Energy - ft-lb	2865	2396	1993	1646	1348	1094
Taylor KO values	16.3	14.9	13.6	12.3	11.2	10.0
Path - inches	-1.5	1.3	0.0	-6.4	-18.9	-38.8
Wind Drift - inches	0.0	0.8	3.2	7.5	14.0	23.0

G1 Ballistic Coefficient = 0.363

Norma 130-grain SP (16902)

Distance - Yards	Muzzle	100	200	300	400	500
Velocity - fps	3140	2862	2601	2354	2122	1903
Energy - ft-lb	2847	2365	1953	1600	1300	1046
Taylor KO values	16.2	14.7	13.4	12.1	10.9	9.8
Path - inches	-1.5	1.3	0.0	-6.5	-19.4	-39.9
Wind Drift - inches	0.0	0.8	3.3	7.8	14.7	24.1

G1 Ballistic Coefficient = 0.359

Federal 130-grain Hi-Shok SP (270A)

Distance - Yards	Muzzle	100	200	300	400	500
Velocity - fps	3060	2880	2560	2330	2110	1900
Energy - ft-lb	2700	2265	1890	1585	1285	1043
Taylor KO values	15.7	14.8	13.2	12.0	10.9	9.8
Path - inches	-1.5	1.5	0.0	-6.8	-20.0	-41.1
Wind Drift - inches	0.0	0.8	3.2	7.6	14.2	23.4

G1 Ballistic Coefficient = 0.371

Federal 130-grain Sierra Pro-Hunter SP (270GS)

Distance - Yards	Muzzle	100	200	300	400	500
Velocity - fps	3060	2830	2600	2390	2190	2000
Energy - ft-lb	2705	2305	1960	1655	1390	1154
Taylor KO values	15.7	14.6	13.4	12.3	11.3	10.3
Path - inches	-1.5	1.4	0.0	-6.4	-19.0	-38.5
Wind Drift - inches	0.0	0.7	2.9	6.8	12.6	20.6

G1 Ballistic Coefficient = 0.411

Federal 130-grain Sierra GameKing BTSP (P270D)

Distance - Yards	Muzzle	100	200	300	400	500
Velocity - fps	3060	2830	2620	2410	2220	2030
Energy - ft-lb	2700	2320	1980	1680	1420	1190
Taylor KO values	15.7	14.6	13.5	12.4	11.4	10.4
Path - inches	-1.5	1.4	0.0	-6.5	-19.0	-38.5
Wind Drift - inches	0.0	0.7	2.8	6.6	12.1	19.8

G1 Ballistic Coefficient = 0.425

Federal 130-grain Nosler Ballistic Tip (P270F)

Distance - Yards	Muzzle	100	200	300	400	500
Velocity - fps	3060	2840	2630	2430	2230	2050
Energy - ft-lb	2700	2325	1990	1700	1440	1210
Taylor KO values	15.7	14.6	13.5	12.5	11.5	10.5
Path - inches	-1.5	1.4	0.0	-6.5	-18.8	-38.2
Wind Drift - inches	0.0	0.7	2.7	6.4	11.8	19.2

G1 Ballistic Coefficient = 0.435

Federal 130-grain Barnes XLC Coated-X Bullet (P270H)

Distance - Yards	Muzzle	100	200	300	400	500
Velocity - fps	3060	2840	2620	2432	2220	2050
Energy - ft-lb	2705	2320	1985	1690	1425	1203
Taylor KO values	15.8	14.7	13.5	12.5	11.5	10.5
Path - inches	-1.5	1.4	0.0	-6.4	-18.9	-38.4
Wind Drift - inches	0.0	0.7	2.8	6.5	12.0	19.5

G1 Ballistic Coefficient = 0.430

Federal 130-grain Trophy Bonded Bear Claw (P270T2)

Distance - Yards	Muzzle	100	200	300	400	500
Velocity - fps	3060	2810	2570	2340	2130	1930
Energy - ft-lb	2785	2275	1905	1585	1310	1070
Taylor KO values	15.7	14.5	13.2	12.0	11.0	9.9
Path - inches	-1.5	1.5	0.0	-6.7	-19.8	-40.5
Wind Drift - inches	0.0	0.8	3.2	7.4	13.8	22.5

G1 Ballistic Coefficient = 0.383

Hornady 130-grain SP (8055)

Distance - Yards	Muzzle	100	200	300	400	500
Velocity - fps	3060	2800	2560	2330	2110	1900
Energy - ft-lb	2700	2265	1890	1565	1285	1045
Taylor KO values	15.7	14.8	13.2	12.0	10.9	9.8
Path - inches	-1.5	1.8	0.0	-7.1	-20.6	-42.0
Wind Drift - inches	0.0	0.8	3.2	7.6	14.2	23.4

G1 Ballistic Coefficient = 0.371

Remington 130-grain Pointed SP (R270W2)

Distance - Yards	Muzzle	100	200	300	400	500
Velocity - fps	3060	2776	2510	2259	2022	1801
Energy - ft-lb	2702	2225	1818	1472	1180	936
Taylor KO values	15.7	14.3	12.9	11.6	10.4	9.3
Path - inches	-1.5	1.5	0.0	-7.0	-20.9	-43.3
Wind Drift - inches	0.0	0.9	3.6	8.5	16.0	26.4

G1 Ballistic Coefficient = 0.337

Winchester 130-grain Power-Point (X2705)

Distance - Yards	Muzzle	100	200	300	400	500
Velocity - fps	3060	2802	2559	2329	2110	1904
Energy - ft-lb	2702	2267	1890	1565	1285	1046
Taylor KO values	15.7	14.4	13.2	12.0	10.9	9.9
Path - inches	-1.5	1.8	0.0	-7.1	-20.6	-42.0
Wind Drift - inches	0.0	0.8	3.2	7.6	14.2	23.3

G1 Ballistic Coefficient = 0.372

Winchester 130-grain Silvertip (X2703)

Distance - Yards	Muzzle	100	200	300	400	500
Velocity - fps	3060	2776	2510	2259	2022	1801
Energy - ft-lb	2702	2225	1818	1472	1180	936
Taylor KO values	15.7	14.3	12.9	11.6	10.4	9.3
Path - inches	-1.5	1.8	0.0	-7.4	-21.6	-44.3
Wind Drift - inches	0.0	0.9	3.6	8.5	16.0	26.4

G1 Ballistic Coefficient = 0.337

PMC 130-grain (270HA)

Distance - Yards	Muzzle	100	200	300	400	500
Velocity - fps	3050	2830	2620	2421	2229	2047
Energy - ft-lb	2685	2312	1982	1691	1435	1209
Taylor KO values	15.7	14.6	13.5	12.5	11.5	10.5
Path - inches	-1.5	1.5	0.0	-6.5	-19.0	-38.5
Wind Drift - inches	0.0	0.7	2.7	6.4	11.8	19.2

G1 Ballistic Coefficient = 0.437

Speer 130-grain Grand Slam (24501)

Distance - Yards	Muzzle	100	200	300	400	500
Velocity - fps	3050	2774	2514	2269	2038	1822
Energy - ft-lb	2685	2221	1824	1485	1200	958
Taylor KO values	15.7	14.3	12.9	11.7	10.5	9.4
Path - inches	-1.5	1.5	0.0	-7.0	-20.9	-43.1
Wind Drift - inches	0.0	0.8	3.5	8.3	15.6	25.6

G1 Ballistic Coefficient = 0.346

Winchester 130-grain Ballistic Silvertip (SBST270)

Distance - Yards	Muzzle	100	200	300	400	500
Velocity - fps	3050	2828	2618	2416	2224	2040
Energy - ft-lb	2685	2309	1978	1685	1428	1202
Taylor KO values	15.7	14.5	13.5	12.4	11.4	10.5
Path - inches	-1.5	1.4	0.0	-6.5	-18.9	-38.4
Wind Drift - inches	0.0	0.7	2.8	6.4	11.9	19.4

G1 Ballistic Coefficient = 0.4334

PMC 130-grain Barnes-X (270XA)

Distance - Yards	Muzzle	100	200	300	400	500
Velocity - fps	2910	2717	2533	2356	2186	2023
Energy - ft-lb	2311	1976	1681	1421	1379	1181
Taylor KO values	15.0	14.0	13.0	12.1	11.2	10.4
Path - inches	-1.5	1.7	0.0	-7.1	-20.4	-41.1
Wind Drift - inches	0.0	0.6	2.6	6.1	11.2	18.2

G1 Ballistic Coefficient = 0.4334

PMC 130-grain Pointed SP (270A)

Distance - Yards	Muzzle	100	200	300	400	500
Velocity - fps	2816	2593	2381	2179	1987	1805
Energy - ft-lb	2288	1941	1636	1370	1139	941
Taylor KO values	14.5	13.3	12.2	11.2	10.2	9.3
Path - inches	-1.5	1.8	0.0	-8.0	-23.2	-47.3
Wind Drift - inches	0.0	0.8	3.3	7.7	14.3	23.4

G1 Ballistic Coefficient = 0.409

Remington 130-grain Bronze Point (R270W3)

Distance - Yards	Muzzle	100	200	300	400	500
Velocity - fps	3060	2802	2559	2329	2110	1904
Energy - ft-lb	2702	2267	1890	1565	1285	1046
Taylor KO values	15.7	14.4	13.2	12.0	10.9	9.8
Path - inches	-1.5	1.5	0.0	-6.8	-20.0	-41.1
Wind Drift - inches	0.0	0.8	3.2	7.6	14.2	23.3

G1 Ballistic Coefficient = 0.371

Federal 140-grain Trophy Bonded Bear Claw (P270T3)

Distance - Yards	Muzzle	100	200	300	400	500
Velocity - fps	3100	2860	2620	2400	2200	2000
Energy - ft-lb	2990	2535	2140	1795	1500	1240
Taylor KO values	17.2	15.8	14.5	13.3	12.2	11.1
Path - inches	-1.5	1.4	0.0	-6.4	-18.9	-38.7
Wind Drift - inches	0.0	0.7	3.0	6.9	12.9	21.0

G1 Ballistic Coefficient = 0.398

Hornady 140-grain SP Boattail-Light Magnum (8556)

Distance - Yards	Muzzle	100	200	300	400	500
Velocity - fps	3100	2894	2697	2508	2327	2155
Energy - ft-lb	2967	2604	2261	1955	1684	1443
Taylor KO values	17.2	16.0	14.9	13.9	12.9	11.9
Path - inches	-1.5	1.4	0.0	-6.3	-18.3	-36.6
Wind Drift - inches	0.0	0.6	2.5	5.7	10.5	17.1

G1 Ballistic Coefficient = 0.473

Remington 140-grain Pointed SP Boattail (PRB270WA)

Distance - Yards	Muzzle	100	200	300	400	500
Velocity - fps	2960	2749	2548	2355	2171	1995
Energy - ft-lb	2723	2349	2018	1724	1465	1237
Taylor KO values	16.4	15.2	14.1	13.0	12.0	11.0
Path - inches	-1.5	1.6	0.0	-6.9	-20.1	-40.7
Wind Drift - inches	0.0	0.7	2.8	6.5	12.0	19.6

G1 Ballistic Coefficient = 0.446

Remington 140-grain Nosler Ballistic Tip (PRT270WB)

Distance - Yards	Muzzle	100	200	300	400	500
Velocity - fps	2969	2754	2557	2368	2187	2014
Energy - ft-lb	2724	2358	2032	1743	1487	1262
Taylor KO values	16.4	15.3	14.2	13.1	12.1	11.2
Path - inches	-1.5	1.6	0.0	-6.9	-20.0	-40.3
Wind Drift - inches	0.0	0.7	2.7	6.4	11.7	19.1

G1 Ballistic Coefficient = 0.456

Federal 140-grain Trophy Bonded Bear Claw (P270T1)

Distance - Yards	Muzzle	100	200	300	400	500
Velocity - fps	2940	2700	2480	2260	2060	1860
Energy - ft-lb	2685	2270	1905	1590	1313	1080
Taylor KO values	16.3	15.0	13.7	12.5	11.4	10.3
Path - inches	-1.5	1.8	0.0	-7.3	-21.5	-43.7
Wind Drift - inches	0.0	0.8	3.2	7.6	14.2	23.2

G1 Ballistic Coefficient = 0.391

Hornady 140-grain SP Boattail (8056)

Distance - Yards	Muzzle	100	200	300	400	500
Velocity - fps	2940	2747	2562	2385	2214	2050
Energy - ft-lb	2688	2346	2041	1769	1524	1307
Taylor KO values	16.3	15.2	14.2	13.2	12.3	11.4
Path - inches	-1.5	1.6	0.0	-6.0	-20.2	-40.3
Wind Drift - inches	0.0	0.6	2.6	6.0	11.0	17.8

G1 Ballistic Coefficient = 0.486

Winchester 150-grain Partition Gold (SPG270)

Distance - Yards	Muzzle	100	200	300	400	500
Velocity - fps	2930	2693	2468	2254	2051	1859
Energy - ft-lb	2860	2416	2030	1693	1402	1152
Taylor KO values	17.5	16.0	14.7	13.4	12.2	11.1
Path - inches	-1.5	1.7	0.0	-7.4	-21.6	-44.1
Wind Drift - inches	0.0	0.8	3.2	7.6	14.2	23.3

G1 Ballistic Coefficient = 0.392

Remington 140-grain Swift A-Frame PSP (RS270WA)

Distance - Yards	Muzzle	100	200	300	400	500
Velocity - fps	2925	2652	2394	2152	1923	1711
Energy - ft-lb	2659	2186	1782	1439	1150	910
Taylor KO values	16.2	14.7	13.3	11.9	10.7	9.5
Path - inches	-1.5	1.7	0.0	-7.8	-23.2	-48.0
Wind Drift - inches	0.0	0.9	3.8	9.0	17.0	28.0

G1 Ballistic Coefficient = 0.339

Winchester 140-grain Fail Safe (S270X)

Distance - Yards	Muzzle	100	200	300	400	500
Velocity - fps	2920	2671	2435	2211	1999	1799
Energy - ft-lb	2651	2218	1843	1519	1242	1007
Taylor KO values	16.2	14.8	13.5	12.2	11.1	10.0
Path - inches	-1.5	1.7	0.0	-7.6	-22.3	-45.7
Wind Drift - inches	0.0	0.8	3.4	8.1	15.2	24.9

G1 Ballistic Coefficient = 0.373

Federal 150-grain Sierra GameKing SP Boattail - HE (P270G)

Distance - Yards	Muzzle	100	200	300	400	500
Velocity - fps	3000	2800	2620	2430	2260	2090
Energy - ft-lb	2995	2615	2275	1975	1700	1460
Taylor KO values	17.9	16.7	15.6	14.5	13.5	12.5
Path - inches	-1.5	1.5	0.0	-6.5	-18.9	-38.3
Wind Drift - inches	0.0	0.6	2.5	5.9	10.8	17.5

G1 Ballistic Coefficient = 0.482

Federal 150-grain Sierra GameKing SP Boattail (P270C)

Distance - Yards	Muzzle	100	200	300	400	500
Velocity - fps	2850	2660	2480	2300	2130	1970
Energy - ft-lb	2705	2355	2040	1760	1510	1290
Taylor KO values	16.9	15.8	14.7	13.7	12.6	11.7
Path - inches	-1.5	1.7	0.0	-7.4	-21.4	-43.0
Wind Drift - inches	0.0	0.6	2.7	6.3	11.6	18.9

G1 Ballistic Coefficient = 0.482

Federal 150-grain Nosler Partition (P270E)

Distance - Yards	Muzzle	100	200	300	400	500
Velocity - fps	2850	2590	2340	2100	1880	1670
Energy - ft-lb	2705	2225	1815	1470	1175	830
Taylor KO values	16.9	15.4	13.9	12.5	11.2	9.9
Path - inches	-1.5	1.9	0.0	9.2	17.3	28.6
Wind Drift - inches	0.0	0.9	3.9	9.2	17.3	28.6

G1 Ballistic Coefficient = 0.344

Federal 150-grain Hi-Shok SP (270B)

Distance - Yards	Muzzle	100	200	300	400	500
Velocity - fps	2850	2500	2180	1890	1620	1390
Energy - ft-lb	2705	2085	1585	1185	870	643
Taylor KO values	16.9	14.8	12.9	11.2	9.6	8.3
Path - inches	-1.5	2.0	0.0	-9.4	-28.6	-61.0
Wind Drift - inches	0.0	1.2	5.3	12.8	24.4	41.1

G1 Ballistic Coefficient = 0.262

PMC 150-grain SP Boattail (270HB)

Distance - Yards	Muzzle	100	200	300	400	500
Velocity - fps	2850	2660	2477	2302	2134	1973
Energy - ft-lb	2705	2355	2043	1765	1516	1296
Taylor KO values	16.9	15.8	14.7	13.7	12.7	11.7
Path - inches	-1.5	1.7	0.0	-7.4	-21.4	-43.0
Wind Drift - inches	0.0	0.6	2.7	6.3	11.6	18.8

G1 Ballistic Coefficient = 0.483

Remington 150-grain SP Core-Lokt (R270W4)

Distance - Yards	Muzzle	100	200	300	400	500
Velocity - fps	2850	2504	2183	1886	1618	1385
Energy - ft-lb	2705	2087	1587	1185	872	639
Taylor KO values	16.9	14.9	13.0	11.2	9.6	8.2
Path - inches	-1.5	2.0	0.0	-9.4	-28.6	-61.2
Wind Drift - inches	0.0	1.2	5.3	12.8	24.5	41.3

G1 Ballistic Coefficient = 0.261

Winchester 150-grain Power-Point (X2704)

Distance - Yards	Muzzle	100	200	300	400	500
Velocity - fps	2850	2585	2344	2108	1886	1673
Energy - ft-lb	2705	2226	1817	1468	1175	932
Taylor KO values	16.9	15.3	13.9	12.5	11.2	9.9
Path - inches	-1.5	2.2	0.0	-8.6	-25.0	-51.4
Wind Drift - inches	0.0	0.9	3.9	9.2	17.3	28.5

G1 Ballistic Coefficient = 0.345

Hornady 150-grain SP (8058)

Distance - Yards	Muzzle	100	200	300	400	500
Velocity - fps	2840	2641	2450	2267	2092	1926
Energy - ft-lb	2686	2322	1999	1712	1458	1235
Taylor KO values	16.9	15.7	14.5	13.5	12.4	11.4
Path - inches	-1.5	2.0	0.0	-7.8	-22.5	-45.0
Wind Drift - inches	0.0	0.7	2.9	6.7	12.4	20.1

G1 Ballistic Coefficient = 0.457

Speer 150-grain Grand Slam (24502)

Distance - Yards	Muzzle	100	200	300	400	500
Velocity - fps	2830	2594	2369	2156	1955	1765
Energy - ft-lb	2667	2240	1869	1548	1273	1038
Taylor KO values	16.8	15.4	14.1	12.8	11.6	10.5
Path - inches	-1.5	1.8	0.0	-8.1	-23.6	-48.3
Wind Drift - inches	0.0	0.8	3.5	8.2	15.2	25.0

G1 Ballistic Coefficient = 0.386

Norma 150-grain SP (16903)

Distance - Yards	Muzzle	100	200	300	400	500
Velocity - fps	2799	2555	2323	2104	1896	1703
Energy - ft-lb	2610	2175	1798	1475	1198	966
Taylor KO values	16.6	15.2	13.8	12.5	11.3	10.1
Path - inches	-1.5	2.0	0.0	-8.6	-24.7	-50.6
Wind Drift - inches	0.0	0.9	3.7	8.7	16.3	26.8

G1 Ballistic Coefficient = 0.370

PMC 150-grain Pointed SP (270B)

Distance - Yards	Muzzle	100	200	300	400	500
Velocity - fps	2547	2368	2197	2032	1875	1727
Energy - ft-lb	2160	1868	1607	1375	1171	993
Taylor KO values	15.1	14.1	13.0	12.1	11.1	10.3
Path - inches	-1.5	2.3	0.0	-9.5	-27.5	-55.3
Wind Drift - inches	0.0	0.8	3.2	7.5	13.8	22.4

G1 Ballistic Coefficient = 0.481

PMC 150-grain Barnes-X HP (270XB)

Distance - Yards	Muzzle	100	200	300	400	500
Velocity - fps	2700	2541	2387	2238	2095	1957
Energy - ft-lb	2428	2150	1897	1668	1461	1275
Taylor KO values	16.0	15.1	14.2	13.3	12.4	11.6
Path - inches	-1.5	2.0	0.0	-8.1	-23.1	-46.0
Wind Drift - inches	0.0	0.6	2.5	5.8	10.6	17.1

G1 Ballistic Coefficient = 0.560

.270 Weatherby Magnum

The .270 Weatherby fills the space between the 7mm Weatherby Magnum and the .257 Weatherby Magnum. From a performance standpoint, it isn't different enough from the 7mm Wby. Mag. for anyone to want both, except perhaps to be able to brag that he has a Weatherby gun in every caliber. It's a screamer; bullet for bullet Weatherby's .270 is 250 to 300 fps faster than the .270 Winchester, and that makes the caliber a great choice for hunting on the high plains. A good selection of bullet weights and styles are available.

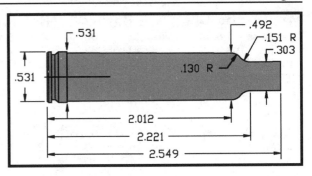

Relative Recoil Factor = 2.05   **Controlling Agency: CIP**

Bullet Weight Grains	Velocity fps	Maximum Average Pressure		Standard barrel for velocity testing:
		Copper Crusher	Transducer	
N/S	N/S	3800 ba	4370 bar	26 inches long - 1 turn in 10 inch twist

Weatherby 100-grain Pointed-Expanding (H 270 100 SP)

Distance - Yards	Muzzle	100	200	300	400	500
Velocity - fps	3760	3396	3061	2751	2462	2190
Energy - ft-lb	3139	2560	2081	1681	1346	1065
Taylor KO values	14.9	13.4	12.1	10.9	9.7	8.7
Path - inches	-1.5	0.8	0.0	-4.5	-13.6	-28.5
Wind Drift - inches	0.0	0.7	3.1	7.2	13.5	22.2

G1 Ballistic Coefficient = 0.307

Weatherby 130-grain Pointed-Expanding (H 270 130 SP)

Distance - Yards	Muzzle	100	200	300	400	500
Velocity - fps	3375	3123	2885	2659	2444	2240
Energy - ft-lb	3288	2815	2402	2041	1724	1448
Taylor KO values	17.4	16.1	14.8	13.7	12.6	11.5
Path - inches	-2.5	1.0	0.0	-5.2	-15.4	-31.4
Wind Drift - inches	0.0	0.6	2.6	6.0	11.1	18.0

G1 Ballistic Coefficient = 0.409

Weatherby 130-grain Nosler Partition (N 270 130 PT)

Distance - Yards	Muzzle	100	200	300	400	500
Velocity - fps	3375	3127	2892	2670	2458	2256
Energy - ft-lb	3288	2822	2415	2058	1744	1470
Taylor KO values	17.4	16.1	14.9	13.7	12.6	11.6
Path - inches	-1.5	1.0	0.0	-5.2	-15.3	-31.1
Wind Drift - inches	0.0	0.6	2.5	5.9	10.8	17.6

G1 Ballistic Coefficient = 0.417

Federal 130-grain Nosler Partition (P270WBA)

Distance - Yards	Muzzle	100	200	300	400	500
Velocity - fps	3200	2960	2740	2520	2320	2120
Energy - ft-lb	2955	2530	2160	1835	1550	1300
Taylor KO values	16.5	15.2	14.1	13.0	11.9	10.9
Path - inches	-1.5	1.2	0.0	-5.9	-17.3	-35.1
Wind Drift - inches	0.0	0.6	2.7	6.3	11.7	19.0

G1 Ballistic Coefficient = 0.416

Federal 130-grain Sierra GameKing SP Boattail (P270WBB)

Distance - Yards	Muzzle	100	200	300	400	500
Velocity - fps	3200	2980	2780	2580	2400	2210
Energy - ft-lb	2955	2570	2230	1925	1655	1415
Taylor KO values	16.5	15.3	14.3	13.3	12.3	11.4
Path - inches	-1.5	1.2	0.0	-5.7	-16.6	-33.7
Wind Drift - inches	0.0	0.6	2.4	5.7	10.4	16.9

G1 Ballistic Coefficient = 0.459

Weatherby 140-grain Nosler Ballistic Tip (N 270 140 BST)

Distance - Yards	Muzzle	100	200	300	400	500
Velocity - fps	3300	3077	2865	2663	2470	2285
Energy - ft-lb	3385	2943	2551	2204	1896	1622
Taylor KO values	18.3	17.0	15.9	14.8	13.7	12.7
Path - inches	-1.5	1.1	0.0	-5.3	-15.6	-31.5
Wind Drift - inches	0.0	0.6	2.4	5.5	10.1	16.3

G1 Ballistic Coefficient = 0.456

Weatherby 140-grain Barnes-X (B 270 140 XS)

Distance - Yards	Muzzle	100	200	300	400	500
Velocity - fps	3250	3032	2825	2628	2438	2257
Energy - ft-lb	3283	2858	2481	2146	1848	1583
Taylor KO values	18.0	16.8	15.7	14.6	13.5	12.5
Path - inches	-1.5	1.1	0.0	-5.5	-16.0	-32.4
Wind Drift - inches	0.0	0.6	2.4	5.5	10.1	16.4

G1 Ballistic Coefficient = 0.463

Federal 140-grain Trophy Bonded Bear Claw (P270WBT1)

Distance - Yards	Muzzle	100	200	300	400	500
Velocity - fps	3100	2840	2600	2370	2150	1950
Energy - ft-lb	2990	2510	2100	1745	1440	1175
Taylor KO values	17.2	15.7	14.4	13.1	11.9	10.8
Path - inches	-1.5	1.4	0.0	-6.6	-19.3	-39.6
Wind Drift - inches	0.0	0.8	3.1	7.4	13.7	22.4

G1 Ballistic Coefficient = 0.xx

Weatherby 150-grain Pointed-Expanding (H 270 150 SP)

Distance - Yards	Muzzle	100	200	300	400	500
Velocity - fps	3245	3028	2821	2623	2434	2253
Energy - ft-lb	3507	3053	2650	2292	1973	1690
Taylor KO values	19.3	18.0	16.7	15.6	14.4	13.4
Path - inches	-1.5	1.2	0.0	-5.5	-16.1	-32.6
Wind Drift - inches	0.0	0.6	2.4	5.5	10.2	16.4

G1 Ballistic Coefficient = 0.462

Weatherby 150-grain Nosler Partition (N 270 150 PT)

Distance - Yards	Muzzle	100	200	300	400	500
Velocity - fps	3245	3029	2823	2627	2439	2259
Energy - ft-lb	3507	3055	2655	2298	1981	1699
Taylor KO values	19.3	18.0	16.8	15.6	14.5	13.4
Path - inches	-1.5	1.2	0.0	-5.5	-16.1	-32.5
Wind Drift - inches	0.0	0.6	2.4	5.5	10.1	16.3

G1 Ballistic Coefficient = 0.466

.280 Remington

Remington introduced their .280 cartridge in 1957. This cartridge has been the source of numerous comparison articles, comparing it with the .30-06 and the .270 Winchester in particular. There really isn't much of a story here. Both the .270 and the .280 are little more than .30-06 cartridges necked to .270 and 7mm respectively. As a result, the performance of these cartridges is so similar that it comes down to exactly which bullet you prefer to use. Both are excellent calibers and if you have a .280 gun there's absolutely no reason to feel you have any more or any less gun than your friend's .270.

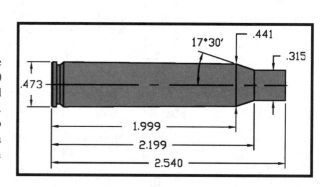

Relative Recoil Factor = 1.95   **Controlling Agency: SAAMI**

Bullet Weight Grains	Velocity fps	Maximum Average Pressure		Standard barrel for velocity testing:
		Copper Crusher	Transducer	
120	3135	52,000 cup	60,000 psi	24 inches long - 1 turn in 10 inch twist
140	2985	52,000 cup	60,000 psi	
150	2875	52,000 cup	60,000 psi	
165	2800	52,000 cup	60,000 psi	

Hornady 139-grain SP Boattail - LM (85583)

Distance - Yards	Muzzle	100	200	300	400	500
Velocity - fps	3110	2888	2675	2473	2280	2096
Energy - ft-lb	2985	2573	2209	1887	1604	1355
Taylor KO values	17.5	16.3	15.1	13.9	12.9	11.8
Path - inches	-1.5	1.4	0.0	-6.5	-18.6	-37.3
Wind Drift - inches	0.0	0.6	2.7	6.2	11.4	18.6

G1 Ballistic Coefficient = 0.438

Federal 140-grain Trophy Bonded Bear Claw - HE (P280T2)

Distance - Yards	Muzzle	100	200	300	400	500
Velocity - fps	3150	2850	2570	2300	2050	1820
Energy - ft-lb	3085	2520	2050	1650	1310	1030
Taylor KO values	17.9	16.2	14.6	13.1	11.6	10.3
Path - inches	-1.5	1.4	0.0	-6.7	-18.4	-41.4
Wind Drift - inches	0.0	0.9	3.6	8.6	16.1	26.7

G1 Ballistic Coefficient = 0.323

Winchester 140-grain Ballistic Silvertip (SBST280)

Distance - Yards	Muzzle	100	200	300	400	500
Velocity - fps	3040	2842	2653	2471	2297	2130
Energy - ft-lb	2872	2511	2187	1898	1640	1410
Taylor KO values	17.3	16.1	15.1	14.0	13.0	12.1
Path - inches	-1.5	1.4	0.0	-6.3	-18.4	-37.0
Wind Drift - inches	0.0	0.6	2.5	5.7	10.5	17.0

G1 Ballistic Coefficient = 0.485

Winchester 140-grain Fail Safe (S280XA)

Distance - Yards	Muzzle	100	200	300	400	500
Velocity - fps	3050	2756	2480	2221	1977	1751
Energy - ft-lb	2893	2362	1913	1533	1216	953
Taylor KO values	17.3	15.7	14.1	12.6	11.2	9.9
Path - inches	-1.5	1.3	0.0	-6.3	-21.5	-44.7
Wind Drift - inches	0.0	0.9	3.8	9.0	16.8	27.9

G1 Ballistic Coefficient = 0.324

Remington 140-grain Pointed SP Boattail (PRB280RA)

Distance - Yards	Muzzle	100	200	300	400	500
Velocity - fps	3000	2789	2588	2395	2211	2035
Energy - ft-lb	2797	2418	2081	1783	1519	1287
Taylor KO values	17.0	15.8	14.7	13.6	12.6	11.6
Path - inches	-1.5	1.5	0.0	-6.7	-19.5	-39.4
Wind Drift - inches	0.0	0.7	2.7	6.3	11.7	19.0

G1 Ballistic Coefficient = 0.450

Remington 140-grain SP (R280R3)

Distance - Yards	Muzzle	100	200	300	400	500
Velocity - fps	3000	2758	2528	2309	2102	1905
Energy - ft-lb	2797	2363	1986	1657	1373	1128
Taylor KO values	17.0	15.7	14.4	13.1	11.9	10.8
Path - inches	-1.5	1.5	0.0	-7.0	-20.5	-42.0
Wind Drift - inches	0.0	0.8	3.2	7.4	13.8	22.5

G1 Ballistic Coefficient = 0.391

Remington 140-grain Nosler Ballistic Tip (PRT280RA)

Distance - Yards	Muzzle	100	200	300	400	500
Velocity - fps	3000	2804	2616	2436	2263	2097
Energy - ft-lb	2799	2445	2128	1846	1593	1368
Taylor KO values	17.0	15.9	14.9	13.8	12.9	11.9
Path - inches	-1.5	1.5	0.0	-6.6	-19.0	-38.2
Wind Drift - inches	0.0	0.6	2.5	5.8	10.7	17.4

G1 Ballistic Coefficient = 0.485

Federal 140-grain Trophy Bonded Bear Claw (P280T1)

Distance - Yards	Muzzle	100	200	300	400	500
Velocity - fps	2990	2630	2310	2040	1730	1480
Energy - ft-lb	2770	2155	1655	1250	925	680
Taylor KO values	17.0	14.9	13.1	11.6	9.8	8.4
Path - inches	-1.5	1.6	0.0	-8.4	-25.4	-54.3
Wind Drift - inches	0.0	1.2	4.9	11.8	22.5	37.8

G1 Ballistic Coefficient = 0.264

Federal 140-grain Sierra Pro-Hunter SP (280CS)

Distance - Yards	Muzzle	100	200	300	400	500
Velocity - fps	2990	2740	2500	2270	2060	1860
Energy - ft-lb	2770	2325	1940	1605	1320	1070
Taylor KO values	16.9	15.6	14.2	12.9	11.7	10.6
Path - inches	-1.5	1.7	0.0	-7.5	-20.8	-42.6
Wind Drift - inches	0.0	0.8	3.3	7.8	14.5	23.8

G1 Ballistic Coefficient = 0.376

Speer 145-grain Grand Slam (24553)

Distance - Yards	Muzzle	100	200	300	400	500
Velocity - fps	2900	2619	2354	2105	1873	1658
Energy - ft-lb	2707	2207	1784	1426	1130	886
Taylor KO values	17.1	15.4	13.8	12.4	11.0	9.8
Path - inches	-1.5	2.1	0.0	-8.4	-24.7	-50.0
Wind Drift - inches	0.0	1.0	4.0	9.5	17.9	29.6

G1 Ballistic Coefficient = 0.328

Federal 150-grain Hi-Shok SP (280B)

Distance - Yards	Muzzle	100	200	300	400	500
Velocity - fps	2890	2670	2460	2260	2060	1880
Energy - ft-lb	2780	2370	2015	1695	1420	1180
Taylor KO values	17.6	16.2	15.0	13.8	12.5	11.4
Path - inches	-1.5	1.7	0.0	-7.5	-21.8	-44.3
Wind Drift - inches	0.0	0.8	3.1	7.3	13.5	22.0

G1 Ballistic Coefficient = 0.417

Federal 150-grain Nosler Partition (P280A)

Distance - Yards	Muzzle	100	200	300	400	500
Velocity - fps	2890	2690	2490	2310	2130	1960
Energy - ft-lb	2780	2405	2070	1770	1510	1275
Taylor KO values	17.6	16.4	15.2	14.1	13.0	11.9
Path - inches	-1.5	1.7	0.0	-7.2	-21.1	-42.5
Wind Drift - inches	0.0	0.7	2.8	6.5	12.1	19.6

G1 Ballistic Coefficient = 0.458

Remington 150-grain Pointed SP Core-Lokt (R280R1)

Distance - Yards	Muzzle	100	200	300	400	500
Velocity - fps	2890	2624	2373	2135	1912	1705
Energy - ft-lb	2781	2293	1875	1518	1217	968
Taylor KO values	17.6	16.0	14.4	13.0	11.6	10.4
Path - inches	-1.5	1.8	0.0	-8.0	-23.6	-48.8
Wind Drift - inches	0.0	0.9	3.8	9.0	16.8	27.8

G1 Ballistic Coefficient = 0.346

Speer 160-grain Grand Slam (24515)

Distance - Yards	Muzzle	100	200	300	400	500
Velocity - fps	2890	2652	2425	2210	2007	1815
Energy - ft-lb	2967	2497	2089	1735	1432	1171
Taylor KO values	18.8	17.2	15.7	14.3	13.0	11.8
Path - inches	-1.5	1.7	0.0	-7.7	-22.4	-45.9
Wind Drift - inches	0.0	0.8	3.4	7.9	14.7	24.1

G1 Ballistic Coefficient = 0.388

Remington 165-grain SP Core-Lokt (R280R2)

Distance - Yards	Muzzle	100	200	300	400	500
Velocity - fps	2820	2510	2220	1950	1701	1479
Energy - ft-lb	2913	2308	1805	1393	1060	801
Taylor KO values	18.9	16.8	14.9	13.1	11.4	9.9
Path - inches	-1.5	2.0	0.0	-9.1	-27.4	-57.8
Wind Drift - inches	0.0	1.1	4.8	11.4	21.7	36.2

G1 Ballistic Coefficient = 0.291

Norma 170-grain Oryx (17049)

Distance - Yards	Muzzle	100	200	300	400	500
Velocity - fps	2890	2416	2159	1918	1694	1492
Energy - ft-lb	2732	2204	1760	1386	1083	841
Taylor KO values	18.6	16.7	14.9	13.2	11.7	10.3
Path - inches	-1.5	2.2	0.0	-9.7	-29.0	-60.4
Wind Drift - inches	0.0	1.0	4.5	10.5	20.6	34.2

G1 Ballistic Coefficient = 0.321

Norma 170-grain Plastic point (17060)

Distance - Yards	Muzzle	100	200	300	400	500
Velocity - fps	2707	2468	2241	2026	1825	1638
Energy - ft-lb	2767	2299	1896	1550	1258	1013
Taylor KO values	18.7	17.0	15.5	14.0	12.6	11.3
Path - inches	-1.5	2.1	0.0	-9.1	-26.6	-54.6
Wind Drift - inches	0.0	0.9	3.9	9.1	17.1	28.1

G1 Ballistic Coefficient = 0.373

Norma 170-grain Vulcan (17051)

Distance - Yards	Muzzle	100	200	300	400	500
Velocity - fps	2592	2346	2113	1894	1692	1507
Energy - ft-lb	2537	2078	1686	1354	1081	857
Taylor KO values	17.9	16.2	14.6	13.1	11.7	10.4
Path - inches	-1.5	2.0	0.0	-9.1	-27.4	-57.8
Wind Drift - inches	0.0	1.0	4.4	10.3	19.5	32.2

G1 Ballistic Coefficient = 0.357

.284 Winchester

Winchester's .284 came on the scene in 1963. In a search for a cartridge case with the .30-06's volume that would work in shorter actions, Winchester went to a larger (0.5008 inch) body with the .30-06's 0.473-inch head size. A cartridge with this form of reduced head size is known as having a "rebated head." The .284 never really set the world on fire as a 7mm but two of its wildcat spin-offs, the 6mm-284 and the 6.5mm-284 have earned a following among long-range target shooters. Only one loading remains in the current catalogs.

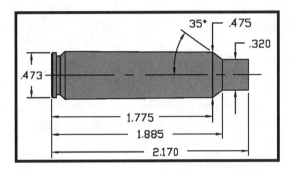

Relative Recoil Factor = 1.93   Controlling Agency: SAAMI

Bullet Weight Grains	Velocity fps	Maximum Average Pressure		Standard barrel for velocity testing:
		Copper Crusher	Transducer	
125	3125	54,000 cup	56,000 psi	24 inches long - 1 turn in 10 inch twist
150	2845	54,000 cup	56,000 psi	

Winchester 150-grain Power-Point (X2842)

Distance - Yards	Muzzle	100	200	300	400	500
Velocity - fps	2860	2595	2344	2108	1886	1680
Energy - ft-lb	2724	2243	1830	1480	1185	940
Taylor KO values	17.4	15.8	14.3	12.8	11.5	10.2
Path - inches	-1.5	2.1	0.0	-8.5	-24.8	-51.0
Wind Drift - inches	0.0	0.9	3.9	9.2	17.2	28.4

G1 Ballistic Coefficient = 0.345

7x57mm Mauser

The 7x57 Mauser is the granddaddy of all modern centerfire rifle cartridges. It was introduced in 1892 for a bolt-action rifle that ultimately became known as the Spanish Mauser. Used in Cuba in the Spanish-American War, the rifle and cartridge so far outperformed the .30-40 Krags used by the US Army at that time that it moved the War Department to expedite development of a new US military rifle and cartridge. The US Army wanted a .30 caliber and started by simply necking the 7x57 to .30 caliber. That's the easiest kind of designing; simply copy what works for someone else and put your own name on it. In any event, the outcome of all this was the 1903 Springfield rifle and the .30-06 cartridge, both classics. The 7x57 has been a commercial cartridge in the U.S. since the early 1900s. It has never been hugely popular but at an age in excess of 100 years it is still a very functional number. Because some old guns that can't stand today's working pressures still exist, factory ammunition for the 7x57 Mauser is loaded to rather mild pressure levels.

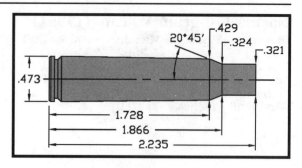

Relative Recoil Factor = 1.68   **Controlling Agency : SAAMI**

Bullet Weight Grains	Velocity fps	Maximum Average Pressure		Standard barrel for velocity testing:
		Copper Crusher	Transducer	24 inches long - 1 turn in 8.75 inch twist
139	2650	46,000 cup	51,000 psi	
145	2680	46,000 cup	51,000 psi	
154	2600	46,000 cup	51,000 psi	
160	2500	46,000 cup	51,000 psi	
175	2420	46,000 cup	51,000 psi	

Hornady 139-grain SP Boattail-Light Magnum (8555)

Distance - Yards	Muzzle	100	200	300	400	500
Velocity - fps	2830	2620	2450	2250	2070	1910
Energy - ft-lb	2475	2135	1835	1565	1330	1115
Taylor KO values	16.0	14.8	13.8	12.7	11.7	10.8
Path - inches	-1.5	1.8	0.0	-7.6	-22.1	-45.0
Wind Drift - inches	0.0	0.7	2.9	6.8	12.5	20.3

G1 Ballistic Coefficient = 0.457

Hornady 139-grain SP-Light Magnum-E (8575)

Distance - Yards	Muzzle	100	200	300	400	500
Velocity - fps	2950	2736	2532	2337	2152	1979
Energy - ft-lb	2686	2310	1978	1686	1429	1209
Taylor KO values	16.6	15.4	14.3	13.2	12.1	11.2
Path - inches	-1.5	2.0	0.0	-7.6	-21.5	-42.2
Wind Drift - inches	0.0	0.7	2.8	6.6	12.2	19.9

G1 Ballistic Coefficient = 0.442

Hornady 139-grain SP Boattail (8155)

Distance - Yards	Muzzle	100	200	300	400	500
Velocity - fps	2700	2504	2316	2137	1965	1802
Energy - ft-lb	2251	1936	1656	1410	1192	1002
Taylor KO values	15.2	14.1	13.1	12.1	11.1	10.2
Path - inches	-1.5	2.0	0.0	-8.5	-24.9	-50.3
Wind Drift - inches	0.0	0.8	3.1	7.3	13.5	22.1

G1 Ballistic Coefficient = 0.453

Federal 140-grain Hi-Shok SP (7B)

Distance - Yards	Muzzle	100	200	300	400	500
Velocity - fps	2660	2450	2260	2070	1890	1730
Energy - ft-lb	2220	1865	1585	1330	1110	930
Taylor KO values	15.1	13.9	12.8	11.8	10.7	9.9
Path - inches	-1.5	2.1	0.0	-9.0	-26.1	-52.9
Wind Drift - inches	0.0	0.8	3.4	7.9	14.7	24.0

G1 Ballistic Coefficient = 0.431

Federal 140-grain Nosler Partition (P7C)

Distance - Yards	Muzzle	100	200	300	400	500
Velocity - fps	2660	2450	2260	2070	1890	1730
Energy - ft-lb	2200	1865	1585	1330	1110	930
Taylor KO values	15.1	13.9	12.8	11.8	10.7	9.9
Path - inches	-1.5	2.1	0.0	-9.0	-26.1	-52.9
Wind Drift - inches	0.0	0.8	3.4	7.9	14.7	24.0

G1 Ballistic Coefficient = 0.431

PMC 140-grain Pointed SP (7MA)

Distance - Yards	Muzzle	100	200	300	400	500
Velocity - fps	2660	2450	2260	2070	1890	1730
Energy - ft-lb	2200	1865	1585	1330	1110	930
Taylor KO values	15.1	13.9	12.8	11.8	10.7	9.9
Path - inches	-1.5	2.1	0.0	-9.0	-26.1	-52.9
Wind Drift - inches	0.0	0.8	3.4	7.9	14.7	24.0

G1 Ballistic Coefficient = 0.431

Remington 140-grain Pointed SP Core-Lokt (R7MSR1)

Distance - Yards	Muzzle	100	200	300	400	500
Velocity - fps	2660	2435	2221	1018	1827	1648
Energy - ft-lb	2199	1843	1533	1266	1037	844
Taylor KO values	15.1	13.8	12.6	11.5	10.4	9.4
Path - inches	-1.5	2.2	0.0	-9.2	-27.4	-55.3
Wind Drift - inches	0.0	0.9	3.8	8.9	16.5	27.1

G1 Ballistic Coefficient = 0.390

Winchester 145-grain Power-Point (X7MM1)

Distance - Yards	Muzzle	100	200	300	400	500
Velocity - fps	2660	2413	2180	1959	1754	1564
Energy - ft-lb	2279	1875	1530	1236	990	788
Taylor KO values	15.6	14.2	12.8	11.5	10.3	9.2
Path - inches	-1.5	2.2	0.0	-9.6	-28.3	-58.3
Wind Drift - inches	0.0	1.0	4.2	9.9	18.5	30.6

G1 Ballistic Coefficient = 0.355

Norma 150-grain SP (17002)

Distance - Yards	Muzzle	100	200	300	400	500
Velocity - fps	2690	2479	2278	2087	1913	1749
Energy - ft-lb	2411	2048	1729	1450	1138	951
Taylor KO values	16.4	15.1	13.9	12.7	11.6	10.6
Path - inches	-1.5	2.0	0.0	-8.8	-25.8	-52.2
Wind Drift - inches	0.0	0.8	3.3	7.7	14.3	23.3

G1 Ballistic Coefficient = 0.441

Federal 175-grain Hi-Shok SP (7A)

Distance - Yards	Muzzle	100	200	300	400	500
Velocity - fps	2440	2140	1860	1600	1380	1200
Energy - ft-lb	2315	1775	1340	1000	740	585
Taylor KO values	17.3	15.2	13.2	11.4	9.8	8.5
Path - inches	-1.5	3.1	0.0	-13.3	-40.1	-84.6
Wind Drift - inches	0.0	1.5	6.4	15.4	29.4	48.9

G1 Ballistic Coefficient = 0.272

PMC 175-grain SP (7MB)

Distance - Yards	Muzzle	100	200	300	400	500
Velocity - fps	2440	2221	2015	1821	1643	1484
Energy - ft-lb	2313	1917	1577	1289	1049	855
Taylor KO values	17.3	15.8	14.3	12.9	11.7	10.5
Path - inches	-1.5	2.8	0.0	-11.4	-33.2	-67.9
Wind Drift - inches	0.0	1.0	4.3	10.1	18.9	31.0

G1 Ballistic Coefficient = 0.388

7mm-08 Remington

It took quite a while for the wildcat 7mm-08 to go commercial. There were 7mm wildcat versions of the .308 as early as about 1956 or 1957, soon after the .308 appeared. Remington announced the 7mm-08 in 1980. All the cartridges based on the .308 Winchester (7.62 NATO) are excellent and the 7mm-08 is certainly no exception. With a volume about 18 percent smaller than the .30-06, the .308 variants work out very nicely for calibers all the way down to the .243. The 7mm-08 and the .260 Remington (6.5 mm-08) are the latest to become commercial but may very well be the best of all.

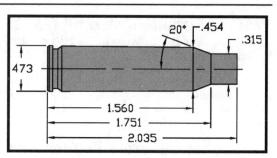

Relative Recoil Factor = 1.80   **Controlling Agency : SAAMI**

Bullet Weight Grains	Velocity fps	Maximum Average Pressure	
		Copper Crusher	Transducer
120	2990	52,000 cup	61,000 psi
140	2845	52,000 cup	61,000 psi

Standard barrel for velocity testing:
24 inches long - 1 turn in 9.5 inch twist

Remington 120-grain HP (R7M082)

Distance - Yards	Muzzle	100	200	300	400	500
Velocity - fps	3000	2725	2467	2223	1992	1778
Energy - ft-lb	2398	1979	1621	1316	1058	842
Taylor KO values	14.6	13.3	12.0	10.8	9.7	8.7
Path - inches	-1.5	1.9	0.0	-7.6	-21.7	-44.9
Wind Drift - inches	0.0	0.9	3.6	8.6	16.0	26.5

G1 Ballistic Coefficient = 0.344

Hornady 139-grain BTSP-Light Magnum (8557)

Distance - Yards	Muzzle	100	200	300	400	500
Velocity - fps	3000	2790	2590	2399	2216	2041
Energy - ft-lb	2777	2403	2071	1776	1515	1285
Taylor KO values	16.9	15.7	14.6	13.5	12.5	7.2
Path - inches	-1.5	1.5	0.0	-6.7	-19.4	-39.2
Wind Drift - inches	0.0	0.6	2.7	6.3	11.6	18.8

G1 Ballistic Coefficient = 0.454

Federal 140-grain Trophy Bonded Bear Claw - HE (P708T1)

Distance - Yards	Muzzle	100	200	300	400	500
Velocity - fps	2950	2660	2390	2140	1900	1680
Energy - ft-lb	2705	2205	1780	1420	1120	875
Taylor KO values	16.8	15.1	13.6	12.2	10.8	9.5
Path - inches	-1.5	1.7	0.0	-7.9	-23.2	-48.6
Wind Drift - inches	0.0	0.9	4.0	9.4	17.7	29.4

G1 Ballistic Coefficient = 0.324

Remington 140-grain Nosler-Ballistic Tip (PRT7M08RA)

Distance - Yards	Muzzle	100	200	300	400	500
Velocity - fps	2860	2670	2488	2313	2145	1984
Energy - ft-lb	2543	2217	1925	1663	1431	1224
Taylor KO values	16.2	15.2	14.1	13.1	12.1	11.3
Path - inches	-1.5	1.7	0.0	-7.3	-21.2	-42.6
Wind Drift - inches	0.0	0.7	2.7	6.3	11.7	19.0

G1 Ballistic Coefficient = 0.471

Remington 140-grain Pointed SP Boattail (PRB7M08RA)

Distance - Yards	Muzzle	100	200	300	400	500
Velocity - fps	2860	2656	2460	2273	2094	1923
Energy - ft-lb	2542	2192	1881	1606	1363	1150
Taylor KO values	16.2	15.1	14.0	12.9	11.9	10.9
Path - inches	-1.5	1.7	0.0	-7.5	-21.7	-43.9
Wind Drift - inches	0.0	0.7	2.9	6.8	12.5	20.4

G1 Ballistic Coefficient = 0.450

Remington 140-grain Pointed SP Core-Lokt (P7M081)

Distance - Yards	Muzzle	100	200	300	400	500
Velocity - fps	2860	2625	2402	2189	1988	1798
Energy - ft-lb	2542	2142	1793	1490	1228	1005
Taylor KO values	16.2	14.9	13.6	12.4	11.3	10.2
Path - inches	-1.5	1.8	0.0	-9.2	-22.9	-46.8
Wind Drift - inches	0.0	0.8	3.4	8.0	14.8	24.3

G1 Ballistic Coefficient = 0.390

Federal 140-grain Nosler Partition (P708A)

Distance - Yards	Muzzle	100	200	300	400	500
Velocity - fps	2800	2590	2396	2200	2020	1840
Energy - ft-lb	2435	2085	1775	1500	1265	1060
Taylor KO values	15.9	14.7	13.6	12.5	11.5	10.5
Path - inches	-1.5	1.8	0.0	-8.0	-23.1	-46.6
Wind Drift - inches	0.0	0.8	3.1	7.3	13.6	22.2

G1 Ballistic Coefficient = 0.431

Federal 140-grain Nosler Ballistic Tip (P708B)

Distance - Yards	Muzzle	100	200	300	400	500
Velocity - fps	2800	2610	2430	2260	2100	1940
Energy - ft-lb	2440	2135	1840	1590	1360	1165
Taylor KO values	15.9	14.8	13.8	12.8	11.9	11.0
Path - inches	-1.5	1.6	0.0	-8.4	-25.4	-44.5
Wind Drift - inches	0.0	0.7	2.7	6.4	11.7	19.0

G1 Ballistic Coefficient = 0.489

Winchester 140-grain Power-Point (X708)

Distance - Yards	Muzzle	100	200	300	400	500
Velocity - fps	2800	2523	2268	2027	1802	1596
Energy - ft-lb	2429	1980	1599	1277	1010	792
Taylor KO values	15.9	14.3	12.9	11.5	10.2	9.0
Path - inches	-1.5	2.0	0.0	-8.8	-26.0	-54.0
Wind Drift - inches	0.0	1.0	4.2	9.9	18.7	30.9

G1 Ballistic Coefficient = 0.331

Winchester 140-grain Ballistic Silvertip (SBST708)

Distance - Yards	Muzzle	100	200	300	400	500
Velocity - fps	2770	2572	2382	2200	2026	1860
Energy - ft-lb	2386	2056	1764	1504	1276	1076
Taylor KO values	15.7	14.6	13.5	12.5	11.5	10.6
Path - inches	-1.5	1.9	0.0	-8.0	-23.2	-46.9
Wind Drift - inches	0.0	0.7	3.0	7.0	13.0	21.1

G1 Ballistic Coefficient = 0.455

Winchester 140-grain Fail Safe (S708)

Distance - Yards	Muzzle	100	200	300	400	500
Velocity - fps	2760	2506	2271	2048	1839	1645
Energy - ft-lb	2360	1953	1603	1304	1051	841
Taylor KO values	15.7	14.2	12.9	11.6	10.4	9.3
Path - inches	-1.5	2.0	0.0	-8.8	-25.9	-53.2
Wind Drift - inches	0.0	0.9	3.9	9.2	17.3	28.6

G1 Ballistic Coefficient = 0.358

Speer 145-grain Grand Slam (24567)

Distance - Yards	Muzzle	100	200	300	400	500
Velocity - fps	2845	2567	2305	2059	1831	1620
Energy - ft-lb	2606	2121	1711	1365	1079	845
Taylor KO values	16.7	15.1	13.6	12.1	10.8	9.5
Path - inches	-1.5	1.9	0.0	-8.4	-25.5	-52.3
Wind Drift - inches	0.0	1.0	4.1	9.8	18.4	30.5

G1 Ballistic Coefficient = 0.328

Federal 150-grain Sierra Pro-Hunter SP (708CS)

Distance - Yards	Muzzle	100	200	300	400	500
Velocity - fps	2650	2440	2230	2040	1860	1690
Energy - ft-lb	2340	1980	1660	1390	1150	950
Taylor KO values	16.1	14.8	13.6	12.4	11.3	10.3
Path - inches	-1.5	2.2	0.0	-9.2	-26.7	-54.4
Wind Drift - inches	0.0	0.8	3.5	8.3	15.5	25.3

G1 Ballistic Coefficient = 0.414

7.21mm (.284) Lazzeroni Firehawk

Here's the 7mm Lazzeroni Magnum cartridge. This big boomer outperforms any other factory 7mm cartridge offered today. The 140-grain bullet has more than a 400 fps velocity edge over the 7mm Remington Magnum.

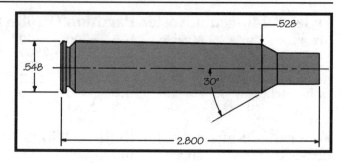

Relative Recoil Factor = 2.27

Controlling Agency : Factory

Lazzeroni 140-grain Nosler Partition (721FH140P)

Distance - Yards	Muzzle	100	200	300	400	500
Velocity - fps	3600	3404	3217	3038	2867	2701
Energy - ft-lb	4030	3604	3219	2871	2555	2269
Taylor KO values	20.4	19.3	18.3	17.3	16.3	15.3
Path - inches	-1.5	0.8	0.0	-4.1	-2.0	-24.1
Wind Drift - inches	0.0	0.4	1.7	3.9	7.2	11.5

G1 Ballistic Coefficient = 0.560

7x64mm Brenneke

This cartridge has been around for a very long time. Wilhelm Brenneke designed the 7x64mm in 1917. It is for all practical purposes a 7mm-06, although Wilhelm undoubtedly used a Mauser cartridge for his development brass. In terms of muzzle velocity the 7x64mm is very close to the .280 Remington, the .270 Winchester, and the .284 Winchester when you compare similar weight bullets, but certainly slower than the 7mm Remington Magnum and the 7mm Weatherby Magnum. It has never been very popular in the US, perhaps because there are too many similar performers in the ammunition catalogs.

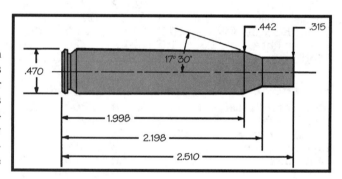

Relative Recoil Factor = 2.11

Controlling Agency: SAAMI

Bullet Weight Grains	Velocity fps	Maximum Average Pressure		Standard barrel for velocity testing:
		Copper Crusher	Transducer	
N/A	N/A	—	60,000 psi (estimated)	24 inches long - 1 turn in 8.66 inch twist

Norma 154-grain SP (17013)

Distance - Yards	Muzzle	100	200	300	400	500
Velocity - fps	2821	2605	2399	2203	2016	1839
Energy - ft-lb	2720	2321	1969	1661	1390	1156
Taylor KO values	17.6	16.3	15.0	13.8	12.6	11.5
Path - inches	-1.5	1.8	0.0	-7.9	-22.9	-46.6
Wind Drift - inches	0.0	0.8	3.2	7.4	13.8	22.4

G1 Ballistic Coefficient = 0.422

Federal 160-grain Nosler Partition (P764A)

Distance - Yards	Muzzle	100	200	300	400	500
Velocity - fps	2650	2480	2310	2150	2000	1850
Energy - ft-lb	2495	2180	1895	1640	1215	970
Taylor KO values	17.2	16.1	15.0	14.0	13.0	12.0
Path - inches	-1.5	2.1	0.0	-8.7	-23.8	-49.4
Wind Drift - inches	0.0	0.7	2.8	6.6	12.1	19.7

G1 Ballistic Coefficient = 0.510

Speer 160-grain Grand Slam (24521)

Distance - Yards	Muzzle	100	200	300	400	500
Velocity - fps	2600	2376	2164	1962	1774	1598
Energy - ft-lb	2401	2006	1663	1368	1118	908
Taylor KO values	16.9	15.4	14.0	12.7	11.5	10.4
Path - inches	-1.5	2.3	0.0	-9.8	-28.6	-58.5
Wind Drift - inches	0.0	0.9	3.9	9.2	17.2	28.3

G1 Ballistic Coefficient = 0.388

Norma 170-grain Plastic Point (17019)

Distance - Yards	Muzzle	100	200	300	400	500
Velocity - fps	2756	2519	2294	2081	1879	1691
Energy - ft-lb	2868	2396	1987	1635	1333	1079
Taylor KO values	19.0	17.4	15.8	14.4	13.0	11.7
Path - inches	-1.5	2.0	0.0	-8.6	-25.3	-51.9
Wind Drift - inches	0.0	0.9	3.7	8.7	16.3	26.7

G1 Ballistic Coefficient = 0.378

Norma 170-grain Oryx SP (17020)

Distance - Yards	Muzzle	100	200	300	400	500
Velocity - fps	2756	2481	2222	1979	1754	1549
Energy - ft-lb	2868	2324	1864	1478	1162	906
Taylor KO values	19.0	17.1	15.3	13.6	12.1	10.7
Path - inches	-1.5	2.1	0.0	-9.2	-27.2	-56.6
Wind Drift - inches	0.0	1.0	4.4	10.4	19.6	32.4

G1 Ballistic Coefficient = 0.325

Norma 170-grain Vulcan HP (17018)

Distance - Yards	Muzzle	100	200	300	400	500
Velocity - fps	2756	2501	2259	2031	1817	1620
Energy - ft-lb	2868	2361	1927	1558	1247	990
Taylor KO values	19.0	17.2	15.6	14.0	12.5	11.2
Path - inches	-1.5	2.0	0.0	-8.8	-26.2	-54.2
Wind Drift - inches	0.0	1.0	4.0	9.5	17.8	29.5

G1 Ballistic Coefficient = 0.350

Speer 175-grain Grand Slam (24522)

Distance - Yards	Muzzle	100	200	300	400	500
Velocity - fps	2650	2461	2280	2106	1941	1784
Energy - ft-lb	2728	2353	2019	1723	1464	1237
Taylor KO values	18.8	17.5	16.2	15.0	13.8	12.7
Path - inches	-1.5	2.4	0.0	-9.2	-26.2	-51.4
Wind Drift - inches	0.0	0.8	3.1	7.3	13.5	21.9

G1 Ballistic Coefficient = 0.466

7mm STW
(Shooting Times Westerner)

The 7mm STW began when Layne Simpson decided that he wanted a high-performance 7mm. His wildcat cartridge started as a 8mm Remington Magnum case necked to 7mm. This provided a case with a little more volume than the 7mm Weatherby, and therefore a little more performance. The idea was that rechambering 7mm Remington Magnums for the 7mm STW cartridge would provide an easy conversion. That is a completely feasible plan if the original chambers are exactly the nominal size, but the real world isn't that way. To make these conversions practical, the 7mm STW shape was "improved" by straightening out the body just a little. The 7mm STW received SAAMI standardization in late 1996.

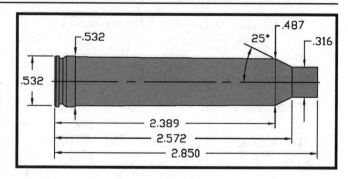

Relative Recoil Factor = 2.34   **Controlling Agency : SAAMI**

Bullet Weight Grains	Velocity fps	Maximum Average Pressure		Standard barrel for velocity testing:
		Copper Crusher	Transducer	
140	3325	54,000 cup	65,000 psi	24 inches long - 1 turn in 10 inch twist
160	3250	54,000 cup	65,000 psi	

A² 140-grain Nosler Ballistic Tip (7STW)

Distance - Yards	Muzzle	100	200	300	400	500
Velocity - fps	3450	3254	3067	2888	2715	2550
Energy - ft-lb	3700	3291	2924	2592	2292	2021
Taylor KO values	19.6	18.5	17.4	16.4	15.4	14.5
Path - inches	-1.5	0.9	0.0	-4.6	-13.4	-26.8
Wind Drift - inches	0.0	0.5	1.9	4.3	7.9	12.6

G1 Ballistic Coefficient = 0.540

Remington 140-grain Pointed SP Core-Lokt (R7MSTW1)

Distance - Yards	Muzzle	100	200	300	400	500
Velocity - fps	3325	3064	2818	2585	2364	2153
Energy - ft-lb	3436	2918	2468	2077	1737	1414
Taylor KO values	18.9	17.4	16.0	14.7	13.4	12.2
Path - inches	-1.5	1.1	0.0	-5.5	-16.2	-33.1
Wind Drift - inches	0.0	0.7	2.8	6.4	11.9	19.4

G1 Ballistic Coefficient = 0.391

Remington 140-grain Swift A-Frame Pointed SP (RS7MSTWA)

Distance - Yards	Muzzle	100	200	300	400	500
Velocity - fps	3325	3020	2735	2467	2215	1978
Energy - ft-lb	3436	2834	2324	1892	1525	1215
Taylor KO values	18.9	17.2	15.5	14.0	12.6	11.2
Path - inches	-1.5	1.2	0.0	-5.8	-17.4	-36.1
Wind Drift - inches	0.0	0.8	3.3	7.7	14.5	23.8

G1 Ballistic Coefficient = 0.332

Winchester 140-grain Ballistic Silvertip (SBST7STW)

Distance - Yards	Muzzle	100	200	300	400	500
Velocity - fps	3320	3100	2890	2690	2499	2315
Energy - ft-lb	3427	2982	2597	2502	1941	1667
Taylor KO values	18.9	17.6	16.4	15.3	14.2	13.1
Path - inches	-1.5	1.1	0.0	-5.2	-15.2	-30.8
Wind Drift - inches	0.0	0.6	2.3	5.3	9.8	15.8

G1 Ballistic Coefficient = 0.464

Speer 145-grain Grand Slam (24566)

Distance - Yards	Muzzle	100	200	300	400	500
Velocity - fps	3300	2992	2704	2435	2183	1945
Energy - ft-lb	3506	2882	2355	1909	1535	1218
Taylor KO values	19.44	17.6	15.9	14.3	12.8	11.5
Path - inches	-1.5	1.2	0.0	-6.0	-17.8	-37.0
Wind Drift - inches	0.0	0.8	3.4	7.9	14.8	24.4

G1 Ballistic Coefficient = 0.328

Federal 150-grain Trophy Bonded Bear Claw (P7STWT1)

Distance - Yards	Muzzle	100	200	300	400	500
Velocity - fps	3250	3010	2770	2560	2350	2150
Energy - ft-lb	3520	3071	2900	2735	1830	1535
Taylor KO values	19.8	18.3	16.9	15.6	14.3	13.1
Path - inches	-1.5	1.2	0.0	-5.7	-16.7	-34.2
Wind Drift - inches	0.0	0.6	2.7	6.2	11.5	18.8

G1 Ballistic Coefficient = 0.413

Winchester 150-grain Power-Point (X7STW1)

Distance - Yards	Muzzle	100	200	300	400	500
Velocity - fps	3250	2957	2683	2424	2181	1951
Energy - ft-lb	3519	2913	2398	1958	1584	1269
Taylor KO values	19.8	18.0	16.3	14.8	13.3	11.9
Path - inches	-1.5	1.2	0.0	-6.1	-18.1	-37.4
Wind Drift - inches	0.0	0.8	3.3	7.7	14.4	23.8

G1 Ballistic Coefficient = 0.341

A² 160-grain Nosler Partition (7STW)

Distance - Yards	Muzzle	100	200	300	400	500
Velocity - fps	3250	3071	2900	2735	2576	2422
Energy - ft-lb	3752	3351	2987	2657	2357	2084
Taylor KO values	21.0	19.9	18.8	17.8	16.7	15.7
Path - inches	-1.5	1.1	0.0	-5.2	-15.1	-30.3
Wind Drift - inches	0.0	0.5	1.9	4.4	8.1	13.0

G1 Ballistic Coefficient = 0.565

A² 160-grain Sierra Boattail (7STW)

Distance - Yards	Muzzle	100	200	300	400	500
Velocity - fps	3250	3087	2930	2778	2631	2490
Energy - ft-lb	3752	3385	3049	2741	2460	2202
Taylor KO values	21.1	20.0	19.0	18.0	17.1	16.2
Path - inches	-1.5	1.1	0.0	-5.1	-14.8	-29.4
Wind Drift - inches	0.0	0.4	1.7	4.0	7.3	11.6

G1 Ballistic Coefficient = 0.622

Federal 160-grain Sierra GameKing SP Boattail (P7STWA)

Distance - Yards	Muzzle	100	200	300	400	500
Velocity - fps	3200	3020	2850	2677	2530	2380
Energy - ft-lb	3640	3245	2890	2570	2275	2010
Taylor KO values	20.8	19.6	18.5	17.3	16.4	15.4
Path - inches	-1.5	1.1	0.0	-5.5	-15.7	-31.3
Wind Drift - inches	0.0	0.5	2.0	4.5	8.2	13.2

G1 Ballistic Coefficient = 0.566

Winchester 160-grain Fail Soft (S7STWX)

Distance - Yards	Muzzle	100	200	300	400	500
Velocity - fps	3150	2894	2652	2422	2204	1998
Energy - ft-lb	3526	2976	2499	2085	1727	1418
Taylor KO values	20.4	18.8	17.2	15.7	14.3	13.0
Path - inches	-1.5	1.3	0.0	-6.3	-18.5	-37.8
Wind Drift - inches	0.0	0.7	3.0	7.1	13.2	21.6

G1 Ballistic Coefficient = 0.382

7mm Remington Magnum

Since it became a standardized cartridge in 1962, the 7mm Remington Magnum has easily been the most popular 7mm cartridge in the inventory. That popularity applies to reloaders as well. The 7mm RM has been in the top ten list of reloading die sales for years. The overall length, slightly smaller than the full length magnums, allows the 7mm RM to be used in standard length actions yet the cartridge case volume is large enough to give excellent ballistics. The caliber is versatile; with the lighter bullets the velocities are right around 3200 fps, and that translates into a flat shooter right out to the longest practical hunting ranges. With the 175-grain bullets in the 2850 fps class, you have a gun that easily outperforms the legendary .30-06.

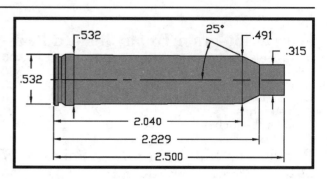

Relative Recoil Factor = 2.13

Controlling Agency: SAAMI

Bullet Weight Grains	Velocity fps	Maximum Average Pressure	
		Copper Crusher	Transducer
125	3290	52,000 cup	61,000 psi
139	3150	52,000 cup	61,000 psi
150	3100	52,000 cup	61,000 psi
154	3035	52,000 cup	61,000 psi
160-162	2940	52,000 cup	61,000 psi
175	2850	52,000 cup	61,000 psi

Standard barrel for velocity testing:
24 inches long - 1 turn in 9.5 inch twist

Hornady 139-grain SP Boattail-Heavy Magnum Moly (85593)

Distance - Yards	Muzzle	100	200	300	400	500
Velocity - fps	3250	3041	2822	2613	2413	2223
Energy - ft-lb	3300	2854	2458	2106	1797	1525
Taylor KO values	18.3	17.1	15.9	14.7	13.6	12.5
Path - inches	-1.5	1.1	0.0	-5.7	-16.6	-33.5
Wind Drift - inches	0.0	0.6	2.5	5.7	10.6	17.2

G1 Ballistic Coefficient = 0.445

Hornady 139-grain SP Boattail (8059)

Distance - Yards	Muzzle	100	200	300	400	500
Velocity - fps	3150	2933	2727	2530	2341	2160
Energy - ft-lb	3063	2656	2296	1976	1692	1440
Taylor KO values	17.8	16.5	15.4	14.3	13.2	12.2
Path - inches	-1.5	1.3	0.0	-6.1	-17.7	-35.5
Wind Drift - inches	0.0	0.6	2.5	5.9	10.8	17.6

G1 Ballistic Coefficient = 0.453

Remington 140-grain Pointed SP Boattail (PRB7MMRA)

Distance - Yards	Muzzle	100	200	300	400	500
Velocity - fps	3175	2956	2747	2547	2356	2174
Energy - ft-lb	3133	2715	2345	2017	1726	1469
Taylor KO values	18.0	16.8	15.6	14.5	13.4	12.3
Path - inches	-1.5	1.2	0.0	-5.9	-17.1	-34.6
Wind Drift - inches	0.0	0.6	2.5	5.8	10.8	17.5

G1 Ballistic Coefficient = 0.450

Remington 140-grain Pointed SP Core-Lokt (R7MM4)

Distance - Yards	Muzzle	100	200	300	400	500
Velocity - fps	3175	2923	2684	2458	2243	2039
Energy - ft-lb	3133	2655	2240	1878	1564	1292
Taylor KO values	18.0	16.6	15.2	14.0	12.7	11.6
Path - inches	-1.5	1.3	0.0	-6.1	-18.0	-36.9
Wind Drift - inches	0.0	0.7	2.9	6.9	12.7	20.8

G1 Ballistic Coefficient = 0.390

Federal 140-grain Nosler Partition (P7RG)

Distance - Yards	Muzzle	100	200	300	400	500
Velocity - fps	3150	2930	2710	2510	2320	2130
Energy - ft-lb	3085	2660	2290	1960	1670	1415
Taylor KO values	17.9	16.6	15.4	14.3	13.2	12.1
Path - inches	-1.5	1.3	0.0	-6.0	-17.5	-35.6
Wind Drift - inches	0.0	0.6	2.6	6.1	11.2	18.2

G1 Ballistic Coefficient = 0.439

Federal 140-grain Trophy Bonded Bear Claw (P7RT3)

Distance - Yards	Muzzle	100	200	300	400	500
Velocity - fps	3150	2910	2680	2460	2250	2060
Energy - ft-lb	3085	2630	2230	1880	1575	1310
Taylor KO values	17.9	16.5	15.2	14.0	12.8	11.7
Path - inches	-1.5	1.3	0.0	-6.1	-18.1	-36.9
Wind Drift - inches	0.0	0.7	2.8	6.6	12.3	20.1

G1 Ballistic Coefficient = 0.405

Winchester 140-grain Fail Safe (S7MAGXB)

Distance - Yards	Muzzle	100	200	300	400	500
Velocity - fps	3150	2861	2589	2333	2092	1866
Energy - ft-lb	3085	2544	2085	1693	1361	1083
Taylor KO values	17.9	16.3	14.7	13.3	11.9	10.6
Path - inches	-1.5	1.4	0.0	-6.6	-19.5	-40.5
Wind Drift - inches	0.0	0.8	3.5	8.2	15.3	25.3

G1 Ballistic Coefficient = 0.337

Winchester 140-grain Ballistic Silvertip (SBST7A)

Distance - Yards	Muzzle	100	200	300	400	500
Velocity - fps	3100	2889	2687	2494	2310	2133
Energy - ft-lb	2988	2595	2245	1934	1659	1414
Taylor KO values	17.6	16.4	15.2	14.2	13.1	12.1
Path - inches	-1.5	1.3	0.0	-6.2	-17.9	-38.1
Wind Drift - inches	0.0	0.6	2.5	5.9	10.9	17.6

G1 Ballistic Coefficient = 0.460

PMC 140-grain SP Boattail (7HA)

Distance - Yards	Muzzle	100	200	300	400	500
Velocity - fps	3125	2891	2669	2457	2255	2063
Energy - ft-lb	3035	2597	2213	1877	1580	1322
Taylor KO values	17.8	16.4	15.2	14.0	12.8	11.7
Path - inches	-1.5	1.4	0.0	-6.3	-18.4	-37.2
Wind Drift - inches	0.0	0.7	2.8	6.5	12.0	19.6

G1 Ballistic Coefficient = 0.417

PMC 140-grain Pointed SP (7A)

Distance - Yards	Muzzle	100	200	300	400	500
Velocity - fps	3099	2878	2668	2469	2279	2097
Energy - ft-lb	2984	2574	2218	1895	1614	1366
Taylor KO values	17.6	16.3	15.2	14.0	12.9	11.9
Path - inches	-1.5	1.4	0.0	-6.2	-18.1	-36.8
Wind Drift - inches	0.0	0.6	2.6	6.2	11.4	18.5

G1 Ballistic Coefficient = 0.443

PMC 140-grain Barnes-X (7XA)

Distance - Yards	Muzzle	100	200	300	400	500
Velocity - fps	3000	2808	2624	2448	2279	2116
Energy - ft-lb	2797	2451	2141	1863	1614	1391
Taylor KO values	17.0	15.9	14.9	13.9	12.9	12.0
Path - inches	-1.5	1.5	0.0	-6.6	-18.9	-38.0
Wind Drift - inches	0.0	0.6	2.4	5.7	10.4	16.9

G1 Ballistic Coefficient = 0.497

Speer 145-grain Grand Slam (24552)

Distance - Yards	Muzzle	100	200	300	400	500
Velocity - fps	3140	2843	2565	2304	2059	1830
Energy - ft-lb	3174	2602	2118	1708	1366	1078
Taylor KO values	18.5	16.7	15.1	13.6	12.1	10.8
Path - inches	-1.5	1.4	0.0	-6.7	-20.0	-41.5
Wind Drift - inches	0.0	0.9	3.6	8.5	15.9	26.3

G1 Ballistic Coefficient = 0.328

Winchester 150-grain Power-Point Plus (SHV7MMR1)

Distance - Yards	Muzzle	100	200	300	400	500
Velocity - fps	3130	2849	2586	2337	2102	1881
Energy - ft-lb	3264	2705	2227	1819	1472	1179
Taylor KO values	19.0	17.3	15.7	14.2	12.8	11.4
Path - inches	-1.5	1.4	0.0	-6.6	-19.6	-40.4
Wind Drift - inches	0.0	0.8	3.4	8.0	15.0	24.7

G1 Ballistic Coefficient = 0.346

Federal 150-grain Sierra GameKing (P7RD)

Distance - Yards	Muzzle	100	200	300	400	500
Velocity - fps	3110	2920	2750	2580	2410	2250
Energy - ft-lb	3220	2850	2510	2210	1930	1690
Taylor KO values	18.9	17.8	16.7	15.7	14.7	13.7
Path - inches	-1.5	1.3	0.0	-5.9	-17.0	-34.2
Wind Drift - inches	0.0	0.5	2.2	5.1	9.3	15.0

G1 Ballistic Coefficient = 0.526

Federal 150-grain Nosler Ballistic Tip (P7RH)

Distance - Yards	Muzzle	100	200	300	400	500
Velocity - fps	3110	2910	2720	2540	2370	2200
Energy - ft-lb	3220	2825	2470	2150	1865	1610
Taylor KO values	18.9	17.7	16.6	15.5	14.4	13.4
Path - inches	-1.5	1.3	0.0	-6.0	-17.4	-35.0
Wind Drift - inches	0.0	0.6	2.4	5.4	10.0	16.2

G1 Ballistic Coefficient = 0.493

Federal 150-grain Hi-Shok SP (7RA)

Distance - Yards	Muzzle	100	200	300	400	500
Velocity - fps	3110	2830	2570	2320	2090	1870
Energy - ft-lb	3220	2670	2200	1790	1450	1160
Taylor KO values	18.9	17.2	15.6	14.1	12.7	11.4
Path - inches	-1.5	1.4	0.0	-6.7	-19.9	-41.0
Wind Drift - inches	0.0	0.8	3.4	8.1	15.1	24.8

G1 Ballistic Coefficient = 0.347

Remington 150-grain Nosler Ballistic Tip (PRT7MMC)

Distance - Yards	Muzzle	100	200	300	400	500
Velocity - fps	3110	2912	2723	2542	2367	2200
Energy - ft-lb	3222	2825	2470	2152	1867	1612
Taylor KO values	18.9	17.7	16.6	15.5	14.4	13.4
Path - inches	-1.5	1.2	0.0	-5.9	-17.3	-34.8
Wind Drift - inches	0.0	0.6	2.4	5.4	10.0	16.2

G1 Ballistic Coefficient = 0.493

Remington 150-grain Pointed SP Core-Lokt (R7MM2)

Distance - Yards	Muzzle	100	200	300	400	500
Velocity - fps	3110	2830	2568	2320	2085	1866
Energy - ft-lb	3221	2667	2196	1792	1448	1160
Taylor KO values	18.9	17.2	15.6	14.1	12.7	11.4
Path - inches	-1.5	1.3	0.0	-6.6	-20.2	-43.4
Wind Drift - inches	0.0	0.8	3.4	8.1	15.1	24.9

G1 Ballistic Coefficient = 0.346

Winchester 150-grain Power-Point (X7MMR1)

Distance - Yards	Muzzle	100	200	300	400	500
Velocity - fps	3090	2812	2551	2304	2071	1852
Energy - ft-lb	3181	2634	2167	1768	1429	1143
Taylor KO values	18.8	17.1	15.5	14.0	12.6	11.3
Path - inches	-1.5	1.5	0.0	-6.8	-20.2	-41.6
Wind Drift - inches	0.0	0.8	3.5	8.2	15.3	25.2

G1 Ballistic Coefficient = 0.346

Winchester 150-grain Ballistic Silvertip (SBST7)

Distance - Yards	Muzzle	100	200	300	400	500
Velocity - fps	3110	2903	2714	2533	2359	2192
Energy - ft-lb	3200	2806	2453	2136	1853	1600
Taylor KO values	18.9	17.7	16.5	15.4	14.4	13.3
Path - inches	-1.5	1.3	0.0	-6.0	-17.5	-35.1
Wind Drift - inches	0.0	0.6	2.4	5.5	10.1	16.3

G1 Ballistic Coefficient = 0.489

Norma 150-grain Full Jacket (17026)

Distance - Yards	Muzzle	100	200	300	400	500
Velocity - fps	2995	2780	2574	2378	2191	2012
Energy - ft-lb	2988	2574	2208	1885	1599	1349
Taylor KO values	18.2	16.9	15.7	14.5	13.3	12.2
Path - inches	-1.5	1.5	0.0	-6.7	-19.7	-39.8
Wind Drift - inches	0.0	0.7	2.8	6.5	12.0	19.5

G1 Ballistic Coefficient = 0.443

Hornady 154-grain SP (8060)

Distance - Yards	Muzzle	100	200	300	400	500
Velocity - fps	3035	2814	2604	2404	2212	2029
Energy - ft-lb	3151	2708	2319	1977	1674	1408
Taylor KO values	19.0	17.6	16.3	15.0	13.8	12.7
Path - inches	-1.5	1.3	0.0	-6.7	-19.3	-39.3
Wind Drift - inches	0.0	0.7	2.8	6.5	12.0	19.5

G1 Ballistic Coefficient = 0.434

Federal 160-grain Nosler Partition (P7RF)

Distance - Yards	Muzzle	100	200	300	400	500
Velocity - fps	2950	2770	2590	2420	2250	2090
Energy - ft-lb	3090	2715	2375	2075	1800	1555
Taylor KO values	19.1	18.0	16.8	15.7	14.6	13.6
Path - inches	-1.5	1.5	0.0	-6.7	-19.4	-39.0
Wind Drift - inches	0.0	0.6	2.4	5.7	10.4	16.9

G1 Ballistic Coefficient = 0.507

Remington 160-grain Nosler Partition (PRP7MMA)

Distance - Yards	Muzzle	100	200	300	400	500
Velocity - fps	2950	2752	2563	2381	2207	2040
Energy - ft-lb	3091	2690	2333	2014	1730	1478
Taylor KO values	19.1	17.7	16.6	15.5	14.3	13.2
Path - inches	-1.5	1.6	0.0	-6.8	-19.8	-40.0
Wind Drift - inches	0.0	0.6	2.6	6.1	11.2	18.2

G1 Ballistic Coefficient = 0.475

Winchester 160-grain Partition Gold (SPG7MAG)

Distance - Yards	Muzzle	100	200	300	400	500
Velocity - fps	2950	2743	2546	2357	2176	2003
Energy - ft-lb	3093	2674	2303	1974	1682	1425
Taylor KO values	19.1	17.8	16.5	15.3	14.1	13.0
Path - inches	-1.5	1.6	0.0	-6.9	-20.1	-40.7
Wind Drift - inches	0.0	0.7	2.7	6.4	11.8	19.2

G1 Ballistic Coefficient = 0.455

Federal 160-grain Trophy Bonded Bear Claw (P7RT2)

Distance - Yards	Muzzle	100	200	300	400	500
Velocity - fps	2940	2660	2390	2140	1900	1680
Energy - ft-lb	3070	2505	2025	1620	1280	1005
Taylor KO values	19.1	17.3	15.5	14.0	12.3	10.9
Path - inches	-1.5	1.7	0.0	-7.9	-23.3	-48.7
Wind Drift - inches	0.0	0.9	4.0	9.4	17.7	29.3

G1 Ballistic Coefficient = 0.326

Federal 160-grain Sierra Pro-Hunter SP (7RJS)

Distance - Yards	Muzzle	100	200	300	400	500
Velocity - fps	2940	2730	2520	2320	2140	1960
Energy - ft-lb	3070	2640	2260	1920	1620	1360
Taylor KO values	19.1	17.7	16.4	15.1	13.9	12.7
Path - inches	-1.5	1.6	0.0	-7.1	-20.6	-42.2
Wind Drift - inches	0.0	0.7	2.9	6.7	12.4	20.3

G1 Ballistic Coefficient = 0.437

Winchester 160-grain Fail Safe (S7MAGX)

Distance - Yards	Muzzle	100	200	300	400	500
Velocity - fps	2920	2678	2449	2331	2025	1830
Energy - ft-lb	3030	2549	2131	1769	1457	1190
Taylor KO values	19.0	17.4	15.9	15.1	13.1	11.9
Path - inches	-1.5	1.7	0.0	-7.5	-22.0	-44.9
Wind Drift - inches	0.0	0.8	3.3	7.8	14.6	23.9

G1 Ballistic Coefficient = 0.385

PMC 160-grain Pointed SP (7B)

Distance - Yards	Muzzle	100	200	300	400	500
Velocity - fps	2914	2748	2586	2428	2276	2130
Energy - ft-lb	3016	2682	2371	2093	1840	1611
Taylor KO values	18.9	17.8	16.8	15.8	14.8	13.8
Path - inches	-1.5	1.6	0.0	-6.7	-19.4	-38.7
Wind Drift - inches	0.0	0.6	2.3	5.2	9.6	15.4

G1 Ballistic Coefficient = 0.556

PMC 160-grain SP Boattail (7HB)

Distance - Yards	Muzzle	100	200	300	400	500
Velocity - fps	2900	2696	2501	2314	2135	1965
Energy - ft-lb	2987	2582	2222	1903	1620	1371
Taylor KO values	18.8	17.5	16.2	15.0	13.9	12.8
Path - inches	-1.5	1.7	0.0	-7.2	-21.0	-42.3
Wind Drift - inches	0.0	0.7	2.8	6.5	12.1	19.6

G1 Ballistic Coefficient = 0.456

Remington 160-grain Swift A-Frame PSP (RS7MMA)

Distance - Yards	Muzzle	100	200	300	400	500
Velocity - fps	2900	2639	2484	2212	2006	1812
Energy - ft-lb	2785	2474	2192	1935	1430	1166
Taylor KO values	18.8	17.1	16.1	14.4	13.0	11.8
Path - inches	-1.5	1.7	0.0	-7.6	-22.4	-44.7
Wind Drift - inches	0.0	0.8	3.4	8.0	14.8	24.3

G1 Ballistic Coefficient = 0.383

PMC 160-grain Barnes-X (7XB)

Distance - Yards	Muzzle	100	200	300	400	500
Velocity - fps	2800	2639	2484	2334	2189	2049
Energy - ft-lb	2785	2478	2192	1935	1703	1492
Taylor KO values	18.2	17.1	16.1	15.2	14.2	13.3
Path - inches	-1.5	1.8	0.0	-7.4	-21.2	-42.3
Wind Drift - inches	0.0	0.6	2.3	5.4	9.9	16.0

G1 Ballistic Coefficient = 0.568

Hornady 162-grain SP Boattail (8063)

Distance - Yards	Muzzle	100	200	300	400	500
Velocity - fps	2940	2757	2582	2413	2251	2094
Energy - ft-lb	3110	2735	2399	2095	1823	1578
Taylor KO values	19.3	18.1	17.0	15.9	14.8	13.8
Path - inches	-1.5	1.5	0.0	-6.7	-19.7	-39.3
Wind Drift - inches	0.0	0.6	2.4	5.6	10.3	16.7

G1 Ballistic Coefficient = 0.515

Federal 165-grain Sierra GameKing BTSP (P7RE)

Distance - Yards	Muzzle	100	200	300	400	500
Velocity - fps	2950	2800	2650	2510	2370	2230
Energy - ft-lb	3190	2865	2570	2300	2050	1825
Taylor KO values	19.7	18.7	17.7	16.8	15.9	14.9
Path - inches	-1.5	1.5	0.0	-6.4	-18.4	-36.6
Wind Drift - inches	0.0	0.5	2.00	4.6	8.4	13.5

G1 Ballistic Coefficient = 0.616

Norma 170-grain Plastic Point (17027)

Distance - Yards	Muzzle	100	200	300	400	500
Velocity - fps	3018	2762	2519	2290	2071	1866
Energy - ft-lb	3439	2880	2394	1980	1620	1315
Taylor KO values	20.8	19.0	17.4	15.8	14.3	12.9
Path - inches	-1.5	1.5	0.0	-7.0	-20.7	-42.5
Wind Drift - inches	0.0	0.8	3.3	7.8	14.6	23.9

G1 Ballistic Coefficient = 0.378

Norma 170-grain Oryx SP (17023)

Distance - Yards	Muzzle	100	200	300	400	500
Velocity - fps	2887	2601	2333	2080	1844	1627
Energy - ft-lb	3147	2555	2055	1634	1284	999
Taylor KO values	19.9	17.9	16.1	14.3	12.7	11.2
Path - inches	-1.5	1.8	0.0	-8.2	-24.6	-51.2
Wind Drift - inches	0.0	1.0	4.1	9.8	18.5	30.7

G1 Ballistic Coefficient = 0.321

Norma 170-grain Vulcan HP (17024)

Distance - Yards	Muzzle	100	200	300	400	500
Velocity - fps	3018	2747	2493	2252	2023	1810
Energy - ft-lb	3439	2850	2346	1914	1546	1237
Taylor KO values	20.8	18.9	17.2	15.5	14.0	12.5
Path - inches	-1.5	1.5	0.0	-7.2	-21.2	-43.8
Wind Drift - inches	0.0	0.8	3.5	8.3	15.6	25.7

G1 Ballistic Coefficient = 0.353

Federal 175-grain Hi-Shok SP (7RB)

Distance - Yards	Muzzle	100	200	300	400	500
Velocity - fps	2860	2650	2440	2240	2060	1880
Energy - ft-lb	3180	2720	2310	1960	1640	1370
Taylor KO values	20.3	18.8	17.3	15.9	14.6	13.3
Path - inches	-1.5	1.7	0.0	-7.6	-22.1	44.9
Wind Drift - inches	0.0	0.7	3.1	7.2	13.3	21.7

G1 Ballistic Coefficient = 0.428

Federal 175-grain Trophy Bonded Bear Claw (P7RT1)

Distance - Yards	Muzzle	100	200	300	400	500
Velocity - fps	2860	2660	2470	2120	1900	1700
Energy - ft-lb	3180	2626	2150	1745	1400	1120
Taylor KO values	20.3	18.9	17.5	15.0	13.5	12.1
Path - inches	-1.5	1.8	0.0	-8.2	-24.0	-49.8
Wind Drift - inches	0.0	0.9	3.8	9.0	16.8	27.7

G1 Ballistic Coefficient = 0.352

Hornady 175-grain SP (8065)

Distance - Yards	Muzzle	100	200	300	400	500
Velocity - fps	2860	2650	2440	2240	2060	1880
Energy - ft-lb	3180	2720	2310	1960	1645	1374
Taylor KO values	20.3	18.8	17.3	15.9	14.6	13.3
Path - inches	-1.5	1.7	0.0	-7.6	-22.1	-44.8
Wind Drift - inches	0.0	0.7	3.1	7.2	13.3	21.7

G1 Ballistic Coefficient = 0.428

PMC 175-grain Pointed SP (7C)

Distance - Yards	Muzzle	100	200	300	400	500
Velocity - fps	2860	2645	2442	2244	2057	1879
Energy - ft-lb	3178	2718	2313	1956	1644	1372
Taylor KO values	20.3	18.8	17.3	15.9	14.6	13.3
Path - inches	-1.5	2.0	0.0	-7.9	22.7	-45.8
Wind Drift - inches	0.0	0.7	3.1	7.2	13.3	21.7

G1 Ballistic Coefficient = 0.428

Remington 175-grain Pointed SP Core-Lokt (R7MM3)

Distance - Yards	Muzzle	100	200	300	400	500
Velocity - fps	2860	2645	2442	2244	2057	1879
Energy - ft-lb	3178	2718	2313	1956	1644	1372
Taylor KO values	20.3	18.8	17.3	15.9	14.6	13.3
Path - inches	-1.5	2.0	0.0	-7.9	22.7	-45.8
Wind Drift - inches	0.0	0.7	3.1	7.2	13.3	21.7

G1 Ballistic Coefficient = 0.428

Winchester 175-grain Power-Point (X7MMR2)

Distance - Yards	Muzzle	100	200	300	400	500
Velocity - fps	2860	2645	2442	2244	2057	1879
Energy - ft-lb	3178	2718	2313	1956	1644	1372
Taylor KO values	20.3	18.8	17.3	15.9	14.6	13.3
Path - inches	-1.5	2.0	0.0	-7.9	22.7	-45.8
Wind Drift - inches	0.0	0.7	3.1	7.2	13.3	21.7

G1 Ballistic Coefficient = 0.428

Speer 175-grain Grand Slam (24503)

Distance - Yards	Muzzle	100	200	300	400	500
Velocity - fps	2850	2653	2463	2282	2105	1937
Energy - ft-lb	3156	2734	2358	2023	1723	1458
Taylor KO values	20.2	18.8	17.5	16.2	14.9	13.8
Path - inches	-1.5	1.7	0.0	-7.5	-21.7	-43.6
Wind Drift - inches	0.0	0.7	2.8	6.6	12.3	20.0

G1 Ballistic Coefficient = 0.458

7mm-30 Waters

The name of the 7-30 Waters could be a bit misleading. This is not a 7x30mm cartridge that you might get fooled into expecting from the designation. Instead it is a 7mm-(.30-30), hence 7-30. Ken Waters reportedly designed this to be a flat shooting round that could be used in 7mm conversions of Winchester Model 94 guns. The pressure limits are, like the .30-30, very mild by today's standards. A word of warning here, the only factory ammunition available today should definitely NOT be used in guns with tubular magazines. If you have a tubular magazine gun chambered for the 7-30 Waters you are stuck with handloading with flat nose bullets.

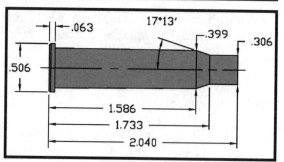

Relative Recoil Factor = 1.46

Controlling Agency: SAAMI

Bullet Weight Grains	Velocity fps	Maximum Average Pressure		Standard barrel for velocity testing:
		Copper Crusher	Transducer	
120	2700	40,000 cup	45,000 psi	24 inches long - 1 turn in 9.5 inch twist

Federal 120-grain Sierra GameKing BTSP (P730A)

Distance - Yards	Muzzle	100	200	300	400	500
Velocity - fps	2700	2300	1930	1600	1330	1140
Energy - ft-lb	1940	1405	990	685	470	345
Taylor KO values	13.1	11.2	9.4	7.8	6.5	5.6
Path - inches	-1.5	2.4	0.0	-9.8	-28.4	-58.2
Wind Drift - inches	0.0	1.6	7.0	17.3	33.6	56.8

G1 Ballistic Coefficient = 0.219

7mm Weatherby Magnum

This cartridge was part of the early family of Weatherby's Magnums, introduced in 1945. The case is considerably shorter than the full-length magnums (2.549 inches vs. 2.850) but slightly longer than the 7mm Remington Magnum (2.500 inches). The 7mm Weatherby is loaded to a higher pressure standard than the 7mm Remington. The combination of greater volume and higher pressure give this cartridge about another 150-200 fps velocity. Using a 26-inch barrel for data collection doesn't hurt either.

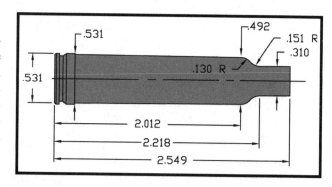

Relative Recoil Factor = 2.20

Controlling Agency : CIP

Bullet Weight Grains	Velocity fps	Maximum Average Pressure		Standard barrel for velocity testing:
		Copper Crusher	Transducer	
N/S	N/S	3800 bar	4370 bar	26 inches long - 1 turn in 10 inch twist

Weatherby 139-grain SP (H 7mm 139 SP)

Distance - Yards	Muzzle	100	200	300	400	500
Velocity - fps	3340	3079	2834	2601	2380	2170
Energy - ft-lb	3443	2926	2478	2088	1748	1453
Taylor KO values	18.8	17.4	16.0	14.7	13.4	12.2
Path - inches	-1.5	0.8	0.0	-5.1	-16.0	-32.8
Wind Drift - inches	0.0	0.7	2.7	6.4	11.8	19.2

G1 Ballistic Coefficient = 0.392

Weatherby 140-grain Nosler Partition (N 7mm 140 PT)

Distance - Yards	Muzzle	100	200	300	400	500
Velocity - fps	3303	3069	2847	2636	2434	2241
Energy - ft-lb	3391	2927	2519	2159	1841	1562
Taylor KO values	18.8	17.4	16.2	15.0	13.8	12.7
Path - inches	-1.5	0.8	0.0	-5.0	-15.8	-32.1
Wind Drift - inches	0.0	0.6	2.5	5.8	10.6	17.3

G1 Ballistic Coefficient = 0.434

Weatherby 150-grain Nosler Ballistic Tip (N 7mm 150 BST)

Distance - Yards	Muzzle	100	200	300	400	500
Velocity - fps	3300	3093	2896	2708	2527	2353
Energy - ft-lb	3627	3187	2793	2442	2127	1844
Taylor KO values	20.1	18.8	17.6	16.5	15.4	14.3
Path - inches	-1.5	1.1	0.0	-5.2	-15.2	-30.6
Wind Drift - inches	0.0	0.5	2.2	5.0	9.2	14.8

G1 Ballistic Coefficient = 0.494

Weatherby 150-grain Barnes-X (B 7mm 150 XS)

Distance - Yards	Muzzle	100	200	300	400	500
Velocity - fps	3100	2901	2710	2527	2352	2183
Energy - ft-lb	3200	2802	2446	2127	1842	1588
Taylor KO values	18.9	17.7	16.5	15.4	14.3	13.3
Path - inches	-1.5	1.3	0.0	-6.1	-17.6	-35.4
Wind Drift - inches	0.0	0.6	2.4	5.5	10.2	16.4

G1 Ballistic Coefficient = 0.488

Weatherby 154-grain Pointed-Expanding (H 7mm 154 SP)

Distance - Yards	Muzzle	100	200	300	400	500
Velocity - fps	3260	3027	2807	2597	2396	2206
Energy - ft-lb	3625	3135	2694	2306	1963	1662
Taylor KO values	20.4	18.9	17.5	16.2	15.0	13.8
Path - inches	-1.5	1.2	0.0	-5.6	-16.3	-33.1
Wind Drift - inches	0.0	0.6	2.5	5.9	10.9	17.6

G1 Ballistic Coefficient = 0.433

Hornady 154-grain SP (8066)

Distance - Yards	Muzzle	100	200	300	400	500
Velocity - fps	3200	2971	2753	2546	2348	2159
Energy - ft-lb	3501	3017	2592	2216	1885	1593
Taylor KO values	20.0	18.6	17.2	15.9	14.7	13.5
Path - inches	-1.5	1.2	0.0	-5.8	-17.0	-34.5
Wind Drift - inches	0.0	0.6	2.6	6.0	11.1	18.1

G1 Ballistic Coefficient = 0.434

Weatherby 160-grain Nosler Partition (N 7mm 160 PT)

Distance - Yards	Muzzle	100	200	300	400	500
Velocity - fps	3200	2991	2791	2600	2417	2241
Energy - ft-lb	3688	3177	2767	2401	2075	1781
Taylor KO values	20.8	19.4	18.1	16.9	15.7	14.5
Path - inches	-1.5	1.2	0.0	-5.7	-16.5	-33.3
Wind Drift - inches	0.0	0.6	2.4	5.5	10.0	16.2

G1 Ballistic Coefficient = 0.475

Federal 160-rain Nosler Partition (P7WBA)

Distance - Yards	Muzzle	100	200	300	400	500
Velocity - fps	3050	2850	2650	2470	2200	2120
Energy - ft-lb	3305	2880	2505	2165	1865	1600
Taylor KO values	19.8	18.5	17.2	16.0	14.3	13.8
Path - inches	-1.5	1.4	0.0	-6.3	-18.4	-37.1
Wind Drift - inches	0.0	0.6	2.5	5.8	10.7	17.4

G1 Ballistic Coefficient = 0.475

Federal 160-grain Trophy Bonded Bear Claw (P7WBT1)

Distance - Yards	Muzzle	100	200	300	400	500
Velocity - fps	3050	2730	2420	2140	1880	1640
Energy - ft-lb	3305	2640	2085	1630	1255	955
Taylor KO values	19.8	17.7	15.7	13.9	12.2	10.6
Path - inches	-1.5	1.6	0.0	-7.6	-22.7	-47.8
Wind Drift - inches	0.0	1.0	4.2	10.1	19.1	31.9

G1 Ballistic Coefficient = 0.293

Federal 160-grain Sierra GameKing SP Boattail (P7WBB)

Distance - Yards	Muzzle	100	200	300	400	500
Velocity - fps	3050	2880	2710	2560	2400	2250
Energy - ft-lb	3305	2945	2615	2320	2055	1805
Taylor KO values	19.8	18.7	17.6	16.6	15.6	14.6
Path - inches	-1.5	1.4	0.0	-6.1	-17.4	-34.9
Wind Drift - inches	0.0	0.5	2.1	4.9	8.9	14.3

G1 Ballistic Coefficient = 0.561

Weatherby 175-grain Pointed-Expanding (H 7mm 175 SP)

Distance - Yards	Muzzle	100	200	300	400	500
Velocity - fps	3070	2861	2662	2471	2288	2113
Energy - ft-lb	3662	3181	2753	2373	2034	1735
Taylor KO Index	21.8	20.3	18.9	17.5	16.2	15.0
Path - Inches	-1.5	1.4	0.0	-6.3	-18.3	-36.9
Wind Drift - Inches	0.0	0.6	2.6	5.9	11.0	17.8

G1 Ballistic Coefficient = 0.462

Hornady 175-grain SP (8067)

Distance - Yards	Muzzle	100	200	300	400	500
Velocity - fps	2910	2709	2516	2331	2154	1985
Energy - ft-lb	3290	2850	2459	2111	1803	1531
Taylor KO values	20.7	19.2	17.9	16.6	15.3	14.1
Path - inches	-1.5	1.6	0.0	-7.1	-20.6	-41.7
Wind Drift - inches	0.0	0.7	2.8	6.4	11.8	19.2

G1 Ballistic Coefficient = 0.463

7.62x39mm Russian

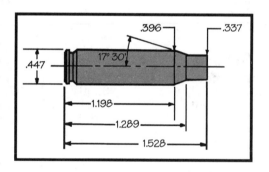

Assault rifles came into general usage during WWII when military authorities recognized that an all-up infantry rifle (the Garand for instance) was not the best weapon for the street fighting requirement. The 7.62x39 mm was the Soviet answer to this need. Introduced in 1943, it has become the standard infantry cartridge for many of the world's armies. Because some guns chambered for this cartridge use a 0.310-inch-groove diameter and some others use 0.308 inches, it's a good idea to know the dimensions of both your gun and your ammunition before you start shooting. The SAAMI standard for this round uses bullets with a diameter tolerance of 0.309 to 0.311 inch.

Relative Recoil Factor = 1.29   **Controlling Agency: SAAMI**

Bullet Weight Grains	Velocity fps	Maximum Average Pressure		Standard barrel for velocity testing:
		Copper Crusher	Transducer	
123	2350	50,000 cup	45,000 psi	20 inches long - 1 turn in 9.45 inch twist

Hansen 123-grain Posi-Feed SP (HCC739B)

Distance - Yards	Muzzle	100	200	300	400	500
Velocity - fps	2400	2110	1843	1599	1387	1213
Energy - ft-lb	1600	1217	928	699	525	402
Taylor KO values	13.0	11.4	10.0	8.7	7.5	6.6
Path - inches	-1.5	2.9	0.0	-14.2	-40.6	-86.0
Wind Drift - inches	0.0	1.5	6.2	15.0	28.5	47.3

G1 Ballistic Coefficient = 0.284

Winchester 123-grain SP (X76239)

Distance - Yards	Muzzle	100	200	300	400	500
Velocity - fps	2365	2033	1731	1465	1248	1093
Energy - ft-lb	1527	1129	878	586	425	327
Taylor KO values	12.8	11.0	9.4	7.9	6.8	5.9
Path - inches	-1.5	3.5	0.0	-15.2	-46.7	-100.6
Wind Drift - inches	0.0	1.8	7.6	18.4	35.2	58.3

G1 Ballistic Coefficient = 0.244

Federal 123-grain Hi-Shok SP (76239B)

Distance - Yards	Muzzle	100	200	300	400	500
Velocity - fps	2300	2030	1780	1550	1350	1200
Energy - ft-lb	1445	1125	860	655	500	395
Taylor KO values	12.4	11.0	9.6	8.4	7.3	6.5
Path - inches	-1.5	3.5	0.0	-14.5	-43.4	-90.6
Wind Drift - inches	0.0	1.5	6.3	15.0	28.4	46.8

G1 Ballistic Coefficient = 0.299

UMC (Remington) 123-grain MC (L762391)

Distance - Yards	Muzzle	100	200	300	400	500
Velocity - fps	2365	2060	1780	1528	1314	1149
Energy - ft-lb	1527	1159	865	638	472	371
Taylor KO values	12.9	11.3	9.7	8.4	7.2	6.3
Path - inches	-1.5	3.4	0.0	-14.4	-43.9	-93.6
Wind Drift - inches	0.0	1.6	6.9	16.6	31.6	52.4

G1 Ballistic Coefficient = 0.266

PMC 123-grain FMJ (7.62A)

Distance - Yards	Muzzle	100	200	300	400	500
Velocity - fps	2350	2072	1817	1583	1368	1171
Energy - ft-lb	1495	1162	894	678	507	371
Taylor KO values	12.7	11.2	9.8	8.6	7.4	6.3
Path - inches	-1.5	3.4	0.0	-14.3	-43.4	-91.9
Wind Drift - inches	0.0	1.6	6.6	15.9	30.3	50.2

G1 Ballistic Coefficient = 0.277

Lapua 123-grain FMJ (4317235)

Distance - Yards	Muzzle	100	200	300	400	500
Velocity - fps	2346	2041	1761	1511	1300	1139
Energy - ft-lb	1493	1130	841	619	462	354
Taylor KO values	12.7	11.0	9.5	8.2	7.0	6.2
Path - inches	-1.5	3.4	0.0	-14.8	-44.8	-95.6
Wind Drift - inches	0.0	1.6	7.0	16.9	32.1	53.1

G1 Ballistic Coefficient = 0.265

Hansen 123-grain FMJ (HCC739A)

Distance - Yards	Muzzle	100	200	300	400	500
Velocity - fps	2320	1997	1708	1459	1250	1099
Energy - ft-lb	1472	1080	790	576	427	330
Taylor KO values	12.6	10.8	9.2	7.9	6.8	5.9
Path - inches	-1.5	3.7	0.0	-15.7	-47.5	-101.8
Wind Drift - inches	0.0	1.7	7.5	18.1	34.5	57.0

G1 Ballistic Coefficient = 0.253

American Eagle (Federal) 124-grain FMJ (AE76239A)

Distance - Yards	Muzzle	100	200	300	400	500
Velocity - fps	2300	2030	1780	1560	1360	1200
Energy - ft-lb	1455	1135	875	670	510	400
Taylor KO values	12.5	11.1	9.7	8.5	7.4	6.5
Path - inches	-1.5	3.5	0.0	-14.6	-42.9	-90.3
Wind Drift - inches	0.0	1.5	6.3	15.1	28.5	47.1

G1 Ballistic Coefficient = 0.295

Remington 125-grain Pointed SP (R762391)

Distance - Yards	Muzzle	100	200	300	400	500
Velocity - fps	2365	2062	1783	1533	1320	1154
Energy - ft-lb	1552	1180	882	652	483	370
Taylor KO values	13.0	11.3	9.8	8.4	7.3	6.3
Path - inches	-1.5	3.1	0.0	-14.1	-43.7	-93.0
Wind Drift - inches	0.0	1.6	6.8	16.4	31.3	51.9

G1 Ballistic Coefficient = 0.268

Lapua 125-grain Mega SP (4317237)

Distance - Yards	Muzzle	100	200	300	400	500
Velocity - fps	2346	2035	1751	1497	1285	1126
Energy - ft-lb	1528	1150	851	623	459	352
Taylor KO values	12.9	11.2	9.6	8.2	7.1	6.2
Path - inches	-1.5	3.5	0.0	-14.9	-45.4	-97.1
Wind Drift - inches	0.0	1.7	7.1	17.2	32.9	54.4

G1 Ballistic Coefficient = 0.260

PMC 125-grain Pointed SP (7.62B)

Distance - Yards	Muzzle	100	200	300	400	500
Velocity - fps	2320	2046	1794	1563	1350	1156
Energy - ft-lb	1493	1161	893	678	505	371
Taylor KO values	12.6	11.1	9.7	8.5	7.3	6.3
Path - inches	-1.5	3.5	0.0	-14.8	-44.6	-94.6
Wind Drift - inches	0.0	1.6	6.7	16.2	30.8	51.0

G1 Ballistic Coefficient = 0.277

Black Hills 150-grain SP (D76239N2)

Distance - Yards	Muzzle	100	200	300	400	500
Velocity - fps	2200	1977	1769	1577	1406	1259
Energy - ft-lb	1612	1302	1042	829	659	528
Taylor KO values	14.5	13.0	11.7	10.4	9.3	8.3
Path - inches	-1.5	3.7	0.0	-14.9	-43.8	-90.3
Wind Drift - inches	0.0	1.3	5.6	13.2	24.7	40.4

G1 Ballistic Coefficient = 0.353

.30 M1 Carbine

Developed shortly before WWII, the .30 M1 Carbine represented the US Army's idea of what was needed in an "assault rifle" cartridge. Today's largely uninformed, but never-the-less highly opinionated press and electronic media have succeeded in making the term "assault rifle" stand for high power, and therefore the guns must be extremely dangerous. The fact is just the reverse. Assault rifles are (and need to be) very low power rifles. They are designed to be controllable by the average soldier in fully automatic fire. The .30 M1 Carbine is not suitable for use on deer-sized game.

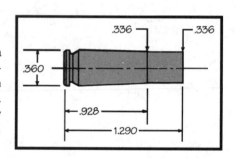

Relative Recoil Factor = 0.99   **Controlling Agency: SAAMI**

Bullet Weight Grains	Velocity fps	Maximum Average Pressure		Standard barrel for velocity testing:
		Copper Crusher	Transducer	
110	1965	40,000 cup	40,000 psi	20 inches long - 1 turn in 20 inch twist

Federal 110-grain Hi-Shok SP (30CA)

Distance - Yards	Muzzle	100	200	300	400	500
Velocity - fps	1990	1570	1240	1040	920	840
Energy - ft-lb	965	600	375	260	210	175
Taylor KO values	9.6	7.6	6.0	5.0	4.5	4.1
Path - inches	-1.5	6.4	0.0	-27.7	-81.8	-167.8
Wind Drift - inches	0.0	3.4	15.1	35.7	63.5	97.2

G1 Ballistic Coefficient = 0.166

Remington 110-grain SP (R30CAR)

Distance - Yards	Muzzle	100	200	300	400	500
Velocity - fps	1990	1567	1236	1035	923	842
Energy - ft-lb	967	600	373	262	208	173
Taylor KO values	9.6	7.6	6.0	5.0	4.5	4.1
Path - inches	-1.5	6.4	0.0	-27.7	-81.8	-167.8
Wind Drift - inches	0.0	3.4	15.0	35.5	63.2	96.6

G1 Ballistic Coefficient = 0.167

Winchester 110-grain Hollow SP (X30M1)

Distance - Yards	Muzzle	100	200	300	400	500
Velocity - fps	1990	1567	1236	1035	923	842
Energy - ft-lb	967	600	373	262	208	173
Taylor KO values	9.6	7.6	6.0	5.0	4.5	4.1
Path - inches	-1.5	6.4	0.0	-27.7	-81.8	-167.8
Wind Drift - inches	0.0	3.4	15.0	35.5	63.2	96.6

G1 Ballistic Coefficient = 0.167

American Eagle (Federal) 110-grain FMJ (AE30CB)

Distance - Yards	Muzzle	100	200	300	400	500
Velocity - fps	1990	1570	1240	1040	920	840
Energy - ft-lb	965	600	375	260	210	175
Taylor KO values	9.6	7.6	6.0	5.0	4.5	4.1
Path - inches	-1.5	6.4	0.0	-27.7	-81.8	-167.8
Wind Drift - inches	0.0	3.4	15.1	35.7	63.5	97.2

G1 Ballistic Coefficient = 0.166

UMC (Remington) 110-grain FMJ (L30CR1)

Distance - Yards	Muzzle	100	200	300	400	500
Velocity - fps	1990	1567	1236	1040	920	840
Energy - ft-lb	965	600	373	260	210	175
Taylor KO values	9.6	7.6	6.0	5.0	4.5	4.1
Path - inches	-1.5	6.4	0.0	-27.7	-81.8	-167.8
Wind Drift - inches	0.0	3.4	15.1	35.7	63.5	97.2

G1 Ballistic Coefficient = 0.166

PMC 110-grain FMJ (30A)

Distance - Yards	Muzzle	100	200	300	400	500
Velocity - fps	1927	1548	1248	1056	945	866
Energy - ft-lb	906	585	380	273	218	183
Taylor KO values	9.3	7.5	6.0	5.1	4.6	4.2
Path - inches	-1.5	6.6	0.0	-29.0	-89.0	-187.9
Wind Drift - inches	0.0	3.2	13.9	32.8	58.4	89.5

G1 Ballistic Coefficient = 0.184

.30-30 Winchester

For nearly 100 years the .30-30 Winchester has been what most hunters would call your basic deer rifle. Despite the black-powder type of designation the .30-30 was the first cartridge of its class loaded with smokeless powder. There are lots of .30 caliber cartridges with better performance but few combine with a carbine-length lever-action rifle to offer a better combination of enough power and a super handy rifle for woods-type hunting. There is a little something to remember when looking at the performance data for the .30-30 Winchester. The velocity specifications are measured in a 24-inch barrel and a lot of guns that are chambered for the .30-30 have 20-inch barrels. This will cost about 100-150 fps in the short barrel. Time has proved that this doesn't make much difference because .30-30's are seldom used where long shots are required.

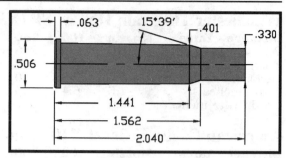

Relative Recoil Factor = 1.68 **Controlling Agency : SAAMI**

Bullet Weight Grains	Velocity fps	Maximum Average Pressure		Standard barrel for velocity testing:
		Copper Crusher	Transducer	
55 (Saboted)	3365	N/S	38,000 psi	24 inches long - 1 turn in 12 inch twist
125	2550	38,000 cup	42,000 psi	
150	2370	38,000 cup	42,000 psi	
170	2180	38,000 cup	42,000 psi	

Remington 55-grain Accelerator SP (R3030A)

Distance - Yards	Muzzle	100	200	300	400	500
Velocity - fps	3400	2693	2085	1570	1187	986
Energy - ft-lb	1412	886	521	301	172	119
Taylor KO values	8.2	6.5	5.0	3.8	2.9	2.4
Path - inches	-1.5	1.7	0.0	-9.9	-34.3	-83.3
Wind Drift - inches	0.0	1.9	8.7	22.4	45.9	79.8

G1 Ballistic Coefficient = 0.139

Federal 125-grain Hi-Shok HP (3030C)

Distance - Yards	Muzzle	100	200	300	400	500
Velocity - fps	2570	2090	1660	1320	1080	960
Energy - ft-lb	1830	1210	770	480	320	260
Taylor KO values	14.1	11.5	9.1	7.3	5.9	5.3
Path - inches	-1.5	3.3	0.0	-16.0	-50.9	-109.5
Wind Drift - inches	0.0	2.2	10.0	25.1	48.9	80.2

G1 Ballistic Coefficient = 0.174

Winchester 150-grain Power-Point Plus (SHV30306)

Distance - Yards	Muzzle	100	200	300	400	500
Velocity - fps	2480	2095	1747	1446	1209	1053
Energy - ft-lb	2049	1462	1017	697	487	369
Taylor KO values	16.4	13.8	11.5	9.5	8.0	6.9
Path - inches	-1.5	3.3	0.0	-14.7	-45.7	-98.4
Wind Drift - inches	0.0	1.9	8.2	20.1	38.9	64.6

G1 Ballistic Coefficient = 0.215

Federal 150-grain Hi-Shok SP Flat Nose (3030A)

Distance - Yards	Muzzle	100	200	300	400	500
Velocity - fps	2390	2020	1680	1400	1180	1040
Energy - ft-lb	1900	1355	945	650	460	355
Taylor KO values	15.8	13.3	11.1	9.2	7.8	6.9
Path - inches	-1.5	3.6	0.0	-15.9	-49.1	-104.5
Wind Drift - inches	0.0	1.9	8.4	20.6	39.6	65.3

G1 Ballistic Coefficient = 0.220

Hornady 150-grain Round Nose (RN) (8080)

Distance - Yards	Muzzle	100	200	300	400	500
Velocity - fps	2390	1973	1605	1303	1095	974
Energy - ft-lb	1902	1296	858	565	399	316
Taylor KO values	15.8	13.0	10.6	8.6	7.2	6.4
Path - inches	-1.5	3.8	0.0	-17.5	-55.6	-122.5
Wind Drift - inches	0.0	2.2	9.8	24.3	46.7	76.0

G1 Ballistic Coefficient = 0.193

Remington 150-grain SP Core-Lokt (R30301)

Distance - Yards	Muzzle	100	200	300	400	500
Velocity - fps	2390	1973	1605	1303	1095	974
Energy - ft-lb	1902	1296	858	565	399	316
Taylor KO values	15.8	13.0	10.6	8.6	7.2	6.4
Path - inches	-1.5	3.8	0.0	-17.5	-55.6	-122.5
Wind Drift - inches	0.0	2.2	9.8	24.3	46.7	76.0

G1 Ballistic Coefficient = 0.193

Winchester 150-grain Power-Point (X30306)

Distance - Yards	Muzzle	100	200	300	400	500
Velocity - fps	2390	2018	1684	1398	1177	1036
Energy - ft-lb	1902	1356	944	651	461	357
Taylor KO values	15.8	13.3	11.1	9.2	7.8	6.8
Path - inches	-1.5	3.6	0.0	-16.0	-49.9	-108.8
Wind Drift - inches	0.0	2.0	8.5	20.9	40.1	66.1

G1 Ballistic Coefficient = 0.218

Winchester 150-grain Silvertip (X30302)

Distance - Yards	Muzzle	100	200	300	400	500
Velocity - fps	2390	2018	1684	1398	1177	1036
Energy - ft-lb	1902	1356	944	651	461	357
Taylor KO values	15.8	13.3	11.1	9.2	7.8	6.8
Path - inches	-1.5	3.6	0.0	-16.0	-49.9	-108.8
Wind Drift - inches	0.0	2.0	8.5	20.9	40.1	66.1

G1 Ballistic Coefficient = 0.218

PMC 150-grain Flat Nose SP (3030A)

Distance - Yards	Muzzle	100	200	300	400	500
Velocity - fps	2159	1819	1544	1242	1073	968
Energy - ft-lb	1552	1102	804	514	383	312
Taylor KO values	14.2	12.0	9.9	8.2	7.1	6.4
Path - inches	-1.5	4.7	0.0	-20.4	-63.5	-136.6
Wind Drift - inches	0.0	2.3	10.1	24.5	46.0	73.6

G1 Ballistic Coefficient = 0.214

Winchester 150-grain HP (X30301)

Distance - Yards	Muzzle	100	200	300	400	500
Velocity - fps	2390	2018	1684	1398	1177	1036
Energy - ft-lb	1902	1356	944	651	461	357
Taylor KO values	15.8	13.3	11.1	9.2	7.8	6.8
Path - inches	-1.5	3.6	0.0	-16.0	-49.9	-108.8
Wind Drift - inches	0.0	2.0	8.5	20.9	40.1	66.1

G1 Ballistic Coefficient = 0.218

Speer 150-grain Flat Nose (24504)

Distance - Yards	Muzzle	100	200	300	400	500
Velocity - fps	2370	2067	1788	1538	1323	1157
Energy - ft-lb	1870	1423	1065	788	583	446
Taylor KO values	15.6	13.6	11.8	10.2	8.7	7.6
Path - inches	-1.5	3.3	0.0	-14.4	-43.7	-92.6
Wind Drift - inches	0.0	1.6	6.8	16.4	31.2	51.7

G1 Ballistic Coefficient = 0.268

PMC 150-grain Starfire HP (C3030SFA)

Distance - Yards	Muzzle	100	200	300	400	500
Velocity - fps	2100	1769	1478	1242	1080	978
Energy - ft-lb	1469	1042	728	514	388	318
Taylor KO values	13.9	11.7	9.8	8.2	7.1	6.5
Path - inches	-1.5	4.9	0.0	-20.9	-64.5	-137.7
Wind Drift - inches	0.0	2.3	9.8	23.8	44.4	70.8

G1 Ballistic Coefficient = 0.226

Federal 170-grain Nosler Partition (P3030D)

Distance - Yards	Muzzle	100	200	300	400	500
Velocity - fps	2200	1900	1620	1380	1190	1060
Energy - ft-lb	1830	1355	990	720	535	425
Taylor KO values	18.5	16.0	13.6	11.6	10.0	8.9
Path - inches	-1.5	4.1	0.0	-17.4	-52.4	-109.4
Wind Drift - inches	0.0	1.9	8.0	19.3	36.6	59.7

G1 Ballistic Coefficient = 0.255

Federal 170-grain Sierra Pro-Hunter (3030FS)

Distance - Yards	Muzzle	100	200	300	400	500
Velocity - fps	2200	1820	1500	1240	1060	960
Energy - ft-lb	1830	1255	845	575	425	345
Taylor KO values	18.5	15.3	12.6	10.4	8.9	8.1
Path - inches	-1.5	4.5	0.0	-20.0	-63.5	-137.4
Wind Drift - inches	0.0	2.4	10.3	25.2	47.5	75.9

G1 Ballistic Coefficient = 0.205

Federal 170-grain Hi-Shok SP Round Nose (3030B)

Distance - Yards	Muzzle	100	200	300	400	500
Velocity - fps	2200	1900	1620	1380	1190	1060
Energy - ft-lb	1830	1355	990	720	535	425
Taylor KO values	18.5	16.0	13.6	11.6	10.0	8.9
Path - inches	-1.5	4.1	0.0	-17.4	-52.4	-109.4
Wind Drift - inches	0.0	1.9	8.0	19.3	36.6	59.7

G1 Ballistic Coefficient = 0.255

Hornady 170-grain Flat Point (8085)

Distance - Yards	Muzzle	100	200	300	400	500
Velocity - fps	2200	1895	1619	1381	1191	1064
Energy - ft-lb	1827	1355	989	720	535	425
Taylor KO values	18.5	16.0	13.6	11.6	10.0	8.9
Path - inches	-1.5	4.1	0.0	-17.4	-53.1	-113.2
Wind Drift - inches	0.0	1.8	8.0	19.2	36.4	59.4

G1 Ballistic Coefficient = 0.256

Remington 170-grain SP Core-Lokt (R30302)

Distance - Yards	Muzzle	100	200	300	400	500
Velocity - fps	2200	1895	1619	1381	1191	1061
Energy - ft-lb	1827	1355	989	720	535	425
Taylor KO values	18.5	16.0	13.6	11.6	10.0	8.9
Path - inches	-1.5	4.1	0.0	-17.5	-53.3	-113.6
Wind Drift - inches	0.0	1.9	8.0	19.3	36.6	59.7

G1 Ballistic Coefficient = 0.255

Winchester 170-grain Power-Point (X30303)

Distance - Yards	Muzzle	100	200	300	400	500
Velocity - fps	2200	1895	1619	1381	1191	1061
Energy - ft-lb	1827	1355	989	720	535	425
Taylor KO values	18.5	16.0	13.6	11.6	10.0	8.9
Path - inches	-1.5	4.1	0.0	-17.5	-53.3	-113.6
Wind Drift - inches	0.0	1.9	8.0	19.3	36.6	59.7

G1 Ballistic Coefficient = 0.255

Winchester 170-grain Silvertip (X30304)

Distance - Yards	Muzzle	100	200	300	400	500
Velocity - fps	2200	1895	1619	1381	1191	1061
Energy - ft-lb	1827	1355	989	720	535	425
Taylor KO values	18.5	16.0	13.6	11.6	10.0	8.9
Path - inches	-1.5	4.1	0.0	-17.5	-53.3	-113.6
Wind Drift - inches	0.0	1.9	8.0	19.3	36.6	59.7

G1 Ballistic Coefficient = 0.255

PMC 170-grain Flat Nose SP (3030B)

Distance - Yards	Muzzle	100	200	300	400	500
Velocity - fps	1965	1680	1480	1278	1129	1028
Energy - ft-lb	1457	1065	827	616	481	399
Taylor KO values	16.5	14.3	12.4	10.7	9.5	8.6
Path - inches	-1.5	5.3	0.0	-21.4	-64.2	-134.2
Wind Drift - inches	0.0	2.0	8.5	20.2	37.4	59.7

G1 Ballistic Coefficient = 0.278

Remington 170-grain HP Core-Lokt (R30303)

Distance - Yards	Muzzle	100	200	300	400	500
Velocity - fps	2200	1895	1619	1381	1191	1061
Energy - ft-lb	1827	1355	989	720	535	425
Taylor KO values	18.5	16.0	13.6	11.6	10.0	8.9
Path - inches	-1.5	4.1	0.0	-17.5	-53.3	-113.6
Wind Drift - inches	0.0	1.9	8.0	19.3	36.6	59.7

G1 Ballistic Coefficient = 0.255

.300 Savage

The .300 Savage cartridge was introduced in 1921 for the Savage Model 99 lever-action rifle. On the basis of case volume it should fall just a little bit short of the .308's performance. But because the .300 Savage was to be used in guns that were not quite as strong as the current standards for bolt-action guns the pressure specifications are about 10% lower than those for the .308. Even with this handicap, the .300 Savage is an entirely adequate hunting cartridge, outperforming the venerable .30-30 by about 250 fps. In spite of the performance advantage, the cartridge has never achieved the popularity of the .30-30.

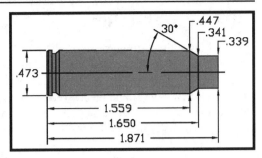

Relative Recoil Factor = 1.78   **Controlling Agency : SAAMI**

Bullet Weight Grains	Velocity fps	Maximum Average Pressure		Standard barrel for velocity testing:
		Copper Crusher	**Transducer**	
150	2615	46,000 cup	47,000 psi	24 inches long - 1 turn in 12 inch twist
180	2340	46,000 cup	47,000 psi	

Federal 150-grain Hi-Shok SP (300A)

Distance - Yards	Muzzle	100	200	300	400	500
Velocity - fps	2630	2350	2100	1850	1630	1430
Energy - ft-lb	2305	1845	1460	1145	885	685
Taylor KO values	17.4	15.5	13.9	12.2	10.8	9.4
Path - inches	-1.5	2.4	0.0	-10.4	-30.9	-64.4
Wind Drift - inches	0.0	1.2	4.9	11.6	22.0	36.6 `

G1 Ballistic Coefficient = 0.313

Remington 150-grain Pointed SP Core-Lokt (R30SV2)

Distance - Yards	Muzzle	100	200	300	400	500
Velocity - fps	2630	2354	2095	1853	1631	1432
Energy - ft-lb	2303	1845	1462	1143	806	685
Taylor KO values	17.4	15.5	13.8	12.2	10.8	9.5
Path - inches	-1.5	2.4	0.0	-10.4	-30.9	-64.6
Wind Drift - inches	0.0	1.2	4.8	11.6	21.9	36.4

G1 Ballistic Coefficient = 0.314

Winchester 150-grain Power-Point (X3001)

Distance - Yards	Muzzle	100	200	300	400	500
Velocity - fps	2630	2311	2015	1743	1500	1295
Energy - ft-lb	2303	1779	1352	1012	749	558
Taylor KO values	17.4	15.3	13.3	11.5	9.9	8.5
Path - inches	-1.5	2.8	0.0	-11.5	-34.4	-73.0
Wind Drift - inches	0.0	1.3	5.7	13.8	26.4	44.2

G1 Ballistic Coefficient = 0.271

Federal 180-grain Hi-Shok SP (300B)

Distance - Yards	Muzzle	100	200	300	400	500
Velocity - fps	2350	2140	1940	1750	1570	1410
Energy - ft-lb	2205	1825	1495	1215	985	800
Taylor KO values	18.6	16.9	15.4	13.9	12.4	11.2
Path - inches	-1.5	3.1	0.0	-12.4	-36.1	-73.8
Wind Drift - inches	0.0	1.1	4.6	10.9	20.4	33.4

G1 Ballistic Coefficient = 0.383

Remington 180-grain SP Core-Lokt (R30SV3)

Distance - Yards	Muzzle	100	200	300	400	500
Velocity - fps	2350	2025	1728	1467	1252	1098
Energy - ft-lb	2207	1639	1193	860	626	482
Taylor KO values	18.6	16.0	13.7	11.6	9.9	8.7
Path - inches	-1.5	3.5	0.0	-15.3	-46.8	-100.6
Wind Drift - inches	0.0	1.7	7.5	18.2	34.8	57.6

G1 Ballistic Coefficient = 0.248

.307 Winchester

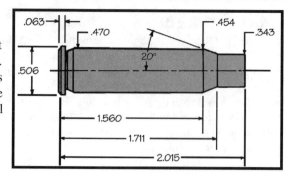

This is an interesting cartridge. If you look at the dimensions you find that the .307 Winchester is externally identical to the .308 except that the .307 has a rim. Introduced in 1982, the .307 was designed to be used in U.S. Repeating Arms Company's new M94 Angle Eject lever-action rifles. Ballistics are similar to the .308 but the .307 has thicker case walls (smaller internal volume) and pays a small performance penalty for that reason.

Relative Recoil Factor = 2.04   **Controlling Agency: SAAMI**

Bullet Weight Grains	Velocity fps	Maximum Average Pressure		Standard barrel for velocity testing:
		Copper Crusher	Transducer	
150	2705	52,000 cup	N/S	24 inches long - 1 turn in 12 inch twist
180	2450	52,000 cup	N/S	

Winchester 180-grain Power-Point (X3076)

Distance - Yards	Muzzle	100	200	300	400	500
Velocity - fps	2510	2179	1874	1599	1362	1177
Energy - ft-lb	2538	1898	1404	1022	742	554
Taylor KO values	19.9	17.3	14.8	12.7	10.8	9.3
Path - inches	-1.5	2.9	0.0	-12.9	-39.6	-85.1
Wind Drift - inches	0.0	1.6	6.6	16.1	30.9	51.7

G1 Ballistic Coefficient = 0.253

.308 Winchester (7.62mm NATO)

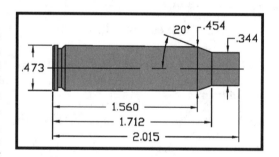

The US Army was working on a potential replacement for the .30-06 cartridge during WWII. The best candidate was called the T65 and by the early 1950s was in the final stages of a serious testing process. While the T65 was not adopted as a standardized military cartridge until 1955, Winchester, who had participated in the development process, jumped the gun (no pun intended) and introduced the .308 Winchester in 1952. Any standardized US military cartridge is almost certain to be "popular" and the .308 has lived up to that expectation. With just a little less recoil than the .30-06 (and a little less performance), the .308 has spawned a series of X-08 neck-downs. The number of different loadings available testify to the popularity of this caliber.

Relative Recoil Factor = 1.93   **Controlling Agency: SAAMI**

Bullet Weight Grains	Velocity fps	Maximum Average Pressure		Standard barrel for velocity testing:
		Copper Crusher	Transducer	
55 (Saboted)	3750	N/S	52,000 psi	24 inches long - 1 turn in 12 inch twist
110	3150	52,000 cup	62,000 psi	
125	3030	52,000 cup	62,000 psi	
150	2800	52,000 cup	62,000 psi	
165-168	2670	52,000 cup	62,000 psi	
180	2600	52,000 cup	62,000 psi	
200	2440	52,000 cup	62,000 psi	

Lapua 123-grain FMJ (4317527)

Distance - Yards	Muzzle	100	200	300	400	500
Velocity - fps	2936	2599	2286	1995	1728	1490
Energy - ft-lb	2355	1845	1428	1087	816	606
Taylor KO values	15.9	14.1	12.4	10.8	9.4	8.1
Path - inches	-1.5	1.8	0.0	-8.5	-25.9	-54.9
Wind Drift - inches	0.0	1.1	4.8	11.6	22.0	37.0

G1 Ballistic Coefficient = 0.274

Hansen 125-grain Posi-Feed SP (HCC308E)

Distance - Yards	Muzzle	100	200	300	400	500
Velocity - fps	3028	2717	2442	2184	1937	1709
Energy - ft-lb	2546	2050	1656	1324	1042	1937
Taylor KO values	16.7	14.9	13.4	12.0	10.7	9.4
Path - inches	-1.5	1.4	0.0	-7.2	-22.2	-46.2
Wind Drift - inches	0.0	0.9	3.9	9.3	17.6	29.2

G1 Ballistic Coefficient = 0.316

Norma 146-grain Full Jacket (17662)

Distance - Yards	Muzzle	100	200	300	400	500
Velocity - fps	2627	2457	2266	2083	1919	1762
Energy - ft-lb	2238	1928	1652	1409	1194	1007
Taylor KO values	16.9	15.8	14.6	13.4	12.3	11.3
Path - inches	-1.5	2.1	0.0	-8.9	-26.0	-52.6
Wind Drift - inches	0.0	0.8	3.3	7.7	13.7	22.3

G1 Ballistic Coefficient = 0.441

PMC 147-grain FMJ - Boattail (308B)

Distance - Yards	Muzzle	100	200	300	400	500
Velocity - fps	2751	2473	2257	2052	1859	1664
Energy - ft-lb	2471	2037	1695	1387	1150	922
Taylor KO values	17.8	16.0	14.6	13.3	12.0	10.8
Path - inches	-1.5	2.3	0.0	-9.3	-27.3	-57.9
Wind Drift - inches	0.0	0.9	3.8	9.0	16.8	27.6

G1 Ballistic Coefficient = 0.369

Hornady 150-grain SP-Light Magnum (8590)

Distance - Yards	Muzzle	100	200	300	400	500
Velocity - fps	3000	2721	2495	2212	1979	1762
Energy - ft-lb	2997	2466	2014	1629	1305	1034
Taylor KO values	19.8	18.0	16.5	14.6	13.1	11.6
Path - inches	-1.5	1.9	0.0	-7.7	-22.5	-46.2
Wind Drift - inches	0.0	0.9	3.7	8.8	16.4	27.1

G1 Ballistic Coefficient = 0.338

Speer 150-grain Grand Slam (24550)

Distance - Yards	Muzzle	100	200	300	400	500
Velocity - fps	2900	2599	2317	2053	1809	1586
Energy - ft-lb	2800	2249	1788	1404	1091	838
Taylor KO values	19.1	17.2	15.3	13.5	11.9	10.5
Path - inches	-1.5	2.1	0.0	-8.6	-24.8	-52.3
Wind Drift - inches	0.0	1.0	4.3	10.3	19.5	32.5

G1 Ballistic Coefficient = 0.306

Winchester 150-grain Partition Gold (SPG308)

Distance - Yards	Muzzle	100	200	300	400	500
Velocity - fps	2900	2645	2405	2177	1962	1760
Energy - ft-lb	2802	2332	1927	1579	1282	1032
Taylor KO values	19.1	17.5	15.9	14.4	12.9	11.6
Path - inches	-1.5	1.7	0.0	-7.8	-22.9	-47.0
Wind Drift - inches	0.0	0.9	3.6	8.5	15.8	26.0

G1 Ballistic Coefficient = 0.363

Winchester 150-grain Power-Point Plus (SHV3085)

Distance - Yards	Muzzle	100	200	300	400	500
Velocity - fps	2900	2558	2241	1946	1678	1441
Energy - ft-lb	2802	2180	1672	1262	938	692
Taylor KO values	19.1	16.9	14.8	12.8	11.1	9.5
Path - inches	-1.5	1.9	0.0	-6.3	-18.3	-37.1
Wind Drift - inches	0.0	1.2	4.9	11.7	22.3	37.3

G1 Ballistic Coefficient = 0.267

Norma 150-grain SP (17624)

Distance - Yards	Muzzle	100	200	300	400	500
Velocity - fps	2861	2537	2235	1954	1695	1466
Energy - ft-lb	2727	2144	1664	1272	957	716
Taylor KO values	18.9	16.7	14.8	12.9	11.2	9.7
Path - inches	-1.5	2.0	0.0	-9.0	-27.1	-57.5
Wind Drift - inches	0.0	1.2	4.9	11.7	22.3	37.3

G1 Ballistic Coefficient = 0.289

Hansen 150-grain Posi-Feed SP (HCC308B)

Distance - Yards	Muzzle	100	200	300	400	500
Velocity - fps	2853	2584	2331	2092	1868	1661
Energy - ft-lb	2717	2225	1811	1459	1163	919
Taylor KO values	18.8	117.1	15.3	13.8	12.3	11.0
Path - inches	-1.5	1.9	0.0	-8.3	-24.6	-50.8
Wind Drift - inches	0.0	0.9	4.0	9.4	17.6	29.0

G1 Ballistic Coefficient = 0.340

Federal 150-grain Nosler Ballistic Tip (P308F)

Distance - Yards	Muzzle	100	200	300	400	500
Velocity - fps	2820	2610	2410	2220	2040	1860
Energy - ft-lb	2650	2270	1935	1640	1380	1155
Taylor KO values	18.6	17.2	15.9	14.7	13.5	12.3
Path - inches	-1.5	1.8	0.0	-7.8	-22.7	-46.0
Wind Drift - inches	0.0	0.7	3.1	7.2	13.4	21.8

G1 Ballistic Coefficient = 0.433

Federal 150-grain Hi-Shok SP (308A)

Distance - Yards	Muzzle	100	200	300	400	500
Velocity - fps	2820	2530	2260	2010	1770	1560
Energy - ft-lb	2650	2140	1705	1345	1050	810
Taylor KO values	18.6	16.7	14.9	13.3	11.7	10.3
Path - inches	-1.5	2.0	0.0	-8.8	-26.3	-54.8
Wind Drift - inches	0.0	1.0	4.4	10.4	19.6	32.6

G1 Ballistic Coefficient = 0.315

Hornady 150-grain Boattail SP (8091)

Distance - Yards	Muzzle	100	200	300	400	500
Velocity - fps	2820	2560	2315	2084	1866	1644
Energy - ft-lb	2648	2183	1785	1447	1160	922
Taylor KO values	18.6	16.9	15.3	13.8	12.3	10.9
Path - inches	-1.5	2.0	0.0	-8.5	-25.2	-51.8
Wind Drift - inches	0.0	1.0	4.0	9.4	17.7	29.3

G1 Ballistic Coefficient = 0.342

PMC 150-grain SP Boattail (308HA)

Distance - Yards	Muzzle	100	200	300	400	500
Velocity - fps	2820	2581	2354	2139	1935	1744
Energy - ft-lb	2648	2218	1846	1523	1247	1013
Taylor KO values	18.6	17.0	15.5	14.1	12.8	11.5
Path - inches	-1.5	1.9	0.0	-8.2	-24.0	-49.0
Wind Drift - inches	0.0	0.8	3.6	8.4	15.6	25.6

G1 Ballistic Coefficient = 0.380

Remington 150-grain Pointed SP Core-Lokt (R308W1)

Distance - Yards	Muzzle	100	200	300	400	500
Velocity - fps	2820	2533	2263	2009	1774	1560
Energy - ft-lb	2649	2137	1705	1344	1048	810
Taylor KO values	18.6	16.7	14.9	13.3	11.7	10.3
Path - inches	-1.5	2.0	0.0	-8.8	-26.2	-54.8
Wind Drift - inches	0.0	1.0	4.4	10.4	19.6	32.6

G1 Ballistic Coefficient = 0.315

Winchester 150-grain Fail Safe (S308XA)

Distance - Yards	Muzzle	100	200	300	400	500
Velocity - fps	2820	2533	2263	2010	1775	1561
Energy - ft-lb	2649	2137	1706	1346	1049	812
Taylor KO values	18.6	16.7	14.9	13.3	11.7	10.3
Path - inches	-1.5	2.0	0.0	-8.8	-26.2	-54.6
Wind Drift - inches	0.0	1.0	4.4	10.4	19.6	32.6

G1 Ballistic Coefficient = 0.316

Winchester 150-grain Power-Point (X3085)

Distance - Yards	Muzzle	100	200	300	400	500
Velocity - fps	2820	2488	2179	1893	1633	1405
Energy - ft-lb	2648	2061	1581	1193	888	657
Taylor KO values	18.6	16.4	14.4	12.5	10.8	9.3
Path - inches	-1.5	2.4	0.0	-9.8	-29.3	-62.0
Wind Drift - inches	0.0	1.2	5.2	12.4	23.8	39.9

G1 Ballistic Coefficient = 0.271

Winchester 150-grain Ballistic Silvertip (SBST308)

Distance - Yards	Muzzle	100	200	300	400	500
Velocity - fps	2810	2601	2401	2211	2028	1856
Energy - ft-lb	2629	2253	1920	1627	1370	1147
Taylor KO values	18.5	17.2	15.8	14.6	13.4	12.2
Path - inches	-1.5	1.8	0.0	-7.8	-22.8	-46.2
Wind Drift - inches	0.0	0.7	3.1	7.2	13.4	21.8

G1 Ballistic Coefficient = 0.435

Lapua 150-grain Mega SP (4317498)

Distance - Yards	Muzzle	100	200	300	400	500
Velocity - fps	2789	2511	2249	2003	1774	1565
Energy - ft-lb	2591	2100	1685	1337	1049	816
Taylor KO values	18.4	16.6	14.8	13.2	11.7	10.3
Path - inches	-1.5	2.0	0.0	-8.9	-26.6	-55.3
Wind Drift - inches	0.0	1.0	4.3	10.3	19.3	32.1

G1 Ballistic Coefficient = 0.323

PMC 150-grain Pointed SP (308A)

Distance - Yards	Muzzle	100	200	300	400	500
Velocity - fps	2643	2417	2203	1999	1807	1632
Energy - ft-lb	2326	1946	1615	1331	1088	887
Taylor KO values	17.4	16.0	14.5	13.2	11.9	10.8
Path - inches	-1.5	2.2	0.0	-9.4	-27.5	-56.2
Wind Drift - inches	0.0	0.9	3.8	9.0	16.7	27.5

G1 Ballistic Coefficient = 0.389

PMC 150-grain Barnes-X (308XA)

Distance - Yards	Muzzle	100	200	300	400	500
Velocity - fps	2700	2504	2316	2135	1964	1801
Energy - ft-lb	2428	2087	1786	1518	1284	1080
Taylor KO values	17.8	16.5	15.3	14.1	13.0	11.9
Path - inches	-1.5	2.0	0.0	-8.6	-24.7	-50.0
Wind Drift - inches	0.0	0.8	3.1	7.3	13.5	22.1

G1 Ballistic Coefficient = 0.453

American Eagle (Federal) 150-grain FMJ Boattail (AE308D)

Distance - Yards	Muzzle	100	200	300	400	500
Velocity - fps	2820	2620	2430	2250	2070	1900
Energy - ft-lb	2650	2285	1965	1680	1430	1205
Taylor KO values	18.6	17.3	16.0	14.9	13.7	12.5
Path - inches	-1.5	1.8	0.0	-7.7	-22.3	-45.1
Wind Drift - inches	0.0	0.7	2.9	6.8	12.6	20.6

G1 Ballistic Coefficient = 0.455

UMC (Remington) 150-grain MC (L308W4)

Distance - Yards	Muzzle	100	200	300	400	500
Velocity - fps	2820	2533	2263	2010	1776	1561
Energy - ft-lb	2649	2137	1707	1347	1050	812
Taylor KO values	18.6	16.7	14.9	13.3	11.7	10.3
Path - inches	-1.5	2.0	0.0	-8.8	-26.2	-54.8
Wind Drift - inches	0.0	1.0	4.4	10.4	19.6	32.6

G1 Ballistic Coefficient = 0.315

Lapua 150-grain Lock Base (4317538)

Distance - Yards	Muzzle	100	200	300	400	500
Velocity - fps	2788	2599	2418	2243	2076	1916
Energy - ft-lb	2591	2251	1947	1676	1435	1223
Taylor KO values	18.4	17.2	16.0	14.8	13.7	12.6
Path - inches	-1.5	1.8	0.0	-7.8	-22.5	-45.3
Wind Drift - inches	0.0	0.7	2.8	6.6	12.1	19.6

G1 Ballistic Coefficient = 0.479

Hansen 150-grain FMJ Boattail (HCC308A)

Distance - Yards	Muzzle	100	200	300	400	500
Velocity - fps	2795	2566	2348	2141	1944	1759
Energy - ft-lb	2603	2193	1837	1527	1259	1031
Taylor KO values	18.4	16.9	15.5	14.1	12.8	11.6
Path - inches	-1.5	1.9	0.0	-8.2	-24.0	-49.1
Wind Drift - inches	0.0	0.8	3.4	8.1	15.1	24.7

G1 Ballistic Coefficient = 0.395

Lapua 155-grain Scenar (4317073)

Distance - Yards	Muzzle	100	200	300	400	500
Velocity - fps	2822	2468	2141	1841	1571	1340
Energy - ft-lb	2729	2088	1572	1161	846	615
Taylor KO values	19.2	16.8	14.6	12.6	10.7	9.1
Path - inches	-1.5	2.1	0.0	-9.8	-29.9	-64.2
Wind Drift - inches	0.0	1.3	5.6	13.4	25.8	43.5

G1 Ballistic Coefficient = 0.254

Federal 155-grain Sierra MatchKing HP Boattail (GM308M3)

Distance - Yards	Muzzle	100	200	300	400	500
Velocity - fps	2950	2740	2540	2350	2170	2000
Energy - ft-lb	2996	2585	2225	1905	1620	1370
Taylor KO values	20.1	18.7	17.3	16.0	14.8	13.6
Path - inches	-1.5	1.6	0.0	-6.9	-20.2	-40.7
Wind Drift - inches	0.0	0.7	2.8	7.4	11.8	19.3

G1 Ballistic Coefficient = 0.455

Hornady 165-grain BTSP-Light Magnum (8598)

Distance - Yards	Muzzle	100	200	300	400	500
Velocity - fps	2880	2655	2441	2237	2043	1859
Energy - ft-lb	3038	2582	2182	1833	1529	1286
Taylor KO values	20.9	19.3	17.7	16.2	14.8	13.5
Path - inches	-1.5	2.0	0.0	-7.9	-22.7	-45.9
Wind Drift - inches	0.0	0.8	3.2	7.4	13.8	22.6

G1 Ballistic Coefficient = 0.410

Federal 165-grain Trophy Bonded Bear Claw - High Energy (P308T2)

Distance - Yards	Muzzle	100	200	300	400	500
Velocity - fps	2870	2600	2350	2120	1890	1690
Energy - ft-lb	3020	2485	2030	1640	1310	1040
Taylor KO values	20.8	18.9	17.1	15.4	13.7	12.3
Path - inches	-1.5	1.8	0.0	-8.2	-24.0	-49.9
Wind Drift - inches	0.0	0.9	3.8	9.1	17.0	28.1

G1 Ballistic Coefficient = 0.346

Hansen 165-grain Posi-Feed SP (HCC308F)

Distance - Yards	Muzzle	100	200	300	400	500
Velocity - fps	2700	2447	2209	1984	1773	1580
Energy - ft-lb	2670	2195	1788	1442	1152	915
Taylor KO values	19.6	17.8	16.0	14.4	12.9	11.5
Path - inches	-1.5	2.2	0.0	-9.3	-27.5	-56.8
Wind Drift - inches	0.0	1.0	4.1	9.8	18.4	30.4

G1 Ballistic Coefficient = 0.350

Federal 165-grain Sierra GameKing SP Boattail (P308C)

Distance - Yards	Muzzle	100	200	300	400	500
Velocity - fps	2700	2520	2330	2160	1990	1830
Energy - ft-lb	2670	2310	1990	1700	1450	1230
Taylor KO values	19.6	18.3	16.9	15.7	14.4	13.3
Path - inches	-1.5	2.0	0.0	-8.4	-24.3	-49.0
Wind Drift - inches	0.0	0.7	3.0	7.0	13.0	21.1

G1 Ballistic Coefficient = 0.470

Federal 165-grain Trophy Bonded Bear Claw (P308T1)

Distance - Yards	Muzzle	100	200	300	400	500
Velocity - fps	2700	2440	2200	1970	1760	1570
Energy - ft-lb	2670	2185	1775	1425	1135	900
Taylor KO values	19.6	17.7	16.0	14.3	12.8	11.3
Path - inches	-1.5	2.2	0.0	-9.4	-27.7	-57.5
Wind Drift - inches	0.0	1.0	4.2	9.9	18.6	30.8

G1 Ballistic Coefficient = 0.347

Hornady 165-grain SP Boattail (8098)

Distance - Yards	Muzzle	100	200	300	400	500
Velocity - fps	2700	2496	2301	2115	1937	1770
Energy - ft-lb	2670	2283	1940	1639	1375	1148
Taylor KO values	19.6	18.1	16.7	15.4	14.1	12.9
Path - inches	-1.5	2.0	0.0	-8.7	-25.2	-51.0
Wind Drift - inches	0.0	0.8	3.3	7.6	14.2	23.2

G1 Ballistic Coefficient = 0.435

Norma 165-grain Swift A-Frame (17612)

Distance - Yards	Muzzle	100	200	300	400	500
Velocity - fps	2700	2459	2231	2015	1811	1623
Energy - ft-lb	2672	2216	1824	1488	1202	965
Taylor KO values	19.6	17.9	16.2	14.6	13.1	11.8
Path - inches	-1.5	2.1	0.0	-9.1	-26.9	-55.3
Wind Drift - inches	0.0	0.9	3.9	9.3	17.4	28.6

G1 Ballistic Coefficient = 0.435

Remington 165-grain Nosler Ballistic Tip (PRT308WB)

Distance - Yards	Muzzle	100	200	300	400	500
Velocity - fps	2700	2513	2333	2161	1996	1839
Energy - ft-lb	2672	2314	1995	1711	1460	1239
Taylor KO values	19.6	18.2	16.9	15.9	14.5	13.4
Path - inches	-1.5	2.0	0.0	-8.4	-24.3	-48.9
Wind Drift - inches	0.0	0.7	3.0	6.9	12.8	20.8

G1 Ballistic Coefficient = 0.475

Remington 165-grain Pointed SP Boattail (PRB308WA)

Distance - Yards	Muzzle	100	200	300	400	500
Velocity - fps	2700	2497	2303	2117	1941	1773
Energy - ft-lb	2670	2284	1942	1642	1379	1152
Taylor KO values	19.6	18.1	16.7	15.4	14.1	12.9
Path - inches	-1.5	2.0	0.0	-8.4	-25.0	-50.6
Wind Drift - inches	0.0	0.8	3.2	7.6	14.1	23.0

G1 Ballistic Coefficient = 0.437

Speer 165-grain Grand Slam (24505)

Distance - Yards	Muzzle	100	200	300	400	500
Velocity - fps	2700	2475	2261	2057	1865	1686
Energy - ft-lb	2670	2243	1872	1550	1275	1041
Taylor KO values	19.6	18.0	16.4	14.9	13.5	12.2
Path - inches	-1.5	2.1	0.0	-8.9	-25.9	-53.2
Wind Drift - inches	0.0	0.9	3.6	8.6	16.0	26.2

G1 Ballistic Coefficient = 0.394

Black Hills 165-grain SP - Boattail (D308N4)

Distance - Yards	Muzzle	100	200	300	400	500
Velocity - fps	2650	2450	2259	2077	1903	1739
Energy - ft-lb	2573	2200	1870	1580	1327	1108
Taylor KO values	19.2	17.8	16.4	15.1	13.8	12.6
Path - inches	-1.5	2.2	0.0	-9.0	-26.0	-52.7
Wind Drift - inches	0.0	0.8	3.3	7.8	14.4	23.5

G1 Ballistic Coefficient = 0.440

PMC 165-grain Barnes-X (308XB)

Distance - Yards	Muzzle	100	200	300	400	500
Velocity - fps	2600	2425	2256	2095	1940	1793
Energy - ft-lb	2476	2154	1865	1608	1379	1177
Taylor KO values	18.9	17.6	16.4	15.2	14.1	13.0
Path - inches	-1.5	2.2	0.0	-9.0	-26.0	-52.4
Wind Drift - inches	0.0	0.7	3.0	7.0	12.9	20.9

G1 Ballistic Coefficient = 0.497

Lapua 167-grain Scenar (4317515)

Distance - Yards	Muzzle	100	200	300	400	500
Velocity - fps	2690	2497	2312	2135	1966	1805
Energy - ft-lb	2684	2313	1983	1691	1433	1209
Taylor KO values	19.8	18.3	17.0	15.7	14.4	13.3
Path - inches	-1.5	2.0	0.0	-8.6	-24.8	-50.0
Wind Drift - inches	0.0	0.8	3.1	7.2	13.4	21.8

G1 Ballistic Coefficient = 0.460

Hornady 168-grain HP - Boattail - Light Magnum (8597)

Distance - Yards	Muzzle	100	200	300	400	500
Velocity - fps	2840	2630	2429	2238	2056	1892
Energy - ft-lb	3008	2597	2201	1868	1577	1335
Taylor KO values	21.0	19.4	18.0	16.5	15.2	14.0
Path - inches	-1.5	1.8	0.0	-7.8	-22.7	-45.2
Wind Drift - inches	0.0	0.7	3.0	7.0	12.9	21.0

G1 Ballistic Coefficient = 0.442

Winchester 168-grain Ballistic Silvertip (SBST308A)

Distance - Yards	Muzzle	100	200	300	400	500
Velocity - fps	2670	2484	2306	2134	1971	1815
Energy - ft-lb	2659	2301	1983	1699	1449	1229
Taylor KO values	19.7	18.4	17.0	15.8	14.6	13.4
Path - inches	-1.5	2.1	0.0	-8.6	-24.8	-50.0
Wind Drift - inches	0.0	0.7	3.0	7.0	13.0	21.12

G1 Ballistic Coefficient = 0.4765

Hornady 168-grain A-Max Match (8096) + Moly (80973)

Distance - Yards	Muzzle	100	200	300	400	500
Velocity - fps	2620	2446	2280	2120	1972	1831
Energy - ft-lb	2560	2232	1939	1677	1450	1251
Taylor KO values	19.4	18.1	16.9	15.7	14.6	13.5
Path - inches	-1.5	2.6	0.0	-9.2	-25.7	-51.9
Wind Drift - inches	0.0	0.7	2.8	6.6	12.2	19.8

G1 Ballistic Coefficient = 0.514

Hornady 168-grain HP Boattail Match (8097)

Distance - Yards	Muzzle	100	200	300	400	500
Velocity - fps	2700	2491	2292	2102	1921	1751
Energy - ft-lb	2719	2315	1959	1648	1377	1149
Taylor KO values	20.0	18.4	16.9	15.5	14.2	12.9
Path - inches	-1.5	2.4	0.0	-9.0	-25.9	-52.2
Wind Drift - inches	0.0	0.8	3.4	7.9	14.6	23.8

G1 Ballistic Coefficient = 0.425

Remington 168-grain HP Boattail Match (R308W7)

Distance - Yards	Muzzle	100	200	300	400	500
Velocity - fps	2680	2496	2314	2143	1979	1823
Energy - ft-lb	2678	2318	1998	1713	1460	1239
Taylor KO values	19.8	18.4	17.1	15.8	14.6	13.5
Path - inches	-1.5	2.1	0.0	-8.6	-24.7	-49.9
Wind Drift - inches	0.0	0.7	3.0	7.0	12.9	21.0

G1 Ballistic Coefficient = 0.476

Black Hills 168-grain Match HP (D308N1)

Distance - Yards	Muzzle	100	200	300	400	500
Velocity - fps	2650	2465	2287	2116	1953	1798
Energy - ft-lb	2620	2267	1951	1671	1423	1207
Taylor KO values	19.6	18.2	16.9	15.6	14.4	13.3
Path - inches	-1.5	2.1	0.0	-8.8	-25.3	-51.0
Wind Drift - inches	0.0	0.7	3.0	7.1	13.2	21.4

G1 Ballistic Coefficient = 0.475

PMC 168-grain HP Boattail (308SMB)

Distance - Yards	Muzzle	100	200	300	400	500
Velocity - fps	2650	2460	2278	2103	1936	1778
Energy - ft-lb	2619	2257	1936	1651	1399	1179
Taylor KO values	19.6	18.2	16.8	15.5	14.3	13.1
Path - inches	-1.5	2.1	0.0	-8.8	-25.6	-51.6
Wind Drift - inches	0.0	0.8	3.1	7.3	13.6	22.1

G1 Ballistic Coefficient = 0.463

Federal 168-grain Sierra MatchKing HP Boattail (GM308M)

Distance - Yards	Muzzle	100	200	300	400	500
Velocity - fps	2600	2410	2230	2060	1890	1740
Energy - ft-lb	2522	2172	1860	1584	1342	1131
Taylor KO values	19.2	17.8	17.2	15.2	14.0	12.9
Path - inches	-1.5	2.2	0.0	-9.2	-26.7	-53.8
Wind Drift - inches	0.0	0.8	3.2	7.5	13.9	22.7

G1 Ballistic Coefficient = 0.464

Hansen 168-grain JHP Match-King (HCC308M)

Distance - Yards	Muzzle	100	200	300	400	500
Velocity - fps	2592	2404	2224	2052	1888	1733
Energy - ft-lb	2506	2157	1846	1572	1330	1121
Taylor KO values	19.2	17.8	16.4	15.2	14.0	13.1
Path - inches	-1.5	2.3	0.0	-9.3	-26.9	-54.2
Wind Drift - inches	0.0	0.8	3.2	7.6	14.0	22.9

G1 Ballistic Coefficient = 0.463

PMC 168-grain FMJ - Boattail (308D)

Distance - Yards	Muzzle	100	200	300	400	500
Velocity - fps	2600	2419	2245	2080	1923	1774
Energy - ft-lb	2522	2182	1881	1614	1380	1173
Taylor KO values	19.2	17.9	16.6	15.4	14.2	13.1
Path - inches	-1.5	2.2	0.0	-9.1	-26.3	-52.9
Wind Drift - inches	0.0	0.8	3.2	7.6	14.0	22.9

G1 Ballistic Coefficient = 0.485

Norma 168-grain HP (17615)

Distance - Yards	Muzzle	100	200	300	400	500
Velocity - fps	2549	2366	2190	2022	1862	1710
Energy - ft-lb	2424	2088	1790	1526	1294	1092
Taylor KO values	18.8	17.5	16.2	14.9	13.8	12.6
Path - inches	-1.5	2.4	0.0	-9.6	-27.8	-56.0
Wind Drift - inches	0.0	0.8	3.3	7.6	14.2	23.0

G1 Ballistic Coefficient = 0.470

Lapua 170-grain Lock Base (4317596)

Distance - Yards	Muzzle	100	200	300	400	500
Velocity - fps	2822	2645	2474	2310	2152	2001
Energy - ft-lb	3007	2641	2260	2090	1749	1512
Taylor KO values	21.1	19.8	18.5	17.3	16.1	15.0
Path - inches	-1.5	1.7	0.0	-7.4	-21.4	-42.8
Wind Drift - inches	0.0	0.6	2.6	5.9	10.9	17.6

G1 Ballistic Coefficient = 0.517

Lapua 170-grain FMJ - Boattail (4317183)

Distance - Yards	Muzzle	100	200	300	400	500
Velocity - fps	2560	2384	2214	2052	1897	1749
Energy - ft-lb	2474	2145	1851	1590	1358	1155
Taylor KO values	19.1	17.8	16.6	15.3	14.2	13.1
Path - inches	-1.5	2.3	0.0	-9.4	-27.1	-54.5
Wind Drift - inches	0.0	0.8	3.1	7.2	13.4	21.8

G1 Ballistic Coefficient = 0.490

Federal 175-grain Sierra MatchKing HP Boattail (GM308M2)

Distance - Yards	Muzzle	100	200	300	400	500
Velocity - fps	2600	2420	2260	2090	1940	1790
Energy - ft-lb	2627	2284	1977	1703	1460	1245
Taylor KO values	20.0	18.6	17.4	16.1	14.9	13.8
Path - inches	-1.5	2.2	0.0	-9.1	-26.1	-52.4
Wind Drift - inches	0.0	0.7	3.0	7.0	12.9	21.0

G1 Ballistic Coefficient = 0.496

Black Hills 175-grain Match HP (D308N5)

Distance - Yards	Muzzle	100	200	300	400	500
Velocity - fps	2600	2420	2260	2090	1940	1790
Energy - ft-lb	2627	2284	1977	1703	1460	1245
Taylor KO values	20.0	18.6	17.4	16.1	14.9	13.8
Path - inches	-1.5	2.2	0.0	-9.1	-26.1	-52.4
Wind Drift - inches	0.0	0.7	3.0	7.0	12.9	21.0

G1 Ballistic Coefficient = 0.496

Hornady 178-grain HP Boattail Match (8105)

Distance - Yards	Muzzle	100	200	300	400	500
Velocity - fps	2610	2439	2274	2116	1964	1819
Energy - ft-lb	2692	2351	2044	1769	1524	1308
Taylor KO values	20.4	19.1	17.8	16.6	15.4	14.2
Path - inches	-1.5	2.5	0.0	-9.2	-26.2	-50.1
Wind Drift - inches	0.0	0.7	2.9	6.7	12.4	20.1

G1 Ballistic Coefficient = 0.511

Federal 180-grain Nosler Partition - HE (P308G)

Distance - Yards	Muzzle	100	200	300	400	500
Velocity - fps	2740	2550	2370	2200	2030	1870
Energy - ft-lb	3000	2600	2245	1925	1645	1395
Taylor KO values	21.7	20.2	18.8	17.4	16.1	14.8
Path - inches	-1.5	1.9	0.0	-8.2	-23.5	-47.1
Wind Drift - inches	0.0	0.7	2.9	6.8	12.5	20.4

G1 Ballistic Coefficient = 0.475

Federal 180-grain Woodleigh Weldcore SP-HE (P308L)

Distance - Yards	Muzzle	100	200	300	400	500
Velocity - fps	2740	2500	2280	2060	1860	1680
Energy - ft-lb	3000	2500	2075	1705	1385	1120
Taylor KO values	21.7	19.8	18.1	16.3	14.7	13.3
Path - inches	-1.5	2.0	0.0	-8.8	-25.6	-52.9
Wind Drift - inches	0.0	0.9	3.7	8.8	16.4	26.9

G1 Ballistic Coefficient = 0.379

Federal 180-grain Hi-Shok SP (308B)

Distance - Yards	Muzzle	100	200	300	400	500
Velocity - fps	2620	2390	2180	1970	1780	1600
Energy - ft-lb	2745	2290	1895	1555	1270	1030
Taylor KO values	21.7	18.9	17.3	15.6	14.1	12.7
Path - inches	-1.5	2.3	0.0	-9.7	-28.3	-57.8
Wind Drift - inches	0.0	0.9	3.9	9.3	17.3	28.5

G1 Ballistic Coefficient = 0.382

Federal 180-grain Woodleigh Weldcore SP (P308J)

Distance - Yards	Muzzle	100	200	300	400	500
Velocity - fps	2620	2390	2170	1960	1770	1590
Energy - ft-lb	2745	2280	1880	1540	1250	1010
Taylor KO values	21.7	18.9	17.2	15.5	14.0	12.6
Path - inches	-1.5	2.3	0.0	-9.7	-28.4	-58.6
Wind Drift - inches	0.0	1.0	4.0	9.4	17.6	28.9

G1 Ballistic Coefficient = 0.378

Federal 180-grain Nosler Partition (P308E)

Distance - Yards	Muzzle	100	200	300	400	500
Velocity - fps	2620	2430	2240	2060	1890	1730
Energy - ft-lb	2745	2355	2005	1700	1430	1200
Taylor KO values	21.7	19.2	17.7	16.3	15.0	13.7
Path - inches	-1.5	2.2	0.0	-9.2	-26.5	-53.6
Wind Drift - inches	0.0	0.8	3.3	7.7	14.4	23.4

G1 Ballistic Coefficient = 0.448

Federal 180-grain Sierra Pro-Hunter SP (308HS)

Distance - Yards	Muzzle	100	200	300	400	500
Velocity - fps	2620	2410	2200	2010	1820	1650
Energy - ft-lb	2745	2315	1940	1610	1330	1090
Taylor KO values	21.7	19.1	17.4	15.9	14.4	13.1
Path - inches	-1.5	2.3	0.0	-9.3	-27.1	-55.8
Wind Drift - inches	0.0	0.9	3.7	8.6	16.1	26.4

G1 Ballistic Coefficient = 0.406

PMC 180-grain SP Boattail (308HC)

Distance - Yards	Muzzle	100	200	300	400	500
Velocity - fps	2620	2446	2278	2117	1962	1815
Energy - ft-lb	2743	2391	2074	1790	1538	1316
Taylor KO values	21.7	19.4	18.0	16.8	15.5	14.4
Path - inches	-1.5	2.2	0.0	-9.0	-25.4	-51.3
Wind Drift - inches	0.0	0.7	2.9	6.8	12.6	20.4

G1 Ballistic Coefficient = 0.502

Remington 180-grain Pointed SP Core-Lokt (R308W3)

Distance - Yards	Muzzle	100	200	300	400	500
Velocity - fps	2620	2393	2178	1974	1782	1604
Energy - ft-lb	2743	2288	1896	1557	1269	1028
Taylor KO values	21.7	19.0	17.2	15.6	14.1	12.7
Path - inches	-1.5	2.3	0.0	-9.7	-28.3	-57.8
Wind Drift - inches	0.0	0.9	3.9	9.2	17.2	28.3

G1 Ballistic Coefficient = 0.384

Remington 180-grain SP Core-Lokt (R308W2)

Distance - Yards	Muzzle	100	200	300	400	500
Velocity - fps	2620	2274	1955	1666	1414	1212
Energy - ft-lb	2743	2066	1527	1109	799	587
Taylor KO values	21.7	18.0	15.5	13.2	11.2	9.6
Path - inches	-1.5	2.6	0.0	-11.8	-36.3	78.2
Wind Drift - inches	0.0	1.5	6.4	15.5	29.8	50.8

G1 Ballistic Coefficient = 0.248

Speer 180-grain Grand Slam (24506)

Distance - Yards	Muzzle	100	200	300	400	500
Velocity - fps	2620	2420	2229	2046	1874	1710
Energy - ft-lb	2743	2340	1985	1674	1403	1169
Taylor KO values	21.7	19.2	17.7	16.2	14.8	13.5
Path - inches	-1.5	2.2	0.0	-9.2	-26.6	-54.3
Wind Drift - inches	0.0	0.8	3.4	8.0	14.8	24.1

G1 Ballistic Coefficient = 0.437

Winchester 180-grain Silvertip (X3083)

Distance - Yards	Muzzle	100	200	300	400	500
Velocity - fps	2620	2393	2178	1974	1782	1604
Energy - ft-lb	2743	2280	1896	1557	1269	1028
Taylor KO values	21.7	19.0	17.2	15.6	14.1	12.7
Path - inches	-1.5	2.6	0.0	-9.9	-28.9	-58.8
Wind Drift - inches	0.0	0.9	3.9	9.2	17.2	28.3

G1 Ballistic Coefficient = 0.384

Winchester 180-grain Power-Point (X3086)

Distance - Yards	Muzzle	100	200	300	400	500
Velocity - fps	2620	2274	1955	1666	1414	1212
Energy - ft-lb	2743	2066	1527	1109	799	587
Taylor KO values	21.7	18.0	15.5	13.2	11.2	9.6
Path - inches	-1.5	2.9	0.0	-12.1	-36.9	-79.1
Wind Drift - inches	0.0	1.5	6.4	15.5	29.8	50.1

G1 Ballistic Coefficient = 0.248

Norma 180-grain Alaska (17636)

Distance - Yards	Muzzle	100	200	300	400	500
Velocity - fps	2612	2269	1953	1667	1420	1215
Energy - ft-lb	2728	2059	1526	1111	802	590
Taylor KO values	20.7	18.0	15.5	13.2	11.2	9.6
Path - inches	-1.5	2.7	0.0	-11.9	-36.3	-78.3
Wind Drift - inches	0.0	1.5	6.4	15.4	29.6	49.8

G1 Ballistic Coefficient = 0.257

Norma 180-grain Oryx (17675)

Distance - Yards	Muzzle	100	200	300	400	500
Velocity - fps	2612	2305	2019	1775	1543	1341
Energy - ft-lb	2728	2124	1629	1232	952	719
Taylor KO values	20.7	18.3	16.0	14.1	12.2	10.6
Path - inches	-1.5	2.5	0.0	-11.1	-33.1	-69.8
Wind Drift - inches	0.0	1.3	5.4	13.0	24.7	41.2

G1 Ballistic Coefficient = 0.288

Norma 180-grain Plastic Point (17628)

Distance - Yards	Muzzle	100	200	300	400	500
Velocity - fps	2612	2365	2131	1911	1705	1518
Energy - ft-lb	2728	2235	1815	1460	1162	921
Taylor KO values	20.7	18.7	16.9	15.1	13.5	12.0
Path - inches	-1.5	2.4	0.0	-10.1	-29.7	-61.4
Wind Drift - inches	0.0	1.0	4.4	10.3	19.4	32.0

G1 Ballistic Coefficient = 0.358

Norma 180-grain Nosler Partition (17635)

Distance - Yards	Muzzle	100	200	300	400	500
Velocity - fps	2612	2414	2225	2044	1873	1711
Energy - ft-lb	2728	2330	1979	1670	1403	1171
Taylor KO values	20.7	19.1	17.6	16.2	14.8	13.6
Path - inches	-1.5	2.2	0.0	-9.3	-26.9	-54.4
Wind Drift - inches	0.0	0.8	3.4	7.9	14.7	24.0

G1 Ballistic Coefficient = 0.442

Hansen 180-grain Posi-Feed SP (HCC308C)

Distance - Yards	Muzzle	100	200	300	400	500
Velocity - fps	2558	2274	2008	1762	1539	1346
Energy - ft-lb	2618	2067	1612	1241	947	724
Taylor KO values	20.3	18.0	15.9	14.0	12.2	10.7
Path - inches	-1.5	2.6	0.0	-11.3	33.9	-71.2
Wind Drift - inches	0.0	1.2	5.3	12.8	24.2	40.3

G1 Ballistic Coefficient = 0.300

113

PMC 180-grain Pointed SP (308C)

Distance - Yards	Muzzle	100	200	300	400	500
Velocity - fps	2410	2223	2044	1874	1714	1561
Energy - ft-lb	2320	1975	1670	1404	1174	973
Taylor KO values	19.1	17.6	16.2	14.8	13.6	12.4
Path - inches	-1.5	2.8	0.0	-11.1	-32.0	-64.8
Wind Drift - inches	0.0	0.9	3.8	8.9	16.5	26.9

G1 Ballistic Coefficient = 0.443

Norma 180-grain Vulcan (17660)

Distance - Yards	Muzzle	100	200	300	400	500
Velocity - fps	2612	2325	2056	1806	1578	1379
Energy - ft-lb	2728	2161	1690	1304	996	760
Taylor KO values	20.7	18.4	16.3	14.3	12.5	10.9
Path - inches	-1.5	2.5	0.0	-10.8	-32.3	-67.8
Wind Drift - inches	0.0	1.2	5.2	12.4	23.4	39.1

G1 Ballistic Coefficient = 0.305

Lapua 185-grain Mega SP (4317189)

Distance - Yards	Muzzle	100	200	300	400	500
Velocity - fps	2510	2238	1983	1746	1532	1345
Energy - ft-lb	2589	2057	1615	1253	964	744
Taylor KO values	20.4	18.2	16.1	14.2	12.5	10.9
Path - inches	-1.5	2.7	0.0	-11.6	-34.7	-72.7
Wind Drift - inches	0.0	1.2	5.3	12.6	23.9	39.7

G1 Ballistic Coefficient = 0.310

Lapua 185-grain Forex (4137214)

Distance - Yards	Muzzle	100	200	300	400	500
Velocity - fps	2575	2100	1681	1336	1099	966
Energy - ft-lb	2724	1812	1161	733	496	384
Taylor KO values	21.0	17.1	13.7	10.9	8.9	7.9
Path - inches	-1.5	3.3	0.0	-15.8	-51.3	-115.4
Wind Drift - inches	0.0	2.2	9.8	24.6	48.0	79.0

G1 Ballistic Coefficient = 0.176

Lapua 185-grain Scenar (4317523)

Distance - Yards	Muzzle	100	200	300	400	500
Velocity - fps	2477	2310	2149	1995	1821	1658
Energy - ft-lb	2521	2193	1898	1636	1363	1129
Taylor KO values	20.2	18.8	17.5	16.2	14.8	13.5
Path - inches	-1.5	2.3	0.0	-9.7	-28.1	-57.1
Wind Drift - inches	0.0	0.9	3.6	8.4	15.6	25.5

G1 Ballistic Coefficient = 0.427

Lapua 185-grain FMJ - Boattail (4317590)

Distance - Yards	Muzzle	100	200	300	400	500
Velocity - fps	2495	2335	2181	2033	1864	1703
Energy - ft-lb	2558	2240	1954	1698	1427	1192
Taylor KO values	20.3	19.0	17.8	16.5	15.2	13.9
Path - inches	-1.5	2.4	0.0	-9.8	-27.2	-55.1
Wind Drift - inches	0.0	0.8	3.4	7.9	14.7	24.0

G1 Ballistic Coefficient = 0.444

Norma 190-grain HP (17616)

Distance - Yards	Muzzle	100	200	300	400	500
Velocity - fps	2559	2404	2255	2111	1973	1840
Energy - ft-lb	2763	2440	2146	1881	1642	1428
Taylor KO values	21.4	20.1	18.9	17.6	16.5	15.4
Path - inches	-1.5	2.3	0.0	-9.1	-26.0	-51.9
Wind Drift - inches	0.0	0.6	2.7	6.3	11.5	18.6

G1 Ballistic Coefficient = 0.560

Norma 200-grain Vulcan (17683)

Distance - Yards	Muzzle	100	200	300	400	500
Velocity - fps	2461	2215	1983	1767	1568	1392
Energy - ft-lb	2690	2179	1747	1387	1092	861
Taylor KO values	21.7	19.5	17.5	15.5	13.8	12.2
Path - inches	-1.5	2.8	0.0	-11.7	-34.6	-71.7
Wind Drift - inches	0.0	1.2	4.9	11.7	22.0	36.3

G1 Ballistic Coefficient = 0.347

Lapua 200-grain Subsonic (4317340)

Distance - Yards	Muzzle	100	200	300	400	500
Velocity - fps	1066	1006	959	918	882	850
Energy - ft-lb	505	450	408	374	346	321
Taylor KO values	9.4	8.9	8.4	8.1	7.8	7.5
Path - inches	-1.5	16.4	0.0	-54.2	-149.7	-289.9
Wind Drift - inches	0.0	1.5	5.8	12.6	21.8	33.3

G1 Ballistic Coefficient = 0.400

.30-06 Springfield

It's over 95 years old, but who's counting. The .30-06 is the standard by which every other US cartridge is judged. Conceived in response to the embarrassment inflicted by the 7x57 mm Mausers in Cuba in the Spanish-American War, the first cut at this cartridge was little more than a 7x57 necked to .30 caliber. In its original form, the 1903 cartridge for the Model 1903 rifle used a 220-grain round-nosed bullet at 2300 fps. Three years later the 1906 version (hence the .30-06 name) adopted a 150-grain pointed bullet at 2700 fps. The basic design of US military rifle ammunition changed very little until the 7.62 NATO cartridge (.308 Winchester) was adopted in 1952. The .30-06 remains the most popular caliber in the inventory in this country. There are nearly 75 different loadings available today. At this rate we might see .30-06s around in the year 2100.

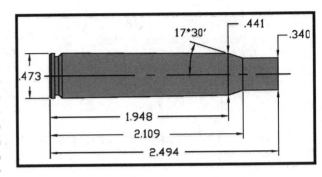

Relative Recoil Factor = 2.19

Controlling Agency : SAAMI

Bullet Weight Grains	Velocity fps	Maximum Average Pressure	
		Copper Crusher	Transducer
110	3300	50,000 cup	60,000 psi
125	3125	50,000 cup	60,000 psi
150	2900	50,000 cup	60,000 psi
165-168	2790	50,000 cup	60,000 psi
180	2690	50,000 cup	60,000 psi
200	2450	50,000 cup	60,000 psi
220	2400	50,000 cup	60,000 psi

Standard barrel for velocity testing:
24 inches long - 1 turn in 10 inch twist

Remington 55-grain Accelerator Pointed SP (R30069)

Distance - Yards	Muzzle	100	200	300	400	500
Velocity - fps	4080	3484	2964	2499	2080	1706
Energy - ft-lb	2033	1482	1073	763	528	355
Taylor KO values	7.2	6.1	5.2	4.4	3.7	3.0
0ath - inches	-1.5	0.7	0.0	-4.7	-15.0	-33.6
Wind Drift - inches	0.0	1.1	4.6	11.1	21.3	36.4

G1 Ballistic Coefficient = 0.197

Lapua 123-grain FMJ (4317577)

Distance - Yards	Muzzle	100	200	300	400	500
Velocity - fps	2936	2599	2286	1995	1728	1490
Energy - ft-lb	2364	1853	1433	1092	819	609
Taylor KO values	15.9	14.1	12.4	10.8	9.4	8.1
Path - inches	-1.5	1.8	0.0	-8.5	-25.9	-54.9
Wind Drift - inches	0.0	1.1	4.8	11.6	22.0	37.0

G1 Ballistic Coefficient = 0.274

Federal 125-grain Sierra Pro-Hunter SP (3006CS)

Distance - Yards	Muzzle	100	200	300	400	500
Velocity - fps	3140	2780	2450	2140	1850	1600
Energy - ft-lb	2735	2145	1680	1270	955	705
Taylor KO values	17.3	15.3	13.5	11.8	10.2	8.8
Path - inches	-1.5	1.5	0.0	-7.3	-22.3	-47.5
Wind Drift - inches	0.0	1.1	4.5	10.7	20.4	34.2

G1 Ballistic Coefficient = 0.269

Remington 125-grain Pointed SP (R30061)

Distance - Yards	Muzzle	100	200	300	400	500
Velocity - fps	3140	2780	2447	2138	1853	1595
Energy - ft-lb	2736	2145	1662	1269	953	706
Taylor KO values	17.3	15.3	13.5	11.8	10.2	8.8
Path - inches	-1.5	1.5	0.0	-7.4	-22.4	-47.6
Wind Drift - inches	0.0	1.1	4.5	10.8	20.5	34.4

G1 Ballistic Coefficient = 0.268

Winchester 125-grain Pointed SP (X30062)

Distance - Yards	Muzzle	100	200	300	400	500
Velocity - fps	3140	2780	2447	2138	1853	1595
Energy - ft-lb	2736	2145	1662	1269	953	706
Taylor KO values	17.3	15.3	13.5	11.8	10.2	8.8
Path - inches	-1.5	1.5	0.0	-7.4	-22.4	-47.6
Wind Drift - inches	0.0	1.1	4.5	10.8	20.5	34.4

G1 Ballistic Coefficient = 0.268

Norma 146-grain Full Jacket (17651)

Distance - Yards	Muzzle	100	200	300	400	500
Velocity - fps	2772	2557	2353	2158	1973	1797
Energy - ft-lb	2492	2121	1796	1511	1262	1048
Taylor KO values	17.8	16.4	15.1	13.9	12.7	11.5
Path - inches	-1.5	1.9	0.0	-8.2	-23.9	-48.5
Wind Drift - inches	0.0	0.8	3.3	7.7	14.2	23.2

G1 Ballistic Coefficient = 0.422

Winchester 150-grain Power-Point Plus (SHV30069)

Distance - Yards	Muzzle	100	200	300	400	500
Velocity - fps	3050	2685	2352	2043	1760	1508
Energy - ft-lb	3089	2402	1843	1391	1032	757
Taylor KO values	20.1	17.7	15.5	13.5	11.6	10.0
Path - inches	-1.5	1.7	0.0	-8.0	-24.3	-51.9
Wind Drift - inches	0.0	1.1	4.8	11.5	22.0	37.1

G1 Ballistic Coefficient = 0.2628

Hornady 150-grain SP - Light Magnum (8510)

Distance - Yards	Muzzle	100	200	300	400	500
Velocity - fps	3100	2815	2548	2295	2059	1835
Energy - ft-lb	3200	2639	2161	1755	1410	1121
Taylor KO values	20.5	18.6	16.8	15.1	13.6	12.1
Path - inches	-1.5	1.4	0.0	-6.8	-20.3	-42.0
Wind Drift - inches	0.0	0.8	3.5	8.4	15.6	25.8

G1 Ballistic Coefficient = 0.339

Speer 150-grain Grand Slam (24551)

Distance - Yards	Muzzle	100	200	300	400	500
Velocity - fps	2975	2669	2383	2114	1863	1634
Energy - ft-lb	2947	2372	1891	1489	1156	889
Taylor KO values	19.6	17.6	15.7	14.0	12.3	10.8
Path - inches	-1.5	1.9	0.0	-8.3	-24.1	-49.3
Wind Drift - inches	0.0	1.0	4.2	10.0	18.8	31.7

G1 Ballistic Coefficient = 0.305

Norma 150-grain SP (17643)

Distance - Yards	Muzzle	100	200	300	400	500
Velocity - fps	2972	2640	2331	1390	1051	787
Energy - ft-lb	2943	2321	1810	1390	1051	787
Taylor KO values	19.6	17.4	15.4	13.5	11.7	10.1
Path - inches	-1.5	1.8	0.0	-8.2	-24.8	-52.5
Wind Drift - inches	0.0	1.1	4.6	11.1	21.0	35.4

G1 Ballistic Coefficient = 0.285

Winchester 150-grain Partition Gold (SPG3006)

Distance - Yards	Muzzle	100	200	300	400	500
Velocity - fps	2960	2705	2464	2235	2019	1815
Energy - ft-lb	2919	2437	2022	1664	1358	1098
Taylor KO values	19.5	17.9	16.3	14.8	13.3	12.0
Path - inches	-1.5	1.6	0.0	-7.4	-21.7	-44.6
Wind Drift - inches	0.0	0.8	3.4	8.1	15.1	24.9

G1 Ballistic Coefficient = 0.367

Hansen 150-grain Posi-Feed SP (HCC306B)

Distance - Yards	Muzzle	100	200	300	400	500
Velocity - fps	2950	2683	2432	2194	1970	1760
Energy - ft-lb	2898	2399	1970	1603	1292	1032
Taylor KO values	19.5	17.7	16.1	14.5	13.0	11.6
Path - inches	-1.5	1.7	0.0	-7.6	-22.4	-46.2
Wind Drift - inches	0.0	0.9	3.6	8.6	16.1	26.6

G1 Ballistic Coefficient = 0.350

Winchester 150-grain Fail Safe (S3006XB)

Distance - Yards	Muzzle	100	200	300	400	500
Velocity - fps	2920	2625	2349	2089	1848	1625
Energy - ft-lb	2841	2296	1838	1455	1137	880
Taylor KO values	19.3	17.3	15.5	13.8	12.2	10.7
Path - inches	-1.5	1.8	0.0	-8.1	-24.3	-50.5
Wind Drift - inches	0.0	1.0	4.2	10.0	18.8	31.2

G1 Ballistic Coefficient = 0.313

Winchester 150-grain Power-Point (X30061)

Distance - Yards	Muzzle	100	200	300	400	500
Velocity - fps	2920	2580	2265	1972	1704	1466
Energy - ft-lb	2839	2217	1708	1295	967	716
Taylor KO values	19.3	17.0	14.9	13.0	11.2	9.7
Path - inches	-1.5	2.2	0.0	-9.0	-27.0	-57.1
Wind Drift - inches	0.0	1.2	4.9	11.9	22.6	38.0

G1 Ballistic Coefficient = 0.270

Federal 150-grain Nosler Ballistic Tip (P3006P)

Distance - Yards	Muzzle	100	200	300	400	500
Velocity - fps	2910	2700	2490	2300	2110	1940
Energy - ft-lb	2820	2420	2070	1760	1485	1240
Taylor KO values	19.2	17.8	16.4	15.2	13.9	12.8
Path - inches	-1.5	1.6	0.0	-7.3	-21.1	-42.8
Wind Drift - inches	0.0	0.7	2.9	6.8	12.6	20.5

G1 Ballistic Coefficient = 0.439

Federal 150-grain Sierra GameKing SP Boattail (P3006G)

Distance - Yards	Muzzle	100	200	300	400	500
Velocity - fps	2910	2690	2480	2270	2070	1880
Energy - ft-lb	2820	2420	2040	1710	1430	1180
Taylor KO values	19.2	17.8	16.4	15.0	13.7	11.2
Path - inches	-1.5	1.7	0.0	-7.4	-21.5	-43.7
Wind Drift - inches	0.0	0.7	3.1	7.2	13.5	22.0

G1 Ballistic Coefficient = 0.410

Federal 150-grain Sierra Pro-Hunter SP (3006SS)

Distance - Yards	Muzzle	100	200	300	400	500
Velocity - fps	2910	2640	2380	2130	1900	1690
Energy - ft-lb	2820	2315	1880	1515	1205	950
Taylor KO values	19.2	17.4	15.7	14.1	12.5	11.2
Path - inches	-1.5	1.7	0.0	-7.0	-23.3	-48.7
Wind Drift - inches	0.0	0.9	3.9	9.2	17.3	28.6

G1 Ballistic Coefficient = 0.336

Federal 150-grain Hi-Shok SP (3006A)

Distance - Yards	Muzzle	100	200	300	400	500
Velocity - fps	2910	2620	2340	2080	1840	1620
Energy - ft-lb	2820	2280	1825	1445	1130	875
Taylor KO values	19.2	17.3	15.4	13.7	12.1	10.7
Path - inches	-1.5	1.8	0.0	-8.2	-24.4	-50.8
Wind Drift - inches	0.0	1.0	4.2	10.0	18.8	31.2

G1 Ballistic Coefficient = 0.314

Hornady 150-grain SP Boattail (8111)

Distance - Yards	Muzzle	100	200	300	400	500
Velocity - fps	2910	2683	2467	2262	2066	1880
Energy - ft-lb	2820	2420	2027	1706	1421	1177
Taylor KO values	19.2	17.7	16.3	14.9	13.6	12.4
Path - inches	-1.5	2.0	0.0	-7.7	-22.2	-44.9
Wind Drift - inches	0.0	0.8	3.1	7.3	13.6	22.2

G1 Ballistic Coefficient = 0.410

Hornady 150-grain SP (8110)

Distance - Yards	Muzzle	100	200	300	400	500
Velocity - fps	2910	2617	2342	2083	1843	1622
Energy - ft-lb	2820	2281	1827	1445	1131	876
Taylor KO values	19.2	17.3	15.5	13.7	12.2	10.7
Path - inches	-1.5	2.1	0.0	-8.5	-25.0	-51.8
Wind Drift - inches	0.0	1.0	4.2	9.9	18.7	31.1

G1 Ballistic Coefficient = 0.315

Remington 150-grain Nosler Ballistic Tip (PRT3006A)

Distance - Yards	Muzzle	100	200	300	400	500
Velocity - fps	2910	2696	2492	2298	2112	1934
Energy - ft-lb	2821	2422	2070	1759	1485	1247
Taylor KO values	19.2	17.8	16.4	15.2	13.9	12.8
Path - inches	-1.5	1.6	0.0	-7.3	-21.1	-42.8
Wind Drift - inches	0.0	0.7	2.9	6.8	12.7	20.6

G1 Ballistic Coefficient = 0.436

Remington 150-grain Bronze Point (R30063)

Distance - Yards	Muzzle	100	200	300	400	500
Velocity - fps	2910	2656	2416	2189	1974	1773
Energy - ft-lb	2820	2349	1944	1596	1298	1047
Taylor KO values	19.2	17.5	15.9	14.4	13.0	11.7
Path - inches	-1.5	1.7	0.0	-7.7	-22.7	-46.6
Wind Drift - inches	0.0	0.8	3.6	8.4	15.6	25.7

G1 Ballistic Coefficient = 0.365

Remington 150-grain Pointed SP Core-Lokt (R30062)

Distance - Yards	Muzzle	100	200	300	400	500
Velocity - fps	2910	2617	2342	2083	1843	1622
Energy - ft-lb	2820	2281	1827	1445	1131	876
Taylor KO values	19.2	17.3	15.5	13.7	12.2	10.7
Path - inches	-1.5	1.8	0.0	-8.2	-24.4	-50.9
Wind Drift - inches	0.0	1.0	4.2	9.9	18.7	31.1

G1 Ballistic Coefficient = 0.315

Winchester 150-grain Silvertip (X30063)

Distance - Yards	Muzzle	100	200	300	400	500
Velocity - fps	2910	2617	2342	2083	1843	1622
Energy - ft-lb	2820	2281	1827	1445	1131	876
Taylor KO values	19.2	17.3	15.5	13.7	12.2	10.7
Path - inches	-1.5	2.1	0.0	-8.5	-25.0	-51.8
Wind Drift - inches	0.0	1.0	4.2	10.0	18.8	31.2

G1 Ballistic Coefficient = 0.314

PMC 150-grain Sierra SP Boattail (3006HA)

Distance - Yards	Muzzle	100	200	300	400	500
Velocity - fps	2900	2657	2427	2208	2000	1805
Energy - ft-lb	2801	2351	1961	1623	1332	1085
Taylor KO values	19.1	17.5	16.0	14.6	13.2	11.9
Path - inches	-1.5	1.7	0.0	-7.7	-22.5	-46.0
Wind Drift - inches	0.0	0.8	3.4	8.0	14.9	24.5

G1 Ballistic Coefficient = 0.381

Winchester 150-grain Ballistic Silvertip (SBST3006)

Distance - Yards	Muzzle	100	200	300	400	500
Velocity - fps	2900	2687	2483	2289	2103	1926
Energy - ft-lb	2801	2404	2054	1745	1473	1236
Taylor KO values	19.1	17.7	16.4	15.1	13.9	12.7
Path - inches	-1.5	1.7	0.0	-7.3	-21.2	-43.0
Wind Drift - inches	0.0	0.7	3.0	6.9	12.8	20.8

G1 Ballistic Coefficient = 0.435

PMC 150-grain Pointed SP (3006A)

Distance - Yards	Muzzle	100	200	300	400	500
Velocity - fps	2773	2542	2322	2113	1916	1730
Energy - ft-lb	2560	2152	1796	1592	1336	1115
Taylor KO values	18.3	16.8	15.3	13.9	12.6	11.4
Path - inches	-1.5	2.4	0.0	-9.7	-28.2	-57.0
Wind Drift - inches	0.0	0.8	3.6	8.4	15.6	25.6

G1 Ballistic Coefficient = 0.389

PMC 150-grain Barnes-X (3006XA)

Distance - Yards	Muzzle	100	200	300	400	500
Velocity - fps	2750	2552	2361	2197	2005	1840
Energy - ft-lb	2518	2168	1857	1582	1340	1128
Taylor KO values	18.2	16.8	15.6	14.5	13.2	12.1
Path - inches	-1.5	2.0	0.0	-8.2	-23.7	-48.0
Wind Drift - inches	0.0	0.7	3.0	7.1	13.2	21.4

G1 Ballistic Coefficient = 0.453

American Eagle (Federal) 150-grain FMJ Boattail (AE3006N)

Distance - Yards	Muzzle	100	200	300	400	500
Velocity - fps	2910	2710	2510	2320	2150	1970
Energy - ft-lb	2820	2440	2100	1800	1535	1300
Taylor KO values	19.2	17.9	16.6	15.3	14.2	13.0
Path - inches	-1.5	1.6	0.0	-7.2	-20.8	-42.0
Wind Drift - inches	0.0	0.7	2.8	6.5	12.1	19.6

G1 Ballistic Coefficient = 0.454

Hansen 150-grain FMJ (HCC306A)

Distance - Yards	Muzzle	100	200	300	400	500
Velocity - fps	2910	2678	2454	2247	2047	1859
Energy - ft-lb	2820	2389	2011	1682	1397	1151
Taylor KO values	19.2	17.7	16.2	14.8	13.5	.12.3
Path - inches	-1.5	1.7	0.0	-7.4	-21.8	-44.5
Wind Drift - inches	0.0	0.8	3.2	7.5	14.0	22.9

G1 Ballistic Coefficient = 0.400

UMC (Remington) 150-grain MC (L30062)

Distance - Yards	Muzzle	100	200	300	400	500
Velocity - fps	2910	2617	2342	2085	1842	1623
Energy - ft-lb	2820	2281	1827	1448	1133	878
Taylor KO values	19.2	17.2	15.4	13.8	12.2	10.7
Path - inches	-1.5	1.8	0.0	-8.2	-24.4	-50.9
Wind Drift - inches	0.0	1.0	4.2	9.9	18.7	31.1

G1 Ballistic Coefficient = 0.315

PMC 150-grain FMJ (3006C)

Distance - Yards	Muzzle	100	200	300	400	500
Velocity - fps	2773	2542	2322	2113	1916	1730
Energy - ft-lb	2560	2152	1796	1487	1222	997
Taylor KO values	18.3	16.8	15.3	13.9	12.6	11.4
Path - inches	-1.5	1.9	0.0	-8.4	-24.6	-50.2
Wind Drift - inches	0.0	0.8	3.6	8.4	15.6	25.6

G1 Ballistic Coefficient = 0.389

Federal 165-grain Sierra GameKing SP Boattail - HE (P3006Y)

Distance - Yards	Muzzle	100	200	300	400	500
Velocity - fps	3140	2900	2670	2450	2240	2050
Energy - ft-lb	3610	3075	2610	2200	1845	1535
Taylor KO values	22.8	21.1	19.4	17.8	16.3	14.9
Path - inches	-1.5	1.5	0.0	-6.9	-20.4	-41.4
Wind Drift - inches	0.0	0.7	2.8	6.7	12.3	20.1

G1 Ballistic Coefficient = 0.406

Federal 165-grain Trophy Bonded Bear Claw - HE (P3006T4)

Distance - Yards	Muzzle	100	200	300	400	500
Velocity - fps	3140	2860	2590	2340	2100	1880
Energy - ft-lb	3610	2990	2460	2010	1625	1300
Taylor KO values	22.8	20.8	18.8	17.0	15.2	13.6
Path - inches	-1.5	1.6	0.0	-7.4	-21.9	-45.2
Wind Drift - inches	0.0	0.8	3.4	8.1	15.1	24.8

G1 Ballistic Coefficient = 0.343

Hornady 165-grain Soft SP Boattail-Light Magnum (8515)

Distance - Yards	Muzzle	100	200	300	400	500
Velocity - fps	3015	2790	2575	2370	2175	1994
Energy - ft-lb	3330	2850	2428	2058	1734	1496
Taylor KO values	21.7	20.1	18.5	19.6	15.6	14.3
Path - inches	-1.5	1.6	0.0	-7.0	-20.1	-39.8
Wind Drift - inches	0.0	0.7	2.9	6.7	12.4	20.3

G1 Ballistic Coefficient = 0.424

Federal 165-grain Nosler Ballistic Tip (P3006Q)

Distance - Yards	Muzzle	100	200	300	400	500
Velocity - fps	2800	2610	2430	2250	2080	1920
Energy - ft-lb	2870	2495	2155	1855	1585	1350
Taylor KO values	20.1	18.8	17.5	16.2	15.0	1350
Path - inches	-1.5	1.8	0.0	-7.7	-22.3	-45.0
Wind Drift - inches	0.0	0.7	2.8	6.6	12.1	19.7

G1 Ballistic Coefficient = 0.476

Federal 165-grain Sierra GameKing SP Boattail (P3006D)

Distance - Yards	Muzzle	100	200	300	400	500
Velocity - fps	2800	2610	2420	2240	2070	1910
Energy - ft-lb	2870	2490	2150	1840	1580	1340
Taylor KO values	20.1	18.8	17.4	16.1	14.9	13.7
Path - inches	-1.5	1.8	0.0	-7.8	-22.4	-45.2
Wind Drift - inches	0.0	0.7	2.8	6.6	12.3	20.0

G1 Ballistic Coefficient = 0.470

Federal 165-grain Sierra Pro-Hunter SP (3006TS)

Distance - Yards	Muzzle	100	200	300	400	500
Velocity - fps	2800	2560	2340	2130	1920	1730
Energy - ft-lb	2875	2410	2005	1655	1360	1100
Taylor KO values	20.1	18.4	16.8	15.3	13.8	12.4
Path - inches	-1.5	1.9	0.0	-8.3	-24.3	-49.8
Wind Drift - inches	0.0	0.9	3.6	8.4	15.7	25.8

G1 Ballistic Coefficient = 0.381

Federal 165-grain Trophy Bonded Bear Claw (P3006T1)

Distance - Yards	Muzzle	100	200	300	400	500
Velocity - fps	2800	2540	2200	2050	1830	1630
Energy - ft-lb	2870	2360	1915	1545	1230	972
Taylor KO values	20.1	18.3	15.8	14.7	13.2	11.7
Path - inches	-1.5	2.0	0.0	-8.7	-25.4	-53.1
Wind Drift - inches	0.0	1.0	4.0	9.5	17.9	29.6

G1 Ballistic Coefficient = 0.342

Hansen 165-grain Posi-Feed SP (HCC306E)

Distance - Yards	Muzzle	100	200	300	400	500
Velocity - fps	2800	2542	2298	2068	1852	1651
Energy - ft-lb	2870	2368	1935	1567	1256	999
Taylor KO values	20.3	18.5	16.7	15.0	13.4	12.0
Path - inches	-1.5	2.0	0.0	-8.6	-25.3	-52.2
Wind Drift - inches	0.0	0.9	3.9	9.3	17.4	28.8

G1 Ballistic Coefficient = 0.350

Hornady 165-grain SP Boattail (8115)

Distance - Yards	Muzzle	100	200	300	400	500
Velocity - fps	2800	2591	2392	2202	2020	1848
Energy - ft-lb	2873	2460	2097	1777	1495	1252
Taylor KO values	20.3	18.7	17.2	15.8	14.5	13.3
Path - inches	-1.5	1.8	0.0	-8.0	-23.3	-47.0
Wind Drift - inches	0.0	0.8	3.1	7.3	13.4	21.9

G1 Ballistic Coefficient = 0.435

Remington 165-grain Nosler Ballistic Tip (PRT3006B)

Distance - Yards	Muzzle	100	200	300	400	500
Velocity - fps	2800	2609	2425	2249	2080	1919
Energy - ft-lb	2873	2494	2155	1854	1588	1350
Taylor KO values	20.3	18.8	17.4	16.2	15.0	13.8
Path - inches	-1.5	1.8	0.0	-7.7	-22.3	-45.0
Wind Drift - inches	0.0	0.7	2.8	6.6	12.1	19.7

G1 Ballistic Coefficient = 0.475

Remington 165-grain Pointed SP Boattail (PRB3006SA)

Distance - Yards	Muzzle	100	200	300	400	500
Velocity - fps	2800	2592	2394	2204	2033	1852
Energy - ft-lb	2872	2462	2100	1780	1500	1256
Taylor KO values	20.3	18.6	17.2	15.8	14.5	13.1
Path - inches	-1.5	1.8	0.0	-7.9	-23.0	-46.6
Wind Drift - inches	0.0	0.7	3.1	7.2	13.4	21.8

G1 Ballistic Coefficient = 0.437

Remington 165-grain Pointed SP Core-Lokt (R3006B)

Distance - Yards	Muzzle	100	200	300	400	500
Velocity - fps	2800	2534	2283	2047	1825	1621
Energy - ft-lb	2872	2352	1909	1534	1220	963
Taylor KO values	20.3	18.2	16.4	14.7	13.1	11.7
Path - inches	-1.5	2.0	0.0	-8.7	-25.9	-53.2
Wind Drift - inches	0.0	1.0	4.1	9.6	18.1	30.0

G1 Ballistic Coefficient = 0.339

Winchester 165-grain Fail Safe (S3006XA)

Distance - Yards	Muzzle	100	200	300	400	500
Velocity - fps	2800	2540	2295	2063	1846	1645
Energy - ft-lb	2873	2365	1930	1560	1249	992
Taylor KO values	20.3	18.3	16.5	14.8	13.3	11.8
Path - inches	-1.5	2.0	0.0	-8.6	-25.3	-52.3
Wind Drift - inches	0.0	0.9	4.0	9.4	17.6	29.0

G1 Ballistic Coefficient = 0.348

Winchester 165-grain Pointed SP (X30065)

Distance - Yards	Muzzle	100	200	300	400	500
Velocity - fps	2800	2573	2357	2151	1956	1772
Energy - ft-lb	2913	2203	1635	1192	859	625
Taylor KO values	20.3	18.5	16.9	15.5	14.1	9.0
Path - inches	-1.5	2.7	0.0	-11.3	-34.4	-73.7
Wind Drift - inches	0.0	1.4	6.1	15.0	28.9	49.0

G1 Ballistic Coefficient = 0.235

Speer 165-grain Grand Slam (24507)

Distance - Yards	Muzzle	100	200	300	400	500
Velocity - fps	2790	2560	2342	2134	1934	1747
Energy - ft-lb	2851	2401	2009	1669	1371	1119
Taylor KO values	20.3	18.6	17.0	15.5	14.0	12.7
Path - inches	-1.5	1.9	0.0	-8.3	-24.1	-49.4
Wind Drift - inches	0.0	0.8	3.5	8.3	15.4	25.3

G1 Ballistic Coefficient = 0.388

PMC 165-grain Barnes-X HP (3006XB)

Distance - Yards	Muzzle	100	200	300	400	500
Velocity - fps	2750	2569	2395	2228	2067	1914
Energy - ft-lb	2770	2418	2101	1818	1565	1342
Taylor KO values	19.8	18.5	17.2	16.0	14.9	13.8
Path - inches	-1.5	1.9	0.0	-8.0	-23.0	-46.1
Wind Drift - inches	0.0	0.7	2.8	6.4	11.8	19.2

G1 Ballistic Coefficient = 0.498

Winchester 168-grain Ballistic Silvertip (SBST3006A)

Distance - Yards	Muzzle	100	200	300	400	500
Velocity - fps	2790	2599	2416	2240	2072	1911
Energy - ft-lb	2903	2520	2177	1872	1601	1362
Taylor KO values	20.6	19.2	17.9	16.6	15.3	14.1
Path - inches	-1.5	1.8	0.0	-7.8	-22.5	-45.2
Wind Drift - inches	0.0	0.7	2.8	6.6	12.2	19.8

G1 Ballistic Coefficient = 0.475

Federal 168-grain Sierra MatchKing HP Boattail (GM3006M)

Distance - Yards	Muzzle	100	200	300	400	500
Velocity - fps	2900	2510	2320	2150	1980	1820
Energy - ft-lb	2720	2347	2016	1722	1463	1236
Taylor KO values	20.0	18.6	17.1	15.9	14.6	13.5
Path - inches	-1.5	2.0	0.0	-8.5	-24.5	-49.4
Wind Drift - inches	0.0	0.7	3.0	7.1	13.2	21.4

G1 Ballistic Coefficient = 0.464

Hornady 168-grain HP Boattail Match (8117)

Distance - Yards	Muzzle	100	200	300	400	500
Velocity - fps	2800	2587	2383	2189	2004	1828
Energy - ft-lb	2924	2496	2118	1787	1497	1247
Taylor KO values	20.7	19.1	17.6	16.2	14.8	13.5
Path - inches	-1.5	2.2	0.0	-8.3	-23.8	-48.6
Wind Drift - inches	0.0	0.8	3.2	7.4	13.8	22.6

G1 Ballistic Coefficient = 0.425

Hornady 180-grain SP Boattail - Light Magnum (8518)

Distance - Yards	Muzzle	100	200	300	400	500
Velocity - fps	2900	2695	2498	2310	2131	1959
Energy - ft-lb	3361	2902	2494	2133	1814	1534
Taylor KO values	23.0	21.3	19.8	18.3	16.9	15.5
Path - inches	-1.5	2.0	0.0	-7.5	-21.6	-43.3
Wind Drift - inches	0.0	0.7	2.8	6.6	12.2	19.8

G1 Ballistic Coefficient = 0.453

Federal 180-grain Nosler Partition - HE (P3006R)

Distance - Yards	Muzzle	100	200	300	400	500
Velocity - fps	2880	2690	2500	2320	2150	1980
Energy - ft-lb	3315	2880	2495	2150	1845	1570
Taylor KO values	22.8	21.3	19.8	18.4	17.0	15.7
Path - inches	-1.5	1.7	0.0	-7.2	-21.0	-42.2
Wind Drift - inches	0.0	0.9	3.6	8.6	16.1	26.5

G1 Ballistic Coefficient = 0.474

Federal 180-grain Woodleigh - HE (P3006X)

Distance - Yards	Muzzle	100	200	300	400	500
Velocity - fps	2880	2640	2400	2180	1970	1780
Energy - ft-lb	3315	2775	2310	1905	1560	1265
Taylor KO values	22.8	20.9	19.0	17.3	15.6	14.1
Path - inches	-1.5	1.7	0.0	-7.8	-23.0	-46.9
Wind Drift - inches	0.0	0.8	3.5	8.2	15.3	25.1

G1 Ballistic Coefficient = 0.377

Federal 180-grain Trophy Bonded Bear Claw - HE (P3006T3)

Distance - Yards	Muzzle	100	200	300	400	500
Velocity - fps	2880	2630	2380	2160	1940	1740
Energy - ft-lb	3315	2755	2270	1855	1505	1210
Taylor KO values	22.8	20.8	18.8	17.1	15.4	13.8
Path - inches	-1.5	1.8	0.0	-8.0	-23.3	-48.2
Wind Drift - inches	0.0	0.9	3.6	8.6	16.1	26.5

G1 Ballistic Coefficient = 0.361

Winchester 180-grain Partition Gold (SPG3006A)

Distance - Yards	Muzzle	100	200	300	400	500
Velocity - fps	2790	2581	2382	2192	2010	1838
Energy - ft-lb	3112	2664	2269	1920	1615	1350
Taylor KO values	22.1	20.4	18.9	17.4	15.9	14.6
Path - inches	-1.5	1.9	0.0	-8.0	-23.2	-47.1
Wind Drift - inches	0.0	0.8	3.1	7.3	13.5	22.0

G1 Ballistic Coefficient = 0.435

Winchester 180-grain Power-Point Plus (SHV30064)

Distance - Yards	Muzzle	100	200	300	400	500
Velocity - fps	2770	2563	2366	2177	1997	1826
Energy - ft-lb	3068	2627	2237	1894	1594	1333
Taylor KO values	21.9	20.3	18.7	17.2	15.8	14.5
Path - inches	-1.5	1.9	0.0	-8.1	-23.6	-47.8
Wind Drift - inches	0.0	0.8	3.1	7.4	13.6	22.2

G1 Ballistic Coefficient = 0.436

A² 180-grain Mono; Dead Tough (None)

Distance - Yards	Muzzle	100	200	300	400	500
Velocity - fps	2700	2365	2054	1769	1524	1310
Energy - ft-lb	2913	2235	1687	1251	928	686
Taylor KO values	21.4	18.7	16.3	14.0	12.1	10.4
Path - inches	-1.5	2.4	0.0	-10.6	-32.4	-69.1
Wind Drift - inches	0.0	1.3	5.7	13.7	26.2	44.1

G1 Ballistic Coefficient = 0.264

Federal 180-grain Sierra GameKing SP Boattail (P3006L)

Distance - Yards	Muzzle	100	200	300	400	500
Velocity - fps	2700	2540	2380	2220	2080	1930
Energy - ft-lb	2915	2570	2260	1975	1720	1495
Taylor KO values	21.4	20.1	18.8	17.6	16.5	15.3
Path - inches	-1.5	1.8	0.0	-7.7	-22.3	-45.0
Wind Drift - inches	0.0	0.6	2.6	6.0	11.1	17.9

G1 Ballistic Coefficient = 0.539

Federal 180-grain Barnes XLC Coated-X Bullet (P3006Z)

Distance - Yards	Muzzle	100	200	300	400	500
Velocity - fps	2700	2530	2360	2200	2040	1890
Energy - ft-lb	2915	2550	2220	1930	1670	1430
Taylor KO values	21.4	20.0	18.7	17.4	16.2	15.0
Path - inches	-1.5	2.0	0.0	-8.3	-23.8	-47.3
Wind Drift - inches	0.0	0.7	2.8	6.4	11.8	19.2

G1 Ballistic Coefficient = 0.509

Federal 180-grain Nosler Partition (P3006F)

Distance - Yards	Muzzle	100	200	300	400	500
Velocity - fps	2700	2500	2320	2140	1970	1810
Energy - ft-lb	2915	2510	2150	1830	1550	1350
Taylor KO values	21.4	19.8	18.4	16.9	15.6	14.3
Path - inches	-1.5	2.0	0.0	-8.6	-24.6	-49.6
Wind Drift - inches	0.0	0.7	3.1	7.2	13.4	21.8

G1 Ballistic Coefficient = 0.458

Federal 180-grain Hi-Shok SP (3006B)

Distance - Yards	Muzzle	100	200	300	400	500
Velocity - fps	2700	2470	2250	2040	1850	1660
Energy - ft-lb	2915	2435	2025	1665	1360	1105
Taylor KO values	21.4	19.6	17.8	16.2	14.7	13.1
Path - inches	-1.5	2.1	0.0	-9.0	-26.4	-54.0
Wind Drift - inches	0.0	0.9	3.8	8.8	16.5	27.1

G1 Ballistic Coefficient = 0.383

Federal 180-grain Woodleigh Weldcore SP (P3006W)

Distance - Yards	Muzzle	100	200	300	400	500
Velocity - fps	2700	2470	2240	2030	1830	1650
Energy - ft-lb	2915	2430	2010	1645	1340	1085
Taylor KO values	21.4	19.6	17.7	16.1	14.5	13.1
Path - inches	-1.5	2.1	0.0	-9.1	-26.4	-54.7
Wind Drift - inches	0.0	0.9	3.8	9.0	16.8	27.6

G1 Ballistic Coefficient = 0.378

Federal 180-grain Trophy Bonded Bear Claw (P3006T2)

Distance - Yards	Muzzle	100	200	300	400	500
Velocity - fps	2700	2460	2220	2000	1800	1610
Energy - ft-lb	2915	2410	1975	1605	1290	1030
Taylor KO values	211.4	19.5	17.6	15.8	14.3	12.8
Path - inches	-1.5	2.2	0.0	-9.2	-27.0	-56.1
Wind Drift - inches	0.0	1.0	4.0	9.4	17.7	29.1

G1 Ballistic Coefficient = 0.362

Federal 180-grain Sierra Pro-Hunter SP Round Nose (3006JS)

Distance - Yards	Muzzle	100	200	300	400	500
Velocity - fps	2700	2350	2020	1730	1470	1250
Energy - ft-lb	2915	2280	1630	1190	860	620
Taylor KO values	21.4	18.6	16.0	13.7	11.6	9.9
Path - inches	-1.5	2.4	0.0	-11.0	-33.6	-71.0
Wind Drift - inches	0.0	1.4	6.1	14.8	28.5	48.0

G1 Ballistic Coefficient = 0.248

Norma 180-grain Nosler (17649)

Distance - Yards	Muzzle	100	200	300	400	500
Velocity - fps	2700	2494	2297	2108	1928	1759
Energy - ft-lb	2914	2486	2108	1777	1487	1237
Taylor KO values	21.4	19.8	18.2	16.7	15.3	13.9
Path - inches	-1.5	2.1	0.0	-8.7	-25.2	-51.0
Wind Drift - inches	0.0	0.8	3.3	7.8	14.4	23.5

G1 Ballistic Coefficient = 0.438

Norma 180-grain TXP Line, Swift (17518)

Distance - Yards	Muzzle	100	200	300	400	500
Velocity - fps	2700	2479	2268	2067	1877	1699
Energy - ft-lb	2914	2456	2056	1708	1408	1158
Taylor KO values	21.4	19.6	18.0	16.4	14.9	13.5
Path - inches	-1.5	2.0	0.0	-8.8	-25.9	-52.8
Wind Drift - inches	0.0	0.9	3.6	8.4	15.7	25.7

G1 Ballistic Coefficient = 0.400

Norma 180-grain Plastic Point (17653)

Distance - Yards	Muzzle	100	200	300	400	500
Velocity - fps	2700	2455	2222	2003	1798	1608
Energy - ft-lb	2914	2409	1974	1603	1293	1034
Taylor KO values	21.4	19.4	17.6	15.9	14.2	12.7
Path - inches	-1.5	2.1	0.0	-9.2	-27.1	-55.8
Wind Drift - inches	0.0	1.0	4.0	9.5	17.7	29.2

G1 Ballistic Coefficient = 0.366

Norma 180-grain Oryx SP (17674)

Distance - Yards	Muzzle	100	200	300	400	500
Velocity - fps	2700	2387	2095	1825	1580	1367
Energy - ft-lb	2914	2278	1755	1332	1580	1367
Taylor KO values	21.4	18.9	16.6	14.5	12.5	10.8
Path - inches	-1.5	2.3	16.6	14.5	12.5	10.8
Wind Drift - inches	0.0	1.2	5.3	12.8	24.3	40.8

G1 Ballistic Coefficient = 0.288

Norma 180-grain Alaska SP (17648)

Distance - Yards	Muzzle	100	200	300	400	500
Velocity - fps	2700	2351	2028	1734	1473	1259
Energy - ft-lb	2914	2209	1645	1202	868	633
Taylor KO values	21.4	18.6	16.1	13.7	11.6	10.0
Path - inches	-1.5	2.4	0.0	-11.0	-33.6	-72.4
Wind Drift - inches	0.0	1.4	6.0	14.7	28.2	47.5

G1 Ballistic Coefficient = 0.257

PMC 180-grain Sierra SP Boattail (3006HC)

Distance - Yards	Muzzle	100	200	300	400	500
Velocity - fps	2700	2523	2352	2188	2030	1879
Energy - ft-lb	2913	2543	2210	1913	1646	1411
Taylor KO values	21.4	20.0	18.6	17.3	16.1	14.9
Path - inches	-1.5	2.0	0.0	-8.3	-23.9	-47.9
Wind Drift - inches	0.0	0.7	2.8	6.5	12.0	19.5

G1 Ballistic Coefficient = 0.502

Remington 180-grain Swift A-Frame Pointed SP (PRP3006A)

Distance - Yards	Muzzle	100	200	300	400	500
Velocity - fps	2700	2465	2243	2032	1833	1648
Energy - ft-lb	2913	2429	2010	1650	1343	1085
Taylor KO values	21.4	19.5	17.8	16.1	14.5	13.1
Path - inches	-1.5	2.1	0.0	-9.1	-26.6	-54.4
Wind Drift - inches	0.0	0.9	3.8	9.0	16.8	27.6

G1 Ballistic Coefficient = 0.378

Remington 180-grain Bronze Point (R30066)

Distance - Yards	Muzzle	100	200	300	400	500
Velocity - fps	2700	2485	2280	2084	1899	1725
Energy - ft-lb	2913	2468	2077	1736	1441	1189
Taylor KO values	21.4	19.7	18.1	16.5	15.0	13.7
Path - inches	-1.5	2.1	0.0	-8.8	25.5	-52.0
Wind Drift - inches	0.0	0.8	3.5	8.1	15.1	24.8

G1 Ballistic Coefficient = 0.412

Remington 180-grain Pointed SP Core-Lokt (R30065)

Distance - Yards	Muzzle	100	200	300	400	500
Velocity - fps	2700	2469	2250	2042	1846	1663
Energy - ft-lb	2913	2436	2023	1666	1362	1105
Taylor KO values	21.4	19.6	17.8	16.2	14.6	13.2
Path - inches	-1.5	2.1	0.0	-9.0	26.3	-54.0
Wind Drift - inches	0.0	0.9	3.7	8.8	16.5	27.0

G1 Ballistic Coefficient = 0.384

Remington 180-grain Swift A-Frame Pointed SP (RS3006A)

Distance - Yards	Muzzle	100	200	300	400	500
Velocity - fps	2700	2465	2243	2032	1833	1648
Energy - ft-lb	2913	2429	2010	1650	1343	1085
Taylor KO values	21.4	19.5	17.8	16.1	14.5	13.0
Path - inches	-1.5	2.1	0.0	-9.1	-26.6	-54.4
Wind Drift - inches	0.0	0.9	3.8	9.0	16.8	27.7

G1 Ballistic Coefficient = 0.377

Remington 180-grain SP Core-Lokt (R30064)

Distance - Yards	Muzzle	100	200	300	400	500
Velocity - fps	2700	2348	2023	1727	1466	1251
Energy - ft-lb	2913	2203	1635	1192	859	625
Taylor KO values	21.4	18.6	16.0	13.7	11.6	9.9
Path - inches	-1.5	2.4	0.0	-11.0	-33.8	-72.8
Wind Drift - inches	0.0	1.4	6.1	14.8	28.5	48.0

G1 Ballistic Coefficient = 0.248

Winchester 180-grain Fail Safe (S3006X)

Distance - Yards	Muzzle	100	200	300	400	500
Velocity - fps	2700	2486	2283	2089	1904	1731
Energy - ft-lb	2914	2472	2083	1744	1450	1198
Taylor KO values	21.4	19.7	18.1	16.5	15.1	13.7
Path - inches	-1.5	2.1	0.0	-8.7	-25.5	-51.8
Wind Drift - inches	0.0	0.8	3.4	8.1	15.0	24.6

G1 Ballistic Coefficient = 0.415

Winchester 180-grain Silvertip (X30066)

Distance - Yards	Muzzle	100	200	300	400	500
Velocity - fps	2700	2469	2250	2042	1846	1663
Energy - ft-lb	2913	2436	1023	1666	1362	1105
Taylor KO values	21.4	19.6	17.8	16.2	14.6	13.2
Path - inches	-1.5	2.4	0.0	-9.3	-27.0	-54.9
Wind Drift - inches	0.0	0.9	3.7	8.8	16.5	27.0

G1 Ballistic Coefficient = 0.384

Winchester 180-grain Power-Point (X30064)

Distance - Yards	Muzzle	100	200	300	400	500
Velocity - fps	2700	2348	2023	1727	1466	1251
Energy - ft-lb	2913	2203	1635	1192	859	625
Taylor KO values	21.4	18.6	16.0	13.7	11.6	9.9
Path - inches	-1.5	2.7	0.0	-11.3	-34.4	-73.7
Wind Drift - inches	0.0	1.4	6.1	14.8	28.5	48.0

G1 Ballistic Coefficient = 0.248

Speer 180-grain Grand Slam (24508)

Distance - Yards	Muzzle	100	200	300	400	500
Velocity - fps	2690	2487	2293	2108	1931	1765
Energy - ft-lb	2892	2472	2101	1775	1491	1245
Taylor KO values	21.3	19.7	18.2	16.7	15.3	14.0
Path - inches	-1.5	2.1	0.0	-8.8	-25.1	-51.1
Wind Drift - inches	0.0	0.8	3.3	7.7	14.2	23.2

G1 Ballistic Coefficient = 0.437

Hansen 180-grain Posi-Feed SP (HCC306C)

Distance - Yards	Muzzle	100	200	300	400	500
Velocity - fps	2670	2469	2277	2094	1919	1755
Energy - ft-lb	2850	2438	2074	1753	1473	1231
Taylor KO values	21.1	19.6	18.0	16.6	15.2	13.9
Path - inches	-1.5	2.1	0.0	-8.8	25.6	-51.8
Wind Drift - inches	0.0	0.8	3.3	7.7	14.3	23.2

G1 Ballistic Coefficient = 0.440

PMC 180-grain Pointed SP (3006B)

Distance - Yards	Muzzle	100	200	300	400	500
Velocity - fps	2550	2357	2172	1996	1829	1671
Energy - ft-lb	2596	2220	1886	1592	1336	1115
Taylor KO values	20.2	18.7	17.2	15.8	14.5	13.2
Path - inches	-1.5	2.4	0.0	-9.7	-28.2	-57.0
Wind Drift - inches	0.0	0.8	3.5	8.1	15.0	24.5

G1 Ballistic Coefficient = 0.446

Hornady 180-grain HP Boattail (8118)

Distance - Yards	Muzzle	100	200	300	400	500
Velocity - fps	2700	2504	2315	2135	1963	1800
Energy - ft-lb	2913	2505	2142	1822	1541	1295
Taylor KO values	21.4	19.8	18.3	16.9	15.5	14.3
Path - inches	-1.5	2.0	0.0	-8.5	-24.7	-49.9
Wind Drift - inches	0.0	0.8	3.1	7.3	13.5	22.1

G1 Ballistic Coefficient = 0.454

Norma 180-grain Vulcan HP (17569)

Distance - Yards	Muzzle	100	200	300	400	500
Velocity - fps	2700	2416	2150	1901	1671	1465
Energy - ft-lb	2914	2334	1848	1445	1116	859
Taylor KO values	21.4	19.1	17.0	15.1	13.2	11.6
Path - inches	-1.5	2.2	0.0	-9.8	-29.3	-61.3
Wind Drift - inches	0.0	1.1	4.7	11.3	21.4	35.6

G1 Ballistic Coefficient = 0.315

PMC 180-grain Barnes-X (3006XC)

Distance - Yards	Muzzle	100	200	300	400	500
Velocity - fps	2650	2487	2331	2179	2034	1894
Energy - ft-lb	2806	2472	2171	1898	1652	1433
Taylor KO values	21.0	19.7	18.5	17.3	16.1	15.0
Path - inches	-1.5	2.1	0.0	-8.5	-24.3	-48.6
Wind Drift - inches	0.0	0.6	2.6	6.2	11.3	18.3

G1 Ballistic Coefficient = 0.543

Lapua 185-grain Mega SP (4317563)

Distance - Yards	Muzzle	100	200	300	400	500
Velocity - fps	2625	2346	2083	1839	1616	1417
Energy - ft-lb	2831	2261	1784	1390	1072	825
Taylor KO values	21.4	19.1	17.0	15.0	13.2	11.5
Path - inches	-1.5	2.4	0.0	-10.5	-31.3	-65.5
Wind Drift - inches	0.0	1.2	4.9	11.8	22.3	37.1

G1 Ballistic Coefficient = 0.310

Lapua 185-grain Forex SP (4317564)

Distance - Yards	Muzzle	100	200	300	400	500
Velocity - fps	2625	2150	1728	1376	1125	983
Energy - ft-lb	2831	1899	1227	778	520	397
Taylor KO values	21.4	17.5	14.1	11.2	9.2	8.0
Path - inches	-1.5	3.1	0.0	-14.9	-48.4	-109.3
Wind Drift - inches	0.0	2.1	9.4	23.6	46.2	76.6

G1 Ballistic Coefficient = 0.178

Norma 200-grain Oryx SP (17677)

Distance - Yards	Muzzle	100	200	300	400	500
Velocity - fps	2625	2362	2155	1883	1670	1477
Energy - ft-lb	3061	2479	1987	1575	1239	969
Taylor KO values	23.1	20.8	18.6	16.6	14.7	13.0
Path - inches	-1.5	2.3	0.0	-10.1	-30.2	-62.7
Wind Drift - inches	0.0	1.1	4.6	10.9	20.6	34.1

G1 Ballistic Coefficient = 0.338

Lapua 200-grain Mega SP (4317567)

Distance - Yards	Muzzle	100	200	300	400	500
Velocity - fps	2543	2284	2040	1813	1604	1417
Energy - ft-lb	2873	2317	1849	1460	1143	892
Taylor KO values	22.4	20.1	18.0	16.0	14.1	12.5
Path - inches	-1.5	2.6	0.0	-11.0	-32.6	-67.8
Wind Drift - inches	0.0	1.2	4.8	11.5	21.8	36.0

G1 Ballistic Coefficient = 0.329

Norma 200-grain Vulcan HP (17684)

Distance - Yards	Muzzle	100	200	300	400	500
Velocity - fps	2641	2385	2143	1916	1707	1515
Energy - ft-lb	3098	2527	2040	1631	1294	1019
Taylor KO values	23.2	21.0	18.9	16.9	15.0	13.3
Path - inches	-1.5	2.3	0.0	-9.9	-29.3	-60.7
Wind Drift - inches	0.0	1.0	4.4	10.4	20.0	32.5

G1 Ballistic Coefficient = 0.347

Federal 220-grain Sierra Pro-Hunter SP Round Nose (3006HS)

Distance - Yards	Muzzle	100	200	300	400	500
Velocity - fps	2410	2130	1870	1630	1420	1250
Energy - ft-lb	2835	2215	1705	1300	985	760
Taylor KO values	19.1	16.9	14.8	12.9	11.2	9.9
Path - inches	-1.5	3.1	0.0	-13.1	-39.3	-82.2
Wind Drift - inches	0.0	1.4	5.9	14.2	26.9	44.6

G1 Ballistic Coefficient = 0.296

Remington 220-grain SP Core-Lokt (R30067)

Distance - Yards	Muzzle	100	200	300	400	500
Velocity - fps	2410	2130	1870	1632	1422	1246
Energy - ft-lb	2837	2216	1708	1301	988	758
Taylor KO values	19.1	16.9	14.8	12.9	11.3	9.9
Path - inches	-1.5	3.1	0.0	-13.1	-39.4	-83.0
Wind Drift - inches	0.0	1.4	6.0	14.3	27.1	45.0

G1 Ballistic Coefficient = 0.294

A² 220-grain Mono (None)

Distance - Yards	Muzzle	100	200	300	400	500
Velocity - fps	2380	2108	1854	1623	1424	1247
Energy - ft-lb	2767	2171	1678	1287	990	760
Taylor KO values	23.0	20.4	17.9	15.7	13.8	12.1
Path - inches	-1.5	3.1	0.0	-13.6	-39.9	-82.8
Wind Drift - inches	0.0	1.4	5.9	14.2	27.0	44.8

G1 Ballistic Coefficient = 0.295

7.82mm (.308) Lazzeroni Patriot

Lazzeroni has two different 30-caliber cartridges. The Patriot is the shorter of the two. A short fireplug of a case, the Patriot uses an unbelted case with a 0.548-inch head diameter to drive a 150-grain bullet to .300 Winchester Magnum velocity.

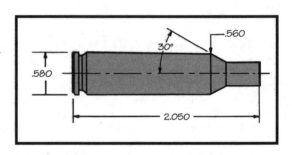

Relative Recoil Factor = 2.23   **Controlling Agency: Factory**

Lazzeroni 150-grain Nosler Partition (782PT150P)

Distance - Yards	Muzzle	100	200	300	400	500
Velocity - fps	3300	3099	2908	2724	2548	2378
Energy - ft-lb	3628	3200	2817	2472	2162	1884
Taylor KO values	21.8	20.5	19.2	18.0	16.8	15.7
Path - inches	-1.5	1.1	0.0	-5.2	-15.0	-30.3
Wind Drift - inches	0.0	0.5	2.1	4.9	8.9	14.4

G1 Ballistic Coefficient = 0.508

Lazzeroni 180-grain Nosler Partition (782PT180P)

Distance - Yards	Muzzle	100	200	300	400	500
Velocity - fps	3100	2934	2774	2620	2471	2327
Energy - ft-lb	3842	3442	3077	2744	2441	2164
Taylor KO values	24.5	23.2	22.0	20.8	19.6	18.4
Path - inches	-1.5	1.3	0.0	-5.6	-16.6	-33.2
Wind Drift - inches	0.0	0.5	2.0	4.5	8.2	13.2

G1 Ballistic Coefficient = 0.585

.300 Winchester Magnum

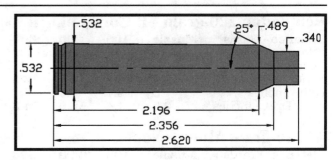

The full-length magnums are too long to chamber in standard length (read .30-06 length) actions. When Winchester introduced the .300 Winchester Magnum in 1963, the idea was to obtain a high performance cartridge that could be chambered in their Model 70 actions. The effort was highly successful. The .300 Win. Mag. sits comfortably in the top 10 of reloading die sales, one place ahead of the 7mm Rem. Mag. Reloading die sales are a pretty good indication of cartridge's popularity. The .300 Win. Mag's popularity is well deserved. It provides performance virtually identical to the .300 H&H in a shorter action. Some factory loads drive 180-grain bullets in excess of 3000 fps.

Relative Recoil Factor = 2.39

Controlling Agency : SAAMI

Bullet Weight Grains	Velocity fps	Maximum Average Pressure	
		Copper Crusher	Transducer
150	3275	54,000 cup	64,000 psi
180	2950	54,000 cup	64,000 psi
190	2875	54,000 cup	64,000 psi
200	2800	54,000 cup	64,000 psi
220	2665	54,000 cup	64,000 psi

Standard barrel for velocity testing:
24 inches long - 1 turn in 10 inch twist

Remington 150-grain Pointed SP Core-Lokt (R300W1)

Distance - Yards	Muzzle	100	200	300	400	500
Velocity - fps	3290	2951	2636	2342	2068	1813
Energy - ft-lb	3605	2900	2314	1827	1424	1095
Taylor KO values	21.7	19.5	17.4	15.5	13.6	12.0
Path - inches	-1.5	1.3	0.0	-6.3	-19.0	-39.8
Wind Drift - inches	0.0	0.9	3.8	9.0	17.0	28.2

G1 Ballistic Coefficient = 0.295

Winchester 150-grain Power-Point (X300WM1)

Distance - Yards	Muzzle	100	200	300	400	500
Velocity - fps	3290	2951	2636	2342	2068	1813
Energy - ft-lb	3605	2900	2314	1827	1424	1095
Taylor KO values	21.7	19.5	17.4	15.5	13.6	12.0
Path - inches	-1.5	1.3	0.0	-6.3	-12.0	-39.8
Wind Drift - inches	0.0	0.9	3.8	9.0	17.0	28.2

G1 Ballistic Coefficient = 0.295

Federal 150-grain Sierra Pro-Hunter SP (300WGS)

Distance - Yards	Muzzle	100	200	300	400	500
Velocity - fps	3280	3030	2800	2570	2360	2160
Energy - ft-lb	3570	3055	2600	2205	1860	1560
Taylor KO values	21.6	20.0	18.5	17.0	15.6	14.3
Path - inches	-1.5	1.1	0.0	-5.6	-16.4	-33.6
Wind Drift - inches	0.0	0.6	2.7	6.3	11.6	18.8

G1 Ballistic Coefficient = 0.407

Federal 150-grain Trophy Bonded Bear Claw (P300WT4)

Distance - Yards	Muzzle	100	200	300	400	500
Velocity - fps	3280	2980	2700	2430	2100	1950
Energy - ft-lb	3580	2960	2420	1970	1590	1270
Taylor KO values	21.6	19.7	17.8	16.0	13.9	12.9
Path - inches	-1.5	1.2	0.0	-6.0	-17.9	-37.1
Wind Drift - inches	0.0	0.8	3.3	7.8	14.6	24.1

G1 Ballistic Coefficient = 0.334

Hornady 150-grain SP Boattail (8201)

Distance - Yards	Muzzle	100	200	300	400	500
Velocity - fps	3275	2988	2718	2469	2224	1998
Energy - ft-lb	3573	2974	2461	2023	1648	1330
Taylor KO values	21.6	19.7	17.9	16.3	14.7	13.2
Path - inches	-1.5	1.2	0.0	-6.0	-17.8	-36.5
Wind Drift - inches	0.0	0.8	3.2	7.4	13.9	22.8

G1 Ballistic Coefficient = 0.350

Winchester 150-grain Fail Safe (S300WBX)

Distance - Yards	Muzzle	100	200	300	400	500
Velocity - fps	3260	2943	2647	2370	2110	1867
Energy - ft-lb	3539	2884	2334	1871	1483	1161
Taylor KO values	21.5	19.4	16.3	15.6	13.9	12.3
Path - inches	-1.5	1.3	0.0	-6.2	-18.7	-38.9

G1 Ballistic Coefficient = 0.314

PMC 150-grain Sierra SP Boattail (300HA)

Distance - Yards	Muzzle	100	200	300	400	500
Velocity - fps	3250	2987	2739	2504	2281	2070
Energy - ft-lb	3517	2970	2498	2088	1733	1426
Taylor KO values	21.4	19.7	18.1	16.5	15.1	13.7
Path - inches	-1.5	1.2	0.0	-6.0	-17.4	-35.6
Wind Drift - inches	0.0	0.7	2.8	6.5	12.1	19.7

G1 Ballistic Coefficient = 0.411

PMC 150-grain Pointed SP (300A)

Distance - Yards	Muzzle	100	200	300	400	500
Velocity - fps	3150	2902	2665	2438	2222	2017
Energy - ft-lb	3304	2804	2364	1979	1644	1355
Taylor KO values	20.8	19.2	17.6	16.1	14.7	13.3
Path - inches	-1.5	1.3	0.0	-6.2	-18.3	-37.4
Wind Drift - inches	0.0	0.7	3.0	6.9	12.9	21.0

G1 Ballistic Coefficient = 0.390

PMC 150-grain Barnes-X (300XA)

Distance - Yards	Muzzle	100	200	300	400	500
Velocity - fps	3135	2918	2712	2515	2327	2146
Energy - ft-lb	3273	2836	2449	2107	1803	1534
Taylor KO values	20.7	19.3	17.9	16.6	15.4	14.2
Path - inches	-1.5	1.3	0.0	-6.1	-17.7	-35.7
Wind Drift - inches	0.0	0.7	2.9	6.7	12.4	20.2

G1 Ballistic Coefficient = 0.406

Winchester 165-grain Fail Safe (S300WXA)

Distance - Yards	Muzzle	100	200	300	400	500
Velocity - fps	3120	2807	2515	2242	1985	1748
Energy - ft-lb	3567	2888	2319	1842	1445	1126
Taylor KO values	22.7	20.4	18.3	16.3	14.4	12.7
Path - inches	-1.5	1.5	0.0	-7.0	-20.9	-43.6
Wind Drift - inches	0.0	0.9	3.9	9.2	17.3	28.7

G1 Ballistic Coefficient = 0.309

Hornady 165-grain SP Boattail (8202)

Distance - Yards	Muzzle	100	200	300	400	500
Velocity - fps	3100	2877	2665	2462	2269	2084
Energy - ft-lb	3522	3033	2603	2221	1887	1592
Taylor KO values	22.5	20.9	19.3	17.8	16.5	15.1
Path - inches	-1.5	1.3	0.0	-6.5	-18.5	-37.3
Wind Drift - inches	0.0	0.6	2.7	6.3	11.6	18.7

G1 Ballistic Coefficient = 0.435

A² 180-grain Monolithic; Dead Tough

Distance - Yards	Muzzle	100	200	300	400	500
Velocity - fps	3120	2756	2420	2108	1820	1559
Energy - ft-lb	3890	3035	2340	1776	1324	972
Taylor KO values	24.7	21.8	19.2	16.7	14.4	12.3
Path - inches	-1.5	1.6	0.0	-7.6	-22.9	-49.0
Wind Drift - inches	0.0	1.1	4.6	11.1	21.2	35.6

G1 Ballistic Coefficient = 0.263

Federal 180-grain Woodleigh Weldcore SP - HE (P300WG)

Distance - Yards	Muzzle	100	200	300	400	500
Velocity - fps	3100	2830	2580	2340	2120	1910
Energy - ft-lb	3840	3210	2685	2185	1705	1450
Taylor KO values	24.6	22.4	20.4	18.5	16.8	15.1
Path - inches	-1.5	1.0	0.0	-6.6	-19.7	-40.2
Wind Drift - inches	0.0	0.8	3.3	7.7	14.3	23.5

G1 Ballistic Coefficient = 0.364

Federal 180-grain Trophy Bonded Bear Claw - HE (P300WT3)

Distance - Yards	Muzzle	100	200	300	400	500
Velocity - fps	3100	2830	2580	2340	2110	1900
Energy - ft-lb	3840	3205	2660	2190	1700	1445
Taylor KO values	24.6	22.4	20.4	18.5	16.7	15.0
Path - inches	-1.5	1.1	0.0	-5.4	-15.8	-32.3
Wind Drift - inches	0.0	0.8	3.3	7.8	14.5	23.8

G1 Ballistic Coefficient = 0.360

Hornady 180-grain SP Boattail - Heavy Magnum (8500)

Distance - Yards	Muzzle	100	200	300	400	500
Velocity - fps	3100	2879	2668	2467	2275	2092
Energy - ft-lb	3840	3313	2845	2431	2068	1772
Taylor KO values	24.6	22.8	21.1	19.5	18.0	16.6
Path - inches	-1.5	1.4	0.0	-6.4	-18.7	-37.5
Wind Drift - inches	0.0	0.6	2.7	6.2	11.5	18.6

G1 Ballistic Coefficient = 0.439

Winchester 180-grain Partition Gold (SPG300WM)

Distance - Yards	Muzzle	100	200	300	400	500
Velocity - fps	3070	2859	2657	2464	2280	2103
Energy - ft-lb	3768	3267	2823	2428	1978	1768
Taylor KO values	24.3	22.6	21.0	19.5	18.1	16.7
Path - inches	-1.5	1.4	0.0	-6.3	-18.3	-37.1
Wind Drift - inches	0.0	0.6	2.6	6.0	11.1	18.0

G1 Ballistic Coefficient = 0.457

Winchester 180-grain Power-Point Plus (SHV30WM2)

Distance - Yards	Muzzle	100	200	300	400	500
Velocity - fps	3070	2846	2633	2430	2236	2051
Energy - ft-lb	3768	3239	2772	2361	1999	1681
Taylor KO values	24.3	22.5	20.9	19.2	17.7	16.2
Path - inches	-1.5	1.4	0.0	-6.4	-18.7	-38.0
Wind Drift - inches	0.0	0.7	2.8	6.4	11.9	19.3

G1 Ballistic Coefficient = 0.431

Norma 180-grain SP (17680)

Distance - Yards	Muzzle	100	200	300	400	500
Velocity - fps	3018	2780	2555	2341	2135	1942
Energy - ft-lb	3641	3091	2610	2190	1823	1507
Taylor KO values	23.9	22.0	20.2	18.3	16.9	15.4
Path - inches	-1.5	1.5	0.0	-7.0	-20.1	-40.9
Wind Drift - inches	0.0	0.7	3.0	7.2	13.3	21.7

G1 Ballistic Coefficient = 0.406

Norma 180-grain Plastic Point (17687)

Distance - Yards	Muzzle	100	200	300	400	500
Velocity - fps	3018	2755	2506	2271	2048	1839
Energy - ft-lb	3641	3034	2512	2062	1677	1352
Taylor KO values	23.9	21.8	19.8	18.0	16.2	14.6
Path - inches	-1.5	1.6	0.0	-6.3	-18.1	-37.1
Wind Drift - inches	0.0	0.8	3.4	8.1	15.1	24.8

G1 Ballistic Coefficient = 0.366

Federal 180-grain Sierra Pro-Hunter SP (300WBS)

Distance - Yards	Muzzle	100	200	300	400	500
Velocity - fps	2960	2750	2540	2340	2160	1980
Energy - ft-lb	3500	3010	2580	2195	1860	1565
Taylor KO values	23.4	21.8	20.1	18.5	17.1	15.7
Path - inches	-1.5	1.6	0.0	-7.0	-20.3	-41.1
Wind Drift - inches	0.0	0.7	2.8	6.6	12.3	20.0

G1 Ballistic Coefficient = 0.439

Federal 180-grain Trophy Bonded Bear Claw (P300WT2)

Distance - Yards	Muzzle	100	200	300	400	500
Velocity - fps	2960	2700	2460	2220	2000	1800
Energy - ft-lb	3500	2915	2410	1875	1605	1295
Taylor KO values	23.4	21.4	19.5	17.6	15.8	14.2
Path - inches	-1.5	1.6	0.0	-7.4	-21.9	-45.0
Wind Drift - inches	0.0	0.8	3.5	8.3	15.4	25.4

G1 Ballistic Coefficient = 0.361

Federal 180-grain Woodleigh Weldcore SP (P300WF)

Distance - Yards	Muzzle	100	200	300	400	500
Velocity - fps	2960	2700	2460	2230	2010	1800
Energy - ft-lb	3500	2915	2415	1980	1610	1300
Taylor KO values	23.4	21.4	19.5	17.7	15.9	14.3
Path - inches	-1.5	1.6	0.0	-7.4	-21.8	-44.8
Wind Drift - inches	0.0	0.8	3.5	8.3	15.4	25.4

G1 Ballistic Coefficient = 0.361

Federal 180-grain Nosler Partition (P300WB2)

Distance - Yards	Muzzle	100	200	300	400	500
Velocity - fps	2960	2700	2450	2210	1990	1780
Energy - ft-lb	3500	2905	2395	1955	1585	1265
Taylor KO values	23.4	21.4	19.4	17.5	15.8	14.1
Path - inches	-1.5	1.6	0.0	-7.5	-22.1	-45.4
Wind Drift - inches	0.0	0.9	3.6	8.4	15.8	26.1

G1 Ballistic Coefficient = 0.354

Hornady 180-grain SP (8200)

Distance - Yards	Muzzle	100	200	300	400	500
Velocity - fps	2960	2745	2540	2344	2157	1979
Energy - ft-lb	3501	3011	2578	2196	1859	1585
Taylor KO values	23.4	21.7	20.1	18.6	17.1	15.7
Path - inches	-1.5	1.9	0.0	-7.3	-20.9	-41.9
Wind Drift - inches	0.0	0.7	2.8	6.6	12.3	20.0

G1 Ballistic Coefficient = 0.438

Remington 180-grain Nosler Ballistic Tip (PRT300WA)

Distance - Yards	Muzzle	100	200	300	400	500
Velocity - fps	2960	2774	2595	2424	2259	2100
Energy - ft-lb	3501	3075	2692	2348	2039	1762
Taylor KO values	23.4	22.0	20.6	19.2	17.9	16.6
Path - inches	-1.5	1.5	0.0	-6.7	-19.3	-38.7
Wind Drift - inches	0.0	0.6	2.4	5.6	10.4	16.8

G1 Ballistic Coefficient = 0.508

Remington 180-grain Pointed SP Core-Lokt (R300W2)

Distance - Yards	Muzzle	100	200	300	400	500
Velocity - fps	2960	2745	2540	2344	2157	1979
Energy - ft-lb	3501	3011	2578	2196	1859	1565
Taylor KO values	23.4	21.7	200.1	18.6	17.1	15.6
Path - inches	-1.5	1.6	0.0	-7.0	-20.2	-41.0
Wind Drift - inches	0.0	0.7	2.8	6.6	12.3	20.1

G1 Ballistic Coefficient = 0.437

Remington 180-grain Nosler Partition (PRP300WA)

Distance - Yards	Muzzle	100	200	300	400	500
Velocity - fps	2960	2725	2503	2291	2089	1898
Energy - ft-lb	3501	2968	2503	2087	1744	1440
Taylor KO values	23.4	21.6	19.8	18.1	16.5	15.0
Path - inches	-1.5	1.6	0.0	-7.2	-20.9	-42.7
Wind Drift - inches	0.0	0.8	3.1	7.3	13.6	22.3

G1 Ballistic Coefficient = 0.401

Winchester 180-grain Power-Point (X300WM2)

Distance - Yards	Muzzle	100	200	300	400	500
Velocity - fps	2960	2745	2540	2344	2157	1979
Energy - ft-lb	3501	3011	2578	2196	1859	1565
Taylor KO values	23.4	21.7	20.1	18.6	17.1	15.7
Path - inches	-1.5	1.9	0.0	-7.3	-20.9	-41.9
Wind Drift - inches	0.0	0.7	2.8	6.6	12.3	20.0

G1 Ballistic Coefficient = 0.438

Winchester 180-grain Fail Safe (S300WX)

Distance - Yards	Muzzle	100	200	300	400	500
Velocity - fps	2960	2732	2514	2307	2110	1923
Energy - ft-lb	3503	2983	2528	2129	1780	1478
Taylor KO values	23.4	21.6	19.9	18.3	16.7	15.2
Path - inches	-1.5	1.6	0.0	-7.1	-20.7	-42.1
Wind Drift - inches	0.0	0.7	3.0	7.1	13.2	21.6

G1 Ballistic Coefficient = 0.411

Speer 180-grain Grand Slam (24509)

Distance - Yards	Muzzle	100	200	300	400	500
Velocity - fps	2950	2735	2530	2335	2149	1971
Energy - ft-lb	3478	2989	2558	2176	1846	1553
Taylor KO values	23.4	21.7	20.0	18.5	17.0	15.6
Path - inches	-1.5	1.6	0.0	-7.0	-20.5	-41.4
Wind Drift - inches	0.0	0.7	2.9	6.7	12.4	20.1

G1 Ballistic Coefficient = 0.438

PMC 180-grain Pointed SP (300B)

Distance - Yards	Muzzle	100	200	300	400	500
Velocity - fps	2853	2643	2446	2258	2077	1906
Energy - ft-lb	3252	2792	2391	2037	1724	1451
Taylor KO values	22.6	20.9	19.4	17.9	16.4	15.1
Path - inches	-1.5	1.7	0.0	-7.5	-21.9	-44.3
Wind Drift - inches	0.0	0.7	3.0	6.9	12.8	20.8

G1 Ballistic Coefficient = 0.444

Winchester 180-grain Ballistic Silvertip (SBST300)

Distance - Yards	Muzzle	100	200	300	400	500
Velocity - fps	2950	2764	2586	2415	2250	2092
Energy - ft-lb	3478	3054	2673	1744	1450	1198
Taylor KO values	23.4	21.9	20.5	19.1	17.8	16.6
Path - inches	-1.5	1.5	0.0	-6.7	-19.4	-38.9
Wind Drift - inches	0.0	0.6	2.4	5.7	10.4	16.8

G1 Ballistic Coefficient = 0.508

Norma 180-grain TXP Line, Swift (17519)

Distance - Yards	Muzzle	100	200	300	400	500
Velocity - fps	2910	2688	2467	2256	2056	1866
Energy - ft-lb	3409	2888	2432	2035	1689	1392
Taylor KO values	23.1	22.7	19.5	17.9	16.3	14.8
Path - inches	-1.5	1.7	0.0	-7.4	-21.6	-44.1
Wind Drift - inches	0.0	0.8	3.2	7.5	13.9	22.8

G1 Ballistic Coefficient = 0.400

PMC 180-grain Barnes-X (300XC)

Distance - Yards	Muzzle	100	200	300	400	500
Velocity - fps	2910	2738	2572	2412	2258	2109
Energy - ft-lb	3384	2995	2644	2325	2037	1778
Taylor KO values	23.0	21.7	20.4	19.1	17.9	16.7
Path - inches	-1.5	1.6	0.0	-6.9	-19.8	-39.4
Wind Drift - inches	0.0	0.6	2.4	5.6	10.2	16.6

G1 Ballistic Coefficient = 0.513

Hornady 190-grain SP Boattail (8220)

Distance - Yards	Muzzle	100	200	300	400	500
Velocity - fps	2900	2711	2529	2365	2187	2026
Energy - ft-lb	3549	3101	2699	2340	2018	1732
Taylor KO values	24.2	22.7	21.1	19.8	18.3	16.9
Path - inches	-1.5	1.6	0.0	-7.1	-20.4	-41.0
Wind Drift - inches	0.0	0.6	2.6	6.0	11.1	18.0

G1 Ballistic Coefficient = 0.492

PMC 190-grain Sierra SP Boattail (300HC)

Distance - Yards	Muzzle	100	200	300	400	500
Velocity - fps	2900	2714	2536	2365	2200	2042
Energy - ft-lb	3361	2944	2571	2235	1935	1666
Taylor KO values	24.2	22.7	21.2	19.8	18.4	17.1
Path - inches	-1.5	1.6	0.0	-7.1	-20.3	-40.8
Wind Drift - inches	0.0	0.6	2.5	5.9	10.8	17.5

G1 Ballistic Coefficient = 0.502

Remington 190-grain Pointed SP Boattail (PRB300WA)

Distance - Yards		Muzzle	100	200	300	400	500
Velocity - fps		2885	2691	2506	2327	2156	1993
Energy - ft-lb		3511	3055	2648	2285	1961	1675
Taylor KO values		24.1	22.5	21.0	19.5	18.0	16.7
Path - inches		-1.5	1.6	0.0	-7.2	-20.8	-41.9
Wind Drift - inches		0.0	0.6	2.7	6.3	11.5	18.7

G1 Ballistic Coefficient = 0.478

Black Hills 190-grain HP Match (D300WMN1)

Distance - Yards	Muzzle	100	200	300	400	500
Velocity - fps	2950	2781	2619	2462	2311	2165
Energy - ft-lb	3672	3265	2894	2559	2254	1978
Taylor KO values	24.7	23.2	21.9	20.6	19.3	18.1
Path - inches	-1.5	1.5	0.0	-6.6	-18.9	-37.7
Wind Drift - inches	0.0	0.5	2.2	5.1	9.3	15.0

G1 Ballistic Coefficient = 0.560

Norma 200-grain Oryx SP (17676)

Distance - Yards	Muzzle	100	200	300	400	500
Velocity - fps	3018	2755	2506	2271	2048	1839
Energy - ft-lb	4046	3371	2791	2292	1863	1502
Taylor KO values	26.6	24.2	22.0	20.0	18.0	16.2
Path - inches	-1.5	1.5	0.0	-7.0	-21.0	-43.2
Wind Drift - inches	0.0	0.8	3.4	8.1	15.1	24.8

G1 Ballistic Coefficient = 0.360

Federal 200-grain Nosler Partition - HE (P300WE)

Distance - Yards	Muzzle	100	200	300	400	500
Velocity - fps	2930	2740	2550	2370	2200	2030
Energy - ft-lb	3810	3325	2885	2495	2145	1840
Taylor KO values	23.2	21.7	20.2	18.0	17.4	16.1
Path - inches	-1.5	1.6	0.0	-6.9	-20.1	-40.4
Wind Drift - inches	0.0	0.6	2.7	6.2	11.5	18.6

G1 Ballistic Coefficient = 0.465

Remington 200-grain Swift A-Frame Pointed SP (RS300WA)

Distance - Yards	Muzzle	100	200	300	400	500
Velocity - fps	2825	2595	2376	2167	1970	1783
Energy - ft-lb	3544	2989	2506	2086	1722	1412
Taylor KO values	24.9	22.8	20.9	19.1	17.3	15.7
Path - inches	-1.5	1.8	0.0	-8.0	-23.5	-47.9
Wind Drift - inches	0.0	0.8	3.4	8.0	14.8	24.8

G1 Ballistic Coefficient = 0.396

Federal 200-grain Sierra GameKing SP Boattail (P300WC)

Distance - Yards	Muzzle	100	200	300	400	500
Velocity - fps	2830	2660	2530	2380	2240	2110
Energy - ft-lb	3500	3180	2830	2520	2230	1870
Taylor KO values	24.9	23.4	22.3	20.9	19.7	18.6
Path - inches	-1.5	1.7	0.0	-7.1	-20.4	-40.5
Wind Drift - inches	0.0	0.5	2.2	5.0	9.2	14.8

G1 Ballistic Coefficient = 0.598

Federal 200-grain Trophy Bonded Bear Claw (P300WT1)

Distance - Yards	Muzzle	100	200	300	400	500
Velocity - fps	2800	2570	2350	2150	1950	1770
Energy - ft-lb	3480	2835	2460	2050	1690	1392
Taylor KO values	24.6	22.6	20.7	18.9	17.2	15.6
Path - inches	-1.5	1.9	0.0	-8.2	-23.9	-48.8
Wind Drift - inches	0.0	0.8	3.4	8.0	14.9	24.5

G1 Ballistic Coefficient = 0.398

Speer 200-grain Grand Slam (24510)

Distance - Yards	Muzzle	100	200	300	400	500
Velocity - fps	2800	2597	2404	2218	2041	1873
Energy - ft-lb	3481	2996	2565	2185	1851	1558
Taylor KO values	24.6	22.9	21.2	19.5	18.0	16.5
Path - inches	-1.5	1.8	0.0	-7.9	-22.9	-46.1
Wind Drift - inches	0.0	0.7	3.0	7.0	13.0	21.1

G1 Ballistic Coefficient = 0.449

Norma 200-grain Vulcan HP (17644)

Distance - Yards	Muzzle	100	200	300	400	500
Velocity - fps	2887	2609	2347	2100	1869	1655
Energy - ft-lb	3702	3023	2447	1960	1551	1217
Taylor KO values	25.4	23.0	20.7	18.5	16.4	14.6
Path - inches	-1.5	1.8	0.0	-8.2	-24.2	-50.3
Wind Drift - inches	0.0	1.0	4.0	9.5	17.9	29.6

G1 Ballistic Coefficient = 0.336

.300 H&H Magnum

The .300 H&H Magnum (introduced about 1920) wasn't the first belted magnum, the .375 H&H actually arrived about 10 years earlier. Still the .300 H&H can be called the father of all the .300 Magnums. Starting with the H&H case, wildcatters improved, reshaped, necked and generally reformed the case into nearly every configuration they, or anyone else, could imagine. The .300 H&H has never been hugely popular in the US but several of its offspring are near the top of the charts. Only two cartridge variations are factory loaded today.

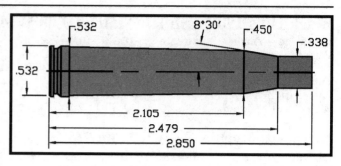

Relative Recoil Factor = 2.34

Controlling Agency: SAAMI

Bullet Weight Grains	Velocity fps	Maximum Average Pressure	
		Copper Crusher	Transducer
150	3110	54,000 cup	N/S
180	2780	54,000 cup	N/S
220	2565	54,000 cup	N/S

Standard barrel for velocity testing:
24 inches long - 1 turn in 10 inch twist

Federal 180-grain Nosler Partition (P300HA)

Distance - Yards	Muzzle	100	200	300	400	500
Velocity - fps	2880	2620	2380	2150	1930	1730
Energy - ft-lb	3315	2750	2260	1840	1480	1190
Taylor KO values	22.8	20.8	18.8	17.0	15.3	13.7
Path - inches	-1.5	1.8	0.0	-8.0	-23.4	-48.6
Wind Drift - inches	0.0	0.9	3.7	8.7	16.2	26.8

G1 Ballistic Coefficient = 0.358

Winchester 180-grain Fail Safe (S300HX)

Distance - Yards	Muzzle	100	200	300	400	500
Velocity - fps	2880	2628	2390	2165	1952	1752
Energy - ft-lb	3316	2762	2284	1873	1523	1227
Taylor KO values	22.8	20.9	18,9	17.1	15.5	13.9
Path - inches	-1.5	1.8	0.0	-7.9	-23.2	-47.6
Wind Drift - inches	0.0	0.9	3.6	8.5	15.8	26.0

G1 Ballistic Coefficient = 0.366

.300 Weatherby Magnum

If you ask most any group of shooters to name one caliber that best describes the term "high-powered rifle," chances are the answer will be the .300 Weatherby Magnum. Until very recently passed by the .30-378 Weatherby, Roy Weatherby's .300 Magnum was the performance leader of the .30-caliber rifles. The design has been around since the WWII years. Perhaps the most obvious identifying feature about Weatherby cartridges is the venturi shoulder. Whether the shoulder adds anything to velocity, the appearance is enough to ensure that most shooters will instantly recognize it as a Weatherby.

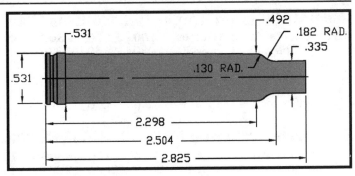

Relative Recoil Factor = 2.63

Controlling Agency : SAAMI*

Bullet Weight Grains	Velocity fps	Maximum Average Pressure	
		Copper Crusher	Transducer
180	3185	N/S	65,000 psi
190	3015	N/S	65,000 psi
220	2835	N/S	65,000 psi

Standard barrel for velocity testing:
24 inches long - 1 turn in 10 inch twist

* Ammunition for the .300 Weatherby Magnum is also manufactured in Europe under CIP standards. Ammunition manufactured to CIP specifications will exhibit somewhat different performance values, but can be safely fired in rifles in good condition.

Weatherby 150-grain Nosler Partition (N 300 150 PT)

Distance - Yards	Muzzle	100	200	300	400	500
Velocity - fps	3540	3263	3004	2759	2528	2307
Energy - ft-lb	4173	3547	3004	2536	2128	1773
Taylor KO values	23.4	21.5	19.8	18.2	16.7	15.2
Path - inches	-1.5	1.0	0.0	-4.9	-14.6	-29.7
Wind Drift - inches	0.0	0.6	2.5	5.8	10.6	17.2

G1 Ballistic Coefficient = 0.414

Weatherby 150-grain Pointed-Expanding (H 300 150 SP)

Distance - Yards	Muzzle	100	200	300	400	500
Velocity - fps	3540	3225	2932	2657	2399	2155
Energy - ft-lb	4173	3462	2862	2351	1916	1547
Taylor KO values	23.4	21.3	19.4	17.5	15.8	14.2
Path - inches	-1.5	1.0	0.0	-5.2	-15.4	-31.8
Wind Drift - inches	0.0	0.7	2.9	6.8	12.6	20.6

G1 Ballistic Coefficient = 0.358

Weatherby 165-grain Hornady Pointed-Expanding (H 300 165 SP)

Distance - Yards	Muzzle	100	200	300	400	500
Velocity - fps	3390	3123	2872	2634	2409	2195
Energy - ft-lb	4210	3573	3021	2542	2126	1765
Taylor KO values	24.6	22.7	20.9	19.1	17.5	15.9
Path - inches	-1.5	1.0	0.0	-5.3	-15.5	-31.8
Wind Drift - inches	0.0	0.6	2.7	6.3	11.7	19.1

G1 Ballistic Coefficient = 0.387

Weatherby 165-grain Nosler Ballistic Tip (N 300 165 BST)

Distance - Yards	Muzzle	100	200	300	400	500
Velocity - fps	3350	3133	2927	2730	2542	2361
Energy - ft-lb	4111	3596	3138	2730	2367	2042
Taylor KO values	24.3	22.7	21.3	19.8	18.5	17.1
Path - inches	-1.5	1.0	0.0	-5.1	-14.8	-30.0
Wind Drift - inches	0.0	0.5	2.2	5.1	9.4	15.2

G1 Ballistic Coefficient = 0.475

Federal 180-grain Nosler Partition - HE (P300WBB)

Distance - Yards	Muzzle	100	200	300	400	500
Velocity - fps	3330	3110	2910	2710	2520	2340
Energy - ft-lb	4430	3875	3375	2835	2540	2180
Taylor KO values	26.4	24.6	23.0	21.5	20.0	18.5
Path - inches	-1.5	1.0	0.0	-5.2	-15.1	-30.4
Wind Drift - inches	0.0	0.6	2.2	5.2	9.6	15.4

G1 Ballistic Coefficient = 0.473

Federal 180-grain Trophy Bonded Bear Claw - HE (P300WBT3)

Distance - Yards	Muzzle	100	200	300	400	500
Velocity - fps	3330	3080	2850	2625	2410	2210
Energy - ft-lb	4430	3790	3235	2750	2320	1950
Taylor KO values	26.4	24.4	22.6	20.8	19.1	17.5
Path - inches	-1.5	1.1	0.0	-5.4	-15.8	-32.3
Wind Drift - inches	0.0	0.6	2.6	6.1	11.2	18.2

G1 Ballistic Coefficient = 0.412

Weatherby 180-grain Nosler Partition (N 300 180 PT)

Distance - Yards	Muzzle	100	200	300	400	500
Velocity - fps	3240	3028	2826	2634	2449	2271
Energy - ft-lb	4195	3665	3194	2772	2396	2062
Taylor KO values	25.7	24.0	22.4	20.9	19.4	18.0
Path - inches	-1.5	1.2	0.0	-5.5	-16.0	-32.4
Wind Drift - inches	0.0	0.6	2.3	5.4	9.9	16.0

G1 Ballistic Coefficient = 0.474

Weatherby 180-grain Hornady Pointed-Expanding (H 300 180 SP)

Distance - Yards	Muzzle	100	200	300	400	500
Velocity - fps	3240	3004	2781	2569	2366	2173
Energy - ft-lb	4195	3607	3091	2637	2237	1886
Taylor KO values	25.7	23.8	22.0	20.3	18.7	17.2
Path - inches	-1.5	1.2	0.0	-5.7	-16.6	-33.8
Wind Drift - inches	0.0	0.6	2.6	6.0	11.2	18.2

G1 Ballistic Coefficient = 0.425

Federal 180-grain Sierra GameKing BTSP (P300WBC)

Distance - Yards	Muzzle	100	200	300	400	500
Velocity - fps	3190	3010	2830	2660	2490	2330
Energy - ft-lb	4065	3610	3195	2820	2480	2175
Taylor KO values	25.3	23.8	22.4	21.1	19.7	18.5
Path - inches	-1.5	1.2	0.0	-5.6	-16.0	-31.0
Wind Drift - inches	0.0	0.5	2.1	4.8	8.8	14.2

G1 Ballistic Coefficient = 0.536

Federal 180-grain Nosler Partition (P300WBA)

Distance - Yards	Muzzle	100	200	300	400	500
Velocity - fps	3190	2980	2780	2590	2400	2230
Energy - ft-lb	4055	3540	3080	2670	2305	1985
Taylor KO values	25.3	23.6	22.0	20.5	19.0	17.7
Path - inches	-1.5	1.2	0.0	-5.7	-16.7	-33.6
Wind Drift - inches	0.0	0.6	2.4	5.5	10.1	16.3

G1 Ballistic Coefficient = 0.474

Federal 180-grain Trophy Bonded Bear Claw (P300WBT1)

Distance - Yards	Muzzle	100	200	300	400	500
Velocity - fps	3190	2850	2720	2500	2290	2100
Energy - ft-lb	4065	3475	2955	2500	2105	1760
Taylor KO values	25.3	22.6	21.5	19.8	18.1	16.6
Path - inches	-1.5	1.3	0.0	-5.9	-17.5	-35.7
Wind Drift - inches	0.0	0.7	2.8	6.4	11.9	19.4

G1 Ballistic Coefficient = 0.411

Speer 180-grain Grand Slam (24516)

Distance - Yards	Muzzle	100	200	300	400	500
Velocity - fps	3185	2948	2722	2508	2305	2110
Energy - ft-lb	4054	3472	2962	2514	2124	1780
Taylor KO values	25.2	23.3	21.6	19.9	18.3	16.7
Path - inches	-1.5	1.3	0.0	-5.9	-17.4	-35.5
Wind Drift - inches	0.0	0.7	2.7	6.3	11.7	19.1

G1 Ballistic Coefficient = 0.417

A² 180-grain Monolithic; Dead Tough (None)

Distance - Yards	Muzzle	100	200	300	400	500
Velocity - fps	3180	2811	2471	2155	1863	1602
Energy - ft-lb	4041	3158	2440	1856	1387	1026
Taylor KO values	25.2	22.3	19.6	17.1	14.8	12.7
Path - inches	-1.5	1.5	0.0	-7.2	-21.8	-46.7
Wind Drift - inches	0.0	1.1	4.5	10.8	20.5	34.4

G1 Ballistic Coefficient = 0.264

Hornady 180-grain SP (8222)

Distance - Yards	Muzzle	100	200	300	400	500
Velocity - fps	3120	2891	2673	2466	2268	2079
Energy - ft-lb	3890	3340	2856	2430	2055	1727
Taylor KO values	24.7	22.9	21.2	19.5	18.0	16.5
Path - inches	-1.5	1.3	0.0	-6.2	-18.1	-36.8
Wind Drift - inches	0.0	0.7	2.7	6.4	11.8	19.2

G1 Ballistic Coefficient = 0.426

Remington 180-grain Pointed SP Core-Lokt (R300WB1)

Distance - Yards	Muzzle	100	200	300	400	500
Velocity - fps	3120	2866	2627	2400	2184	1976
Energy - ft-lb	3890	3284	2758	2301	1905	1565
Taylor KO values	24.7	22.7	20.8	19.0	17.3	15.7
Path - inches	-1.5	1.4	0.0	-6.4	-18.9	-38.7
Wind Drift - inches	0.0	0.7	3.1	7.2	13.3	21.8

G1 Ballistic Coefficient = 0.383

Weatherby 180-grain Barnes-X (B 300 180 XS)

Distance - Yards	Muzzle	100	200	300	400	500
Velocity - fps	3190	2995	2809	2631	2459	2294
Energy - ft-lb	4067	3586	3154	2766	2417	2103
Taylor KO values	25.3	23.7	22.2	20.8	19.5	18.2
Path - inches	-1.5	1.2	0.0	-5.6	-16.2	-32.6
Wind Drift - inches	0.0	0.5	2.2	5.1	9.3	15.0

G1 Ballistic Coefficient = 0.511

Remington 190-grain Pointed SP Boattail (PRB300WBA)

Distance - Yards	Muzzle	100	200	300	400	500
Velocity - fps	3030	2830	2638	2455	2279	2110
Energy - ft-lb	3873	3378	2936	2542	2190	1878
Taylor KO values	25.3	23.7	22.1	20.5	19.1	17.6
Path - inches	-1.5	1.4	0.0	-6.4	-18.6	-37.6
Wind Drift - inches	0.0	0.6	2.5	5.8	10.7	17.4

G1 Ballistic Coefficient = 0.479

Weatherby 200-grain Nosler Partition (N 300 200 PT)

Distance - Yards	Muzzle	100	200	300	400	500
Velocity - fps	3060	2860	2668	2485	2308	2139
Energy - ft-lb	4158	3631	3161	2741	2366	2032
Taylor KO values	26.9	25.2	23.5	21.9	20.3	18.8
Path - inches	-1.5	1.4	0.0	-6.3	-18.2	-36.6
Wind Drift - inches	0.0	0.6	2.5	5.7	10.5	17.0

G1 Ballistic Coefficient = 0.481

Remington 200-grain Swift A-Frame Pointed SP (RS300WBB)

Distance - Yards	Muzzle	100	200	300	400	500
Velocity - fps	2925	2690	2467	2254	2052	1861
Energy - ft-lb	3799	3213	2701	2256	1870	1538
Taylor KO values	24.5	22.5	20.6	18.8	17.2	15.6
Path - inches	-1.5	1.7	0.0	-7.4	-21.6	-44.2
Wind Drift - inches	0.0	0.8	3.2	7.6	14.1	23.0

G1 Ballistic Coefficient = 0.396

Federal 200-grain Trophy Bonded Bear Claw (P300WBT2)

Distance - Yards	Muzzle	100	200	300	400	500
Velocity - fps	2900	2670	2440	2230	2030	1830
Energy - ft-lb	3735	3150	2645	2200	1820	1490
Taylor KO values	24.2	22.3	20.4	18.6	17.0	15.3
Path - inches	-1.5	1.7	0.0	-7.6	-22.2	-45.1
Wind Drift - inches	0.0	0.8	3.3	7.8	14.5	23.7

G1 Ballistic Coefficient = 0.391

Weatherby 220-grain Hornady Round Nose-Expanding (H 300 220 RN)

Distance - Yards	Muzzle	100	200	300	400	500
Velocity - fps	2845	2543	2260	1996	1751	1530
Energy - ft-lb	3954	3158	2495	1946	1497	1143
Taylor KO values	23.8	21.3	18.9	16.7	14.6	12.8
Path - inches	-1.5	2.0	0.0	-8.8	-26.4	-55.2
Wind Drift - inches	0.0	1.1	4.5	10.8	20.5	34.2

G1 Ballistic Coefficient = 0.300

A² 220-grain Monolithic (None)

Distance - Yards	Muzzle	100	200	300	400	500
Velocity - fps	2700	2407	2133	1877	1653	1447
Energy - ft-lb	3561	2830	2223	1721	1334	1023
Taylor KO values	22.6	20.1	17.8	15.7	13.8	12.1
Path - inches	-1.5	2.3	0.0	-9.8	-29.8	-62.1
Wind Drift - inches	0.0	1.1	4.8	11.6	21.9	36.5

G1 Ballistic Coefficient = 0.304

.300 Remington Ultra Mag

It's clear that just plain old "magnum" isn't good enough any more. Now (1999) we have the .300 ULTRA Mag. This is Remington's entry into the .30-caliber class, where they have been absent for many years. The .300 RUM (now that's an unfortunate abbreviation) is something a little different from the standard belted magnum. For openers, it's beltless. It is actually based on a .404 Jeffery case necked to .308 and with a rebated head. It follows a recent trend to do away with the belt on magnum cartridges. While the data below is based on what is expected to be the SAAMI standard barrel length of 24 inches, you may find 26-inch data quoted by various sources. That extra 2 inches makes about a 50 fps difference in muzzle velocity.

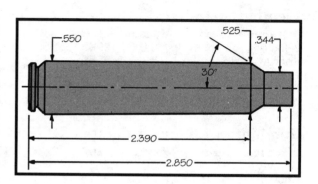

Relative Recoil Factor = 2.64   **Controlling Agency : SAAMI (Standardization pending)**

Bullet Weight Grains	Velocity fps	Maximum Average Pressure		Standard barrel for velocity testing:
		Copper Crusher	Transducer	
180	3250	N/A	65,000 psi	24 inches long - 1 turn in 10 inch twist

Remington 180-grain Nosler Partition (PR300UM1)

Distance - Yards	Muzzle	100	200	300	400	500
Velocity - fps	3250	3037	2834	2640	2454	2276
Energy - ft-lb	4221	3686	3201	2786	2407	2071
Taylor KO values	25.7	24.1	22.4	20.9	19.4	18.0
Path - inches	-1.5	1.1	0.0	-5.5	-15.9	-32.2
Wind Drift - inches	0.0	0.6	2.3	5.4	9.9	16.0

G1 Ballistic Coefficient = 0.473

7.82mm (.308) Lazzeroni Warbird

If the 7.82mm Patriot is Lazzeroni's "short" magnum, the Warbird is certainly a "long" magnum. This cartridge shares the lead in the .30 caliber velocity derby with the .30-378 Weatherby. It is an extremely potent cartridge, and one with rather specialized applications.

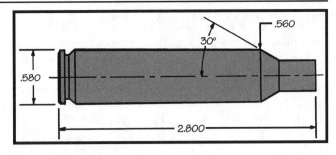

Relative Recoil Factor = 2.80

Controlling Agency: Factory

Lazzeroni 150-grain Nosler Partition (782WB150P)

Distance - Yards	Muzzle	100	200	300	400	500
Velocity - fps	3700	3477	3266	3064	2872	2688
Energy - ft-lb	4561	4028	3553	3128	2748	2407
Taylor KO values	24.4	22.9	21.6	20.2	19.0	17.7
Path - inches	-1.5	0.7	0.0	-4.0	-11.6	-23.5
Wind Drift - inches	0.0	0.4	1.8	4.3	7.8	12.5

G1 Ballistic Coefficient = 0.503

Lazzeroni 180-grain Nosler Partition (782WB180P)

Distance - Yards	Muzzle	100	200	300	400	500
Velocity - fps	3450	3269	3096	2929	2768	2613
Energy - ft-lb	4758	4273	3831	3430	3064	2731
Taylor KO values	27.3	25.9	24.5	23.2	21.9	20.7
Path - inches	-1.5	0.9	0.0	-4.5	-13.1	-26.2
Wind Drift - inches	0.0	0.4	1.77	4.0	7.2	11.5

G1 Ballistic Coefficient = 0.585

Lazzeroni 200-grain Swift A-Frame (782WB200A)

Distance - Yards	Muzzle	100	200	300	400	500
Velocity - fps	3300	3126	2959	2799	2644	2494
Energy - ft-lb	4837	4342	3891	3480	3105	2762
Taylor KO values	29.0	27.5	26.0	24.6	23.3	21.9
Path - inches	-1.5	1.0	0.0	-5.0	-14.4	-28.9
Wind Drift - inches	0.0	0.4	1.8	4.2	7.6	12.1

G1 Ballistic Coefficient = 0.589

.30-378 Weatherby Magnum

Whenever a new cartridge case is introduced the wildcat builders have a field day. The basic case is necked down, necked up, improved, and otherwise modified to conform to the whims of the wildcat "designer." The .378 Weatherby offered a tremendous opportunity. This big case was necked to both .338 and .30 calibers soon after its introduction. The wildcat versions have been around for a long time. I fired a .30-378 in about 1965 and that certainly wasn't the first gun in this caliber. Recently Weatherby has begun offering guns and ammunition in both .30-378 and .333-378 calibers. The .30-378 is the hottest .30 caliber in the standard inventory.

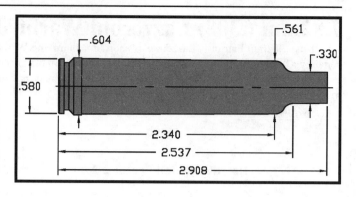

Relative Recoil Factor = 2.55

Controlling Agency : Factory

Standard barrel for velocity testing:
26 inches long - 1 turn in 10 inch twist

Weatherby 165-grain Nosler Ballistic Tip (N 303 165 BST)

Distance - Yards	Muzzle	100	200	300	400	500
Velocity - fps	3500	3275	3062	2859	2665	2480
Energy - ft-lb	4488	3930	3435	2995	2603	2253
Taylor KO values	25.4	23.8	22.2	20.8	19.3	18.0
Path - inches	-1.5	0.9	0.0	-4.6	-13.4	-27.2
Wind Drift - inches	0.0	0.5	2.1	4.7	8.9	14.3

G1 Ballistic Coefficient = 0.475

Weatherby 180-grain Barnes-X (B 303 180 XS)

Distance - Yards	Muzzle	100	200	300	400	500
Velocity - fps	3450	3243	3046	2858	2678	2504
Energy - ft-lb	4757	4204	3709	3264	2865	2506
Taylor KO values	27.3	25.7	24.1	22.6	21.2	19.8
Path - inches	-1.5	0.9	0.0	-4.7	-13.6	-27.4
Wind Drift - inches	0.0	0.5	2.0	4.6	8.4	13.5

G1 Ballistic Coefficient = 0.511

Weatherby 200-grain Nosler Partition (N 303 200 PT)

Distance - Yards	Muzzle	100	200	300	400	500
Velocity - fps	3160	2955	2759	2572	2392	2220
Energy - ft-lb	4434	3877	3381	2938	2541	2188
Taylor KO values	27.8	26.0	24.3	22.6	21.0	19.5
Path - inches	-1.5	1.2	0.0	-5.8	-16.9	-34.1
Wind Drift - inches	0.0	0.6	2.4	5.5	10.1	116.3

G1 Ballistic Coefficient = 0.481

.303 British

The .303 British was Britain's service rifle cartridge from 1888 until replaced, in about 1957, by the 7.62 NATO round (.308). It started life as a black-powder number firing a 215-grain bullet. When smokeless powder came into service use, the black powder was replaced with Cordite. Cordite is a tubular "powder" that was manufactured for this cartridge in sticks about 0.040 inches in diameter and 1.625 inches long, like pencil leads. Since it would have been almost impossible to load the Cordite sticks into the 0.310-inch-diameter case mouth, a flock of little old ladies in tennis shoes loaded the sticks into the cases by hand before the neck and shoulder were formed. After the propellant was inserted, the case forming was completed and the bullet seated. Talk about hard ways to do easy things.

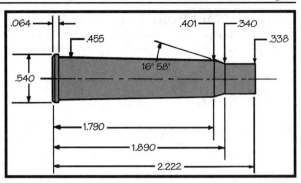

Relative Recoil Factor = 1.98   **Controlling Agency : SAAMI**

Bullet Weight Grains	Velocity fps	Maximum Average Pressure	
		Copper Crusher	Transducer
150	2685	45,000 cup	49,000 psi
180	2450	45,000 cup	49,000 psi
215	2155	45,000 cup	49,000 psi

Standard barrel for velocity testing:
24 inches long - 1 turn in 10 inch twist

Hornady 150-grain SP-Light Magnum (8525)

Distance - Yards	Muzzle	100	200	300	400	500
Velocity - fps	2830	2570	2325	2094	1884	1690
Energy - ft-lb	2667	2199	1800	1461	1185	952
Taylor KO values	19.0	17.3	15.6	14.1	12.7	11.4
Path - inches	-1.5	2.0	0.0	-8.4	-24.6	-50.3
Wind Drift - inches	0.0	0.9	3.8	9.0	16.8	27.7

G1 Ballistic Coefficient = 0.356

Norma 150-grain SP (17712)

Distance - Yards	Muzzle	100	200	300	400	500
Velocity - fps	2723	2440	2174	1920	1691	1484
Energy - ft-lb	2470	1983	1574	1235	953	733
Taylor KO values	18.3	16.4	14.6	12.9	11.4	10.0
Path - inches	-1.5	2.2	0.0	-9.6	-28.7	-60.0
Wind Drift - inches	0.0	1.1	4.7	11.1	21.0	35.0

G1 Ballistic Coefficient = 0.316

Federal 150-grain Hi-Shok SP (303B)

Distance - Yards	Muzzle	100	200	300	400	500
Velocity - fps	2690	2440	2210	1980	1780	1590
Energy - ft-lb	2400	1980	1620	1310	1055	840
Taylor KO values	18.1	16.4	14.9	13.3	12.0	10.7
Path - inches	-1.5	2.2	0.0	-9.4	-27.6	-56.8
Wind Drift - inches	0.0	1.0	4.1	9.6	18.1	29.8

G1 Ballistic Coefficient = 0.215

Hornady 150-grain SP (8225)

Distance - Yards	Muzzle	100	200	300	400	500
Velocity - fps	2685	2441	2210	1992	1767	1598
Energy - ft-lb	2401	1984	1627	1321	1064	850
Taylor KO values	18.1	16.4	14.9	13.4	11.9	10.8
Path - inches	-1.5	2.2	0.0	-9.3	-27.4	-56.5
Wind Drift - inches	0.0	1.0	4.0	9.5	17.9	29.5

G1 Ballistic Coefficient = 0.361

PMC 174-grain HP Boattail Match (303SMA)

Distance - Yards	Muzzle	100	200	300	400	500
Velocity - fps	2425	2254	2091	1936	1788	1651
Energy - ft-lb	2272	1963	1690	1448	1235	1053
Taylor KO values	16.3	15.2	14.1	13.0	12.0	11.1
Path - inches	-1.5	2.7	0.0	-10.6	-30.6	-61.3
Wind Drift - inches	0.0	0.8	3.3	7.8	14.4	23.3

G1 Ballistic Coefficient = 0.495

UMC (Remington) 174-grain MC (L303B1)

Distance - Yards	Muzzle	100	200	300	400	500
Velocity - fps	2475	2209	1960	1729	1520	1337
Energy - ft-lb	2366	1885	1484	1155	892	691
Taylor KO values	19.1	17.1	15.2	13.4	11.8	10.3
Path - inches	-1.5	2.8	0.0	-11.9	-35.6	-74.3
Wind Drift - inches	0.0	1.2	5.3	1.2.7	23.9	39.7

G1 Ballistic Coefficient = 0.495

Federal 180-grain Trophy Bonded Bear Claw - HE (P303T1)

Distance - Yards	Muzzle	100	200	300	400	500
Velocity - fps	2590	2350	2120	1900	1700	1520
Energy - ft-lb	2680	2205	1795	1445	1160	920
Taylor KO values	20.9	19.0	17.1	15.3	13.7	12.3
Path - inches	-1.5	2.4	0.0	-10.0	-30.0	-61.9
Wind Drift - inches	0.0	1.0	4.3	10.2	19.1	31.6

G1 Ballistic Coefficient = 0.357

Federal 180-grain Sierra Pro-Hunter SP (303AS)

Distance - Yards	Muzzle	100	200	300	400	500
Velocity - fps	2460	2230	2020	1820	1630	1460
Energy - ft-lb	2420	1985	1625	1315	1060	850
Taylor KO values	19.9	18.0	16.3	14.7	13.2	11.8
Path - inches	-1.5	2.8	0.0	-11.3	-33.2	-68.1
Wind Drift - inches	0.0	1.1	4.5	10.6	20.0	32.6

G1 Ballistic Coefficient = 0.370

Remington 180-grain SP Core-Lokt (R303B1)

Distance - Yards	Muzzle	100	200	300	400	500
Velocity - fps	2460	2124	1817	1542	1311	1137
Energy - ft-lb	2418	1803	1319	950	690	517
Taylor KO values	19.9	17.1	14.7	12.5	10.6	9.2
Path - inches	-1.5	2.9	0.0	-13.6	-42.2	-91.0
Wind Drift - inches	0.0	1.6	7.0	17.1	32.8	54.8

G1 Ballistic Coefficient = 0.247

Winchester 180-grain Power-Point (X303B1)

Distance - Yards	Muzzle	100	200	300	400	500
Velocity - fps	2460	2233	2018	1816	1629	1459
Energy - ft-lb	2418	1993	1627	1318	1060	851
Taylor KO values	19.9	18.0	16.3	14.7	13.2	11.8
Path - inches	-1.5	2.8	0.0	-11.3	-33.2	-68.2
Wind Drift - inches	0.0	1.1	4.5	10.6	19.8	32.6

G1 Ballistic Coefficient = 0.370

PMC 180-grain SP Boattail (303HB)

Distance - Yards	Muzzle	100	200	300	400	500
Velocity - fps	2450	2276	2110	1951	1799	1656
Energy - ft-lb	2399	2071	1780	1521	1294	1096
Taylor KO values	19.8	18.4	17.0	15.8	14.5	13.4
Path - inches	-1.5	2.6	0.0	-10.4	-30.1	-60.2
Wind Drift - inches	0.0	0.8	3.3	7.8	14.4	23.5

G1 Ballistic Coefficient = 0.486

.32-20 Winchester

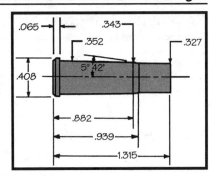

The .32-20 dates back to 1882. That's 117 years ago. Winchester designed the .32-20 to be a midpower rifle cartridge but it was also useful in revolvers. As is true with many of these old designations, the .32-20 isn't a .32 at all. The bore diameter is 0.305 inch. Today two companies make ammunition for this old-timer. Velocities and pressures are very low. The .32-20 isn't the caliber you would choose if you wanted a flat shooting varmint rifle.

Relative Recoil Factor = 0.55   **Controlling Agency : SAAMI**

Bullet Weight Grains	Velocity fps	Maximum Average Pressure		Standard barrel for velocity testing:
		Copper Crusher	Transducer	
100	1200	16,000 cup	N/S	24 inches long - 1 turn in 20 inch twist

---

Remington 100-grain Lead (R32201)

Distance - Yards	Muzzle	100	200	300	400	500
Velocity - fps	1210	1021	913	834	769	712
Energy - ft-lb	325	231	185	154	131	113
Taylor KO values	5.4	4.5	4.1	3.7	3.4	3.2
Path - inches	-1.5	15.8	0.0	-57.5	-165.1	-331.5
Wind Drift - inches	0.0	4.2	15.5	32.4	54.8	82.6

G1 Ballistic Coefficient = 0.167

Winchester 100-grain Lead (X32201)

Distance - Yards	Muzzle	100	200	300	400	500
Velocity - fps	1210	1021	913	834	769	712
Energy - ft-lb	325	231	185	154	131	113
Taylor KO values	5.4	4.5	4.1	3.7	3.4	3.2
Path - inches	-1.5	15.8	0.0	-57.5	-165.1	-331.5
Wind Drift - inches	0.0	4.2	15.5	32.4	54.8	82.6

G1 Ballistic Coefficient = 0.167

.32 Winchester Special

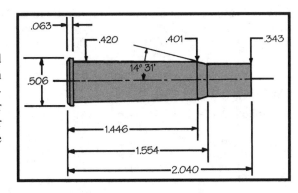

Winchester's .32 Winchester Special cartridge is another very old number. This cartridge is a real .32, using bullets that are 0.321 inch in diameter. It can be thought of as the .30-30 necked up to .32 caliber. Starting in 1895, Winchester's Model 94 rifles were available chambered for the .32 Win. Special. There have not been any guns built in this caliber since about 1960 and you can expect the caliber to be dropped from the inventory in the near future.

Relative Recoil Factor = 1.95   **Controlling Agency : SAAMI**

Bullet Weight Grains	Velocity fps	Maximum Average Pressure		Standard barrel for velocity testing:
		Copper Crusher	Transducer	
170	2235	38,000 cup	42,000 psi	24 inches long - 1 turn in 16 inch twist

---

Federal 170-grain Hi-Shok SP (32A)

Distance - Yards	Muzzle	100	200	300	400	500
Velocity - fps	2250	1920	1630	1370	1180	1040
Energy - ft-lb	1910	1395	1000	710	520	375
Taylor KO values	17.5	14.9	12.7	10.6	9.2	8.1
Path - inches	-1.5	4.00	0.0	-17.2	-52.3	-109.8
Wind Drift - inches	0.0	1.9	8.4	20.4	38.8	63.3

G1 Ballistic Coefficient = 0.238

Remington 170-grain SP Core-Lokt (R32WS2)

Distance - Yards	Muzzle	100	200	300	400	500
Velocity - fps	2250	1921	1626	1372	1175	1044
Energy - ft-lb	1910	1393	998	710	521	411
Taylor KO values	17.5	14.9	12.6	10.7	9.1	8.1
Path - inches	-1.5	4.0	0.0	-17.3	-53.2	-114.2
Wind Drift - inches	0.0	1.9	8.4	20.3	38.6	63.0

G1 Ballistic Coefficient = 0.239

Winchester 170-grain Power-Point (X32WS2)

Distance - Yards	Muzzle	100	200	300	400	500
Velocity - fps	2250	1870	1537	1267	1082	971
Energy - ft-lb	1911	1320	892	606	442	356
Taylor KO values	17.5	14.5	11.9	9.8	8.4	7.5
Path - inches	-1.5	4.3	0.0	-19.2	-60.2	-130.8
Wind Drift - inches	0.0	2.3	10.0	24.5	46.4	74.7

G1 Ballistic Coefficient = 0.205

8x57mm Mauser

The 8x57 mm Mauser was adopted as the standard German military cartridge in 1888. It has been around for a long time, and so have some of the guns that use this caliber. Exactly because some of these old guns still exist, the SAAMI pressure specifications are very modest (see below). Interestingly, the CIP (European) specifications allow the European manufacturers to load to considerably better performance. If you have an old gun it might be prudent to use only ammunition made in the USA although the European ammunition is entirely satisfactory in modern guns.

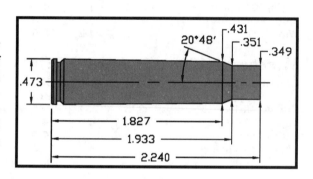

Relative Recoil Factor = 1.81   **Controlling Agency : SAAMI (see above)**

Bullet Weight Grains	Velocity fps	Maximum Average Pressure		Standard barrel for velocity testing:
		Copper Crusher	Transducer	
170	2340	37,000 cup	53,000 psi	24 inches long - 1 turn in 9.5 inch twist

Federal 170-grain Hi-Shok SP (8A)

Distance - Yards	Muzzle	100	200	300	400	500
Velocity - fps	2360	1970	1620	1330	1120	1000
Energy - ft-lb	2100	1465	995	670	475	375
Taylor KO values	18.5	15.5	12.7	10.4	8.8	7.8
Path - inches	-1.5	3.8	0.0	-17.1	-52.9	-111.9
Wind Drift - inches	0.0	2.1	9.2	22.7	43.5	71.0

G1 Ballistic Coefficient = 0.207

PMC 170-grain Pointed SP (8MA)

Distance - Yards	Muzzle	100	200	300	400	500
Velocity - fps	2360	2116	1888	1673	1493	1330
Energy - ft-lb	2102	1690	1345	1063	842	668
Taylor KO values	18.5	16.6	14.8	11.7	10.0	8.8
Path - inches	-1.5	3.2	0.0	-12.9	-38.2	-79.2
Wind Drift - inches	0.0	1.7	7.2	17.5	33.4	55.3

G1 Ballistic Coefficient = 0.255

Winchester 170-grain Power-Point (X8MM)

Distance - Yards	Muzzle	100	200	300	400	500
Velocity - fps	2360	1969	1622	1333	1123	997
Energy - ft-lb	2102	1463	993	671	476	375
Taylor KO values	18.5	15.4	12.7	10.5	8.8	7.8
Path - inches	-1.5	3.8	0.0	-17.2	-54.1	-118.6
Wind Drift - inches	0.0	2.1	9.3	23.0	44.0	71.8

G1 Ballistic Coefficient = 0.205

Norma 196-grain SP (18003)

Distance - Yards	Muzzle	100	200	300	400	500
Velocity - fps	2526	2244	1981	1737	1517	1327
Energy - ft-lb	2778	2192	1708	1314	1001	766
Taylor KO values	22.8	20.3	17.9	15.7	13.7	12.0
Path - inches	-1.5	2.7	0.0	-11.6	-34.9	-73.3
Wind Drift - inches	0.0	1.3	5.4	13.0	24.7	41.0

G1 Ballistic Coefficient = 0.305

Norma 196-grain Vulcan (18020)

Distance - Yards	Muzzle	100	200	300	400	500
Velocity - fps	2526	2278	2041	1821	1617	1434
Energy - ft-lb	2778	2256	1813	1443	1138	896
Taylor KO values	22.8	20.6	18.5	16.5	14.6	13.0
Path - inches	-1.5	2.6	0.0	-11.0	-32.6	-67.5
Wind Drift - inches	0.0	1.1	4.7	11.2	21.4	34.9

G1 Ballistic Coefficient = 0.347

8mm Remington Magnum

The 8mm Remington Magnum is a "full length" magnum cartridge. That is, it is the same length as the .375 H&H, the grandfather of all belted magnums. This gives the 8mm enough case volume to produce some impressive ballistics. While the SAAMI standards list two bullet weights, the 185-grain bullet has been dropped by Remington and replaced with a 200-grain load. This makes some sense since the .300 Magnums can all handle 180-grain bullets with ease. This cartridge is at least enough for all North American game, even the big bears.

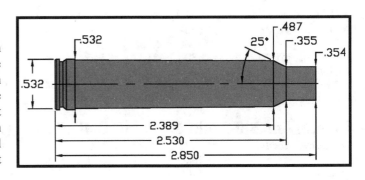

Relative Recoil Factor = 2.77   **Controlling Agency: SAAMI**

Bullet Weight Grains	Velocity fps	Maximum Average Pressure	
		Copper Crusher	Transducer
185	3065	54,000 cup	65,000 psi
220	2815	54,000 cup	65,000 psi

Standard barrel for velocity testing:
24 inches long - 1 turn in 9.5 inch twist

Remington 200-grain Swift A-Frame PSP (RS8MMRA)

Distance - Yards	Muzzle	100	200	300	400	500
Velocity - fps	2900	2623	2361	2115	1884	1671
Energy - ft-lb	3734	3054	2476	1987	1577	1240
Taylor KO values	26.8	24.2	21.8	19.5	17.4	15.4
Path - inches	-1.5	1.8	0.0	-8.0	-23.9	-49.6
Wind Drift - inches	0.0	0.9	4.0	9.4	17.6	29.2

G1 Ballistic Coefficient = 0.332

A² 220-grain Monolithic Solid (None)

Distance - Yards	Muzzle	100	200	300	400	500
Velocity - fps	2800	2501	2221	1959	1716	1499
Energy - ft-lb	3829	3055	2409	1875	1439	1097
Taylor KO values	28.4	25.4	22.5	19.9	17.4	15.2
Path - inches	-1.5	2.0	0.0	-9.1	-27.4	-57.6
Wind Drift - inches	0.0	1.1	4.7	11.1	21.1	35.2

G1 Ballistic Coefficient = 0.300

.338 Winchester Magnum

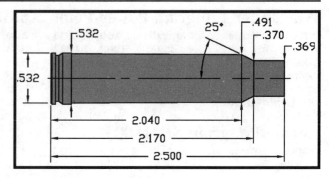

The .338 Winchester Magnum and the .264 Winchester Magnum were both introduced in 1958. The .338 is still going great while the .264 is on its last legs. That may well be because the .338 Win. Mag. filled a big void in the power spectrum of cartridges available at that time. The .338 is enough cartridge for any North American game including the big bears. At the same time, it can't realistically be called an "African" caliber. The .338 Winchester Magnum is one of the family of shortened magnums designed to fit into a standard length Model 70 action. The nearest competition comes from the 8mm Remington Magnum, which never achieved the popularity of the .338 Win. Mag.

Relative Recoil Factor = 2.93   **Controlling Agency : SAAMI**

Bullet Weight Grains	Velocity fps	Maximum Average Pressure	
		Copper Crusher	Transducer
200	2940	54,000 cup	64,000 psi
210	2855	54,000 cup	64,000 psi
225	2770	54,000 cup	64,000 psi
250	2645	54,000 cup	64,000 psi
300	2415	54,000 cup	64,000 psi

Standard barrel for velocity testing:
24 inches long - 1 turn in 10 inch twist

Winchester 200-grain Power-Point (X3381)

Distance - Yards	Muzzle	100	200	300	400	500
Velocity - fps	2960	2658	2375	2110	1862	1635
Energy - ft-lb	3890	3137	2505	1977	1539	1187
Taylor KO values	28.6	25.7	22.9	20.4	18.0	15.8
Path - inches	-1.5	2.0	0.0	-8.2	-24.3	-50.4
Wind Drift - inches	0.0	1.0	4.2	9.9	18.8	31.2

G1 Ballistic Coefficient = 0.308

Remington 200-grain PS Point, Ballistic Tip (PRT338WB)

Distance - Yards	Muzzle	100	200	300	400	500
Velocity - fps	2950	2724	2509	2303	2108	1922
Energy - ft-lb	3866	3295	2795	2357	1973	1641
Taylor KO values	28.5	26.3	24.2	22.2	20.4	18.6
Path - inches	-1.5	1.6	0.0	-7.1	-20.8	-42.4
Wind Drift - inches	0.0	0.7	3.0	7.1	13.2	21.5

G1 Ballistic Coefficient = 0.415

Winchester 200-grain Ballistic Silvertip (SBST338)

Distance - Yards	Muzzle	100	200	300	400	500
Velocity - fps	2950	2724	2509	2303	2108	1922
Energy - ft-lb	3866	3295	2795	2357	1973	1641
Taylor KO values	28.5	26.3	24.2	22.2	20.4	18.6
Path - inches	-1.5	1.6	0.0	-7.1	-20.8	-42.4
Wind Drift - inches	0.0	0.7	3.0	7.1	13.2	21.5

G1 Ballistic Coefficient = 0.415

Federal 210-grain Nosler Partition (P338A2)

Distance - Yards	Muzzle	100	200	300	400	500
Velocity - fps	2830	2600	2390	2180	1980	1800
Energy - ft-lb	3735	3160	2655	2215	1835	1505
Taylor KO values	28.7	26.4	24.2	22.1	20.1	18.3
Path - inches	-1.5	1.8	0.0	-8.0	-23.3	-47.3
Wind Drift - inches	0.0	0.8	3.3	7.8	14.6	23.8

G1 Ballistic Coefficient = 0.401

Remington 210-grain Nosler Partition (PRP338WC)

Distance - Yards	Muzzle	100	200	300	400	500
Velocity - fps	2830	2602	2385	2179	1983	1798
Energy - ft-lb	3734	3157	2653	2214	1834	1508
Taylor KO values	28.7	26.4	24.2	22.1	20.1	18.2
Path - inches	-1.5	1.8	0.0	-7.9	-23.2	-47.4
Wind Drift - inches	0.0	0.8	3.3	7.8	14.6	23.9

G1 Ballistic Coefficient = 0.400

Hornady 225-grain SP - Heavy Magnum (8505)

Distance - Yards	Muzzle	100	200	300	400	500
Velocity - fps	2950	2714	2491	2278	2075	1884
Energy - ft-lb	4347	3680	3098	2591	2151	1772
Taylor KO values	32.0	29.5	27.1	24.7	22.5	20.5
Path - inches	-1.5	1.9	0.0	-7.5	-21.8	-44.1
Wind Drift - inches	0.0	0.8	3.2	7.4	13.8	22.6

G1 Ballistic Coefficient = 0.398

Federal 225-grain Trophy Bonded Bear Claw - HE (P338T2)

Distance - Yards	Muzzle	100	200	300	400	500
Velocity - fps	2940	2690	2450	2230	2010	1810
Energy - ft-lb	4320	3610	3000	2475	2025	1640
Taylor KO values	31.9	29.2	26.6	24.2	21.8	19.7
Path - inches	-1.5	1.7	0.0	-7.5	-22.0	-45.0
Wind Drift - inches	0.0	0.8	3.4	8.1	15.1	24.8

G1 Ballistic Coefficient = 0.371

Federal 225-grain Trophy Bonded Bear Claw (P338T1)

Distance - Yards	Muzzle	100	200	300	400	500
Velocity - fps	2800	2560	2330	2110	1900	1710
Energy - ft-lb	3915	3265	2700	2220	1800	1455
Taylor KO values	30.4	27.8	25.3	22.9	20.6	18.6
Path - inches	-1.5	1.9	0.0	-8.4	-24.5	-50.6
Wind Drift - inches	0.0	0.9	3.7	8.6	16.1	26.5

G1 Ballistic Coefficient = 0.373

Remington 225-grain Swift A-Frame Pointed SP (RS338WA)

Distance - Yards	Muzzle	100	200	300	400	500
Velocity - fps	2785	2517	2266	2029	1808	1605
Energy - ft-lb	3871	3165	2565	2057	1633	1286
Taylor KO values	30.3	27.3	24.6	22.0	19.6	17.4
Path - inches	-1.5	2.0	0.0	-8.8	-25.2	-54.1
Wind Drift - inches	0.0	1.0	4.1	9.8	18.4	30.5

G1 Ballistic Coefficient = 0.337

Federal 225-grain Sierra Pro-Hunter SP (338ES)

Distance - Yards	Muzzle	100	200	300	400	500
Velocity - fps	2780	2570	2380	2170	1980	1800
Energy - ft-lb	3860	3290	2780	2340	1960	1630
Taylor KO values	30.2	27.9	25.9	23.6	21.5	119.6
Path - inches	-1.5	1.9	0.0	-8.2	-23.7	-48.2
Wind Drift - inches	0.0	0.8	3.2	7.6	14.2	23.1

G1 Ballistic Coefficient = 0.420

Remington 225-grain Pointed SP Core-Lokt (R338W1)

Distance - Yards	Muzzle	100	200	300	400	500
Velocity - fps	2780	2572	2374	2184	2003	1832
Energy - ft-lb	3860	3305	2837	2389	1999	1663
Taylor KO values	30.2	27.9	25.8	23.7	21.8	19.9
Path - inches	-1.5	1.9	0.0	-8.1	-23.4	-47.5
Wind Drift - inches	0.0	0.8	3.1	7.3	13.6	22.2

G1 Ballistic Coefficient = 0.435

PMC 225-grain Barnes-X (338XA)

Distance - Yards	Muzzle	100	200	300	400	500
Velocity - fps	2780	2619	2464	2313	2168	2028
Energy - ft-lb	3860	3426	3032	2673	2348	2054
Taylor KO values	30.2	28.5	26.8	25.1	23.6	22.0
Path - inches	-1.5	1.8	0.0	-7.6	-21.6	-43.1
Wind Drift - inches	0.0	0.6	2.4	5.5	10.1	16.3

G1 Ballistic Coefficient = 0.523

Winchester 230-grain Fail Safe (S338XA)

Distance - Yards	Muzzle	100	200	300	400	500
Velocity - fps	2780	2573	2375	2186	2005	1834
Energy - ft-lb	3948	3382	1881	2441	2054	1719
Taylor KO values	30.9	28.6	26.4	24.3	22.3	20.4
Path - inches	-1.5	1.9	0.0	-8.1	-23.4	-47.4
Wind Drift - inches	0.0	0.8	3.1	7.3	13.5	22.1

G1 Ballistic Coefficient = 0.437

Federal 250-grain Nosler Partition - HE (P338D)

Distance - Yards	Muzzle	100	200	300	400	500
Velocity - fps	2800	2610	2420	2250	2080	1920
Energy - ft-lb	4350	3775	3260	2805	2395	2035
Taylor KO values	33.8	31.5	29.2	27.2	25.1	23.2
Path - inches	-1.5	1.8	0.0	-7.8	-22.5	-44.9
Wind Drift - inches	0.0	0.7	2.8	6.6	12.1	19.7

G1 Ballistic Coefficient = 0.476

Federal 250-grain Woodleigh Weldcore - HE (P338G)

Distance - Yards	Muzzle	100	200	300	400	500
Velocity - fps	2800	2610	2420	2240	2070	1910
Energy - ft-lb	4350	3770	3255	2795	2385	2025
Taylor KO values	33.8	31.5	29.2	27.0	25.0	23.1
Path - inches	-1.5	1.8	0.0	-7.8	-22.5	-45.0
Wind Drift - inches	0.0	0.7	2.8	6.6	12.3	20.0

G1 Ballistic Coefficient = 0.470

A² 250-grain Triad (None)

Distance - Yards	Muzzle	100	200	300	400	500
Velocity - fps	2700	2407	2133	1877	1653	1447
Energy - ft-lb	4046	3216	2526	1956	1516	1162
Taylor KO values	32.6	29.1	25.7	22.7	20.0	17.5
Path - inches	-1.5	2.3	0.0	-9.8	-29.8	-62.1
Wind Drift - inches	0.0	1.1	4.8	11.6	21.9	36.5

G1 Ballistic Coefficient = 0.304

A² 250-grain Sierra Spitzer Boattail (None)

Distance - Yards	Muzzle	100	200	300	400	500
Velocity - fps	2700	2568	2439	2314	2193	2075
Energy - ft-lb	4046	3659	3302	2972	2669	2390
Taylor KO values	32.6	31.0	29.4	27.9	26.5	25.0
Path - inches	-1.5	1.9	0.0	-7.7	-22.0	-43.4
Wind Drift - inches	0.0	0.5	2.0	4.7	8.6	13.8

G1 Ballistic Coefficient = 0.677

Federal 250-grain Woodleigh Weldcore (P338F)

Distance - Yards	Muzzle	100	200	300	400	500
Velocity - fps	2660	2470	2290	2120	1960	1800
Energy - ft-lb	3925	3395	2920	2495	2120	1785
Taylor KO values	32.1	29.8	27.6	25.6	23.7	21.7
Path - inches	-1.5	2.1	0.0	-8.8	-25.2	-50.7
Wind Drift - inches	0.0	0.7	3.1	7.2	13.2	21.5

G1 Ballistic Coefficient = 0.471

Federal 250-grain Nosler Partition (P338B2)

Distance - Yards	Muzzle	100	200	300	400	500
Velocity - fps	2660	2470	2290	2120	1960	1800
Energy - ft-lb	3925	3395	2920	2495	2120	1785
Taylor KO values	32.1	29.8	27.6	25.6	23.7	21.7
Path - inches	-1.5	2.1	0.0	-8.8	-25.2	-50.7
Wind Drift - inches	0.0	0.7	3.1	7.2	13.2	21.5

G1 Ballistic Coefficient = 0.471

Remington 250-grain Pointed SP Core-Lokt (R338W2)

Distance - Yards	Muzzle	100	200	300	400	500
Velocity - fps	2660	2456	2261	2075	1898	1731
Energy - ft-lb	3927	3348	2837	2389	1999	1663
Taylor KO values	32.1	29.6	27.3	25.0	22.9	20.9
Path - inches	-1.5	2.1	0.0	-8.9	-26.0	-52.7
Wind Drift - inches	0.0	0.8	3.4	7.9	14.6	23.9

G1 Ballistic Coefficient = 0.432

Norma 250-grain Nosler (18502)

Distance - Yards	Muzzle	100	200	300	400	500
Velocity - fps	2657	2470	2290	2118	1954	1797
Energy - ft-lb	3920	3387	2912	2490	2119	1797
Taylor KO values	32.1	29.8	27.6	25.6	23.6	21.7
Path - inches	-1.5	2.1	0.0	-8.7	-25.3	-50.9
Wind Drift - inches	0.0	0.8	3.1	7.2	13.3	21.6

G1 Ballistic Coefficient = 0.478

Winchester 250-grain Partition Gold (SPG338WM)

Distance - Yards	Muzzle	100	200	300	400	500
Velocity - fps	2650	2467	2291	2122	1960	1807
Energy - ft-lb	3899	3378	2914	2500	2134	1812
Taylor KO values	32.0	29.8	27.7	25.6	23.7	21.8
Path - inches	-1.5	2.1	0.0	-8.7	-25.2	-50.7
Wind Drift - inches	0.0	0.7	3.0	7.0	13.0	21.2

G1 Ballistic Coefficient = 0.480

Speer 250-grain Grand Slam (24511)

Distance - Yards	Muzzle	100	200	300	400	500
Velocity - fps	2645	2442	2247	2062	1886	1720
Energy - ft-lb	3883	3309	2803	2360	1976	1644
Taylor KO values	31.9	29.5	27.1	24.9	22.8	20.8
Path - inches	-1.5	2.2	0.0	-9.1	-26.2	-53.4
Wind Drift - inches	0.0	0.8	3.4	8.0	14.8	24.1

G1 Ballistic Coefficient = 0.432x

.338 A-Square

Developed in 1978, the .338 A^2 is a .338 caliber variation on the .378 Weatherby cartridge. Performance is similar to the .338-378, muzzle velocities being a little higher for two of the three bullet weights and a bit slower for the third. This cartridge was designed to fill the need for a flat-shooting round for long-range hunting of large game.

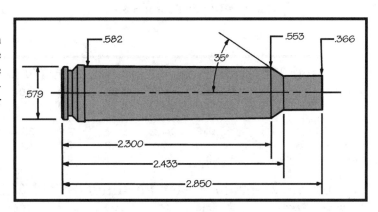

Relative Recoil Factor = 3.15

Controlling Agency : Factory

Standard barrel for velocity testing:
26 inches long - 1 turn in 10 inch twist

A^2 200-grain Nosler Ballistic Tip (None)

Distance - Yards	Muzzle	100	200	300	400	500
Velocity - fps	3500	3266	3045	2835	2634	2442
Energy - ft-lb	5440	4737	4117	3568	3081	2648
Taylor KO values	33.8	31.5	29.4	27.4	25.4	23.6
Path - Inch	-1.5	0.9	0.0	-4.6	-13.6	-27.6
Wind Drift - inches	0.0	0.5	2.2	5.1	9.3	15.0

G1 Ballistic Coefficient = 0.457

A^2 250-grain SBT (None)

Distance - Yards	Muzzle	100	200	300	400	500
Velocity - fps	3120	2974	2834	2697	2565	2436
Energy - ft-lb	5403	4911	4457	4038	3652	3295
Taylor KO values	37.7	35.9	34.2	32.6	31.0	29.4
Path - inches	-1.5	1.2	0.0	-5.6	-15.9	-31.5
Wind Drift - inches	0.0	0.4	1.7	3.8	7.0	11.2

G1 Ballistic Coefficient = 0.676

A² 250-grain Triad (None)

Distance - Yards	Muzzle	100	200	300	400	500
Velocity - fps	3120	2799	2500	2220	1938	1715
Energy - ft-lb	5403	4348	3469	2736	2128	1634
Taylor KO values	37.7	33.8	30.2	26.8	23.6	20.7
Path - inches	-1.5	1.5	0.0	-7.1	-21.2	-44.6
Wind Drift - inches	0.0	1.0	4.0	9.5	17.9	29.8

G1 Ballistic Coefficient = 0.300

8.59mm (.338) Lazzeroni Titan

Lazzeroni's 8.59mm Titan is a very large capacity .338 with performance to match the case volume. This cartridge significantly out-performs the .338 Winchester Magnum. In fact, it is the performance leader in the .338 class. The gun is certainly adequate for any North American game, including the large bears.

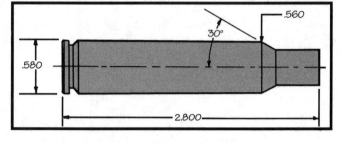

Relative Recoil Factor = 3.34

Controlling Agency: Factory

Lazzeroni 200-grain Nosler Partition (859TN200P)

Distance - Yards	Muzzle	100	200	300	400	500
Velocity - fps	3450	3230	3020	2820	2629	2445
Energy - ft-lb	5287	4633	4051	3533	3070	2656
Taylor KO values	33.3	31.2	29.2	27.2	25.4	23.6
Path - Inch	-1.5	0.9	0.0	-4.7	-13.8	-28.0
Wind Drift - inches	0.0	0.5	2.1	4.9	9.0	28.0

G1 Ballistic Coefficient = 0.478

Lazzeroni 225-grain Nosler Partition (859TN225P)

Distance - Yards	Muzzle	100	200	300	400	500
Velocity - fps	3300	3110	2927	2752	2584	2421
Energy - ft-lb	5422	4832	4282	3785	3336	2929
Taylor KO values	35.9	33.8	31.8	29.9	28.1	26.3
Path - inches	-1.5	1.0	0.0	-5.1	-14.8	-29.7
Wind Drift - inches	0.0	0.5	2.0	4.6	8.4	13.5

G1 Ballistic Coefficient = 0.536

Lazzeroni 250-grain Swift A-Frame (859TN250A)

Distance - Yards	Muzzle	100	200	300	400	500
Velocity - fps	3150	2977	2810	2649	2494	2344
Energy - ft-lb	5510	4920	4384	3896	3453	3050
Taylor KO values	38.0	35.9	33.9	32.0	30.1	28.3
Path - inches	-1.5	1.2	0.0	-5.6	-16.2	-32.4
Wind Drift - inches	0.0	0.5	2.0	4.6	8.3	13.4

G1 Ballistic Coefficient = 0.570

.338-378 Weatherby Magnum

As with the .30-378, Weatherby has responded to what wildcatters have been doing for years and "formalized" the .338-378. This is a very potent cartridge, one that is suitable for African game except for the most dangerous beasties. Driving a 250-grain bullet in excess of 3000 fps produces a recoil that certainly gets your attention. This is hardly a caliber for plinking tin cans.

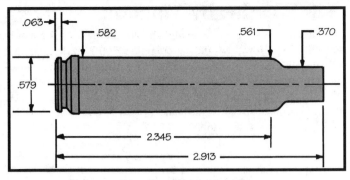

Relative Recoil Factor = 3.22

Controlling Agency: Factory

Standard barrel for velocity testing:
26 inches long - 1 turn in 10 inch twist

Weatherby 200-grain Nosler Ballsitic Tip (N 333 200 BST)

Distance - Yards	Muzzle	100	200	300	400	500
Velocity - fps	3350	3145	2949	2761	2582	2409
Energy - ft-lb	4983	4391	3861	3386	2959	2576
Taylor KO values	32.4	30.4	28.5	26.7	24.9	23.3
Path - inches	-1.5	1.0	0.0	-5.0	-14.6	-29.4
Wind Drift - inches	0.0	0.5	2.1	4.8	8.9	14.3

G1 Ballistic Coefficient = 0.502

Weatherby 225-grain Barnes-X (B 333 225 XS)

Distance - Yards	Muzzle	100	200	300	400	500
Velocity - fps	3180	2874	2778	2591	2410	2238
Energy - ft-lb	5052	4420	3856	3353	2902	2501
Taylor KO values	34.5	31.2	30.2	28.1	26.2	24.3
Path - inches	-1.5	1.2	0.0	-5.7	-16.6	-33.5
Wind Drift - inches	0.0	0.6	2.3	5.4	9.9	16.0

G1 Ballistic Coefficient = 0.482

Weatherby 250-grain Nosler Partition (N 333 250 PT)

Distance - Yards	Muzzle	100	200	300	400	500
Velocity - fps	3060	2856	2662	2478	2297	2125
Energy - ft-lb	5197	4528	3933	3401	2927	2507
Taylor KO values	36.9	34.5	32.1	29.9	27.7	25.7
Path - inches	-1.5	1.4	0.0	-6.3	-18.3	-36.9
Wind Drift - inches	0.0	0.6	2.5	5.8	10.7	17.4

G1 Ballistic Coefficient = 0.473

.340 Weatherby Magnum

The .340 Weatherby Magnum was Weatherby's 1962 entry in the .338 derby. It follows the pattern of the .300 Wby. Mag., being little more than the .300 necked up to .340. Until the recent introduction of the .338-378, the .340 Weatherby was the king of the .338s in terms of performance. As with many other cartridge names, the .340 number has no significance. This is a .338 caliber cartridge, and a potent one, too.

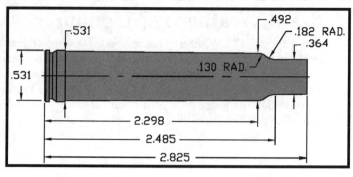

Relative Recoil Factor = 3.33

Controlling Agency : CIP

Bullet Weight Grains	Velocity fps	Maximum Average Pressure		Standard barrel for velocity testing:
		Copper Crusher	**Transducer**	
N/S	N/S	3800 bar	4370 bar	26 inches long - 1 turn in 10 inch twist

Weatherby 200-grain Nosler Ballistic Tip (N 340 200 BST)

Distance - Yards	Muzzle	100	200	300	400	500
Velocity - fps	3221	2980	2753	2536	2329	2133
Energy - ft-lb	4607	3944	3364	2856	2409	2020
Taylor KO values	31.1	29.2	27.3	25.6	23.9	22.3
Path - inches	-1.5	1.2	0.0	-5.8	-17.0	-34.7
Wind Drift - inches	0.0	0.6	2.7	6.3	11.6	18.9

G1 Ballistic Coefficient = 0.414

Weatherby 200-grain Hornady SP (H 340 200 SP)

Distance - Yards	Muzzle	100	200	300	400	500
Velocity - fps	3221	2946	2688	2444	2213	1995
Energy - ft-lb	4607	3854	3208	2652	2174	1767
Taylor KO values	31.1	28.4	26.0	23.6	21.4	19.3
Path - inches	-1.5	2.3	0.0	-6.1	-18.0	-37.0
Wind Drift - inches	0.0	0.8	3.1	7.3	13.6	22.4

G1 Ballistic Coefficient = 0.361

Weatherby 210-grain Nosler Partition (H 340 210 PT)

Distance - Yards	Muzzle	100	200	300	400	500
Velocity - fps	3211	2963	2728	2505	2293	2092
Energy - ft-lb	4807	4093	3470	2927	2452	2040
Taylor KO values	32.6	30.0	27.7	25.4	23.3	21.2
Path - inches	-1.5	1.2	0.0	-5.9	-17.4	-35.5
Wind Drift - inches	0.0	0.7	2.8	6.6	12.1	19.8

G1 Ballistic Coefficient = 0.400

Weatherby 225-grain Hornady SP (H 340 225 SP)

Distance - Yards	Muzzle	100	200	300	400	500
Velocity - fps	3066	2824	2595	2377	2170	1973
Energy - ft-lb	4696	3984	3364	2822	2352	1944
Taylor KO values	33.3	30.7	28.2	25.8	23.6	21.4
Path - inches	-1.5	1.4	0.0	-6.6	-19.4	-39.6
Wind Drift - inches	0.0	1.4	3.0	7.0	13.1	21.4

G1 Ballistic Coefficient = 0.397

Weatherby 225-grain Barnes-X (B 340 225 XS)

Distance - Yards	Muzzle	100	200	300	400	500
Velocity - fps	3001	2804	2615	2434	2260	2093
Energy - ft-lb	4499	3927	3416	2959	2551	2189
Taylor KO values	32.6	30.5	28.4	26.4	24.6	22.7
Path - inches	-1.5	1.5	0.0	-6.6	-19.0	-38.3
Wind Drift - inches	0.0	0.6	2.5	5.9	10.8	17.5

G1 Ballistic Coefficient = 0.482

Weatherby 250-grain Nosler Partition (N 340 250 PT)

Distance - Yards	Muzzle	100	200	300	400	500
Velocity - fps	2941	2743	2553	2371	2197	2029
Energy - ft-lb	4801	4176	3618	3120	2678	2286
Taylor KO values	35.5	33.1	30.8	28.6	26.5	24.5
Path - inches	-1.5	1.6	0.0	-6.9	-20.0	-40.4
Wind Drift - inches	0.0	0.6	2.6	6.2	11.4	18.4

G1 Ballistic Coefficient = 0.473

Weatherby 200-grain Hornady SP (H 340 250 SP)

Distance - Yards	Muzzle	100	200	300	400	500
Velocity - fps	2963	2745	2537	2338	2149	1968
Energy - ft-lb	4873	4182	3572	3035	2563	2150
Taylor KO values	35.8	33.1	30.6	28.2	25.9	23.8
Path - inches	-1.5	1.6	0.0	-7.0	-20.3	-41.2
Wind Drift - inches	0.0	0.7	2.9	6.8	12.5	20.4

G1 Ballistic Coefficient = 0.431

A² 250-grain Sierra Spitzer Boattail (None)

Distance - Yards	Muzzle	100	200	300	400	500
Velocity - fps	2820	2684	2552	2424	2299	2179
Energy - ft-lb	4414	3999	3615	3261	2935	2635
Taylor KO values	34.0	32.4	30.8	29.3	27.6	26.3
Path - inches	-1.5	1.7	0.0	-7.2	-20.7	-41.3
Wind Drift - inches	0.0	0.6	2.3	5.2	9.6	15.5

G1 Ballistic Coefficient = 0.579

A² 250-grain Triad (None)

Distance - Yards	Muzzle	100	200	300	400	500
Velocity - fps	2820	2520	2238	1976	1741	1522
Energy - ft-lb	4414	3524	2781	2166	1683	1286
Taylor KO values	34.0	30.4	27.0	23.9	21.0	18.4
Path - inches	-1.5	2.0	0.0	-9.0	-26.8	-56.2
Wind Drift - inches	0.0	1.1	4.6	10.9	20.6	34.3

G1 Ballistic Coefficient = 0.303

.35 Remington

When Remington introduced their new .35 caliber in 1908 it was intended as a mild round for the Model 6 semi-automatic rifle. Later it was offered in a number of slide-action and lever-action guns. Even with the pressure levels very low by modern standards, this cartridge offers more punch than the .30-30 but falls considerably short of what can be achieved by the .35 Whelen. While this cartridge is adequate for deer-sized game under brush hunting conditions, it's popularity is slowly declining except for the single shot pistol (one-hand rifle) market.

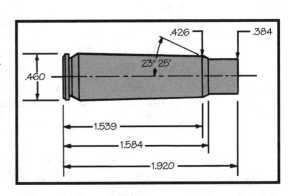

Relative Recoil Factor = 1.87

Controlling Agency: SAAMI

Bullet Weight Grains	Velocity fps	Maximum Average Pressure	
		Copper Crusher	Transducer
150	2275	35,000 cup	33,500 psi
200	2055	35,000 cup	33,500 psi

Standard barrel for velocity testing:
24 inches long - 1 turn in 16 inch twist

Remington 150-grain Pointed SP Core-Lokt (R35R1)

Distance - Yards	Muzzle	100	200	300	400	500
Velocity - fps	2300	1874	1506	1218	1039	934
Energy - ft-lb	1762	1169	755	494	359	291
Taylor KO values	17.7	14.4	11.6	9.4	8.0	7.2
Path - inches	-1.5	4.3	0.0	-19.9	-63.2	-138.7
Wind Drift - inches	0.0	2.5	11.0	27.2	51.6	82.4

G1 Ballistic Coefficient = 0.184

Federal 200-grain Hi-Shok SP (35A)

Distance - Yards	Muzzle	100	200	300	400	500
Velocity - fps	2080	1700	1380	1140	1000	910
Energy - ft-lb	1920	1280	840	575	445	368
Taylor KO values	21.3	17.4	14.2	11.7	10.3	9.3
Path - inches	-1.5	5.4	0.0	-23.3	-70.0	-144.0
Wind Drift - inches	0.0	2.7	12.0	29.0	53.3	83.4

G1 Ballistic Coefficient = 0.193

Remington 200-grain SP Core-Lokt (R35R2)

Distance - Yards	Muzzle	100	200	300	400	500
Velocity - fps	2080	1698	1376	1140	1001	911
Energy - ft-lb	1921	1280	841	577	445	369
Taylor KO values	21.3	17.4	14.1	11.7	10.3	9.3
Path - inches	-1.5	5.4	0.0	-23.3	-70.0	-144.0
Wind Drift - inches	0.0	2.7	12.0	29.0	53.3	83.4

G1 Ballistic Coefficient = 0.193

Winchester 200-grain Power-Point (X35R1)

Distance - Yards	Muzzle	100	200	300	400	500
Velocity - fps	2020	1646	1335	1114	985	901
Energy - ft-lb	1812	1203	791	551	431	366
Taylor KO values	20.7	16.9	13.7	11.4	10.1	9.2
Path - inches	-1.5	5.8	0.0	-25.4	-78.8	-168.0
Wind Drift - inches	0.0	2.8	12.4	29.8	54.3	84.4

G1 Ballistic Coefficient = 0.193

.35 Whelen

Named for Col. Townsend Whelen, this cartridge is nothing but a .30-06 necked to .35 caliber. There is some disagreement whether Col. Whelen or gunmaker James Howe developed the cartridge in the early 1920s, but that matters little since in all probability they worked together. Besides, necking an existing cartridge to another caliber is hardly the epitome of the cartridge designer's art. The .35 Whelen can handle bullets up to 250 grains and that produces some impressive Taylor KO values numbers, especially for a cartridge based on the .30-06 case.

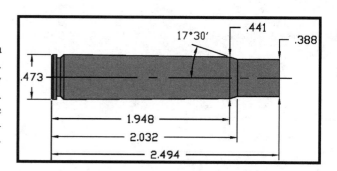

Relative Recoil Factor = 2.64   **Controlling Agency: SAAMI**

Bullet Weight Grains	Velocity fps	Maximum Average Pressure		Standard barrel for velocity testing:
		Copper Crusher	Transducer	
200	2660	52,000 cup	N/S	24 inches long - 1 turn in 12 inch twist

Remington 200-grain Pointed SP (R35WH1)

Distance - Yards	Muzzle	100	200	300	400	500
Velocity - fps	2675	2378	2100	1842	1606	1399
Energy - ft-lb	3177	2510	1968	1506	1146	869
Taylor KO values	27.3	24.3	21.4	18.8	16.4	14.3
Path - inches	-1.5	2.3	0.0	-10.3	-30.9	-65.0
Wind Drift - inches	0.0	1.2	5.1	12.2	23.2	38.7

G1 Ballistic Coefficient = 0.294

Federal 225-grain Trophy Bonded Bear Claw (P35WT1)

Distance - Yards	Muzzle	100	200	300	400	500
Velocity - fps	2600	2400	2200	2020	1846	1670
Energy - ft-lb	3378	2879	2429	2041	1703	1414
Taylor KO values	29.8	27.5	25.2	23.2	21.2	19.2
Path - inches	-1.5	2.3	0.0	-9.4	-27.3	-56.0
Wind Drift - inches	0.0	0.8	3.6	8.4	15.5	25.4

G1 Ballistic Coefficient = 0.423

Remington 250-grain Pointed SP (R35WH3)

Distance - Yards	Muzzle	100	200	300	400	500
Velocity - fps	2400	2196	2005	1823	1653	1497
Energy - ft-lb	3197	2680	2230	1844	1570	1244
Taylor KO values	30.6	28.0	25.6	23.2	21.1	19.1
Path - inches	-1.5	2.9	0.0	-11.5	-33.6	-68.3
Wind Drift - inches	0.0	1.0	4.2	9.8	18.2	29.8

G1 Ballistic Coefficient = 0.410

.356 Winchester

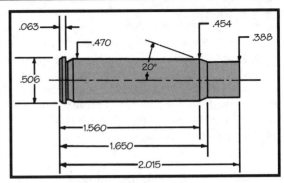

Designed as a rimmed version of the .358 Winchester for use in lever-action rifles, the .356 Winchester is a .35-caliber version of the .307 Winchester. The internal ballistics of this cartridge suffer a little because of the lower pressures allowable to be compatible with the lever-action guns. The exterior ballistics also suffer from the flat-nosed bullet that is needed for use in tubular magazines. Still, the .356 is a an excellent choice for deer-sized game, especially in eastern type conditions where game is nearly always taken at very modest ranges. In very light rifles the .356's recoil gets to be a problem for recoil sensitive shooters. Like the .307, short-barreled guns will yield lower muzzle velocities.

Relative Recoil Factor = 2.22   **Controlling Agency : SAAMI**

Bullet Weight Grains	Velocity fps	Maximum Average Pressure		Standard barrel for velocity testing:
		Copper Crusher	Transducer	
200	2370	52,000 cup	N/S	24 inches long - 1 turn in 12 inch twist
250	2075	52,000 cup	N/S	

Winchester 200-grain Power-Point (X3561)

Distance - Yards	Muzzle	100	200	300	400	500
Velocity - fps	2460	2114	1797	1517	1284	1113
Energy - ft-lb	2688	1985	1434	1022	732	550
Taylor KO values	25.2	21.6	18.4	15.5	13.1	11.4
Path - inches	-1.5	3.2	0.0	-14.0	-43.3	-93.7
Wind Drift - inches	0.0	1.7	7.3	17.8	34.3	57.1

G1 Ballistic Coefficient = 0.239

.357 Magnum (Rifle Data)

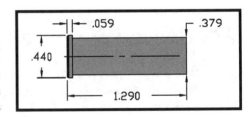

The high performance pistol cartridges, especially the .357 Magnum and the .44 Remington Magnum, can be effectively shot from rifle length barrels. They are especially useful for carbine-size rifles, since they have light recoil and provide good effectiveness at short ranges. The loads shown below have the same product numbers as the comparable pistol loads produced by these same companies. They represent identical loading levels. While all pistol ammunition in this caliber is suitable for use in rifles chambered for this cartridge, you can occasionally find some ammunition marked for "Rifles Only." See the .357 Magnum pistol listing for more information.

Relative Recoil Factor = 1.30   **Controlling Agency : SAAMI***

* See pistol data section for detailed specifications.
The data below was taken in the barrel lengths listed with each loading.

Winchester 158-grain JSP (X3575P) [20-inch barrel data]

Distance - Yards	Muzzle	100	200	300	400	500
Velocity - fps	1830	1427	1138	980	883	809
Energy - ft-lb	1175	715	454	337	274	229
Taylor KO values	14.8	11.5	9.2	7.9	7.1	6.5
Path - inches	-1.5	7.9	0.0	-34.6	-105.4	-220.7
Wind Drift - inches	0.0	3.9	16.7	38.2	66.2	100.0

G1 Ballistic Coefficient = 0.163

Federal 180-grain Hi-Shok HP (357G) [18-inch barrel data]

Distance - Yards	Muzzle	100	200	300	400	500
Velocity - fps	1550	1160	980	860	770	680
Energy - ft-lb	960	535	385	295	235	185
Taylor KO values	14.3	10.7	9.0	7.9	7.1	6.3
Path - inches	-1.5	12.5	0.0	-50.9	-151.5	-313.7
Wind Drift - inches	0.0	6.0	23.1	48.4	81.0	120.9

G1 Ballistic Coefficient = 0.125

.375 Winchester

In 1978 Winchester introduced the .375 Winchester. This cartridge is certainly not a .375 Magnum. In terms of both energy and Taylor KO values, the .375 is inferior to the .356 Winchester. This cartridge can be thought of as a .30-30 necked to .375 caliber. The only bullet that is factory loaded is a 200-grain Power-Point. It is intended for the Model 94 Big Bore lever action that tolerates high pressures. No full size rifles are currently being chambered for this cartridge, but it is chambered in some single shot pistols.

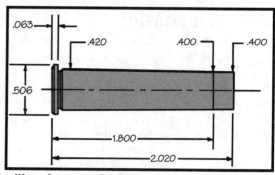

Relative Recoil Factor = 1.98

Controlling Agency: SAAMI

Bullet Weight Grains	Velocity fps	Maximum Average Pressure	
		Copper Crusher	Transducer
200	2180	52,000 cup	N/S
250	1885	52,000 cup	N/S

Standard barrel for velocity testing:
24 inches long - 1 turn in 12 inch twist

Winchester 200-grain Power-Point (X375W)

Distance - Yards	Muzzle	100	200	300	400	500
Velocity - fps	2200	1841	1526	1268	1089	980
Energy - ft-lb	2150	1506	1034	714	527	427
Taylor KO values	23.6	19.8	16.4	13.6	11.7	10.5
Path - inches	-1.5	4.4	0.0	-19.5	-60.7	-131.1
Wind Drift - inches	0.0	2.2	9.8	23.8	44.9	72.2

G1 Ballistic Coefficient = 0.215

.375 Holland & Holland Magnum

The British rifle-making firm of Holland and Holland wanted something new and different in 1912 when they introduced their .375 H&H. It was common for gunmakers in those days to have their own proprietary cartridges. Of course we don't do that any more, not much. The names Weatherby, Lazeroni, A², and Dakota come to mind as carrying on that practice, at least to a degree. The .375 H&H is the smallest "African" cartridge allowed in many countries. It has proved its worth with nearly 90 years of exemplary field history. A few years after its introduction the .375 H&H led to the .300 H&H and that number begat nearly all the other belted magnums we use today. The .375 H&H has a well earned place in cartridge history.

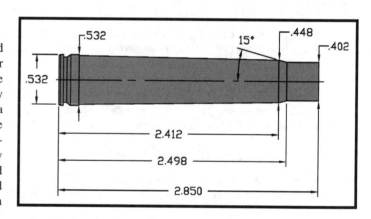

Relative Recoil Factor = 3.42

Controlling Agency: SAAMI*

Bullet Weight Grains	Velocity fps	Maximum Average Pressure	
		Copper Crusher	Transducer
270	2680	53,000 cup	62,000 psi
300	2515	53,000 cup	62,000 psi

Standard barrel for velocity testing:
24 inches long - 1 turn in 12 inch twist

* Some ammunition that is available in this caliber is manufactured to CIP (European) specifications.

Hornady 270-grain SP - Heavy Magnum (8508)

Distance - Yards	Muzzle	100	200	300	400	500
Velocity - fps	2870	2620	2385	2162	1957	1767
Energy - ft-lb	4937	4116	3408	2802	2296	1871
Taylor KO values	41.6	38.0	34.6	31.4	28.4	25.6
Path - inches	-1.5	2.2	0.0	-8.4	-23.9	-48.8
Wind Drift - inches	0.0	0.8	3.5	8.3	15.5	25.5

G1 Ballistic Coefficient = 0.374

Federal 270-grain Hi-Shok SP (375A)

Distance - Yards	Muzzle	100	200	300	400	500
Velocity - fps	2690	2420	2170	1920	1700	1500
Energy - ft-lb	4340	3510	2810	2220	1740	1351
Taylor KO values	39.0	35.1	31.5	27.8	24.7	21.8
Path - inches	-1.5	2.4	0.0	-10.9	-33.3	-71.2
Wind Drift - inches	0.0	1.1	4.5	10.8	20.4	33.8

G1 Ballistic Coefficient = 0.324

Remington 270-grain SP (R375M1)

Distance - Yards	Muzzle	100	200	300	400	500
Velocity - fps	2690	2420	2166	1928	1707	1507
Energy - ft-lb	4337	3510	2812	2228	1747	1361
Taylor KO values	39.0	35.1	31.4	28.0	24.8	21.9
Path - inches	-1.5	2.2	0.0	-9.7	-28.7	-59.8
Wind Drift - inches	0.0	1.1	4.5	10.7	20.2	33.5

G1 Ballistic Coefficient = 0.326

Winchester 270-grain Fail Safe (S375HX)

Distance - Yards	Muzzle	100	200	300	400	500
Velocity - fps	2670	2447	2344	2033	1842	1664
Energy - ft-lb	4275	3570	2994	2478	2035	1662
Taylor KO values	38.7	35.5	32.4	29.5	26.7	24.1
Path - inches	-1.5	2.0	0.0	-9.1	-28.7	-54.5
Wind Drift - inches	0.0	0.9	3.7	8.8	16.4	26.8

G1 Ballistic Coefficient = 0.388

Kynoch 270-grain Soft Nose

Distance - Yards	Muzzle	100	200	300	400	500
Velocity - fps	2650	2415	2189	1977	1778	1594
Energy - ft-lb	4210	3496	2874	2344	1895	1524
Taylor KO values	38.4	35.0	31.7	28.7	25.8	23.1
Path - inches	-1.5	2.2	0.0	-9.5	-28.0	-57.5
Wind Drift - inches	0.0	1.0	4.0	9.5	17.7	29.2

G1 Ballistic Coefficient = 0.370

PMC 270-grain Barnes-X (375XA)

Distance - Yards	Muzzle	100	200	300	400	500
Velocity - fps	2690	2528	2372	2221	2076	1936
Energy - ft-lb	4337	3831	3371	2957	2582	2247
Taylor KO values	39.0	36.7	34.4	32.2	30.1	28.1
Path - inches	-1.5	2.0	0.0	-8.2	-23.4	-28.1
Wind Drift - inches	0.0	0.6	2.6	5.9	10.9	17.6

G1 Ballistic Coefficient = 0.549

Speer 285-grain Grand Slam (24512)

Distance - Yards	Muzzle	100	200	300	400	500
Velocity - fps	2610	2365	2134	1916	1712	1527
Energy - ft-lb	4310	3540	2883	2323	1856	1475
Taylor KO values	40.0	36.2	32.7	29.3	26.2	23.4
Path - inches	-1.5	2.4	0.0	-9.9	-29.6	-61.0
Wind Drift - inches	0.0	1.0	4.3	10.2	19.1	31.6

G1 Ballistic Coefficient = 0.354

Federal 300-grain Trophy Bonded Bear Claw - HE (P375T3)

Distance - Yards	Muzzle	100	200	300	400	500
Velocity - fps	2700	2440	2190	1960	1740	1540
Energy - ft-lb	4855	3960	3195	2550	2020	1585
Taylor KO values	43.5	39.3	35.3	31.6	28.0	24.8
Path - inches	-1.5	2.2	0.0	-9.4	-28.0	-58.3
Wind Drift - inches	0.0	1.0	4.4	10.4	19.6	32.4

G1 Ballistic Coefficient = 0.333

Norma 300-grain TXP Line, Swift (19503)

Distance - Yards	Muzzle	100	200	300	400	500
Velocity - fps	2560	2296	2049	1818	1607	1418
Energy - ft-lb	4363	3513	2798	2203	1720	1339
Taylor KO values	41.3	37.0	33.0	29.3	25.9	22.9
Path - inches	-1.5	2.6	0.0	-10.9	-32.3	-67.3
Wind Drift - inches	0.0	1.2	4.9	11.6	21.9	36.3

G1 Ballistic Coefficient = 0.325

A² 300-grain Sierra Spitzer Boattail (None)

Distance - Yards	Muzzle	100	200	300	400	500
Velocity - fps	2550	2415	2284	2157	2034	1914
Energy - ft-lb	4331	3884	3474	3098	2755	2441
Taylor KO values	41.1	38.9	36.8	34.8	32.8	30.8
Path - inches	-1.5	2.2	0.0	-8.9	-25.3	-50.1
Wind Drift - inches	0.0	0.6	2.4	5.4	9.9	16.0

G1 Ballistic Coefficient = 0.641

A² 300-grain Triad (None)

Distance - Yards	Muzzle	100	200	300	400	500
Velocity - fps	2550	2251	1973	1717	1496	1302
Energy - ft-lb	4331	3375	2592	1964	1491	1130
Taylor KO values	41.1	36.3	31.8	27.7	24.1	21.0
Path - inches	-1.5	2.7	0.0	-11.7	-35.1	-75.1
Wind Drift - inches	0.0	1.3	5.6	13.5	25.7	42.9

G1 Ballistic Coefficient = 0.287

Norma 300-grain SP (19502)

Distance - Yards	Muzzle	100	200	300	400	500
Velocity - fps	2550	2211	1900	1619	1377	1185
Energy - ft-lb	4329	3258	2406	1747	1263	936
Taylor KO values	41.1	35.6	30.6	26.1	22.2	19.1
Path - inches	-1.5	2.8	0.0	-12.6	-38.5	-82.8
Wind Drift - inches	0.0	1.5	6.6	16.0	30.7	51.4

G1 Ballistic Coefficient = 0.257

Federal 300-grain Nosler Partition (P375F)

Distance - Yards	Muzzle	100	200	300	400	500
Velocity - fps	2530	2320	2120	1930	1750	1590
Energy - ft-lb	4265	3585	2995	2475	2040	1675
Taylor KO values	40.8	37.4	34.2	31.1	28.2	25.6
Path - inches	-1.5	2.5	0.0	-10.3	-29.9	-60.8
Wind Drift - inches	0.0	0.9	3.8	9.0	16.8	27.6

G1 Ballistic Coefficient = 0.409

Federal 300-grain Trophy Bonded Bear Claw (P375T1)

Distance - Yards	Muzzle	100	200	300	400	500
Velocity - fps	2530	2280	2040	1810	1610	1425
Energy - ft-lb	4265	3450	2765	2190	1725	1350
Taylor KO values	40.8	366.7	32.9	29.2	25.9	23.0
Path - inches	-1.5	2.6	0.0	-10.9	-32.8	-67.8
Wind Drift - inches	0.0	1.1	4.8	11.4	21.4	35.5

G1 Ballistic Coefficient = 0.335

Federal 300-grain Hi-Shok SP (375B)

Distance - Yards	Muzzle	100	200	300	400	500
Velocity - fps	2530	2270	2020	1790	1580	1400
Energy - ft-lb	4265	3425	2720	2135	1665	1308
Taylor KO values	40.8	36.6	32.6	28.8	25.5	22.6
Path - inches	-1.5	2.6	0.0	-11.2	-33.3	-69.1
Wind Drift - inches	0.0	1.2	4.9	11.8	22.2	36.8

G1 Ballistic Coefficient = 0.326

Remington 300-grain Swift A-Frame Pointed SP (RS375MA)

Distance - Yards	Muzzle	100	200	300	400	500
Velocity - fps	2530	2245	1979	1733	1512	1321
Energy - ft-lb	4262	3357	2608	2001	1523	1163
Taylor KO values	40.8	36.2	31.9	27.9	24.4	21.3
Path - inches	-1.5	2.7	0.0	-11.7	-35.0	-73.6
Wind Drift - inches	0.0	1.3	5.5	13.1	24.9	41.5

G1 Ballistic Coefficient = 0.297

Winchester 300-grain Fail Safe (S375HXA)

Distance - Yards	Muzzle	100	200	300	400	500
Velocity - fps	2530	2336	2151	1974	1806	1649
Energy - ft-lb	4265	3636	3082	2596	2174	1812
Taylor KO values	40.8	37.6	34.7	31.8	29.1	26.6
Path - inches	-1.5	2.4	0.0	-10.0	-26.9	-58.4
Wind Drift - inches	0.0	0.8	3.5	8.3	15.4	25.2

G1 Ballistic Coefficient = 0.441

PMC 300-grain Barnes-X (375XB)

Distance - Yards	Muzzle	100	200	300	400	500
Velocity - fps	2530	2389	2252	2120	1993	1870
Energy - ft-lb	4263	3801	3378	2994	2644	2329
Taylor KO values	40.8	38.5	36.3	34.2	32.1	30.1
Path - inches	-1.5	2.3	0.0	-9.2	-26.1	-51.8
Wind Drift - inches	0.0	0.6	2.5	5.8	10.6	17.1

G1 Ballistic Coefficient = 0.610

Hornady 300-grain FMJ Round Nose - Heavy Magnum (8509)

Distance - Yards	Muzzle	100	200	300	400	500
Velocity - fps	2705	2376	2072	1804	1560	1356
Energy - ft-lb	4873	3760	2861	2167	1621	1222
Taylor KO values	43.6	38.3	33.4	29.1	25.1	21.9
Path - inches	-1.5	2.7	0.0	-10.8	-32.1	-68.4
Wind Drift - inches	0.0	1.3	5.4	13.0	24.7	41.4

G1 Ballistic Coefficient = 0.276

Speer 300-grain African Grand Slam Tungsten Solid (24517)

Distance - Yards	Muzzle	100	200	300	400	500
Velocity - fps	2609	2277	1970	1690	1443	1241
Energy - ft-lb	4534	3453	2585	1903	1387	1025
Taylor KO values	42.0	36.7	31.7	27.2	23.3	20.0
Path - inches	-1.5	2.6	0.0	-11.7	-35.6	-76.4
Wind Drift - inches	0.0	1.4	6.1	14.9	28.5	47.8

G1 Ballistic Coefficient = 0.258

Federal 300-grain Trophy Bonded Sledgehammer (P375T2)

Distance - Yards	Muzzle	100	200	300	400	500
Velocity - fps	2530	2160	1820	1520	1280	1100
Energy - ft-lb	4265	3105	2210	1550	1090	810
Taylor KO values	40.8	34.8	29.3	24.5	20.6	17.7
Path - inches	-1.5	3.0	0.0	-13.7	-42.5	-92.9
Wind Drift - inches	0.0	1.7	7.5	18.4	35.6	59.6

G1 Ballistic Coefficient = 0.225

.375 A-Square

The .375 A² is Art Alphin's high-performance vision for this caliber. Driving a 300-grain bullet at better than 2900 fps, the .375 A² stands between the .375 H&H and the .378 Weatherby. This is generally more rifle than is needed for North American hunting use, but easily fills the African medium rifle requirement.

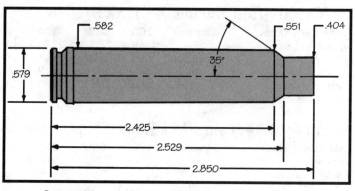

Relative Recoil Factor = 3.94

Controlling Agency : Factory

A² 300 grain SBT (None)

Distance - Yards	Muzzle	100	200	300	400	500
Velocity - fps	2920	2773	2631	2494	2360	2231
Energy - ft-lb	5679	5123	4611	4142	3710	3314
Taylor KO values	47.1	44.7	42.4	40.2	38.0	36.0
Path - Inch	-1.5	1.5	0.0	-6.5	-18.7	-37.0
Wind Drift - inches	0.0	0.5	1.9	4.5	8.1	13.1

G1 Ballistic Coefficient = 0.641

A² 300 grain Triad (None)

Distance - Yards	Muzzle	100	200	300	400	500
Velocity - fps	2920	2598	2294	2012	1762	1531
Energy - ft-lb	5679	4488	3505	2698	2068	1582
Taylor KO values	47.1	41.9	37.0	32.4	28.4	24.7
Path - inches	-1.5	1.8	0.0	-8.4	-25.5	-53.7
Wind Drift - inches	0.0	1.1	4.6	11.0	20.9	35.0

G1 Ballistic Coefficient = 0.287

.378 Weatherby Magnum

The .378 Weatherby Magnum goes back quite a long way. Its story starts in about 1953. Roy Weatherby wanted something that was significantly more potent than the .375 H&H. His .375 Weatherby Magnum was better than the H&H but not enough better to satisfy Roy. Being very well aware that in cartridge design there's no substitute for case volume for producing velocity and bullet energy the Weatherby company developed the .378. This cartridge takes a larger action than the standard full-length magnums like the .375. It's a big boomer and kills at both ends. If you are recoil sensitive you would be well advised to pick a different caliber. Since its introduction, the .378 Wby. Mag. has become the basic cartridge case for the .30-378 and the .338-378 as well as numerous wildcats.

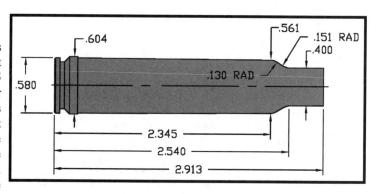

Relative Recoil Factor = 3.95

Controlling Agency: CIP

Bullet Weight Grains	Velocity fps	Maximum Average Pressure		Typical barrel for velocity testing:
		Copper Crusher	Transducer	
N/S	N/S	3800 bar	4370 bar	26 inches long - 1 turn in 12 inch twist

Weatherby 270-grain Pointed Expanding (H 378 270 SP)

Distance - Yards	Muzzle	100	200	300	400	500
Velocity - fps	3180	2921	2677	2445	2225	2017
Energy - ft-lb	6062	5115	4295	3583	2968	2438
Taylor KO values	46.4	42.6	39.0	35.6	322.4	29.4
Path - inches	-1.5	1.3	0.0	-6.1	-18.1	-37.1
Wind Drift - inches	0.0	0.7	3.0	7.0	13.1	21.4

G1 Ballistic Coefficient = 0.380

Weatherby 270-grain Barnes-X (B 378 270XS)

Distance - Yards	Muzzle	100	200	300	400	500
Velocity - fps	3150	2954	2767	2587	2415	2249
Energy - ft-lb	5948	5238	4589	4013	3495	3031
Taylor KO values	45.9	43.1	40.3	37.7	35.2	32.8
Path - inches	-1.5	1.2	0.0	-5.8	-16.7	-33.7
Wind Drift - inches	0.0	0.6	2.3	5.2	9.6	15.5

G1 Ballistic Coefficient = 0.503

Weatherby 300-grain Round Nose-Expanding (H 378 300 RN)

Distance - Yards	Muzzle	100	200	300	400	500
Velocity - fps	2925	2558	2220	1908	1627	1383
Energy - ft-lb	5699	4360	3283	2424	1764	1274
Taylor KO values	47.4	41.4	36.0	30.9	26.4	22.4
Path - inches	-1.5	1.9	0.0	-9.0	-27.8	-60.0
Wind Drift - inches	0.0	1.3	5.4	13.0	24.9	42.2

G1 Ballistic Coefficient = 0.250

A² 300-grain Sierra Spitzer Boattail (None)

Distance - Yards	Muzzle	100	200	300	400	500
Velocity - fps	2900	2754	2612	2475	2342	2214
Energy - ft-lb	5602	5051	4546	4081	3655	3264
Taylor KO values	47.0	44.6	42.3	40.1	37.9	35.9
Path - inches	-1.5	1.5	0.0	-6.6	-19.0	-37.6
Wind Drift - inches	0.0	0.5	2.0	4.5	8.2	13.2

G1 Ballistic Coefficient = 0.640

A² 300-grain Triad (None)

Distance - Yards	Muzzle	100	200	300	400	500
Velocity - fps	2900	2577	2276	1997	1747	1518
Energy - ft-lb	5602	4424	3452	2656	2034	1535
Taylor KO values	47.0	441.7	36.9	32.4	28.3	24.6
Path - inches	-1.5	1.9	0.0	-8.6	-25.9	-54.6
Wind Drift - inches	0.0	1.1	4.6	11.1	21.1	35.4

G1 Ballistic Coefficient = 0.287

Weatherby 300-grain FMJ (H 378 300 FMJ)

Distance - Yards	Muzzle	100	200	300	400	500
Velocity - fps	2925	2591	2280	1991	1725	1489
Energy - ft-lb	5699	4470	3461	2640	1983	1476
Taylor KO values	47.4	42.0	36.9	32.3	27.9	24.1
Path - inches	-1.5	1.8	0.0	-8.6	-26.1	-55.4
Wind Drift - inches	0.0	1.1	4.8	11.5	21.9	36.8

G1 Ballistic Coefficient = 0.275

.38-40 Winchester

Perhaps the first thing you should know about the .38-40 is that it isn't. Isn't a .38 caliber round, that is. The .38-40 uses bullets 0.4005 inches in diameter and is really a .40 caliber. I suppose that doesn't matter too much because the .38 Special isn't a .38 either. The .38-40 goes back to the beginning of centerfire cartridges; it was introduced clear back in 1874. At the time of its introduction the idea of using the same cartridge in both rifles and pistols had lots of support. Today, only Winchester makes ammunition in this caliber.

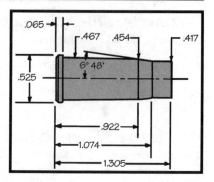

Relative Recoil Factor = 0.95   **Controlling Agency: SAAMI**

Bullet Weight Grains	Velocity fps	Maximum Average Pressure Copper Crusher	Transducer	Standard barrel for velocity testing:
180	1150	14,000 cup	N/S	24 inches long - 1 turn in 36 inch twist

Winchester 180-grain SP (X3840)

Distance - Yards	Muzzle	100	200	300	400	500
Velocity - fps	1160	999	901	827	764	710
Energy - ft-lb	538	3999	324	273	233	201
Taylor KO values	11.9	10.3	9.3	8.5	7.9	7.3
Path - inches	-1.5	16.6	0.0	-59.4	-169.8	-339.6
Wind Drift - inches	0.0	3.9	14.2	29.9	50.8	77.0

G1 Ballistic Coefficient = 0.173

.38-55 Winchester

This is another example of an old, old cartridge, originally designed for use with black powder. Unlike the .38-40, this was a rifle cartridge from it's introduction. The cases (not complete rounds) have been used for many years in Schutzen rifle competition where they have established a fine record for accuracy. The cartridge is nearing the end of its useful life, After all it has only been around since about 1884.

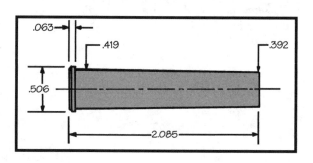

Relative Recoil Factor = 1.51   **Controlling Agency: SAAMI**

Bullet Weight Grains	Velocity fps	Maximum Average Pressure Copper Crusher	Transducer	Standard barrel for velocity testing:
2550	1320	30,000 cup	N/S	24 inches long - 1 turn in 18 inch twist

Winchester 255-grain SP (X3855)

Distance - Yards	Muzzle	100	200	300	400	500
Velocity - fps	1320	1190	1091	1018	963	917
Energy - ft-lb	987	802	674	587	525	476
Taylor KO values	18.1	16.3	15.0	14.0	13.2	12.6
Path - inches	-1.5	11.5	0.0	-40.7	-114.8	-226.5
Wind Drift - inches	0.0	2.2	8.6	18.8	32.2	48.4

G1 Ballistic Coefficient = 0.355

.44-40 Winchester

The .44-40 was developed for Winchester's Model 1873 rifle. It is another example of an early centerfire black powder cartridge that has been used in both rifles and pistols. While it is greatly outperformed by the .44 Remington Magnum, this caliber is making a comeback in Cowboy Action Shooting events. The Cowboy Action ammunition is loaded to a very much milder standard than the current SAAMI specification.

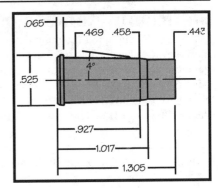

Relative Recoil Factor = 1.07

Controlling Agency: SAAMI

Bullet Weight Grains	Velocity fps	Maximum Average Pressure		Standard barrel for velocity testing:
		Copper Crusher	Transducer	
200	1175	13,000 cup	N/S	24 inches long - 1 turn in 36 inch twist

Remington 200-grain SP (R4440W)

Distance - Yards	Muzzle	100	200	300	400	500
Velocity - fps	1190	1006	900	822	756	699
Energy - ft-lb	629	449	360	300	254	217
Taylor KO values	14.5	12.3	11.0	10.0	9.2	8.5
Path - inches	-1.5	16.4	0.0	-59.3	-170.3	-342.3
Wind Drift - inches	0.0	4.3	15.6	32.8	55.5	84.0

G1 Ballistic Coefficient = 0.161

Winchester 200-grain SP (X4440)

Distance - Yards	Muzzle	100	200	300	400	500
Velocity - fps	1190	1006	900	822	756	699
Energy - ft-lb	629	449	360	300	254	217
Taylor KO values	14.5	12.3	11.0	10.0	9.2	8.5
Path - inches	-1.5	16.4	0.0	-59.3	-170.3	-342.3
Wind Drift - inches	0.0	4.3	15.6	32.8	55.5	84.0

G1 Ballistic Coefficient = 0.161

Black Hills 200-grain Cowboy Action Round Nose Flat Point (DCB4440N1)

Distance - Yards	Muzzle	100	200	300	400	500
Velocity - fps	800	733	673	620	571	527
Energy - ft-lb	284	238	201	171	145	123
Taylor KO values	9.8	8.9	8.2	7.6	7.0	6.4
Path - inches	-1.5	31.7	0.0	-108.5	-307.7	-614.2
Wind Drift - inches	0.0	3.0	12.2	28.0	50.9	81.5

G1 Ballistic Coefficient = 0.150

.44 Remington Magnum (Rifle Data)

The .44 Remington Magnum defined the high-powered pistol from its introduction in 1956 until the .454 Casull came into being a few years ago. As a pistol, there are few shooters who can get more than a few shots out of the .44 Rem. Mag. without beginning to flinch. Pistol shooting is one thing, and rifle shooting is another. In carbine-style guns, the .44 Rem. Mag. becomes a good choice for deer-sized game. The comparison with the .30-30 is interesting. On an energy basis, the .30-30 is a little better. But when Taylor KO indices are compared, the .44 Rem. Mag. is the clear choice. It comes down to whether you believe energy (lighter bullet, higher velocity) is "everything" or if you like heavy bullets at modest velocity. It becomes "shooters choice." All the cartridges listed here can be used in pistols and any pistol cartridge in this caliber can be used in properly chambered modern rifles in good condition. See the pistol listing for more information.

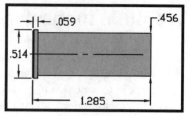

Relative Recoil Factor = 1.90

Controlling Agency: SAAMI

See pistol data section for detailed specifications.

All data in this section taken in 20-inch barrels.

Remington 210-grain Semi-JHP (R44MG6)

Distance - Yards	Muzzle	100	200	300	400	500
Velocity - fps	1920	1477	1155	982	880	802
Energy - ft-lb	1719	1017	622	450	361	300
Taylor KO values	24.7	19.0	14.9	12.6	11.3	10.3
Path - inches	-1.5	7.4	0.0	-33.3	-102.4	-216.4
Wind Drift - inches	0.0	3.9	17.0	39.0	68.9	104.3

G1 Ballistic Coefficient = 0.154

Winchester 210-grain Silvertip HP (X44MS)

Distance - Yards	Muzzle	100	200	300	400	500
Velocity - fps	1580	1198	993	879	795	725
Energy - ft-lb	1164	670	460	361	295	245
Taylor KO values	20.3	15.4	12.8	11.3	10.2	9.3
Path - inches	-1.5	11.4	0.0	-46.4	-137.8	-284.1
Wind Drift - inches	0.0	5.2	20.6	43.9	73.6	109.8

G1 Ballistic Coefficient = 0.142

Remington 240-grain SP (R44MG2)

Distance - Yards	Muzzle	100	200	300	400	500
Velocity - fps	1760	1380	1114	970	878	806
Energy - ft-lb	1650	1015	661	501	411	346
Taylor KO values	25.9	20.3	16.4	14.3	12.9	11.9
Path - inches	-1.5	8.5	0.0	-36.3	-109.5	-227.8
Wind Drift - inches	0.0	4.0	16.8	37.9	65.2	98.1

G1 Ballistic Coefficient = 0.167

Federal 240-grain Hi-Shok HP (C44A)

Distance - Yards	Muzzle	100	200	300	400	500
Velocity - fps	1760	1380	1090	950	860	790
Energy - ft-lb	1650	1015	640	485	395	330
Taylor KO values	25.9	20.3	16.0	14.0	12.6	11.3
Path - inches	-1.5	8.7	0.0	-37.5	-113.1	-235.5
Wind Drift - inches	0.0	4.2	17.7	39.6	68.0	102.0

G1 Ballistic Coefficient = 0.159

Remington 240-grain Semi-JHP (R44MG3)

Distance - Yards	Muzzle	100	200	300	400	500
Velocity - fps	1760	1380	1114	970	878	806
Energy - ft-lb	1650	1015	661	501	411	346
Taylor KO values	25.9	20.3	16.4	14.3	12.9	11.9
Path - inches	-1.5	8.5	0.0	-36.3	-109.5	-227.8
Wind Drift - inches	0.0	4.0	16.8	37.9	65.2	98.1

G1 Ballistic Coefficient = 0.167

Winchester 240-grain Hollow SP (X44MHSP2)

Distance - Yards	Muzzle	100	200	300	400	500
Velocity - fps	1760	1362	1094	953	861	789
Energy - ft-lb	1651	988	638	484	395	332
Taylor KO values	25.9	20.0	16.1	14.0	12.7	10.3
Path - inches	-1.5	10.2	0.0	-44.7	-135.4	-284.2
Wind Drift - inches	0.0	5.6	23.1	50.0	84.4	126.3

G1 Ballistic Coefficient = 0.122

Remington 275-grain JHP Core-Lokt (RH44MGA)

Distance - Yards	Muzzle	100	200	300	400	500
Velocity - fps	1580	1293	1093	976	896	832
Energy - ft-lb	1524	1020	730	582	490	422
Taylor KO values	26.6	21.5	18.4	16.4	15.1	14.0
Path - inches	-1.5	9.7	0.0	-38.6	-113.8	-232.2
Wind Drift - inches	0.0	3.6	14.8	32.7	55.9	83.8

G1 Ballistic Coefficient = 0.200

.444 Marlin

In 1964, Marlin reopened their production line for their Model 1895 Lever Action. To make the new offering more attractive, Marlin chambered the gun for a new cartridge that had been developed by Remington, the .444. The .444 and the .45-70 are near enough in physical size to make you wonder why bother. The answer is that the .444 and the new Model 1895 were designed for a pressure level of 42,000 psi compared with the .45-70's 28,000 psi limit. While the .444 makes an excellent brush gun, the caliber never caught on with the American hunter.

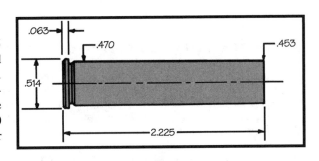

Relative Recoil Factor = 2.54

Controlling Agency: SAAMI

Bullet Weight Grains	Velocity fps	Maximum Average Pressure	
		Copper Crusher	Transducer
240	2320	44,000 cup	42,000 psi
265	2100	44,000 cup	42,000 psi

Standard barrel for velocity testing:
24 inches long - 1 turn in 38 inch twist

Remington 240-grain SP (R444M)

Distance - Yards	Muzzle	100	200	300	400	500
Velocity - fps	2350	1815	1377	1087	941	846
Energy - ft-lb	2942	1755	1010	630	472	381
Taylor KO values	34.6	26.8	20.3	16.0	13.9	12.5
Path - inches	-1.5	4.7	0.0	-23.4	-76.0	-168.1
Wind Drift - inches	0.0	3.1	14.2	35.4	65.5	102.5

G1 Ballistic Coefficient = 0.146

.45-70 Government

The .45-70 Government was originally manufactured for the Model 1873 Springfield rifle. In 1866, Erskine Allin developed a way to convert 1865 Springfield muzzleloading rifles to fire a .58 caliber rimfire cartridge. By 1873, an Allin-style rifle won a competition for a new breechloading rifle. Those rifles became known as "Trapdoors" because of their breeching mechanism. Today's factory loadings are held to very mild levels because of these old guns but handloaders push pressures up to as high as 50,000 psi in modern guns.

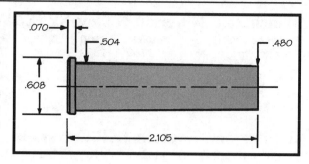

Relative Recoil Factor = 2.43

Controlling Agency: SAAMI

Bullet Weight Grains	Velocity fps	Maximum Average Pressure		Standard barrel for velocity testing:
		Copper Crusher	Transducer	
300	1830	28,000 cup	28,000 psi	24 inches long - 1 turn in 20 inch twist
405	1320	28,000 cup	28,000 psi	

Winchester 300-grain JHP (X4570H)

Distance - Yards	Muzzle	100	200	300	400	500
Velocity - fps	1880	1650	1425	1235	1105	1010
Energy - ft-lb	2355	1815	1355	1015	810	680
Taylor KO values	36.9	32.4	28.0	24.2	21.7	19.8
Path - inches	-1.5	5.8	0.0	-23.3	-69.4	-144.1
Wind Drift - inches	0.0	2.1	8.8	20.7	38.0	60.1

G1 Ballistic Coefficient = 0.287

Winchester 300-grain Partition Gold (SPGX4570)

Distance - Yards	Muzzle	100	200	300	400	500
Velocity - fps	1880	1558	1292	1103	988	910
Energy - ft-lb	2355	1616	1112	811	651	551
Taylor KO values	36.9	30.6	25.4	21.7	19.4	17.9
Path - inches	-1.5	6.5	0.0	-27.3	-83.0	-174.2
Wind Drift - inches	0.0	2.8	12.0	28.2	50.8	78.4

G1 Ballistic Coefficient = 0.215

Remington 300-grain JHP (R4570L)

Distance - Yards	Muzzle	100	200	300	400	500
Velocity - fps	1810	1497	1244	1073	969	895
Energy - ft-lb	2182	1492	1031	767	625	533
Taylor KO values	35.5	29.4	24.4	21.1	19.0	17.6
Path - inches	-1.5	7.1	0.0	-29.6	-89.3	-186.0
Wind Drift - inches	0.0	2.9	12.6	29.3	52.1	79.8

G1 Ballistic Coefficient = 0.213

Remington 405-grain SP (R4570G)

Distance - Yards	Muzzle	100	200	300	400	500
Velocity - fps	1330	1168	1055	977	918	869
Energy - ft-lb	1590	1227	1001	858	758	679
Taylor KO values	35.2	30.9	28.0	25.9	24.3	23.0
Path - inches	-1.5	12.0	0.0	-43.1	-122.7	-243.5
Wind Drift - inches	0.0	2.8	10.8	23.2	39.3	58.8

G1 Ballistic Coefficient = 0.281

.50 BMG
(Browning Machine Gun)

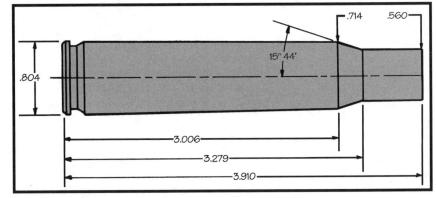

Early in the American participation in WWI John Browning was approached by the US War Department to develop a .50-caliber heavy machine gun. Browning worked at the Colt plant on the gun while Winchester worked on developing the ammunition. Although the gun and ammunition were developed too late to see any significant action in WWI, the gun, in a variety of forms, became a classic military weapon. In the last 15 years or so a .50 Caliber Shooters Association has been formed to fire bolt-action and semi-automatic guns in long-range target competition. The bolt-action guns are all equipped with rather exotic muzzle brakes to reduce the recoil, which is formidable. These guns always draw a crowd when fired on a public range.

Relative Recoil Factor = 9.16   **Controlling Agency: Factory**

Hansen 650-grain Ball FMJ (HCC55A)

Distance - Yards	Muzzle	100	200	300	400	500
Velocity - fps	2910	2695	2489	2292	2105	1927
Energy - ft-lb	12,225	10,482	8945	7590	6400	5362
Taylor KO values	138.3	128.1	118.3	109.0	100.1	91.6
Path - inches	-1.5	1.6	0.0	-7.3	-21.2	-42.9
Wind Drift - inches	0.0	0.7	3.0	6.9	12.8	20.9

G1 Ballistic Coefficient = 0.432

Hansen 650-grain Match FMJ (HCC55M)

Distance - Yards	Muzzle	100	200	300	400	500
Velocity - fps	2910	2695	2489	2292	2105	1927
Energy - ft-lb	12,225	10,482	8945	7590	6400	5362
Taylor KO values	138.3	128.1	118.3	109.0	100.1	91.6
Path - inches	-1.5	1.6	0.0	-7.3	-21.2	-42.9
Wind Drift - inches	0.0	0.7	3.0	6.9	12.8	20.9

G1 Ballistic Coefficient = 0.432

Hansen 800-grain Super Match FMJ (HCC55S)

Distance - Yards	Muzzle	100	200	300	400	500
Velocity - fps	2660	2493	2332	2177	2088	1886
Energy - ft-lb	12,572	11,044	9666	8425	7311	6319
Taylor KO values	155.6	145.9	136.5	127.4	122.2	110.4
Path - inches	-1.5	2.0	0.0	-8.4	-24.2	-48.5
Wind Drift - inches	0.0	0.6	2.7	6.3	11.6	18.7

G1 Ballistic Coefficient = 0.530

THE DANGEROUS GAME DIFFERENCE

by

Colonel Craig T. Boddington

Some animals classed as dangerous game are terrifyingly huge. It is awe-inspiring to see an elephant loom out of the dense bush at close range, and if the experience doesn't inspire more than a little fear, there's something wrong with you. However, some "dangerous game" is not necessarily huge. Few leopards outweigh the average white-tailed buck, but no one disputes the leopard's deadliness. By the same token, an Alaskan moose will outweigh Cape buffalo. A rutting moose can be silly enough to turn the tables, but it's a stretch to call it dangerous, and no one questions the Cape buffalo's right to that title!

It isn't size that places game in the dangerous category. The difference is very simple. Dangerous game is dangerous, and if you mess up, somebody is very likely to get hurt. It could be you, which is a bad thing. Personally, I think it's worse if the one who's hurt turns out to be a guide who is there to help you, an unarmed tracker, or an innocent bystander who gets run over by a wounded beast you allowed to escape.

With all game, we as responsible hunters have the obligation to choose sound hunting arms that are adequate for the job at hand, and use them with enough skill to get the job done cleanly and quickly. That's sportsmanship, but with dangerous game, it is also just plain common sense. I know that the rich body of African literature would be much poorer without tales of hair-raising charges stopped at bayonet range, but you don't need to go out of your way to add your

The big double's strong point is handling qualities and the instantaneous second shot. Extra cartridges in the hand look good, but during a charge the chances of actually using them are very slim.

escapade to Africana. I do not claim to be an expert on dangerous game in the way that John Taylor or Karamojo Bell were, but I've done a great deal of African hunting, a lot of bear hunting, and some hunting of Asian water buffalo and such. It is possible to get into trouble innocently, such as getting upwind of a poacher-harassed herd of elephant cows, or running into a bad-tempered hippo in a reedbed. Mostly, however, the way you get into trouble with dangerous game is by making a mistake.

Mistakes tend to compound themselves. Very few people get hurt by unwounded animals. This means that the first mistake happened with the first shot. Every other shot that fails to anchor the animal is also a mistake, and failing to stop a charge is a huge mistake. Often, tactical errors get mixed in—moving in too fast, reacting too slowly, approaching a downed animal from the front rather than the rear, and so forth. Sometimes it's out of your control. The animal decides where he will wait for you, and sometimes the cover is so thick that the result is inevitable. None of this will happen if the first shot does its job.

And that, in essence, is what choosing a rifle and cartridge for dangerous game is all about. There are four considerations. First, the rifle must allow you to place that first shot with precision. Second, the cartridge must have adequate power for the game. Third, the bullet must be constructed so it will penetrate to the vitals. Depending somewhat on the game and circumstances, powerful handguns, muzzleloaders, and archery tackle can meet these criteria. I have

no issue with dedicated handgun hunters, black-powder hunters, and bow hunters who wish to test their mettle against some varieties of dangerous game under some conditions. However, it is my studied opinion that only a centerfire rifle of adequate caliber can be considered a proper firearm for dangerous game. This is because of the fourth consideration: Despite the best planning and the best intentions, sometimes things go wrong, so a suitable firearm for dangerous game simply must be capable of stopping a serious charge.

When we think of dangerous game, Africa generally comes to mind. Dangerous game in

Shot placement is most important on buffalo. They can be taken with anything from a .375 on up, although larger calibers are more dramatic. This bull was taken with a Rogue River double in .470.

A very big brown bear can be almost as heavy as a Cape buffalo. Outfitter Bob Kern, Joe Bishop, and I pose with a good Russian bear taken by Joe with his .416 Remington Magnum. On very big bears, a .416 makes a lot of sense.

Africa runs the gamut from a 130-pound leopard to a 14,000-pound elephant. Between those two extremes, the continent holds rhino weighing two or three tons, several varieties of buffalo ranging from less than a half-ton to about 1,500 pounds, and lion weighing between 350 and 500 pounds. The Dark Continent holds the greatest variety of dangerous game, but it doesn't have an exclusive on game that bites back. Australia holds two varieties of wild bovine—water buffalo, bigger than Cape buffalo but probably not as aggressive, and banteng, which are smaller than Cape buffalo, but more aggressive. Then there are the big bears, found not only in North America, but also parts of Europe and much of Asia. I tend to think of grizzlies, brown bears, and polar bears as dangerous, and the black bear as not dangerous, but it must be recognized that a big black bear can outweigh a medium grizzly and is capable of turning the tables quickly!

Africa's dangerous game can be hunted in the plains, the swamps, or the thickest forest. Big bears may be hunted on wide-open polar ice, in dense alder thickets, or in high alpine basins. With this diversity of country as well as game, a dangerous-game rifle is not easy to describe. In Alaska or in Africa's rain forest, a strong case could be made for stainless steel and synthetic stocks. In alder thickets and forests, open sights are all you need. In mountains and plains a scope of modest power is a great advantage.

One thing all dangerous-game rifles have in common is that a high level of accuracy is not necessary to satisfy my first characteristic of enabling shot placement. Nobody in their right mind shoots at dangerous game at long range. Overall, you need the most precise accuracy in leopard hunting, but the range will usually be no more than 70 yards. If you can hit a grapefruit at that distance, you're in business. In this context, a very bright scope is generally far more important than benchrest accuracy.

The longest shots in the world of hunting dangerous game probably come on the big bears, especially grizzlies in high country. You only need enough accuracy to hit a volleyball, but the strength and tenacity of the animal is such that 200 yards is long and 250 yards is risky. From there the shots get closer. A shot at 100 yards is extreme on buffalo, and almost unheard of on elephant. Because of their better eyesight, I think the "normal" shot on a buffalo is probably about 60 yards. With elephant, cut that in half. Dangerous game rifles don't have to be tackdrivers, but they must be dependable, and their owners must have absolute confidence in them. Cartridges for dangerous game are just as varied as the rifles and the animals themselves. It is an absolute that the rifle must be adequate for the game, but that varies a great deal between leopard and elephant! The excellent tables in this book offer a chance to compare ballistics among many cartridges. You can go back and forth between Knock-out Values and foot-pounds, and compare downrange energies and bullet weights. This is fascinating stuff, but never forget that, as Karamojo Bell more or less said, the important thing is to get whatever energy, KO value, or foot-pounds you have in

the right place. Shot placement is always and forever more important than raw power on all game. That said, common sense and conventional wisdom are worth a lot when you compare cartridges for dangerous game.

Again, this varies greatly with the animal. In some African countries you may be obligated by law to use a minimum of .375 caliber on leopard. That's the law, and you should adhere to it, but you don't have to be a ballistic genius to figure out that you don't need a .375 for even the largest leopard in Africa. The ability to shoot coolly and precisely under extreme excitement and in poor light is far more important. Common sense should tell you that your "light" or favorite deer rifle—whether .270, .30-06, or 7mm magnum—is probably ideal for shooting a leopard, but is not the ideal firearm for following up a wounded leopard. However, the vast majority of leopard are shot deliberately over bait. If you must follow one up, you have time to change guns. For the record, I'd choose an open-sighted double rifle, despite the general preference for buckshot. I once failed to stop a leopard with two charges of good 00 Buck, and Russ Broom's double .500 saved the day.

Lion are much bigger than leopard. We hunters love to exaggerate, but I suspect the

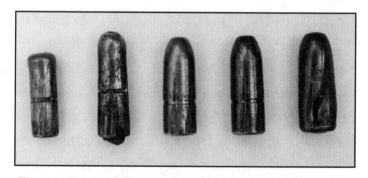

These solids were all recovered from buffalo. The two Speer African Grand Slams (third and fourth from left) look pretty good, while the rest are beaten up a bit. These were all very good solids that did their work, but their appearance is testimony to the toughness of Cape buffalo.

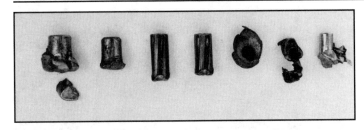

These bullets recovered from African game include: Speer Grand Slam, Sierra boattails (2), Winchester Fail Safe (2), and Speer African Grand Slams (2). Depending on the game, these are all good bullets. None of them look quite like the advertisements, but each penetrated to the vitals and did its job.

wild lion that weighs 500 pounds is very rare. Even so, 350 to 400 pounds is a lot of cat—very fast cat with big teeth and long claws. You could theorize that something like a .30-06 or .300 magnum is plenty of gun for a 400-pound animal, and that may be so. But things happen very fast when you open the ballgame on a lion, and it's no place for half measures. Here I defer to the conventional wisdom built on generations of African hunting. Most African countries impose a .375 minimum on lion, and I think that's sound. You don't need a cannon, but after all these years the .375 remains ideal with the various .416s just as good.

I feel much the same about the biggest bears. They are much larger than the biggest lions, and can be just as fast and deadly. A big difference, however, is that excepting coastal Alaska, bears are often shot at a somewhat longer distance than any professional hunter in his right mind would allow if it were a lion. In thick country I believe in the .375s and .416s for the big bears. Many Alaskan guides who are interested in stopping bears, not shooting them, carry .458's, and a few use big doubles. In more open country, a fast .33 or .35 makes a fine choice. Due to the higher sectional density which this book will allow you to compare, a 250-grain .338 bullet will outpenetrate a 300-grain .375. On

the biggest bears you need much more penetration than you do on any lion.

When you get into the wild bovines, I think it's time to leave the medium bores behind. Once again, you can make the ballistic argument that in energy figures and even in penetration, a .338 Winchester Magnum will do what a .375 will do. There is truth to that if everything goes right, but if things go wrong, a heavier bullet of larger caliber will always do a better job of making them right. Conventional wisdom and most African game laws suggest a minimum of .375 for buffalo, and I think this is sound. I also think the word "minimum" is apt. The .375 will do the job, but assuming identical shot placement, larger calibers are generally more decisive.

This fact is somewhat relative. Buffalo are only impressed by shot placement, not brute force. A single .375 bullet in the right place will do much more good than a half-dozen .500 slugs in the wrong place. I have absolutely no qualms about hunting buffalo with a .375, but I believe a .416 or similar cartridge does a better job, and a true big bore, a .450 and up, is even more dramatic.

The .375 is generally considered the minimum for all the thick-skinned dangerous game. In cool hands it will surely do the job on the likes of rhino, elephant, and hippo, but for game larger than buffalo I think a bigger gun is in order. This is especially true in the heavy cover where most elephant hunting is done today. To me, the various .416s are a more sensible minimum, and a true big bore is better yet. Whether you choose a big bolt action or a double depends largely on personal preference and budget. The traditional Nitro Express cartridges are wonderful, but a bolt action in .458 or, even better, a more powerful

Geoff Miller and Norm Bridge regulating a Rogue River double. Precise accuracy is not important in this kind of rifle. Power, handling qualities, and reliability in a tight spot are what the double is all about.

cartridge like a .458 Lott or .450 Dakota will do the job with equal aplomb.

On the largest game, the sound rule is to choose the most powerful cartridge you can shoot well. Keep that last part in mind. The energy figures delivered by powerhouses like the .460 Weatherby, .600 Nitro Express, and A-Square's behemoth .577 Tyrannosaur are as effective as they are impressive, but these levels of recoil are not for everybody. If .375 recoil is the limit that you are comfortable with, you will do far better work with a .375 than with a rifle that hurts you.

Although rifles and calibers are important, never forget that the third consideration—a bullet that will reach the vitals—is perhaps the most important of all. When all is said and done, it is the bullet that does the work, not the rifle or the cartridge. In different times, W. D. M. Bell

shot more than a thousand elephant with cartridges such as the 7mm Mauser, .303 British, and .318 Westley Richards. He did this with shot placement and bullet performance, not raw power.

There is bullet performance, and there is bullet performance. Selecting the right bullet is more difficult than ever these days with a bewildering assortment available. But that's not all bad because today's bullets are better than ever. The problem is knowing which type of bullet to choose for different kinds of game. Expanding bullets vary from those that open up very rapidly to extremely tough bullets that control expansion through various design features. The thing to keep in mind is that expansion limits penetration. If a bullet expands radically it will do tremendous tissue damage, but its increased diameter will cause it to slow more rapidly and eventually stop.

If it comes apart it will do even more damage, but will penetrate less. On the other hand, a bullet that expands less will not open as large a wound channel, but will penetrate farther. The ultimate extension of this is the full-metal jacket or "solid" bullet that will not expand at all, but will penetrate an elephant's skull from any angle.

Both leopard and lion, like all cats, are thin-skinned animals with relatively light bones. The really tough controlled-expansion bullets are probably not the best choice, as they are likely to pass through without doing the kind of damage you want done. Obviously you need a lot more penetration on lion than you do on leopard, but in both cases the amount of penetration required is not extreme. For cats, I like a bullet that will open up and do some damage.

The big bears are a different story. Bears have massive shoulders and corded muscles, and a really big Alaskan brown bear could weigh almost as much as a buffalo. You need a really tough controlled-expansion bullet, and the best is none too good.

Having said that, bullet performance is also a function of velocity. A standard .375 bullet may deliver ideal performance at .375 H&H velocity, but the same bullet may become an unreliable bomb when loaded to maximum velocity in a .378 Weatherby. Cartridges that are especially fast for caliber need tougher bullets, and they are available today.

The great dilemma in bullets for dangerous game comes with buffalo. The old school has it that solids are the only choice. Indeed they were back in the days when softpoints were much less reliable than they are today. On buffalo you simply must have penetration, and you can surely get it with full-metal-jacket bullets. However, today we have a great many truly fabulous expanding bullets that will hold together and penetrate, even on game as large and tough as buffalo. You can definitely kill buffalo with solids, but I am absolutely certain that you can achieve a much more rapid first-shot effect with an expanding bullet. It must be a good bullet, but I absolutely believe in a softpoint for the first shot on buffalo.

After that it's solids all the way. Buffalo are tough creatures, and only rarely do they succumb rapidly to even a well-placed bullet. It isn't common for a buffalo to receive a bullet and charge; he is much more likely to head for the brush. If you placed your shot well and the bullet did its work, you'll find him there. If you didn't, he'll find you there, so when you open the ballgame on buffalo, you keep shooting. After the first softpoint, which will be fatal if you placed it right, you want solids so you can get an insurance shot or shots into the vitals from any angle.

On hippo, rhino, and elephant there should be no discussion. This is work for solid bullets, period. It's true that you can easily brain a hippo with a softpoint from a .30-06, and I once saw a game scout kill an elephant with a 500-grain Hornady softpoint from a .458, but a solid is the only way to go. Even a 500-grain bullet is just a small speck against the great bulk of an elephant, so shot placement is absolutely paramount.

The fourth consideration when selecting a rifle, cartridge, and bullet for dangerous game is that it must be able to stop a charge. This is not something you want to have to do, but the capability simply must be there. It is not just a matter of raw power, although you'd best have enough at your disposal. It isn't altogether a matter of bullet performance, although your bullet must still penetrate. Stopping a charge remains a game of shot placement, but the distance is measured in yards or feet, so the rifle must fit perfectly and handle like a good quail gun. This has always been the strong suit of the double rifle, along with its instantaneous second shot. A bolt-action can fit just as well and be just as lively, and so can a single shot, but whatever you choose, the big difference between a dangerous-game rifle and any other is that your life may depend on it.

Data for
African Calibers

For most hunters, the ultimate experience is an African hunt. Somehow, bagging a white-tailed deer doesn't seem to come up to the same standard as a lion or a Cape buffalo. The professional hunters in Africa learned early on that if they wanted to stay in the business (read alive) they wanted guns with reliable stopping power. That led to large calibers, and generally to rather heavy rifles. The cartridges listed here represent a good selection of what cartridges are most suitable for someone planning (or just dreaming about) a hunt for dangerous game.

.416 Remington Magnum

When Remington wanted to get onto the .416 bandwagon they simply necked up their 8mm magnum to make the .416 Remington Magnum (introduced in 1988). If you have to pick a single gun for your next African safari, this caliber should be on your short list. When the major factories began offering premium hunting bullets, obtained from outside suppliers, the terminal performance of factory ammo took a huge jump. All the loadings available today feature premium-style bullets. For all practical purposes the .416 Remington Magnum offers the same performance as the legendary .416 Rigby.

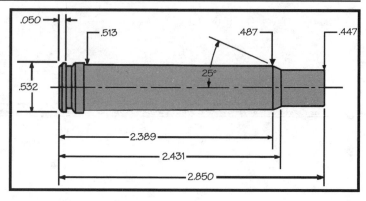

Relative Recoil Factor = 4.32

Controlling Agency : SAAMI

Bullet Weight Grains	Velocity fps	Maximum Average Pressure	
		Copper Crusher	Transducer
350	2525	54,000 cup	65,000 psi
400	2400	54,000 cup	65,000 psi

Standard barrel for velocity testing:
24 inches long - 1 turn in 14 inch twist

Federal 400-grain Trophy Bonded Bear Claw (P416RT1)

Distance - Yards	Muzzle	50	100	150	200	250
Velocity - fps	2400	2287	2180	2071	1970	1867
Energy - ft-lb	5115	4648	4215	3810	3440	3096
Taylor KO values	57.1	54.3	51.8	49.2	46.8	44.4
Path - inches	-0.9	1.1	1.5	0.0	-3.5	-9.3
Wind Drift - inches	0.0	0.3	1.1	2.5	4.6	7.4

G1 Ballistic Coefficient = 0.372

Remington 400-grain Swift A-Frame Pointed SP (R416RA)

Distance - Yards	Muzzle	50	100	150	200	250
Velocity - fps	2400	2286	2175	2067	1962	1861
Energy - ft-lb	5115	4643	4201	3797	3419	3078
Taylor KO values	57.1	54.3	51.7	49.1	46.6	44.2
Path - inches	-0.9	1.1	1.5	0.0	-3..5	-9.3
Wind Drift - inches	0.0	0.3	1.1	2.6	4.7	7.5

G1 Ballistic Coefficient = 0.368

Federal 400-grain Trophy Bonded Sledgehammer (P416T2)

Distance - Yards	Muzzle	50	100	150	200	250
Velocity - fps	2400	2274	2150	2032	1920	1806
Energy - ft-lb	5115	4592	4110	3668	3260	2899
Taylor KO values	57.1	54.0	51.1	48.3	45.6	42.9
Path - inches	-0.9	1.1	1.5	0.0	-3..6	-9.6
Wind Drift - inches	0.0	0.3	1.2	2.9	5.2	8.4

G1 Ballistic Coefficient = 0.331

A² 400-grain Dead Tough SP, Monolithic Solid, Lion Load SP (None)

Distance - Yards	Muzzle	50	100	150	200	250
Velocity - fps	2380	2249	2121	1998	1880	1766
Energy - ft-lb	5031	4492	3998	3548	3139	2770
Taylor KO values	56.6	53.5	50.4	47.5	44.7	42.0
Path - inches	-0.9	1.2	1.6	0.0	-3.7	-9.9
Wind Drift - inches	0.0	0.3	1.3	3.0	5.6	9.0

G1 Ballistic Coefficient = 0.317

.416 Rigby

This cartridge represented what the British thought of as a minimum African cartridge when it was introduced in 1911. The .416 soon showed that it really wasn't minimum at all. It's a large case, roughly the same volume as the .378 and the .460 Weatherby Magnums. The .416 Rigby has always been loaded to a much more modest pressure level than the more modern cartridges of similar caliber. Today, there are other cartridges that offer similar performance in slightly smaller cases, but none of these is really a whole lot "better" in the field (where performance really counts) than the .416 Rigby.

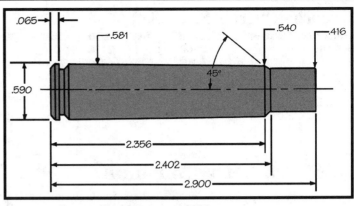

Relative Recoil Factor = 4.27

Controlling Agency: CIP*

Bullet Weight Grains	Velocity fps	Maximum Average Pressure		Typical barrel for velocity testing:
		Copper Crusher	**Transducer**	
N/S	N/S	52,000 bar	N/A	26 inches long - 1 turn in 16.5 inch twist

*SAAMI standards apply to Federal's loadings. Factory standards to A²'s

A² 400-grain Dead Tough SP, Monolithic Solid, Lion Load SP (None)

Distance - Yards	Muzzle	50	100	150	200	250
Velocity - fps	2400	2268	2140	2016	1897	1782
Energy - ft-lb	5115	4570	4069	3612	3194	2823
Taylor KO values	57.1	53.9	50.9	47.9	45.1	42.4
Path - inches	-0.9	1.2	1.5	0.0	-3.7	-9.8
Wind Drift - inches	0.0	0.3	1.3	3.0	5.5	8.6

G1 Ballistic Coefficient = 0.317

Federal 400-grain Trophy Bonded Bear Claw (P416T1)

Distance - Yards	Muzzle	50	100	150	200	250
Velocity - fps	2370	2259	2150	2046	1940	1845
Energy - ft-lb	4990	4533	4110	3718	3350	3023
Taylor KO values	56.3	53.7	51.1	48.6	46.1	43.9
Path - inches	-0.9	1.2	1.5	0.0	-3.6	-9.5
Wind Drift - inches	0.0	0.3	1.1	2.6	4.7	7.5

G1 Ballistic Coefficient = 0.375

Federal 400-grain Trophy Bonded Sledgehammer (P416T2)

Distance - Yards	Muzzle	50	100	150	200	250
Velocity - fps	2370	2241	2110	1995	1880	1766
Energy - ft-lb	4990	4462	3975	3535	3130	2771
Taylor KO values	56.3	53.3	50.2	47.4	44.7	42.0
Path - inches	-0.9	1.2	1.6	0.0	-3.8	-10.0
Wind Drift - inches	0.0	0.3	1.3	3.0	5.5	8.9

G1 Ballistic Coefficient = 0.322

Federal 410-grain Woodleigh Weldcore SP (P416A)

Distance - Yards	Muzzle	50	100	150	200	250
Velocity - fps	2370	2239	2110	1989	1870	1757
Energy - ft-lb	5115	4565	4050	3603	3165	2812
Taylor KO values	57.7	54.6	51.4	48.5	45.6	42.8
Path - inches	-0.9	1.2	1.6	0.0	-3.8	-10.0
Wind Drift - inches	0.0	0.3	1.3	3.1	5.6	9.0

G1 Ballistic Coefficient = 0.317

Federal 410-grain Solid (P416B)

Distance - Yards	Muzzle	50	100	150	200	250
Velocity - fps	2370	2239	2110	1989	1870	1757
Energy - ft-lb	5115	4565	4050	3603	3165	2812
Taylor KO values	57.7	54.6	51.4	48.5	45.6	42.8
Path - inches	-0.9	1.2	1.6	0.0	-3.8	-10.0
Wind Drift - inches	0.0	0.3	1.3	3.1	5.6	9.0

G1 Ballistic Coefficient = 0.317

Kynoch 410-grain Solid; Soft Nose

Distance - Yards	Muzzle	50	100	150	200	250
Velocity - fps	2300	2204	2110	2018	1929	1842
Energy - ft-lb	4817	4422	4053	3708	3387	3090
Taylor KO values	56.0	53.7	51.4	49.2	47.0	44.9
Path - inches	-0.9	1.2	1.6	0.0	-3.7	-9.8
Wind Drift - inches	0.0	1.0	4.2	9.9	18.4	30.1

G1 Ballistic Coefficient = 0.426

.416 Weatherby Magnum

The .416 Weatherby was Weatherby's answer to the popularity of the .416 caliber generally. Introduced in 1989, it is really a .416-378, that is, a .378 Weatherby case necked to .416. That puts this cartridge's performance between the .378 Weatherby and the .460 Weatherby. That's pretty awesome company. The .416 WM is a truly "African" caliber, suitable for any game anywhere.

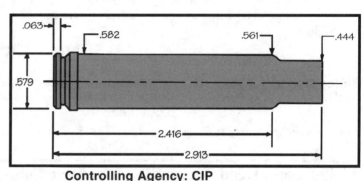

Relative Recoil Factor = 4.77

Controlling Agency: CIP

Bullet Weight Grains	Velocity fps	Maximum Average Pressure		Standard barrel for velocity testing:
		Copper Crusher	Transducer	
N/S	N/S	3800 bar	4370 bar	26 inches long - 1 turn in 14 inch twist

Weatherby 350-grain Barnes-X (B 416 350 XS)

Distance - Yards	Muzzle	50	100	150	200	250
Velocity - fps	2850	2761	2673	2587	2503	2420
Energy - ft-lb	6312	5924	5553	5203	4870	4553
Taylor KO values	59.3	57.4	55.6	53.8	52.1	50.3
Path - inches	-0.9	0.6	0.9	0.0	-2.2	-5.7
Wind Drift - inches	0.0	0.2	0.6	1.4	2.5	4.0

G1 Ballistic Coefficient = 0.521

Weatherby 400-grain Hornady SP (H 416 400 RN)

Distance - Yards	Muzzle	50	100	150	200	250
Velocity - fps	2700	2556	2417	2282	2152	2025
Energy - ft-lb	6474	5805	5189	4626	4113	3642
Taylor KO values	64.2	60.8	57.5	54.2	51.2	48.1
Path - inches	-0.9	0.8	1,1	0.0	-2.8	-7.5
Wind Drift - inches	0.0	0.3	1.1	2.6	4.7	7.6

G1 Ballistic Coefficient = 0.311

Weatherby 400-grain Swift A-Frame (W 416 400 PT)

Distance - Yards	Muzzle	50	100	150	200	250
Velocity - fps	2650	2536	2426	2318	2213	2110
Energy - ft-lb	6237	5716	5227	4773	4350	3955
Taylor KO values	63.0	60.3	57.7	55.1	52.6	50.1
Path - inches	-0.9	0.8	1.1	0.0	-2.8	-7.3
Wind Drift - inches	0.0	0.2	0.9	2.1	3.8	6.0

G1 Ballistic Coefficient = 0.391

A² 400-grain Dead Tough SP, Monolithic Solid, Lion Load SP (None)

Distance - Yards	Muzzle	50	100	150	200	250
Velocity - fps	2600	2463	2328	2202	2073	1957
Energy - ft-lb	6004	5390	4813	4307	3834	3402
Taylor KO values	61.8	58.5	55.3	52.3	49.3	46.5
Path - inches	-0.9	0.9	1.2	0.0	-3.0	-8.1
Wind Drift - inches	0.0	0.3	1.1	2.6	4.8	7.8

G1 Ballistic Coefficient = 0.320

Weatherby 400-grain A-Square Monolithic Solid (A 416 400 SD)

Distance - Yards	Muzzle	50	100	150	200	250
Velocity - fps	2700	2553	2411	2273	2140	2010
Energy - ft-lb	6457	5790	5162	4589	4068	3591
Taylor KO values	64.2	60.7	57.3	54.0	50.9	47.8
Path - inches	-0.9	0.8	1.1	0.0	-2.8	-7.6
Wind Drift - inches	0.0	0.3	1.1	2.6	4.8	7.8

G1 Ballistic Coefficient = 0.304

10.57mm (.416) Lazzeroni Meteor

The 10.57mm Meteor is the largest caliber in the Lazzeroni line. As is true of all the Lazzeroni line, the 10.57 has performance considerably better than most of the older, more traditional cartridges in the same caliber. There's nothing mild about the Meteor. In fact, it drives a 400-grain bullet 100 fps faster than any other .416 cartridge. This is a cartridge for serious African hunters.

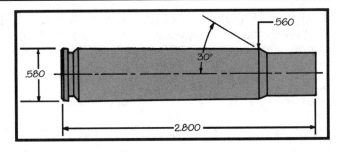

Relative Recoil Factor = 4.95

Controlling Agency : Factory

Lazzeroni 400-grain Swift A-Frame (1057MR400A)

Distance - Yards	Muzzle	50	100	150	200	250
Velocity - fps	2750	2651	2554	2460	2367	2277
Energy - ft-lb	6719	6244	5796	5376	4976	4605
Taylor KO values	65.4	63.0	60.7	58.5	56.3	54.1
Path - inches	-0.9	0.7	1.0	0.0	-2.4	-6.4
Wind Drift - inches	0.0	0.2	0.7	1.6	3.0	4.8

G1 Ballistic Coefficient = 0.460

.458 Winchester Magnum

The .458 Winchester Magnum is the largest of Winchester's slightly shortened belted magnum calibers. It was introduced in 1956, and its adaptability to standard length actions made it popular in the US. The question of relative popularity between this cartridge and the British "African" cartridges is that the British cartridges are nearly always utilized in custom-made (read very expensive) rifles, while the .458 Win. Mag. is available in the more or less over-the-counter Model 70 African. Performance-wise the .458 Win. Mag. is bullet-for-bullet about 450 fps slower than the .460 Weatherby Magnum, which is based on the .378 Wby. Mag. case.

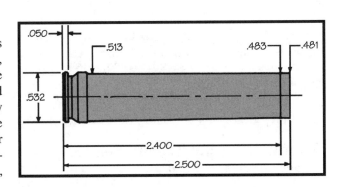

Relative Recoil Factor = 4.36

Controlling Agency: SAAMI

Bullet Weight Grains	Velocity fps	Maximum Average Pressure		Standard barrel for velocity testing:
		Copper Crusher	Transducer	
500	2025	53,000 cup	N/S	24 inches long - 1 turn in 14 inch twist
510	2025	53,000 cup	N/S	

Federal 350-grain SP (P458A)

Distance - Yards	Muzzle	50	100	150	200	250
Velocity - fps	2470	2225	1990	1778	1570	1402
Energy - ft-lb	4740	3847	3065	2456	1915	1529
Taylor KO values	56.6	51.0	45.6	40.7	36.0	32.1
Path - inches	-0.9	1.3	1.8	0.0	-4.5	-12.5
Wind Drift - inches	0.0	0.6	2.3	5.8	10.8	17.9

G1 Ballistic Coefficient = 0.178

Federal 400-grain Trophy Bonded Bear Claw (P458T1)

Distance - Yards	Muzzle	50	100	150	200	250
Velocity - fps	2380	2271	2170	2061	1960	1862
Energy - ft-lb	5030	4581	4185	3772	3415	3081
Taylor KO values	62.3	59.4	56.8	53.9	51.3	48.7
Path - inches	-0.9	1.1	1.5	0.0	-3.6	-9.4
Wind Drift - inches	0.0	0.3	1.1	2.5	4.5	7.3

G1 Ballistic Coefficient = 0.382

Remington 450-grain Swift A-Frame Pointed SP (RS458WA)

Distance - Yards	Muzzle	50	100	150	200	250
Velocity - fps	2150	2023	1901	1784	1671	1585
Energy - ft-lb	4618	4091	3609	3179	2789	2449
Taylor KO values	63.3	59.6	56.0	52.5	49.2	46.7
Path - inches	-0.9	1.6	2.0	0.0	-4.8	-12.6
Wind Drift - inches	0.0	0.4	1.6	3.6	6.6	10.7

G1 Ballistic Coefficient = 0.310

A² 465-grain Dead Tough SP, Monolithic Solid, Lion Load SP (None)

Distance - Yards	Muzzle	50	100	150	200	250
Velocity - fps	2220	2108	1999	1894	1791	1694
Energy - ft-lb	5088	4589	4127	3704	3312	2965
Taylor KO values	67.5	64.1	60.8	57.6	54.5	51.5
Path - inches	-0.9	1.4	1.8	0.0	-4.2	-11.2
Wind Drift - inches	0.0	0.3	1.3	3.0	5.4	8.7

G1 Ballistic Coefficient = 0.358

Speer 500-grain African GS SP (24518)

Distance - Yards	Muzzle	50	100	150	200	250
Velocity - fps	2120	1984	1853	1729	1609	1500
Energy - ft-lb	4989	4371	3810	3318	2875	2497
Taylor KO values	69.3	64.9	60.6	56.6	52.6	49.1
Path - inches	-0.9	1.7	2.1	0.0	-5.1	-13.4
Wind Drift - inches	0.0	0.4	1.7	3.0	7.4	12.0

G1 Ballistic Coefficient = 0.286

Speer 500-grain African GS Tungsten Solid (24519)

Distance - Yards	Muzzle	50	100	150	200	250
Velocity - fps	2120	1980	1845	1717	1596	1482
Energy - ft-lb	4989	4352	3780	3273	2828	2440
Taylor KO values	69.3	64.8	60.4	56.2	52.2	48.5
Path - inches	-0.9	1.7	2.2	0.0	-5.1	-13.0
Wind Drift - inches	0.0	0.4	1.8	3.4	7.7	9.9

G1 Ballistic Coefficient = 0.277

Federal 500-grain Trophy Bonded Bear Claw (P458T2)

Distance - Yards	Muzzle	50	100	150	200	250
Velocity - fps	2090	1977	1870	1762	1660	1565
Energy - ft-lb	4850	4340	3870	3448	3065	2721
Taylor KO values	68.3	64.7	61.2	57.6	54.3	51.2
Path - inches	-0.9	1.7	2.1	0.0	-4.9	-13.0
Wind Drift - inches	0.0	0.4	1.5	3.4	6.2	9.9

G1 Ballistic Coefficient = 0.342

Federal 500-grain Trophy Bonded Sledgehammer (P458T3)

Distance - Yards	Muzzle	50	100	150	200	250
Velocity - fps	2090	1975	1860	1757	1650	1557
Energy - ft-lb	4850	4331	3845	3427	3025	2692
Taylor KO values	68.4	64.6	60.2	57.5	54.0	50.9
Path - inches	-0.9	1.7	2.1	0.0	-4.9	-13.0
Wind Drift - inches	0.0	0.4	1.5	3.5	6.3	10.1

G1 Ballistic Coefficient = 0.336

Federal 500-grain Solid (P458C)

Distance - Yards	Muzzle	50	100	150	200	250
Velocity - fps	2090	1960	1870	1714	1670	1494
Energy - ft-lb	4850	4264	3880	3264	3085	2480
Taylor KO values	68.4	64.1	61.2	56.1	54.6	48.9
Path - inches	-,0.9	1.8	2.2	0.0	-5.1	-13.7
Wind Drift - inches	0.0	0.4	1.7	4.0	7.3	11.7

G1 Ballistic Coefficient = 0.296

Federal 510-grain SP (P458B)

Distance - Yards	Muzzle	50	100	150	200	250
Velocity - fps	2090	1954	1820	1700	1570	1473
Energy - ft-lb	4845	4325	3730	3273	2790	2458
Taylor KO values	69.7	65.2	60.7	56.7	52.4	49.2
Path - inches	-0.9	1.8	2.2	0.0	-5.2	-13.9
Wind Drift - inches	0.0	0.4	1.8	4.2	7.6	12.3

G1 Ballistic Coefficient = 0.284

.460 Weatherby Magnum

In terms of muzzle energy, the .460 Weatherby until recently was the most "powerful" cartridge available to the serious hunter. Weatherby introduced the .460 in 1958. The cartridge case is from the same basic head size as the .378. With factory loadings that produce in excess of 7500 ft-lb of muzzle energy, this is enough gun for any game, anywhere. The .460 Wby. Mag. is a caliber that very few people shoot for "fun." The recoil is fearsome even with a heavy gun.

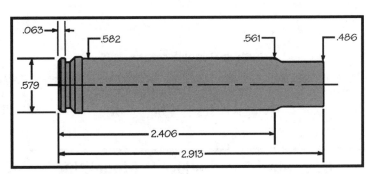

Relative Recoil Factor = 5.86

Controlling Agency: CIP

Bullet Weight Grains	Velocity fps	Maximum Average Pressure		Standard barrel for velocity testing:
		Copper Crusher	Transducer	
N/S	N/S	3800 bar	4370 bar	26 inches long - 1 turn in 16 inch twist

Weatherby 450-grain Barnes-X (B 460 450 XS)

Distance - Yards	Muzzle	50	100	150	200	250
Velocity - fps	2700	2608	2518	2429	2343	2257
Energy - ft-lb	7284	6797	6333	5897	5482	5092
Taylor KO values	79.5	76.8	74.1	71.5	69.0	66.5
Path - inches	-0.9	0.7	1.0	0.0	-2.5	-6.6
Wind Drift - inches	0.0	0.2	0.7	1.6	2.9	4.6

G1 Ballistic Coefficient = 0.488

Weatherby 500-grain Round Nose-Expanding (H 460 500 RN)

Distance - Yards	Muzzle	50	100	150	200	250
Velocity - fps	2600	2448	2301	2158	2022	1890
Energy - ft-lb	7504	6654	5877	5174	4539	3965
Taylor KO values	85.1	80.1	75.3	70.6	66.1	61.8
Path - inches	-0.9	0.9	1.3	0.0	-3.2	-8.4
Wind Drift - inches	0.0	0.3	1.3	3.0	5.4	8.8

G1 Ballistic Coefficient = 0.287

A² 500-grain Dead Tough SP, Monolithic Solid, Lion Load SP (None)

Distance - Yards	Muzzle	50	100	150	200	250
Velocity - fps	2580	2464	2349	2241	2131	2030
Energy - ft-lb	7389	6743	6126	5578	5040	4576
Taylor KO values	84.4	80.6	76.8	73.3	69.7	66.4
Path - inches	-0.9	0.9	1.2	0.0	-3.0	-7.8
Wind Drift - inches	0.0	0.2	1.0	2.2	4.1	6.5

G1 Ballistic Coefficient = 0.377

Weatherby 500-grain FMJ (B 460 500 FJ)

Distance - Yards	Muzzle	50	100	150	200	250
Velocity - fps	2600	2452	2309	2170	2037	1907
Energy - ft-lb	7504	6676	5917	5229	4605	4039
Taylor KO values	85.1	80.2	75.5	71.0	66.6	62.4
Path - inches	0.9	0.9	1.3	0.0	-3.1	-8.3
Wind Drift - inches	0.0	0.3	1.2	2.9	5.3	8.5

G1 Ballistic Coefficient = 0.295

.500-465 Nitro Express

The most common practice in the US when naming "necked to" cartridges is to put the caliber first and the cartridge of origin second. An example would be the .30-378 WM which is a .378 WM case necked to .30 caliber. The Brits seem to do just the opposite. The .500-465 Nitro Express is basically a .500 Nitro Express (it's actually closer to a .470 NE case) necked to .465 caliber. This cartridge was introduced in 1906 or 1907 by Holland and Holland when the British government outlawed .450 caliber guns in India.

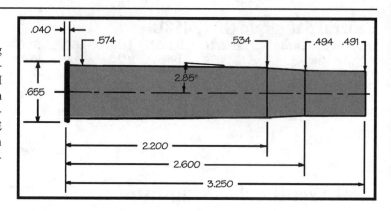

Relative Recoil Factor = 1.98

Controlling Agency: CIP

Bullet Weight Grains	Velocity fps	Maximum Average Pressure		Standard barrel for velocity testing:
		Copper Crusher	Transducer	
N/S	N/S	2200 bar	2450 bar	26 inches long - 1 turn in 30 inch twist

A² 480-grain Dead Tough SP, Monolithic Solid, Lion Load SP (None)

Distance - Yards	Muzzle	50	100	150	200	250
Velocity - fps	2150	2038	1926	1823	1722	1626
Energy - ft-lb	4926	4426	3960	3545	3160	2817
Taylor KO values	63.8	60.5	57.2	54.1	51.1	48.3
Path - inches	-0.9	1.6	2.0	0.0	-4.6	-12.1
Wind Drift - inches	0.0	0.3	1.4	3.2	5.8	9.3

G1 Ballistic Coefficient = 0.350

Kynoch 480-grain SP

Distance - Yards	Muzzle	50	100	150	200	250
Velocity - fps	2150	2054	1962	1872	1784	1700
Energy - ft-lb	4930	4490	4100	3735	3394	3091
Taylor KO values	63.8	61.0	58.3	55.6	53.0	50.5
Path - inches	-0.9	1.5	1.9	0.0	-4.4	-11.5
Wind Drift - inches	0.0	0.3	1.2	2.6	4.8	7.7

G1 Ballistic Coefficient = 0.414

.470 Nitro Express

The .470 Nitro Express is a large rimmed cartridge in the British tradition. It is intended primarily for double rifles. Most of the traditional British cartridges have one thing in common. They drive a large caliber, heavy bullet at velocities in the 2000 to 2300 fps range. When you have a 500-grain bullet humping along at about 2150 fps you have tremendous stopping power, and the double rifle provides the shooter with a reserve shot without any manipulating of the gun. While the recoil of these cartridges is formidable, the weight of double rifles tames down the worst of the jolt. Besides, who feels recoil in the face of a charging buffalo.

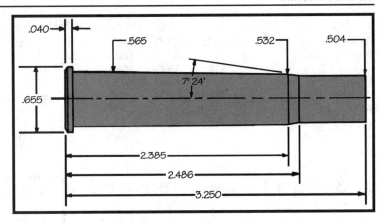

Relative Recoil Factor = 4.84

Controlling Agency: CIP*

Bullet Weight Grains	Velocity fps	Maximum Average Pressure		Standard barrel for velocity testing:
		Copper Crusher	**Transducer**	
N/S	N/S	2400 bar	2700 bar	26 inches long - 1 turn in 21 inch twist

*SAAMI standards apply to Federal's loadings. Factory standards to A²'s

A² 500-grain Dead Tough SP, Monolithic Solid, Lion Load SP (None)

Distance - Yards	Muzzle	50	100	150	200	250
Velocity - fps	2150	2029	1912	1800	1693	1590
Energy - ft-lb	5132	4572	4058	3597	3182	2806
Taylor KO values	74.2	70.0	66.0	62.1	58.4	54.9
Path - inches	-0.9	1.6	2.0	0.0	-4.7	-12.4
Wind Drift - inches	0.0	0.4	1.5	3.4	6.3	10.1

G1 Ballistic Coefficient = 0.325

Kynoch 500-grain Solid or Soft Nose

Distance - Yards	Muzzle	50	100	150	200	250
Velocity - fps	2125	2023	1923	1827	1734	1644
Energy - ft-lb	5015	4543	4107	3706	3338	3003
Taylor KO values	73.3	69.8	66.3	63.0	59.8	56.7
Path - inches	-0.9	1.6	2.0	0.0	-4.6	-12.0
Wind Drift - inches	0.0	0.3	1.3	2.9	5.4	8.6

G1 Ballistic Coefficient = 0.382

Federal 500-grain Woodleigh Weldcore SP (P470A)

Distance - Yards	Muzzle	100	200	300	400	500
Velocity - fps	2150	2018	1890	1769	1650	1543
Energy - ft-lb	5130	4521	3969	3473	3033	2644
Taylor KO values	72.8	68.3	64.0	59.9	55.9	52.2
Path - inches	-0.9	1.6	2.0	0.0	-4.8	-12.8
Wind Drift - inches	0.0	0.4	1.6	3.8	7.0	11.2

G1 Ballistic Coefficient = 0.297

Federal 500-grain Trophy Bonded Bear Claw (P470T1)

Distance - Yards	Muzzle	100	200	300	400	500
Velocity - fps	2150	2043	1940	1838	1740	1649
Energy - ft-lb	5130	4635	4175	3753	3368	3018
Taylor KO values	72.8	69.2	65.7	62.2	58.9	55.8
Path - inches	-0.9	3.9	0.0	-15.4	-45.0	-92.4
Wind Drift - inches	0.0	0.3	1.3	3.0	5.5	8.8

G1 Ballistic Coefficient = 0.370

Federal 500-grain Trophy Bonded Sledgehammer (P470T2)

Distance - Yards	Muzzle	100	200	300	400	500
Velocity - fps	2150	2043	1940	1838	1740	1649
Energy - ft-lb	5130	4635	4175	3753	3368	3018
Taylor KO values	72.8	69.2	65.7	62.2	58.9	55.8
Path - inches	-0.9	3.9	0.0	-15.4	-45.0	-92.4
Wind Drift - inches	0.0	0.3	1.3	3.0	5.5	8.8

G1 Ballistic Coefficient = 0.370

Federal 500-grain Woodleigh Weldcore SP (P470B)

Distance - Yards	Muzzle	100	200	300	400	500
Velocity - fps	2150	2018	1890	1769	1650	1543
Energy - ft-lb	5130	4521	3969	3473	3033	2644
Taylor KO values	72.8	68.3	64.0	59.9	55.9	52.2
Path - inches	-0.9	1.6	2.0	0.0	-4.8	-12.8
Wind Drift - inches	0.0	0.4	1.6	3.8	7.0	11.2

G1 Ballistic Coefficient = 0.297

.475 Nitro Express Number 2

The .475 Nitro Express Number 2 was, like many other British cartridges, introduced in 1907. This cartridge has a case head somewhat larger than the .470 and .500 NE cartridges and has a case length of 3.500 inches. It's a big one. There were a variety of loadings (some very mild and some pretty hot) for this cartridge so care must be used when selecting ammunition for an old gun.

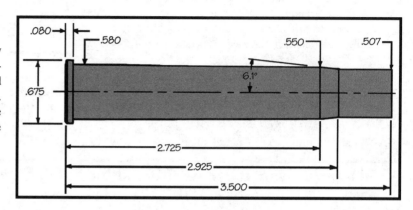

Relative Recoil Factor = 4.95

Controlling Agency: CIP

Bullet Weight Grains	Velocity fps	Maximum Average Pressure		Standard barrel for velocity testing:
		Copper Crusher	Transducer	
N/S	N/S	2450 bar	2750 bar	26 inches long - 1 turn in 18 inch twist

Kynoch 480-grain Solid or Soft Nose

Distance - Yards	Muzzle	50	100	150	200	250
Velocity - fps	2200	2084	1974	1867	1763	1664
Energy - ft-lb	5160	4636	4155	3716	3315	2953
Taylor KO values	71.8	68.0	64.0	60.9	57.4	54.3
Path - inches	-0.9	1.5	1.8	0.0	-4.4	-11.5
Wind Drift - inches	0.0	0.3	1.3	3.1	5.6	9.0

G1 Ballistic Coefficient = 0.348

A² 500-grain Dead Tough SP, Monolithic Solid, Lion Load SP (None)

Distance - Yards	Muzzle	50	100	150	200	250
Velocity - fps	2200	2080	1964	1852	1744	1641
Energy - ft-lb	5375	4804	4283	3808	3378	2991
Taylor KO values	74.8	70.7	66.8	63.0	59.3	55.8
Path - inches	-0.9	1.5	1.9	0.0	-4.4	-11.7
Wind Drift - inches	0.0	0.3	1.4	3.2	5.9	9.6

G1 Ballistic Coefficient = 0.332

.495 A-Square

Art Alphin's .495 A² cartridge is basically a slightly shortened .460 Weatherby case necked to hold a 0.510-diameter bullet. When it was designed in 1977 it was intended to provide a cartridge firing .50-caliber bullets that could be adapted to existing bolt-actions. Performancewise, this cartridge is more powerful than either the .500 Nitro Express or the .505 Gibbs.

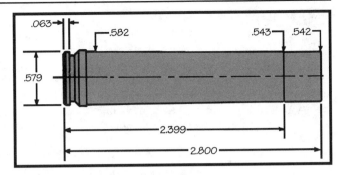

Relative Recoil Factor = 6.03

Controlling Agency: Factory

Standard barrel for velocity testing:
26 inches long - 1 turn in 10 inch twist

A² 570-grain Dead Tough SP, Monolithic Solid, Lion Load SP (None)

Distance - Yards	Muzzle	50	100	150	200	250
Velocity - fps	2350	2231	2117	2003	1896	1790
Energy - ft-lb	6989	6302	5671	5081	4552	4058
Taylor KO values	97.6	92.7	87.9	83.2	78.7	73.9
Path - inches	-0.9	1.2	1.6	0.0	-3.8	-9.9
Wind Drift - inches	0.0	0.3	1.2	2.8	5.1	8.2

G1 Ballistic Coefficient = 0.348

.500 Nitro Express 3-Inch

This cartridge was first introduced as a black-powder version (the .500 Express) in about 1880. The smokeless powder version came along about 1890. While it is an excellent cartridge and was highly respected by some of the professional hunters, the .500 NE never reached the popularity of the .470 NE.

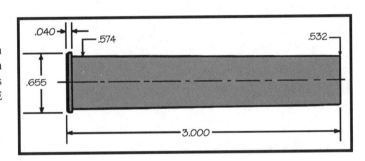

Relative Recoil Factor = 5.52

Controlling Agency: CIP

Bullet Weight Grains	Velocity fps	Maximum Average Pressure		Standard barrel for velocity testing:
		Copper Crusher	Transducer	
N/S	N/S	2500 bar	2800 bar	26 inches long - 1 turn in 15 inch twist

A² 570-grain Dead Tough SP, Monolithic Solid, Lion Load SP (None)

Distance - Yards	Muzzle	50	100	150	200	250
Velocity - fps	2150	2038	1928	1823	1722	1626
Energy - ft-lb	5850	5256	4703	4209	3752	3345
Taylor KO values	89.3	84.6	80.1	75.7	71.5	67.5
Path - inches	-0.9	1.6	2.0	0.0	-4.6	-12.1
Wind Drift - inches	0.0	0.3	1.4	3.2	5.8	9.3

G1 Ballistic Coefficient = 0.350

Kynoch 570-grain Solid or Soft Nose

Distance - Yards	Muzzle	50	100	150	200	250
Velocity - fps	2150	2048	1948	1851	1758	1688
Energy - ft-lb	5850	5300	4800	4337	3911	3521
Taylor KO values	89.3	85.0	80.9	76.9	73.0	70.1
Path - inches	-0.9	1.6	1.9	0.0	-4.5	-11.7
Wind Drift - inches	0.0	0.3	1.2	2.9	5.2	8.4

G1 Ballistic Coefficient = 0.384

.500 Jeffery

While the British hunters tended to prefer the big double rifles which used rimmed cartridges, German hunters preferred bolt-action rifles. This cartridge originated as the 12.7x70 mm Schuler. Jeffery picked it up and offered it in his line. For many years it was the most powerful cartridge available for bolt-action rifles.

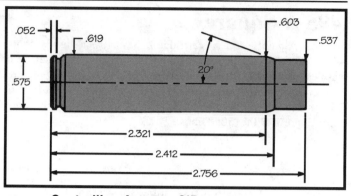

Controlling Agency: CIP

Relative Recoil Factor = 5.78

Bullet Weight Grains	Velocity fps	Maximum Average Pressure		Standard barrel for velocity testing:
		Copper Crusher	Transducer	
N/S	N/S	2850 bar	3250 bar	26 inches long - 1 turn in 10 inch twist

Kynoch 535-grain Solid or Soft Nose

Distance - Yards	Muzzle	50	100	150	200	250
Velocity - fps	2400	2280	2164	2051	1942	1836
Energy - ft-lb	6844	6179	5565	4999	4480	4006
Taylor KO values	93.5	88.9	84.3	79.9	75.7	71.6
Path - inches	-0.9	1.1	1.5	0.0	-3.6	-9.4
Wind Drift - inches	0.0	0.3	1.2	2.7	4.9	7.9

G1 Ballistic Coefficient = 0.350

A² 570-grain Dead Tough SP, Monolithic Solid, Lion Load SP (None)

Distance - Yards	Muzzle	50	100	150	200	250
Velocity - fps	2300	2183	2070	1960	1853	1751
Energy - ft-lb	6697	6034	5422	4861	4348	3881
Taylor KO values	95.5	90.7	86.0	81.4	77.0	72.7
Path - inches	-0.9	1.3	1.7	0.0	-3.9	-10.4
Wind Drift - inches	0.0	0.3	1.2	2.9	5.2	8.4

G1 Ballistic Coefficient = 0.350

.500 A-Square

Companion cartridge to the .495 A², the .500 can be thought of as an "improved" .495. The case is 0.1 inch longer and the body is blown out to 0.568 just at the shoulder. These changes allow the .500 A² to produce well over 100 ft-lb more muzzle energy than the .495. It is a potent round for bolt-action rifles.

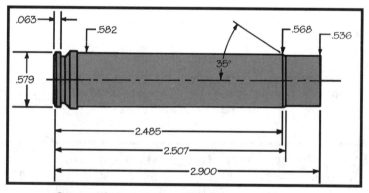

Controlling Agency: Factory

Relative Recoil Factor = 6.68

Standard barrel for velocity testing:
26 inches long - 1 turn in 10 inch twist

A² 600-grain Dead Tough SP, Monolithic Solid, Lion Load SP (None)

Distance - Yards	Muzzle	50	100	150	200	250
Velocity - fps	2470	2351	2235	2122	2031	1907
Energy - ft-lb	8127	7364	6654	6001	5397	4844
Taylor KO values	108.0	102.8	97.7	92.8	88.0	83.4
Path - inches	-0.9	1.0	1.4	0.0	-3.3	-8.8
Wind Drift - inches	0.0	0.3	1.1	2.5	4.6	7.4

G1 Ballistic Coefficient = 0.357

.505 Rimless Magnum (Gibbs)

Introduced about 1913, the .505 Gibbs was a proprietary cartridge designed for use in bolt-action rifles. Ammunition is a little hard to get for this caliber but it is available from the two sources listed below. The ballistics of this cartridge are such that it's doubtful that anyone would chamber a new rifle for it today, but the cartridge was certainly well respected in the pre-WWII period.

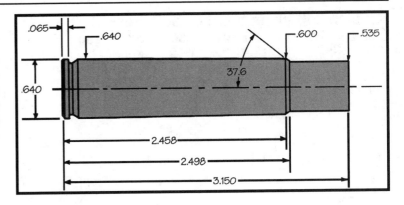

Relative Recoil Factor = 5.44

Controlling Agency: CIP

Bullet Weight Grains	Velocity fps	Maximum Average Pressure		Standard barrel for velocity testing:
		Copper Crusher	Transducer	
N/S	N/S	2400 bar	2700 bar	26 inches long - 1 turn in 16 inch twist

A² 525-grain Dead Tough SP, Monolithic Solid, Lion Load SP (None)

Distance - Yards	Muzzle	50	100	150	200	250
Velocity - fps	2300	2179	2063	1949	1840	1735
Energy - ft-lb	6166	5539	4962	4430	3948	3510
Taylor KO values	87.1	82.5	78.1	73.8	69.7	65.7
Path - inches	-0.9	1.3	1.7	0.0	-4.0	-10.5
Wind Drift - inches	0.0	0.3	1.3	3.0	5.4	8.7

G1 Ballistic Coefficient = 0.339

Kynoch 525-grain Solid or Soft Nose

Distance - Yards	Muzzle	50	100	150	200	250
Velocity - fps	2300	2183	2070	1960	1853	1751
Energy - ft-lb	6168	5558	4995	4478	4005	3575
Taylor KO values	87.1	82.7	78.4	74.2	70.2	66.3
Path - inches	-0.9	1.3	1.7	0.0	-3.9	-10.4
Wind Drift - inches	0.0	0.3	1.2	2.9	5.2	8.4

G1 Ballistic Coefficient = 0.350

.577 Nitro Express 3-Inch

The .577 Nitro Express started life in about 1880 as a black powder cartridge (obviously not called "Nitro" then). Even before 1900, in the very dawning of the smokeless powder era, the .577 was introduced as a Nitro version. There was also a 2¾-inch version. With all these variations, any owner of a .577 caliber gun would be well advised to be very sure he knows just exactly which cartridges are suitable for use in his gun. The consequences of getting the wrong ammo are just too severe.

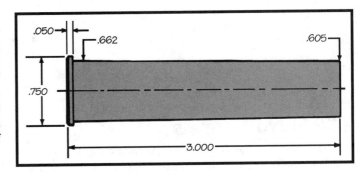

Relative Recoil Factor = 6.93

Controlling Agency: CIP

Bullet Weight Grains	Velocity fps	Maximum Average Pressure		Standard barrel for velocity testing:
		Copper Crusher	Transducer	
N/S	N/S	2200 bar	2450 bar	26 inches long - 1 turn in 30 inch twist

A² 750-grain Dead Tough SP, Monolithic Solid, Lion Load SP (None)

Distance - Yards	Muzzle	50	100	150	200	250
Velocity - fps	2050	1929	1811	1701	1595	1495
Energy - ft-lb	6998	6197	5463	4817	4234	3721
Taylor KO values	128.5	120.8	113.5	106.6	100.0	93.7
Path - inches	-0.9	1.8	2.2	0.0	-5.2	-13.9
Wind Drift - inches	0.0	0.4	1.6	3.8	7.0	11.2

G1 Ballistic Coefficient = 0.315

Kynoch 750-grain Solid or Soft Nose

Distance - Yards	Muzzle	50	100	150	200	250
Velocity - fps	2050	1960	1874	1790	1708	1630
Energy - ft-lb	7010	6400	5860	5335	4860	4424
Taylor KO values	128.5	122.8	117.5	112.2	107.1	102.2
Path - inches	-0.9	1.7	2.1	0.0	-4.8	-12.6
Wind Drift - inches	0.0	0.3	1.2	2.7	5.0	7.9

G1 Ballistic Coefficient = 0.430

.577 Tyrannosaur

The .577 Tyrannosaur is an A^2 development, designed (in about 1993) to produce a "big stopper" cartridge for a bolt-action rifle. The cartridge certainly achieves that goal, falling only about one Taylor KO index point (154 to 155) short of the legendary .600 NE. The case has a huge volume, holding something on the order of 150-grains of propellant. I think Art Alphin wins the naming award for this cartridge.

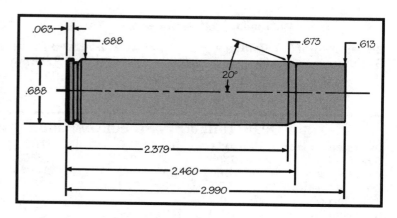

Relative Recoil Factor = 8.31

Controlling Agency: Factory

Bullet Weight Grains	Velocity fps	Maximum Average Pressure		Standard barrel for velocity testing:
		Copper Crusher	Transducer	
N/S	N/S	53,000 cup	65,000 psi	26 inches long - 1 turn in 12 inch twist

A^2 750-grain Dead Tough SP, Monolithic Solid, Lion Load SP (None)

Distance - Yards	Muzzle	50	100	150	200	250
Velocity - fps	2460	2327	2197	2072	1950	1835
Energy - ft-lb	10,077	9018	8039	7153	6335	5609
Taylor KO values	154.2	145.9	137.7	129.9	122.2	115.0
Path - inches	-0.9	1.1	1.4	0.0	-3.5	-9.2
Wind Drift - inches	0.0	0.3	1.2	2.9	5.2	8.5

G1 Ballistic Coefficient = 0.318

.600 Nitro Express

Developed by Jeffery in 1903, the .600 Nitro Express has long held the position of the ultimate "elephant gun." If John "Pondoro" Taylor's KO index has any meaning, the .600 Nitro is more potent as a stopper than the .50 BMG. That comparison puts us right into the center of the energy vs. momentum argument, and the .600 NE is one of the foremost examples for the momentum advocates. Guns are still being built for this cartridge.

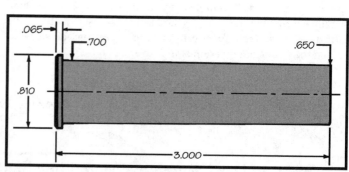

Relative Recoil Factor = 7.91

Controlling Agency: CIP

Bullet Weight Grains	Velocity fps	Maximum Average Pressure		Standard barrel for velocity testing:
		Copper Crusher	Transducer	
N/S	N/S	2200 bar	2450 bar	26 inches long - 1 turn in 30 inch twist

A² 900-grain Dead Tough SP, Monolithic Solid, Lion Load SP (None)

Distance - Yards	Muzzle	50	100	150	200	250
Velocity - fps	1950	1814	1680	1564	1452	1349
Energy - ft-lb	7596	6581	5634	4891	4212	3635
Taylor KO values	155.9	145.1	134.4	125.1	116.1	107.9
Path - inches	-0.9	2.2	2.6	0.0	-6.2	-16.5
Wind Drift - inches	0.0	0.5	2.1	4.8	8.8	16.5

G1 Ballistic Coefficient = 0.272

Kynoch 900-grain Solid or Soft Nose

Distance - Yards	Muzzle	50	100	150	200	250
Velocity - fps	1950	1807	1676	1551	1435	1390
Energy - ft-lb	7600	6330	5620	4808	4117	3596
Taylor KO values	155.9	144.5	134.0	124.0	114.8	111.1
Path - inches	-0.9	2.2	2.6	0.0	-6.3	-16.8
Wind Drift - inches	0.0	0.5	2.1	5.0	9.1	14.7

G1 Ballistic Coefficient = 0.262

.700 Nitro Express

The .700 Nitro Express first appeared in about 1988. As near as I can tell, the main reason for a .700 Nitro Express is that there already was a .600 Nitro Express. The .700 NE gives its owner a great "My gun is bigger than your gun" position. One wonders if it is really all that much "better." Because there are very few rifles chambered for this caliber, they are all custom-made and very, very, expensive.

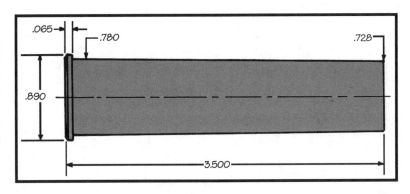

Relative Recoil Factor = 9.00

Controlling Agency: CIP

Bullet Weight Grains	Velocity fps	Maximum Average Pressure		Standard barrel for velocity testing:
		Copper Crusher	Transducer	
N/S	N/S	2200 bar*	2450 bar*	26 inches long*
*Estimated				

Kynoch 1000-grain Solid

Distance - Yards	Muzzle	50	100	150	200	250
Velocity - fps	2000	1879	1762	1651	1547	1448
Energy - ft-lb	8900	7842	6902	6061	5316	4663
Taylor KO values	206.3	193.8	181.7	170.3	159.6	149.4
Path - inches	-0.9	2.0	2.4	0.0	-5.6	-14.8
Wind Drift - inches	0.0	0.4	1.7	4.0	7.3	11.8

G1 Ballistic Coefficient = 0.310

A² 1000-grain Monolithic (None)

Distance - Yards	Muzzle	50	100	150	200	250
Velocity - fps	1900	1782	1669	1562	1461	1369
Energy - ft-lb	8015	7950	6188	5419	4740	4166
Taylor KO values	196.0	183.8	172.1	161.1	150.7	141.1
Path - inches	-0.9	2.3	2.7	0.0	-6.3	-16.6
Wind Drift - inches	0.0	0.5	1.9	4.3	7.9	12.7

G1 Ballistic Coefficient = 0.307

DEFENSIVE HANDGUN AMMO SELECTION

by

Massad Ayoob

Triton's 135-grain at 1325 fps velocity is the most potent conventional hollow point available in .40 pistols like this Beretta 94D Centurion.

Cor-Bon was the first company to make 9mm+P+ ballistics available to the private citizen.

Feedback from actual incidents shows that some handgun rounds are more reliable "manstoppers" than others.

A defensive handgun is intended to be used in the gravest extreme of deadly danger. Therefore, those who decide to own or even carry one put a lot of importance on selecting carry loads. As combat handgun guru Jeff Cooper has noted, the projectile is probably more important than the launcher when you must immediately stop lethal hostility with defensive handgun fire.

This issue has become bitterly hostile in recent years. Retired Detroit homicide investigator Evan Marshal has kept a running tally of "one-shot stops" with various rounds over the years. His colleague Ed Sanow brought dual backgrounds in engineering and law enforcement to the table, and they jointly authored two books—*Handgun Stopping Power* and *Street Stoppers*. The leading voice for the other side of the debate, Marty Fackler's

International Wound Ballistics Association, took more of a laboratory approach. Although I respect the views of many members of the IWBA, information from the field combined with the input I get from cops as chair of the firearms/deadly force committee of the American Society of Law Enforcement Trainers convinces me that Marshal and Sanow are on the right track.

A wide spectrum of defensive handgun rounds is available, so wide that a complete treatment does indeed require a book or two, not an article. Therefore, let's limit the discussion to the half-dozen most popular self-protection calibers. In any defensive round, we're looking for five factors. One is reliability. The defensive firearm is safety rescue equipment, and reliable function in a given weapon is a non-negotiable starting point. (Hint: In older "milspec" pistols that feed only ball ammunition, use Remington's standard line of jacketed hollowpoint [JHP] ammo. It was expressly designed to work reliably in any pistol that functions 100 percent with ball ammo, and will still open up reasonably well). Other factors we want are optimum penetration, reduced ricochet potential, and a proven street record as a manstopper. All these will cry out for a hollowpoint bullet. Last but not least, we want controllable recoil.

The .45 ACP is our most popular largebore defensive handgun caliber. Even with its relatively inefficient round-nose, full-metal-jacket design, it amassed a military history over most of this century as a proven fight-ender. The .45 ACP is even more potent with good hollowpoint bullets.

Federal Hydra-Shok is always a top choice in .45 ACP.

A hollowpoint expands from the inside of its cavity outward, and the larger cavity of the .45 caliber bullet promotes expansion if the projectile is correctly designed. A 165-grain .45 JHP is now on the market, loaded to velocities ranging from a "Lite" 1,050 fps to a screaming 1,250 fps. This bullet weight is too new to have a track record, but there exist three other proven options.

One option that makes sense for home and store defense is a 185-grain hollowpoint at a velocity of 935 to 1,000 fps. This bullet weight has lighter recoil than GI hardball and tends

to be very accurate. One good choice is the Winchester Silvertip, which usually expands well and stays in a human body.

Another option, one preferred by many police who choose the .45 ACP, is the 230-grain hollow point. Because it duplicates the bullet weight and velocity of hardball, one can practice with cheap GI ammo and have the same recoil and point-of-aim/point-of-impact coordinates as the duty load. Federal Hydra-Shok is the most thoroughly proven, but PMC StarFire, Remington Golden Saber, Speer Gold Dot, and Winchester SXT also perform well in flesh.

A third .45 ACP choice is +P. The greatest volume of field experience has been with the 185-grain JHP at 1,140 to 1,150 fps. It delivers more recoil than the above-mentioned standard pressure rounds, but its performance is right up there with the best loads in the caliber. Those who carry very short barrel guns like +P. This is because a 3 inch .45 barrel loses significant velocity with standard pressure cartridges, but will still send a +P out of its barrel at about 1,070 fps—more power than the standard pressure 185-grain hollowpoint—even when fired from a full-length Government Model. For ranchers, rural police, and others who might anticipate a long-range shot with their .45-caliber belt gun, the 185-grain +P offers a significantly flatter trajectory.

The .40 S&W, introduced jointly by Winchester and Smith & Wesson in 1990, has achieved enormous popularity with unprecedented speed. In its first generation, it used a 180-grain bullet at 950 fps. This roughly duplicated the ballistics of a .45 Silvertip, and not surprisingly, did well in the field. The second generation, popularized by the Border Patrol, is a 155-grain hollowpoint in the 1,200 fps velocity range. It delivers more recoil, but also a wider wound channel. This load in the Federal Classic brand has been enormously successful for the Border Patrol. The third generation round is a 135-grain hollowpoint in the 1,300 fps range, and this may provide the greatest volume of wounding the caliber offers. Gunshot injuries inflicted with it resemble those of a 125-grain .357 Magnum, penetrating about 8 to 10 inches in flesh, but with a remarkably wide wound channel.

A 165-grain "Lite" load at 950 fps is available, but the wounds inflicted by this load resemble .38 Special wounds more than the .357 Magnum-class wounds of the hot 135s, or those inflicted by the .45-like ballistics of the 180-grain JHP. I load my backup Glock 27 and my other off-duty .40s with the hot 135-grain Triton, and would probably go with something like the 155-grain Federal Classic or Winchester Silvertip if I carried a .40 S&W as a uniform sidearm.

The .357 Magnum has been in use since 1935, and one round in the caliber stands out above all others in every objective survey of gunfight results—the 125-grain hollowpoint at 1,400 to 1,450 fps. Recoil is fierce, and until low-flash gunpowder became the norm in the mid-1980s, it had blinding muzzle flash. You can learn to control this load, but you have to pay your dues with proper training and lots of shooting.

Most shooters prefer semi-jacketed bullets (Winchester, Federal, Remington, Speer) because their exposed lead tips open quickly, even when they encounter heavy clothing. Some shooters prefer full-jacketed hollowpoints, at least for their spare ammo, because soft lead bullet mouths can become deformed over time if you carry a speedloader

or Speed Strip in a pocket. Pro-Load offers 125-grain .357 Magnum ammo with a full jacketed bullet (the Hornady XTP) and so does Triton Cartridge (the Rainier Funnel Point).

The .38 Special ammo will work in a .357 Magnum revolver, but the reverse is not true. Today, the .38 Special's niche is in small, lightweight, pocket-size, carry revolvers with short barrels. Although a plethora of different .38 Special loads is available, the general consensus is that the 158-grain lead semi-wadcutter hollowpoint (LSWCHP) is the single most efficient round. All the big manufacturers produce such a load. Because it was first developed by Winchester with input from the FBI—which immediately adopted it—the 158-grain LSWCHP is now known as the "FBI round."

Loaded to +P velocity (some 950 to 1,000 fps from a four-inch-barrel revolver, perhaps 850 fps from a two-inch snubby) this round is manageable in a service revolver, but a bit snappy in a very small, light .38. Because it has no tough copper jacket to peel back, the lead hollowpoint almost always deforms in the opponent's body, even when fired from the short-barreled gun.

Although the FBI load is the near-unanimous choice of experts who have studied gunfights it just kicks too hard for some people. The best compromise is probably the Federal Nyclad 125-grain "Chief's Special" load at standard pressure. Recoil is mild, and the very soft lead inside the nylon jacket generally expands in living tissue.

The 9mm Parabellum (9mm Luger) has been in wide use since the beginning of the century. Military 9mm ball ammunition quickly earned a reputation as an impotent manstopper, but hollowpoint rounds developed in the latter third of the twentieth century have allowed the 9mm to equal or exceed the best hollowpoint .38 Specials.

Laboratory-based testing in 1988 created an enormous groundswell of interest in the 147-grain subsonic (950 fps) 9mm hollowpoint, but the round achieved mixed results in the field. Many cases of overpenetration occurred because of bullets expanding too late or not at all, and resulted in individuals taking a large number of hits before they went down. A great many of the agencies that adopted this round have forsaken the 9mm entirely and either adopted or approved more powerful .40 and/or .45 caliber pistols as replacements.

Far more successful was the "Illinois State Police" (ISP) load, a 115-grain hollowpoint at 1,300 fps. The ISP still issues it, and is enormously pleased with the proven effectiveness of this hot 9mm load in gunfights. The bullet almost always stays in the offender's body, and in Marshal's study had a 90 percent probability of stopping a fight with a single, solid torso hit. I saw one autopsy of a felon killed with such a round. The cause of death was listed as "cardiac maceration"; the heart had literally been shredded like burrito filling.

Because of high +P+ pressures, major manufacturers were reluctant to sell it to the public.

Remington's standard line of jacketed hollow points will work in any pistol that feeds ball.

Cor-Bon stepped into the breach, offering a 115-grain Sierra JHP factory round, loaded to 1,350 fps. Triton and Pro-Load followed, using Rainier Funnel Point and Speer Gold Dot projectiles, respectively. These are the most effective 9mm combat rounds available.

These +P and +P+ 9mm rounds have more recoil than standard loads, and they can be hard on older gun designs like the Browning Hi-Power. In a standard pressure 9mm round, the Federal Classic, coded 9BP, is a standout. Its 115-grain bullet at a little more than 1,100 fps always seems to mushroom, and it is a particularly accurate round.

The .380 ACP is extremely popular because many small, concealable guns are made in this caliber. It is right at the razor's edge of acceptable potency. Some authorities consider the .380 to be the absolute minimum, while some of us feel that it falls below the cut.

The best .380 hollowpoints harness all of its power, but all of a .380's power isn't much. If the bullet mushrooms, it may not penetrate far enough and may lack the power to smash major bone complexes, such as the pelvis. Deeper-penetrating rounds produce little damage around the wound track, and a full-metal-jacket, roundnose .380 can ricochet off a human skull or pelvis.

I have spent a lot of time in a slaughterhouse testing all six of these calibers on live animals. It should surprise no one that the .380 had the highest failure rate, while the .45 had the lowest failure rate.

In standard .380 hollowpoints, the PMC Starfire seemed to cause the most soft tissue damage. The wound track was short, but somewhat wider than the others. The most violent disruption came with 1,050 fps +P ammo, but this load also sometimes failed to go as deep as I'd have liked. A 90-grain JHP at that velocity roughly equals the potency of the 9mm Makarov, a cartridge the Russians developed to split the difference between the .380 and the 9mm Luger. If I had to carry a .380, I would load it with +P Triton or Cor-Bon.

However, I feel a better bet would be to purchase a Colt Pocket Nine. This pistol is exactly the size and thickness of a Walther PPK .380, and is actually lighter, but holds the same number of full power 9mm Luger rounds.

Compromise Rounds

When people read the writings of qualified experts who disagree vehemently, they may suffer a crisis of confidence. The .40 S&W cartridge was successful largely because it split the difference between 9mm and .45 ACP. When some officers wanted the sixteen-shot capacity of a 9mm but others wanted the per-shot stopping power of an eight-shot .45, the twelve-shot .40 gave one side enough additional capacity and the other side enough bullet diameter that everyone was satisfied, if grudgingly.

Compromise is likewise possible within most calibers for those who haven't yet figured out whether to believe Fackler or Marshall and Sanow. This is because some rounds have received the blessing of both sides.

In .45 ACP, both sides agree that the 230-grain hollowpoint can't be beat. Marshal

The 125-grain full power Magnum loads give maximum "stopping power" even in shorter barrel .357s like this Ruger SP-101.

prefers the Federal Hydra-Shok, and Fackler gave his highest accolades to the Black Talon, Winchester's predecessor to the current SXT. Frankly, you won't go wrong with either or with the Gold Dot, StarFire, or Golden Saber.

In .40 S&W, the load of compromise is the 180-grain subsonic hollowpoint. Marshal and Sanow report a one-shot stop rate in the high 80th percentile with the Federal Hydra-Shok in this configuration, and the 180-grain subsonic is likewise recommended by Fackler and his followers.

Both sides similarly agree on the 158-grain lead SWC +P hollowpoint as being a top choice in caliber .38 Special.

Neither side agrees with the other on .357 Magnum or 9mm loads. However, the .38 Special round they both recommend will work fine in the .357, and most 9mm pistols can be had in functionally identical size and shape, chambered for the .40 S&W cartridge. If experts can't even agree on whether the .380 is an acceptable minimum self-defense caliber, it is no wonder they can't agree on a favorite self-defense load.

The Bottom Line

Today, we have the best range of defensive ammunition choices that has existed in the history of handguns. No handgun round is powerful enough to vaporize an offender with a single hit. Reality tells us to find rounds that have been field-proven to do the best that handguns can do, then focus on developing tactics and marksmanship under stress—the two things that are far more likely to win gunfights than "magic guns," "magic calibers," or "magic bullets."

About the Author

Voted by his peers as the Outstanding American Handgunner of the Year in 1998, Massad Ayoob won Senior Class at the IDPA midwinter National Championships of 1999. He has investigated dozens of shootings as an expert for the courts, and has studied hundreds as a researcher in Officer Survival. A trustee of the Second Amendment Foundation for more than a decade, he has been head of firearms and deadly force training for the American Society of Law Enforcement Trainers since the organization was founded. Massad, in his twenty-fifth year as a sworn police officer, reports to work with a department-issue Ruger .45 and Black Hills 230-grain Gold Dot ammunition, and with 135-grain Triton .40 in his personally owned backup Glock. The pistol he keeps in his bedroom is a Beretta 9mm loaded with 115-grain Cor-Bon.

HANDGUNS FOR HUNTING
by
Wayne van Zwoll

It probably started with a .22, this notion that handguns could be used for hunting. In the late 19th century, when black powder cartridges relieved shooters of cap-and-ball loading, pistols were guns of convenience. Policemen and soldiers, cowboys and gamblers, Pinkerton detectives and Texas Rangers carried pistols when they didn't want people to see they were carrying guns at all, or when rifles and shotguns would be too awkward for quick use. Pistols weighed less and could be carried all the time. They could be tucked under a pillow or a shirt. Holsters snugged them to saddles, belts, and even garters.

But convenience was the only advantage pistols held over rifles and shotguns. Short-barreled guns chambered for powerful cartridges were necessarily bulky, and the recoil made them hard to control. They developed less velocity than long-barreled guns. Take the .44-40 caliber, a great favorite following the development of Colt's Single Action Army revolver and the Winchester 1873 rifle. It was chambered in both types of firearms. The rifle

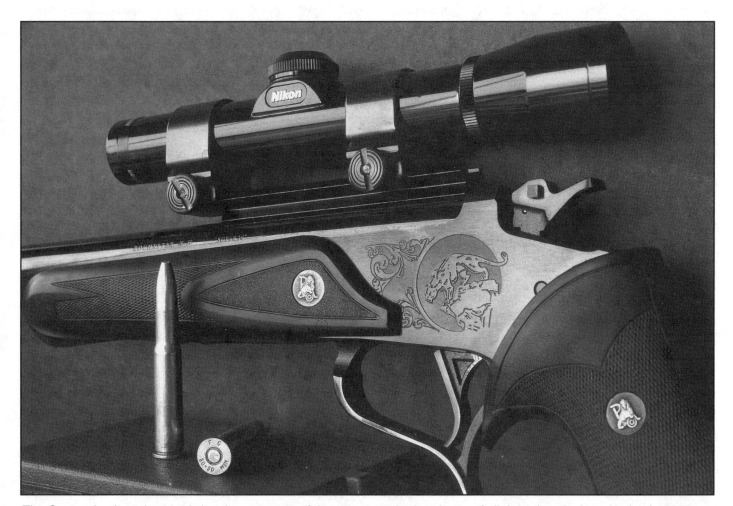

The Contender, here in .30-30, has become one of the most popular handguns of all time since its introduction in 1967.

gave shooters a decided edge in both ballistic performance and accuracy.

After smokeless powder replaced black in the 1890s, pistols and long guns both became more efficient. By the advent of the First World War, autoloading pistols and double-action revolvers had all but replaced single-action Colts among law enforcement agencies and military groups. Smith & Wesson's .38 Military and Police double-action had earned plaudits within the U.S. Revolver Association (USRA), then the largest competitive handgun association in the world. In 1913, twenty-seven of the forty USRA records were shot with Smith & Wessons, no doubt almost all of them with the M&P Target model.

In the late 1920s Smith & Wesson solicited suggestions from shooters for the development of another target gun. The consensus: Build a .22 just like the .38. In 1930 the firm introduced its K22 Outdoorsman, cannily named to draw sportsmen as well as target shooters to the counter. The six-shot revolver featured a six-inch barrel, checkered grips of Circassian walnut, target sights, and a crisp trigger that broke at about three pounds. It weighed thirty-five ounces and was advertised to keep bullets in an inch and a half at fifty yards. The gun sold well, but in 1939, after a production run of just 17,000, S&W gave it a makeover. A faster action and micrometer rear sight improved the K22. The new model called the K22 Masterpiece, retailed for just $40 in 1940. Shortly thereafter it was discontinued as Smith & Wesson geared up for military production.

Despite its success with this new .22 and other revolvers, the company was ailing. Diversification during the 1930s—handcuffs, razor blade sharpeners, washing machines,

and flush valves for toilets—failed to bring better financial news. Doggedly, S&W poured more resources into new revolver designs. The .38-44 Heavy Duty, which appeared with the original K22 in 1930, was the answer to law enforcement demands for a cartridge with more power than the .38 Special (a potent round for those times). Built on the massive "N" frame, this new revolver had the strength to bottle pressure from the .38-44—essentially a .38 Special loaded to higher performance levels. The gun sold well, and more than 11,000 units were produced before it was discontinued in 1941.

A year after the .38-44 Heavy Duty came along, S&W offered a refined version, the .38-44 Outdoorsman. It had target sights, a longer barrel (6½ inches compared to 5 inches for the Heavy Duty) and walnut grips that extended farther up the frame. Like its plain-Jane sister, the Outdoorsman was discontinued in 1941. It was a beautiful revolver. For the hunters who had shot rabbits with a K22, the .38-44 Outdoorsmen no doubt seemed a natural companion in the woods. Some surely found their way to deer camps.

During the 1930s, gun authority Philip B. Sharpe, who had worked on loads for the .38-44, urged the development of a more potent revolver round. Smith & Wesson took the idea to Winchester Repeating Arms. Winchester came up with a case an eighth-inch longer than that of the .38 Special but the same diameter. It held a heavier powder charge that would drive a 158-grain bullet over 1,500 fps.

Using the N frame of the .38-44, S&W designed a revolver for Winchester's lively round. Company market analysts predicted limited demand, so they advertised the first .357 Magnum revolvers as custom guns,

The .30-30 and 7-30 Waters are mild rifle rounds, but they're giants among handgun cartridges. The Thompson-Center's Contender can handle them.

available with a variety of sight and barrel options. Each gun would be zeroed by the factory at 200 yards, and each owner would get a registration certificate numbered to the gun. For such high-falutin' treatment, buyers would have to shell out $60, or about $15 more than they'd pay for any other Smith & Wesson revolver.

Demand for the powerful new gun far exceeded expectations. In 1938, after 5,500 revolvers, the company dropped the registration certificate. At 120 guns a month, it could barely keep up with orders. When the war diverted production efforts, 6,642 Magnums had been built. Part of the .357's appeal was its extraordinary reach. In the hands of pistol wizard Ed McGivern (who had used a S&W .38 to rattle five bullets into a playing card in ²/₅ of a second) the .357 Magnum revolver could hit man-sized targets at 600 yards! If shooters hadn't thought of the K22 Masterpiece or .38-44 Outdoorsman as hunting guns, many saw the .357 Magnum as having potential beyond law enforcement, defense, and target shooting.

But in the dust of the Depression, no civilian gun or cartridge could pull S&W from its economic hole. In desperation, the company turned to Great Britain with a proposal to build a 9mm assault rifle. The British government responded favorably, with a $1 million advance. But the 1940 Light Rifle did not please either party, and eventually Smith & Wesson consulting engineer Carl Hellstrom persuaded the firm to scrap the project and return the advance in pistols! Great Britain grudgingly accepted the settlement. Hellstrom became S&W's fifth president in 1946.

Hellstrom pushed for aggressive expansion of the company in the postwar era. He wisely focused on handguns, allowing only handcuffs as peripheral products. In 1950, profits from civilian revolvers paid for a new 270,000-square-foot factory. About this time, a stocky frontiersman with a big cowboy hat began

As early as 1953 Dick Casull was experimenting with stout single action revolvers and hot-loaded .45 Long Colt cartridges.

201

urging development of a new handgun cartridge even more powerful than the .357. Elmer Keith had handloaded the .44 Special in the S&W 1950 N-frame Target revolver to perform well beyond traditional expectations. "Give the .44 what you gave the .38 in 1935, and sales of that gun will climb," he said. Carl Hellstrom asked Remington's R. H. Coleman to research the idea.

In the summer of 1954, Remington delivered a new .44 cartridge to Smith & Wesson, an eighth-inch longer than the .44 Special. Tests in rechambered Model 1950 Target revolvers showed that the guns needed more beef. A heavier barrel and modified frame followed, boosting weight from 40 to 47 ounces. The gun was named the Model 29. The first commercial .44 Magnum revolver went to R. H. Coleman at Remington in January, 1956. Julian Hatcher of the NRA Technical Division got the second gun, and Elmer Keith got the third. More than 3,100 Model 29s sold the first year of production.

By this time, Dick Casull, a pistol shooter of experimental bent, was loading the .45 Long Colt to higher pressures than were safe in the cylinders of the early single-actions for which it had been developed. He began his work on a more potent .45 in 1953, and in 1959 P. O. Ackley wrote about a new .454 Casull Magnum cartridge. That year Ruger began offering its stout "Super Blackhawk" revolvers in .44 Magnum, and the "Blackhawk" in .45 Long Colt. Dick Casull latched onto the Blackhawk, replacing its six-shot cylinder with a five-shot cylinder bored for his new round. After a long life as a wildcat, the .454 became commercially available in 1985 with the introduction of the Freedom Arms single-action revolver. The use of small rifle primers strengthened the case. With a 260-grain jacketed bullet at 1,800 fps

and a 300-grain at 1,625, factory ammunition now loaded by Winchester outperforms .44 Magnum cartridges by quite a stretch.

The Freedom Arms revolver is still widely acclaimed as the best-made single-action in production. The fit and finish of these guns, with the muscle of the .454 Casull cartridge, endear them to serious hunters. They're more expensive than the Smith & Wesson Model 29, but owners say they're worth every penny.

The .44 Magnum soon found its way out of the S&W fold as other gunmakers developed mechanisms big and strong enough to handle it. Ruger's Super Blackhawk became a favorite, partly because it was a well-engineered single-action and partly because it looked good with the unmistakable Old West lines that would later be adopted by Freedom Arms. After Ruger got into the double-action business, it designed the "Redhawk" specifically for hunters. This .44 Magnum with 5½- and 7½-inch barrels competed directly with the Smith & Wesson 29. The "Super Redhawk" with 7½ and 9½-inch barrels has a rib machined as an integral scope base. This Ruger is most certainly a revolver built expressly for big game hunting.

Like Ruger, Colt now has a .44 Magnum double-action revolver, the Anaconda. It also comes in .45 Long Colt, with barrel lengths of four, six and eight inches.

During the 1960s, when I was growing up, the Smith & Wesson Model 29 became popular as a backup gun with guides and hunters chasing brown bears in alder thickets. One guide laughed off the .44 magnum as a bear stopper. "It's hard to hit with," he told me. "You can't shoot it fast because there's too much recoil. If the bear is close and coming, you can't count on stopping it. I remember one big boar that charged out of a tangle and ran right over me as I emptied the cylinder into it. I'd have been dead if he'd stopped to chew on me.

"Oh, I suppose a revolver is better than nothing, but only if you are a very fast and cool shot. Even then, a bear can unhinge you up close. Things happen so quickly you think the world is blowing up around you. The best plan for bear hunters is to make one good shot with a powerful rifle. Then the bear dies with no fuss."

Using a handgun as a primary firearm for big game was still a novel idea to most hunters in the 1960s. Remington's XP-100 bolt-action pistol, chambered for the .221 Fireball, was not intended for big game, but the bullet's high speed and the XP's inherent accuracy earned the allegiance of hunters beyond the chuck pasture. A friend of mine has killed several moose with the Fireball. Conceding that shots must be surgically placed, he tells me he has never lost an animal. Given the success of Inuits using .22 rimfires on caribou, there's no doubt that the .221 can be deadly on these animals and on deer of all sorts. The .221, essentially a shortened .222, did not survive Remington's abandonment of the XP-100. It is no longer loaded at Ilion.

During this era, Smith & Wesson offered a hunting revolver chambered for the .22 Remington Jet. Cylinder inserts converted this gun to shoot .22 rimfire cartridges. The Jet was neither powerful enough for big game nor accurate enough to compete with the likes of the XP-100.

In 1965, gun designer Warren Center joined the K. W. Thompson Tool Company in Rochester, New Hampshire. Ken Thompson was struggling to keep the investment casting foundry going year round, so when Center came up with a single-shot pistol in his basement workshop, the company began manufacturing the gun to supplement its cast parts business. The "Contender" pistol, announced in 1967, could easily have failed. It cost more than many revolvers, yet it used an old break-action design. It was hardly a handsome gun, and it weighed a lot.

But Warren Center made the Contender marketable with easily switched barrels. You could buy one pistol, then equip it with several barrels that could be installed in the manner of assembling a double shotgun. A new 2,500-square-foot factory was soon built to manufacture only the pistol. Chamberings were expanded to include a tremendous assortment of pistol and small rifle cartridges, plus wildcats that Center thought would be popular with hunters. Shot barrels (.410) with interchangeable chokes followed. Now the Contender is chambered for rounds ranging in size from the .22 Long Rifle to the .45-70. The most popular include some that have traditionally appeared in woods rifles—the .30-30, 7mm-30 Waters, and .35 Remington. These numbers make the .44 Magnum cartridge, also on the list, look anemic. Barrels of 10 to 16 inches snag most of their potential. A break-action single-shot can accommodate a long barrel without being cumbersome—a significant advantage over autoloaders and revolvers.

Part of the Contender's continued appeal is its adaptability to scopes. Cartridges with lots of reach have little utility if you can't aim precisely at long range. By the 1970s, optics firms were offering scopes with long eye relief. The market in pistol glass has grown fast, and now includes variable as well as fixed-power scopes.

This hunter wisely rests his pistol on a fence post after padding the forestock with his hand.

To extend the reach of pistoleers still farther, a couple of years ago Thompson-Center introduced another single-shot break-action gun. Chambered for such cartridges as the .260, 7mm-08, .270, .308, and .30-06, the "Encore" is really a rifle without a buttstock. It comes with a 10-inch or 15-inch barrel and is available with a 2–7X scope installed.

Continued strong sales for the Contender, a warm reception for the Encore, and a booming market in long-range rifles and cartridges no doubt influenced Savage Arms to develop its bolt-action "Striker" pistols, now in their second year. Reminiscent of Remington's XP-100, the Striker comes with a laminated or synthetic stock, the grip well under the action so the substantial weight (five pounds plus) is somewhat balanced over the web of your hand. The pistol is still muzzle-heavy with its 14-inch barrel, now chambered in

your choice of .223, .22-250, .243, 7mm-08, .260, or .308. There are no sights. Almost everyone will scope this pistol. There's a provision for a bipod too. Some models come with an adjustable muzzle brake to tame barrel jump.

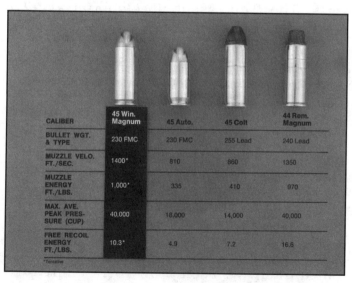

CALIBER	45 Win. Magnum	45 Auto.	45 Colt	44 Rem. Magnum
BULLET WGT. & TYPE	230 FMC	230 FMC	255 Lead	240 Lead
MUZZLE VELO. FT./SEC.	1400*	810	860	1350
MUZZLE ENERGY FT./LBS.	1,000*	335	410	970
MAX. AVE. PEAK PRES-SURE (CUP)	40,000	18,000	14,000	40,000
FREE RECOIL ENERGY FT./LBS.	10.3*	4.9	7.2	16.8

*Tentative

The .45 Winchester Magnum is one of several cartridges designed for autoloading pistols that is also potent enough for big game.

During the late 1970s the competitive pastime of metallic silhouette shooting became a pistol game with the formation, by Elgin Gates, of the International Handgun Metallic Silhouette Association. Gates convinced Roy Weatherby to build a pistol for the sport. Roy adapted his svelte .224 Varmintmaster rifle action by moving the trigger mechanism forward and eliminating the magazine. At that time, alas, Weatherby rifles were being made in Japan. After production of only 200 handguns, the Japanese government announced that Howa (the manufacturer) could no longer export "pistols." Though final assembly and fitting was done in the U.S. by Weatherby, the 15-inch barrels were not legal for shipment from Japan. Those pistols already exported—150 in .308 and 50 in .22-250—immediately became collectors' items.

That was the last of Weatherby handguns until 1997, when the company trotted out a new centerfire pistol, this time with the grip behind the bolt action. The pistol, now available in .22-250, .243, 7mm-08, and .308, was meant to be fired from a bipod. Its magazine holds three shots, one more than that of Savage's Striker. Like the Weatherby pistol of 1980, this one wears a 15-inch barrel.

A number of other handguns merit attention from serious hunters. The Wichita Silhouette Pistol in .308, 7mm IHMSA, and 7mm08 is a single-shot bolt-action. Its rear grip looks like that of the Weatherby. The 11-inch barrel has adjustable sights. Wichita also makes a top-break single-shot called the International. It's available with 10- and 14-inch barrels chambered in a variety of cartridges from .22 Long Rifle to .30-30.

Wildey manufactures an autoloading pistol for hunters. Chamberings include the .41, .44, and .475 Wildey Magnums, the .45 and .475 Winchester Magnums. The gas-operated mechanism features a three-lug rotating bolt. Barrels from 5 to 14 inches long have ventilated ribs. These guns are heavy—four pounds with the shortest barrel—but have a seven-shot capacity.

Another autoloader with the power for big game is the LAR Grizzly, available in .44 Magnum, .45 Winchester Magnum, and .50 Action Express, as well as in lesser chamberings. Barrel lengths are 5½ and 6½ inches. The Grizzly looks and handles much like a Colt 1911. Magazine capacity is seven rounds (one less for the .50 AE).

Almost more interesting than the evolution of handguns for hunters has been the development of cartridges suitable for handgun mechanisms and efficient in short barrels.

J. D. Jones is perhaps the most prolific of designers in this field. His wildcats have proven so useful that they've been offered as standard chamberings in some models. J. D. now earns part of his living fitting custom barrels to the Thompson-Center Contender, a gun that has served him well on the hunt.

The increasing interest in handgun hunting has forced state wildlife agencies to adopt regulations specific to handguns. Minimum caliber restrictions emerged right away as a controversial issue. In handguns even more than in rifles, bore diameter means little. Modern small-bore cartridges like the 7mm-08 Remington have far more punch than traditional pistol rounds with bigger bullets. The chambering of rifle cartridges in pistols all but mandates that minimum cartridges be designated by delivered energy in combination with bullet weight.

What is a reasonable minimum? That depends on the game being hunted and the proficiency of the hunter, as well as on the type of handgun, cartridge, and bullet. A scoped Weatherby pistol in .308, fired from a bipod, is certainly effective on deer and even elk out to ordinary rifle ranges. An S&W 29 with iron sights, fired from the sit, is probably a 50-yard deer gun in the hands of most shooters.

Most pistol cartridges deliver plenty of energy to kill deer-sized game cleanly from up close. When you get beyond 75 yards a rifle cartridge has an edge over traditional handgun rounds. Part of the difference lies in bullet design. Short, blunt pistol bullets can't carry their energy very far.

As with rifles, the main cause for missing and crippling game lies in the shooter's inability to hold the sights still and trigger the shot gently. A softpoint bullet (or large-caliber cast bullet) that centers the vitals doesn't have to be screaming along at 3000 fps. It doesn't have to weigh 250 grains or boast elaborate devices for controlling expansion. It just has to land in the right place. Because it lacks a buttstock, a pistol is harder to aim than a rifle.

If I were to buy a new handgun for big-game hunting, it would be a Freedom Arms revolver in .454 Casull. I'm impressed by the cartridge, having used it in a carbine last year to kill a pronghorn. But in choosing a hunting handgun, I'm not after efficiency. If I were,

I'd pick a Savage Striker or Weatherby Mark V pistol chambered for a rifle round, or perhaps a Thompson-Center Encore. I just like certain kinds of pistols, and none of them look best or handle well with a scope.

The bolt-action pistol, pioneered by Remington and taken a step farther by Savage and Weatherby, is one of the most accurate and ballistically efficient of all big-game guns for its size. No doubt hunters after top performance will ensure continued brisk sales of these and the Thompson-Center single-shots. But powerful, accurate guns are only deadly on game when they're properly aimed, and when hunters choose their shots with care. Those caveats have applied ever since Elmer Keith started handloading the .44 Special.

Hunters who carry traditional handguns with iron sights must get closer to game than they would if they carried rifles or handguns with scopes and bipods. That's part of the fun of handgun hunting, as I see it. I'll hunt with my Smith & Wesson .44 Magnum or my single-action Ruger in .45 Long Colt and without killing anything, have as much fun as the fellow with the most far-reaching pistol on the market. It seems to me that Smith & Wesson had it right in 1930, naming the K22 the Outdoorsman. There's a lot of pleasure to be had just taking a traditional revolver into the woods.

Data for
Pistol and Revolver
Ammunition

.25 Auto (ACP)

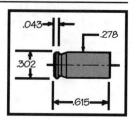

The smallest of the current factory production centerfire pistol rounds, the great virtue of the .25 Auto is that it fits very small pistols. The power is so low, much lower than a .22 WMR that its use for self-defense is limited to the deterrent effect that the mere showing of any gun provides. This cartridge has been around since 1908. That's a long time and there are still 10 different loadings available, so someone must be buying this ammunition.

Relative Recoil Factor = 0.17   **Controlling Agency: SAAMI**

Bullet Weight Grains	Velocity fps	Maximum Average Pressure		Standard barrel for velocity testing:
		Copper Crusher	Transducer	2 inches long - 1 turn in 16 inch twist
35XTP-HP	900	18,000 cup	25,000 psi	
45XP	805	18,000 cup	25,000 psi	
50MC-FMC	755	18,000 cup	25,000 psi	

Hornady 35-grain JHP (9001 and 9001c)

Distance - Yards	Muzzle	25	50	75	100
Velocity - fps	900	854	813	777	742
Energy - ft/lb	63	57	51	47	43
Taylor KO values	1.1	1.1	1.0	1.0	0.9
Mid-Range Trajectory Height - inches	0.0	0.3	1.5	3.5	6.6
Drop - inches	0.0	-1.4	-5.8	-13.4	-24.6

G1 Ballistic Coefficient = 0.073

Speer 35-grain Gold Dot (23602)

Distance - Yards	Muzzle	25	50	75	100
Velocity - fps	900	856	816	781	747
Energy - ft/lb	62	57	52	47	43
Taylor KO values	1.1	1.1	1.0	1.0	0.9
Mid-Range Trajectory Height - inches	0.0	0.3	1.5	3.5	6.5
Drop - inches	0.0	-1.4	-5.7	-13.4	-24.5

G1 Ballistic Coefficient = 0.076

Winchester 45-grain Expanding Point (X25AXP)

Distance - Yards	Muzzle	25	50	75	100
Velocity - fps	815	770	729	690	655
Energy - ft/lb	66	59	53	48	42
Taylor KO values	1.3	1.2	1.2	1.1	1.1
Mid-Range Trajectory Height - inches	0.0	0.4	1.8	4.4	8.2
Drop - inches	0.0	-1.7	-7.1	-16.5	-30.6

G1 Ballistic Coefficient = 0.059

CCI 50-grain FMJ (3501)

Distance - Yards	Muzzle	25	50	75	100
Velocity - fps	800	773	755	724	700
Energy - ft/lb	73	66	63	58	54
Taylor KO values	1.4	1.4	1.3	1.3	1.3
Mid-Range Trajectory Height - inches	0.0	0.4	1.8	4.2	7.7
Drop - inches	0.0	-1.7	-7.1	-16.4	-29.8

G1 Ballistic Coefficient = 0.098

American Eagle (Federal) 50-grain FMJ (AE25AP)

Distance - Yards	Muzzle	25	50	75	100
Velocity - fps	760	750	730	720	700
Energy - ft/lb	65	60	60	55	55
Taylor KO values	1.4	1.3	1.3	1.3	1.3
Mid-Range Trajectory Height - inches	0.0	0.5	1.9	4.5	8.1
Drop - inches	0.0	-1.9	-7.7	-17.6	-31.8

G1 Ballistic Coefficient = 0.155

Federal 50-grain FMJ (C25AP)

Distance - Yards	Muzzle	25	50	75	100
Velocity - fps	760	750	730	720	700
Energy - ft/lb	65	60	60	55	55
Taylor KO values	1.4	1.3	1.3	1.3	1.3
Mid-Range Trajectory Height - inches	0.0	0.5	1.9	4.5	8.1
Drop - inches	0.0	-1.9	-7.7	-17.6	-31.8

G1 Ballistic Coefficient = 0.155

Fiocchi 50-grain Metal Case (25AP)

Distance - Yards	Muzzle	25	50	75	100
Velocity - fps	760	750	730	720	700
Energy - ft/lb	65	60	60	55	55
Taylor KO values	1.4	1.3	1.3	1.3	1.3
Mid-Range Trajectory Height - inches	0.0	0.5	1.9	4.5	8.1
Drop - inches	0.0	-1.9	-7.7	-17.6	-31.8

G1 Ballistic Coefficient = 0.155

Magech 50-grain Full Metal Case (25A)

Distance - Yards	Muzzle	25	50	75	100
Velocity - fps	760	733	707	682	659
Energy - ft/lb	64	60	56	52	48
Taylor KO values	1.4	1.3	1.3	1.2	1.2
Mid-Range Trajectory Height - inches	0.0	0.5	2.0	4.7	8.7
Drop - inches	0.0	-1.9	-7.9	-18.2	-33.2

G1 Ballistic Coefficient = 0.089

Remington 50-grain Metal Case (R25AP)

Distance - Yards	Muzzle	25	50	75	100
Velocity - fps	760	733	707	682	659
Energy - ft/lb	64	60	56	52	48
Taylor KO values	1.4	1.3	1.3	1.2	1.2
Mid-Range Trajectory Height - inches	0.0	0.5	2.0	4.7	8.7
Drop - inches	0.0	-1.9	-7.9	-18.2	-33.2

G1 Ballistic Coefficient = 0.089

UMC (Remington) 50-grain Metal Case (L25AP)

Distance - Yards	Muzzle	25	50	75	100
Velocity - fps	760	733	707	682	659
Energy - ft/lb	64	60	56	52	48
Taylor KO values	1.4	1.3	1.3	1.2	1.2
Mid-Range Trajectory Height - inches	0.0	0.5	2.0	4.7	8.7
Drop - inches	0.0	-1.9	-7.9	-18.2	-33.2

G1 Ballistic Coefficient = 0.089

USA (Winchester) 50-grain FMJ (Q4203)

Distance - Yards	Muzzle	25	50	75	100
Velocity - fps	760	736	713	690	669
Energy - ft/lb	64	60	56	53	50
Taylor KO values	1.4	1.3	1.3	1.2	1.2
Mid-Range Trajectory Height - inches	0.0	0.5	2.0	4.6	8.6
Drop - inches	0.0	-1.9	-7.9	-18.1	-32.8

G1 Ballistic Coefficient = 0.100

PMC 50-grain FMJ (25A)

Distance - Yards	Muzzle	25	50	75	100
Velocity - fps	754	730	707	685	663
Energy - ft/lb	63	59	55	52	49
Taylor KO values	1.4	1.3	1.3	1.2	1.2
Mid-Range Trajectory Height - inches	0.0	0.5	2.0	4.7	8.7
Drop - inches	0.0	-2.0	-8.0	-18.4	-33.4

G1 Ballistic Coefficient = 0.099

.30 Luger (7.65mm)

The .30 Luger actually predates the 9mm Luger, having been introduced in 1900. It is very similar to the .30 Mauser but is not interchangeable. The design is a rimless bottlenecked case that anticipated the .357 Sig design by nearly 100 years. Winchester has recently started making this ammunition. They must think that they can sell enough to pay for tooling up the line or they wouldn't bother.

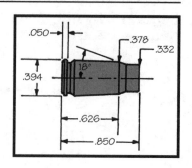

Relative Recoil Factor = 0.52   **Controlling Agency : SAAMI**

Bullet Weight Grains	Velocity fps	Maximum Average Pressure		Standard barrel for velocity testing:
		Copper Crusher	Transducer	
93	1190	28000 cup	N/S	4.5 inches long - 1 turn in 11 inch twist

Winchester 93-grain FMJ (X30LP)

Distance - Yards	Muzzle	25	50	75	100
Velocity - fps	1220	1165	1110	1075	1040
Energy - ft/lb	305	280	255	239	225
Taylor KO values	5.1	4.9	4.7	4.5	4.4
Mid-Range Trajectory Height - inches	0.0	0.1	0.9	2.0	3.5
Drop - inches	0.0	-0.8	-3.1	-7.2	-13.2

G1 Ballistic Coefficient = 0.184

.32 Short Colt

Here's another oldie (vintage of about 1875) that's been recently reintroduced into manufacturing. As with the .30 Luger, it's hard to see where the sales potential comes from, but since I know practically nothing about that part of the business, I hope the factory folks are smarter than I am.

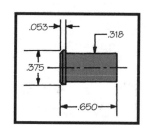

Relative Recoil Factor = 0.27   **Controlling Agency: SAAMI**

Bullet Weight Grains	Velocity fps	Maximum Average Pressure		Standard barrel for velocity testing:
		Copper Crusher	Transducer	
80 L	700	13,000 cup	N/S	4 inches long, vented- 1 turn in 16 inch twist

Winchester 80-grain Lead Round Nose (LRN) (X32SCP)

Distance - Yards	Muzzle	25	50	75	100
Velocity - fps	745	702	665	625	590
Energy - ft/lb	100	88	79	69	62
Taylor KO values	2.6	2.5	2.4	2.2	2.1
Mid-Range Trajectory Height - inches	0.0	0.5	2.2	5.0	9.9
Drop - inches	0.0	-2.0	-8.5	-19.9	-36.8

G1 Ballistic Coefficient = 0.054

.32 Smith & Wesson (S&W)

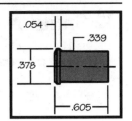

The little .32 Smith & Wesson cartridge dates clear back to 1878. It was designed when "pocket" pistols were all the rage. This is a meek and mild cartridge and can't be considered for any serious self-defense role. Both the muzzle energy and the Taylor KO indices are far too low to be effective.

Relative Recoil Factor = 0.27   **Controlling Agency: SAAMI**

Bullet Weight Grains	Velocity fps	Maximum Average Pressure		Standard barrel for velocity testing:
		Copper Crusher	Transducer	
85-88 L	700	12,000 cup	N/S	4 inches long, Vented - 1 turn in 18.75 inch twist

Magtech 85-grain LRN (32SWA)

Distance - Yards	Muzzle	25	50	75	100	
Velocity - fps	680	662	645	627	610	
Energy - ft/lb	87	83	78	74	70	
Taylor KO values	2.6	2.5	2.5	2.4	2.3	
Mid-Range Trajectory Height - inches	0.0	0.2	2.1	5.3	10.1	
Drop - inches	0.0	-2.4	-9.8	-22.3	-40.5	G1 Ballistic Coefficient = 0.115

Winchester 85-grain LRN (X32SWP)

Distance - Yards	Muzzle	25	50	75	100	
Velocity - fps	680	662	645	627	610	
Energy - ft/lb	87	83	78	74	70	
Taylor KO values	2.6	2.5	2.5	2.4	2.3	
Mid-Range Trajectory Height - inches	0.0	0.2	2.1	5.3	10.1	
Drop - inches	0.0	-2.4	-9.8	-22.3	-40.5	G1 Ballistic Coefficient = 0.115

Remington 88-grain Lead (R32SW)

Distance - Yards	Muzzle	25	50	75	100	
Velocity - fps	680	662	645	627	610	
Energy - ft/lb	90	86	81	77	73	
Taylor KO values	2.8	2.6	2.5	2.5	24	
Mid-Range Trajectory Height - inches	0.0	0.2	2.1	5.3	10.1	
Drop - inches	0.0	-2.4	-9.8	-22.3	-40.5	G1 Ballistic Coefficient = 0.115

.32 Smith & Wesson Long

This is a very old cartridge (introduced in 1896). While it originally was considered a self-defense round for pocket pistols, today's use of this caliber is almost exclusively for target pistols. In some competitions, .32-caliber pistols meet the rules and have the virtue of very light recoil and fine accuracy. The use of this caliber in competition seems more common in Europe than in the US.

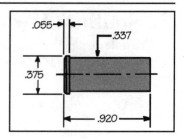

Relative Recoil Factor = 0.35   **Controlling Agency: SAAMI**

Bullet Weight Grains	Velocity fps	Maximum Average Pressure Copper Crusher	Transducer	Standard barrel for velocity testing:
98 L	775	12,000 cup	15,000 psi	4 inches long - 1 turn in 18.75 inch twist

Lapua 83-grain Lead Wadcutter (LWC) (4318023)

Distance - Yards	Muzzle	25	50	75	100
Velocity - fps	787	688	604	530	463
Energy - ft/lb	114	87	67	52	40
Taylor KO values	2.9	2.6	2.3	2.0	1.7
Mid-Range Trajectory Height - inches	0.0	0.5	2.3	6.0	12.2
Drop - inches	0.0	-1.9	-8.5	-21.0	-41.3

G1 Ballistic Coefficient = 0.029

Federal 98-grain LWC (C32LA)

Distance - Yards	Muzzle	25	50	75	100
Velocity - fps	780	700	630	560	500
Energy - ft/lb	130	105	85	70	55
Taylor KO values	3.4	3.0	2.7	2.4	2.2
Mid-Range Trajectory Height - inches	0.0	0.5	2.2	5.8	11.1
Drop - inches	0.0	-1.9	-8.4	-20.5	-39.6

G1 Ballistic Coefficient = 0.028

PMC 98-grain LRN (32SWLA)

Distance - Yards	Muzzle	25	50	75	100
Velocity - fps	789	770	751	733	716
Energy - ft/lb	135	129	123	117	112
Taylor KO values	3.4	3.4	3.3	3.2	3.1
Mid-Range Trajectory Height - inches	0.0	0.4	1.8	4.2	7.7
Drop - inches	0.0	-1.8	-7.2	-16.5	-29.8

G1 Ballistic Coefficient = 0.134

Norma 98-grain LWC (17810)

Distance - Yards	Muzzle	25	50	75	100
Velocity - fps	787	759	732	707	683
Energy - ft/lb	136	126	118	109	102
Taylor KO values	3.4	3.3	3.2	3.1	3.0
Mid-Range Trajectory Height - inches	0.0	0.4	1.9	4.4	8.1
Drop - inches	0.0	-1.8	-7.4	-17.0	-31.0

G1 Ballistic Coefficient = 0.091

Lapua 98-grain LWC (4318026)

Distance - Yards	Muzzle	25	50	75	100
Velocity - fps	787	727	673	623	578
Energy - ft/lb	135	115	98	85	73
Taylor KO values	3.4	3.2	2.9	2.7	2.5
Mid-Range Trajectory Height - inches	0.0	0.5	2.1	5.0	9.7
Drop - inches	0.0	-1.8	-7.8	-18.6	-35.0

G1 Ballistic Coefficient = 0.041

Federal 98-grain LRN (C32LB)

Distance - Yards	Muzzle	25	50	75	100
Velocity - fps	710	690	630	560	500
Energy - ft/lb	130	105	85	70	55
Taylor KO values	33.1	2.8	2.6	2.4	2.2
Mid-Range Trajectory Height - inches	0.0	0.6	2.3	5.3	9.6
Drop - inches	0.0	-2.3	-9.7	-23.3	-44.1

G1 Ballistic Coefficient = 0.036

Magtech 98-grain LWC (32SWLB)

Distance - Yards	Muzzle	25	50	75	100
Velocity - fps	682	628	578	533	491
Energy - ft/lb	102	86	73	62	52
Taylor KO values	3.0	2.8	2.5	2.3	2.2
Mid-Range Trajectory Height - inches	0.0	0.6	2.3	6.7	12.6
Drop - inches	0.0	-2.5	-10.4	-24.9	-47.1

G1 Ballistic Coefficient = 0.038

Magtech 98-grain LRN (32SWLA)

Distance - Yards	Muzzle	25	50	75	100
Velocity - fps	705	687	670	651	635
Energy - ft/lb	108	103	98	92	88
Taylor KO values	3.1	3.0	2.9	2.8	2.8
Mid-Range Trajectory Height - inches	0.0	0.5	2.3	5.3	10.5
Drop - inches	0.0	-2.2	-9.1	-20.8	-37.6

G1 Ballistic Coefficient = 0.119

Remington 98-grain LRN (R32SWL)

Distance - Yards	Muzzle	25	50	75	100
Velocity - fps	705	687	670	651	635
Energy - ft/lb	108	103	98	92	88
Taylor KO values	3.1	3.0	2.9	2.8	2.8
Mid-Range Trajectory Height - inches	0.0	0.5	2.3	5.3	10.5
Drop - inches	0.0	-2.2	-9.1	-20.8	-37.6

G1 Ballistic Coefficient = 0.119

Winchester 98-grain LRN (X32SWLP)

Distance - Yards	Muzzle	25	50	75	100
Velocity - fps	705	687	670	651	635
Energy - ft/lb	108	103	98	92	88
Taylor KO values	3.1	3.0	2.9	2.8	2.8
Mid-Range Trajectory Height - inches	0.0	0.5	2.3	5.3	10.5
Drop - inches	0.0	-2.2	-9.1	-20.8	-37.6

G1 Ballistic Coefficient = 0.119

Fiocchi 100-grain LWC (32LA)

Distance - Yards	Muzzle	25	50	75	100
Velocity - fps	730	678	631	587	545
Energy - ft/lb	118	102	88	76	66
Taylor KO values	3.3	3.0	2.8	2.6	2.4
Mid-Range Trajectory Height - inches	0.0	0.5	2.8	2.6	2.4
Drop - inches	0.0	-2.1	-9.0	-21.4	-40.0

G1 Ballistic Coefficient = 0.043

PMC 100-grain LWC (32SWLB)

Distance - Yards	Muzzle	25	50	75	100
Velocity - fps	683	652	623	595	569
Energy - ft/lb	104	94	86	79	72
Taylor KO values	3.1	2.9	2.8	2.7	2.5
Mid-Range Trajectory Height - inches	0.0	0.6	2.6	6.0	11.2
Drop - inches	0.0	-2.4	-9.9	-23.0	-42.3

G1 Ballistic Coefficient = 0.068

.32 H&R Magnum

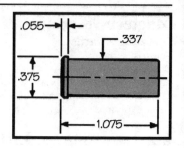

Designed in 1983, the .32 H&R (Harrington and Richardson) Magnum brings modern technology and high velocity to the .32-caliber pistol market. This cartridge is sometimes touted for hunting use but can't be taken seriously for that purpose. The .32-caliber guns have long been more popular in Europe as target pistols. This is still a new cartridge and it will take more time before its true worth is established by active shooters.

Relative Recoil Factor = 0.42   **Controlling Agency: SAAMI**

Bullet Weight Grains	Velocity fps	Maximum Average Pressure Copper Crusher	Transducer	Standard barrel for velocity testing:
85 JHP	1120	21,000 cup	N/S	24 inches long - 1 turn in 12 inch twist
95 LSWC	1020	21,000 cup	N/S	

Federal 85-grain Hi-Shok JHP (C32HRB)

Distance - Yards	Muzzle	25	50	75	100
Velocity - fps	1100	1050	1020	970	930
Energy - ft/lb	230	210	195	175	165
Taylor KO values	4.2	4.0	3.8	3.7	3.5
Mid-Range Trajectory Height - inches	0.0	0.2	1.0	2.3	4.3
Drop - inches	0.0	-0.9	-3.8	-8.9	-16.4

G1 Ballistic Coefficient = 0.127

Federal 95-grain Lead Semi-Wadcutter (LSWC) (C32HRA)

Distance - Yards	Muzzle	25	50	75	100
Velocity - fps	1030	1000	940	930	900
Energy - ft/lb	225	210	195	185	170
Taylor KO values	4.4	4.2	4.1	3.9	3.8
Mid-Range Trajectory Height - inches	0.0	0.3	1.1	2.5	4.7
Drop - inches	0.0	-1.0	-4.3	-10.0	-18.1

G1 Ballistic Coefficient = 0.138

.32 Auto (7.65mm Browning)

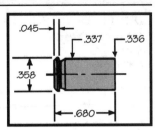

John Browning designed this little cartridge in 1899. The fact that it is still around proves that some shooters find it useful. There is some good news and some bad news about the .32 Auto. The good news is that the cartridge design allows very lightweight and compact guns. Since concealed carry has been legalized in many states, the .32 Auto finds many advocates. The bad news is that the .32 Auto isn't really enough cartridge to provide serious self-defense. It's a difficult trade-off to get just right, and it's one that's made only slightly easier with the availability of high-performance bullets.

Relative Recoil Factor = 0.29   **Controlling Agency: SAAMI**

Bullet Weight Grains	Velocity fps	Maximum Average Pressure		Standard barrel for velocity testing:
		Copper Crusher	Transducer	
60 STHP	960	15,000 cup	20,500 psi	4 inches long - 1 turn in 16 inch twist
71 MC	900	15,000 cup	20,500 psi	

Fiocchi 60-grain JHP (32APHP)

Distance - Yards	Muzzle	25	50	75	100	
Velocity - fps	1200	1108	1039	985	940	
Energy - ft/lb	205	164	144	129	118	
Taylor KO values	3.2	3.0	2.8	2.6	2.5	
Mid-Range Trajectory Height - inches	0.0	0.2	0.9	2.1	4.0	
Drop - inches	0.0	-0.8	-3.4	-7.9	-14.8	G1 Ballistic Coefficient = 0.100

Hornady 60-grain HP/XTP (9006c)

Distance - Yards	Muzzle	25	50	75	100	
Velocity - fps	1000	951	917	873	849	
Energy - ft/lb	133	120	112	101	96	
Taylor KO values	2.7	2.6	2.5	2.3	2.2	
Mid-Range Trajectory Height - inches	0.0	0.3	1.2	2.8	5.2	
Drop - inches	0.0	-1.1	-4.6	-10.8	-19.8	G1 Ballistic Coefficient = 0.095

PMC 60-grain JHP (32B)

Distance - Yards	Muzzle	25	50	75	100	
Velocity - fps	980	849	820	791	763	
Energy - ft/lb	117	111	98	87	78	
Taylor KO values	2.7	2.6	2.5	2.4	2.3	
Mid-Range Trajectory Height - inches	0.0	0.2	0.9	2.7	5.5	
Drop - inches	0.0	-1.2	-5.0	-11.8	-21.9	G1 Ballistic Coefficient = 0.098

Winchester 60-grain Silvertip HP (X32ASHP)

Distance - Yards	Muzzle	25	50	75	100	
Velocity - fps	970	930	895	864	835	
Energy - ft/lb	125	115	107	99	93	
Taylor KO values	2.6	2.5	2.4	2.3	2.2	
Mid-Range Trajectory Height - inches	0.0	0.3	1.3	2.9	5.4	
Drop - inches	0.0	-1.2	-4.9	-11.3	-20.6	G1 Ballistic Coefficient = 0.107

CCI 60-grain Gold Dot (23604)

Distance - Yards	Muzzle	25	50	75	100	
Velocity - fps	960	911	868	831	796	
Energy - ft/lb	123	111	100	92	84	
Taylor KO values	2.6	2.4	2.3	2.2	2.1	
Mid-Range Trajectory Height - inches	0.0	0.3	0.7	3.1	5.1	
Drop - inches	0.0	-1.2	-5.1	-11.8	-21.6	G1 Ballistic Coefficient = 0.082

Federal 65-grain Hydra-Shok JHP (P32HS1)

Distance - Yards	Muzzle	25	50	75	100	
Velocity - fps	950	920	890	860	830	
Energy - ft/lb	130	120	115	105	100	
Taylor KO values	2.8	2.7	2.6	2.5	2.4	
Mid-Range Trajectory Height - inches	0.0	0.3	1.3	3.0	5.6	
Drop - inches	0.0	-1.2	-5.1	-11.7	-21.2	G1 Ballistic Coefficient = 0.116

American Eagle (Federal) 65-grain FMJ (AE32BP)

Distance - Yards	Muzzle	25	50	75	100
Velocity - fps	1000	960	930	900	870
Energy - ft/lb	145	135	125	115	110
Taylor KO values	2.9	2.8	2.7	2.6	2.5
Mid-Range Trajectory Height - inches	0.0	0.3	1.2	2.8	5.1
Drop - inches	0.0	-1.1	-4.6	-10.6	-19.3

G1 Ballistic Coefficient = 0.123

Magtech 71-grain JHP (32B)

Distance - Yards	Muzzle	25	50	75	100
Velocity - fps	905	879	855	831	810
Energy - ft/lb	129	122	115	109	103
Taylor KO values	2.9	2.8	2.7	2.6	2.6
Mid-Range Trajectory Height - inches	0.0	0.3	1.4	3.2	5.8
Drop - inches	0.0	-1.4	-5.5	-12.7	-23.0

G1 Ballistic Coefficient = 0.132

Federal 71-grain FMJ (32AP)

Distance - Yards	Muzzle	25	50	75	100
Velocity - fps	910	880	860	830	810
Energy - ft/lb	130	120	115	110	105
Taylor KO values	2.9	2.8	2.7	2.6	2.6
Mid-Range Trajectory Height - inches	0.0	0.3	1.4	3.2	5.9
Drop - inches	0.0	-1.3	-5.5	-12.6	-22.8

G1 Ballistic Coefficient = 0.127

Magtech 71-grain Full Metal Case (32A)

Distance - Yards	Muzzle	25	50	75	100
Velocity - fps	905	879	855	831	810
Energy - ft/lb	129	122	115	109	103
Taylor KO values	2.9	2.8	2.7	2.6	2.6
Mid-Range Trajectory Height - inches	0.0	0.3	1.4	3.2	5.8
Drop - inches	0.0	-1.4	-5.5	-12.7	-23.0

G1 Ballistic Coefficient = 0.132

Remington 71-grain Metal Case (R32AP)

Distance - Yards	Muzzle	25	50	75	100
Velocity - fps	905	879	855	831	810
Energy - ft/lb	129	122	115	109	103
Taylor KO values	2.9	2.8	2.7	2.6	2.6
Mid-Range Trajectory Height - inches	0.0	0.3	1.4	3.2	5.8
Drop - inches	0.0	-1.4	-5.5	-12.7	-23.0

G1 Ballistic Coefficient = 0.132

UMC (Remington) 71-grain Metal Case (L32AP)

Distance - Yards	Muzzle	25	50	75	100
Velocity - fps	905	879	855	831	810
Energy - ft/lb	129	122	115	109	103
Taylor KO values	2.9	2.8	2.7	2.6	2.6
Mid-Range Trajectory Height - inches	0.0	0.3	1.4	3.2	5.8
Drop - inches	0.0	-1.4	-5.5	-12.7	-23.0

G1 Ballistic Coefficient = 0.132

USA (Winchester) 71-grain FMJ (Q4255)

Distance - Yards	Muzzle	25	50	75	100
Velocity - fps	905	879	855	831	810
Energy - ft/lb	129	122	115	109	103
Taylor KO values	2.9	2.8	2.7	2.6	2.6
Mid-Range Trajectory Height - inches	0.0	0.3	1.4	3.2	5.8
Drop - inches	0.0	-1.4	-5.5	-12.7	-23.0

G1 Ballistic Coefficient = 0.132

CCI 71-grain FMJ (3503)

Distance - Yards	Muzzle	25	50	75	100
Velocity - fps	900	875	855	831	810
Energy - ft/lb	129	121	115	109	103
Taylor KO values	2.8	2.8	2.7	2.6	2.6
Mid-Range Trajectory Height - inches	0.0	0.3	1.4	3.3	5.8
Drop - inches	0.0	-1.4	-5.6	-12.8	-23.1

G1 Ballistic Coefficient = 0.139

Hornady 71-grain FMJ-RN (9007c)

Distance - Yards	Muzzle	25	50	75	100
Velocity - fps	900	871	845	820	797
Energy - ft/lb	128	120	112	106	100
Taylor KO values	2.8	2.8	2.7	2.6	2.5
Mid-Range Trajectory Height - inches	0.0	0.3	1.4	3.3	6.1
Drop - inches	0.0	-1.4	-5.6	-12.9	-23.4

G1 Ballistic Coefficient = 0.119

PMC 71-grain FMJ (32A)

Distance - Yards	Muzzle	25	50	75	100
Velocity - fps	870	841	814	788	764
Energy - ft/lb	119	111	104	98	92
Taylor KO values	2.8	2.7	2.6	2.5	2.4
Mid-Range Trajectory Height - inches	0.0	0.4	1.5	3.6	6.6
Drop - inches	0.0	-1.5	-6.0	-13.8	-25.2

G1 Ballistic Coefficient = 0.107

Fiocchi 73-grain Metal Case (32AP)

Distance - Yards	Muzzle	25	50	75	100
Velocity - fps	980	940	905	873	845
Energy - ft/lb	155	143	133	124	116
Taylor KO values	3.2	3.1	2.9	2.8	2.7
Mid-Range Trajectory Height - inches	0.0	0.3	1.2	2.9	5.3
Drop - inches	0.0	-1.2	-4.8	-11.1	-20.2

G1 Ballistic Coefficient = 0.110

Norma 77-grain Full Jacket, Round Nose (17614)

Distance - Yards	Muzzle	25	50	75	100
Velocity - fps	899	884	871	857	845
Energy - ft/lb	138	134	130	126	122
Taylor KO values	3.1	3.0	3.0	2.9	2.9
Mid-Range Trajectory Height - inches	0.0	0.3	1.4	3.2	5.7
Drop - inches	0.0	-1.4	-5.5	-12.5	-22.4

G1 Ballistic Coefficient = 0.241

.357 Magnum

At the time of its introduction in 1935, the .357 Magnum (sometimes called the .357 Smith & Wesson Magnum) was the world's most powerful revolver cartridge. Credit for its development is usually given to Col. D. B. Wesson of Smith & Wesson and to Phil Sharpe. The .357 design is essentially a lengthened .38 Special but the working pressure level has been pushed up to 35,000 psi, which more than doubles the .38 Special's 17,000 psi level, producing much better performance. Before the .357 was introduced, the .38 Special was the standard police sidearm in the US, almost the universal choice. It wasn't very long until the increased effectiveness of the .357 Magnum became known. Today, factories are offering over 50 different loadings in this caliber. In the law enforcement application today, revolvers are gradually being replaced by semi-automatic pistols.

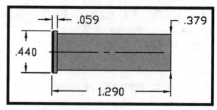

Relative Recoil Factor = 0.89   **Controlling Agency: SAAMI**

Bullet Weight Grains	Velocity fps	Maximum Average Pressure		Standard barrel for velocity testing:
		Copper Crusher	Transducer	
110 JHP	1270	45,000 cup	35,000 psi	4 inches long [vented];
125 SJHP	1500	45,000 cup	35,000 psi	12.493 inch alternate one piece barrel
125 JSP	1400	45,000 cup	35,000 psi	- 1 turn in 18.75 inch twist
140 SJHP	1330	45,000 cup	35,000 psi	
145 STHP	1270	45,000 cup	35,000 psi	
158 MP-L	1220	45,000 cup	35,000 psi	
158 SWC	1220	45,000 cup	35,000 psi	
158 SJHP	1220	45,000 cup	35,000 psi	
180 STHP	1400	45,000 cup	35,000 psi	

Winchester 105-grain JSP (SC357NT)

Distance - Yards	Muzzle	25	50	75	100
Velocity - fps	1650	1532	1422	1323	356
Energy - ft/lb	635	547	472	408	356
Taylor KO values	8.8	8.2	7.6	7.1	6.6
Mid-Range Trajectory Height - inches	0.0	0.1	0.3	0.7	1.8
Drop - inches	0.0	-0.4	-1.8	-4.2	-7.8

G1 Ballistic Coefficient = 0.137

CCI 109-grain Shotshell (3709)

Muzzle Velocity = 1000 fps — Loaded with #9 Shot

Federal 110-grain Hi-Shok JHP (C357D)

Distance - Yards	Muzzle	25	50	75	100
Velocity - fps	1300	1180	1090	1040	990
Energy - ft/lb	410	340	290	260	235
Taylor KO values	7.3	6.6	6.1	5.8	5.5
Mid-Range Trajectory Height - inches	0.0	0.2	0.8	1.9	3.5
Drop - inches	0.0	-0.7	-2.9	-6.9	-12.8

G1 Ballistic Coefficient = 0.106

Remington 110-grain Semi-JHP (R357M7)

Distance - Yards	Muzzle	25	50	75	100
Velocity - fps	1295	1182	1094	1027	975
Energy - ft/lb	410	341	292	258	232
Taylor KO values	7.2	6.6	6.1	5.7	5.5
Mid-Range Trajectory Height - inches	0.0	0.2	0.8	1.9	3.5
Drop - inches	0.0	-0.7	-2.9	-7.0	-13.1

G1 Ballistic Coefficient = 0.099

USA (Winchester) 110-grain JHP (Q4204)

Distance - Yards	Muzzle	25	50	75	100
Velocity - fps	1295	1183	1095	1029	977
Energy - ft/lb	410	342	292	259	233
Taylor KO values	7.2	6.6	6.1	5.7	5.5
Mid-Range Trajectory Height - inches	0.0	0.2	0.8	1.9	3.5
Drop - inches	0.0	-0.7	-2.9	-7.0	-13.1

G1 Ballistic Coefficient = 0.100

Norma 123-grain Security Cartridge (19104) [Until Stock Exhausted]

Distance - Yards	Muzzle	25	50	75	100	
Velocity - fps	1312	1248	1191	1142	1098	
Energy - ft/lb	472	427	389	356	330	
Taylor KO values	8.2	7.8	7.5	7.1	6.9	
Mid-Range Trajectory Height - inches	0.0	0.2	0.7	1.6	3.1	
Drop - inches	0.0	-0.6	-2.7	-6.3	-11.5	G1 Ballistic Coefficient = 0.191

Hornady 125-grain JFP/XTP (9053)

Distance - Yards	Muzzle	25	50	75	100	
Velocity - fps	1500	1401	1311	1230	1161	
Energy - ft/lb	624	545	477	420	374	
Taylor KO values	9.5	8.9	8.3	7.8	7.4	
Mid-Range Trajectory Height - inches	0.0	0.1	0.6	1.3	2.5	
Drop - inches	0.0	-0.5	-2.1	-5.0	-9.3	G1 Ballistic Coefficient = 0.148

UMC (Remington) 125-grain JSP (L357M2)

Distance - Yards	Muzzle	25	50	75	100	
Velocity - fps	1450	1339	1240	1158	1090	
Energy - ft/lb	584	497	427	372	330	
Taylor KO values	9.2	8.5	7.9	7.4	6.9	
Mid-Range Trajectory Height - inches	0.0	0.1	0.2	1.1	2.4	
Drop - inches	0.0	-0.6	-2.3	-5.5	-10.3	G1 Ballistic Coefficient = 0.125

Black Hills 125-grain JHP-Gold Dot (M357N2)

Distance - Yards	Muzzle	25	50	75	100	
Velocity - fps	1500	1402	1313	1233	1164	
Energy - ft/lb	625	546	478	422	376	
Taylor KO values	9.5	8.9	8.3	7.8	7.4	
Mid-Range Trajectory Height - inches	0.0	0.1	0.6	1.3	2.5	
Drop - inches	0.0	-0.5	-2.1	-5.0	-9.3	G1 Ballistic Coefficient = 0.150

Hornady 125-grain JHP/XTP (9050)

Distance - Yards	Muzzle	25	50	75	100	
Velocity - fps	1500	1403	1314	1234	1166	
Energy - ft/lb	625	546	476	423	377	
Taylor KO values	9.5	8.9	8.4	7.8	7.4	
Mid-Range Trajectory Height - inches	0.0	0.1	0.6	1.3	2.5	
Drop - inches	0.0	-0.5	-2.1	-5.0	-9.3	G1 Ballistic Coefficient = 0.151

Federal 125-grain Hi-Shok JHP (C357B)

Distance - Yards	Muzzle	25	50	75	100	
Velocity - fps	1450	1350	1240	1160	1100	
Energy - ft/lb	580	495	430	370	335	
Taylor KO values	9.2	8.6	7.9	7.4	7.0	
Mid-Range Trajectory Height - inches	0.0	0.1	0.6	1.5	2.8	
Drop - inches	0.0	-0.5	-2.3	-5.4	-10.2	G1 Ballistic Coefficient = 0.130

Remington 125-grain Semi-JHP (R357M1)

Distance - Yards	Muzzle	25	50	75	100	
Velocity - fps	1450	1339	1240	1158	1090	
Energy - ft/lb	583	497	427	372	330	
Taylor KO values	9.2	8.5	7.9	7.4	6.9	
Mid-Range Trajectory Height - inches	0.0	0.1	0.6	1.5	2.8	
Drop - inches	0.0	-0.6	-2.3	-5.5	-10.3	G1 Ballistic Coefficient = 0.125

Speer 125-grain Gold Dot (23920)

Distance - Yards	Muzzle	25	50	75	100	
Velocity - fps	1450	1339	1240	1158	1090	
Energy - ft/lb	583	497	427	372	330	
Taylor KO values	9.2	8.5	7.9	7.4	6.9	
Mid-Range Trajectory Height - inches	0.0	0.1	0.6	1.5	2.8	
Drop - inches	0.0	-0.6	-2.3	-5.5	-10.3	G1 Ballistic Coefficient = 0.125

Remington 125-grain Brass-JHP (GS357MA)

Distance - Yards	Muzzle	25	50	75	100
Velocity - fps	1220	1152	1095	1049	1009
Energy - ft/lb	413	369	333	305	283
Taylor KO values	7.8	7.3	7.0	6.7	6.4
Mid-Range Trajectory Height - inches	0.0	0.2	0.8	1.9	3.5
Drop - inches	0.0	-0.8	-3.2	-7.4	-13.5

G1 Ballistic Coefficient = 0.148

PMC 125-grain JHP (357B)

Distance - Yards	Muzzle	25	50	75	100
Velocity - fps	1194	1117	1057	1008	967
Energy - ft/lb	396	347	310	282	260
Taylor KO values	7.6	7.1	6.7	6.4	6.1
Mid-Range Trajectory Height - inches	0.0	0.2	0.9	2.1	3.9
Drop - inches	0.0	-0.8	-3.3	-7.8	-14.4

G1 Ballistic Coefficient = 0.121

Federal 130-grain Hydra-Shok JHP (PD357HS2)

Distance - Yards	Muzzle	25	50	75	100
Velocity - fps	1300	1210	1130	1070	1020
Energy - ft/lb	490	420	370	330	300
Taylor KO values	8.6	8.0	7.5	7.1	6.7
Mid-Range Trajectory Height - inches	0.0	0.2	0.7	1.8	3.4
Drop - inches	0.0	-0.7	-2.8	-6.7	-12.5

G1 Ballistic Coefficient = 0.125

Hornady 140-grain JHP/XTP (9055)

Distance - Yards	Muzzle	25	50	75	100
Velocity - fps	1400	1320	1249	1185	1130
Energy - ft/lb	609	542	485	436	397
Taylor KO values	10.0	9.4	8.9	8.4	8.0
Mid-Range Trajectory Height - inches	0.0	0.1	0.6	1.5	2.8
Drop - inches	0.0	-0.6	-2.4	-5.6	-10.4

G1 Ballistic Coefficient = 0.169

Federal 140-grain Hi-Shok JHP (C357H)

Distance - Yards	Muzzle	25	50	75	100
Velocity - fps	1360	1270	1200	1130	1080
Energy - ft/lb	575	500	445	395	360
Taylor KO values	9.7	9.0	8.5	8.0	7.7
Mid-Range Trajectory Height - inches	0.0	0.2	0.7	1.6	3.0
Drop - inches	0.0	-0.6	-2.6	-6.0	-11.2

G1 Ballistic Coefficient = 0.148

Fiocchi 142-grain Truncated Cone Point (357F)

Distance - Yards	Muzzle	25	50	75	100
Velocity - fps	1420	1329	1247	1176	1116
Energy - ft/lb	650	557	491	436	393
Taylor KO values	10.3	9.6	491	436	393
Mid-Range Trajectory Height - inches	0.0	0.1	0.6	1.5	2.8
Drop - inches	0.0	-0.6	-2.4	-5.6	-10.3

G1 Ballistic Coefficient = 0.150

Winchester 145-grain Silvertip HP (X357SHP)

Distance - Yards	Muzzle	25	50	75	100
Velocity - fps	1290	1219	1155	1104	1060
Energy - ft/lb	535	478	428	393	361
Taylor KO values	9.5	9.0	8.5	8.1	7.8
Mid-Range Trajectory Height - inches	0.0	0.2	0.8	1.7	3.5
Drop - inches	0.0	-0.7	-2.8	-6.6	-12.1

G1 Ballistic Coefficient = 0.163

Fiocchi 148-grain JHP (357E)

Distance - Yards	Muzzle	25	50	75	100
Velocity - fps	1500	1411	1328	1254	1188
Energy - ft/lb	720	654	580	517	464
Taylor KO values	11.3	10.6	10.0	8.3	8.0
Mid-Range Trajectory Height - inches	0.0	0.2	0.8	1.7	3.5
Drop - inches	0.0	-0.7	-2.8	-6.6	-12.1

G1 Ballistic Coefficient = 0.165

PMC 150-grain JHP (357C)

Distance - Yards	Muzzle	25	50	75	100
Velocity - fps	1234	1156	1093	1042	1000
Energy - ft/lb	507	446	398	362	333
Taylor KO values	9.4	8.8	8.3	7.9	7.6
Mid-Range Trajectory Height - inches	0.0	0.2	0.8	1.9	3.6
Drop - inches	0.0	-0.8	-3.1	-7.3	-13.5

G1 Ballistic Coefficient = 0.133

PMC 150-grain Starfire HP (357SFA)

Distance - Yards	Muzzle	25	50	75	100
Velocity - fps	1205	1129	1069	1020	980
Energy - ft/lb	484	425	381	347	320
Taylor KO values	9.2	8.6	8.2	7.8	7.5
Mid-Range Trajectory Height - inches	0.0	0.2	0.8	2.0	3.8
Drop - inches	0.0	-0.8	-3.3	-7.6	-14.1

G1 Ballistic Coefficient = 0.127

Lapua 150-grain CEPP SUPER (4319213)

Distance - Yards	Muzzle	25	50	75	100
Velocity - fps	1214	1152	1100	1056	1019
Energy - ft/lb	491	442	403	372	346
Taylor KO values	9.3	8.8	8.4	8.1	7.8
Mid-Range Trajectory Height - inches	0.0	0.2	0.8	1.9	3.6
Drop - inches	0.0	-0.8	-3.2	-7.4	-13.5

G1 Ballistic Coefficient = 0.162

Lapua 150-grain Semi-Jacketed Flat Nose (4319214)

Distance - Yards	Muzzle	25	50	75	100
Velocity - fps	1542	1448	1361	1282	1211
Energy - ft/lb	834	736	650	577	515
Taylor KO values	12.4	11.6	10.9	10.3	9.7
Mid-Range Trajectory Height - inches	0.0	0.1	0.5	1.2	2.4
Drop - inches	0.0	-0.5	-2.0	-4.7	-8.7

G1 Ballistic Coefficient = 0.162

Hornady 158-grain JFP/XTP (9058)

Distance - Yards	Muzzle	25	50	75	100
Velocity - fps	1250	1195	1147	1105	1068
Energy - ft/lb	548	501	461	428	400
Taylor KO values	10.0	9.6	9.2	8.9	8.6
Mid-Range Trajectory Height - inches	0.0	0.2	0.8	1.8	3.3
Drop - inches	0.0	-0.7	-3.0	-6.8	-12.5

G1 Ballistic Coefficient = 0.200

American Eagle (Federal) 158-grain JSP (AE357A)

Distance - Yards	Muzzle	25	50	75	100
Velocity - fps	1240	1160	1100	1060	1020
Energy - ft/lb	535	475	430	395	365
Taylor KO values	10.0	9.3	8.8	8.5	8.2
Mid-Range Trajectory Height - inches	0.0	0.2	0.8	1.9	3.5
Drop - inches	0.0	-0.7	-3.1	-7.1	-13.2

G1 Ballistic Coefficient = 0.149

Federal 158-grain Hi-Shok JSP (C357A)

Distance - Yards	Muzzle	25	50	75	100
Velocity - fps	1240	1160	1100	1060	1020
Energy - ft/lb	535	475	430	395	365
Taylor KO values	10.0	9.3	8.8	8.5	8.2
Mid-Range Trajectory Height - inches	0.0	0.2	0.8	1.9	3.5
Drop - inches	0.0	-0.7	-3.1	-7.1	-13.2

G1 Ballistic Coefficient = 0.149

Federal 158-grain Nyclad Semi-Wadcutter-HP (P357E)

Distance - Yards	Muzzle	25	50	75	100
Velocity - fps	1240	1160	1100	1060	1020
Energy - ft/lb	535	475	430	395	365
Taylor KO values	10.0	9.3	8.8	8.5	8.2
Mid-Range Trajectory Height - inches	0.0	0.2	0.8	1.9	3.5
Drop - inches	0.0	-0.7	-3.1	-7.1	-13.2

G1 Ballistic Coefficient = 0.149

Federal 158-grain LSWC (C357C)

Distance - Yards	Muzzle	25	50	75	100
Velocity - fps	1240	1160	1100	1060	1020
Energy - ft/lb	535	475	430	395	365
Taylor KO values	10.0	9.3	8.8	8.5	8.2
Mid-Range Trajectory Height - inches	0.0	0.2	0.8	1.9	3.5
Drop - inches	0.0	-0.7	-3.1	-7.1	-13.2

G1 Ballistic Coefficient = 0.149

Remington 158-grain LSWC (R357M5)

Distance - Yards	Muzzle	25	50	75	100
Velocity - fps	1235	1164	1104	1056	1015
Energy - ft/lb	535	475	428	391	361
Taylor KO values	9.9	9.4	8.9	8.5	8.2
Mid-Range Trajectory Height - inches	0.0	0.2	0.8	1.9	3.5
Drop - inches	0.0	-0.7	-3.1	-7.2	-13.3

G1 Ballistic Coefficient = 0.146

Magtech 158-grain LSWC (357C)

Distance - Yards	Muzzle	25	50	75	100
Velocity - fps	1235	1164	1104	1056	1015
Energy - ft/lb	535	475	428	391	361
Taylor KO values	9.9	9.4	8.9	8.5	8.2
Mid-Range Trajectory Height - inches	0.0	0.2	0.8	1.9	3.5
Drop - inches	0.0	-0.7	-3.1	-7.2	-13.3

G1 Ballistic Coefficient = 0.146

Norma 158-grain Full Jacket SWC (19106)

Distance - Yards	Muzzle	25	50	75	100
Velocity - fps	1214	1155	1105	1062	1026
Energy - ft/lb	515	466	427	396	368
Taylor KO values	9.8	9.3	8.9	8.5	8.2
Mid-Range Trajectory Height - inches	0.0	0.4	0.8	1.9	3.6
Drop - inches	0.0	-1.0	-4.2	-9.6	-17.4

G1 Ballistic Coefficient = 0.170

Black Hills 158-grain SWC (M357N1)

Distance - Yards	Muzzle	25	50	75	100
Velocity - fps	1050	1011	977	948	921
Energy - ft/lb	387	359	335	315	298
Taylor KO values	8.4	8.1	7.9	7.6	7.4
Mid-Range Trajectory Height - inches	0.0	0.3	1.1	2.5	4.5
Drop - inches	0.0	-1.0	-4.2	-9.6	-17.4

G1 Ballistic Coefficient = 0.150

Magtech 158-grain SJSP (357A)

Distance - Yards	Muzzle	25	50	75	100
Velocity - fps	1235	1164	1104	1056	1015
Energy - ft/lb	535	475	428	391	361
Taylor KO values	9.9	9.4	8.9	8.5	8.2
Mid-Range Trajectory Height - inches	0.0	0.2	0.8	1.9	3.5
Drop - inches	0.0	-0.7	-3.1	-7.2	-13.3

G1 Ballistic Coefficient = 0.146

Remington 158-grain SP (R357M3)

Distance - Yards	Muzzle	25	50	75	100
Velocity - fps	1235	1164	1104	1056	1015
Energy - ft/lb	535	475	428	391	361
Taylor KO values	9.9	9.4	8.9	8.5	8.2
Mid-Range Trajectory Height - inches	0.0	0.2	0.8	1.9	3.5
Drop - inches	0.0	-0.7	-3.1	-7.2	-13.3

G1 Ballistic Coefficient = 0.146

Winchester 158-grain JSP (X3575P)

Distance - Yards	Muzzle	25	50	75	100
Velocity - fps	1235	1164	1104	1056	1015
Energy - ft/lb	535	475	428	391	361
Taylor KO values	9.9	9.4	8.9	8.5	8.2
Mid-Range Trajectory Height - inches	0.0	0.2	0.8	1.9	3.5
Drop - inches	0.0	-0.7	-3.1	-7.2	-13.3

G1 Ballistic Coefficient = 0.146

Hansen 158-grain JSP "Combat" (HCC357C)

Distance - Yards	Muzzle	25	50	75	100
Velocity - fps	1220	1153	1097	1050	1011
Energy - ft/lb	522	467	422	387	359
Taylor KO values	9.8	9.3	8.8	8.4	8.1
Mid-Range Trajectory Height - inches	0.0	0.2	0.8	1.9	3.6
Drop - inches	0.0	-0.8	-3.2	-7.4	-13.5

G1 Ballistic Coefficient = 0.150

PMC 158-grain JSP (357A)

Distance - Yards	Muzzle	25	50	75	100
Velocity - fps	1194	1122	1063	1016	977
Energy - ft/lb	500	442	397	363	335
Taylor KO values	9.6	9.0	8.5	8.2	7.9
Mid-Range Trajectory Height - inches	0.0	0.2	0.9	2.0	3.8
Drop - inches	0.0	-0.8	-3.3	-7.8	-14.3

G1 Ballistic Coefficient = 0.129

Norma 158-grain SP Flat Nose (19107)

Distance - Yards	Muzzle	25	50	75	100
Velocity - fps	1214	1158	1110	1069	1034
Energy - ft/lb	515	469	431	401	374
Taylor KO values	9.8	9.3	8.9	8.6	8.3
Mid-Range Trajectory Height - inches	0.0	0.4	0.8	1.9	3.5
Drop - inches	0.0	-0.8	-3.1	-7.3	-13.3

G1 Ballistic Coefficient = 0.181

Lapua 158-grain Semi-JHP (4319218)

Distance - Yards	Muzzle	25	50	75	100
Velocity - fps	1542	1447	1359	1279	1208
Energy - ft/lb	834	735	648	574	512
Taylor KO values	12.4	11.6	10.9	10.3	9.7
Mid-Range Trajectory Height - inches	0.0	0.1	0.5	1.2	2.4
Drop - inches	0.0	-0.5	-2.0	-4.7	-8.7

G1 Ballistic Coefficient = 0.160

Black Hills 158-grain JHP-Gold Dot (M357N3)

Distance - Yards	Muzzle	25	50	75	100
Velocity - fps	1250	1188	1134	1088	1049
Energy - ft/lb	548	495	451	416	386
Taylor KO values	10.0	9.5	9.1	8.7	8.4
Mid-Range Trajectory Height - inches	0.0	0.2	0.8	1.8	3.4
Drop - inches	0.0	-0.7	-3.0	-6.9	-12.7

G1 Ballistic Coefficient = 0.175

Hansen 158-grain JHP "Combat" HP (HCC357C)

Distance - Yards	Muzzle	25	50	75	100
Velocity - fps	1250	1188	1134	1088	1049
Energy - ft/lb	548	495	451	416	386
Taylor KO values	10.0	9.5	9.1	8.7	8.4
Mid-Range Trajectory Height - inches	0.0	0.2	0.8	1.8	3.4
Drop - inches	0.0	-0.7	-3.0	-6.9	-12.7

G1 Ballistic Coefficient = 0.175

Hornady 158-grain JHP/XTP (9056)

Distance - Yards	Muzzle	25	50	75	100
Velocity - fps	1250	1197	1150	1109	1073
Energy - ft/lb	548	503	464	431	404
Taylor KO values	10.0	9.6	9.2	8.9	8.6
Mid-Range Trajectory Height - inches	0.0	0.2	0.8	1.8	3.3
Drop - inches	0.0	-0.7	-3.0	-6.8	-12.5

G1 Ballistic Coefficient = 0.207

Federal 158-grain Hydra-Shok JHP (P357HS1)

Distance - Yards	Muzzle	25	50	75	100
Velocity - fps	1240	1160	1100	1060	1020
Energy - ft/lb	535	475	430	395	365
Taylor KO values	10.0	9.3	8.8	8.5	8.2
Mid-Range Trajectory Height - inches	0.0	0.2	0.8	1.9	3.5
Drop - inches	0.0	-0.7	-3.1	-7.1	-13.2

G1 Ballistic Coefficient = 0.149

Federal 158-grain Hi-Shok JHP (C357E)

Distance - Yards	Muzzle	25	50	75	100
Velocity - fps	1240	1160	1100	1060	1020
Energy - ft/lb	535	475	430	395	365
Taylor KO values	10.0	9.3	8.8	8.5	8.2
Mid-Range Trajectory Height - inches	0.0	0.2	0.8	1.9	3.5
Drop - inches	0.0	-0.7	-3.1	-7.1	-13.2

G1 Ballistic Coefficient = 0.149

Speer 158-grain Gold Dot (23960)

Distance - Yards	Muzzle	25	50	75	100
Velocity - fps	1235	1164	1104	1056	1015
Energy - ft/lb	535	475	428	391	361
Taylor KO values	9.9	9.4	8.9	8.5	8.2
Mid-Range Trajectory Height - inches	0.0	0.2	0.8	1.9	3.5
Drop - inches	0.0	-0.7	-3.1	-7.2	-13.3

G1 Ballistic Coefficient = 0.146

Magtech 158-grain Semi-JHP (357B)

Distance - Yards	Muzzle	25	50	75	100
Velocity - fps	1235	1164	1104	1056	1015
Energy - ft/lb	535	475	428	391	361
Taylor KO values	9.9	9.4	8.9	8.5	8.2
Mid-Range Trajectory Height - inches	0.0	0.2	0.8	1.9	3.5
Drop - inches	0.0	-0.7	-3.1	-7.2	-13.3

G1 Ballistic Coefficient = 0.146

Remington 158-grain Semi-JHP (R357M2)

Distance - Yards	Muzzle	25	50	75	100
Velocity - fps	1235	1164	1104	1056	1015
Energy - ft/lb	535	475	428	391	361
Taylor KO values	9.9	9.4	8.9	8.5	8.2
Mid-Range Trajectory Height - inches	0.0	0.2	0.8	1.9	3.5
Drop - inches	0.0	-0.7	-3.1	-7.2	-13.3

G1 Ballistic Coefficient = 0.146

Winchester 158-grain JHP (X3574P)

Distance - Yards	Muzzle	25	50	75	100
Velocity - fps	1235	1164	1104	1056	1015
Energy - ft/lb	535	475	428	391	361
Taylor KO values	9.9	9.4	8.9	8.5	8.2
Mid-Range Trajectory Height - inches	0.0	0.2	0.8	1.9	3.5
Drop - inches	0.0	-0.7	-3.1	-7.2	-13.3

G1 Ballistic Coefficient = 0.146

Norma 158-grain HP (19101) [Until Stock Exhausted]

Distance - Yards	Muzzle	25	50	75	100
Velocity - fps	1214	1158	1110	1069	1034
Energy - ft/lb	515	468	431	401	374
Taylor KO values	9.8	9.3	8.9	8.6	8.3
Mid-Range Trajectory Height - inches	0.0	0.4	0.8	1.9	3.5
Drop - inches	0.0	-0.8	-3.1	-7.3	-13.3

G1 Ballistic Coefficient = 0.181

Hansen 158-grain FMJ "Combat" (HCC357A)

Distance - Yards	Muzzle	25	50	75	100
Velocity - fps	1250	1188	1134	1088	1049
Energy - ft/lb	549	495	451	416	386
Taylor KO values	10.0	9.5	9.1	8.7	8.4
Mid-Range Trajectory Height - inches	0.0	0.2	0.8	1.8	3.4
Drop - inches	0.0	-0.7	-3.0	-6.9	-12.7

`G1 Ballistic Coefficient = 0.175

CCI 158-grain JHP (3542)

Distance - Yards	Muzzle	25	50	75	100
Velocity - fps	1150	1109	1074	1043	1015
Energy - ft/lb	464	432	405	382	361
Taylor KO values	9.2	8.9	8.6	8.4	8.2
Mid-Range Trajectory Height - inches	0.0	0.2	0.8	2.0	3.5
Drop - inches	0.0	-0.8	-3.5	-7.9	-14.4

G1 Ballistic Coefficient = 0.211

Remington 165-grain JHP Core-Lokt (RH357MA)

Distance - Yards	Muzzle	25	50	75	100	
Velocity - fps	1290	1237	1189	1146	1108	
Energy - ft/lb	610	561	518	481	450	
Taylor KO values	10.4	9.9	9.6	9.2	8.9	
Mid-Range Trajectory Height - inches	0.0	0.2	0.7	1.7	3.1	
Drop - inches	0.0	-0.7	-2.8	-6.4	-11.7	G1 Ballistic Coefficient = 0.223

Federal 180-grain Cast Core (P357J)

Distance - Yards	Muzzle	25	50	75	100	
Velocity - fps	1250	1200	1160	1120	1060	
Energy - ft/lb	675	575	535	495	465	
Taylor KO values	11.4	11.0	10.6	10.3	9.7	
Mid-Range Trajectory Height - inches	0.0	0.2	0.8	1.8	3.3	
Drop - inches	0.0	-0.7	-3.0	-6.9	-12.6	G1 Ballistic Coefficient = 0.189

Winchester 180-grain Partition Gold (S357P)

Distance - Yards	Muzzle	25	50	75	100	
Velocity - fps	1180	1131	1088	1052	1020	
Energy - ft/lb	557	511	473	442	416	
Taylor KO values	10.8	10.4	10.0	9.6	9.3	
Mid-Range Trajectory Height - inches	0.0	0.2	0.8	2.0	3.6	
Drop - inches	0.0	-0.8	-3.3	-7.6	-13.9	G1 Ballistic Coefficient = 0.188

Remington 180-grain Semi-JHP (R357M10)

Distance - Yards	Muzzle	25	50	75	100	
Velocity - fps	1145	1095	1053	1017	985	
Energy - ft/lb	524	479	443	413	388	
Taylor KO values	10.5	10.0	9.6	9.3	9.0	
Mid-Range Trajectory Height - inches	0.0	0.2	0.9	2.1	3.9	
Drop - inches	0.0	-0.8	-3.5	-8.1	-14.9	G1 Ballistic Coefficient = 0.165

Federal 180-grain Hi-Shok JHP (C357G)

Distance - Yards	Muzzle	25	50	75	100	
Velocity - fps	1090	1030	980	930	890	
Energy - ft/lb	475	425	385	350	320	
Taylor KO values	10.0	9.4	9.0	8.5	8.1	
Mid-Range Trajectory Height - inches	0.0	0.2	1.0	2.4	4.5	
Drop - inches	0.0	-1.0	-4.0	-9.3	-17.2	G1 Ballistic Coefficient = 0.098

──── Cowboy Action Loads ────

Hornady 140 grain L (9054)

Distance - Yards	Muzzle	25	50	75	100	
Velocity - fps	800	783	767	750	735	
Energy - Ft-lbs	199	191	183	175	168	
Taylor KO Index	5.7	5.6	5.5	5.4	5.2	
Mid-Range Trajectory Height - Inches	0.0	0.1	1.4	3.6	7.0	
Drop - Inches	0.0	-1.7	-7.0	-16.0	-28.8	G1 Ballistic Coefficient = 0.150

Black Hills 158-grain CNL (DCB357N1)

Distance - Yards	Muzzle	25	50	75	100	
Velocity - fps	800	782	765	749	733	
Energy - ft/lb	225	215	205	197	188	
Taylor KO values	6.4	6.3	6.1	6.0	5.9	
Mid-Range Trajectory Height - inches	0.0	0.4	1.8	4.1	7.4	
Drop - inches	0.0	-1.7	-7.0	-16.0	-28.8	G1 Ballistic Coefficient = 0.150

PMC 158-grain Lead Flat Point (357CA)

Distance - Yards	Muzzle	25	50	75	100	
Velocity - fps	800	780	761	743	725	
Energy - ft/lb	225	214	203	194	185	
Taylor KO values	6.4	6.3	6.1	6.0	5.8	
Mid-Range Trajectory Height - inches	0.0	0.4	1.8	4.1	7.5	
Drop - inches	0.0	-1.7	-7.0	-16.1	-29.0	G1 Ballistic Coefficient = 0.134

.357 SIG

This cartridge was developed in 1994 especially for the Sig P229 pistol. Designwise, the .357 SIG comes pretty close to being a 10mm Auto cartridge necked to .357 caliber. The design follows the concept of the wildcat .38-45 cartridge that received some interest in the early 1960s. The case volume gives the .357 SIG performance approaching that of the .357 Magnum.

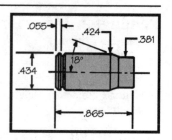

Relative Recoil Factor = 0.76   Controlling Agency: SAAMI

Bullet Weight Grains	Velocity fps	Maximum Average Pressure		Standard barrel for velocity testing:
		Copper Crusher	Transducer	
125 FMJ	1350	N/S	40,000 psi	4 inches long - 1 turn in 16 inch twist

Hornady 124-grain JHP/XTP (9130)

Distance - Yard	Muzzle	25	50	75	100	
Velocity - fps	1350	1278	1208	1157	1108	
Energy - ft/lb	502	450	405	369	338	
Taylor KO values	8.4	7.9	7.5	7.2	6.9	
Mid-Range Trajectory Height - inches	0.0	0.1	0.5	1.4	2.8	
Drop - inches	0.0	-0.6	-2.6	-6.2	-11.5	G1 Ballistic Coefficient = 0.177

Federal 125-grain JHP (P357S1)

Distance - Yards	Muzzle	25	50	75	100	
Velocity - fps	1350	1270	1190	1130	1080	
Energy - ft/lb	510	445	395	355	325	
Taylor KO values	8.6	8.1	7.6	7.2	6.9	
Mid-Range Trajectory Height - inches	0.0	0.1	0.5	1.4	2.9	
Drop - inches	0.0	-0.6	-2.6	-6.1	-11.3	G1 Ballistic Coefficient = 0.177

CCI 125-grain FMJ (3580)

Distance - Yards	Muzzle	25	50	75	100	
Velocity - fps	1350	1257	1177	1111	1057	
Energy - ft/lb	502	439	381	343	307	
Taylor KO values	8.6	8.0	7.5	7.0	6.7	
Mid-Range Trajectory Height - inches	0.0	0.2	0.5	1.6	2.9	
Drop - inches	0.0	-0.6	-2.6	-6.2	-11.5	G1 Ballistic Coefficient = 0.135

Federal 125-grain FMJ (C357S2)

Distance - Yards	Muzzle	25	50	75	100	
Velocity - fps	1350	1270	1190	1130	1080	
Energy - ft/lb	510	445	395	355	325	
Taylor KO values	8.6	8.1	7.6	7.2	6.9	
Mid-Range Trajectory Height - inches	0.0	0.1	0.5	1.4	2.9	
Drop - inches	0.0	-0.6	-2.6	-6.1	-11.3	G1 Ballistic Coefficient = 0.153

Speer 125-grain FMJ (53919)

Distance - Yards	Muzzle	25	50	75	100	
Velocity - fps	1350	1257	1177	1111	1057	
Energy - ft/lb	502	439	381	343	307	
Taylor KO values	8.6	8.0	7.5	7.0	6.7	
Mid-Range Trajectory Height - inches	0.0	0.2	0.5	1.6	2.9	
Drop - inches	0.0	-0.6	-2.6	-6.2	-11.5	G1 Ballistic Coefficient = 0.135

Remington 125-grain JHP (R357S1)

Distance - Yards	Muzzle	25	50	75	100	
Velocity - fps	1350	1246	1157	1088	1032	
Energy - ft/lb	506	431	372	329	296	
Taylor KO values	8.6	7.9	7.4	6.9	6.6	
Mid-Range Trajectory Height - inches	0.0	0.2	0.5	1.6	2.9	
Drop - inches	0.0	-0.6	-2.7	-6.3	-11.8	G1 Ballistic Coefficient = 0.119

USA (Winchester) 125-grain FMJ-Flat Nose (Q4209)

Distance - Yards	Muzzle	25	50	75	100
Velocity - fps	1350	1262	1185	1120	1067
Energy - ft/lb	506	442	390	348	316
Taylor KO values	8.6	8.0	7.6	7.1	6.8
Mid-Range Trajectory Height - inches	0.0	0.1	0.5	1.5	2.9
Drop - inches	0.0	-0.6	-2.6	-6.2	-11.4

G1 Ballistic Coefficient = 0.142

Hornady 147-grain JHP/XTP (9131)

Distance - Yards	Muzzle	25	50	75	100
Velocity - fps	1225	1180	1138	1104	1072
Energy - ft/lb	490	455	422	398	375
Taylor KO values	9.2	8.8	8.5	8.3	8.0
Mid-Range Trajectory Height - inches	0.0	0.2	0.6	1.6	3.1
Drop - inches	0.0	-0.7	-3.0	-7.0	-12.8

G1 Ballistic Coefficient = 0.233

Federal 150-grain JHP (P357S3)

Distance - Yards	Muzzle	25	50	75	100
Velocity - fps	1130	1080	1030	1000	970
Energy - ft/lb	420	385	355	330	3310
Taylor KO values	8.6	7.9	7.5	7.2	6.9
Mid-Range Trajectory Height - inches	0.0	0.2	0.9	2.1	4.0
Drop - inches	0.0	-0.9	-3.6	-8.4	-15.3

G1 Ballistic Coefficient = 0.155

.380 Auto (9mm Browning Short)

Another of the John Browning designs, the .380 Auto was first introduced as the 9mm Browning Short in 1908. Most decisions involving ballistics involve trade-offs. The .380 Auto makes an interesting example. The cartridge is far better than the .32 Auto in terms of energy and stopping power, but still falls considerably short of either the 9mm Luger or the .38 Special. At the same time, the modest power lends itself to simple and very compact guns that are easier to carry than the more powerful calibers. The trade does not have an obvious "perfect" choice. The .380 Auto is generally accepted as "enough" gun by persons wanting a gun that's comfortable to carry (for occasional use, and perhaps never), but not "enough" gun by the law enforcement types who want all the power they can handle.

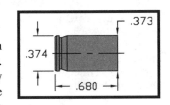

Relative Recoil Factor = 0.41   **Controlling Agency: SAAMI**

Bullet Weight Grains	Velocity fps	Maximum Average Pressure		Standard barrel for velocity testing:
		Copper Crusher	Transducer	
85 STHP	990	17,000 cup	21,500 psi	3.75 inches long - 1 turn in 16 inch twist
88-90 JHP	980	17,000 cup	21,500 psi	
95 MC	945	17,000 cup	21,500 psi	
100 FMJ	910	17,000 cup	21,500 psi	

Federal 60-grain Ballisticlean JSP (BC380NT1)

Distance - Yards	Muzzle	25	50	75	100
Velocity - fps	1050	970	900	847	801
Energy - ft/lb	170	140	120	109	98
Taylor KO values	3.5	3.2	3.0	2.8	2.6
Mid-Range Trajectory Height - inches	0.0	0.2	1.8	2.6	5.2
Drop - inches	0.0	-1.0	-4.4	-10.5	-19.6

G1 Ballistic Coefficient = 0.062

Winchester 85-grain Silvertip HP (X380ASHP)

Distance - Yards	Muzzle	25	50	75	100
Velocity - fps	1000	958	921	890	860
Energy - ft/lb	189	173	160	149	140
Taylor KO values	4.3	4.1	4.0	3.8	3.7
Mid-Range Trajectory Height - inches	0.0	0.3	1.2	2.8	5.1
Drop - inches	0.0	-1.1	-4.6	-10.6	-19.4

G1 Ballistic Coefficient = 0.113

Remington 88-grain JHP (R380A1)

Distance - Yards	Muzzle	25	50	75	100
Velocity - fps	990	954	920	894	868
Energy - ft/lb	191	178	165	156	146
Taylor KO values	4.4	4.2	4.1	4.0	3.8
Mid-Range Trajectory Height - inches	0.0	0.3	1.2	2.8	5.1
Drop - inches	0.0	-1.1	-4.7	-10.7	-19.5

G1 Ballistic Coefficient = 0.129

CCI 88-grain JHP (3504)

Distance - Yards	Muzzle	25	50	75	100
Velocity - fps	950	928	920	888	870
Energy - ft/lb	176	168	161	154	148
Taylor KO values	4.2	4.1	4.1	4.0	3.9
Mid-Range Trajectory Height - inches	0.0	0.3	1.2	2.9	5.3
Drop - inches	0.0	-1.1	-5.0	-11.4	-20.5

G1 Ballistic Coefficient = 0.185

Black Hills 90-grain JHP (M380M1)

Distance - Yards	Muzzle	25	50	75	100
Velocity - fps	1000	953	913	878	846
Energy - ft/lb	200	182	167	154	143
Taylor KO values	4.6	4.3	4.2	4.0	3.9
Mid-Range Trajectory Height - inches	0.0	0.3	1.2	2.8	5.2
Drop - inches	0.0	-1.1	-44.6	-10.8	-19.7

G1 Ballistic Coefficient = 0.100

Fiocchi Black Hills 90-grain JHP (380APHP)

Distance - Yards	Muzzle	25	50	75	100
Velocity - fps	1000	953	913	878	846
Energy - ft/lb	200	182	167	154	143
Taylor KO values	4.6	4.3	4.2	4.0	3.9
Mid-Range Trajectory Height - inches	0.0	0.3	1.2	2.8	5.2
Drop - inches	0.0	-1.1	-44.6	-10.8	-19.7

G1 Ballistic Coefficient = 0.100

Hansen 90-grain JHP "Combat" (HCC380B)

Distance - Yards	Muzzle	25	50	75	100
Velocity - fps	1000	953	913	878	846
Energy - ft/lb	200	182	167	154	143
Taylor KO values	4.6	4.3	4.2	4.0	3.9
Mid-Range Trajectory Height - inches	0.0	0.3	1.2	2.8	5.2
Drop - inches	0.0	-1.1	-44.6	-10.8	-19.7

G1 Ballistic Coefficient = 0.100

Hornady 90-grain JHP/XTP (9010) & (9010c)

Distance - Yards	Muzzle	25	50	75	100
Velocity - fps	1000	945	902	859	823
Energy - ft/lb	200	179	163	148	135
Taylor KO values	4.6	4.3	4.1	3.9	3.7
Mid-Range Trajectory Height - inches	0.0	0.3	1.2	2.9	5.4
Drop - inches	0.0	-1.1	-4.7	-10.9	-20.1

G1 Ballistic Coefficient = 0.084

Federal 90-grain Hydra-Shok JHP (PD380HS1)

Distance - Yards	Muzzle	25	50	75	100
Velocity - fps	1000	940	890	840	800
Energy - ft/lb	200	175	160	140	130
Taylor KO values	4.6	4.3	4.1	3.8	3.6
Mid-Range Trajectory Height - inches	0.0	0.3	1.2	2.9	5.5
Drop - inches	0.0	-1.1	-4.8	-11.1	-20.6

G1 Ballistic Coefficient = 0.072

Federal 90-grain Hi-Shok JHP (C380BP)

Distance - Yards	Muzzle	25	50	75	100
Velocity - fps	1000	940	890	840	800
Energy - ft/lb	200	175	160	140	130
Taylor KO values	4.6	4.3	4.1	3.8	3.6
Mid-Range Trajectory Height - inches	0.0	0.3	1.2	2.9	5.5
Drop - inches	0.0	-1.1	-4.8	-11.1	-20.6

G1 Ballistic Coefficient = 0.072

Speer 90-grain Gold Dot (23606)

Distance - Yards	Muzzle	25	50	75	100
Velocity - fps	950	911	877	846	817
Energy - ft/lb	180	166	154	143	133
Taylor KO values	4.3	4.1	4.0	3.9	3.7
Mid-Range Trajectory Height - inches	0.0	0.3	1.1	3.0	5.4
Drop - inches	0.0	-1.2	-5.1	-11.8	-21.5

G1 Ballistic Coefficient = 0.102

PMC 90-grain JHP (380B)

Distance - Yards	Muzzle	25	50	75	100
Velocity - fps	917	878	844	812	782
Energy - ft/lb	168	154	142	132	122
Taylor KO values	4.2	4.0	3.8	3.7	3.6
Mid-Range Trajectory Height - inches	0.0	0.3	1.4	3.3	6.1
Drop - inches	0.0	-1.3	-5.5	-12.9	-23.2

G1 Ballistic Coefficient = 0.092

PMC 90-grain FMJ (380A)

Distance - Yards	Muzzle	25	50	75	100
Velocity - fps	910	872	838	807	778
Energy - ft/lb	165	152	140	130	121
Taylor KO values	4.1	4.0	3.8	3.7	3.5
Mid-Range Trajectory Height - inches	0.0	0.3	1.4	3.3	6.2
Drop - inches	0.0	-1.4	-5.6	-12.8	-23.5

G1 Ballistic Coefficient = 0.092

Winchester 95-grain SXT (S380)

Distance - Yards	Muzzle	25	50	75	100
Velocity - fps	955	920	889	861	835
Energy - ft/lb	192	179	167	156	147
Taylor KO values	4.6	4.4	4.3	4.1	4.0
Mid-Range Trajectory Height - inches	0.0	0.3	1.3	3.0	5.5
Drop - inches	0.0	-1.2	05.0	-11.5	-21.0

G1 Ballistic Coefficient = 0.117

Magtech 95-grain JHP (380B)

Distance - Yards	Muzzle	25	50	75	100
Velocity - fps	951	900	861	817	781
Energy - ft/lb	190	171	156	141	128
Taylor KO values	4.6	4.3	4.1	3.9	3.8
Mid-Range Trajectory Height - inches	0.0	0.3	1.4	3.2	5.9
Drop - inches	0.0	-1.2	-5.2	-12.1	-22.2

G1 Ballistic Coefficient = 0.076

PMC 95-grain Starfire HP (380SFA)

Distance - Yards	Muzzle	25	50	75	100
Velocity - fps	925	884	847	813	783
Energy - ft/lb	180	165	151	140	129
Taylor KO values	4.4	4.2	4.1	3.9	3.8
Mid-Range Trajectory Height - inches	0.0	0.3	1.4	3.3	6.1
Drop - inches	0.0	-1.3	-5.4	-12.5	-22.9

G1 Ballistic Coefficient = 0.088

Fiocchi 95-grain Metal Case (380AP)

Distance - Yards	Muzzle	25	50	75	100
Velocity - fps	1000	943	885	854	817
Energy - ft/lb	211	187	169	154	141
Taylor KO values	4.8	4.6	4.3	4.1	3.9
Mid-Range Trajectory Height - inches	0.0	0.2	1.0	2.7	5.2
Drop - inches	0.0	-1.1	-4.7	-11.0	-20.3

G1 Ballistic Coefficient = 0.080

American Eagle (Federal) 95-grain FMJ (AE380AP)

Distance - Yards	Muzzle	25	50	75	100
Velocity - fps	960	910	870	830	790
Energy - ft/lb	190	175	160	145	130
Taylor KO values	4.6	4.4	4.2	4.0	3.8
Mid-Range Trajectory Height - inches	0.0	0.3	1.3	3.1	5.8
Drop - inches	0.0	-1.2	-5.1	-11.8	-21.8

G1 Ballistic Coefficient = 0.078

Federal 95-grain FMJ (C80AP)

Distance - Yards	Muzzle	25	50	75	100
Velocity - fps	960	910	870	830	790
Energy - ft/lb	190	175	160	145	130
Taylor KO values	4.6	4.4	4.2	4.0	3.8
Mid-Range Trajectory Height - inches	0.0	0.3	1.3	3.1	5.8
Drop - inches	0.0	-1.2	-5.1	-11.8	-21.8

G1 Ballistic Coefficient = 0.078

Remington 95-grain Metal Case (R380AP)

Distance - Yards	Muzzle	25	50	75	100
Velocity - fps	955	904	865	821	785
Energy - ft/lb	190	172	160	142	130
Taylor KO values	4.6	4.4	4.2	4.0	3.8
Mid-Range Trajectory Height - inches	0.0	0.3	1.4	3.1	5.9
Drop - inches	0.0	-1.2	-5.1	-122.0	-22.0

G1 Ballistic Coefficient = 0.077

UMC (Remington) 95-grain Metal Case (L380AP)

Distance - Yards	Muzzle	25	50	75	100
Velocity - fps	955	904	865	821	785
Energy - ft/lb	190	172	160	142	130
Taylor KO values	4.6	4.4	4.2	4.0	3.8
Mid-Range Trajectory Height - inches	0.0	0.3	1.4	3.1	5.9
Drop - inches	0.0	-1.2	-5.1	-122.0	-22.0

G1 Ballistic Coefficient = 0.077

USA (Winchester) 95-grain FMJ (Q4206)

Distance - Yards	Muzzle	25	50	75	100
Velocity - fps	955	907	865	828	794
Energy - ft/lb	190	173	160	145	133
Taylor KO values	4.6	4.4	4.2	4.0	3.8
Mid-Range Trajectory Height - inches	0.0	0.3	1.3	3.1	5.8
Drop - inches	0.0	-1.2	-5.1	-11.9	-21.8

G1 Ballistic Coefficient = 0.082

Magtech 95-grain Full Metal Case (380A)

Distance - Yards	Muzzle	25	50	75	100
Velocity - fps	951	900	861	817	781
Energy - ft/lb	190	171	156	141	128
Taylor KO values	4.6	4.3	4.1	3.9	3.7
Mid-Range Trajectory Height - inches	0.0	0.3	1.4	3.2	5.9
Drop - inches	0.0	-1.2	-5.2	-12.1	-22.2

G1 Ballistic Coefficient = 0.078

Black Hills 95-grain FMJ (M380N2)

Distance - Yards	Muzzle	25	50	75	100
Velocity - fps	950	901	859	822	787
Energy - ft/lb	190	171	156	142	131
Taylor KO values	4.6	4.3	4.1	3.9	3.8
Mid-Range Trajectory Height - inches	0.0	0.3	1.4	3.2	5.9
Drop - inches	0.0	-1.2	-5.2	-12.0	-22.1

G1 Ballistic Coefficient = 0.080

Speer 95-grain FMJ (53608)

Distance - Yards	Muzzle	25	50	75	100
Velocity - fps	950	911	877	846	817
Energy - ft/lb	190	175	162	151	143
Taylor KO values	4.6	4.4	4.2	4.1	3.9
Mid-Range Trajectory Height - inches	0.0	0.2	1.1	3.0	5.4
Drop - inches	0.0	-1.2	-5.1	-11.8	-21.5

G1 Ballistic Coefficient = 0.081

CCI 95-grain FMJ (3505)

Distance - Yards	Muzzle	25	50	75	100	
Velocity - fps	945	898	865	820	785	
Energy - ft/lb	190	170	160	142	130	
Taylor KO values	4.5	4.3	4.1	3.9	3.8	
Mid-Range Trajectory Height - inches	0.0	0.3	1.4	3.2	5.9	
Drop - inches	0.0	-1.3	-5.2	-12.1	-22.2	G1 Ballistic Coefficient = 0.081

Hansen 95-grain FMJ "Combat" (HCC380A)

Distance - Yards	Muzzle	25	50	75	100	
Velocity - fps	925	880	840	804	771	
Energy - ft/lb	181	163	149	137	126	
Taylor KO values	4.4	4.2	4.0	3.9	3.7	
Mid-Range Trajectory Height - inches	0.0	0.3	1.4	3.3	6.2	
Drop - inches	0.0	-1.3	-5.4	-12.6	-23.2	G1 Ballistic Coefficient = 0.080

Remington 102-grain Brass-JHP (GS380B)

Distance - Yards	Muzzle	25	50	75	100	
Velocity - fps	940	920	901	883	866	
Energy - ft/lb	200	192	184	177	170	
Taylor KO values	4.8	4.7	4.6	4.6	4.5	
Mid-Range Trajectory Height - inches	0.0	0.3	1.2	2.9	5.1	
Drop - inches	0.0	-1.2	-5.1	-11.6	-20.8	G1 Ballistic Coefficient = 0.195

9mm Makarov (9x18mm)

During the cold war days, 9mm Makarov cartridge was the standard military and police cartridge for the USSR and several Eastern Block countries. Since the collapse of the USSR, Makarov pistols have begun to appear in the US, both new and surplus. Powerwise, this cartridge falls in the gap between the .380 Auto and the 9mm Luger. The dimensions are such that these rounds won't fit Luger chambers, and it isn't a good idea to try to use either .380 or 9mm cartridges in the Makarov. Three companies in the US make ammunition for Makarov pistols.

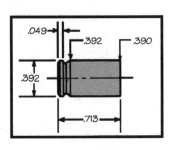

Relative Recoil Factor = 0.41   **Controlling Agency: Factory**

Standard barrel for velocity testing:
3.75 inches long - 1 turn in 9.45 inch twist

CCI 90-grain HP (3512)

Distance - Yards	Muzzle	25	50	75	100	
Velocity - fps	1050	997	952	915	881	
Energy - ft/lb	220	199	181	167	155	
Taylor KO values	4.8	4.5	4.3	4.2	4.0	
Mid-Range Trajectory Height - inches	0.0	0.2	1.1	2.6	4.8	
Drop - inches	0.0	-1.0	-4.2	-9.8	-18.0	G1 Ballistic Coefficient = 0.106

Federal 90-grain Hi-Shok JHP (C9MKB)

Distance - Yards	Muzzle	25	50	75	100	
Velocity - fps	990	950	910	880	850	
Energy - ft/lb	195	180	165	155	145	
Taylor KO values	4.5	4.3	4.2	4.0	3.9	
Mid-Range Trajectory Height - inches	0.0	0.3	1.2	2.9	5.3	
Drop - inches	0.0	-1.1	-4.7	-10.9	-19.8	G1 Ballistic Coefficient = 0.109

Hornady 95-grain JHP/XTP (9100c)

Distance - Yards	Muzzle	25	50	75	100
Velocity - fps	1000	963	930	901	874
Energy - ft/lb	211	196	182	171	161
Taylor KO values	4.8	4.7	4.5	4.3	4.2
Mid-Range Trajectory Height - inches	0.0	0.3	1.2	2.7	5.0
Drop - inches	0.0	-1.1	-4.6	-10.5	-19.2

G1 Ballistic Coefficient = 0.128

American Eagle (Federal) 95-grain FMJ (AE9MK)

Distance - Yards	Muzzle	25	50	75	100
Velocity - fps	990	960	920	900	870
Energy - ft/lb	205	190	180	170	160
Taylor KO values	4.8	4.7	4.5	4.4	4.2
Mid-Range Trajectory Height - inches	0.0	0.3	1.2	2.8	5.1
Drop - inches	0.0	-1.1	-4.6	-10.7	-19.5

G1 Ballistic Coefficient = 0.131

9mm Luger
(9mm Parabellum)
(9x19mm)

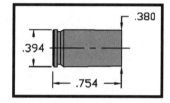

When he first introduced his 9mm pistol cartridge in 1902, Georgi Luger couldn't have even imagined what was going to happen to his brainchild. The German Navy adopted the cartridge in 1904 and the German Army in 1908. That in itself would be a pretty glowing resume for any cartridge design, but its history was just starting. By WW2 the 9mm Luger had gone on to become the standard military and police pistol cartridge in most of Western Europe. Metric cartridges weren't very popular in the US before WW2 and the cartridge didn't get a lot of use here. With the increased popularity of semi-automatic pistols in the US the 9mm caliber ended up on more and more shooter's ammo shelves. Then in 1985, the US army adopted the M-9 Beretta pistol as a "replacement" for the 1911A1 .45 Auto and guaranteed the 9mm Luger at least another 50 years of useful life. Performancewise, the 9mm Luger packs a little more punch than the .38 Special but falls well short of the .357 Magnum.

Relative Recoil Factor = 0.65   **Controlling Agency: SAAMI**

Bullet Weight Grains	Velocity fps	Maximum Average Pressure		Standard barrel for velocity testing:
		Copper Crusher	Transducer	
88 JHP	1500	33,000 cup	35,000 psi	4 inches long - 1 turn in 10 inch twist
95 JSP	1330	33,000 cup	35,000 psi	
100 JHP	1210	33,000 cup	35,000 psi	
115 MC	1125	33,000 cup	35,000 psi	
115 JHP	1145	33,000 cup	35,000 psi	
115 STHP	1210	33,000 cup	35,000 psi	
124 NC	1090	33,000 cup	35,000 psi	
147 MC	985	33,000 cup	35,000 psi	

Fiocchi 63-grain Compound Plastic (9CPB)

Distance - Yards	Muzzle	25	50	75	100
Velocity - fps	1883	1662	1463	1293	1157
Energy - ft/lb	495	386	300	234	187
Taylor KO values	6.0	5.3	4.7	4.1	3.7
Mid-Range Trajectory Height - inches	0.0	0.1	0.4	1.0	2.1
Drop - inches	0.0	-0.3	-1.5	-3.6	-7.1

G1 Ballistic Coefficient = 0.080

CCI 64-grain Shotshell (3706)

Shot cartridge using # 11 Shot @ 1450 fps muzzle velocity.

Fiocchi 82-grain Compound Plastic (9CPBJ)

Distance - Yards	Muzzle	25	50	75	100
Velocity - fps	1532	1391	1268	1166	1086
Energy - ft/lb	425	352	293	247	215
Taylor KO values	6.4	5.8	5.3	4.8	4.5
Mid-Range Trajectory Height - inches	0.0	0.1	0.6	1.4	2.7
Drop - inches	0.0	-0.5	-2.1	-5.1	-9.6

G1 Ballistic Coefficient = 0.105

Hornady 90-grain JHP/XTP (9020)

Distance - Yards	Muzzle	25	50	75	100
Velocity - fps	1360	1235	1134	1058	999
Energy - ft/lb	370	305	257	224	200
Taylor KO values	6.2	5.6	5.2	4.8	4.6
Mid-Range Trajectory Height - inches	0.0	0.2	0.7	1.7	3.4
Drop - inches	0.0	-0.6	-2.7	-6.4	-12.1

G1 Ballistic Coefficient = 0.099

Magtech 95-grain JSP - FLAT (9D)

Distance - Yards	Muzzle	25	50	75	100
Velocity - fps	1345	1253	1174	1108	1055
Energy - ft/lb	380	331	291	259	235
Taylor KO values	6.5	6.0	5.7	5.3	5.1
Mid-Range Trajectory Height - inches	0.0	0.2	0.8	1.7	3.4
Drop - inches	0.0	-0.6	-2.6	-6.2	-11.6

G1 Ballistic Coefficient = 0.135

Magtech 95-grain JSP - FLAT Clean Range (9K)

Distance - Yards	Muzzle	25	50	75	100
Velocity - fps	1345	1253	1174	1108	1055
Energy - ft/lb	380	331	291	259	235
Taylor KO values	6.5	6.0	5.7	5.3	5.1
Mid-Range Trajectory Height - inches	0.0	0.2	0.8	1.7	3.4
Drop - inches	0.0	-0.6	-2.6	-6.2	-11.6

G1 Ballistic Coefficient = 0.135

PMC 95-grain Starfire HP (9SFL)

Distance - Yards	Muzzle	25	50	75	100
Velocity - fps	1250	1179	1118	1068	1026
Energy - ft/lb	330	293	264	241	222
Taylor KO values	6.0	5.7	5.4	5.1	4.9
Mid-Range Trajectory Height - inches	0.0	0.3	0.9	1.8	3.9
Drop - inches	0.0	-0.6	-2.6	-6.2	-11.6

G1 Ballistic Coefficient = 0.150

Federal 100-grain JSP (BC9NT1)

Distance - Yards	Muzzle	25	50	75	100
Velocity - fps	1180	1120	1080	1041	1007
Energy - ft/lb	305	280	255	240	225
Taylor KO values	6.0	5.7	5.5	5.3	5.1
Mid-Range Trajectory Height - inches	0.0	0.2	0.9	2.0	3.7
Drop - inches	0.0	-0.8	-3.3	-7.7	-14.1

G1 Ballistic Coefficient = 0.169

Winchester 105-grain JSP/NT (SC9NT)

Distance - Yards	Muzzle	25	50	75	100
Velocity - fps	1200	1131	1074	1028	989
Energy - ft/lb	336	298	269	246	228
Taylor KO values	6.4	6.0	5.7	5.5	5.3
Mid-Range Trajectory Height - inches	0.0	0.2	0.8	2.0	3.7
Drop - inches	0.0	-0.8	-3.3	-7.6	-14.1

G1 Ballistic Coefficient = 0.137

Remington 101-grain Disintegrator Plated Frangible (LF9MMA)

Distance - Yards	Muzzle	25	50	75	100
Velocity - fps	1100	1055	1016	983	954
Energy - ft/lb	282	259	241	226	212
Taylor KO values	5.9	5.6	5.4	5.2	5.1
Mid-Range Trajectory Height - inches	0.0	0.2	1.0	2.3	4.3
Drop - inches	0.0	-0.9	-3.8	-8.8	-16.0

G1 Ballistic Coefficient = 0.156

Black Hills 115-grain JHP + P (M9N8)

Distance - Yards	Muzzle	25	50	75	100
Velocity - fps	1300	1222	1155	1098	1052
Energy - ft/lb	431	381	340	308	282
Taylor KO values	7.6	7.1	6.7	6.4	6.1
Mid-Range Trajectory Height - inches	0.0	0.2	0.7	1.7	3.3
Drop - inches	0.0	-0.7	-2.8	-6.6	-12.1

G1 Ballistic Coefficient = 0.150

Black Hills 115-grain (Extra Power) JHP (M9N6)

Distance - Yards	Muzzle	25	50	75	100
Velocity - fps	1250	1179	1118	1068	1026
Energy - ft/lb	400	355	319	291	269
Taylor KO values	7.3	6.9	6.5	6.2	6.0
Mid-Range Trajectory Height - inches	0.0	0.2	0.8	1.8	3.5
Drop - inches	0.0	-0.7	-3.0	-7.0	-13.0

G1 Ballistic Coefficient = 0.150

Fiocchi 115-grain JHP (9APHP)

Distance - Yards	Muzzle	25	50	75	100
Velocity - fps	1250	1176	1114	1063	1021
Energy - ft/lb	400	353	317	289	266
Taylor KO values	7.3	6.9	6.5	6.2	6.0
Mid-Range Trajectory Height - inches	0.0	0.2	0.8	1.8	3.5
Drop - inches	0.0	-0.7	-3.0	-7.1	-13.0

G1 Ballistic Coefficient = 0.145

Remington 115-grain JHP + P (R9MM6)

Distance - Yards	Muzzle	25	50	75	100
Velocity - fps	1250	1175	1113	1061	1019
Energy - ft/lb	399	353	315	288	265
Taylor KO values	7.3	6.9	6.5	6.2	5.9
Mid-Range Trajectory Height - inches	0.0	0.2	0.8	1.9	3.5
Drop - inches	0.0	-0.7	-3.0	-7.1	-13.0

G1 Ballistic Coefficient = 0.143

Magtech 115-grain JHP + P + (9H)

Distance - Yards	Muzzle	25	50	75	100
Velocity - fps	1246	1193	1145	1105	1069
Energy - ft/lb	397	364	335	312	292
Taylor KO values	7.3	7.0	6.7	6.4	6.2
Mid-Range Trajectory Height - inches	0.0	0.2	0.8	1.8	3.3
Drop - inches	0.0	-0.7	-3.0	-6.9	-12.5

G1 Ballistic Coefficient = 0.205

Winchester 115-grain Silvertip HP (X9MMSHP)

Distance - Yards	Muzzle	25	50	75	100
Velocity - fps	1225	1154	1095	1047	1007
Energy - ft/lb	383	340	306	280	259
Taylor KO values	7.1	6.7	6.4	6.1	5.9
Mid-Range Trajectory Height - inches	0.0	0.2	0.8	1.9	3.6
Drop - inches	0.0	-0.8	-3.1	-7.3	-13.5

G1 Ballistic Coefficient = 0.143

Speer 115-grain Gold Dot (23614)

Distance - Yards	Muzzle	25	50	75	100
Velocity - fps	1200	1123	1047	1012	971
Energy - ft/lb	341	322	280	262	241
Taylor KO values	7.0	6.5	6.2	6.0	5.7
Mid-Range Trajectory Height - inches	0.0	0.2	0.9	2.0	3.9
Drop - inches	0.0	-0.8	-3.3	-7.7	-14.3

G1 Ballistic Coefficient = 0.122

PMC 115-grain JHP (9B)

Distance - Yards	Muzzle	25	50	75	100
Velocity - fps	1167	1098	1044	999	961
Energy - ft/lb	350	308	278	255	236
Taylor KO values	6.8	6.4	6.1	5.8	5.6
Mid-Range Trajectory Height - inches	0.0	0.2	0.9	2.1	4.0
Drop - inches	0.0	-0.8	-3.5	-8.1	-14.9

G1 Ballistic Coefficient = 0.126

Norma 115-grain HP (19021)

Distance - Yards	Muzzle	25	50	75	100
Velocity - fps	1165	1099	1046	1003	966
Energy - ft/lb	344	306	277	257	236
Taylor KO values	6.8	6.4	6.1	5.8	5.6
Mid-Range Trajectory Height - inches	0.0	0.2	0.9	2.1	4.0
Drop - inches	0.0	-0.8	-3.5	-8.1	-14.8

G1 Ballistic Coefficient = 0.131

Federal 115-grain Hi-Shok JHP (C9BP)

Distance - Yards	Muzzle	25	50	75	100
Velocity - fps	1160	1100	1060	1020	990
Energy - ft/lb	345	310	285	270	250
Taylor KO values	6.8	6.4	6.2	5.9	5.8
Mid-Range Trajectory Height - inches	0.0	0.2	0.9	2.1	3.8
Drop - inches	0.0	-0.8	-3.4	-8.0	-14.6

G1 Ballistic Coefficient = 0.161

Hansen 115-grain JHP "Combat" (HCC9C)

Distance - Yards	Muzzle	25	50	75	100
Velocity - fps	1160	1100	1060	1020	990
Energy - ft/lb	345	310	285	270	250
Taylor KO values	6.8	6.4	6.2	5.9	5.8
Mid-Range Trajectory Height - inches	0.0	0.2	0.9	2.1	3.8
Drop - inches	0.0	-0.8	-3.4	-8.0	-14.6

G1 Ballistic Coefficient = 0.161

Hornady 115-grain JHP/XTP (9025)

Distance - Yards	Muzzle	25	50	75	100
Velocity - fps	1155	1095	1047	1006	971
Energy - ft/lb	341	306	280	258	241
Taylor KO values	6.7	6.4	6.1	5.9	5.7
Mid-Range Trajectory Height - inches	0.0	0.2	0.9	2.1	4.0
Drop - inches	0.0	-0.8	-3.5	-8.1	-14.9

G1 Ballistic Coefficient = 0.141

Magtech 115-grain JHP (9C)

Distance - Yards	Muzzle	25	50	75	100
Velocity - fps	1155	1095	1047	1006	971
Energy - ft/lb	341	306	280	258	241
Taylor KO values	6.7	6.4	6.1	5.9	5.7
Mid-Range Trajectory Height - inches	0.0	0.2	0.9	2.1	4.0
Drop - inches	0.0	-0.8	-3.5	-8.1	-14.9

G1 Ballistic Coefficient = 0.141

Remington 115-grain JHP (R9MM1)

Distance - Yards	Muzzle	25	50	75	100
Velocity - fps	1155	1095	1047	1006	971
Energy - ft/lb	341	306	280	258	241
Taylor KO values	6.7	6.4	6.1	5.9	5.7
Mid-Range Trajectory Height - inches	0.0	0.2	0.9	2.1	4.0
Drop - inches	0.0	-0.8	-3.5	-8.1	-14.9

G1 Ballistic Coefficient = 0.141

CCI 115-grain JHP (3508)

Distance - Yards	Muzzle	25	50	75	100
Velocity - fps	1145	1078	1024	981	943
Energy - ft/lb	335	297	268	246	227
Taylor KO values	6.7	6.3	6.0	5.7	5.5
Mid-Range Trajectory Height - inches	0.0	0.2	1.0	2.2	4.1
Drop - inches	0.0	-0.9	3.6	-8.4	-15.5

G1 Ballistic Coefficient = 0.119

Fiocchi 115-grain Metal Case (9AP)

Distance - Yards	Muzzle	25	50	75	100
Velocity - fps	1250	1179	1118	1068	1026
Energy - ft/lb	400	355	319	291	269
Taylor KO values	7.3	6.9	6.5	6.2	6.0
Mid-Range Trajectory Height - inches	0.0	0.2	0.8	1.8	3.5
Drop - inches	0.0	-0.7	-3.0	-7.0	-13.0

G1 Ballistic Coefficient = 0.150

USA (Winchester) 115-grain Brass Enclosed Base (WC91)

Distance - Yards	Muzzle	25	50	75	100
Velocity - fps	1190	1135	1088	1048	1014
Energy - ft/lb	362	329	302	281	262
Taylor KO values	6.9	6.6	6.3	6.1	5.9
Mid-Range Trajectory Height - inches	0.0	0.2	0.9	2.1	3.7
Drop - inches	0.0	-0.8	-3.3	-7.6	-13.9

G1 Ballistic Coefficient = 0.171

Winchester 115-grain FMJ (Q4172)

Distance - Yards	Muzzle	25	50	75	100
Velocity - fps	1190	1125	1071	1027	990
Energy - ft/lb	362	323	293	270	250
Taylor KO values	6.9	6.6	6.2	6.0	5.8
Mid-Range Trajectory Height - inches	0.0	0.2	0.9	2.0	3.8
Drop - inches	0.0	-0.8	-3.3	-7.7	-14.2

G1 Ballistic Coefficient = 0.143

Hansen 115-grain FMJ "Black Tip" + P (HCC9G)

Distance - Yards	Muzzle	25	50	75	100
Velocity - fps	1180	1115	1063	1019	982
Energy - ft/lb	355	318	288	265	246
Taylor KO values	6.9	6.5	6.2	5.9	5.7
Mid-Range Trajectory Height - inches	0.0	0.2	0.9	2.1	3.8
Drop - inches	0.0	-0.8	-3.4	-7.8	-14.4

G1 Ballistic Coefficient = 0.140

American Eagle (Federal) 115-grain FMJ (AE9DP)

Distance - Yards	Muzzle	25	50	75	100
Velocity - fps	1160	1100	1060	1020	990
Energy - ft/lb	344	313	288	267	250
Taylor KO values	6.8	6.4	6.2	5.9	5.8
Mid-Range Trajectory Height - inches	0.0	0.2	0.9	2.1	3.9
Drop - inches	0.0	-0.8	-3.4	-8.0	-14.6

G1 Ballistic Coefficient = 0.161

PMC 115-grain FMJ (9A)

Distance - Yards	Muzzle	25	50	75	100
Velocity - fps	1157	1100	1053	1013	979
Energy - ft/lb	344	309	283	262	245
Taylor KO values	6.7	6.4	6.1	5.9	5.7
Mid-Range Trajectory Height - inches	0.0	0.2	0.9	2.1	3.9
Drop - inches	0.0	-0.8	-3.5	-8.1	-14.8

G1 Ballistic Coefficient = 0.149

Hansen 115-grain FMJ "Combat" (HCC9A)

Distance - Yards	Muzzle	25	50	75	100
Velocity - fps	1155	1095	1046	1005	970
Energy - ft/lb	340	306	279	258	240
Taylor KO values	6.7	6.4	6.1	5.9	5.7
Mid-Range Trajectory Height - inches	0.0	0.2	0.9	2.1	4.0
Drop - inches	0.0	-0.8	-3.5	-8.1	-14.9

G1 Ballistic Coefficient = 0.140

Black Hills 115-grain FMJ (M9N1)

Distance - Yards	Muzzle	25	50	75	100
Velocity - fps	1150	1091	1042	1002	967
Energy - ft/lb	336	304	278	256	239
Taylor KO values	6.7	6.4	6.1	5.8	5.6
Mid-Range Trajectory Height - inches	0.0	0.2	0.9	2.1	4.0
Drop - inches	0.0	-0.8	-3.5	-8.2	-15.0

G1 Ballistic Coefficient = 0.140

CCI 115-grain FMJ (3509)

Distance - Yards	Muzzle	25	50	75	100
Velocity - fps	1145	1089	1047	1005	971
Energy - ft/lb	341	303	280	258	241
Taylor KO values	6.7	6.4	6.1	5.9	5.7
Mid-Range Trajectory Height - inches	0.0	0.2	0.9	2.1	3.9
Drop - inches	0.0	-0.9	-3.5	-8.2	-15.1

G1 Ballistic Coefficient = 0.147

Speer 115-grain FMJ (53615)

Distance - Yards	Muzzle	25	50	75	100
Velocity - fps	1145	1089	1047	1005	971
Energy - ft/lb	341	303	280	258	241
Taylor KO values	6.7	6.4	6.1	5.9	5.7
Mid-Range Trajectory Height - inches	0.0	0.2	0.9	2.1	3.9
Drop - inches	0.0	-0.9	-3.5	-8.2	-15.1

G1 Ballistic Coefficient = 0.147

Magtech 115-grain FMC (9A)

Distance - Yards	Muzzle	25	50	75	100
Velocity - fps	1135	1079	1027	994	961
Energy - ft/lb	330	297	270	253	235
Taylor KO values	6.6	6.3	6.0	5.8	5.6
Mid-Range Trajectory Height - inches	0.0	0.2	0.9	2.1	4.0
Drop - inches	0.0	-0.9	-3.6	-8.4	-15.4

G1 Ballistic Coefficient = 0.141

Remington 115-grain Metal Case (R9MM3)

Distance - Yards	Muzzle	25	50	75	100
Velocity - fps	1135	1084	1041	1005	973
Energy - ft/lb	329	300	277	258	242
Taylor KO values	6.6	6.3	6.1	5.9	5.7
Mid-Range Trajectory Height - inches	0.0	0.2	0.9	2.1	4.0
Drop - inches	0.0	-0.9	-3.6	-8.3	-15.2

G1 Ballistic Coefficient = 0.156

UMC (Remington) 115-grain Metal Case (L9MM3)

Distance - Yards	Muzzle	25	50	75	100
Velocity - fps	1135	1084	1041	1005	973
Energy - ft/lb	329	300	277	258	242
Taylor KO values	6.6	6.3	6.1	5.9	5.7
Mid-Range Trajectory Height - inches	0.0	0.2	0.9	2.1	4.0
Drop - inches	0.0	-0.9	-3.6	-8.3	-15.2

G1 Ballistic Coefficient = 0.156

Norma 116-grain SP Flat Nose (19026)

Distance - Yards	Muzzle	25	50	75	100
Velocity - fps	1165	1094	1038	992	954
Energy - ft/lb	349	308	278	254	235
Taylor KO values	6.9	6.4	6.1	5.8	5.6
Mid-Range Trajectory Height - inches	0.0	0.2	0.9	2.1	4.0
Drop - inches	0.0	-0.8	-3.5	-8.2	-15.0

G1 Ballistic Coefficient = 0.120

Lapua 116-grain FMJ (4319200)

Distance - Yards	Muzzle	25	50	75	100
Velocity - fps	1198	1118	1056	1006	964
Energy - ft/lb	300	322	287	261	240
Taylor KO values	7.0	6.6	6.2	5.9	5.7
Mid-Range Trajectory Height - inches	0.0	0.2	0.9	2.1	3.8
Drop - inches	0.0	-0.8	-3.3	-7.8	-14.4

G1 Ballistic Coefficient = 0.117

Lapua 120-grain CEPP SUPER (4319175)

Distance - Yards	Muzzle	25	50	75	100
Velocity - fps	1181	1111	1055	1010	971
Energy - ft/lb	372	329	297	272	251
Taylor KO values	7.2	6.8	6.4	6.1	5.9
Mid-Range Trajectory Height - inches	0.0	0.2	0.9	2.1	3.9
Drop - inches	0.0	-0.8	-3.4	-7.9	-14.6

G1 Ballistic Coefficient = 0.129

Lapua 120-grain CEPP EXTRA (4319174)

Distance - Yards	Muzzle	25	50	75	100
Velocity - fps	1181	1111	1055	1010	971
Energy - ft/lb	372	329	297	272	251
Taylor KO values	7.2	6.8	6.4	6.1	5.9
Mid-Range Trajectory Height - inches	0.0	0.2	0.9	2.1	3.9
Drop - inches	0.0	-0.8	-3.4	-7.9	-14.6

G1 Ballistic Coefficient = 0.129

Lapua 123-grain HP Megashock (4319185)

Distance - Yards	Muzzle	25	50	75	100
Velocity - fps	1165	1097	1042	997	959
Energy - ft/lb	371	328	297	272	251
Taylor KO values	7.3	6.8	6.5	6.2	6.0
Mid-Range Trajectory Height - inches	0.0	0.2	0.9	2.1	4.0
Drop - inches	0.0	-0.8	-3.5	-8.1	-14.9

G1 Ballistic Coefficient = 0.125

Lapua 123-grain FMJ (4319230)

Distance - Yards	Muzzle	25	50	75	100
Velocity - fps	1312	1225	1151	1090	1040
Energy - ft/lb	470	410	362	324	296
Taylor KO values	8.2	7.6	7.2	6.8	6.5
Mid-Range Trajectory Height - inches	0.0	0.2	0.7	1.7	3.3
Drop - inches	0.0	-0.7	-2.8	-6.5	-12.1

G1 Ballistic Coefficient = 0.136

Fiocchi 123-grain Metal Case (9APB)

Distance - Yards	Muzzle	25	50	75	100
Velocity - fps	1250	1174	1110	1059	1016
Energy - ft/lb	425	376	337	306	282
Taylor KO values	7.8	7.3	6.9	6.6	6.3
Mid-Range Trajectory Height - inches	0.0	0.2	0.8	1.9	3.5
Drop - inches	0.0	-0.7	-3.0	-7.1	-13.1

G1 Ballistic Coefficient = 0.140

Lapua 123-grain FMJ Combat (4319163)

Distance - Yards	Muzzle	25	50	75	100
Velocity - fps	1165	1102	1050	1007	971
Energy - ft/lb	371	331	301	277	258
Taylor KO values	7.3	6.9	6.5	6.3	6.1
Mid-Range Trajectory Height - inches	0.0	0.2	0.9	2.1	3.9
Drop - inches	0.0	-0.8	-3.4	-8.0	-14.8

G1 Ballistic Coefficient = 0.140

Norma 123-grain Security Cartridge (19027)

Distance - Yards	Muzzle	25	50	75	100
Velocity - fps	1165	1074	1007	955	910
Energy - ft/lb	372	315	278	249	227
Taylor KO values	7.3	6.7	6.3	6.0	5.7
Mid-Range Trajectory Height - inches	0.0	0.2	0.9	2.2	4.3
Drop - inches	0.0	-0.8	-3.6	-8.4	-15.7

G1 Ballistic Coefficient = 0.091

Hansen 123-grain FMJ NATO Military (HCC9B)

Distance - Yards	Muzzle	25	50	75	100
Velocity - fps	1092	1032	983	943	907
Energy - ft/lb	328	291	264	243	225
Taylor KO values	6.8	6.4	6.1	5.9	5.7
Mid-Range Trajectory Height - inches	0.0	0.2	1.0	2.4	4.5
Drop - inches	0.0	-1.0	-3.9	-9.2	-16.8

G1 Ballistic Coefficient = 0.110

Lapua 123-grain FMJ (4319177)

Distance - Yards	Muzzle	25	50	75	100
Velocity - fps	1050	1007	970	938	909
Energy - ft/lb	301	277	257	240	226
Taylor KO values	6.5	6.3	6.1	5.9	5.7
Mid-Range Trajectory Height - inches	0.0	0.2	1.1	2.5	4.6
Drop - inches	0.0	-1.0	-4.2	-9.6	-17.6

G1 Ballistic Coefficient = 0.134

Federal 124-grain Nyclad Ball (P9BNL)

Distance - Yards	Muzzle	25	50	75	100
Velocity - fps	1120	1070	1030	990	960
Energy - ft/lb	345	315	290	270	255
Taylor KO values	7.0	6.7	6.5	6.2	6.0
Mid-Range Trajectory Height - inches	0.0	0.2	0.9	2.2	4.1
Drop - inches	0.0	-0.9	-3.7	-8.5	-15.6

G1 Ballistic Coefficient = 0.149

Magtech 124-grain LRN (9E)

Distance - Yards	Muzzle	25	50	75	100
Velocity - fps	1109	1067	1030	999	971
Energy - ft/lb	339	313	292	275	259
Taylor KO values	7.0	6.7	6.5	6.3	6.1
Mid-Range Trajectory Height - inches	0.0	0.2	1.0	2.2	4.1
Drop - inches	0.0	-0.9	-3.7	-8.6	-15.6

G1 Ballistic Coefficient = 0.174

Remington 124-grain Brass-JHP + P (GS9MMD)

Distance - Yards	Muzzle	25	50	75	100
Velocity - fps	1180	1131	1089	1053	1021
Energy - ft/lb	384	352	327	305	287
Taylor KO values	7.4	7.1	6.8	6.6	6.4
Mid-Range Trajectory Height - inches	0.0	0.2	0.8	2.0	3.8
Drop - inches	0.0	-0.8	-3.3	-7.6	-13.9

G1 Ballistic Coefficient = 0.174

Black Hills 124-grain JHP (M9N3)

Distance - Yards	Muzzle	25	50	75	100
Velocity - fps	1150	1103	1063	1028	998
Energy - ft/lb	363	335	311	291	274
Taylor KO values	7.2	6.9	6.7	6.5	6.3
Mid-Range Trajectory Height - inches	0.0	0.2	0.9	2.1	3.8
Drop - inches	0.0	-0.8	-3.5	08.0	-14.6

G1 Ballistic Coefficient = 0.180

Speer 124-grain Gold Dot (23618)

Distance - Yards	Muzzle	25	50	75	100
Velocity - fps	1150	1083	1030	985	948
Energy - ft/lb	367	323	292	267	247
Taylor KO values	7.2	6.8	6.5	6.2	6.0
Mid-Range Trajectory Height - inches	0.0	0.2	0.9	2.2	3.9
Drop - inches	0.0	-0.9	-3.6	-8.3	-15.3

G1 Ballistic Coefficient = 0.121

Federal 124-grain Hydra-Shok JHP (P9HS1)

Distance - Yards	Muzzle	25	50	75	100
Velocity - fps	1120	1070	1030	990	960
Energy - ft/lb	345	315	290	270	255
Taylor KO values	7.0	6.7	6.5	6.2	6.0
Mid-Range Trajectory Height - inches	0.0	0.2	0.9	2.2	4.1
Drop - inches	0.0	-0.9	-3.7	-8.5	-15.6

G1 Ballistic Coefficient = 0.149

Federal 124-grain Nyclad HP (P9BP)

Distance - Yards	Muzzle	25	50	75	100
Velocity - fps	1120	1070	1030	990	960
Energy - ft/lb	345	315	290	270	255
Taylor KO values	7.0	6.7	6.5	6.2	6.0
Mid-Range Trajectory Height - inches	0.0	0.2	0.9	2.2	4.1
Drop - inches	0.0	-0.9	-3.7	-8.5	-15.6

G1 Ballistic Coefficient = 0.149

Remington 124-grain Brass JHP (GS9MMB)

Distance - Yards	Muzzle	25	50	75	100
Velocity - fps	1125	1074	1031	995	963
Energy - ft/lb	349	318	293	273	255
Taylor KO values	7.1	6.8	6.5	6.3	6.1
Mid-Range Trajectory Height - inches	0.0	0.2	1.0	2.2	4.0
Drop - inches	0.0	-0.9	-3.7	-8.5	-15.5

G1 Ballistic Coefficient = 0.149

Remington 124-grain JHP (R9MM10)

Distance - Yards	Muzzle	25	50	75	100
Velocity - fps	1120	1070	1030	990	960
Energy - ft/lb	345	315	290	270	255
Taylor KO values	7.0	6.7	6.5	6.2	6.0
Mid-Range Trajectory Height - inches	0.0	0.2	0.9	2.2	4.1
Drop - inches	0.0	-0.9	-3.7	-8.5	-15.6

G1 Ballistic Coefficient = 0.149

Hornady 124-grain JHP/XTP (9024)

Distance - Yards	Muzzle	25	50	75	100
Velocity - fps	1110	1067	1030	999	971
Energy - ft/lb	339	314	292	275	250
Taylor KO values	7.0	6.7	6.5	6.3	6.1
Mid-Range Trajectory Height - inches	0.0	0.2	1.0	2.2	4.1
Drop - inches	0.0	-0.9	-3.7	-8.6	-15.6

G1 Ballistic Coefficient = 0.173

PMC 124-grain Starfire HP (9SFB)

Distance - Yards	Muzzle	25	50	75	100
Velocity - fps	1090	1043	1003	969	939
Energy - ft/lb	327	299	277	259	243
Taylor KO values	6.9	6.6	6.3	6.1	5.9
Mid-Range Trajectory Height - inches	0.0	0.2	1.0	2.3	4.3
Drop - inches	0.0	-0.9	-3.9	-9.0	-16.4

G1 Ballistic Coefficient = 0.143

Federal 124-grain FMJ (C9AP)

Distance - Yards	Muzzle	25	50	75	100
Velocity - fps	1120	1070	1030	990	960
Energy - ft/lb	345	315	290	270	255
Taylor KO values	7.0	6.7	6.5	6.2	6.0
Mid-Range Trajectory Height - inches	0.0	0.2	0.9	2.2	4.1
Drop - inches	0.0	-0.9	-3.7	-8.5	-15.6

G1 Ballistic Coefficient = 0.149

Federal 124-grain Truncated FMJ Match (GM9MP)

Distance - Yards	Muzzle	25	50	75	100
Velocity - fps	1120	1070	1030	990	960
Energy - ft/lb	345	315	290	270	255
Taylor KO values	7.0	6.7	6.5	6.2	6.0
Mid-Range Trajectory Height - inches	0.0	0.2	0.9	2.2	4.1
Drop - inches	0.0	-0.9	-3.7	-8.5	-15.6

G1 Ballistic Coefficient = 0.149

American Eagle (Federal) 124-grain FMJ (AE9MP)

Distance - Yards	Muzzle	25	50	75	100
Velocity - fps	1120	1070	1030	990	960
Energy - ft/lb	345	315	290	270	255
Taylor KO values	7.0	6.7	6.5	6.2	6.0
Mid-Range Trajectory Height - inches	0.0	0.2	0.9	2.2	4.1
Drop - inches	0.0	-0.9	-3.7	-8.5	-15.6

G1 Ballistic Coefficient = 0.149

Hornady 124-grain FMJ-Vector (9327c)

Distance - Yards	Muzzle	25	50	75	100
Velocity - fps	1110	1071	1038	1007	981
Energy - ft/lb	339	316	297	279	265
Taylor KO values	7.0	6.7	6.5	6.3	6.2
Mid-Range Trajectory Height - inches	0.0	0.2	1.0	2.2	4.0
Drop - inches	0.0	-0.9	-3.7	-8.5	-15.5

G1 Ballistic Coefficient = 0.190

PMC 124-grain FMJ (9G)

Distance - Yards	Muzzle	25	50	75	100
Velocity - fps	1110	1059	1017	980	949
Energy - ft/lb	339	309	285	265	248
Taylor KO values	7.0	6.7	6.4	6.2	6.0
Mid-Range Trajectory Height - inches	0.0	0.2	1.0	2.3	4.2
Drop - inches	0.0	-0.9	-3.8	-8.7	-15.9

G1 Ballistic Coefficient = 0.142

Remington 124-grain Metal Case (R9MM2)

Distance - Yards	Muzzle	25	50	75	100
Velocity - fps	1110	1067	1030	999	971
Energy - ft/lb	339	314	292	275	250
Taylor KO values	7.0	6.7	6.5	6.3	6.1
Mid-Range Trajectory Height - inches	0.0	0.2	1.0	2.2	4.1
Drop - inches	0.0	-0.9	-3.7	-8.6	-15.6

G1 Ballistic Coefficient = 0.173

Magtech 124-grain FMJ Clean-Range (9J)

Distance - Yards	Muzzle	25	50	75	100
Velocity - fps	1109	1067	1030	999	971
Energy - ft/lb	339	313	292	275	259
Taylor KO values	7.0	6.7	6.5	6.3	6.1
Mid-Range Trajectory Height - inches	0.0	0.2	1.0	2.2	4.1
Drop - inches	0.0	-0.9	-3.7	-8.6	-15.6

G1 Ballistic Coefficient = 0.174

Magtech 124-grain FMC (9B)

Distance - Yards	Muzzle	25	50	75	100
Velocity - fps	1109	1067	1030	999	971
Energy - ft/lb	339	314	292	275	250
Taylor KO values	7.0	6.7	6.5	6.3	6.1
Mid-Range Trajectory Height - inches	0.0	0.2	1.0	2.2	4.1
Drop - inches	0.0	-0.9	-3.7	-8.6	-15.6

G1 Ballistic Coefficient = 0.174

CCI 124-grain Clean-Fire - FMJ (3578)

Distance - Yards	Muzzle	25	50	75	100
Velocity - fps	1090	1034	989	950	917
Energy - ft/lb	327	295	269	249	231
Taylor KO values	6.9	6.5	6.2	6.0	5.8
Mid-Range Trajectory Height - inches	0.0	0.2	1.0	2.4	4.4
Drop - inches	0.0	-1.0	-3.9	-9.1	-16.7

G1 Ballistic Coefficient = 0.119

CCI 124-grain Clean-Fire - FMJ (3064)

Distance - Yards	Muzzle	25	50	75	100
Velocity - fps	1090	1034	989	950	917
Energy - ft/lb	327	295	269	249	231
Taylor KO values	6.9	6.5	6.2	6.0	5.8
Mid-Range Trajectory Height - inches	0.0	0.2	1.0	2.4	4.4
Drop - inches	0.0	-1.0	-3.9	-9.1	-16.7

G1 Ballistic Coefficient = 0.119

Speer 124-grain Clean-Fire - FMJ (53824)

Distance - Yards	Muzzle	25	50	75	100
Velocity - fps	1090	1034	989	950	917
Energy - ft/lb	327	295	269	249	231
Taylor KO values	6.9	6.5	6.2	6.0	5.8
Mid-Range Trajectory Height - inches	0.0	0.2	1.0	2.4	4.4
Drop - inches	0.0	-1.0	-3.9	-9.1	-16.7

G1 Ballistic Coefficient = 0.119

Speer 124-grain FMJ (53616)

Distance - Yards	Muzzle	25	50	75	100
Velocity - fps	1090	1033	987	948	913
Energy - ft/lb	327	294	268	247	230
Taylor KO values	6.9	6.5	6.2	6.0	5.7
Mid-Range Trajectory Height - inches	0.0	0.2	1.0	2.4	4.5
Drop - inches	0.0	-1.0	-3.9	-9.2	-16.8

G1 Ballistic Coefficient = 0.119

Fiocchi 125-grain FMJ Truncated (9APC)

Distance - Yards	Muzzle	25	50	75	100
Velocity - fps	1250	1183	1125	1077	1036
Energy - ft/lb	425	388	351	322	298
Taylor KO values	7.9	7.5	7.1	6.8	6.6
Mid-Range Trajectory Height - inches	0.0	0.2	0.8	1.8	3.4
Drop - inches	0.0	-0.7	-3.0	-7.0	-12.8

G1 Ballistic Coefficient = 0.160

Federal 135-grain Hydra-Shok JHP (PD9HS5)

Distance - Yards	Muzzle	25	50	75	100
Velocity - fps	1050	1030	1010	980	970
Energy - ft/lb	330	315	300	290	280
Taylor KO values	7.2	7.1	6.9	6.7	6.6
Mid-Range Trajectory Height - inches	0.0	0.4	1.2	2.4	4.3
Drop - inches	0.0	-1.0	-4.1	-9.3	-16.7

G1 Ballistic Coefficient = 0.268

Winchester 147-grain Silvertip HP (X9MMST147)

Distance - Yards	Muzzle	25	50	75	100
Velocity - fps	1010	985	962	940	921
Energy - ft/lb	333	317	302	289	277
Taylor KO values	7.5	7.3	7.2	7.0	6.9
Mid-Range Trajectory Height - inches	0.0	0.3	1.1	2.6	4.7
Drop - inches	0.0	-1.1	-4.4	-10.1	-18.2

G1 Ballistic Coefficient = 0.268

Federal 147-grain Hydra-Shok JHP (P9MS2)

Distance - Yards	Muzzle	25	50	75	100
Velocity - fps	1000	960	920	890	860
Energy - ft/lb	325	300	275	260	240
Taylor KO values	7.5	7.2	6.9	6.6	6.4
Mid-Range Trajectory Height - inches	0.0	0.3	1.2	2.8	5.1
Drop - inches	0.0	-1.1	-4.6	-10.6	-19.4

G1 Ballistic Coefficient = 0.113

Remington 147-grain JHP (Subsonic) (R9MM8)

Distance - Yards	Muzzle	25	50	75	100
Velocity - fps	990	964	941	920	900
Energy - ft/lb	320	304	289	276	264
Taylor KO values	7.4	7.2	7.0	6.9	6.7
Mid-Range Trajectory Height - inches	0.0	0.3	1.1	2.7	4.9
Drop - inches	0.0	-1.1	-4.6	-10.5	-19.0

G1 Ballistic Coefficient = 0.184

Remington 147-grain Brass-JHP (GS9MMC)

Distance - Yards	Muzzle	25	50	75	100
Velocity - fps	990	964	941	920	900
Energy - ft/lb	320	304	289	276	264
Taylor KO values	7.4	7.2	7.0	6.9	6.7
Mid-Range Trajectory Height - inches	0.0	0.3	1.1	2.7	4.9
Drop - inches	0.0	-1.1	-4.6	-10.5	-19.0

G1 Ballistic Coefficient = 0.184

Winchester 147-grain JHP (Subsonic) (XSUB9MM)

Distance - Yards	Muzzle	25	50	75	100
Velocity - fps	990	967	945	926	907
Energy - ft/lb	320	305	292	280	268
Taylor KO values	7.4	7.2	7.0	6.9	6.8
Mid-Range Trajectory Height - inches	0.0	0.3	1.2	2.7	4.8
Drop - inches	0.0	-1.1	-4.6	-10.5	-18.9

G1 Ballistic Coefficient = 0.204

Winchester 147-grain SXT (S9)

Distance - Yards	Muzzle	25	50	75	100
Velocity - fps	990	967	947	927	909
Energy - ft/lb	320	306	293	281	270
Taylor KO values	7.4	7.2	7.1	6.9	6.8
Mid-Range Trajectory Height - inches	0.0	0.3	1.2	2.7	4.8
Drop - inches	0.0	-1.1	-4.6	-10.4	-18.8

G1 Ballistic Coefficient = 0.210

Speer 147-grain Gold Dot (23619)

Distance - Yards	Muzzle	25	50	75	100
Velocity - fps	985	968	960	938	924
Energy - ft/lb	326	306	300	287	279
Taylor KO values	7.3	7.2	7.1	7.0	6.9
Mid-Range Trajectory Height - inches	0.0	0.3	0.5	2.6	4.0
Drop - inches	0.0	-1.1	-4.6	-10.4	-18.7

G1 Ballistic Coefficient = 0.281

Federal 147-grain Hi-Shok JHP (C9MS)

Distance - Yards	Muzzle	25	50	75	100
Velocity - fps	980	950	930	900	880
Energy - ft/lb	310	295	285	265	255
Taylor KO values	7.3	7.1	6.9	6.7	6.6
Mid-Range Trajectory Height - inches	0.0	0.3	1.2	2.8	5.1
Drop - inches	0.0	-1.2	-4.7	-10.8	-19.6

G1 Ballistic Coefficient = 0.158

Black Hills 147-grain JHP Subsonic (M9N5)

Distance - Yards	Muzzle	25	50	75	100
Velocity - fps	975	959	943	928	914
Energy - ft/lb	309	300	290	281	273
Taylor KO values	7.3	7.1	7.0	6.9	6.8
Mid-Range Trajectory Height - inches	0.0	0.3	1.2	2.7	4.9
Drop - inches	0.0	-1.2	-4.7	-10.6	-19.1

G1 Ballistic Coefficient = 0.275

Fiocchi 147-grain JHP (9APDHP)

Distance - Yards	Muzzle	25	50	75	100
Velocity - fps	975	953	932	913	895
Energy - ft/lb	310	296	284	272	261
Taylor KO values	7.3	7.1	6.9	6.8	6.7
Mid-Range Trajectory Height - inches	0.0	0.3	1.2	2.7	5.0
Drop - inches	0.0	-1.2	-4.7	-10.8	-19.4

G1 Ballistic Coefficient = 0.200

Hornady 147-grain JHP/XTP (9028)

Distance - Yards	Muzzle	25	50	75	100
Velocity - fps	975	954	935	916	899
Energy - ft/lb	310	297	285	274	264
Taylor KO values	7.3	7.1	6.9	6.8	6.7
Mid-Range Trajectory Height - inches	0.0	0.3	1.2	2.7	5.0
Drop - inches	0.0	-1.2	-4.7	-10.7	-19.4

G1 Ballistic Coefficient = 0.214

Magtech 147-grain Full Metal Case - FLAT (Subsonic) (9G)

Distance - Yards	Muzzle	25	50	75	100
Velocity - fps	990	967	945	926	907
Energy - ft/lb	320	305	292	280	268
Taylor KO values	7.4	7.2	7.0	6.9	6.8
Mid-Range Trajectory Height - inches	0.0	0.3	1.2	2.7	4.8
Drop - inches	0.0	-1.1	-4.6	-10.5	-18.9

G1 Ballistic Coefficient = 0.204

Remington 147-grain Metal Case (Match) (R9MM9)

Distance - Yards	Muzzle	25	50	75	100
Velocity - fps	990	964	941	920	900
Energy - ft/lb	320	304	289	276	264
Taylor KO values	7.4	7.2	7.0	6.9	6.7
Mid-Range Trajectory Height - inches	0.0	0.3	1.1	2.7	4.9
Drop - inches	0.0	-1.1	-4.6	-10.5	-19.0

G1 Ballistic Coefficient = 0.184

CCI 147-grain FMJ (3582)

Distance - Yards	Muzzle	25	50	75	100
Velocity - fps	985	968	953	938	924
Energy - ft/lb	326	306	300	287	279
Taylor KO values	7.3	7.2	7.1	7.0	6.9
Mid-Range Trajectory Height - inches	0.0	0.3	0.5	2.6	4.0
Drop - inches	0.0	-1.1	-4.6	-10.4	-18.7

G1 Ballistic Coefficient = 0.285

CCI 147-grain Clean-Fire - FMJ (3462)

Distance - Yards	Muzzle	25	50	75	100
Velocity - fps	985	968	953	938	924
Energy - ft/lb	326	306	300	287	279
Taylor KO values	7.3	7.2	7.1	7.0	6.9
Mid-Range Trajectory Height - inches	0.0	0.3	0.5	2.6	4.0
Drop - inches	0.0	-1.1	-4.6	-10.4	-18.7

G1 Ballistic Coefficient = 0.285

Speer 147-grain Clean-Fire - FMJ (53826)

Distance - Yards	Muzzle	25	50	75	100
Velocity - fps	985	968	953	938	924
Energy - ft/lb	326	306	300	287	279
Taylor KO values	7.3	7.2	7.1	7.0	6.9
Mid-Range Trajectory Height - inches	0.0	0.3	0.5	2.6	4.0
Drop - inches	0.0	-1.1	-4.6	-10.4	-18.7

G1 Ballistic Coefficient = 0.285

Speer 147-grain FMJ (53620)

Distance - Yards	Muzzle	25	50	75	100	
Velocity - fps	985	963	943	923	906	
Energy - ft/lb	317	303	290	278	268	
Taylor KO values	7.3	7.2	7.0	6.9	6.8	
Mid-Range Trajectory Height - inches	0.0	0.2	1.1	2.7	4.7	
Drop - inches	0.0	-1.1	-4.6	-10.5	-19.0	G1 Ballistic Coefficient = 0.210

Hansen 147-grain FMJ "Subsonic" (HCC9E)

Distance - Yards	Muzzle	25	50	75	100	
Velocity - fps	985	968	953	938	924	
Energy - ft/lb	326	306	300	287	279	
Taylor KO values	7.3	7.2	7.1	7.0	6.9	
Mid-Range Trajectory Height - inches	0.0	0.3	0.5	2.6	4.0	
Drop - inches	0.0	-1.1	-4.6	-10.4	-18.7	G1 Ballistic Coefficient = 0.285

Black Hills 147-grain FMJ Subsonic (M9N4)

Distance - Yards	Muzzle	25	50	75	100	
Velocity - fps	975	954	935	916	899	
Energy - ft/lb	310	297	285	274	264	
Taylor KO values	7.3	7.1	6.9	6.8	6.7	
Mid-Range Trajectory Height - inches	0.0	0.3	1.2	2.7	5.0	
Drop - inches	0.0	-1.2	-4.7	-10.7	-19.4	G1 Ballistic Coefficient = 0.214

American Eagle (Federal) 147-grain FMJ Flat Point (AE9FP)

Distance - Yards	Muzzle	25	50	75	100	
Velocity - fps	960	930	910	890	870	
Energy - ft/lb	295	280	270	260	250	
Taylor KO values	7.2	6.9	6.8	6.6	6.5	
Mid-Range Trajectory Height - inches	0.0	0.3	1.3	2.9	0.3	
Drop - inches	0.0	-1.2	-4.9	11.2	-20.2	G1 Ballistic Coefficient = 0.214

Fiocchi 158-grain Metal Case (9APE) [Until Stock Exhausted]

Distance - Yards	Muzzle	25	50	75	100	
Velocity - fps	950	934	918	903	889	
Energy - ft/lb	317	306	296	286	277	
Taylor KO values	7.6	7.5	7.4	7.2	7.1	
Mid-Range Trajectory Height - inches	0.0	0.3	1.3	2.8	5.2	
Drop - inches	0.0	-1.2	-4.9	-11.2	-20.2	G1 Ballistic Coefficient = 0.250

9mm Largo (9x23mm*)

The 9mm Largo is a lengthened version of the 9mm Luger. It originated in Spain in about 1913 as a variation on the earlier Bergmann-Bayard. The CCI ammunition loaded for this caliber was originally manufactured to support surplus Spanish military pistols. This cartridge has a potential for mixing with the Winchester 9x23mm.

* Several cautions apply here. While several European 9mms are sometimes called 9x23mm, they are loaded to a much lower pressure specification than the current Winchester 9x23mm loadings. The Winchester ammunition should never be used in any 9mm Largo guns. The Largo is very similar to the .380 Super Auto, but again, the two are not interchangeable.

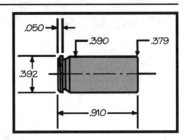

Relative Recoil Factor = 0.82

Controlling Agency: Factory

Barrel used for velocity testing:
4 inches long - 1 turn in 10 inch twist

CCI 124-grain HP (3513)

Distance - Yards	Muzzle	25	50	75	100
Velocity - fps	1190	1114	1055	1006	966
Energy - ft/lb	390	342	306	279	257
Taylor KO values	7.5	7.0	6.6	6.3	6.1
Mid-Range Trajectory Height - inches	0.0	0.2	0.7	2.1	3.7
Drop - inches	0.0	-0.8	-3.4	-7.9	-14.5

G1 Ballistic Coefficient = 0.121

9x23mm Winchester

Please review the comments for the 9mm Largo. This is high pressure ammunition that meets the performance specifications of the USPSA/IPSC competition rules. It should NOT be used in pistols that might also be marked 9x23mm, but were not designed for the high pressures. If your 9x23mm gun is not a competition gun it probably was not designed for this ammunition.
CAUTION: There is a real potential for a mixup here!

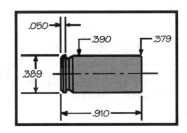

Relative Recoil Factor = 0.82

Controlling Agency: Factory

Barrel used for velocity testing:
5 inches long - The twist rate is not available

Winchester 124-grain JSP (Q4304)

Distance - Yards	Muzzle	25	50	75	100
Velocity - fps	1460	1381	1308	1242	1183
Energy - ft/lb	587	525	471	425	385
Taylor KO values	9.2	8.7	8.2	7.8	7.4
Mid-Range Trajectory Height - inches	0.0	0.1	0.6	1.3	2.5
Drop - inches	0.0	-0.5	-2.2	-5.1	-9.5

G1 Ballistic Coefficient = 0.181

Winchester 125-grain Silvertip HP (X923W)

Distance - Yards	Muzzle	25	50	75	100
Velocity - fps	1450	1344	1249	1170	1103
Energy - ft/lb	583	502	433	380	338
Taylor KO values	9.2	8.5	7.9	7.4	7.0
Mid-Range Trajectory Height - inches	0.0	0.1	0.6	1.5	2.8
Drop - inches	0.0	-0.5	-2.3	-5.4	-10.2

G1 Ballistic Coefficient = 0.132

.38 Short Colt

The history of the .38 Short Colt is rather cloudy. This cartridge seems to have appeared on the scene sometime along about the 1880s. It has the same dimensions as the .38 Long Colt except for the case length and the overall length. Why it is still in the inventory is a mystery. Perhaps the best excuse for this cartridge is that if there hadn't been a .38 SHORT Colt there couldn't have been a .38 LONG Colt.

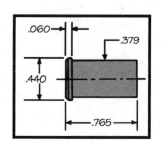

Relative Recoil Factor = 0.17   **Controlling Agency : SAAMI**

Bullet Weight Grains	Velocity fps	Maximum Average Pressure	
		Copper Crusher	Transducer
125 L	775	12,000 cup	N/S

Standard barrel for velocity testing:
4 inches long (vented)
- 1 turn in 16 inch twist

Remington 125-grain Lead (R38CS)

Distance - Yards	Muzzle	25	50	75	100
Velocity - fps	730	707	685	665	645
Energy - ft/lb	150	140	130	123	115
Taylor KO values	4.7	4.5	4.4	4.2	4.1
Mid-Range Trajectory Height - inches	0.0	0.5	2.1	5.0	9.2
Drop - inches	0.0	-2.1	-8.5	-19.5	-35.5

G1 Ballistic Coefficient = 0.102

.38 Smith & Wesson

The .38 Smith & Wesson might be thought of as a forerunner of the .38 Special. Designed in 1877, it was once very popular as a police cartridge. Today it is loaded only by Remington and Winchester. The very modest performance (145 to 146 grains at 685 fps) is about like the mildest wadcutter target loads for the .38 Special.

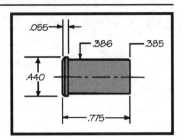

Relative Recoil Factor = 0.45   **Controlling Agency: SAAMI**

Bullet Weight Grains	Velocity fps	Maximum Average Pressure		Standard barrel for velocity testing:
		Copper Crusher	Transducer	
145-146	680	13,000 cup	14,500 psi	4 inches long - 1 turn in 18.75 inch twist

Remington 146-grain Lead (R38SW)

Distance - Yards	Muzzle	25	50	75	100
Velocity - fps	685	668	650	635	620
Energy - ft/lb	150	145	138	131	125
Taylor KO values	5.1	5.0	4.9	4.8	4.6
Mid-Range Trajectory Height - inches	0.0	0.6	2.4	5.6	10.2
Drop - inches	0.0	-2.4	-9.6	-21.9	-39.6

G1 Ballistic Coefficient = 0.125

Winchester 145-grain Lead (X38SWP)

Distance - Yards	Muzzle	25	50	75	100
Velocity - fps	685	668	650	635	620
Energy - ft/lb	150	145	138	131	125
Taylor KO values	5.1	5.0	4.9	4.8	4.6
Mid-Range Trajectory Height - inches	0.0	0.6	2.4	5.6	10.2
Drop - inches	0.0	-2.4	-9.6	-21.9	-39.6

G1 Ballistic Coefficient = 0.125

.38 Super Auto Colt

The .38 Super Auto Colt was introduced clear back in 1929 as an improved version of the even older (1900) .38 Auto. The very minimal rim feeds much better from automatic pistol magazines than ammunition with a more standard rim size, like the .38 Special. This cartridge should NOT be used in pistols chambered for .38 ACP. Performance is good, better than the .38 Special but nowhere near the .357 Magnum with the same bullet weights. The performance of the .38 Super Auto Colt is approximately equal to the 9mm, which may explain why its popularity seems to be in decline.

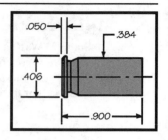

Relative Recoil Factor = 0.71   **Controlling Agency: SAAMI**

Bullet Weight Grains	Velocity fps	Maximum Average Pressure		Standard barrel for velocity testing:
		Copper Crusher	Transducer	
115 JHP	1280	33,000 cup	36,500 psi	5 inches long - 1 turn in 16 inch twist
125 JHP	1230	33,000 cup	36,500 psi	
130 FMC	1200	33,000 cup	36,500 psi	

PMC 115-grain JHP (38SB)

Distance - Yards	Muzzle	25	50	75	100	
Velocity - fps	1116	1052	1001	959	923	
Energy - ft/lb	318	283	256	235	217	
Taylor KO values	6.5	6.2	5.8	5.6	5.4	
Mid-Range Trajectory Height - inches	0.0	0.2	1.0	2.3	4.3	
Drop - inches	0.0	-0.9	-3.8	-8.8	-16.2	G1 Ballistic Coefficient = 0.113

Winchester 125-grain Silvertip HP [+ P Load] (X38ASHP)

Distance - Yards	Muzzle	25	50	75	100	
Velocity - fps	1240	1182	1130	1087	1050	
Energy - ft/lb	427	388	354	328	306	
Taylor KO values	7.9	7.5	7.2	6.9	66.7	
Mid-Range Trajectory Height - inches	0.0	0.2	0.8	1.8	3.4	
Drop - inches	0.0	-0.7	-3.0	-7.0	-12.8	G1 Ballistic Coefficient = 0.183

PMC 130-grain FMJ (38SA)

Distance - Yards	Muzzle	25	50	75	100	
Velocity - fps	1092	1038	994	957	924	
Energy - ft/lb	344	311	285	264	246	
Taylor KO values	7.2	6.9	6.6	6.3	6.1	
Mid-Range Trajectory Height - inches	0.0	0.2	1.0	2.4	4.4	
Drop - inches	0.0	-0.9	-3.9	-9.1	-16.6	G1 Ballistic Coefficient = 0.125

.38 Special (.38 Smith & Wesson Special)

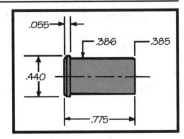

Like the .30-06 cartridge in rifles, the .38 Special is the standard by which pistol cartridges are compared. The .38 Special was introduced by Smith & Wesson in 1902, and at that time it was loaded with black powder. For many years this cartridge was the cartridge used by most police officers. That began to change in the 1950s as other, more potent, cartridges came into general use. The +P loads were introduced in an attempt to "soup-up" the .38 Special, but even the +Ps fall well short of the performance obtainable with the .357 Magnum. Just a glance at the SAAMI pressure levels shows why this is true. Still, with a 148-grain wadcutter bullet, the .38 Special continues to be the most popular caliber for target revolvers. There are more different factory loadings offered for this cartridge than for any other pistol ammunition.

Relative Recoil Factor = 0.53   **Controlling Agency: SAAMI**

Bullet Weight Grains	Velocity fps	Maximum Average Pressure Copper Crusher	Transducer
110 STHP	945	17,000 cup	17,000 psi
158 LSWC	750	17,000 cup	17,000 psi
200 L	630	17,000 cup	17,000 psi
+P Loads			
95 STHP	1080	20,000 cup	18,500 psi
110 JHP	980	20,000 cup	18,500 psi
125 JHP	940	20,000 cup	18,500 psi
147 JHP	855	20,000 cup	18,500 psi
150 L	840	20,000 cup	18,500 psi
158 LSWC	880	20,000 cup	18,500 psi

Standard barrel for velocity testing:
4 inches long (vented)
Alternate one piece barrel - 7.710 inches
- 1 turn in 18.75 inch twist.

CCI 109-grain - Shotshell (3709)
Number 9 Shot at 1000 fps

Winchester 110-grain JSP - NT (SC38NT)

Distance - Yards	Muzzle	25	50	75	100
Velocity - fps	975	938	906	876	849
Energy - ft/lb	222	205	191	179	168
Taylor KO values	5.2	5.0	4.9	4.7	4.5
Mid-Range Trajectory Height - inches	0.0	0.3	1.2	2.9	5.3
Drop - inches	0.0	-1.2	-4.8	-11.1	-20.2

G1 Ballistic Coefficient = 0.118

Federal 110-grain Hydra-Shok JHP (PD38HS3)

Distance - Yards	Muzzle	25	50	75	100
Velocity - fps	1000	970	930	910	880
Energy - ft/lb	245	225	215	200	190
Taylor KO values	5.6	5.4	5.2	5.1	4.9
Mid-Range Trajectory Height - inches	0.0	0.3	1.2	2.7	5.0
Drop - inches	0.0	-1.1	-4.6	10.5	-19.1

G1 Ballistic Coefficient = 0.136

Federal 110-grain Hi-Shok JHP (C38F)

Distance - Yards	Muzzle	25	50	75	100
Velocity - fps	1000	970	930	910	880
Energy - ft/lb	245	225	215	200	190
Taylor KO values	5.6	5.4	5.2	5.1	4.9
Mid-Range Trajectory Height - inches	0.0	0.3	1.2	2.7	5.0
Drop - inches	0.0	-1.1	-4.6	10.5	-19.1

G1 Ballistic Coefficient = 0.136

Remington 110-grain Semi-JHP + P (R38S10)

Distance - Yards	Muzzle	25	50	75	100
Velocity - fps	995	959	926	898	871
Energy - ft/lb	242	224	210	197	185
Taylor KO values	5.6	5.4	5.2	5.0	4.9
Mid-Range Trajectory Height - inches	0.0	0.3	1.2	2.7	5.1
Drop - inches	0.0	-1.1	-4.6	-10.6	-19.4

G1 Ballistic Coefficient = 0.129

Remington 110-grain Semi-JHP (R38S16)

Distance - Yards	Muzzle	25	50	75	100
Velocity - fps	950	919	890	864	840
Energy - ft/lb	220	206	194	182	172
Taylor KO values	5.3	5.2	5.0	4.8	4.7
Mid-Range Trajectory Height - inches	0.0	0.3	1.4	3.0	5.4
Drop - inches	0.0	-1.2	-5.0	-11.6	-21.0

G1 Ballistic Coefficient = 0.128

Winchester 110-grain Silvertip HP (X38S9HP)

Distance - Yards	Muzzle	25	50	75	100
Velocity - fps	945	918	894	871	850
Energy - ft/lb	218	206	195	185	176
Taylor KO values	5.3	5.1	5.0	4.9	4.8
Mid-Range Trajectory Height - inches	0.0	0.3	1.3	3.0	5.4
Drop - inches	0.0	-1.2	-5.1	-11.6	-21.0

G1 Ballistic Coefficient = 0.128

Lapua 123-grain HP Megashock (4319187)

Distance - Yards	Muzzle	25	50	75	100
Velocity - fps	1165	1097	1042	997	959
Energy - ft/lb	371	328	297	272	251
Taylor KO values	7.3	6.9	6.5	6.3	6.0
Mid-Range Trajectory Height - inches	0.0	0.2	0.9	2.1	4.0
Drop - inches	0.0	-0.8	-3.5	-8.1	-14.9

G1 Ballistic Coefficient = 0.128

Norma 123-grain Security Cartridge (19130)

Distance - Yards	Muzzle	25	50	75	100
Velocity - fps	886	868	852	836	821
Energy - ft/lb	215	207	199	191	185
Taylor KO values	5.6	5.4	5.3	5.2	5.1
Mid-Range Trajectory Height - inches	0.0	0.3	1.4	3.3	6.0
Drop - inches	0.0	-1.4	-5.7	-13.0	-23.3

G1 Ballistic Coefficient = 0.192

Federal 125-grain Hi-Shok JSP + P (C38J)

Distance - Yards	Muzzle	25	50	75	100
Velocity - fps	950	920	900	880	860
Energy - ft/lb	250	235	225	215	205
Taylor KO values	6.1	5.9	5.7	5.6	5.5
Mid-Range Trajectory Height - inches	0.0	0.3	1.3	2.9	5.4
Drop - inches	0.0	-1.2	-5.0	-11.4	-20.7

G1 Ballistic Coefficient = 0.162

Magtech 125-grain Semi-JSP + P (38D)

Distance - Yards	Muzzle	25	50	75	100
Velocity - fps	938	914	891	870	851
Energy - ft/lb	245	232	220	210	200
Taylor KO values	6.0	5.8	5.7	5.5	5.4
Mid-Range Trajectory Height - inches	0.0	0.3	1.3	3.0	5.4
Drop - inches	0.0	-1.3	-5.1	-11.7	-21.2

G1 Ballistic Coefficient = 0.161

Federal 125-grain JSP - Non-Toxic + P (BC38NT1)

Distance - Yards	Muzzle	25	50	75	100
Velocity - fps	950	920	900	878	857
Energy - ft/lb	251	237	225	214	204
Taylor KO values	6.1	5.9	5.7	5.6	5.5
Mid-Range Trajectory Height - inches	0.0	0.3	1.3	2.9	5.3
Drop - inches	0.0	-1.2	-5.0	-11.4	-20.7

G1 Ballistic Coefficient = 0.161

Winchester 125-grain JSP (WC381)

Distance - Yards	Muzzle	25	50	75	100
Velocity - fps	775	758	742	727	712
Energy - ft/lb	167	160	153	147	141
Taylor KO values	4.9	4.8	4.7	4.6	4.5
Mid-Range Trajectory Height - inches	0.0	0.5	1.5	5.3	8.7
Drop - inches	0.0	-1.8	-7.4	-17.0	-30.7

G1 Ballistic Coefficient = 0.152

Magtech 125-grain LRN (38G)

Distance - Yards	Muzzle	25	50	75	100
Velocity - fps	686	671	659	642	628
Energy - ft/lb	130	125	120	114	109
Taylor KO values	4.4	4.3	4.2	4.1	4.0
Mid-Range Trajectory Height - inches	0.0	0.6	2.0	5.5	9.7
Drop - inches	0.0	-2.3	-9.5	-21.7	-39.2

G1 Ballistic Coefficient = 0.142

Black Hills 125-grain JHP - Gold Dot + P (M38N2)

Distance - Yards	Muzzle	25	50	75	100
Velocity - fps	1050	1008	973	942	914
Energy - ft/lb	306	282	263	246	232
Taylor KO values	6.7	6.4	6.2	6.0	5.8
Mid-Range Trajectory Height - inches	0.0	0.2	1.1	2.5	4.6
Drop - inches	0.0	-1.0	-4.2	-9.6	-17.5

G1 Ballistic Coefficient = 0.140

Remington 125-grain Brass-JHP + P (GS38SB)

Distance - Yards	Muzzle	25	50	75	100
Velocity - fps	975	950	929	905	885
Energy - ft/lb	264	250	238	227	218
Taylor KO values	6.2	6.0	5.9	5.8	5.2
Mid-Range Trajectory Height - inches	0.0	0.3	1.0	2.8	5.2
Drop - inches	0.0	-1.2	-4.7	-10.8	-19.6

G1 Ballistic Coefficient = 0.175

PMC 125-grain JHP + P (38D)

Distance - Yards	Muzzle	25	50	75	100
Velocity - fps	974	938	906	878	851
Energy - ft/lb	266	244	228	214	201
Taylor KO values	6.2	6.0	5.8	5.6	5.4
Mid-Range Trajectory Height - inches	0.0	0.3	1.2	2.9	5.3
Drop - inches	0.0	-1.2	-4.8	-11.1	-20.2

G1 Ballistic Coefficient = 0.121

Federal 125-grain Hi-Shok JHP + P (38E)

Distance - Yards	Muzzle	25	50	75	100
Velocity - fps	950	920	900	880	860
Energy - ft/lb	250	235	225	215	205
Taylor KO values	6.1	5.9	5.7	5.6	5.5
Mid-Range Trajectory Height - inches	0.0	0.3	1.3	2.9	5.4
Drop - inches	0.0	-1.2	-5.0	-11.4	-20.7

G1 Ballistic Coefficient = 0.162

Federal 125-grain Nyclad HP + P (P38N)

Distance - Yards	Muzzle	25	50	75	100
Velocity - fps	950	920	900	880	860
Energy - ft/lb	250	235	225	215	205
Taylor KO values	6.1	5.9	5.7	5.6	5.5
Mid-Range Trajectory Height - inches	0.0	0.3	1.3	2.9	5.4
Drop - inches	0.0	-1.2	-5.0	-11.4	-20.7

G1 Ballistic Coefficient = 0.162

PMC 125-grain Starfire HP + P (38SFA)

Distance - Yards	Muzzle	25	50	75	100
Velocity - fps	950	918	889	863	838
Energy - ft/lb	251	234	219	206	195
Taylor KO values	6.1	5.9	5.7	5.5	5.3
Mid-Range Trajectory Height - inches	0.0	0.3	1.3	3.0	5.5
Drop - inches	0.0	-1.2	-5.0	-11.6	-21.1

G1 Ballistic Coefficient = 0.125

CCI 125-grain JHP + P (3514)

Distance - Yards	Muzzle	25	50	75	100
Velocity - fps	945	921	898	878	858
Energy - ft/lb	248	235	224	214	204
Taylor KO values	6.0	5.9	5.7	5.6	5.5
Mid-Range Trajectory Height - inches	0.0	0.3	1.3	3.0	5.4
Drop - inches	0.0	-1.2	-5.0	-11.5	-20.8

G1 Ballistic Coefficient = 0.125

Speer 125-grain Gold Dot + P (23720)

Distance - Yards	Muzzle	25	50	75	100
Velocity - fps	945	921	898	878	858
Energy - ft/lb	248	235	224	214	204
Taylor KO values	6.0	5.9	5.7	5.6	5.5
Mid-Range Trajectory Height - inches	0.0	0.3	1.3	3.0	5.4
Drop - inches	0.0	-1.2	-5.0	-11.5	-20.8

G1 Ballistic Coefficient = 0.165

Remington 125-grain Semi-JHP + P (R38S2)

Distance - Yards	Muzzle	25	50	75	100
Velocity - fps	945	921	898	878	858
Energy - ft/lb	248	235	224	214	204
Taylor KO values	6.0	5.9	5.7	5.6	5.5
Mid-Range Trajectory Height - inches	0.0	0.3	1.3	3.0	5.4
Drop - inches	0.0	-1.2	-5.0	-11.5	-20.8

G1 Ballistic Coefficient = 0.165

Winchester 125-grain JHP + P (X38S7PH)

Distance - Yards	Muzzle	25	50	75	100
Velocity - fps	945	921	898	878	858
Energy - ft/lb	248	235	224	214	204
Taylor KO values	6.0	5.9	5.7	5.6	5.5
Mid-Range Trajectory Height - inches	0.0	0.3	1.3	3.0	5.4
Drop - inches	0.0	-1.2	-5.0	-11.5	-20.8

G1 Ballistic Coefficient = 0.165

Winchester 125-grain Silvertip HP + P (X38S8HP)

Distance - Yards	Muzzle	25	50	75	100
Velocity - fps	945	921	898	878	858
Energy - ft/lb	248	235	224	214	204
Taylor KO values	6.0	5.9	5.7	5.6	5.5
Mid-Range Trajectory Height - inches	0.0	0.3	1.3	3.0	5.4
Drop - inches	0.0	-1.2	-5.0	-11.5	-20.8

G1 Ballistic Coefficient = 0.165

Hansen 125-grain JHP "Combat" + P (HCC38H)

Distance - Yards	Muzzle	25	50	75	100
Velocity - fps	940	916	894	874	854
Energy - ft/lb	245	233	222	212	203
Taylor KO values	6.0	5.8	5.7	5.6	5.4
Mid-Range Trajectory Height - inches	0.0	0.3	1.3	3.0	5.4
Drop - inches	0.0	-1.2	-5.1	-11.6	-21.0

G1 Ballistic Coefficient = 0.165

Magtech 125-grain Semi-JHP + P (38F)

Distance - Yards	Muzzle	25	50	75	100
Velocity - fps	938	914	891	870	851
Energy - ft/lb	245	232	220	210	200
Taylor KO values	6.0	5.8	5.7	5.5	5.4
Mid-Range Trajectory Height - inches	0.0	0.3	1.3	3.0	5.4
Drop - inches	0.0	-1.3	-5.1	-11.7	-21.2

G1 Ballistic Coefficient = 0.161

Hornady 125-grain JHP/XTP (9032)

Distance - Yards	Muzzle	25	50	75	100
Velocity - fps	900	877	856	836	817
Energy - ft/lb	225	214	203	194	185
Taylor KO values	5.7	5.6	5.5	5.3	5.2
Mid-Range Trajectory Height - inches	0.0	0.3	1.4	3.2	5.9
Drop - inches	0.0	-1.4	-5.6	-12.7	-23.0

G1 Ballistic Coefficient = 0.161

Federal 125-grain Nyclad HP (P38M)

Distance - Yards	Muzzle	25	50	75	100
Velocity - fps	830	780	730	690	650
Energy - ft/lb	190	170	150	130	115
Taylor KO values	5.3	5.0	4.7	4.4	4.1
Mid-Range Trajectory Height - inches	0.0	0.4	1.8	4.3	8.1
Drop - inches	0.0	-1.6	-6.9	-16.2	-30.1

G1 Ballistic Coefficient = 0.053

Federal 129-grain Hydra-Shok JHP + P (P38HS1)

Distance - Yards	Muzzle	25	50	75	100
Velocity - fps	950	930	910	890	870
Energy - ft/lb	255	245	235	225	215
Taylor KO values	6.3	6.1	6.0	5.9	5.7
Mid-Range Trajectory Height - inches	0.0	0.3	1.3	2.9	5.3
Drop - inches	0.0	-1.2	-5.0	-11.4	-20.5

G1 Ballistic Coefficient = 0.184

Winchester 130-grain SXT (S38SP)

Distance - Yards	Muzzle	25	50	75	100
Velocity - fps	925	905	887	869	852
Energy - ft/lb	247	237	227	218	210
Taylor KO values	6.1	6.0	5.9	5.8	5.6
Mid-Range Trajectory Height - inches	0.0	0.3	1.3	3.0	5.5
Drop - inches	0.0	-1.3	-5.2	-11.9	-21.5

G1 Ballistic Coefficient = 0.190

American Eagle (Federal) 130-grain FMJ (AE38K)

Distance - Yards	Muzzle	25	50	75	100
Velocity - fps	950	920	890	870	840
Energy - ft/lb	260	245	230	215	205
Taylor KO values	6.3	6.1	5.9	5.8	5.6
Mid-Range Trajectory Height - inches	0.0	0.3	1.3	3.0	5.5
Drop - inches	0.0	-1.2	-5.0	-11.6	-21.0

G1 Ballistic Coefficient = 0.128

UMC (Remington) 130-grain Metal Case (L38S11)

Distance - Yards	Muzzle	25	50	75	100
Velocity - fps	950	931	913	895	879
Energy - ft/lb	261	250	240	231	223
Taylor KO values	6.3	6.2	6.1	5.9	5.8
Mid-Range Trajectory Height - inches	0.0	0.3	1.2	2.9	4.8
Drop - inches	0.0	-1.2	-5.0	-11.3	-20.3

G1 Ballistic Coefficient = 0.211

USA (Winchester) 130-grain FMJ (Q4171)

Distance - Yards	Muzzle	25	50	75	100
Velocity - fps	800	782	765	749	733
Energy - ft/lb	185	177	169	162	155
Taylor KO values	5.3	5.2	5.1	5.0	4.9
Mid-Range Trajectory Height - inches	0.0	0.4	1.8	4.1	7.4.
Drop - inches	0.0	-1.7	-7.0	-16.0	-28.8

G1 Ballistic Coefficient = 0.150

Hansen 132-grain FMJ "Combat" (HCC38A)

Distance - Yards	Muzzle	25	50	75	100
Velocity - fps	853	833	814	795	778
Energy - ft/lb	213	203	194	185	177
Taylor KO values	5.7	5.6	5.5	5.4	5.2
Mid-Range Trajectory Height - inches	0.0	0.4	1.6	3.6	6.6
Drop - inches	0.0	-1.5	-6.2	-14.1	-25.5

G1 Ballistic Coefficient = 0.150

PMC 132-grain FMJ (38G)

Distance - Yards	Muzzle	25	50	75	100
Velocity - fps	841	820	799	780	761
Energy - ft/lb	206	197	187	178	170
Taylor KO values	5.7	5.5	5.4	5.3	5.1
Mid-Range Trajectory Height - inches	0.0	0.4	1.6	3.7	6.8
Drop - inches	0.0	-1.6	-6.4	-14.6	-26.3

G1 Ballistic Coefficient = 0.137

Hornady 140-grain JHP/XTP (9035)

Distance - Yards	Muzzle	25	50	75	100
Velocity - fps	900	874	850	828	806
Energy - ft/lb	252	238	225	213	202
Taylor KO values	6.4	6.2	6.1	5.9	5.8
Mid-Range Trajectory Height - inches	0.0	0.3	1.4	3.3	6.0
Drop - inches	0.0	-1.4	-5.6	-12.8	-23.2

G1 Ballistic Coefficient = 0.133

Hansen 148-grain Wadcutter Target Grade (HCC38C)

Distance - Yards	Muzzle	25	50	75	100
Velocity - fps	890	832	782	737	695
Energy - ft/lb	260	228	201	178	159
Taylor KO values	6.7	6.3	5.9	5.6	5.2
Mid-Range Trajectory Height - inches	0.0	0.4	1.6	3.8	7.1
Drop - inches	0.0	-1.4	-6.0	-14.1	-26.3

G1 Ballistic Coefficient = 0.055

Hornady 148-grain Hollow Base Wadcutter (HBWC) (Match) (9043)

Distance - Yards	Muzzle	25	50	75	100
Velocity - fps	800	746	697	652	610
Energy - ft/lb	210	183	160	140	122
Taylor KO values	6.0	5.6	5.3	4.9	4.6
Mid-Range Trajectory Height - inches	0.0	0.4	2.0	4.7	9.0
Drop - inches	0.0	-1.8	-7.5	-17.6	-32.9

G1 Ballistic Coefficient = 0.047

Lapua 148-grain LWC (4319025)

Distance - Yards	Muzzle	25	50	75	100
Velocity - fps	755	712	672	635	600
Energy - ft/lb	187	167	149	133	118
Taylor KO values	5.7	5.4	5.1	4.8	4.5
Mid-Range Trajectory Height - inches	0.0	0.5	2.1	5.1	9.6
Drop - inches	0.0	-2.0	-8.2	-19.3	-35.8

G1 Ballistic Coefficient = 0.055

PMC 148-grain LWC (38C)

Distance - Yards	Muzzle	25	50	75	100
Velocity - fps	728	694	662	631	602
Energy - ft/lb	175	158	144	131	119
Taylor KO values	5.5	5.2	5.0	4.8	4.5
Mid-Range Trajectory Height - inches	0.0	0.5	2.3	5.3	10.0
Drop - inches	0.0	-2.1	-8.8	-20.4	-37.4

G1 Ballistic Coefficient = 0.066

CCI 148-grain HBWC (3517)

Distance - Yards	Muzzle	25	50	75	100
Velocity - fps	710	670	634	599	566
Energy - ft/lb	166	148	132	118	105
Taylor KO values	5.4	5.1	4.8	4.5	4.3
Mid-Range Trajectory Height - inches	0.0	0.6	2.4	5.7	10.9
Drop - inches	0.0	-2.2	-9.3	-21.8	-40.4

G1 Ballistic Coefficient = 0.053

Federal 148-grain LWC Match (GM38A)

Distance - Yards	Muzzle	25	50	75	100
Velocity - fps	710	670	630	600	560
Energy - ft/lb	165	150	130	115	105
Taylor KO values	5.4	5.1	4.8	4.5	4.2
Mid-Range Trajectory Height - inches	0.0	0.6	2.4	5.7	10.8
Drop - inches	0.0	-2.2	-9.3	-21.9	-40.6

G1 Ballistic Coefficient = 0.053

Magtech 148-grain LWC (38B)

Distance - Yards	Muzzle	25	50	75	100
Velocity - fps	710	670	634	599	566
Energy - ft/lb	166	148	132	118	105
Taylor KO values	5.4	5.1	4.8	4.5	4.3
Mid-Range Trajectory Height - inches	0.0	0.6	2.4	5.7	10.8
Drop - inches	0.0	-2.2	-9.3	-21.8	-40.4

G1 Ballistic Coefficient = 0.055

Remington 148-grain Targetmaster LWC Match (R38S3)

Distance - Yards	Muzzle	25	50	75	100
Velocity - fps	710	670	634	599	566
Energy - ft/lb	166	148	132	118	105
Taylor KO values	5.4	5.1	4.8	4.5	4.3
Mid-Range Trajectory Height - inches	0.0	0.6	2.4	5.7	10.8
Drop - inches	0.0	-2.2	-9.3	-21.8	-40.4

G1 Ballistic Coefficient = 0.055

Winchester 148-grain LWC (X38SMRP)

Distance - Yards	Muzzle	25	50	75	100
Velocity - fps	710	670	634	599	566
Energy - ft/lb	166	148	132	118	105
Taylor KO values	5.4	5.1	4.8	4.5	4.3
Mid-Range Trajectory Height - inches	0.0	0.6	2.4	5.7	10.8
Drop - inches	0.0	-2.2	-9.3	-21.8	-40.4

G1 Ballistic Coefficient = 0.055

Norma 148-grain Bly Wadcutter (19110)

Distance - Yards	Muzzle	25	50	75	100
Velocity - fps	705	691	671	662	649
Energy - ft/lb	164	157	150	144	138
Taylor KO values	5.3	5.2	5.1	5.0	4.9
Mid-Range Trajectory Height - inches	0.0	0.5	2.3	5.2	9.5
Drop - inches	0.0	-2.2	-9.0	-20.5	-37.0

G1 Ballistic Coefficient = 0.151

Fiocchi 148-grain JHP (38E)

Distance - Yards	Muzzle	25	50	75	100
Velocity - fps	950	920	890	870	840
Energy - ft/lb	260	245	230	215	205
Taylor KO values	6.3	6.1	5.9	5.8	5.6
Mid-Range Trajectory Height - inches	0.0	0.3	1.3	3.0	5.5
Drop - inches	0.0	-1.2	-5.0	-11.6	-21.0

G1 Ballistic Coefficient = 0.120

Lapua 150-grain Semi-Jacketed Flat Nose (4319242)

Distance - Yards	Muzzle	25	50	75	100
Velocity - fps	1066	1023	987	955	927
Energy - ft/lb	374	344	320	300	282
Taylor KO values	8.2	7.8	7.6	7.3	7.1
Mid-Range Trajectory Height - inches	0.0	0.3	1.3	3.0	4.3
Drop - inches	0.0	-1.0	-4.0	-9.3	-17.0

G1 Ballistic Coefficient = 0.145

Winchester 150-grain Lead (Q4196)

Distance - Yards	Muzzle	25	50	75	100
Velocity - fps	845	828	812	796	781
Energy - ft/lb	238	228	219	211	203
Taylor KO values	6.5	6.3	6.2	6.1	6.0
Mid-Range Trajectory Height - inches	0.0	0.3	1.2	2.9	4.5
Drop - inches	0.0	-1.5	-6.2	-14.3	-25.7

G1 Ballistic Coefficient = 0.175

Lapua 158-grain LRN (4319137)

Distance - Yards	Muzzle	25	50	75	100
Velocity - fps	837	818	799	781	764
Energy - ft/lb	246	235	224	214	205
Taylor KO values	6.7	6.6	6.4	6.3	6.2
Mid-Range Trajectory Height - inches	0.0	0.4	1.6	3.7	6.8
Drop - inches	0.0	-1.6	-6.4	-14.6	-26.4

G1 Ballistic Coefficient = 0.150

PMC 158-grain LRN (38A)

Distance - Yards	Muzzle	25	50	75	100
Velocity - fps	820	801	783	765	749
Energy - ft/lb	235	225	215	206	197
Taylor KO values	6.6	6.5	6.3	6.2	6.0
Mid-Range Trajectory Height - inches	0.0	0.4	1.7	3.9	7.1
Drop - inches	0.0	-1.6	-6.7	-15.2	-27.5

G1 Ballistic Coefficient = 0.147

Federal 158-grain Nyclad Round Nose (P38B)

Distance - Yards	Muzzle	25	50	75	100
Velocity - fps	760	740	720	710	690
Energy - ft/lb	200	190	185	175	170
Taylor KO values	6.1	6.0	5.8	5.7	5.6
Mid-Range Trajectory Height - inches	0.0	0.5	2.0	4.6	8.3
Drop - inches	0.0	-1.9	-77.8	-17.8	-32.1

G1 Ballistic Coefficient = 0.133

Federal 158-grain LRN (C8B)

Distance - Yards	Muzzle	25	50	75	100
Velocity - fps	760	740	720	710	690
Energy - ft/lb	200	190	185	175	170
Taylor KO values	6.1	6.0	5.8	5.7	5.6
Mid-Range Trajectory Height - inches	0.0	0.5	2.0	4.6	8.3
Drop - inches	0.0	-1.9	-7.8	-17.8	-32.1

G1 Ballistic Coefficient = 0.133

American Eagle (Federal) 158-grain LRN (AE38B)

Distance - Yards	Muzzle	25	50	75	100
Velocity - fps	760	740	720	710	690
Energy - ft/lb	200	190	185	175	170
Taylor KO values	6.1	6.0	5.8	5.7	5.6
Mid-Range Trajectory Height - inches	0.0	0.5	2.0	4.6	8.3
Drop - inches	0.0	-1.9	-7.8	-17.8	-32.1

G1 Ballistic Coefficient = 0.133

CCI 158-grain LRN (3522)

Distance - Yards	Muzzle	25	50	75	100
Velocity - fps	755	739	723	707	692
Energy - ft/lb	200	191	183	175	168
Taylor KO values	6.1	6.0	5.8	5.7	5.6
Mid-Range Trajectory Height - inches	0.0	0.5	2.0	4.6	8.3
Drop - inches	0.0	-1.9	-7.8	-17.8	-32.4

G1 Ballistic Coefficient = 0.147

Hansen 158-grain LRN (HCC38B)

Distance - Yards	Muzzle	25	50	75	100
Velocity - fps	755	739	723	707	692
Energy - ft/lb	200	191	183	175	168
Taylor KO values	6.1	6.0	5.8	5.7	5.6
Mid-Range Trajectory Height - inches	0.0	0.5	2.0	4.6	8.3
Drop - inches	0.0	-1.9	-7.8	-17.8	-32.4

G1 Ballistic Coefficient = 0.147

Magtech 158-grain LRN (38A)

Distance - Yards	Muzzle	25	50	75	100
Velocity - fps	755	739	723	707	693
Energy - ft/lb	200	191	183	175	168
Taylor KO values	6.1	6.0	5.8	5.7	5.6
Mid-Range Trajectory Height - inches	0.0	0.5	2.0	4.6	8.3
Drop - inches	0.0	-1.9	-7.8	-17.8	-32.4

G1 Ballistic Coefficient = 0.147

Norma 158-grain Bly, Ogival (19112) [Until Stock Exhausted]

Distance - Yards	Muzzle	25	50	75	100
Velocity - fps	755	741	729	717	705
Energy - ft/lb	199	192	186	180	174
Taylor KO values	6.1	6.0	5.9	5.8	5.7
Mid-Range Trajectory Height - inches	0.0	0.5	2.0	4.5	8.2
Drop - inches	0.0	-1.9	-7.8	-17.8	-31.9

G1 Ballistic Coefficient = 0.186

Remington 158-grain LRN (R38S5)

Distance - Yards	Muzzle	25	50	75	100
Velocity - fps	755	739	723	707	692
Energy - ft/lb	200	191	183	175	168
Taylor KO values	6.1	6.0	5.8	5.7	5.6
Mid-Range Trajectory Height - inches	0.0	0.5	2.0	4.6	8.3
Drop - inches	0.0	-1.9	-7.8	-17.8	-32.4

G1 Ballistic Coefficient = 0.147

UMC (Remington) 158-grain LRN (L38S5)

Distance - Yards	Muzzle	25	50	75	100
Velocity - fps	755	738	723	707	692
Energy - ft/lb	200	191	183	175	168
Taylor KO values	6.1	6.0	5.8	5.7	5.6
Mid-Range Trajectory Height - inches	0.0	0.5	2.0	4.6	8.3
Drop - inches	0.0	-1.9	-7.8	-17.8	-32.4

G1 Ballistic Coefficient = 0.146

Winchester 158-grain LRN (X38S1P)

Distance - Yards	Muzzle	25	50	75	100	
Velocity - fps	755	739	723	707	693	
Energy - ft/lb	200	191	183	175	168	
Taylor KO values	6.1	6.0	5.8	5.7	5.6	
Mid-Range Trajectory Height - inches	0.0	0.5	2.0	4.6	8.3	
Drop - inches	0.0	-1.9	-7.8	-17.8	-32.4	G1 Ballistic Coefficient = 0.147

Federal 158-grain Semi-Wadcutter HP + P (C38G)

Distance - Yards	Muzzle	25	50	75	100	
Velocity - fps	890	870	860	840	820	
Energy - ft/lb	270	265	260	245	235	
Taylor KO values	7.2	7.0	6.9	6.8	6.6	
Mid-Range Trajectory Height - inches	0.0	0.3	1.4	3.3	5.9	
Drop - inches	0.0	-1.4	-5.6	-12.9	-23.2	G1 Ballistic Coefficient = 0.180

Federal 158-grain Lead Semi-Wadcutter + P (C38H)

Distance - Yards	Muzzle	25	50	75	100	
Velocity - fps	890	870	860	840	820	
Energy - ft/lb	270	265	260	245	235	
Taylor KO values	7.2	7.0	6.9	6.8	6.6	
Mid-Range Trajectory Height - inches	0.0	0.3	1.4	3.3	5.9	
Drop - inches	0.0	-1.4	-5.6	-12.9	-23.2	G1 Ballistic Coefficient = 0.180

Federal 158-grain Nyclad Semi-Wadcutter HP + P (P38G)

Distance - Yards	Muzzle	25	50	75	100	
Velocity - fps	890	870	860	840	820	
Energy - ft/lb	270	265	260	245	235	
Taylor KO values	7.2	7.0	6.9	6.8	6.6	
Mid-Range Trajectory Height - inches	0.0	0.3	1.4	3.3	5.9	
Drop - inches	0.0	-1.4	-5.6	-12.9	-23.2	G1 Ballistic Coefficient = 0.180

Remington 158-grain Lead HP + P (R38S12)

Distance - Yards	Muzzle	25	50	75	100	
Velocity - fps	890	872	855	839	823	
Energy - ft/lb	278	267	257	247	238	
Taylor KO values	7.2	7.0	6.9	6.8	6.6	
Mid-Range Trajectory Height - inches	0.0	0.3	1.4	3.3	6.6	
Drop - inches	0.0	-1.4	-5.6	-12.8	-23.2	G1 Ballistic Coefficient = 0.188

Remington 158-grain Semi-Wadcutter + P (R38S14)

Distance - Yards	Muzzle	25	50	75	100	
Velocity - fps	890	872	855	838	823	
Energy - ft/lb	278	267	257	247	238	
Taylor KO values	7.2	7.0	6.9	6.8	6.6	
Mid-Range Trajectory Height - inches	0.0	0.3	1.4	3.3	6.0	
Drop - inches	0.0	-1.4	-5.6	-12.9	-23.2	G1 Ballistic Coefficient = 0.186

Winchester 158-grain LWC HP + P (X38SPD)

Distance - Yards	Muzzle	25	50	75	100	
Velocity - fps	890	872	855	839	823	
Energy - ft/lb	278	267	257	247	238	
Taylor KO values	7.2	7.0	6.9	6.8	6.6	
Mid-Range Trajectory Height - inches	0.0	0.3	1.4	3.3	6.6	
Drop - inches	0.0	-1.4	-5.6	-12.8	-23.2	G1 Ballistic Coefficient = 0.188

Federal 158-grain Lead Semi-Wadcutter (C38C)

Distance - Yards	Muzzle	25	50	75	100	
Velocity - fps	760	740	720	710	690	
Energy - ft/lb	200	190	185	175	170	
Taylor KO values	6.1	6.0	5.8	5.7	5.6	
Mid-Range Trajectory Height - inches	0.0	0.5	2.0	4.6	8.3	
Drop - inches	0.0	-1.9	-77.8	-17.8	-32.1	G1 Ballistic Coefficient = 0.133

Hansen 158-grain Lead Semi-Wadcutter Target Grade (HCC38F)

Distance - Yards	Muzzle	25	50	75	100
Velocity - fps	760	743	726	709	694
Energy - ft/lb	200	193	185	177	169
Taylor KO values	6.1	6.0	5.9	5.7	5.6
Mid-Range Trajectory Height - inches	0.0	0.5	2.0	4.5	8.2
Drop - inches	0.0	-1.9	-7.8	-17.7	-32.0

G1 Ballistic Coefficient = 0.140

Magtech 158-grain Lead Semi-Wadcutter (38J)

Distance - Yards	Muzzle	25	50	75	100
Velocity - fps	755	738	721	705	689
Energy - ft/lb	200	191	182	174	167
Taylor KO values	6.1	5.9	5.8	5.7	5.6
Mid-Range Trajectory Height - inches	0.0	0.5	2.0	4.6	8.4
Drop - inches	0.0	-1.9	-7.9	-18.0	-32.4

G1 Ballistic Coefficient = 0.140

Remington 158-grain Semi-Wadcutter (R38S6)

Distance - Yards	Muzzle	25	50	75	100
Velocity - fps	755	739	723	707	692
Energy - ft/lb	200	191	183	176	168
Taylor KO values	6.1	6.0	5.8	5.7	5.6
Mid-Range Trajectory Height - inches	0.0	0.5	2.0	4.6	8.3
Drop - inches	0.0	-1.9	-7.8	-17.9	-32.3

G1 Ballistic Coefficient = 0.148

Winchester 158-grain Lead Semi-Wadcutter (X38WCPSV)

Distance - Yards	Muzzle	25	50	75	100
Velocity - fps	755	738	721	705	689
Energy - ft/lb	200	191	182	174	167
Taylor KO values	6.1	5.9	5.8	5.7	5.6
Mid-Range Trajectory Height - inches	0.0	0.5	2.0	4.6	8.4
Drop - inches	0.0	-1.9	-7.9	-18.0	-32.4

G1 Ballistic Coefficient = 0.140

PMC 158-grain JSP (38N)

Distance - Yards	Muzzle	25	50	75	100
Velocity - fps	835	816	797	779	762
Energy - ft/lb	245	233	223	213	204
Taylor KO values	6.7	6.6	6.4	6.3	6.1
Mid-Range Trajectory Height - inches	0.0	0.4	1.6	3.8	6.8
Drop - inches	0.0	-1.6	-6.4	-14.7	-26.6

G1 Ballistic Coefficient = 0.140

Magtech 158-grain Semi-JSP (38C)

Distance - Yards	Muzzle	25	50	75	100
Velocity - fps	807	793	779	766	753
Energy - ft/lb	230	221	213	206	199
Taylor KO values	6.5	6.4	6.3	6.2	6.1
Mid-Range Trajectory Height - inches	0.0	0.4	1.7	3.9	7.2
Drop - inches	0.0	-1.7	-6.8	-15.6	-28.0

G1 Ballistic Coefficient = 0.192

Norma 158-grain SP Flat Nose (19124) [Until Stock Exhausted]

Distance - Yards	Muzzle	25	50	75	100
Velocity - fps	804	789	774	760	747
Energy - ft/lb	226	217	210	203	195
Taylor KO values	6.5	6.4	6.2	6.1	6.0
Mid-Range Trajectory Height - inches	0.0	0.4	1.7	4.0	7.2
Drop - inches	0.0	-1.7	-6.9	-15.7	-28.3

G1 Ballistic Coefficient = 0.180

Hornady 158-grain JHP (9036)

Distance - Yards	Muzzle	25	50	75	100
Velocity - fps	800	782	765	747	731
Energy - ft/lb	225	214	205	196	188
Taylor KO values	6.4	6.3	6.2	6.0	5.9
Mid-Range Trajectory Height - inches	0.0	0.4	1.8	4.1	7.4
Drop - inches	0.0	-1.7	-7.0	-16.0	-28.9

G1 Ballistic Coefficient = 0.145

Magtech 158-grain Semi-JHP (38E)

Distance - Yards	Muzzle	25	50	75	100
Velocity - fps	807	793	779	766	753
Energy - ft/lb	230	221	213	206	199
Taylor KO values	6.5	6.4	6.3	6.2	6.1
Mid-Range Trajectory Height - inches	0.0	0.4	1.7	3.9	7.2
Drop - inches	0.0	-1.7	-6.8	-15.6	-28.0

G1 Ballistic Coefficient = 0.145

Fiocchi 158-grain FMJ (38G)

Distance - Yards	Muzzle	25	50	75	100
Velocity - fps	960	934	910	888	867
Energy - ft/lb	320	306	290	276	264
Taylor KO values	7.7	7.5	7.3	7.2	7.0
Mid-Range Trajectory Height - inches	0.0	0.3	1.2	2.9	5.2
Drop - inches	0.0	-1.2	-4.9	-11.2	-20.3

G1 Ballistic Coefficient = 0.160

CCI 158-grain FMJ + P (3519)

Distance - Yards	Muzzle	25	50	75	100
Velocity - fps	900	878	852	837	818
Energy - ft/lb	278	270	255	246	235
Taylor KO values	7.3	7.1	6.9	6.7	6.6
Mid-Range Trajectory Height - inches	0.0	0.3	1.4	3.2	5.9
Drop - inches	0.0	-1.4	-5.6	-12.7	-22.9

G1 Ballistic Coefficient = 0.160

CCI 158-grain Clean-Fire - FMJ + P (3475)

Distance - Yards	Muzzle	25	50	75	100
Velocity - fps	900	878	852	837	818
Energy - ft/lb	278	270	255	246	235
Taylor KO values	7.3	7.1	6.9	6.7	6.6
Mid-Range Trajectory Height - inches	0.0	0.3	1.4	3.2	5.9
Drop - inches	0.0	-1.4	-5.6	-12.7	-22.9

G1 Ballistic Coefficient = 0.155

Speer 158-grain FMJ + P (53750)

Distance - Yards	Muzzle	25	50	75	100
Velocity - fps	900	878	852	837	818
Energy - ft/lb	278	270	255	246	235
Taylor KO values	7.3	7.1	6.9	6.7	6.6
Mid-Range Trajectory Height - inches	0.0	0.3	1.4	3.2	5.9
Drop - inches	0.0	-1.4	-5.6	-12.7	-22.9

G1 Ballistic Coefficient = 0.155

Speer 158-grain Clean-Fire - FMJ + P (53833)

Distance - Yards	Muzzle	25	50	75	100
Velocity - fps	900	878	852	837	818
Energy - ft/lb	278	270	255	246	235
Taylor KO values	7.3	7.1	6.9	6.7	6.6
Mid-Range Trajectory Height - inches	0.0	0.3	1.4	3.2	5.9
Drop - inches	0.0	-1.4	-5.6	-12.7	-22.9

G1 Ballistic Coefficient = 0.155

Lapua 158-grain FMJ (4319143)

Distance - Yards	Muzzle	25	50	75	100
Velocity - fps	837	819	801	785	769
Energy - ft/lb	246	235	225	216	207
Taylor KO values	6.7	6.6	6.5	6.3	6.2
Mid-Range Trajectory Height - inches	0.0	0.4	1.6	3.7	6.8
Drop - inches	0.0	-1.6	-6.4	-14.6	-26.3

G1 Ballistic Coefficient = 0.160

Norma 158-grain FMJ Semi-Wadcutter (19114)

Distance - Yards	Muzzle	25	50	75	100
Velocity - fps	804	790	777	765	752
Energy - ft/lb	226	218	211	205	198
Taylor KO values	6.5	6.4	6.3	6.2	6.1
Mid-Range Trajectory Height - inches	0.0	0.4	1.7	4.0	7.2
Drop - inches	0.0	-1.7	-6.9	-15.6	-28.1

G1 Ballistic Coefficient = 0.160

Magtech 158-grain FMJ (38K)

Distance - Yards	Muzzle	25	50	75	100
Velocity - fps	755	738	723	707	692
Energy - ft/lb	200	191	183	175	168
Taylor KO values	6.1	6.0	5.8	5.7	5.6
Mid-Range Trajectory Height - inches	0.0	0.5	2.0	4.6	8.3
Drop - inches	0.0	-1.9	-7.8	-17.8	-32.4

G1 Ballistic Coefficient = 0.146

Cowboy Action Loads

Hornady 140-grain Cowboy (9034)

Distance - Yards	Muzzle	25	50	75	100
Velocity - fps	800	782	765	747	731
Energy - ft/lb	225	214	205	196	188
Taylor KO values	6.4	6.3	6.1	6.0	5.9
Mid-Range Trajectory Height - inches	0.0	0.4	1.8	4.1	7.5
Drop - inches	0.0	-1.7	-7.0	-16.0	-28.9

G1 Ballistic Coefficient = 0.146

Black Hills 158-grain CNL (DCB38N1)

Distance - Yards	Muzzle	25	50	75	100
Velocity - fps	800	781	763	745	728
Energy - ft/lb	225	214	204	195	186
Taylor KO values	6.4	6.3	6.1	6.0	5.9
Mid-Range Trajectory Height - inches	0.0	0.4	1.8	4.1	7.5
Drop - inches	0.0	-1.7	-7.0	-16.0	-29.0

G1 Ballistic Coefficient = 0.140

Magtech 158-grain Lead Flat Nose (38L)

Distance - Yards	Muzzle	25	50	75	100
Velocity - fps	800	781	763	745	728
Energy - ft/lb	225	214	204	195	186
Taylor KO values	6.4	6.3	6.1	6.0	5.9
Mid-Range Trajectory Height - inches	0.0	0.4	1.8	4.1	7.5
Drop - inches	0.0	-1.7	-7.0	-16.0	-29.0

G1 Ballistic Coefficient = 0.140

PMC 158-grain Lead Flat Nose (38CA)

Distance - Yards	Muzzle	25	50	75	100
Velocity - fps	800	780	761	743	725
Energy - ft/lb	225	214	203	193	185
Taylor KO values	6.4	6.3	6.1	6.0	5.8
Mid-Range Trajectory Height - inches	0.0	0.4	1.8	4.1	7.5
Drop - inches	0.0	-1.7	-7.0	-16.1	-29.1

G1 Ballistic Coefficient = 0.133

Winchester 158-grain Cast Lead (CB38SP)

Distance - Yards	Muzzle	25	50	75	100
Velocity - fps	800	780	761	743	725
Energy - ft/lb	225	214	203	193	185
Taylor KO values	6.4	6.3	6.1	6.0	5.8
Mid-Range Trajectory Height - inches	0.0	0.4	1.8	4.1	7.5
Drop - inches	0.0	-1.7	-7.0	-16.1	-29.1

G1 Ballistic Coefficient = 0.133

.40 Smith & Wesson

This cartridge came on the scene (1990) just after the 10mm Auto was announced. It's easy to guess that some bright lad recognized that if the 10mm cartridge was simply shortened by 0.140 inches, the resulting ammunition would fit in many 9mm pistol frames and still retain enough volume to have plenty of power for the personal defense task. This conversion resulted in an effective round in a more compact pistol than what was needed for the 10mm. The .40 S&W has become the cartridge of choice for many law enforcement groups in the US.

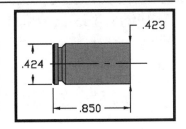

Relative Recoil Factor = 0.74   **Controlling Agency: SAAMI**

Bullet Weight Grains	Velocity fps	Maximum Average Pressure		Standard barrel for velocity testing:
		Copper Crusher	Transducer	
155 STHP	1195	N/S	35,000 psi	4 inches long - 1 turn in 16 inch twist
155 FMJ	1115	N/S	35,000 psi	
180 JHP	985	N/S	35,000 psi	

CCI 105-grain Shotshell (0420)

Number 9 shot at 1250 fps.

Federal 135-grain JSP - Non-Toxic (BC40NT1)

Distance - Yards	Muzzle	25	50	75	100
Velocity - fps	1140	1100	1070	1040	1014
Energy - ft/lb	390	365	345	325	309
Taylor KO values	8.8	8.5	8.3	8.0	7.8
Mid-Range Trajectory Height - inches	0.0	0.2	0.9	2.1	3.8
Drop - inches	0.0	-0.8	-3.5	-8.0	-14.6

G1 Ballistic Coefficient = 0.222

Federal 135-grain Hydra-Shok JHP (PD40HS4)

Distance - Yards	Muzzle	25	50	75	100
Velocity - fps	1190	1050	970	900	850
Energy - ft/lb	420	330	280	245	215
Taylor KO values	9.2	8.1	7.5	6.9	6.6
Mid-Range Trajectory Height - inches	0.0	0.2	1.0	2.4	4.0
Drop - inches	0.0	-0.8	-3.4	-8.0	-14.7

G1 Ballistic Coefficient = 0.109

Winchester 140-grain JSP (SC40NT)

Distance - Yards	Muzzle	25	50	75	100
Velocity - fps	1155	1091	1039	996	960
Energy - ft/lb	415	370	336	309	286
Taylor KO values	9.2	8.7	8.3	8.0	7.7
Mid-Range Trajectory Height - inches	0.0	0.2	0.9	2.1	4.0
Drop - inches	0.0	-0.8	-3.5	-8.2	-15.1

G1 Ballistic Coefficient = 0.130

Remington 141-grain Disintegrator Plated Frangible (LF40SWA)

Distance - Yards	Muzzle	25	50	75	100
Velocity - fps	1135	1093	1056	1024	996
Energy - ft/lb	403	374	349	328	311
Taylor KO values	9.4	9.0	8.7	8.5	8.2
Mid-Range Trajectory Height - inches	0.0	0.2	1.0	2.0	3.9
Drop - inches	0.0	-0.9	-3.2	-8.2	-14.9

G1 Ballistic Coefficient = 0.196

Fiocchi 145-grain JHP (40SWB)

Distance - Yards	Muzzle	25	50	75	100
Velocity - fps	1150	1091	1042	1002	967
Energy - ft/lb	411	370	338	312	291
Taylor KO values	9.2	8.7	8.3	8.0	7.7
Mid-Range Trajectory Height - inches	0.0	0.2	0.9	2.1	4.0
Drop - inches	0.0	-0.8	-3.5	-8.2	-15.0

G1 Ballistic Coefficient = 0.140

Magtech 155-grain JHP (40D)

Distance - Yards	Muzzle	25	50	75	100	
Velocity - fps	1205	1146	1096	1054	1018	
Energy - ft/lb	500	452	414	382	357	
Taylor KO values	10.7	10.2	9.7	9.3	9.0	
Mid-Range Trajectory Height - inches	0.0	0.2	0.8	1.9	3.6	
Drop - inches	0.0	-0.8	-3.2	-7.4	-13.6	G1 Ballistic Coefficient = 0.166

Remington 155-grain JHP (R40SW1)

Distance - Yards	Muzzle	25	50	75	100	
Velocity - fps	1205	1146	1095	1053	1017	
Energy - ft/lb	499	452	413	382	356	
Taylor KO values	10.7	10.2	9.7	9.3	9.0	
Mid-Range Trajectory Height - inches	0.0	0.2	0.8	1.9	3.6	
Drop - inches	0.0	-0.8	-3.2	-7.4	-13.6	G1 Ballistic Coefficient = 0.165

Winchester 155-grain Silvertip HP (X40SWSTHP)

Distance - Yards	Muzzle	25	50	75	100	
Velocity - fps	1205	1146	1096	1054	1018	
Energy - ft/lb	500	452	414	382	357	
Taylor KO values	10.7	10.2	9.7	9.3	9.0	
Mid-Range Trajectory Height - inches	0.0	0.2	0.8	1.9	3.6	
Drop - inches	0.0	-0.8	-3.2	-7.4	-13.6	G1 Ballistic Coefficient = 0.166

Hornady 155-grain JHP/XTP (9132)

Distance - Yards	Muzzle	25	50	75	100	
Velocity - fps	1180	1115	1061	1017	980	
Energy - ft/lb	479	428	388	356	331	
Taylor KO values	10.5	9.9	9.4	9.0	8.7	
Mid-Range Trajectory Height - inches	0.0	0.2	0.9	2.1	3.8	
Drop - inches	0.0	-0.8	-3.4	-7.9	-14.4	G1 Ballistic Coefficient = 0.138

Speer 155-grain Gold Dot (23961)

Distance - Yards	Muzzle	25	50	75	100	
Velocity - fps	1175	1104	1047	1001	963	
Energy - ft/lb	475	420	377	345	319	
Taylor KO values	10.4	9.8	9.3	8.9	8.5	
Mid-Range Trajectory Height - inches	0.0	0.2	0.9	2.1	4.0	
Drop - inches	0.0	-0.8	-3.4	-8.0	-14.8	G1 Ballistic Coefficient = 0.124

PMC 155-grain Starfire HP (40SFB)

Distance - Yards	Muzzle	25	50	75	100	
Velocity - fps	1160	1092	1039	994	957	
Energy - ft/lb	463	411	371	340	315	
Taylor KO values	10.3	9.7	9.2	8.8	8.5	
Mid-Range Trajectory Height - inches	0.0	0.2	0.9	2.1	4.0	
Drop - inches	0.0	-0.8	-33.5	-8.2	-15.0	G1 Ballistic Coefficient = 0.125

Black Hills 155-grain JHP - Gold Dot (D40N1)

Distance - Yards	Muzzle	25	50	75	100	
Velocity - fps	1150	1085	1032	989	952	
Energy - ft/lb	450	405	367	337	312	
Taylor KO values	10.2	9.6	9.1	8.8	8.4	
Mid-Range Trajectory Height - inches	0.0	0.2	0.9	2.2	4.1	
Drop - inches	0.0	-0.9	-3.6	-8.3	-15.2	G1 Ballistic Coefficient = 0.125

Federal 155-grain Hydra-Shok JHP (P40HS2)

Distance - Yards	Muzzle	25	50	75	100	
Velocity - fps	1140	1080	1030	990	850	
Energy - ft/lb	445	400	365	335	315	
Taylor KO values	10.1	9.6	9.1	8.8	7.5	
Mid-Range Trajectory Height - inches	0.0	0.2	0.9	2.2	4.1	
Drop - inches	0.0	-0.9	-3.8	-9.1	-17.1	G1 Ballistic Coefficient = 0.067

Federal 155-grain Hi-Shok JHP (C40SWB)

Distance - Yards	Muzzle	25	50	75	100
Velocity - fps	1140	1080	1030	990	850
Energy - ft/lb	445	400	365	335	315
Taylor KO values	10.1	9.6	9.1	8.8	7.5
Mid-Range Trajectory Height - inches	0.0	0.2	0.9	2.2	4.1
Drop - inches	0.0	-0.9	-3.8	-9.1	-17.1

G1 Ballistic Coefficient = 0.067

CCI 155-grain FMJ (3587)

Distance - Yards	Muzzle	25	50	75	100
Velocity - fps	1175	1104	1047	1001	963
Energy - ft/lb	475	420	377	345	319
Taylor KO values	10.4	9.8	9.3	8.9	8.5
Mid-Range Trajectory Height - inches	0.0	0.2	0.9	2.1	4.0
Drop - inches	0.0	-0.8	-3.4	-8.0	-14.8

G1 Ballistic Coefficient = 0.124

Speer 155-grain FMJ (53957)

Distance - Yards	Muzzle	25	50	75	100
Velocity - fps	1175	1104	1047	1001	963
Energy - ft/lb	475	420	377	345	319
Taylor KO values	10.4	9.8	9.3	8.9	8.5
Mid-Range Trajectory Height - inches	0.0	0.2	0.9	2.1	4.0
Drop - inches	0.0	-0.8	-3.4	-8.0	-14.8

G1 Ballistic Coefficient = 0.124

American Eagle (Federal) 155-grain FMJ Ball (AE40R2)

Distance - Yards	Muzzle	25	50	75	100
Velocity - fps	1140	1080	1030	990	960
Energy - ft/lb	445	400	365	335	315
Taylor KO values	10.1	9.6	9.1	8.8	8.5
Mid-Range Trajectory Height - inches	0.0	0.2	0.9	2.2	4.1
Drop - inches	0.0	-0.9	-3.6	-8.3	-15.3

G1 Ballistic Coefficient = 0.150

Magtech 160-grain Lead Semi-Wadcutter (40C)

Distance - Yards	Muzzle	25	50	75	100
Velocity - fps	1165	1107	1059	1018	984
Energy - ft/lb	484	435	398	369	343
Taylor KO values	10.7	10.1	9.7	9.3	9.0
Mid-Range Trajectory Height - inches	0.0	0.2	0.9	2.1	3.9
Drop - inches	0.0	-0.8	-3.4	-8.0	-14.6

G1 Ballistic Coefficient = 0.150

Remington 165-grain Brass-JHP (GS40SWA)

Distance - Yards	Muzzle	25	50	75	100
Velocity - fps	1150	1089	1040	999	964
Energy - ft/lb	485	435	396	366	340
Taylor KO values	10.8	10.3	9.8	9.4	9.1
Mid-Range Trajectory Height - inches	0.0	0.2	0.9	2.1	4.0
Drop - inches	0.0	-0.8	-3.5	-8.2	-15.1

G1 Ballistic Coefficient = 0.136

Winchester 165-grain Brass Enclosed Base (WC401)

Distance - Yards	Muzzle	25	50	75	100
Velocity - fps	1130	1089	1054	1024	996
Energy - ft/lb	468	435	407	384	364
Taylor KO values	10.5	10.0	9.7	9.4	9.1
Mid-Range Trajectory Height - inches	0.0	0.2	0.9	2.1	3.9
Drop - inches	0.0	-0.9	-3.6	-8.2	-15.0

G1 Ballistic Coefficient = 0.197

Winchester 165-grain SXT (S401)

Distance - Yards	Muzzle	25	50	75	100
Velocity - fps	1130	1082	1041	1007	977
Energy - ft/lb	468	429	397	372	349
Taylor KO values	10.7	10.2	9.8	9.5	9.2
Mid-Range Trajectory Height - inches	0.0	0.2	0.9	2.1	4.0
Drop - inches	0.0	-0.9	-3.6	-8.3	-15.2

G1 Ballistic Coefficient = 0.165

PMC 165-grain JHP (40B)

Distance - Yards	Muzzle	25	50	75	100
Velocity - fps	1040	1002	970	922	899
Energy - ft/lb	396	364	338	316	296
Taylor KO values	9.8	9.4	9.1	8.7	8.5
Mid-Range Trajectory Height - inches	0.0	0.2	1.1	2.5	4.0
Drop - inches	0.0	-1.0	-4.2	-9.8	-17.9

G1 Ballistic Coefficient = 0.129

Federal 165-grain Hydra-Shok JHP (P40HS3)

Distance - Yards	Muzzle	25	50	75	100
Velocity - fps	980	950	930	910	890
Energy - ft/lb	350	330	315	300	290
Taylor KO values	9.2	9.0	8.8	8.6	8.4
Mid-Range Trajectory Height - inches	0.0	0.3	1.2	2.7	5.1
Drop - inches	0.0	-1.2	-4.7	-10.7	-19.4

G1 Ballistic Coefficient = 0.178

Speer 165-grain Gold Dot (23970)

Distance - Yards	Muzzle	25	50	75	100
Velocity - fps	978	944	911	887	862
Energy - ft/lb	345	327	304	289	272
Taylor KO values	9.2	8.9	8.6	8.4	8.1
Mid-Range Trajectory Height - inches	0.0	0.3	1.0	2.8	5.0
Drop - inches	0.0	-1.2	-4.8	-11.0	-19.9

G1 Ballistic Coefficient = 0.132

Speer 165-grain FMJ (53955)

Distance - Yards	Muzzle	25	50	75	100
Velocity - fps	1150	1089	1040	999	964
Energy - ft/lb	484	435	396	366	340
Taylor KO values	10.8	10.2	9.8	9.4	9.1
Mid-Range Trajectory Height - inches	0.0	0.2	1.0	2.2	4.1
Drop - inches	0.0	-0.8	-3.5	-8.2	-15.1

G1 Ballistic Coefficient = 0.136

UMC (Remington) 165-grain Metal Case (L40SW4)

Distance - Yards	Muzzle	25	50	75	100
Velocity - fps	1150	1090	1040	1002	964
Energy - ft/lb	485	435	396	366	340
Taylor KO values	10.8	10.2	9.8	9.4	9.1
Mid-Range Trajectory Height - inches	0.0	0.2	1.0	2.1	4.0
Drop - inches	0.0	-0.8	-3.5	-8.2	-15.1

G1 Ballistic Coefficient = 0.137

PMC 165-grain FMJ (40D)

Distance - Yards	Muzzle	25	50	75	100
Velocity - fps	1010	977	948	922	899
Energy - ft/lb	374	350	330	312	296
Taylor KO values	9.5	9.2	8.9	8.7	8.5
Mid-Range Trajectory Height - inches	0.0	0.3	1.1	2.6	4.8
Drop - inches	0.0	-1.1	-4.4	-10.2	-18.6

G1 Ballistic Coefficient = 0.137

American Eagle (Federal) 165-grain FMJ Ball (AE40R3)

Distance - Yards	Muzzle	25	50	75	100
Velocity - fps	980	950	920	900	880
Energy - ft/lb	350	330	310	295	280
Taylor KO values	9.2	9.0	8.8	8.5	8.3
Mid-Range Trajectory Height - inches	0.0	0.3	1.2	2.8	5.1
Drop - inches	0.0	-1.2	-4.7	-10.8	-19.6

G1 Ballistic Coefficient = 0.158

CCI 165-grain FMJ (3589)

Distance - Yards	Muzzle	25	50	75	100
Velocity - fps	970	939	911	886	862
Energy - ft/lb	345	323	304	288	270
Taylor KO values	9.1	8.9	8.6	8.4	8.1
Mid-Range Trajectory Height - inches	0.0	0.3	1.2	2.8	5.2
Drop - inches	0.0	-1.2	-4.8	-11.1	-20.1

G1 Ballistic Coefficient = 0.140

Fiocchi 170-grain FMJ Truncated Cone (40SWA)

Distance - Yards	Muzzle	25	50	75	100
Velocity - fps	1050	1011	977	948	921
Energy - ft/lb	416	386	361	339	320
Taylor KO values	10.2	9.8	9.5	9.2	8.9
Mid-Range Trajectory Height - inches	0.0	0.2	1.1	2.5	4.5
Drop - inches	0.0	-1.0	-4.2	-9.6	-17.4

G1 Ballistic Coefficient = 0.150

Winchester 180-grain SXT (S40)

Distance - Yards	Muzzle	25	50	75	100
Velocity - fps	1015	985	959	935	912
Energy - ft/lb	412	388	367	349	333
Taylor KO values	10.4	10.1	9.9	9.6	9.4
Mid-Range Trajectory Height - inches	0.0	0.3	1.1	2.6	4.7
Drop - inches	0.0	-1.1	-4.4	-10.1	-18.2

G1 Ballistic Coefficient = 0.173

American Eagle (Federal) 180-grain High Antimony Lead (AE40)

Distance - Yards	Muzzle	25	50	75	100
Velocity - fps	990	960	930	910	890
Energy - ft/lb	390	365	345	330	315
Taylor KO values	10.2	9.9	9.6	9.4	9.2
Mid-Range Trajectory Height - inches	0.0	0.3	1.2	2.8	5.0
Drop - inches	0.0	-1.1	-4.6	-10.6	-19.1

G1 Ballistic Coefficient = 0.164

Federal 180-grain Hi-Shok JHP (C40SWA)

Distance - Yards	Muzzle	25	50	75	100
Velocity - fps	990	960	930	910	890
Energy - ft/lb	390	365	345	330	315
Taylor KO values	10.2	9.9	9.6	9.4	9.2
Mid-Range Trajectory Height - inches	0.0	0.3	1.2	2.8	5.0
Drop - inches	0.0	-1.1	-4.6	-10.6	-19.1

G1 Ballistic Coefficient = 0.164

Winchester 180-grain Brass Enclosed Base (WC402)

Distance - Yards	Muzzle	25	50	75	100
Velocity - fps	990	965	943	922	902
Energy - ft/lb	392	372	356	340	325
Taylor KO values	10.2	9.9	9.7	9.5	9.3
Mid-Range Trajectory Height - inches	0.0	0.3	1.2	2.7	5.0
Drop - inches	0.0	-1.1	-4.6	-10.6	-19.2

G1 Ballistic Coefficient = 0.190

Remington 180-grain Brass-JHP (GS40SWB)

Distance - Yards	Muzzle	25	50	75	100
Velocity - fps	1015	986	960	936	914
Energy - ft/lb	412	389	368	350	334
Taylor KO values	10.4	10.1	9.9	9.6	9.4
Mid-Range Trajectory Height - inches	0.0	0.3	1.3	2.6	4.5
Drop - inches	0.0	-1.1	-4.4	-10.0	-18.2

G1 Ballistic Coefficient = 0.190

Remington 180-grain JHP (R40SW2)

Distance - Yards	Muzzle	25	50	75	100
Velocity - fps	1015	986	960	936	914
Energy - ft/lb	412	389	368	350	334
Taylor KO values	10.4	10.1	9.9	9.6	9.4
Mid-Range Trajectory Height - inches	0.0	0.3	1.3	2.6	4.5
Drop - inches	0.0	-1.1	-4.4	-10.0	-18.2

G1 Ballistic Coefficient = 0.190

Winchester 180-grain JHP (XSUB40SW)

Distance - Yards	Muzzle	25	50	75	100
Velocity - fps	1010	981	954	931	909
Energy - ft/lb	408	385	364	347	330
Taylor KO values	10.4	10.1	9.8	9.6	9.3
Mid-Range Trajectory Height - inches	0.0	0.3	1.1	2.6	4.8
Drop - inches	0.0	-1.1	-4.4	-10.2	-18.4

G1 Ballistic Coefficient = 0.174

Black Hills 180-grain JHP - Gold Dot (D40N2)

Distance - Yards	Muzzle	25	50	75	100
Velocity - fps	1000	972	947	924	903
Energy - ft/lb	400	378	359	341	326
Taylor KO values	10.3	10.0	9.7	9.5	9.3
Mid-Range Trajectory Height - inches	0.0	0.3	1.2	2.6	4.8
Drop - inches	0.0	-1.1	-4.5	-10.3	-18.7

G1 Ballistic Coefficient = 0.175

Fiocchi 180-grain JHP (40SWE)

Distance - Yards	Muzzle	25	50	75	100
Velocity - fps	1000	972	947	924	903
Energy - ft/lb	400	378	359	341	326
Taylor KO values	10.3	10.0	9.7	9.5	9.3
Mid-Range Trajectory Height - inches	0.0	0.3	1.2	2.6	4.8
Drop - inches	0.0	-1.1	-4.5	-10.3	-18.7

G1 Ballistic Coefficient = 0.175

Federal 180-grain Hydra-Shok JHP (P40HS1)

Distance - Yards	Muzzle	25	50	75	100
Velocity - fps	990	960	930	910	890
Energy - ft/lb	390	365	345	330	315
Taylor KO values	10.2	9.9	9.6	9.4	9.2
Mid-Range Trajectory Height - inches	0.0	0.3	1.2	2.8	5.0
Drop - inches	0.0	-1.1	-4.6	-10.6	-19.1

G1 Ballistic Coefficient = 0.164

Magtech 180-grain JHP (40A)

Distance - Yards	Muzzle	25	50	75	100
Velocity - fps	990	960	933	909	886
Energy - ft/lb	390	368	348	330	314
Taylor KO values	10.2	9.9	9.6	9.3	9.1
Mid-Range Trajectory Height - inches	0.0	0.3	1.2	2.7	5.0
Drop - inches	0.0	-1.1	-4.6	-10.6	-19.2

G1 Ballistic Coefficient = 0.156

Hansen 180-grain JHP "Combat" (HCC40B)

Distance - Yards	Muzzle	25	50	75	100
Velocity - fps	987	960	936	914	893
Energy - ft/lb	390	369	350	334	319
Taylor KO values	10.2	9.9	9.6	9.4	9.2
Mid-Range Trajectory Height - inches	0.0	0.3	1.2	2.7	5.0
Drop - inches	0.0	-1.1	-4.6	-10.6	-19.2

G1 Ballistic Coefficient = 0.175

CCI 180-grain HP (3590)

Distance - Yards	Muzzle	25	50	75	100
Velocity - fps	985	964	951	926	909
Energy - ft/lb	400	371	361	343	330
Taylor KO values	10.1	9.9	9.8	9.5	9.3
Mid-Range Trajectory Height - inches	0.0	0.3	1.2	2.7	4.9
Drop - inches	0.0	-1.1	-4.6	-10.5	-19.0

G1 Ballistic Coefficient = 0.220

Speer 180-grain Gold Dot (23962)

Distance - Yards	Muzzle	25	50	75	100
Velocity - fps	985	964	951	926	909
Energy - ft/lb	400	371	361	343	330
Taylor KO values	10.1	9.9	9.8	9.5	9.3
Mid-Range Trajectory Height - inches	0.0	0.3	1.2	2.7	4.9
Drop - inches	0.0	-1.1	-4.6	-10.5	-19.0

G1 Ballistic Coefficient = 0.220

PMC 180-grain Starfire HP (40SFA)

Distance - Yards	Muzzle	25	50	75	100
Velocity - fps	985	958	933	910	889
Energy - ft/lb	388	367	348	331	316
Taylor KO values	10.1	9.9	9.6	9.4	9.1
Mid-Range Trajectory Height - inches	0.0	0.3	1.2	2.7	5.0
Drop - inches	0.0	-1.1	-4.6	-10.7	-19.3

G1 Ballistic Coefficient = 0.168

Hornady 180-grain JHP/XTP (9136)

Distance - Yards	Muzzle	25	50	75	100
Velocity - fps	950	926	903	882	862
Energy - ft/lb	361	342	326	311	297
Taylor KO values	9.8	9.5	9.3	9.1	8.9
Mid-Range Trajectory Height - inches	0.0	0.3	1.3	2.9	5.3
Drop - inches	0.0	-1.2	-5.0	-11.4	-20.61

G1 Ballistic Coefficient = 0.166

CCI 180-grain Clean-Fire - FMJ (3477)

Distance - Yards	Muzzle	25	50	75	100
Velocity - fps	1000	974	951	929	909
Energy - ft/lb	400	379	361	345	330
Taylor KO values	10.3	10.0	9.8	9.6	9.3
Mid-Range Trajectory Height - inches	0.0	0.3	1.1	2.6	4.8
Drop - inches	0.0	-1.1	-4.5	-10.3	-18.6

G1 Ballistic Coefficient = 0.190

CCI 180-grain FMJ (53958)

Distance - Yards	Muzzle	25	50	75	100
Velocity - fps	1000	974	951	929	909
Energy - ft/lb	400	379	361	345	330
Taylor KO values	10.3	10.0	9.8	9.6	9.3
Mid-Range Trajectory Height - inches	0.0	0.3	1.1	2.6	4.8
Drop - inches	0.0	-1.1	-4.5	-10.3	-18.6

G1 Ballistic Coefficient = 0.190

CCI 180-grain Clean-Fire - FMJ (53880)

xDistance - Yards	Muzzle	25	50	75	100
Velocity - fps	1000	974	951	929	909
Energy - ft/lb	400	379	361	345	330
Taylor KO values	10.3	10.0	9.8	9.6	9.3
Mid-Range Trajectory Height - inches	0.0	0.3	1.1	2.6	4.8
Drop - inches	0.0	-1.1	-4.5	-10.3	-18.6

G1 Ballistic Coefficient = 0.190

Fiocchi 180-grain FMJ Flat Nose (40SWD)

Distance - Yards	Muzzle	25	50	75	100
Velocity - fps	1000	972	947	924	903
Energy - ft/lb	400	378	359	341	326
Taylor KO values	10.3	10.0	9.7	9.5	9.3
Mid-Range Trajectory Height - inches	0.0	0.3	1.2	2.6	4.8
Drop - inches	0.0	-1.1	-4.5	-10.3	-18.7

G1 Ballistic Coefficient = 0.175

Magtech 180-grain Full Metal Case (40B)

Distance - Yards	Muzzle	25	50	75	100
Velocity - fps	990	960	933	909	886
Energy - ft/lb	390	368	348	330	314
Taylor KO values	10.2	9.9	9.6	9.3	9.1
Mid-Range Trajectory Height - inches	0.0	0.3	1.2	2.7	5.0
Drop - inches	0.0	-1.1	-4.6	-10.6	-19.2

G1 Ballistic Coefficient = 0.156

American Eagle (Federal) 180-grain FMJ Ball (AE40R1)

Distance - Yards	Muzzle	25	50	75	100
Velocity - fps	990	960	930	910	890
Energy - ft/lb	390	365	345	330	315
Taylor KO values	10.2	9.9	9.6	9.4	9.2
Mid-Range Trajectory Height - inches	0.0	0.3	1.2	2.8	5.0
Drop - inches	0.0	-1.1	-4.6	-10.6	-19.2

G1 Ballistic Coefficient = 0.164

PMC 180-grain FMJ/FP (40E)

Distance - Yards	Muzzle	25	50	75	100
Velocity - fps	990	962	936	913	891
Energy - ft/lb	390	370	350	333	317
Taylor KO values	10.2	9.9	9.6	9.4	9.2
Mid-Range Trajectory Height - inches	0.0	0.3	1.2	2.7	5.0
Drop - inches	0.0	-1.1	-4.6	-10.6	-19.1

G1 Ballistic Coefficient = 0.164

USA (Winchester) 180-grain FMJ (Q4238)

Distance - Yards	Muzzle	25	50	75	100
Velocity - fps	990	962	936	912	891
Energy - ft/lb	390	370	350	333	317
Taylor KO values	10.2	9.9	9.6	9.4	9.2
Mid-Range Trajectory Height - inches	0.0	0.3	1.2	2.7	5.0
Drop - inches	0.0	-1.1	-4.6	-10.6	-19.1

G1 Ballistic Coefficient = 0.165

Hansen 180-grain FMJ "Combat" (HCC40A)

Distance - Yards	Muzzle	25	50	75	100
Velocity - fps	987	960	936	914	893
Energy - ft/lb	390	369	350	334	319
Taylor KO values	10.2	9.9	9.6	9.4	9.2
Mid-Range Trajectory Height - inches	0.0	0.3	1.2	2.7	5.0
Drop - inches	0.0	-1.1	-4.6	-10.6	-19.2

G1 Ballistic Coefficient = 0.175

CCI 180-grain FMJ (3591)

Distance - Yards	Muzzle	25	50	75	100
Velocity - fps	985	964	951	926	909
Energy - ft/lb	400	371	361	343	330
Taylor KO values	10.1	9.9	9.8	9.5	9.3
Mid-Range Trajectory Height - inches	0.0	0.3	1.2	2.7	4.9
Drop - inches	0.0	-1.1	-4.6	-10.5	-19.0

G1 Ballistic Coefficient = 0.221

UMC (Remington) 180-grain Metal Case (L40SW3)

Distance - Yards	Muzzle	25	50	75	100
Velocity - fps	985	959	936	913	893
Energy - ft/lb	388	368	350	333	319
Taylor KO values	9.8	9.5	9.3	9.1	8.9
Mid-Range Trajectory Height - inches	0.0	0.3	1.3	2.9	5.1
Drop - inches	0.0	-1.1	-4.6	-10.6	-19.2

G1 Ballistic Coefficient = 0.177

Hornady 180-grain FMJ/FP (9337)

Distance - Yards	Muzzle	25	50	75	100
Velocity - fps	950	926	906	884	865
Energy - ft/lb	361	343	328	312	299
Taylor KO values	9.8	9.5	9.3	9.1	8.9
Mid-Range Trajectory Height - inches	0.0	0.3	1.3	2.9	5.3
Drop - inches	0.0	-1.2	-5.0	-11.4	-20.6

G1 Ballistic Coefficient = 0.177

10mm Auto

First chambered in the Bren Ten pistol in 1983, the 10mm Auto was a powerful pistol. The first ammo was manufactured by Norma. The Bren Ten went nowhere and it wasn't until 1989, when the FBI announced the selection of the 10mm Auto as their officially favored sidearm that the 10mm Auto took off. The best performance overall as a pistol round came at velocities near 1000 fps. The cartridge case has lots more volume than is needed for that kind of performance, leaving room for a considerable jump in performance as a submachine cartridge. The .40 Smith & Wesson Auto is a spin-off design.

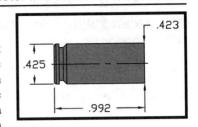

Relative Recoil Factor = 0.96   **Controlling Agency: SAAMI**

Bullet Weight Grains	Velocity fps	Maximum Average Pressure Copper Crusher	Transducer	Standard barrel for velocity testing:
155 HP/XP	1410	N/S	37,500 psi	5 inches long - 1 turn in 16 inch twist
155 FMJ	1115	N/S	37,500 psi	
170 HP/XP	1320	N/S	37,500 psi	
175 STHP	1275	N/S	37,500 psi	
200 FMJ/FP	1150	N/S	37,500 psi	
200	SXT	985	37,500 psi	

Federal 155-grain Hi-Shok JHP (C10E)

Distance - Yards	Muzzle	25	50	75	100
Velocity - fps	1330	1230	1140	1080	1030
Energy - ft/lb	605	515	450	400	360
Taylor KO values	11.8	10.9	10.1	9.6	9.1
Mid-Range Trajectory Height - inches	0.0	0.2	0.7	1.8	3.3
Drop - inches	0.0	-0.6	-2.7	-6.4	-12.0

G1 Ballistic Coefficient = 0.123

Hornady 155-grain JHP/XTP (9122)

Distance - Yards	Muzzle	25	50	75	100
Velocity - fps	1265	1186	1119	1065	1020
Energy - ft/lb	551	484	431	390	358
Taylor KO values	11.2	10.5	9.9	9.4	9.0
Mid-Range Trajectory Height - inches	0.0	0.2	0.8	1.8	3.5
Drop - inches	0.0	-0.7	-3.0	-4.0	-12.8

G1 Ballistic Coefficient = 0.138

Norma 170-grain HP (11002)   [Until Supply Exhausted]

Distance - Yards	Muzzle	25	50	75	100
Velocity - fps	1299	1215	1145	1088	1040
Energy - ft/lb	636	557	494	447	407
Taylor KO values	12.6	11.8	11.1	10.6	10.1
Mid-Range Trajectory Height - inches	0.0	0.2	0.7	1.8	3.3
Drop - inches	0.0	-0.7	-2.8	-6.6	-12.2

G1 Ballistic Coefficient = 0.141

PMC 170-grain JHP (10B)

Distance - Yards	Muzzle	25	50	75	100
Velocity - fps	1200	1117	1052	1000	958
Energy - ft/lb	544	471	418	378	347
Taylor KO values	11.7	10.9	10.2	9.7	9.3
Mid-Range Trajectory Height - inches	0.0	0.2	0.9	22.1	3.9
Drop - inches	0.0	-0.8	-3.3	-7.8	-14.5

G1 Ballistic Coefficient = 0.112

Winchester 175-grain Silvertip HP (X10MMSTHP)

Distance - Yards	Muzzle	25	50	75	100
Velocity - fps	1290	1209	1141	1084	1037
Energy - ft/lb	649	568	506	457	418
Taylor KO values	12.9	12.1	11.4	10.8	10.4
Mid-Range Trajectory Height - inches	0.0	0.2	0.7	1.8	3.3
Drop - inches	0.0	-0.7	-2.8	-6.7	-12.4

G1 Ballistic Coefficient = 0.142

American Eagle (Federal) 180-grain High Antimony Lead (AE10)

Distance - Yards	Muzzle	25	50	75	100
Velocity - fps	1030	1000	970	950	920
Energy - ft/lb	425	400	375	355	340
Taylor KO values	10.6	10.3	10.0	9.8	9.5
Mid-Range Trajectory Height - inches	0.0	0.3	1.1	2.5	4.7
Drop - inches	0.0	-1.0	-4.3	-9.8	-17.8

G1 Ballistic Coefficient = 0.169

Hornady 180-grain JHP/XTP - Full Load (9126)

Distance - Yards	Muzzle	25	50	75	100
Velocity - fps	1180	1124	1077	1038	1004
Energy - ft/lb	556	505	464	431	403
Taylor KO values	12.1	11.6	11.1	10.7	10.3
Mid-Range Trajectory Height - inches	0.0	0.2	0.9	2.0	3.7
Drop - inches	0.0	-0.8	-3.3	-7.7	-14.1

G1 Ballistic Coefficient = 0.165

Federal 180-grain Hydra-Shok JHP (P10HS1)

Distance - Yards	Muzzle	25	50	75	100
Velocity - fps	1030	1000	970	950	920
Energy - ft/lb	425	400	375	355	340
Taylor KO values	10.6	10.3	10.0	9.8	9.5
Mid-Range Trajectory Height - inches	0.0	0.3	1.1	2.5	4.7
Drop - inches	0.0	-1.0	-4.3	-9.8	-17.8

G1 Ballistic Coefficient = 0.169

Federal 180-grain Hi-Shok JHP (C10E)

Distance - Yards	Muzzle	25	50	75	100
Velocity - fps	1030	1000	970	950	920
Energy - ft/lb	425	400	375	355	340
Taylor KO values	10.6	10.3	10.0	9.8	9.5
Mid-Range Trajectory Height - inches	0.0	0.3	1.1	2.5	4.7
Drop - inches	0.0	-1.0	-4.3	-9.8	-17.8

G1 Ballistic Coefficient = 0.169

PMC 180-grain Starfire HP (10SFA)

Distance - Yards	Muzzle	25	50	75	100
Velocity - fps	950	926	903	882	862
Energy - ft/lb	360	342	326	311	297
Taylor KO values	9.8	9.5	9.3	9.1	8.9
Mid-Range Trajectory Height - inches	0.0	0.3	1.3	2.9	5.3
Drop - inches	0.0	-1.2	-5.0	-11.4	-20.6

G1 Ballistic Coefficient = 0.165

UMC (Remington) 180-grain Metal Case (L10MM6)

Distance - Yards	Muzzle	25	50	75	100
Velocity - fps	1150	1103	1063	1023	998
Energy - ft/lb	529	486	452	423	398
Taylor KO values	11.8	11.3	10.9	10.6	10.3
Mid-Range Trajectory Height - inches	0.0	0.2	0.9	2.0	3.7
Drop - inches	0.0	-0.8	-3.5	-8.0	-14.6

G1 Ballistic Coefficient = 0.180

Hornady 200-grain JHP/XTP (9129)

Distance - Yards	Muzzle	25	50	75	100
Velocity - fps	1050	1020	994	970	948
Energy - ft/lb	490	462	439	418	399
Taylor KO values	12.0	11.7	11.4	11.1	10.8
Mid-Range Trajectory Height - inches	0.0	0.2	1.0	2.4	4.4
Drop - inches	0.0	-1.0	-4.1	-9.4	-17.0

G1 Ballistic Coefficient = 0.200

Norma 200-grain Full Jacket Flat Nose (11001)

Distance - Yards	Muzzle	25	50	75	100
Velocity - fps	1115	1074	1038	1007	979
Energy - ft/lb	554	513	480	450	427
Taylor KO values	12.7	12.3	11.9	11.5	11.2
Mid-Range Trajectory Height - inches	0.0	0.2	0.9	2.2	4.0
Drop - inches	0.0	-0.9	-3.7	-8.5	-15.4

G1 Ballistic Coefficient = 0.182

CCI 200-grain FMJ (3597)

Distance - Yards	Muzzle	25	50	75	100
Velocity - fps	1050	1006	968	935	906
Energy - ft/lb	490	449	416	388	364
Taylor KO values	12.0	11.5	11.1	10.7	10.4
Mid-Range Trajectory Height - inches	0.0	0.3	1.1	2.5	4.6
Drop - inches	0.0	-1.0	-4.2	-9.7	-17.6

G1 Ballistic Coefficient = 0.130

PMC 200-grain Truncated Cone - FMJ (10A)

Distance - Yards	Muzzle	25	50	75	100
Velocity - fps	1050	1008	972	941	912
Energy - ft/lb	490	451	420	393	370
Taylor KO values	12.0	11.5	11.1	10.8	10.4
Mid-Range Trajectory Height - inches	0.0	0.2	1.1	2.5	4.6
Drop - inches	0.0	-1.0	-4.2	-9.6	-17.5

G1 Ballistic Coefficient = 0.138

.41 Remington Magnum

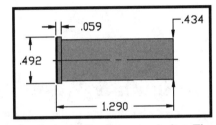

Remington announced the .41 Remington Magnum in 1964 at the same time that Smith & Wesson announced a Model 57 pistol chambered .41 Rem. Mag. The idea in offering the .41 was a simple one. The .357 Mag. wasn't quite enough gun for some shooters, but the .44 Rem. Mag. was too much. The .41 Rem. Mag. was supposed to be "Just Right." While the .41 Rem. Mag. does just what it was designed to do, a couple things happened on the way to the gun shop. The first was that the .41 Rem. Mag. was a little too much for many shooters. The second was that the caliber arrived just about the time that semi-automatic pistols were experiencing a big jump in popularity. The .41 Remington Magnum is still a powerful cartridge, one that fills the hunting application very easily.

Relative Recoil Factor = 1.23   **Controlling Agency: SAAMI**

Bullet Weight Grains	Velocity fps	Maximum Average Pressure		Standard barrel for velocity testing:
		Copper Crusher	Transducer	
170 STHP	1400	40,000 cup	36,000 psi	4 inches long (vented)
175 STHP	1250	40,000 cup	36,000 psi	10.135 inches alternate one piece barrel length
210 L	955	40,000 cup	36,000 psi	- 1 turn in 18.75 inch twist.
210 SP-HP	1280	40,000 cup	36,000 psi	

Winchester 175-grain Silvertip HP (X41MSTHP2)

Distance - Yards	Muzzle	25	50	75	100
Velocity - fps	1250	1180	1120	1071	1029
Energy - ft/lb	607	541	488	446	412
Taylor KO values	12.8	12.1	11.5	11.0	10.5
Mid-Range Trajectory Height - inches	0.0	0.2	0.8	1.8	3.4
Drop - inches	0.0	-0.7	-3.0	-7.0	-12.9

G1 Ballistic Coefficient = 0.163

Remington 210-grain JSP (R41MG)

Distance - Yards	Muzzle	25	50	75	100
Velocity - fps	1300	1226	1162	1108	1062
Energy - ft/lb	788	702	630	573	526
Taylor KO values	16.0	15.1	14.3	13.6	13.1
Mid-Range Trajectory Height - inches	0.0	0.2	0.7	1.7	3.2
Drop - inches	0.0	-0.7	-2.8	-6.5	-12.0

G1 Ballistic Coefficient = 0.160

PMC 210-grain Truncated Cone SP (41C)

Distance - Yards	Muzzle	25	50	75	100
Velocity - fps	1290	1201	1128	1040	958
Energy - ft/lb	774	637	542	476	427
Taylor KO values	15.9	14.8	13.9	12.8	11.8
Mid-Range Trajectory Height - inches	0.0	0.2	0.5	1.9	3.7
Drop - inches	0.0	-0.7	-3.0	-7.1	-13.4

G1 Ballistic Coefficient = 0.091

Federal 210-grain Hi-Shok JHP (C41A)

Distance - Yards	Muzzle	25	50	75	100
Velocity - fps	1300	1210	1130	1070	1030
Energy - ft/lb	790	680	595	540	495
Taylor KO values	16.0	14.9	13.9	13.2	12.7
Mid-Range Trajectory Height - inches	0.0	0.2	0.7	1.8	3.3
Drop - inches	0.0	-0.7	-2.8	-6.6	-12.3

G1 Ballistic Coefficient = 0.133

Federal 250-grain Cast Core (P41B)

Distance - Yards	Muzzle	25	50	75	100
Velocity - fps	1250	1200	1150	1110	1080
Energy - ft/lb	865	795	735	685	645
Taylor KO values	18.3	17.6	16.8	16.3	15.8
Mid-Range Trajectory Height - inches	0.0	0.2	0.8	1.8	3.3
Drop - inches	0.0	-0.7	-2.9	-6.8	-12.4

G1 Ballistic Coefficient = 0.218

.44 Smith & Wesson Special

The .44 S&W is one of the first generation pistol cartridges designed to use smokeless powder. At the time of its introduction the working pressures were kept very low, pretty much a duplication of black-powder pressure levels. As a result, the performance is certainly modest when compared with .44 Remington Magnum performance levels (although very potent compared with calibers like .38 Special). Like the .38 Special in a .357 Magnum revolver, the .44 S&W Special can be fired in modern guns in good condition that are chambered for the .44 Rem. Mag. This provides a way for the nonreloader to get modestly powered ammo for use in the .44 Rem. Mag. Using .44 Rem. Mag. ammo in a gun chambered for the .44 S&W Special is definitely NOT recommended.

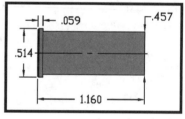

Relative Recoil Factor = 0.81   **Controlling Agency: SAAMI**

Bullet Weight Grains	Velocity fps	Maximum Average Pressure		Standard barrel for velocity testing:
		Copper Crusher	Transducer	
200 STHP	900	14,000 cup	N/S	4 inches long [Vented] -
200 SWCHP	1025	14,000 cup	N/S	8.15 inches long alternate one piece barrel
246 L	800	N/S	15,500 psi	- 1 turn in 20 inch twist - Several

manufacturers are using 6 or 6.5 inch vented barrels to obtain their velocity data.

CCI 140-grain Magnum Shotshell (3979)

Shot load using #9 shot - Muzzle Velocity = 1000 fps.

Hornady 180 grain JHP/XTP (9070)

Distance - Yards	Muzzle	25	50	75	100
Velocity - fps	1000	965	935	907	882
Energy - ft/lb	400	373	350	329	311
Taylor KO values	11.1	10.7	10.3	10.0	9.8
Mid-Range Trajectory Height - inches	0.0	0.3	1.2	2.7	5.0
Drop - inches	0.0	-1.1	-4.6	-10.5	-19.0

G1 Ballistic Coefficient = 0.139

PMC 180-grain JHP (44SB)

Distance - Yards	Muzzle	25	50	75	100
Velocity - fps	980	938	902	869	839
Energy - ft/lb	383	352	325	302	282
Taylor KO values	10.8	10.4	10.0	9.6	9.3
Mid-Range Trajectory Height - inches	0.0	0.3	1.2	2.9	5.3
Drop - inches	0.0	-1.2	-4.8	-11.1	-20.3

G1 Ballistic Coefficient = 0.105

Remington 200-grain Semi-Wadcutter (R44SW1)

Distance - Yards	Muzzle	25	50	75	100
Velocity - fps	1035	982	938	900	866
Energy - ft/lb	476	428	391	360	333
Taylor KO values	12.7	12.1	11.5	11.1	10.6
Mid-Range Trajectory Height - inches	0.0	0.3	1.1	2.6	4.9
Drop - inches	0.0	-1.0	-4.4	-10.1	-18.6

G1 Ballistic Coefficient = 0.100

Federal 200-grain Semi-Wadcutter HP (C44SA)

Distance - Yards	Muzzle	25	50	75	100
Velocity - fps	900	860	830	800	770
Energy - ft/lb	360	330	305	285	260
Taylor KO values	11.1	10.6	10.2	9.8	9.5
Mid-Range Trajectory Height - inches	0.0	0.3	1.4	3.4	6.3
Drop - inches	0.0	-1.4	-5.7	-13.1	-24.0

G1 Ballistic Coefficient = 0.091

Winchester 200-grain Silvertip HP (X44STHPS2)

Distance - Yards	Muzzle	25	50	75	100
Velocity - fps	900	879	860	840	822
Energy - ft/lb	360	343	328	313	300
Taylor KO values	11.1	10.8	10.6	10.3	10.1
Mid-Range Trajectory Height - inches	0.0	0.3	1.4	3.2	5.9
Drop - inches	0.0	-1.4	-5.5	-12.7	-22.9

G1 Ballistic Coefficient = 0.162

CCI 200-grain HP (3556)

Distance - Yards	Muzzle	25	50	75	100
Velocity - fps	875	849	825	802	780
Energy - ft/lb	340	320	302	286	270
Taylor KO values	10.8	10.4	10.1	9.9	9.6
Mid-Range Trajectory Height - inches	0.0	0.4	1.5	3.5	6.4
Drop - inches	0.0	-1.4	-5.9	-13.6	-24.6

G1 Ballistic Coefficient = 0.123

PMC 240-grain Semi-Wadcutter - Copper Plated (44SA)

Distance - Yards	Muzzle	25	50	75	100
Velocity - fps	764	744	724	706	687
Energy - ft/lb	311	295	280	265	252
Taylor KO values	11.3	11.0	10.7	10.4	10.1
Mid-Range Trajectory Height - inches	0.0	0.5	2.0	4.5	8.3
Drop - inches	0.0	-1.9	-7.7	-17.7	-32.0

G1 Ballistic Coefficient = 0.121

Remington 246-grain Lead (R44SW)

Distance - Yards	Muzzle	25	50	75	100
Velocity - fps	755	739	725	709	695
Energy - ft/lb	310	299	285	275	265
Taylor KO values	11.4	11.2	11.0	10.7	10.5
Mid-Range Trajectory Height - inches	0.0	0.5	2.0	4.6	8.3
Drop - inches	0.0	-1.9	-7.8	-17.9	-32.3

G1 Ballistic Coefficient = 0.154

Winchester 246-grain LRN (X44SP)

Distance - Yards	Muzzle	25	50	75	100
Velocity - fps	755	739	725	709	695
Energy - ft/lb	310	299	285	275	265
Taylor KO values	11.4	11.2	11.0	10.7	10.5
Mid-Range Trajectory Height - inches	0.0	0.5	2.0	4.6	8.3
Drop - inches	0.0	-1.9	-7.8	-17.9	-32.3

G1 Ballistic Coefficient = 0.154

Cowboy Action Loads

Black Hills 210-grain FPL (DCB44SPLN1)

Distance - Yards	Muzzle	25	50	75	100
Velocity - fps	700	678	657	637	618
Energy - ft/lb	229	215	202	189	178
Taylor KO values	9.0	8.7	8.5	8.2	8.0
Mid-Range Trajectory Height - inches	0.0	0.6	2.4	5.5	10.1
Drop - inches	0.0	-2.3	-9.2	-21.3	-38.6

G1 Ballistic Coefficient = 0.100

PMC 240-grain Lead Flat Point (44D)

Distance - Yards	Muzzle	25	50	75	100
Velocity - fps	750	734	719	704	690
Energy - ft/lb	300	287	276	264	254
Taylor KO values	11.0	10.8	10.6	10.4	10.1
Mid-Range Trajectory Height - inches	0.0	0.5	2.1	4.8	8.4
Drop - inches	0.0	-2.0	-7.9	-18.1	-32.7

G1 Ballistic Coefficient = 0.153

Winchester 240-grain Cast Lead (CB44SP)

Distance - Yards	Muzzle	25	50	75	100
Velocity - fps	750	734	719	704	690
Energy - ft/lb	300	287	276	264	254
Taylor KO values	11.0	10.8	10.6	10.4	10.1
Mid-Range Trajectory Height - inches	0.0	0.5	2.1	4.8	8.4
Drop - inches	0.0	-2.0	-7.9	-18.1	-32.7

G1 Ballistic Coefficient = 0.153

.44 Remington Magnum (Pistol Data)

The .44 Remington Magnum cartridge was introduced in 1956. From its inception, it has been the stuff of legends. Much of the world's dangerous game has been killed at one time or another by a hunter equipped with a .44 Magnum revolver (backed up, usually, by a professional hunter equipped with a suitable large rifle). As a pistol cartridge, the .44 Magnum kills at both ends. Few shooters can get off more than 5 or 6 shots without beginning to flinch. Ammunition in .44 S&W Special caliber can be used in revolvers chambered for .44 Remington Magnum, a condition similar to firing .38 Special in a .357 Magnum. See the data in the rifle section for further information. (.44 S&W Special ammunition generally can't be used in tubular magazine rifles designed for the .44 RM because the shorter cartridge promotes feeding problems that aren't present in a revolver).

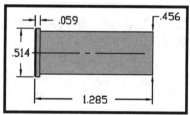

Relative Recoil Factor = 1.45   **Controlling Agency: SAAMI**

Bullet Weight Grains	Velocity fps	Maximum Average Pressure		Standard barrel for velocity testing:
		Copper Crusher	Transducer	
180 JHP	1400	40,000 cup	36,000 psi	4 inches long [vented]
210 STHP	1250	40,000 cup	36,000 psi	- 1 turn in 20 inch twist
240 L-SWC	995	40,000 cup	36,000 psi	Some velocities listed below are taken
240 L	1335	40,000 cup	36,000 psi	with "non-standard" barrel lengths

CCI 140-grain Shotshell (3979)

Shotshell load using # 9 shot at 1000 fps.

Federal 180-grain Hi-Shok JHP (C44B)

Distance - Yards	Muzzle	25	50	75	100
Velocity - fps	1610	1480	1370	1270	1180
Energy - ft/lb	1035	875	750	640	555
Taylor KO values	17.9	16.4	15.2	14.1	13.1
Mid-Range Trajectory Height - inches	0.0	0.1	0.5	1.2	2.3
Drop - inches	0.0	-0.4	-1.9	-4.5	-8.4

G1 Ballistic Coefficient = 0.125

Hansen 180-grain JHP "Combat" HP (HCC44B)

Distance - Yards	Muzzle	25	50	75	100
Velocity - fps	1610	1482	1365	1262	1175
Energy - ft/lb	1036	878	745	637	551
Taylor KO values	17.9	16.5	15.2	14.0	13.1
Mid-Range Trajectory Height - inches	0.0	0.1	0.5	1.2	2.3
Drop - inches	0.0	-0.4	-1.9	-4.5	-8.4

G1 Ballistic Coefficient = 0.125

Remington 180-grain Semi-JHP (R44MG5)

Distance - Yards	Muzzle	25	50	75	100
Velocity - fps	1610	1482	1365	1262	1175
Energy - ft/lb	1036	878	745	637	551
Taylor KO values	17.9	16.5	15.2	14.0	13.1
Mid-Range Trajectory Height - inches	0.0	0.1	0.5	1.2	2.3
Drop - inches	0.0	-0.4	-1.9	-4.5	-8.4

G1 Ballistic Coefficient = 0.125

UMC (Remington) 180-grain Semi-JHP (L44MG5)

Distance - Yards	Muzzle	25	50	75	100
Velocity - fps	1610	1482	1365	1262	1175
Energy - ft/lb	1036	878	745	637	551
Taylor KO values	17.9	16.5	15.2	14.0	13.1
Mid-Range Trajectory Height - inches	0.0	0.1	0.5	1.2	2.3
Drop - inches	0.0	-0.4	-1.9	-4.5	-8.4

G1 Ballistic Coefficient = 0.125

Hornady 180-grain JHP/XTP (9081)

Distance - Yards	Muzzle	25	50	75	100
Velocity - fps	1550	1440	1340	1250	1173
Energy - ft/lb	960	829	717	624	550
Taylor KO values	17.2	16.0	14.9	13.9	13.0
Mid-Range Trajectory Height - inches	0.0	0.1	0.5	1.3	2.4
Drop - inches	0.0	-0.5	-2.0	-4.7	-8.9

G1 Ballistic Coefficient = 0.138

PMC 180-grain JHP (44B)

Distance - Yards	Muzzle	25	50	75	100
Velocity - fps	1392	1263	1157	1076	1015
Energy - ft/lb	772	639	537	465	413
Taylor KO values	15.4	14.0	12.8	11.9	11.2
Mid-Range Trajectory Height - inches	0.0	0.2	0.7	1.7	3.2
Drop - inches	0.0	-0.6	-2.6	-6.1	-11.6

G1 Ballistic Coefficient = 0.101

Hornady 200-grain JHP/XTP (9080)

Distance - Yards	Muzzle	25	50	75	100
Velocity - fps	1500	1389	1284	1202	1128
Energy - ft/lb	999	856	732	641	565
Taylor KO values	18.4	17.1	15.8	14.8	13.9
Mid-Range Trajectory Height - inches	0.0	0.1	0.6	1.4	2.6
Drop - inches	0.0	-0.5	-2.2	-5.1	-9.5

G1 Ballistic Coefficient = 0.131

Fiocchi 200-grain JHP (44B)

Distance - Yards	Muzzle	25	50	75	100
Velocity - fps	1475	1365	1267	1183	1113
Energy - ft/lb	966	826	713	622	551
Taylor KO values	18.1	16.8	15.6	14.5	13.7
Mid-Range Trajectory Height - inches	0.0	0.1	0.6	1.4	2.7
Drop - inches	0.0	-0.5	-2.2	-5.3	-9.9

G1 Ballistic Coefficient = 0.130

Winchester 210-grain Silvertip HP (X44MS)

Distance - Yards	Muzzle	25	50	75	100
Velocity - fps	1250	1171	1106	1053	1010
Energy - ft/lb	729	640	570	518	475
Taylor KO values	16.1	15.1	14.3	13.6	13.0
Mid-Range Trajectory Height - inches	0.0	0.2	0.8	1.9	3.7
Drop - inches	0.0	-0.7	-3.0	-7.1	-13.2

G1 Ballistic Coefficient = 0.135

Fiocchi 240-grain JSP (44A)

Distance - Yards	Muzzle	25	50	75	100
Velocity - fps	1375	1283	1202	1133	1077
Energy - ft/lb	1008	877	770	685	620
Taylor KO values	17.7	16.6	15.5	14.6	13.9
Mid-Range Trajectory Height - inches	0.0	0.2	0.7	1.6	3.0
Drop - inches	0.0	-0.6	-2.5	-6.0	-11.1

G1 Ballistic Coefficient = 0.140

PMC 240-grain Truncated Cone - SP (44D)

Distance - Yards	Muzzle	25	50	75	100
Velocity - fps	1300	1216	1145	1086	1038
Energy - ft/lb	900	788	699	629	575
Taylor KO values	16.8	15.7	14.8	14.0	13.4
Mid-Range Trajectory Height - inches	0.0	0.2	0.7	1.8	3.3
Drop - inches	0.0	-0.7	-2.8	-6.6	-12.2

G1 Ballistic Coefficient = 0.139

Hansen 240-grain JSP "Combat" (HCC44F)

Distance - Yards	Muzzle	25	50	75	100
Velocity - fps	1180	1115	1063	1019	982
Energy - ft/lb	740	663	602	554	514
Taylor KO values	15.2	14.4	13.7	13.1	12.7
Mid-Range Trajectory Height - inches	0.0	0.2	0.9	2.1	3.8
Drop - inches	0.0	-0.8	-3.4	-7.8	-14.4

G1 Ballistic Coefficient = 0.140

Magtech 240-grain Semi-JSP (44A)

Distance - Yards	Muzzle	25	50	75	100
Velocity - fps	1180	1127	1081	1043	1010
Energy - ft/lb	741	677	624	580	544
Taylor KO values	15.2	14.5	13.9	13.5	13.0
Mid-Range Trajectory Height - inches	0.0	0.2	0.9	2.0	3.7
Drop - inches	0.0	-0.8	-3.3	-7.7	-14.1

G1 Ballistic Coefficient = 0.173

Remington 240-grain SP (R44MG2)

Distance - Yards	Muzzle	25	50	75	100
Velocity - fps	1180	1127	1081	1043	1010
Energy - ft/lb	741	677	624	580	544
Taylor KO values	15.2	14.5	13.9	13.5	13.0
Mid-Range Trajectory Height - inches	0.0	0.2	0.9	2.0	3.7
Drop - inches	0.0	-0.8	-3.3	-7.7	-14.1

G1 Ballistic Coefficient = 0.173

USA (Winchester) 240-grain JSP (Q4240)

Distance - Yards	Muzzle	25	50	75	100
Velocity - fps	1180	1127	1081	1043	1010
Energy - ft/lb	741	677	624	580	544
Taylor KO values	15.2	14.5	13.9	13.5	13.0
Mid-Range Trajectory Height - inches	0.0	0.2	0.9	2.0	3.7
Drop - inches	0.0	-0.8	-3.3	-7.7	-14.1

G1 Ballistic Coefficient = 0.173

PMC 240-grain Lead Semi-Wadcutter - Gas Check (44A)

Distance - Yards	Muzzle	25	50	75	100
Velocity - fps	1225	1143	1077	1025	982
Energy - ft/lb	240	697	619	561	515
Taylor KO values	15.8	14.7	13.9	13.2	12.7
Mid-Range Trajectory Height - inches	0.0	0.2	0.8	2.0	3.7
Drop - inches	0.0	-0.8	-3.2	-7.5	-13.8

G1 Ballistic Coefficient = 0.122

Hornady 240-grain JHP/XTP (9085)

Distance - Yards	Muzzle	25	50	75	100
Velocity - fps	1350	1266	1188	1130	1078
Energy - ft/lb	971	854	753	680	619
Taylor KO values	17.4	16.3	15.3	14.6	13.9
Mid-Range Trajectory Height - inches	0.0	0.2	0.7	1.6	3.1
Drop - inches	0.0	-0.6	-2.6	-6.1	-11.3

G1 Ballistic Coefficient = 0.150

PMC 240-grain JHP (44C)

Distance - Yards	Muzzle	25	50	75	100
Velocity - fps	1301	1218	1147	1088	1041
Energy - ft/lb	902	791	702	632	578
Taylor KO values	19.1	17.9	16.8	16.0	15.3
Mid-Range Trajectory Height - inches	0.0	0.2	0.7	1.8	3.3
Drop - inches	0.0	-0.7	-2.8	-6.6	-12.2

G1 Ballistic Coefficient = 0.141

PMC 240-grain Starfire HP (44SFA)

Distance - Yards	Muzzle	25	50	75	100
Velocity - fps	1300	1212	1138	1079	1030
Energy - ft/lb	900	784	692	621	566
Taylor KO values	16.8	15.6	14.7	13.9	13.3
Mid-Range Trajectory Height - inches	0.0	0.2	0.7	1.8	3.3
Drop - inches	0.0	-0.7	-2.8	-6.6	-12.3

G1 Ballistic Coefficient = 0.133

Norma 240-grain "Power Cavity" (11103)

Distance - Yards	Muzzle	25	50	75	100
Velocity - fps	1280	1208	1147	1095	1052
Energy - ft/lb	875	780	703	640	591
Taylor KO values	16.5	15.6	14.8	14.1	13.6
Mid-Range Trajectory Height - inches	0.0	0.2	0.7	1.8	3.3
Drop - inches	0.0	-0.7	-2.9	-6.7	-12.3

G1 Ballistic Coefficient = 0.160

Remington 240-grain JHP Core-Lokt (RH44MGA)

Distance - Yards	Muzzle	25	50	75	100
Velocity - fps	1235	1186	1142	1104	1070
Energy - ft/lb	813	750	695	649	610
Taylor KO values	15.9	15.3	14.7	14.2	13.8
Mid-Range Trajectory Height - inches	0.0	0.2	0.8	1.8	3.3
Drop - inches	0.0	-0.7	-3.0	-7.0	-12.7

G1 Ballistic Coefficient = 0.217

Black Hills 240-grain JHP (D44MN2)

Distance - Yards	Muzzle	25	50	75	100
Velocity - fps	1260	1187	1125	1074	1031
Energy - ft/lb	848	751	675	615	567
Taylor KO values	16.2	15.3	14.5	13.9	13.3
Mid-Range Trajectory Height - inches	0.0	0.2	0.8	1.8	3.4
Drop - inches	0.0	-0.7	-3.0	-6.9	-12.8

G1 Ballistic Coefficient = 0.150

American Eagle (Federal) 240-grain JHP (AE44A)

Distance - Yards	Muzzle	25	50	75	100
Velocity - fps	1180	1127	1081	1043	1010
Energy - ft/lb	741	677	624	580	544
Taylor KO values	15.2	14.5	13.9	13.5	13.0
Mid-Range Trajectory Height - inches	0.0	0.2	0.9	2.0	3.7
Drop - inches	0.0	-0.8	-3.3	-7.7	-14.1

G1 Ballistic Coefficient = 0.173

Federal 240-grain Hydra-Shok JHP (P44HS1)

Distance - Yards	Muzzle	25	50	75	100
Velocity - fps	1180	1127	1081	1043	1010
Energy - ft/lb	741	677	624	580	544
Taylor KO values	15.2	14.5	13.9	13.5	13.0
Mid-Range Trajectory Height - inches	0.0	0.2	0.9	2.0	3.7
Drop - inches	0.0	-0.8	-3.3	-7.7	-14.1

G1 Ballistic Coefficient = 0.173

Federal 240-grain Hi-Shok JHP (C44A)

Distance - Yards	Muzzle	25	50	75	100
Velocity - fps	1180	1127	1081	1043	1010
Energy - ft/lb	741	677	624	580	544
Taylor KO values	15.2	14.5	13.9	13.5	13.0
Mid-Range Trajectory Height - inches	0.0	0.2	0.9	2.0	3.7
Drop - inches	0.0	-0.8	-3.3	-7.7	-14.1

G1 Ballistic Coefficient = 0.173

Hansen 240-grain JHP "Combat" HP (HCC44C)

Distance - Yards	Muzzle	25	50	75	100
Velocity - fps	1180	1115	1063	1019	982
Energy - ft/lb	740	663	602	554	514
Taylor KO values	15.2	14.4	13.7	13.1	12.7
Mid-Range Trajectory Height - inches	0.0	0.2	0.9	2.1	3.8
Drop - inches	0.0	-0.8	-3.4	-7.8	-14.4

G1 Ballistic Coefficient = 0.140

CCI 240-grain JHP (3564)

Distance - Yards	Muzzle	25	50	75	100
Velocity - fps	1200	1142	1092	1051	1015
Energy - ft/lb	767	695	636	589	549
Taylor KO values	15.5	14.7	14.1	13.6	13.1
Mid-Range Trajectory Height - inches	0.0	0.2	0.8	2.0	3.3
Drop - inches	0.0	-0.8	-3.2	-7.5	-13.7

G1 Ballistic Coefficient = 0.166

Remington 240-grain Semi-JHP (R44MG3)

Distance - Yards	Muzzle	25	50	75	100
Velocity - fps	1180	1127	1081	1043	1010
Energy - ft/lb	741	677	624	580	544
Taylor KO values	15.2	14.5	13.9	13.5	13.0
Mid-Range Trajectory Height - inches	0.0	0.2	0.9	2.0	3.7
Drop - inches	0.0	-0.8	-3.3	-7.7	-14.1

G1 Ballistic Coefficient = 0.173

Winchester 240-grain HSP (X44MHSP2)

Distance - Yards	Muzzle	25	50	75	100
Velocity - fps	1180	1127	1081	1043	1010
Energy - ft/lb	741	677	624	580	544
Taylor KO values	15.2	14.5	13.9	13.5	13.0
Mid-Range Trajectory Height - inches	0.0	0.2	0.9	2.0	3.7
Drop - inches	0.0	-0.8	-3.3	-7.7	-14.1

G1 Ballistic Coefficient = 0.173

Federal 250-grain Metal Case Profile Match (GM44D)

Distance - Yards	Muzzle	25	50	75	100
Velocity - fps	1180	1140	1100	1070	1040
Energy - ft/lb	775	715	670	630	600
Taylor KO values	18.1	17.5	16.9	16.4	15.9
Mid-Range Trajectory Height - inches	0.0	0.2	0.8	1.9	3.6
Drop - inches	0.0	-0.8	-3.3	-7.5	-13.7

G1 Ballistic Coefficient = 0.224

Winchester 250-grain Partition Gold (S44MP)

Distance - Yards	Muzzle	25	50	75	100
Velocity - fps	1230	1178	1132	1092	1057
Energy - ft/lb	840	770	711	662	620
Taylor KO values	18.9	18.1	17.4	16.8	16.2
Mid-Range Trajectory Height - inches	0.0	0.2	0.8	1.8	3.4
Drop - inches	0.0	-0.7	-3.0	-7.0	-12.9

G1 Ballistic Coefficient = 0.201

Speer 270-grain Gold Dot SP (23968)

Distance - Yards	Muzzle	25	50	75	100
Velocity - fps	1250	1192	1142	1098	1060
Energy - ft/lb	937	853	781	723	674
Taylor KO values	20.7	19.8	18.9	18.2	17.6
Mid-Range Trajectory Height - inches	0.0	0.2	0.8	1.8	3.3
Drop - inches	0.0	-0.7	-3.0	-6.9	-12.6

G1 Ballistic Coefficient = 0.189

Black Hills 300-grain JHP (D44MN3)

Distance - Yards	Muzzle	25	50	75	100
Velocity - fps	1225	1173	1127	1088	1053
Energy - ft/lb	1002	917	847	789	739
Taylor KO values	22.6	21.6	20.8	20.1	19.4
Mid-Range Trajectory Height - inches	0.0	0.2	0.8	1.9	3.4
Drop - inches	0.0	-0.8	-3.1	-7.1	-13.0

G1 Ballistic Coefficient = 0.200

Federal 300-grain Cast Core (P44E)

Distance - Yards	Muzzle	25	50	75	100
Velocity - fps	1250	1200	1160	1120	1080
Energy - ft/lb	1040	940	885	825	773
Taylor KO values	23.0	22.1	21.3	20.6	19.9
Mid-Range Trajectory Height - inches	0.0	0.2	0.8	1.9	3.4
Drop - inches	0.0	-0.7	-2.9	-6.8	-12.4

G1 Ballistic Coefficient = 0.219

Hornady 300-grain JHP/XTP (9088)

Distance - Yards	Muzzle	25	50	75	100
Velocity - fps	1150	1111	1084	1047	1021
Energy - ft/lb	881	823	782	731	708
Taylor KO values	21.3	20.5	20.0	19.3	18.8
Mid-Range Trajectory Height - inches	0.0	0.2	0.9	2.0	3.7
Drop - inches	0.0	-0.8	-3.4	-7.9	-14.4

G1 Ballistic Coefficient = 0.222

.45 Auto (.45 ACP)

Born in the flurry of gun and cartridge design following the end of the Spanish-American War (1905), the .45 Auto cartridge was designed by John Browning to be fired in his automatic pistol. The first cut at the gun's design didn't do well, so the gun was modified (some might say improved) into what became the M1911 pistol. The original loading for that pistol used a 230-grain bullet at 850 fps. Here we are, nearly 90 years later and the 230-grain bullet at 850 fps is still pretty close to the standard load for the .45. Like most calibers that have been adopted by the US military, the .45 Auto remains a very popular caliber, and certainly a very effective defensive weapon.

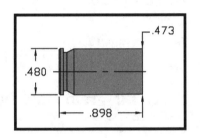

Relative Recoil Factor = 0.93   **Controlling Agency: SAAMI**

Bullet Weight Grains	Velocity fps	Maximum Average Pressure		Standard barrel for velocity testing:
		Copper Crusher	Transducer	
180 JHP	995	18,000 cup	21,000 psi	5 inches long - 1 turn in 16 inch twist
180 JHP	930	18,000 cup	21,000 psi	
230 FMC	830	18,000 cup	21,000 psi	
+ P Loads				
185 JHP	1130	N/S	23,000 psi	

CCI 117-grain Shotshell (3567)

Number 9 shot at 1100 fps

Federal 165-grain Jacketed Soft Point - Non-Toxic (JSP-NT) (BC45NT1)

Distance - Yards	Muzzle	25	50	75	100
Velocity - fps	1030	970	930	891	856
Energy - ft/lb	385	345	315	291	269
Taylor KO values	11.0	10.3	9.9	9.5	9.1
Mid-Range Trajectory Height - inches	0.0	0.3	1.1	2.7	5.0
Drop - inches	0.0	-1.1	-4.4	-10.3	-18.9

G1 Ballistic Coefficient = 0.095

Federal 165-grain Hydra-Shok JHP (PD45HS3)

Distance - Yards	Muzzle	25	50	75	100
Velocity - fps	1060	1020	980	948	920
Energy - ft/lb	410	375	350	330	310
Taylor KO values	11.3	10.9	10.4	10.1	9.8
Mid-Range Trajectory Height - inches	0.0	0.2	1.1	2.5	4.5
Drop - inches	0.0	-1.0	-4.1	-9.4	-17.2

G1 Ballistic Coefficient = 0.140

Winchester 170-grain JSP - NT (SC45NT)

Distance - Yards	Muzzle	25	50	75	100
Velocity - fps	1050	1013	982	954	928
Energy - ft/lb	416	388	364	343	325
Taylor KO values	11.5	11.1	10.8	10.5	10.2
Mid-Range Trajectory Height - inches	0.0	0.2	0.9	2.4	4.0
Drop - inches	0.0	-1.0	-4.1	-9.5	-17.3

G1 Ballistic Coefficient = 0.161

Remington 175-grain Disintegrator Plated Frangible (LF45APA)

Distance - Yards	Muzzle	25	50	75	100
Velocity - fps	1020	970	928	892	859
Energy - ft/lb	404	366	335	309	286
Taylor KO values	11.5	11.0	10.5	10.1	9.7
Mid-Range Trajectory Height - inches	0.0	0.3	1.2	2.7	5.1
Drop - inches	0.0	-1.1	-4.5	-10.4	-19.0

G1 Ballistic Coefficient = 0.101

Remington 185-grain Brass-JHP + P (GS45APC)

Distance - Yards	Muzzle	25	50	75	100
Velocity - fps	1140	1086	1042	1004	971
Energy - ft/lb	534	485	446	414	388
Taylor KO values	13.6	13.0	12.4	12.0	11.6
Mid-Range Trajectory Height - inches	0.0	0.2	1.0	2.2	4.0
Drop - inches	0.0	-0.9	-3.6	-8.3	-15.1

G1 Ballistic Coefficient = 0.150

Speer 185-grain Gold Dot (23964)

Distance - Yards	Muzzle	25	50	75	100
Velocity - fps	1050	998	956	919	886
Energy - ft/lb	453	409	375	347	322
Taylor KO values	12.5	11.9	11.4	11.0	10.6
Mid-Range Trajectory Height - inches	0.0	0.3	1.1	2.6	4.6
Drop - inches	0.0	-1.0	-4.2	-9.8	-18.0

G1 Ballistic Coefficient = 0.110

Remington 185-grain Brass-JHP (GS45APA)

Distance - Yards	Muzzle	25	50	75	100
Velocity - fps	1015	981	951	924	899
Energy - ft/lb	423	395	372	35'	332
Taylor KO values	12.1	11.7	11.4	11.0	10.7
Mid-Range Trajectory Height - inches	0.0	0.3	1.1	2.6	4.5
Drop - inches	0.0	-1.1	-4.4	-10.2	-18.4

G1 Ballistic Coefficient = 0.150

Black Hills 185-grain JHP - Gold Dot (D45N4)

Distance - Yards	Muzzle	25	50	75	100
Velocity - fps	1000	963	931	902	875
Energy - ft/lb	411	381	356	334	315
Taylor KO values	11.9	11.5	11.1	10.8	10.5
Mid-Range Trajectory Height - inches	0.0	0.3	1.2	2.7	5.0
Drop - inches	0.0	-1.1	-4.6	-10.5	-19.2

G1 Ballistic Coefficient = 0.130

Remington 185-grain JHP (R45AP2)

Distance - Yards	Muzzle	25	50	75	100
Velocity - fps	1000	968	939	913	889
Energy - ft/lb	411	385	362	342	324
Taylor KO values	11.9	11.6	11.2	10.9	10.6
Mid-Range Trajectory Height - inches	0.0	0.3	1.1	2.7	4.9
Drop - inches	0.0	-1.1	-4.5	-10.4	-18.9

G1 Ballistic Coefficient = 0.149

Winchester 185-grain Silvertip HP (X45ASHP2)

Distance - Yards	Muzzle	25	50	75	100
Velocity - fps	1000	967	938	912	888
Energy - ft/lb	411	384	362	342	324
Taylor KO values	11.9	11.6	11.2	10.9	10.6
Mid-Range Trajectory Height - inches	0.0	0.3	1.2	2.7	4.9
Drop - inches	0.0	-1.1	-4.5	-10.4	-19.0

G1 Ballistic Coefficient = 0.148

Federal 185-grain Hi-Shok JHP (C45C)

Distance - Yards	Muzzle	25	50	75	100
Velocity - fps	950	920	900	880	860
Energy - ft/lb	370	350	335	320	300
Taylor KO values	11.3	11.0	10.8	10.5	10.3
Mid-Range Trajectory Height - inches	0.0	0.4	1.6	3.7	6.7
Drop - inches	0.0	-1.2	-5.0	-111.4	-20.7

G1 Ballistic Coefficient = 0.162

Hornady 185-grain JHP/XTP (9090)

Distance - Yards	Muzzle	25	50	75	100
Velocity - fps	950	912	880	847	819
Energy - ft/lb	371	342	318	295	276
Taylor KO values	11.3	10.9	10.5	10.1	9.8
Mid-Range Trajectory Height - inches	0.0	0.3	1.3	3.0	5.6
Drop - inches	0.0	-1.2	-5.1	-11.8	-21.4

G1 Ballistic Coefficient = 0.104

Hansen 185-grain JHP "Combat" (HCC453)

Distance - Yards	Muzzle	25	50	75	100
Velocity - fps	930	903	878	855	833
Energy - ft/lb	355	335	317	300	285
Taylor KO values	11.1	10.8	10.5	10.2	10.0
Mid-Range Trajectory Height - inches	0.0	0.3	1.3	3.0	5.6
Drop - inches	0.0	-1.3	-5.2	-12.0	-21.7

G1 Ballistic Coefficient = 0.140

PMC 185-grain JHP (45B)

Distance - Yards	Muzzle	25	50	75	100
Velocity - fps	903	870	839	811	785
Energy - ft/lb	339	311	290	270	253
Taylor KO values	10.8	10.4	10.0	9.7	9.4
Mid-Range Trajectory Height - inches	0.0	0.3	1.4	3.3	6.2
Drop - inches	0.0	-1.4	-5.6	-12.9	-23.9

G1 Ballistic Coefficient = 0.103

Winchester 185-grain Brass Enclosed Base (WC451)

Distance - Yards	Muzzle	25	50	75	100
Velocity - fps	910	870	835	802	772
Energy - ft/lb	340	311	286	264	245
Taylor KO values	11.0	10.5	10.1	9.7	9.3
Mid-Range Trajectory Height - inches	0.0	0.3	1.4	3.2	5.9
Drop - inches	0.0	-1.4	-5.6	-12.9	-23.6

G1 Ballistic Coefficient = 0.087

Federal 185-grain FMJ - Semi-Wadcutter Match (GM45B)

Distance - Yards	Muzzle	25	50	75	100
Velocity - fps	780	730	700	660	620
Energy - ft/lb	245	220	200	175	160
Taylor KO values	9.3	8.7	8.4	7.9	7.4
Mid-Range Trajectory Height - inches	0.0	0.5	2.0	4.8	9.0
Drop - inches	0.0	-1.9	-7.7	-18.1	-33.6

G1 Ballistic Coefficient = 0.055

Hansen 185-grain Semi-Wadcutter - FMJ Match (HCC45C)

Distance - Yards	Muzzle	25	50	75	100
Velocity - fps	775	730	689	651	615
Energy - ft/lb	243	219	195	174	156
Taylor KO values	9.3	8.7	8.2	7.8	7.3
Mid-Range Trajectory Height - inches	0.0	0.5	2.0	4.8	9.2
Drop - inches	0.0	-1.9	-7.8	-18.4	-34.0

G1 Ballistic Coefficient = 0.055

Remington 185-grain Targetmaster Metal Case Wadcutter Match (R45AP1)

Distance - Yards	Muzzle	25	50	75	100
Velocity - fps	770	737	707	677	650
Energy - ft/lb	244	223	205	189	174
Taylor KO values	9.3	8.9	8.6	8.2	7.9
Mid-Range Trajectory Height - inches	0.0	0.5	2.0	4.6	8.7
Drop - inches	0.0	-1.9	-7.8	-18.0	-33.0

G1 Ballistic Coefficient = 0.075

Magtech 200-grain Lead Semi-Wadcutter (45C)

Distance - Yards	Muzzle	25	50	75	100
Velocity - fps	950	929	910	891	874
Energy - ft/lb	401	383	368	353	339
Taylor KO values	12.3	12.0	11.8	11.5	11.3
Mid-Range Trajectory Height - inches	0.0	0.3	0.8	2.9	4.8
Drop - inches	0.0	-1.2	-5.0	-11.3	-20.4

G1 Ballistic Coefficient = 0.195

Black Hills 200-grain Match Semi-Wadcutter (D45N1)

Distance - Yards	Muzzle	25	50	75	100
Velocity - fps	875	854	833	814	796
Energy - ft/lb	340	324	309	294	280
Taylor KO values	11.3	11.0	10.8	10.5	10.3
Mid-Range Trajectory Height - inches	0.0	0.4	1.5	3.4	6.2
Drop - inches	0.0	-1.4	-5.9	-13.4	-24.2

G1 Ballistic Coefficient = 0.150

Hornady 200-grain JHP/XTP + P (9113)

Distance - Yards	Muzzle	25	50	75	100
Velocity - fps	1055	1015	982	952	925
Energy - ft/lb	494	458	428	402	380
Taylor KO values	13.6	13.1	12.7	12.3	11.9
Mid-Range Trajectory Height - inches	0.0	0.2	1.0	2.4	4.5
Drop - inches	0.0	-1.0	-4.1	-9.5	-17.2

G1 Ballistic Coefficient = 0.151

CCI 200-grain JHP (3568)

Distance - Yards	Muzzle	25	50	75	100
Velocity - fps	975	942	917	885	860
Energy - ft/lb	421	394	372	348	328
Taylor KO values	12.6	12.2	11.8	11.4	11.1
Mid-Range Trajectory Height - inches	0.0	0.3	1.4	2.8	5.0
Drop - inches	0.0	-1.2	-4.8	-11.0	-20.0

G1 Ballistic Coefficient = 0.131

Speer 200-grain Gold Dot + P (23969)

Distance - Yards	Muzzle	25	50	75	100
Velocity - fps	975	942	917	885	860
Energy - ft/lb	421	394	372	348	328
Taylor KO values	12.6	12.2	11.8	11.4	11.1
Mid-Range Trajectory Height - inches	0.0	0.3	1.4	2.8	5.0
Drop - inches	0.0	-1.2	-4.8	-11.0	-20.0

G1 Ballistic Coefficient = 0.131

Fiocchi 200-grain JHP (45B)

Distance - Yards	Muzzle	25	50	75	100
Velocity - fps	900	877	855	835	816
Energy - ft/lb	360	342	325	310	296
Taylor KO values	11.6	11.3	11.0	10.8	10.5
Mid-Range Trajectory Height - inches	0.0	0.3	1.4	3.2	5.8
Drop - inches	0.0	-1.4	-5.6	-12.7	-23.0

G1 Ballistic Coefficient = 0.131

Hornady 200-grain JHP/XTP (9112)

Distance - Yards	Muzzle	25	50	75	100
Velocity - fps	900	877	855	835	815
Energy - ft/lb	358	342	325	310	295
Taylor KO values	11.6	11.3	11.0	10.8	10.5
Mid-Range Trajectory Height - inches	0.0	0.3	1.4	3.2	5.9
Drop - inches	0.0	-1.4	-5.6	-12.7	-23.0

G1 Ballistic Coefficient = 0.149

PMC 200-grain FMJ - Semi-Wadcutter (45C)

Distance - Yards	Muzzle	25	50	75	100
Velocity - fps	850	818	788	761	734
Energy - ft/lb	321	297	276	257	239
Taylor KO values	11.0	10.6	10.2	9.8	9.5
Mid-Range Trajectory Height - inches	0.0	0.4	1.6	3.8	7.0
Drop - inches	0.0	-1.5	-6.3	-14.6	-26.7

G1 Ballistic Coefficient = 0.092

Hornady 230-grain JHP/XTP + P (9096)

Distance - Yards	Muzzle	25	50	75	100
Velocity - fps	950	926	904	884	865
Energy - ft/lb	462	438	418	399	382
Taylor KO values	14.1	13.8	13.4	13.1	12.8
Mid-Range Trajectory Height - inches	0.0	0.3	1.3	2.9	5.3
Drop - inches	0.0	-1.2	-5.0	-11.4	-20.6

G1 Ballistic Coefficient = 0.172

Black Hills 230-grain JHP - Gold Dot (D45N5)

Distance - Yards	Muzzle	25	50	75	100
Velocity - fps	900	879	859	841	823
Energy - ft/lb	412	395	377	361	346
Taylor KO values	13.8	13.1	12.8	12.5	12.2
Mid-Range Trajectory Height - inches	0.0	0.3	1.4	3.2	5.9
Drop - inches	0.0	-1.4	-5.5	-12.6	-22.8

G1 Ballistic Coefficient = 0.165

Winchester 230-grain JHP (S45)

Distance - Yards	Muzzle	25	50	75	100
Velocity - fps	880	863	846	831	816
Energy - ft/lb	396	380	366	353	340
Taylor KO values	13.2	13.0	12.7	12.5	12.3
Mid-Range Trajectory Height - inches	0.0	0.3	1.5	3.4	6.1
Drop - inches	0.0	-1.4	-5.8	-13.1	-23.6

G1 Ballistic Coefficient = 0.192

Winchester 230-grain JHP (XSUB45A)

Distance - Yards	Muzzle	25	50	75	100
Velocity - fps	880	863	846	831	816
Energy - ft/lb	396	380	366	353	340
Taylor KO values	13.2	13.0	12.7	12.5	12.3
Mid-Range Trajectory Height - inches	0.0	0.3	1.5	3.4	6.1
Drop - inches	0.0	-1.4	-5.8	-13.1	-23.6

G1 Ballistic Coefficient = 0.192

Remington 230-grain Brass-JHP (GS45APB)

Distance - Yards	Muzzle	25	50	75	100
Velocity - fps	875	853	833	813	795
Energy - ft/lb	391	372	355	338	323
Taylor KO values	13.0	12.7	12.4	12.1	11.8
Mid-Range Trajectory Height - inches	0.0	0.3	1.5	3.4	6.1
Drop - inches	0.0	-1.4	-5.9	-13.4	-24.3

G1 Ballistic Coefficient = 0.148

Federal 230-grain Hi-Shok JHP (C45D)

Distance - Yards	Muzzle	25	50	75	100
Velocity - fps	850	830	810	790	770
Energy - ft/lb	370	350	335	320	305
Taylor KO values	12.6	12.3	12.0	11.7	11.4
Mid-Range Trajectory Height - inches	0.0	0.4	1.6	3.6	6.6
Drop - inches	0.0	-1.5	-6.2	-14.2	-25.8

G1 Ballistic Coefficient = 0.148

Federal 230-grain Hydra-Shok JHP (P45HS1)

Distance - Yards	Muzzle	25	50	75	100
Velocity - fps	850	830	810	790	770
Energy - ft/lb	370	350	335	320	305
Taylor KO values	12.6	12.3	12.0	11.7	11.4
Mid-Range Trajectory Height - inches	0.0	0.4	1.6	3.6	6.6
Drop - inches	0.0	-1.5	-6.2	-14.2	-25.8

G1 Ballistic Coefficient = 0.140

PMC 230-grain Starfire HP (45SFA)

Distance - Yards	Muzzle	25	50	75	100
Velocity - fps	850	830	811	792	775
Energy - ft/lb	369	352	336	321	307
Taylor KO values	12.6	12.3	12.0	11.8	11.5
Mid-Range Trajectory Height - inches	0.0	0.4	1.6	3.6	6.6
Drop - inches	0.0	-1.5	-6.2	-14.2	-25.6

G1 Ballistic Coefficient = 0.150

Remington 230-grain JHP (Subsonic) (R45AP7)

Distance - Yards	Muzzle	25	50	75	100
Velocity - fps	835	817	800	783	767
Energy - ft/lb	356	341	326	313	300
Taylor KO values	12.4	21.1	11.9	11.6	11.4
Mid-Range Trajectory Height - inches	0.0	0.4	1.6	3.7	6.8
Drop - inches	0.0	-1.6	-6.4	-14.6	-26.4

G1 Ballistic Coefficient = 0.160

Speer 230-grain Gold Dot (23966)

Distance - Yards	Muzzle	25	50	75	100
Velocity - fps	830	810	791	774	756
Energy - ft/lb	352	335	320	306	292
Taylor KO values	12.3	12.0	11.7	11.5	11.2
Mid-Range Trajectory Height - inches	0.0	0.4	1.7	3.8	6.9
Drop - inches	0.0	-1.6	-6.5	-14.9	-26.9

G1 Ballistic Coefficient = 0.145

PMC 230-grain FMJ (45A)

Distance - Yards	Muzzle	25	50	75	100
Velocity - fps	895	872	851	831	811
Energy - ft/lb	411	389	370	352	336
Taylor KO values	13.3	13.0	12.6	12.3	12.0
Mid-Range Trajectory Height - inches	0.0	0.3	1.4	3.3	6.0
Drop - inches	0.0	-11.4	-5.6	-12.8	-23.2

G1 Ballistic Coefficient = 0.149

Hansen 230-grain FMJ Military (HCC45A)

Distance - Yards	Muzzle	25	50	75	100
Velocity - fps	880	858	838	818	800
Energy - ft/lb	395	376	359	342	327
Taylor KO values	13.1	12.7	12.4	12.1	11.9
Mid-Range Trajectory Height - inches	0.0	0.3	1.5	3.4	6.2
Drop - inches	0.0	-1.4	-5.8	-13.3	-24.0

G1 Ballistic Coefficient = 0.149

Fiocchi 230-grain Metal Case (45A)

Distance - Yards	Muzzle	25	50	75	100
Velocity - fps	875	854	833	814	796
Energy - ft/lb	390	372	355	339	324
Taylor KO values	13.0	12.7	12.4	12.1	11.8
Mid-Range Trajectory Height - inches	0.0	0.3	1.5	3.4	6.3
Drop - inches	0.0	-1.4	-5.9	-13.4	-24.2

G1 Ballistic Coefficient = 0.150

American Eagle (Federal) 230-grain FMJ (AE45A)

Distance - Yards	Muzzle	25	50	75	100
Velocity - fps	850	830	810	790	770
Energy - ft/lb	370	350	335	320	305
Taylor KO values	12.6	12.3	12.0	11.7	11.4
Mid-Range Trajectory Height - inches	0.0	0.4	1.6	3.6	6.6
Drop - inches	0.0	-1.5	-6.2	-14.2	-25.8

G1 Ballistic Coefficient = 0.140

Black Hills 230-grain FMJ (D45N3)

Distance - Yards	Muzzle	25	50	75	100
Velocity - fps	850	830	811	793	775
Energy - ft/lb	368	352	336	321	307
Taylor KO values	12.6	12.3	12.0	11.8	11.5
Mid-Range Trajectory Height - inches	0.0	0.4	1.6	3.6	6.6
Drop - inches	0.0	-1.5	-6.2	-14.2	-25.6

G1 Ballistic Coefficient = 0.150

Federal 230-grain FMJ (C45A)

Distance - Yards	Muzzle	25	50	75	100
Velocity - fps	850	830	810	790	770
Energy - ft/lb	370	350	335	320	305
Taylor KO values	12.6	12.3	12.0	11.7	11.4
Mid-Range Trajectory Height - inches	0.0	0.4	1.6	3.6	6.6
Drop - inches	0.0	-1.5	-6.2	-14.2	-25.8

G1 Ballistic Coefficient = 0.140

Hornady 230-grain FMJ - Flat Point (9098)

Distance - Yards	Muzzle	25	50	75	100
Velocity - fps	850	829	809	790	771
Energy - ft/lb	369	351	334	319	304
Taylor KO values	12.6	12.3	12.0	11.7	11.4
Mid-Range Trajectory Height - inches	0.0	0.4	1.6	3.6	6.6
Drop - inches	0.0	-1.5	-6.2	-14.2	-25.7

G1 Ballistic Coefficient = 0.142

Hornady 230-grain FMJ - Round Nose (9397)

Distance - Yards	Muzzle	25	50	75	100
Velocity - fps	850	829	809	790	771
Energy - ft/lb	369	351	334	319	304
Taylor KO values	12.6	12.3	12.0	11.7	11.4
Mid-Range Trajectory Height - inches	0.0	0.4	1.6	3.6	6.6
Drop - inches	0.0	-1.5	-6.2	-14.2	-25.7

G1 Ballistic Coefficient = 0.142

CCI 230-grain FMJ (3570)

Distance - Yards	Muzzle	25	50	75	100
Velocity - fps	845	826	804	792	775
Energy - ft/lb	363	349	329	320	304
Taylor KO values	12.5	12.3	11.9	11.8	11.5
Mid-Range Trajectory Height - inches	0.0	0.4	1.6	3.6	6.6
Drop - inches	0.0	-1.5	-6.3	-14.3	-25.8

G1 Ballistic Coefficient = 0.160

CCI 230-grain Clean-Fire - FMJ (3480)

Distance - Yards	Muzzle	25	50	75	100
Velocity - fps	845	826	804	792	775
Energy - ft/lb	363	349	329	320	304
Taylor KO values	12.5	12.3	11.9	11.8	11.5
Mid-Range Trajectory Height - inches	0.0	0.4	1.6	3.6	6.6
Drop - inches	0.0	-1.5	-6.3	-14.3	-25.8

G1 Ballistic Coefficient = 0.160

Speer 230-grain FMJ (53967)

Distance - Yards	Muzzle	25	50	75	100
Velocity - fps	845	826	804	792	775
Energy - ft/lb	363	349	329	320	304
Taylor KO values	12.5	12.3	11.9	11.8	11.5
Mid-Range Trajectory Height - inches	0.0	0.4	1.6	3.6	6.6
Drop - inches	0.0	-1.5	-6.3	-14.3	-25.8

G1 Ballistic Coefficient = 0.160

Speer 230-grain Clean-Fire - FMJ (53885)

Distance - Yards	Muzzle	25	50	75	100
Velocity - fps	845	826	804	792	775
Energy - ft/lb	363	349	329	320	304
Taylor KO values	12.5	12.3	11.9	11.8	11.5
Mid-Range Trajectory Height - inches	0.0	0.4	1.6	3.6	6.6
Drop - inches	0.0	-1.5	-6.3	-14.3	-25.8

G1 Ballistic Coefficient = 0.160

Hornady 230-grain FMJ - Flat Point Vector (9097)

Distance - Yards	Muzzle	25	50	75	100
Velocity - fps	850	831	814	795	779
Energy - ft/lb	369	353	338	323	310
Taylor KO values	12.6	12.3	12.1	11.8	11.6
Mid-Range Trajectory Height - inches	0.0	0.4	1.6	3.6	6.6
Drop - inches	0.0	-1.5	-6.2	-14.2	-25.6

G1 Ballistic Coefficient = 0.158

Hansen 230-grain FMJ Match (HCC45E)

Distance - Yards	Muzzle	25	50	75	100
Velocity - fps	850	830	811	793	775
Energy - ft/lb	368	352	336	321	307
Taylor KO values	12.6	12.3	12.0	11.8	11.5
Mid-Range Trajectory Height - inches	0.0	0.4	1.6	3.6	6.6
Drop - inches	0.0	-1.5	-6.2	-14.2	-25.6

G1 Ballistic Coefficient = 0.150

Magtech 230-grain FMC (45A)

Distance - Yards	Muzzle	25	50	75	100
Velocity - fps	837	818	800	783	767
Energy - ft/lb	356	342	326	313	300
Taylor KO values	12.4	12.1	11.9	11.6	11.4
Mid-Range Trajectory Height - inches	0.0	0.4	1.6	3.7	6.8
Drop - inches	0.0	-1.6	-6.4	-14.6	-26.4

G1 Ballistic Coefficient = 0.155

Remington 230-grain Metal Case (Subsonic) (R45AP4)

Distance - Yards	Muzzle	25	50	75	100
Velocity - fps	835	817	800	783	767
Energy - ft/lb	356	341	326	313	300
Taylor KO values	12.4	21.1	11.9	11.6	11.4
Mid-Range Trajectory Height - inches	0.0	0.4	1.6	3.7	6.8
Drop - inches	0.0	-1.6	-6.4	-14.6	-26.4

G1 Ballistic Coefficient = 0.160

UMC (Remington) 230-grain Metal Case (L45AP4)

Distance - Yards	Muzzle	25	50	75	100
Velocity - fps	835	817	800	783	767
Energy - ft/lb	356	341	326	313	300
Taylor KO values	12.4	21.1	11.9	11.6	11.4
Mid-Range Trajectory Height - inches	0.0	0.4	1.6	3.7	6.8
Drop - inches	0.0	-1.6	-6.4	-14.6	-26.4

G1 Ballistic Coefficient = 0.160

USA (Winchester) 230-grain FMJ (Q4170)

Distance - Yards	Muzzle	25	50	75	100
Velocity - fps	835	817	800	783	767
Energy - ft/lb	356	341	326	313	300
Taylor KO values	12.4	21.1	11.9	11.6	11.4
Mid-Range Trajectory Height - inches	0.0	0.4	1.6	3.7	6.8
Drop - inches	0.0	-1.6	-6.4	-14.6	-26.4

G1 Ballistic Coefficient = 0.160

Winchester 230-grain Brass Enclosed Base (WC452)

Distance - Yards	Muzzle	25	50	75	100
Velocity - fps	835	818	802	786	771
Energy - ft/lb	356	342	329	315	303
Taylor KO values	12.6	12.3	12.1	11.8	11.6
Mid-Range Trajectory Height - inches	0.0	0.4	1.6	3.7	6.8
Drop - inches	0.0	-1.6	-6.4	-14.6	-26.3

G1 Ballistic Coefficient = 0.160

Magtech 230-grain Full Metal Case - Semi-Wadcutter (45B)

Distance - Yards	Muzzle	25	50	75	100
Velocity - fps	780	747	720	687	660
Energy - ft/lb	310	285	265	241	220
Taylor KO values	11.6	11.1	10.7	10.2	9.8
Mid-Range Trajectory Height - inches	0.0	0.4	1.8	4.6	7.8
Drop - inches	0.0	-1.8	-7.6	-17.5	-32.1

G1 Ballistic Coefficient = 0.076

.45 Smith & Wesson Schofield

The .45 Schofield is a cartridge that had nearly disappeared into the mists of obsolescence, only to have been given a new life by the introduction of Cowboy Action shooting. It was introduced in 1875 as a competitor for the .45 Colt. The Schofield is about 0.2 inches shorter than the .45 Colt, otherwise very nearly identical in dimensions. For a while in the 1870s, the Army had both guns and both calibers of ammunition in the inventory. Can you imagine how many units got the wrong ammunition ?

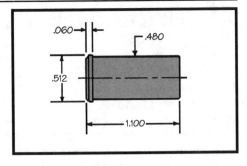

Relative Recoil Factor = 0.76

Controlling Agency: Factory

Standard barrel for velocity testing:
6 inches long - 1 turn in 12 inch twist

Cowboy Action Loads

Black Hills 180-grain SP (DCB45SCHON2)

Distance - Yards	Muzzle	25	50	75	100
Velocity - fps	730	713	696	680	665
Energy - ft/lb	213	203	195	185	177
Taylor KO values	8.6	8.4	8.2	8.0	7.8
Mid-Range Trajectory Height - inches	0.0	0.5	2.1	4.9	9.0
Drop - inches	0.0	-2.1	-8.4	-19.2	-34.8

G1 Ballistic Coefficient = 0.135

Black Hills 230-grain SP (DCB45SCHON1)

Distance - Yards	Muzzle	25	50	75	100
Velocity - fps	730	715	700	685	671
Energy - ft/lb	272	261	250	240	230
Taylor KO values	10.9	10.7	10.5	10.3	10.1
Mid-Range Trajectory Height - inches	0.0	0.5	2.1	4.9	8.9
Drop - inches	0.0	-2.1	-8.4	-19.2	-34.5

G1 Ballistic Coefficient = 0.150

.45 Colt (Often called .45 Long Colt)

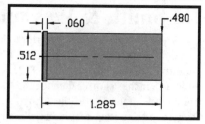

The name of this cartridge is interesting. It is often called .45 Long Colt or .45 Colt Long. Neither name is correct because there never was a .45 Short Colt. The name that gets used today relates to the .45 S&W Schofield. The .45 Colt was adopted by the Army in 1873 for the legendary Colt Single Action Army revolver. That made it the first centerfire pistol round in the US inventory. A couple years later the Army adopted the .45 S&W Schofield in a Smith & Wesson revolver as an alternate. That put the Army in the position of having two very similar rounds in the inventory at the same time. Guaranteed chaos. The .45 Schofield would fit the Colt revolver but the Colt ammo wouldn't fit the Smith. Besides, the quartermasters in outfits that used the Colt revolver didn't want any of that shorter ammo (thought of as inferior). They were careful to specify .45 Colt (LONG) when they ordered ammo. While the standard factory ammo is pretty mild by today's standards (because there are still a lot of very old guns in circulation) the advent of Cowboy Action shooting is adding new life to this great old cartridge.

Relative Recoil Factor = 0.45   **Controlling Agency: SAAMI**

Bullet Weight Grains	Velocity fps	Maximum Average Pressure Copper Crusher	Transducer	Standard barrel for velocity testing:
225 STHP	915	14,000 cup	14,000 psi	4 inches long [vented]
225 SWC	950	14,000 cup	14,000 psi	- 1 turn in 16 inch twist
250-255 L	900	14,000 cup	14,000 psi	

CCI 200-grain JHP (3584)

Distance - Yards	Muzzle	25	50	75	100
Velocity - fps	1000	968	938	913	889
Energy - ft/lb	444	416	391	370	351
Taylor KO values	13.0	12.6	12.2	11.9	11.6
Mid-Range Trajectory Height - inches	0.0	0.3	1.3	2.7	4.8
Drop - inches	0.0	-1.1	-4.5	-10.4	-18.9

G1 Ballistic Coefficient = 0.150

Remington 225-grain Semi-Wadcutter [Kieth] (R45C1)

Distance - Yards	Muzzle	25	50	75	100
Velocity - fps	960	923	890	859	832
Energy - ft/lb	460	425	395	369	346
Taylor KO values	14.1	13.5	13.0	12.6	12.2
Mid-Range Trajectory Height - inches	0.0	0.3	1.3	3.0	5.5
Drop - inches	0.0	-1.2	-5.0	-11.5	-20.9

G1 Ballistic Coefficient = 0.110

Winchester 225-grain Silvertip HP (X45CSHP2)

Distance - Yards	Muzzle	25	50	75	100
Velocity - fps	920	898	877	857	839
Energy - ft/lb	423	403	384	367	352
Taylor KO values	13.5	13.2	12.9	12.6	12.3
Mid-Range Trajectory Height - inches	0.0	0.3	1.4	3.1	5.6
Drop - inches	0.0	-1.3	-5.3	-12.1	-21.9

G1 Ballistic Coefficient = 0.165

Federal 225-grain JHP (45CLCA)

Distance - Yards	Muzzle	25	50	75	100
Velocity - fps	900	880	860	840	820
Energy - ft/lb	405	385	370	355	340
Taylor KO values	13.2	12.9	12.6	12.3	12.0
Mid-Range Trajectory Height - inches	0.0	0.3	1.4	3.2	5.8
Drop - inches	0.0	-1.4	-5.5	-12.7	-22.9

G1 Ballistic Coefficient = 0.159

Remington 250-grain Lead (R45C)

Distance - Yards	Muzzle	25	50	75	100
Velocity - fps	860	838	820	798	780
Energy - ft/lb	410	390	375	354	340
Taylor KO values	14.0	13.6	13.4	13.0	12.7
Mid-Range Trajectory Height - inches	0.0	0.4	1.6	3.6	6.6
Drop - inches	0.0	-1.5	-6.1	-13.9	-25.2

G1 Ballistic Coefficient = 0.152

Winchester 255-grain Lead-Round Nose (X45CP2)

Distance - Yards	Muzzle	25	50	75	100
Velocity - fps	860	838	820	798	780
Energy - ft/lb	420	398	380	361	344
Taylor KO values	14.3	13.9	13.6	133.3	13.0
Mid-Range Trajectory Height - inches	0.0	0.4	1.5	3.5	6.1
Drop - inches	0.0	-1.5	-6.1	-13.9	-25.2

G1 Ballistic Coefficient = 0.153

Cowboy Action Loads

Magtech 250-grain Lead Flate Nose (45D)

Distance - Yards	Muzzle	25	50	75	100
Velocity - fps	750	733	717	702	687
Energy - ft/lb	312	299	286	274	262
Taylor KO values	12.3	12.0	11.7	11.5	11.2
Mid-Range Trajectory Height - inches	0.0	0.4	2.0	4.6	8.0
Drop - inches	0.0	-2.0	-8.0	-18.2	-32.8

G1 Ballistic Coefficient = 0.145

Black Hills 250-grain Round Nose Flat Point (DCB45CLTN1)

Distance - Yards	Muzzle	25	50	75	100
Velocity - fps	725	709	693	677	663
Energy - ft/lb	292	279	267	255	244
Taylor KO values	11.8	11.5	11.3	11.0	10.8
Mid-Range Trajectory Height - inches	0.0	0.5	2.2	5.0	9.1
Drop - inches	0.0	-2.1	-8.5	-19.5	-35.2

G1 Ballistic Coefficient = 0.140

PMC 250-grain Lead Flat Point (45LA)

Distance - Yards	Muzzle	25	50	75	100
Velocity - fps	800	783	767	751	736
Energy - ft/lb	355	341	331	313	309
Taylor KO values	13.0	12.8	12.5	12.2	12.0
Mid-Range Trajectory Height - inches	0.0	0.4	1.8	4.1	7.4
Drop - inches	0.0	-1.7	-7.0	-15.9	-28.8

G1 Ballistic Coefficient = 0.158

Hornady 255-grain Cowboy (9115)

Distance - Yards	Muzzle	25	50	75	100
Velocity - fps	725	708	692	676	660
Energy - ft/lb	298	284	271	259	247
Taylor KO values	12.0	11.8	11.5	11.2	11.0
Mid-Range Trajectory Height - inches	0.0	0.5	2.2	5.0	9.1
Drop - inches	0.0	-2.1	-8.5	-19.5	-35.2

G1 Ballistic Coefficient = 0.134

.45 Winchester Magnum

In 1979, Winchester introduced their .45 Winchester Magnum cartridge. The round was intended for the gas-operated Wildey pistol. The buying public never took to the Wildey gun but the cartridge was a real performer. At the time of its introduction it was the most powerful pistol cartridge in the inventory. While the .45 Casull and the .50 Action Express have pushed it out of first place in the power derby, the .45 Win. Mag. is still a very potent pistol round. It makes a great hunting cartridge in the single-shot, long-barrel pistols.

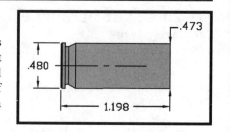

Relative Recoil Factor = 0.1.46   **Controlling Agency: SAAMI**

Bullet Weight Grains	Velocity fps	Maximum Average Pressure		Standard barrel for velocity testing:
		Copper Crusher	Transducer	
230 MC	1380	40,000 cup	N/S	5 inches long - 1 turn in 16 inch twist

Winchester 260-grain Partition Gold (SPG45WM)

Distance - Yards	Muzzle	25	50	75	100
Velocity - fps	1200	1149	1105	1066	1033
Energy - ft/lb	832	762	705	656	617
Taylor KO values	20.1	19.3	18.6	17.9	17.3
Mid-Range Trajectory Height - inches	0.0	0.2	0.8	1.9	3.5
Drop - inches	0.0	-0.8	-3.2	-7.4	-13.5

G1 Ballistic Coefficient = 0.190

Winchester 260-grain JHP (X45MWA)

Distance - Yards	Muzzle	25	50	75	100
Velocity - fps	1200	1146	1099	1060	1026
Energy - ft/lb	831	758	698	649	607
Taylor KO values	20.4	19.5	18.7	18.0	17.5
Mid-Range Trajectory Height - inches	0.0	0.2	0.8	1.9	3.5
Drop - inches	0.0	-0.8	-3.2	-7.4	-13.6

G1 Ballistic Coefficient = 0.180

.454 Casull

If you look carefully at their dimensions, the .454 Casull is really a long version of the .45 Colt (which is often called Long Colt). The Casull is 0.100 inch longer but the real performance improvement comes from using chamber pressures that approach 50,000 psi. The .454 Casull is one of just a few cartridges factory manufactured in the US that have not been standardized by either SAAMI or CIP (the European agency). If a milder loading is desired, .45 Colt ammunition can be fired in .454 Casull chambers. The result is pretty much the same as firing .38 Special in a .357 Magnum.

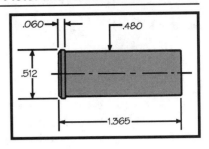

Relative Recoil Factor = 2.20

Controlling Agency: Factory

Standard barrel for velocity testing:

7.5 inches long [Vented] - 1 turn in N/S inch twist

Winchester 250-grain Jacketed Flat Point (X454C3)

Distance - Yards	Muzzle	25	50	75	100
Velocity - fps	1300	1220	1151	1094	1047
Energy - ft/lb	938	826	735	665	608
Taylor KO values	22.1	20.8	19.6	18.6	17.8
Mid-Range Trajectory Height - inches	0.0	0.2	0.8	0.8	3.2
Drop - inches	0.0	-0.7	-2.8	-6.6	-12.2

G1 Ballistic Coefficient = 0.146

Winchester 260-grain Jacketed Flat Point (X454C11)

Distance - Yards	Muzzle	25	50	75	100
Velocity - fps	1800	1686	1577	1476	1381
Energy - ft/lb	1871	1641	1436	1258	1101
Taylor KO values	30.2	28.3	26.5	24.8	23.2
Mid-Range Trajectory Height - inches	0.0	0.1	0.4	0.9	1.8
Drop - inches	0.0	-0.4	-1.5	-3.5	-6.4

G1 Ballistic Coefficient = 0.153

Winchester 300-grain Jacketed Flat Point (X454C22)

Distance - Yards	Muzzle	25	50	75	100
Velocity - fps	1625	1538	1451	1380	1308
Energy - ft/lb	1759	1577	1413	1268	1141
Taylor KO values	31.5	29.8	28.1	26.7	25.3
Mid-Range Trajectory Height - inches	0.0	0.1	0.5	1.1	2.0
Drop - inches	0.0	-0.4	-1.8	-4.1	-7.6

G1 Ballistic Coefficient = 0.186

.50 Action Express

This is the current "big boomer" of the pistol rounds. The .50 Action Express, which was introduced in 1991, packs about the same muzzle energy as a .30-30 with much higher Taylor KO values. This is because the .50 AE pushes a much heavier bullet at a lower velocity. This is one of those calibers for the macho pistol shooter. Like the .44 Remington Magnum and the .454 Casull, there are few shooters who can shoot the .50 AE really well. The .50 AE cartridge chambered into a carbine-style gun would make an interesting deer rifle for brushy hunting conditions where long shots aren't normally encountered.

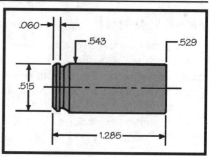

Relative Recoil Factor = 2.05   **Controlling Agency: SAAMI**

Bullet Weight Grains	Velocity fps	Maximum Average Pressure		Standard barrel for velocity testing:
		Copper Crusher	Transducer	
300 PHP	1400	N/S	35,000 psi	6 inches long - 1 turn in 20 inch twist

Hansen 300-grain JSP "Combat" (HCC50C)

Distance - Yards	Muzzle	25	50	75	100
Velocity - fps	1195	1121	1061	1013	973
Energy - ft/lb	951	837	750	694	631
Taylor KO values	27.1	25.4	24.1	23.0	22.1
Mid-Range Trajectory Height - inches	0.0	0.2	0.9	2.1	3.8
Drop - inches	0.0	-0.8	-3.3	-7.8	-14.3

G1 Ballistic Coefficient = 0.125

Hansen 300-grain JHP (HCC50B)

Distance - Yards	Muzzle	25	50	75	100
Velocity - fps	1195	1118	1057	1008	967
Energy - ft/lb	951	833	744	677	623
Taylor KO values	27.1	25.2	24.0	22.9	21.9
Mid-Range Trajectory Height - inches	0.0	0.2	0.9	2.1	3.9
Drop - inches	0.0	-0.8	-3.3	-7.8	-14.4

G1 Ballistic Coefficient = 0.120

Speer 325-grain Gold Dot (3977)

Distance - Yards	Muzzle	25	50	75	100
Velocity - fps	1400	1299	1209	1136	1075
Energy - ft/lb	1414	1217	1055	932	834
Taylor KO values	34.4	31.9	29.7	27.9	26.4
Mid-Range Trajectory Height - inches	0.0	0.1	0.2	1.6	2.3
Drop - inches	0.0	-0.6	-2.5	-5.8	-10.8

G1 Ballistic Coefficient = 0.131

THE .22 RIMFIRE: REALLY OLD, REALLY GOOD!

by
Wayne van Zwoll

The best isn't always the biggest or the newest. Among rifle cartridges, one of the smallest and mildest rounds remains one of the most popular after more than a century. The accuracy, economy, and versatility of the .22 Long Rifle has made it an all-time best-seller. Its quiet report and low recoil, as well as the trim rifles and pistols in which it is chambered, keep it chugging along while more potent center-fires come and go.

The .22 rimfire clan is so old that it makes the .30-30 look like a newcomer. These diminutive cartridges first popped up just before the Civil War, but their origin dates to the beginning of the eighteenth century, when chemists discovered fulminates—compounds that detonated under a sharp blow. For the next 100 years, that discovery was of no benefit to shooters. Then, in 1807, Scottish clergyman Alexander John Forsyth patented the application of percussion ignition to firearms. Seven years later, an immigrant sea captain named Joshua Shaw devised a percussion cap in his Philadelphia shop. After that, the race to perfect and market internal ignition accelerated as fast as flintlocks were becoming obsolete. By the time Shaw had discarded steel and pewter caps in favor of copper, flint shooters were ready for the quicker, more reliable percussion spark.

To modern marksmen, designing a mechanism to fire fulminates seems a simple task. It was not. Many inventors spent many years deciding where to put the sensitive charge, then building guns around their ideas. In 1808, a Geneva gunmaker named

Pauly devised a paper percussion cap that fired when pierced by a long-nosed pin. Because of the internal location of the priming charge, this seemed a prudent notion even after Shaw's copper cap came along. Lefaucheux's breechloading "pinfire," with the firing pin set inside the cartridge at right angles to its axis, evolved from the Pauly gun in 1836. Two years later, Dreyse of Sommerda introduced a unique breechloading "needle gun," in

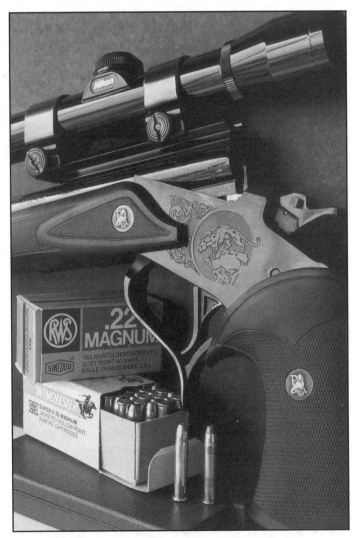

Thompson-Center's popular Contender handgun is chambered in .22 Long Rifle and .22 Magnum. Interchangeable barrels add versatility.

which the firing pin penetrated the paper case and powder charge to strike the fulminate on a shot wad or bullet base.

Much of the early work on breechloading guns should be called cartridge development because inventors were trying to build mechanisms that would accommodate paper cases and to find better case material at the same time. First used in the late sixteenth century, paper cases were vulnerable to moisture, varied in dimension, bent or broke if forced by steel parts, and played no part in containing breech pressures. When percussion caps became available, LePage, a Frenchman, tried to fit one to a paper case. The primer and its thick wad proved too difficult to extract after firing. Shortly thereafter, in 1847, a Parisian named Houllier fashioned a metal case for use in Lefaucheux's pinfire gun. The metal slid smoothly into the chamber, expanded on firing to help seal gas, and extracted easily. About this time in the U.S., Steven Taylor patented a hollow-base bullet housing its own powder charge. A perforated end cap admitted sparks from an outside primer. A year later, Walter Hunt developed a similar bullet with cork sealing the base. Hunt, a New Yorker who was over 50 years old at the time, had impressive credentials as an inventor, but no interest in business. He developed but did not patent a lockstitch needle that would spawn the sewing machine. His inventions ranged from stoves to the safety pin.

Hunt's "rocket ball" cartridge was really only one step on the road to a more ambitious goal. In 1849 the prolific inventor was awarded a patent for an ingenious breechloading rifle: the "Volitional" repeater, but he lacked money to further develop it. Fellow New Yorker George Arrowsmith

chipped in with some cash and business savvy, hiring skilled gun mechanic Lewis Jennings to troubleshoot the complex rifle. The brilliantly conceived tubular magazine and delicate pill-lock primer advance had glaring weaknesses, but by year's end Jennings had made several improvements. He assigned patent rights to Arrowsmith, who had decided to sell the rifle. Arrowsmith found a buyer in Courtlandt Palmer, a leading New York hardware merchant and financier. Palmer paid $100,000 for all rights and immediately sought a manufacturer to assemble 5,000 guns so he could recoup his investment. The Vermont firm of Robbins & Lawrence contracted to build the

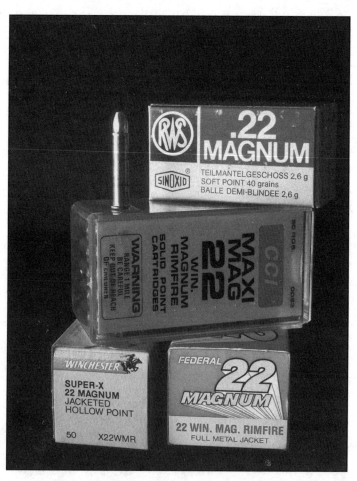

The .22 WMR (Winchester Magnum Rimfire) is a third faster than the .22 Long rifle, but is also more expensive, less widely chambered, and not nearly as popular.

Hunt-Jennings repeater. Soon the project unveiled several problems. Company mechanic Horace Smith solved some, but by completion of the contracted production run in 1851, many flaws remained. In fact, feeding inconsistencies prompted Robbins & Lawrence to modify the mechanism slightly and market part of the run as single-shots!

That year a Washington dentist, Dr. Edward Maynard, introduced a cylindrical brass cartridge case with a wide, flat base soldered to one end. There was a hole in the middle of the base. Maynard's own "tape primer," advanced on a spool, shot sparks through this hole to ignite the main powder charge. Previously the tape primer had been used on an external nipple, the sparks blasting into paper or linen cases; later it was resurrected for use in toy cap guns. Maynard's case had an advantage over Hunt's rocket ball: It came out after firing, leaving no base wad residue in the bore. It could also be made in any size to hold more powder.

Meanwhile, sales of Hunt-Jennings rifles were so slow that Palmer decided not to build more, and there the project might have died. But in 1852 Horace Smith met Daniel Wesson while both were working at the Massachusetts plant of Allen, Brown, and Luther. They discussed an alternative to the Volitional repeater. Wesson, who had studied the work of French gun designer Flobert, considered using Flobert's self-contained ammunition in the Hunt-Jennings mechanism. Seating a ball atop a metallic primer, Flobert had produced ammunition that worked in French parlor pistols. Incorporating the primer in the case would eliminate the repeater's troublesome primer feed. Adding powder in a case longer than Flobert's would adapt the idea to repeating rifles.

Smith and Wesson explored this idea with Palmer's backing. Patents issued to Flobert in 1846 and 1849 limited the partners in their work, but by 1853 they had patented a disc to cover the priming compound in such a cartridge. The disc would also serve as an anvil against which the fulminate could be pinched by the blow of the striker. Two weeks after that filing, Smith and Wesson sought patents on an extractor for the Flobert-style case and a cocking mechanism that readied the hammer on the bolt's rearward travel.

The first guns built for Smith and Wesson's new cartridge were pistols, partly because the small size of the case was most suitable for short ranges and partly because the Hunt-Jennings rifle had become a public failure. The pistols must not have worked well because none of the 250 built in 1853 and 1854 are known to exist. The partners adapted a few to a modified rocket ball that featured a fulminate of mercury primer in a glass cap in the cork cap's inner face. The cap rested on an iron anvil. However, cork crumbs remained in the bore after firing, and the cork cushioned the striker, sometimes causing misfires.

Although Smith and Wesson found the Flobert-style cartridge hard to make, they considered it to be the most promising of any design in their day. By 1857 they were working on it again, and later that year designed what we still know as the .22 Short. Its case was made much as it is now: A disc punched from thin sheet metal was drawn into a tube with one closed end. Next, a rim was "bumped" onto that end, and the fold filled from the inside with fulminate of mercury. This fulminate exploded when the case rim was crushed against the chamber by the striker. Smith and Wesson adapted the cartridge to a new revolver and went on to establish a revolver company. But that .22 rimfire round proved to be one of their most important contributions to the firearms industry. It became the prototype for a tide of rimfire rounds during the 1860s. The .44 Henry cartridge in a modified Hunt-Jennings rifle and the huge .56 Spencer in another repeater brought battle to a deadlier level in the Civil War. These and other rimfires fueled the development of repeating rifles and new companies like Winchester Repeating Arms.

By 1900, 75 rimfire cartridges had been loaded by American ammunition firms. But center-fire priming and smokeless powder eventually killed off many big rimfire rounds. The thin, soft, folded head of a rimfire case could not contain the pressures bottled in a center-fire with a solid case head. By the end of World War I, Remington was listing only 32 rimfires; by the middle of the Great Depression Winchester was down to 17. Now only a handful of rimfire cartridges remain, and most are .22s.

The smallest .22 is the BB Cap (BB for "bullet breech"). It is essentially the Flobert round that prompted Smith and Wesson to experiment with bigger cases. Several American companies loaded the BB Cap until World War II, but now I believe it is marketed only by the German firm of RWS. Intended for indoor target shooting, BB Caps launch bullets of 16 grains at 750 fps, for a muzzle energy of 26 foot/pounds. They can penetrate up to an inch of soft pine at close range. Conical bullets replaced the original round ball before U.S. ammunition firms dropped this cartridge, but it still packs only one fifth the energy of a .22 Long Rifle.

The .22 CB ("conical bullet") cap is a grownup BB Cap, born in 1888. The original loading called for a 29-grain .22 Short bullet in a BB Cap case, with a pinch of black powder.

You don't have to worry about flinching when you're around a .22. This young rifleman is learning how to zero from a bench.

But most CB Cap cases were longer than the BB Cap's. Still loaded by RWS, the CB Cap has about the same velocity as its little brother, but gets 10 foot/pounds more energy because of the heavier bullet.

The .22 Short that Smith and Wesson pioneered was initially charged with four grains of black powder. In 1887 it became available with semismokeless powder, to be followed shortly by a smokeless loading. Remington announced "Kleanbore" priming for the .22 Short in 1927, several years after German cartridges had first featured "rostfrei" (rust-free) noncorrosive priming. All ammunition companies that load rimfire rounds still list the .22 Short today. Its

The .22 Long Rifle is as popular with pistoleers as with riflemen. This hunter hefts a Kansas cottontail and a Model 18 Smith & Wesson.

high-speed 29-grain solid bullet leaves a rifle muzzle at 1,125 fps, high-speed hollowpoints fractionally faster. Energy is about 80 foot/pounds. A 15-grain gallery load chronographs at 1,750 fps.

When I was a shy lad ogling gingham-skirted girls at county fairs, I lost a lot of quarters at shooting booths, trying to punch diamonds out of cards with battered Remington pump guns so I could win a teddy bear and a girl. The bears were dusty enough to have perched above those galleries for months. I've since determined that you can't draw three .22 bullet holes on one of those diamonds without missing a corner.

But I digress. Some shooters claim that the .22 Long derived from a marriage of the Short bullet and the Long Rifle case. They're half right. The bullets and cases do check out dimensionally. But the Long, introduced in 1871, predated the Long Rifle by 16 years. The .22 Long's original loading of five grains of black powder gave its 29-grain bullet a little more sauce than the Short, though the difference did not pull the Long past its parent in the market. A high-speed .22 Long now generates 1,240 fps and 99 ft-lb from a rifle. It is generally considered less accurate than the .22 Long Rifle; surely it is less powerful. Like the .22 Short, it can be used in many rifles built primarily for the Long Rifle. However, I don't know of any rifles chambered specifically for the .22 Long, and few gun shops now carry the ammunition.

The proliferation of special-purpose Long Rifle loads for hunting and competition has all but killed off the .22 Long. Announced in 1887, the .22 Long Rifle was first loaded with a 40-grain bullet in front of five grains of black powder. Semismokeless and smokeless loads followed quickly, as did a crimp for the heeled bullet. Peters is said to have been the first manufacturer to list this cartridge; Remington is credited with the first high-velocity load (in 1930). For as long as I can remember, high-speed solids from the .22 Long Rifle have been leaving rifles at 1335 fps, delivering 158 ft-lb at the muzzle. That's twice the energy claimed by the .22 Short, and 60 percent more than you'll get with the Long. Flatter flight is a bonus, with listed drop of 3.3 inches at 100 yards, given a 75-yard zero. The Short bullet drops 4.3 inches, the Long bullet 3.8. Long Rifle bullets I've shot don't quite meet factory specs. High-speed ammunition from three manufacturers recently averaged 1247 fps from a 22-inch barrel over my Oehler screens. I have no recent data for Short and Long cartridges, but I expect a similar discrepancy. Incidentally, rifles chambered in .22 Long Rifle are generally given a 1-in-16 rifling twist, while .22 Short barrels are commonly rifled 1-in-24. Button rifling is by far the most common type in .22 rimfire guns.

Compared to center-fire varmint cartridges, any .22 rimfire looks puny. The blunt lead bullets, which may be plated, waxed, or greased to prevent barrel leading, have low ballistic coefficients—.083 for the 29-grain Short and .115 for the 40-grain Long Rifle. (Compare those figures with .400 for a sleek hunting bullet from a .270 or .30-06.) Wind blows .22 rimfire bullets around like scraps of newspaper. Gentle, oblique puffs of air, loafing across the range during a match, have kicked my bullets three inches out at 100 yards. Higher speeds are not the answer; extra velocity is only a benefit if it can be sustained. Low ballistic coefficient guarantees a quick deceleration, and "hyper-velocity" Long Rifle rounds that look good on ballistics charts get much of their speed from lighter bullets with low ballistic coefficients. Besides, match bullets must be loaded modestly to keep them subsonic. Accuracy suffers when bullets break the sound barrier.

Whatever their shortcomings, the .22 rimfires still have a lot going for them. First, they're inexpensive. Someone once wrote that a disadvantage of rimfires is that you cannot reload them. That may be a disadvantage for someone with a .44 Henry. But with cartridges at two or three cents a round, why would you want to reload? Even if you could reassemble rimfires, you'd hardly achieve the accuracy of top-grade match ammunition (the best rifles can put

competition-class bullets into quarter-inch groups at 50 yards all day long). You might not even equal the accuracy of the least expensive plinking loads.

Another credit for the .22 rimfire is its light report and recoil. The older I get, the more I like gentle rifles. And lots of places with good small-game hunting are on farms where noise, reach, and penetration can be liabilities. However, the standard caution about safe backstops still applies to rimfires. A .22 Long Rifle bullet will travel over 1600 yards if you elevate the gun 31 degrees. A .22 Short bullet will go 1200. Each will be clocking over 200 fps when it noses into the ground or anything else it finds. Because of its construction and relatively low velocity, a .22 bullet will also ricochet more readily than one from a center-fire varmint gun.

Still another, often-overlooked benefit of the .22 rimfire is how it treats your rifle's bore. The small powder charges and low bullet speeds won't erode rifling. The spartan dose of priming mix and fast-burning powder leaves little bore residue. Because they are not moving at high speed (compared to center-fire varmint and big-game bullets), rimfire bullets need not wear jackets that can coat the bore with copper fouling. The thin plating, grease, and wax typically used on the rimfires actually helps preserve the bore. While I clean my .22 match rifle frequently during competition to guarantee gilt-edge accuracy, I usually leave the bores of sporting .22s alone for a year unless they get wet. An annual cleaning seems enough. More frequent brushings just subject the bore to more friction from the cleaning rod and attachments.

The most versatile of .22 rimfires is surely the Long Rifle. This classic round is even better in some ways than the more potent and now-defunct .22 Special and that recent (1960s) scorcher, the .22 Winchester Magnum Rimfire (WMR). The .22 WMR shoots a 40-grain bullet at 2000 fps from a case that is longer but in other respects the same as the .22 Long Rifle hull. This mighty little round makes more noise than the Long Rifle and costs several times as much to shoot. It is available in nowhere near as many rifles and handguns.

A surprising number of load and bullet combinations are offered in .22 Long Rifle ammo. For hunting squirrels in the October beech woods, where you can make a head or lung shot, the standard- or high-velocity

Prairie dogs are challenging game for .22 rimfires, with their practical effective range of less than 100 yards.

rounds with solid bullets usually suffice. The slightly more expensive hollowpoints work best if you're walking up rabbits and taking body shots. Hollowpoints are more destructive than solids, so you'll lose more meat, but quick kills should be the first priority. New "hyper-velocity" rounds with lightweight hollowpoints kill with authority at normal ranges. Some feature scored noses that erupt violently and fragment in soft tissue. These bullets are a good choice for shooting in areas where penetration or ricocheting could be dangerous.

It is sometimes a good idea to trade a little snap for smaller groups, even when you're hunting. Match-grade .22 ammunition not only churns up less energy, it costs more than high-speed fodder, but it affords greater precision. Pairing it with a medium-weight competition gun should give you half-inch accuracy at 50 yards. You can pick up heavier Winchester 52s and Remington 37 and 40x rifles second-hand, trim them down to field dimensions, and use them both for hunting and for metallic silhouette competition. Their fine triggers are worth as much as their exceptional barrels. Over the last decade a cottage industry has developed around the Ruger 10/22 autoloading rifle, which gunshops rebarrel with a heavy, high-quality tube. Special stocks and trigger jobs make the best of these rifles not only competition-worthy, but expensive. They are also fine hunting rifles. Classy alternatives of entirely different style are the traditional lever-actions produced by Marlin (on its Model 39) mechanism and Winchester (on its 9422 frame).

For most hunting, sporting-weight .22s are sufficiently accurate. I grew up shooting barn rats in Michigan with a lovely Remington 121. Later I used a prewar

Winchester 52A with a 10x Fecker scope to shoot hundreds of alfalfa-chomping ground squirrels in eastern Oregon. My most memorable game shot with a .22 killed a crow at 147 paces. The rifle was a Browning lever-action with a receiver sight. Although one hit proves neither equipment nor ability, it is easy to shoot well with a .22. Both rifles and handguns behave civilly. You're less likely to horse the trigger or flinch than with a more violent centerfire. Besides, the .22 rimfire cartridges are so inexpensive that you can shoot a lot. Practice, and not bullet speed, barrel quality, or optics, is the key to better target shooting and small-game hunting.

No matter which rifle or handgun you choose, hunting with a .22 will hone your stalking skills as well as your shooting and wind-doping abilities. If you're a bit gray around the edges like I am, it might bring you memories of cottontails or fox squirrels from seasons long past, of hunters who cannot be with you anymore. And it might remind you how much fun it was to put a hole in a soda can, or get really close to your quarry. The .22 rimfires are a piece of American history, gentle rounds that shoot straight and kill efficiently for any marksman or hunter bold enough to embrace their limitations. They don't have to reach 400 yards. They've already spanned more than a century.

Data for

.22 Rimfire Ammunition

This section covers .22 Rimfire ammunition in its various forms. While some of this ammunition is used primarily in pistols, the SAAMI specifications for all .22 Rimfire variations call for testing in 24-inch barrels. Some manufacturers also report performance in pistol-length barrels, but because this data is completely unstandardized in terms of barrel lengths used, the results can not be used for any meaningful comparison. The data below is confined to values obtained in standard 24-inch barrel.

There's an interesting situation regarding some brands of match and training ammunition. These manufacturers make their match and training ammo on the same production line, using identical components, the same everything. In fact, they don't know which grade they are making until it is tested, then the best becomes the match grade. Quite often the ammo is so good that there's more match quality ammo than can be sold so the excess supply simply becomes the training grade. It could be just as good as the match-quality grade but of course there's no guarantee. There is at least one manufacturer that makes three grades on the same line.

.22 Short

The .22 Short has the distinction of being the cartridge that has been in continuous production for longer than any other. Introduced in 1857 (loaded with black powder, of course) the short today has been relegated, for the most part, to specialized applications.

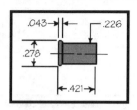

Relative Recoil Factor = 0.13   **Controlling Agency: SAAMI**

Bullet Weight Grains	Velocity fps	Maximum Average Pressure		Standard barrel for velocity testing:
		Copper Crusher	Transducer	
29 CB	710	N/S	21,000 psi	24 inches long - 1 turn in 16 inch twist
29 SV	1035	N/S	21,000 psi	
27 HP	1105	N/S	21,000 psi	
29 HV	1080	N/S	21,000 psi	

CCI 27-grain Short HP (0028)

Distance - Yards	Muzzle	25	50	75	100
Velocity - fps	1164	1062	1013	960	920
Energy - ft/lb	81	73	62	57	50
Path - inches	-1.5	2.0	3.5	3.0	0.0
Wind Drift - inches	0.0	0.4	1.6	3.4	5.8

G1 Ballistic Coefficient = 0.105

CCI 27-grain Short High Speed Solid (0027)

Distance - Yards	Muzzle	25	50	75	100
Velocity - fps	1132	1060	1004	959	920
Energy - ft/lb	83	72	65	59	54
Path - inches	-1.5	2.0	3.6	3.0	0.0
Wind Drift - inches	0.0	0.4	1.6	3.4	5.8

G1 Ballistic Coefficient = 0.105

Remington 29-grain Short Solid (1022)

Distance - Yards	Muzzle	25	50	75	100
Velocity - fps	1095	1032	981	939	903
Energy - ft/lb	77	69	62	57	52
Path - inches	-1.5	2.2	3.8	3.1	0.0
Wind Drift - inches	0.0	0.4	1.4	3.2	5.4

G1 Ballistic Coefficient = 0.105

Winchester 29-grain Short Standard Velocity Solid (X22S)

Distance - Yards	Muzzle	25	50	75	100
Velocity - fps	1095	1032	981	939	903
Energy - ft/lb	77	69	62	57	52
Path - inches	-1.5	2.2	3.8	3.1	0.0
Wind Drift - inches	0.0	0.4	1.4	3.2	5.4

G1 Ballistic Coefficient = 0.105

CCI 29-grain Short Target Solid (0037)

Distance - Yards	Muzzle	25	50	75	100
Velocity - fps	830	792	752	725	695
Energy - ft/lb	44	40	36	34	31
Path - inches	-1.5	4.4	6.8	5.5	0.0
Wind Drift - inches	0.0	0.4	1.5	3.4	6.1

G1 Ballistic Coefficient = 0.074

CCI 29-grain Short CB Solid (0026)

Distance - Yards	Muzzle	25	50	75	100
Velocity - fps	727	696	667	638	610
Energy - ft/lb	33	31	28	26	24
Path - inches	-1.5	6.0	9.1	7.2	0.0
Wind Drift - inches	0.0	0.4	1.6	3.8	6.8

G1 Ballistic Coefficient = 0.072

Fiocchi 29-grain Short Round Nose Compensated Solid (22SM200)

Distance - Yards	Muzzle	25	50	75	100
Velocity - fps	650	632	614	597	580
Energy - ft/lb	27	26	24	23	22
Path - inches	-1.5	7.4	10.8	8.4	0.0
Wind Drift - inches	0.0	0.3	1.2	2.7	4.8

G1 Ballistic Coefficient = 0.110

.22 Long

The .22 Long has just about dropped from the inventory. There was a time when not all the .22 caliber rifles were cambered for .22 Long Rifle. Since today's .22 Long Rifle ammunition will do everything the .22 Long cartridges will do, and most of it a lot better, the .22 Long is sliding quickly down the chute to the scrap pile of history.

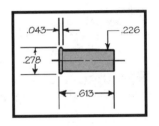

Relative Recoil Factor = 0.14   **Controlling Agency: SAAMI**

Bullet Weight Grains	Velocity fps	Maximum Average Pressure		Standard barrel for velocity testing:
		Copper Crusher	Transducer	
29 HV	1215	N/S	24,000 psi	24 inches long - 1 turn in 16 inch twist

CCI 29-grain Long High Speed (0029)

Distance - Yards	Muzzle	25	50	75	100
Velocity - fps	1180	1099	1038	987	946
Energy - ft/lb	90	78	69	63	57
Path - inches	-1.5	1.8	3.3	2.8	0.0
Wind Drift - inches	0.0	0.4	1.6	3.5	6.0

G1 Ballistic Coefficient = 0.109

CCI 29-grain Long CB Solid (0038)

Distance - Yards	Muzzle	25	50	75	100
Velocity - fps	727	696	667	638	610
Energy - ft/lb	33	31	28	26	24
Path - inches	-1.5	6.0	9.1	7.2	0.0
Wind Drift - inches	0.0	0.4	1.6	3.8	6.8

G1 Ballistic Coefficient = 0.072

.22 Long Rifle Standard Velocity and Match Ammunition

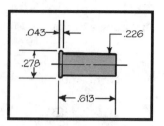

This is what the .22 Rimfire does best. Even the most expensive .22 Long Rifle match ammunition is inexpensive when compared to centerfire ammo. It's not reloadable, but that's not a factor since the .22 Rimfire case is so inexpensive that there just isn't anything worth saving. On an accuracy basis, it is sometimes very difficult to tell the difference in performance between "regular" standard-velocity ammo and match ammo, especially since match ammo comes in at least three grades: club or practice, match grade, and the super match grade. That's a good class of problem. Unless you have a pretty high quality target rifle you probably won't notice any improvement if you buy better than the standard velocity or the practice grade. In competition, you should use whatever you think works best for you. Mental attitude is an elemental part of competition.

Relative Recoil Factor = 0.19   **Controlling Agency : SAAMI**

Bullet Weight Grains	Velocity fps	Maximum Average Pressure		Standard barrel for velocity testing:
		Copper Crusher	Transducer	
40 SV	1135	N/S	24,000 psi	24 inches long - 1 turn in 16 inch twist

Lapua 36-grain Long Rifle (LR) Subsonic HP (4312246)

Distance - Yards	Muzzle	25	50	75	100
Velocity - fps	1033	1010	988	968	950
Energy - ft/lb	85	81	78	75	72
Path - inches	-1.5	2.2	3.7	3.0	0.0
Wind Drift - inches	0.0	0.2	0.6	1.3	2.3

G1 Ballistic Coefficient = 0.240

Remington 38-grain LR Subsonic HP (SUB22HP)

Distance - Yards	Muzzle	25	50	75	100
Velocity - fps	1050	1004	965	932	901
Energy - ft/lb	93	85	79	73	69
Path - inches	-1.5	2.3	3.9	3.2	0.0
Wind Drift - inches	0.0	0.3	1.1	2.5	4.3

G1 Ballistic Coefficient = 0.125

PMC 38-grain LR Subsonic Vel. (22SS)

Distance - Yards	Muzzle	25	50	75	100
Velocity - fps	1000	957	921	886	854
Energy - ft/lb	84	77	71	66	62
Path - inches	-1.5	2.6	4.4	3.6	0.0
Wind Drift - inches	0.0	0.3	1.2	2.7	4.6

G1 Ballistic Coefficient = 0.107

Winchester 40-grain Lead HP (W22LRB)

Distance - Yards	Muzzle	25	50	75	100
Velocity - fps	1150	1094	1048	1010	976
Energy - ft/lb	117	106	98	91	85
Path - inches	-1.5	1.8	3.2	2.7	0.0
Wind Drift - inches	0.0	0.3	1.2	2.5	4.3

G1 Ballistic Coefficient = 0.143

Federal 40-grain LR Target Solid (711)

Distance - Yards	Muzzle	25	50	75	100
Velocity - fps	1150	1090	1050	1010	970
Energy - ft/lb	115	105	95	90	80
Path - inches	-1.5	1.8	3.2	2.7	0.0
Wind Drift - inches	0.0	0.3	1.2	2.6	4.5

G1 Ballistic Coefficient = 0.143

Remington 40-grain LR Target Solid (6122)

Distance - Yards	Muzzle	25	50	75	100
Velocity - fps	1150	1094	1048	1009	976
Energy - ft/lb	117	106	98	90	85
Path - inches	-1.5	1.8	3.2	2.7	0.0
Wind Drift - inches	0.0	0.3	1.2	2.5	4.4

G1 Ballistic Coefficient = 0.149

Winchester 40-grain T22 LR Standard Velocity Solid (XT22LR)

Distance - Yards	Muzzle	25	50	75	100
Velocity - fps	1150	1094	1048	1009	976
Energy - ft/lb	117	106	98	90	85
Path - inches	-1.5	1.8	3.2	2.7	0.0
Wind Drift - inches	0.0	0.3	1.2	2.5	4.4

G1 Ballistic Coefficient = 0.149

Federal 40-grain LR Ultramatch Solid (UM1)

Distance - Yards	Muzzle	25	50	75	100
Velocity - fps	1140	1090	1040	1000	970
Energy - ft/lb	115	105	95	90	80
Path - inches	-1.5	1.8	3.2	2.7	0.0
Wind Drift - inches	0.0	0.3	1.1	2.5	4.3

G1 Ballistic Coefficient = 0.149

Federal 40-grain LR Match Solid (900)

Distance - Yards	Muzzle	25	50	75	100
Velocity - fps	1140	1090	1040	1000	970
Energy - ft/lb	115	105	95	90	80
Path - inches	-1.5	1.8	3.2	2.7	0.0
Wind Drift - inches	0.0	0.3	1.1	2.5	4.3

G1 Ballistic Coefficient = 0.149

PMC 40-grain Scoremaster LR Standard Velocity Solid (22SM)

Distance - Yards	Muzzle	25	50	75	100
Velocity - fps	1135	1071	1019	977	941
Energy - ft/lb	114	102	92	85	79
Path - inches	-1.5	1.9	3.4	2.8	0.0
Wind Drift - inches	0.0	0.4	1.4	3.0	5.1

G1 Ballistic Coefficient = 0.121

Fiocchi 40-grain LR Biathlon Match Solid (22SM340)

Distance - Yards	Muzzle	25	50	75	100
Velocity - fps	1116	1063	1020	983	950
Energy - ft/lb	111	100	92	86	80
Path - inches	-1.5	1.9	3.4	2.8	0.0
Wind Drift - inches	0.0	0.3	1.2	2.5	4.4

G1 Ballistic Coefficient = 0.140

Lapua 40-grain LR Polar Biathlon Solid (4317023)

Distance - Yards	Muzzle	25	50	75	100
Velocity - fps	1100	1037	987	945	909
Energy - ft/lb	107	96	87	79	73
Path - inches	-1.5	2.1	3.7	3.1	0.0
Wind Drift - inches	0.0	0.4	1.4	3.1	5.4

G1 Ballistic Coefficient = 0.108

Federal 40-grain LR Ultramatch Solid (UM1B)

Distance - Yards	Muzzle	25	50	75	100
Velocity - fps	1080	1030	1000	960	930
Energy - ft/lb	105	95	90	80	75
Path - inches	-1.5	2.1	3.6	3.0	0.0
Wind Drift - inches	0.0	0.3	1.1	2.4	4.1

G1 Ballistic Coefficient = 0.139

Federal 40-grain LR Match Solid (900B)

Distance - Yards	Muzzle	25	50	75	100
Velocity - fps	1080	1030	1000	960	930
Energy - ft/lb	105	95	90	80	75
Path - inches	-1.5	2.1	3.6	3.0	0.0
Wind Drift - inches	0.0	0.3	1.1	2.4	4.1

G1 Ballistic Coefficient = 0.139

CCI 40-grain LR Standard Velocity Solid (0032)

Distance - Yards	Muzzle	25	50	75	100
Velocity - fps	1070	1012	970	925	890
Energy - ft/lb	100	91	80	76	70
Path - inches	-1.5	2.3	3.9	3.2	0.0
Wind Drift - inches	0.0	0.4	1.4	3.0	5.2

G1 Ballistic Coefficient = 0.105

CCI 40-grain LR Green Tag Comp. Solid (0033)

Distance - Yards	Muzzle	25	50	75	100
Velocity - fps	1070	1012	970	925	890
Energy - ft/lb	100	91	80	76	70
Path - inches	-1.5	2.3	3.9	3.2	0.0
Wind Drift - inches	0.0	0.4	1.4	3.0	5.2

G1 Ballistic Coefficient = 0.105

CCI 40-grain LR Pistol Match Solid (0051)

Distance - Yards	Muzzle	25	50	75	100
Velocity - fps	1070	1012	970	925	890
Energy - ft/lb	100	91	80	76	70
Path - inches	-1.5	2.3	3.9	3.2	0.0
Wind Drift - inches	0.0	0.4	1.4	3.0	5.2

G1 Ballistic Coefficient = 0.105

Lapua 40-grain LR Master Solid (4317033)

Distance - Yards	Muzzle	25	50	75	100
Velocity - fps	1066	1020	981	947	917
Energy - ft/lb	101	92	85	80	75
Path - inches	-1.5	2.2	3.8	3.1	0.0
Wind Drift - inches	0.0	0.3	1.1	2.4	4.3

G1 Ballistic Coefficient = 0.132

Lapua 40-grain LR Midas L Solid (4317022)

Distance - Yards	Muzzle	25	50	75	100
Velocity - fps	1066	1020	981	947	917
Energy - ft/lb	101	92	85	80	75
Path - inches	-1.5	2.2	3.8	3.1	0.0
Wind Drift - inches	0.0	0.3	1.1	2.4	4.3

G1 Ballistic Coefficient = 0.132

Lapua 40-grain LR Midas M Solid (4317021)

Distance - Yards	Muzzle	25	50	75	100
Velocity - fps	1066	1020	981	947	917
Energy - ft/lb	101	92	85	80	75
Path - inches	-1.5	2.2	3.8	3.1	0.0
Wind Drift - inches	0.0	0.3	1.1	2.4	4.3

G1 Ballistic Coefficient = 0.132

Norma 1 - 40-grain LRN (15613)

Distance - Yards	Muzzle	25	50	75	100
Velocity - fps	1066	1020	981	947	917
Energy - ft/lb	101	92	85	80	75
Path - inches	-1.5	2.2	3.8	3.1	0.0
Wind Drift - inches	0.0	0.3	1.1	2.4	4.3

G1 Ballistic Coefficient = 0.132

Norma 2 - 40-grain LRN (15614)

Distance - Yards	Muzzle	25	50	75	100
Velocity - fps	1066	1020	981	947	917
Energy - ft/lb	101	92	85	80	75
Path - inches	-1.5	2.2	3.8	3.1	0.0
Wind Drift - inches	0.0	0.3	1.1	2.4	4.3

G1 Ballistic Coefficient = 0.132

Norma 3 - 40-grain LRN (15615)

Distance - Yards	Muzzle	25	50	75	100
Velocity - fps	1066	1020	981	947	917
Energy - ft/lb	101	92	85	80	75
Path - inches	-1.5	2.2	3.8	3.1	0.0
Wind Drift - inches	0.0	0.3	1.1	2.4	4.3

G1 Ballistic Coefficient = 0.132

Fiocchi 40-grain LR - Rifle Match Solid (22SM320)

Distance - Yards	Muzzle	25	50	75	100
Velocity - fps	1050	1008	973	942	914
Energy - ft/lb	98	90	84	79	74
Path - inches	-1.5	2.2	3.8	3.1	0.0
Wind Drift - inches	0.0	0.3	1.0	2.2	3.9

G1 Ballistic Coefficient = 0.140

Fiocchi 40-grain LR Match Training Solid (22M320)

Distance - Yards	Muzzle	25	50	75	100
Velocity - fps	1050	1006	968	935	906
Energy - ft/lb	98	90	83	78	73
Path - inches	-1.5	2.3	3.9	3.2	0.0
Wind Drift - inches	0.0	0.3	1.1	2.4	4.2

G1 Ballistic Coefficient = 0.130

Lapua 40-grain LR Super Club Solid (4317066)

Distance - Yards	Muzzle	25	50	75	100
Velocity - fps	1050	1000	958	922	891
Energy - ft/lb	98	89	82	76	70
Path - inches	-1.5	2.3	4.0	3.3	0.0
Wind Drift - inches	0.0	0.3	1.2	2.7	4.7

G1 Ballistic Coefficient = 0.114

Lapua 40-grain LR Standard Rifle Club Solid (43122420)

Distance - Yards	Muzzle	25	50	75	100
Velocity - fps	1050	1000	958	922	891
Energy - ft/lb	98	89	82	76	70
Path - inches	-1.5	2.3	4.0	3.3	0.0
Wind Drift - inches	0.0	0.3	1.2	2.7	4.7

G1 Ballistic Coefficient = 0.114

PMC 40-grain LR Pistol King Solid (22MR)

Distance - Yards	Muzzle	25	50	75	100
Velocity - fps	1050	1000	956	919	885
Energy - ft/lb	98	89	81	75	70
Path - inches	-1.5	2.3	4.0	3.3	0.0
Wind Drift - inches	0.0	0.3	1.3	2.8	4.9

G1 Ballistic Coefficient = 0.110

Lapua 40-grain Long Rifle Pistol King Solid (4317031)

Distance - Yards	Muzzle	25	50	75	100
Velocity - fps	1033	991	956	924	896
Energy - ft/lb	95	87	81	76	71
Path - inches	-1.5	2.4	4.0	3.3	0.0
Wind Drift - inches	0.0	0.3	1.1	2.3	4.1

G1 Ballistic Coefficient = 0.130

Lapua 40-grain LR Pistol Trainer Solid (4312260)

Distance - Yards	Muzzle	25	50	75	100
Velocity - fps	1033	991	956	924	896
Energy - ft/lb	95	87	81	76	71
Path - inches	-1.5	2.4	4.0	3.3	0.0
Wind Drift - inches	0.0	0.3	1.1	2.3	4.1

G1 Ballistic Coefficient = 0.130

Fiocchi 40-grain LR Match Training Solid (22M300)

Distance - Yards	Muzzle	25	50	75	100
Velocity - fps	984	948	916	887	861
Energy - ft/lb	86	80	75	70	66
Path - inches	-1.5	2.7	4.4	3.6	0.0
Wind Drift - inches	0.0	0.3	1.0	2.2	3.9

G1 Ballistic Coefficient = 0.125

Fiocchi 40-grain LR - Pistol Match Solid (22SM300)

Distance - Yards	Muzzle	25	50	75	100
Velocity - fps	984	949	918	891	865
Energy - ft/lb	86	80	75	70	66
Path - inches	-1.5	2.6	4.4	3.6	0.0
Wind Drift - inches	0.0	0.3	1.0	2.2	3.8

G1 Ballistic Coefficient = 0.130

Winchester 40-grain LR Lead HP (W22LRB)

Distance - Yards	Muzzle	25	50	75	100
Velocity - fps	1150	1094	1048	1010	976
Energy - ft/lb	117	106	98	91	85
Path - inches	-1.5	1.8	3.2	2.7	0.0
Wind Drift - inches	0.0	0.3	1.2	2.5	4.3

G1 Ballistic Coefficient = 0.150

Lapua 48-grain LR Scoremax Solid (4317030)

Distance - Yards	Muzzle	25	50	75	100
Velocity - fps	1033	995	962	933	907
Energy - ft/lb	114	106	99	93	88
Path - inches	-1.5	2.3	3.9	3.2	0.0
Wind Drift - inches	0.0	0.2	1.0	2.1	3.7

G1 Ballistic Coefficient = 0.144

Lapua 48-grain LR Multi Match Solid (4317020)

Distance - Yards	Muzzle	25	50	75	100
Velocity - fps	1100	1048	1005	969	937
Energy - ft/lb	129	117	108	100	94
Path - inches	-1.5	2.0	3.5	2.9	0.0
Wind Drift - inches	0.0	0.3	1.2	2.6	4.4

G1 Ballistic Coefficient = 0.134

.22 Long Rifle High Velocity and Hyper Velocity

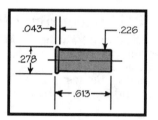

This ammunition is the generic form of the .22 Long Rifle caliber. There is more of this ammo made than any other basic performance category. The bullets are available in a variety of forms and weights. In general, the high speed ammunition is not quite as accurate as the standard velocity form but from time to time you will run across a gun and ammo combination that shoots extremely well with high velocity ammunition.

Relative Recoil Factor = 0.22   **Controlling Agency: SAAMI**

Bullet Weight Grains	Velocity fps	Maximum Average Pressure		
		Copper Crusher	Transducer	
36 HVHP	1260	N/S	24,000 psi	
37 HVHP	1260	N/S	24,000 psi	
40 HV	1235	N/S	24,000 psi	
33 Hyper HP	1465	N/S	24,000 psi	
36 Hyper	1385	N/S	24,000 psi	

Standard barrel for velocity testing:
24 inches long - 1 turn in 16 inch twist

Federal 27-grain LR Ballisticlean (BC22NT1)

Distance - Yards	Muzzle	25	50	75	100
Velocity - fps	1300	1187	1098	1031	978
Energy - ft/lb	100	84	72	64	57
Path - inches	-1.5	1.4	2.8	2.4	0.0
Wind Drift - inches	0.0	0.5	1.9	4.2	7.2

G1 Ballistic Coefficient = 0.100

Federal 31-grain LR Hyper Velocity HP Copper Plated (724)

Distance - Yards	Muzzle	25	50	75	100
Velocity - fps	1550	1410	1280	1182	1100
Energy - ft/lb	165	137	115	96	85
Path - inches	-1.5	0.7	1.9	1.7	0.0
Wind Drift - inches	0.0	0.4	1.7	3.9	7.0

G1 Ballistic Coefficient = 0.107

CCI 32-grain LR Stinger HP (0050)

Distance - Yards	Muzzle	25	50	75	100
Velocity - fps	1640	1486	1348	1229	1132
Energy - ft/lb	191	157	129	107	91
Path - inches	-1.5	0.6	1.9	1.6	0.0
Wind Drift - inches	0.0	0.4	1.7	3.9	7.1

G1 Ballistic Coefficient = 0.103

Remington 33-grain LR Yellow JHP (1722)

Distance - Yards	Muzzle	25	50	75	100
Velocity - fps	1500	1365	1247	1151	1075
Energy - ft/lb	165	137	114	97	85
Path - inches	-1.5	0.9	2.0	1.8	0.0
Wind Drift - inches	0.0	0.4	1.8	4.0	7.0

G1 Ballistic Coefficient = 0.107

Remington 36-grain LR Viper Solid (1922)

Distance - Yards	Muzzle	25	50	75	100
Velocity - fps	1410	1296	1198	1119	1056
Energy - ft/lb	159	134	115	100	89
Path - inches	-1.5	1.0	2.3	2.0	0.0
Wind Drift - inches	0.0	0.4	1.6	3.7	6.5

G1 Ballistic Coefficient = 0.139

Lapua 36-grain LR HP (4312245)

Distance - Yards	Muzzle	25	50	75	100
Velocity - fps	1345	1244	1159	1090	1036
Energy - ft/lb	145	124	107	95	86
Path - inches	-1.5	1.2	2.5	2.2	0.0
Wind Drift - inches	0.0	0.4	1.6	3.5	6.2

G1 Ballistic Coefficient = 0.122

CCI 36-grain LR Mini-Mag HP (0031)

Distance - Yards	Muzzle	25	50	75	100
Velocity - fps	1280	1191	1125	1060	1012
Energy - ft/lb	135	113	101	90	84
Path - inches	-1.5	1.4	2.7	2.3	0.0
Wind Drift - inches	0.0	0.4	1.5	3.3	5.8

G1 Ballistic Coefficient = 0.126

Remington 36-grain LR Cyclone HP (CY22HP)

Distance - Yards	Muzzle	25	50	75	100
Velocity - fps	1280	1190	1117	1057	1010
Energy - ft/lb	131	113	100	89	82
Path - inches	-1.5	1.4	2.7	2.3	0.0
Wind Drift - inches	0.0	0.4	1.5	3.4	5.9

G1 Ballistic Coefficient = 0.124

Remington 36-grain LR HP (1622)

Distance - Yards	Muzzle	25	50	75	100
Velocity - fps	1280	1190	1117	1057	1010
Energy - ft/lb	131	113	100	89	82
Path - inches	-1.5	1.4	2.7	2.3	0.0
Wind Drift - inches	0.0	0.4	1.5	3.4	5.9

G1 Ballistic Coefficient = 0.124

Winchester 37-grain LR HP (X22LRH)

Distance - Yards	Muzzle	25	50	75	100
Velocity - fps	1280	1193	1120	1062	1015
Energy - ft/lb	135	117	103	93	85
Path - inches	-1.5	1.4	2.7	2.3	0.0
Wind Drift - inches	0.0	0.4	1.5	3.3	5.7

G1 Ballistic Coefficient = 0.128

Federal 38-grain LR HP Copper-Plated (712)

Distance - Yards	Muzzle	25	50	75	100
Velocity - fps	1280	1195	1120	1067	1020
Energy - ft/lb	140	121	105	96	90
Path - inches	-1.5	1.4	2.7	2.3	0.0
Wind Drift - inches	0.0	0.4	1.4	3.2	5.6

G1 Ballistic Coefficient = 0.132

American Eagle (Federal) 38-grain LR HP Copper-Plated (AE22)

Distance - Yards	Muzzle	25	50	75	100
Velocity - fps	1280	1195	1120	1067	1020
Energy - ft/lb	140	121	105	96	90
Path - inches	-1.5	1.4	2.7	2.3	0.0
Wind Drift - inches	0.0	0.4	1.4	3.2	5.6

G1 Ballistic Coefficient = 0.132

PMC 38-grain LR Zapper HP (22D)

Distance - Yards	Muzzle	25	50	75	100
Velocity - fps	1280	1187	1112	1052	1004
Energy - ft/lb	138	119	104	93	85
Path - inches	-1.5	1.4	2.8	2.4	0.0
Wind Drift - inches	0.0	0.4	1.6	3.5	6.0

G1 Ballistic Coefficient = 0.120

Winchester 40-grain LR Power-Point HP (X22LRPP)

Distance - Yards	Muzzle	25	50	75	100
Velocity - fps	1280	1186	1110	1049	1001
Energy - ft/lb	146	125	109	98	89
Path - inches	-1.5	1.4	2.8	2.4	0.0
Wind Drift - inches	0.0	0.4	1.6	3.6	6.1

G1 Ballistic Coefficient = 0.118

Lapua 40-grain LR Speed Ace Solid (4312243)

Distance - Yards	Muzzle	25	50	75	100
Velocity - fps	1345	1286	1231	1182	1139
Energy - ft/lb	161	147	135	124	115
Path - inches	-1.5	1.0	2.1	1.8	0.0
Wind Drift - inches	0.0	0.2	0.9	2.0	3.6

G1 Ballistic Coefficient = 0.215

American Eagle (Federal) 40-grain LR Solid (AE5022)

Distance - Yards	Muzzle	25	50	75	100
Velocity - fps	1260	1182	1100	1064	1020
Energy - ft/lb	140	124	110	101	90
Path - inches	-1.5	1.4	2.7	2.3	0.0
Wind Drift - inches	0.0	0.4	1.4	3.0	5.2

G1 Ballistic Coefficient = 0.138

Federal 40-grain LR Solid (710)

Distance - Yards	Muzzle	25	50	75	100
Velocity - fps	1260	1182	1100	1064	1020
Energy - ft/lb	140	124	110	101	90
Path - inches	-1.5	1.4	2.7	2.3	0.0
Wind Drift - inches	0.0	0.4	1.4	3.0	5.2

G1 Ballistic Coefficient = 0.138

CCI 40-grain LR Silhouette (0065)

Distance - Yards	Muzzle	25	50	75	100
Velocity - fps	1255	1177	1110	1060	1016
Energy - ft/lb	140	123	109	100	92
Path - inches	-1.5	1.4	2.8	2.3	0.0
Wind Drift - inches	0.0	0.4	1.4	3.0	5.2

G1 Ballistic Coefficient = 0.138

CCI 40-grain LR Mini-Mag Solid (0030)

Distance - Yards	Muzzle	25	50	75	100
Velocity - fps	1255	1177	1110	1060	1016
Energy - ft/lb	140	123	109	100	92
Path - inches	-1.5	1.4	2.8	2.3	0.0
Wind Drift - inches	0.0	0.4	1.4	3.0	5.2

G1 Ballistic Coefficient = 0.138

PMC 40-grain LR Zapper Solid (22CC)

Distance - Yards	Muzzle	25	50	75	100
Velocity - fps	1255	1167	1096	1040	994
Energy - ft/lb	140	121	107	96	88
Path - inches	-1.5	1.5	2.9	2.4	0.0
Wind Drift - inches	0.0	0.4	1.6	3.4	5.9

G1 Ballistic Coefficient = 0.121

Remington 40-grain LR Solid (1522)

Distance - Yards	Muzzle	25	50	75	100
Velocity - fps	1255	1167	1113	1061	1017
Energy - ft/lb	140	123	110	100	92
Path - inches	-1.5	1.4	2.8	2.3	0.0
Wind Drift - inches	0.0	0.4	1.4	3.0	5.2

`G1 Ballistic Coefficient = 0.138

Remington 40-grain LR Thunderbolt Solid (TB22A)

Distance - Yards	Muzzle	25	50	75	100
Velocity - fps	1255	1167	1113	1061	1017
Energy - ft/lb	140	123	110	100	92
Path - inches	-1.5	1.4	2.8	2.3	0.0
Wind Drift - inches	0.0	0.4	1.4	3.0	5.2

G1 Ballistic Coefficient = 0.138

Winchester 40-grain LR Wildcat Solid (WW22LR)

Distance - Yards	Muzzle	25	50	75	100
Velocity - fps	1255	1167	1113	1061	1017
Energy - ft/lb	140	123	110	100	92
Path - inches	-1.5	1.4	2.8	2.3	0.0
Wind Drift - inches	0.0	0.4	1.4	3.0	5.2

G1 Ballistic Coefficient = 0.139

Winchester 40-grain LR Solid (X22LR)

Distance - Yards	Muzzle	25	50	75	100
Velocity - fps	1255	1167	1113	1061	1017
Energy - ft/lb	140	123	110	100	92
Path - inches	-1.5	1.4	2.8	2.3	0.0
Wind Drift - inches	0.0	0.4	1.4	3.0	5.2

G1 Ballistic Coefficient = 0.139

PMC 40-grain LR Sidewinder Solid (22SC)

Distance - Yards	Muzzle	25	50	75	100
Velocity - fps	1250	1163	1092	1037	992
Energy - ft/lb	139	120	106	96	87
Path - inches	-1.5	1.5	2.9	2.5	0.0
Wind Drift - inches	0.0	0.4	1.6	3.4	5.9

G1 Ballistic Coefficient = 0.121

.22 Winchester Magnum Rimfire (WMR)

The .22 WMR cartridge can be thought of as a .22 Long Rifle on steroids. The bad news is that the .22 WMR is a significantly larger cartridge and will NOT fit into standard .22 guns chambered for .22 Long Rifle (nor for that matter can the .22 Long Rifle cartridge be fired in a .22 WMR chamber). The good news is that in the fastest loadings the .22 WMR begins to approach the performance of the .22 Hornet. That's a lot of performance from a rimfire cartridge.

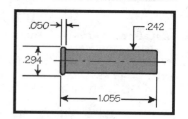

Relative Recoil Factor = 0.34   **Controlling Agency: SAAMI**

Bullet Weight Grains	Velocity fps	Maximum Average Pressure		Standard barrel for velocity testing:
		Copper Crusher	Transducer	
40	1875	N/S	24,000 psi	24 inches long - 1 turn in 16 inch twist

CCI 30-grain WMR Maxi-Mag. + V HP (0059)

Distance - Yards	Muzzle	25	50	75	100
Velocity - fps	2200	1966	1750	1550	1373
Energy - ft/lb	322	258	203	160	127
Path - inches	-1.5	-0.1	0.7	0.8	0.0
Wind Drift - inches	0.0	0.4	1.5	3.5	6.5

G1 Ballistic Coefficient = 0.084

Federal 30-grain WMR JHP (767)

Distance - Yards	Muzzle	25	50	75	100
Velocity - fps	2200	1977	1760	1576	1400
Energy - ft/lb	325	260	205	166	130
Path - inches	-1.5	-0.1	0.7	0.8	0.0
Wind Drift - inches	0.0	0.3	1.4	3.3	6.2

G1 Ballistic Coefficient = 0.088

Remington 33-grain WMR Premier V-Max Boattail (R22M1)

Distance - Yards	Muzzle	25	50	75	100
Velocity - fps	2000	1836	1730	1609	1495
Energy - ft/lb	293	254	219	190	164
Path - inches	-1.5	-0.1	0.7	0.8	0.0
Wind Drift - inches	0.0	0.2	1.0	2.3	4.2

G1 Ballistic Coefficient = 0.137

Winchester 33-grain WMR JHP (S22WM)

Distance - Yards	Muzzle	25	50	75	100
Velocity - fps	2120	1931	1753	1537	1435
Energy - ft/lb	338	282	232	190	155
Path - inches	-1.5	-0.1	0.7	0.8	0.0
Wind Drift - inches	0.0	0.3	1.2	2.9	5.5

G1 Ballistic Coefficient = 0.102

CCI 40-grain WMR Maxi-Mag HP (0024)

Distance - Yards	Muzzle	25	50	75	100
Velocity - fps	1910	1746	1592	1452	1326
Energy - ft/lb	324	271	225	187	156
Path - inches	-1.5	0.1	1.0	1.0	0.0
Wind Drift - inches	0.0	0.3	1.3	3.1	5.4

G1 Ballistic Coefficient = 0.110

Remington 40-grain WMR JHP (R22M2)

Distance - Yards	Muzzle	25	50	75	100
Velocity - fps	1910	1754	1610	1472	1350
Energy - ft/lb	324	273	230	193	162
Path - inches	-1.5	0.1	1.0	1.0	0.0
Wind Drift - inches	0.0	0.3	1.2	2.9	5.4

G1 Ballistic Coefficient = 0.116

Winchester 40-grain WMR JHP (X22MH)

Distance - Yards	Muzzle	25	50	75	100
Velocity - fps	1910	1746	1592	1452	1326
Energy - ft/lb	324	271	225	187	156
Path - inches	-1.5	0.1	1.0	1.0	0.0
Wind Drift - inches	0.0	0.3	1.3	3.1	5.4

G1 Ballistic Coefficient = 0.110

CCI 40-grain WMR Maxi-Mag Solid (0023)

Distance - Yards	Muzzle	25	50	75	100
Velocity - fps	1910	1746	1592	1452	1326
Energy - ft/lb	324	271	225	187	156
Path - inches	-1.5	0.1	1.0	1.0	0.0
Wind Drift - inches	0.0	0.3	1.3	3.1	5.4

G1 Ballistic Coefficient = 0.110

Federal 40-grain WMR FMJ Solid (737)

Distance - Yards	Muzzle	25	50	75	100
Velocity - fps	1910	1747	1600	1455	1330
Energy - ft/lb	325	271	225	188	155
Path - inches	-1.5	0.1	1.0	1.0	0.0
Wind Drift - inches	0.0	0.3	1.3	3.1	5.6

G1 Ballistic Coefficient = 0.111

Remington 40-grain WMR Pointed SP Solid (R22M2)

Distance - Yards	Muzzle	25	50	75	100
Velocity - fps	1910	1751	1600	1466	1340
Energy - ft/lb	324	272	227	191	159
Path - inches	-1.5	0.1	1.0	1.0	0.0
Wind Drift - inches	0.0	0.3	1.3	3.0	5.5

G1 Ballistic Coefficient = 0.114

Winchester 40-grain WMR FMJ Solid (X22M)

Distance - Yards	Muzzle	25	50	75	100
Velocity - fps	1910	1746	1592	1452	1326
Energy - ft/lb	324	271	225	187	156
Path - inches	-1.5	0.1	1.0	1.0	0.0
Wind Drift - inches	0.0	0.3	1.3	3.1	5.4

G1 Ballistic Coefficient = 0.110

Federal 50-grain WMR JHP (757)

Distance - Yards	Muzzle	25	50	75	100
Velocity - fps	1650	1547	1450	1361	1280
Energy - ft/lb	302	266	234	206	182
Path - inches	-1.5	0.4	1.3	1.2	0.0
Wind Drift - inches	0.0	0.3	1.1	2.5	4.5

G1 Ballistic Coefficient = 0.158

.22 Rimfire Shotshells (Long Rifle Size)

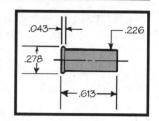

In the 1940s my father took me to some outdoor shows. One of the booths that got my interest was a trap-shooting game that used .22 Rimfire shotshells and miniature clay targets. The backstop was nothing more than a sheet of heavy canvas hung from the ceiling of the hall. That was enough to stop the very fine shot. It's hard to imagine anyone getting away with that today but I never heard of any accident resulting from those shows. The .22 Rimfire shotshells also make a fine load for a snake gun.

Relative Recoil Factor = 0.14   **Controlling Agency: SAAMI**

Bullet Weight Grains	Velocity fps	Maximum Average Pressure Copper Crusher	Transducer	Standard barrel for velocity testing:
25 #12 Shot	1000	N/S	24,000 psi	24 inches long - 1 turn in 16 inch twist

Federal 25-grain Long Rifle Bird Shot (710)
This load uses #10 shot. No performance data is given.

CCI 31-grain Long Rifle Shotshell (0039)
This load uses #12 shot.
Muzzle Velocity is listed at 950 fps.

Winchester Long Rifle Shot (X22LRS)
This load uses #12 shot. No performance data is given.

.22 Rimfire Shotshells (WMR Size)

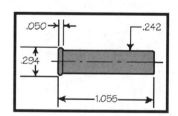

The .22 WMR case offers a slightly more potent shotshell capability than can be found in the standard .22 Long Rifle size, but it is still no match for even the 2½ inch .410.

Relative Recoil = 0.23   **Controlling Agency : SAAMI**

There is no separate SAAMI specification for this loading.

CCI 52-grain WMR Shotshell (0025)
This load uses #11 shot.
Muzzle velocity is listed at 1000 fps.